Canadian Cities in Transition | second edition |

the twenty-first century

Edited by

OXFORD
UNIVERSITY PRESS

OXFORD
UNIVERSITY PRESS

70 Wynford Drive, Don Mills, Ontario M3C 1J9
www.oup.com/ca

Oxford University Press is a department of the University of Oxford.
It furthers the University's objective of excellence in research, scholarship,
and education by publishing worldwide in

Oxford New York

Auckland Bangkok Buenos Aires Cape Town Chennai
Dar es Salaam Delhi Hong Kong Istanbul Karachi Kolkata
Kuala Lumpur Madrid Melbourne Mexico City Mumbai Nairobi
São Paulo Shanghai Taipei Tokyo Toronto

Oxford is a trade mark of Oxford University Press
in the UK and in certain other countries

Published in Canada
by Oxford University Press

Canadian Cataloguing in Publication Data

Main entry under title:
Canadian cities in transition : the twenty-first century
2nd ed.
ISBN 0-19-541288-5

1. Cities and towns—Canada. I. Bunting, Trudi E., 1944– . II. Filion, Pierre, 1952– .

HT127.C32 2000   307.76'0971   C99-932964-2

Cover Design: Tearney McMurtry
Text Design: Brett Miller

5 6 7 - 06 05 04

This book is printed on permanent (acid-free) paper ∞.
Printed in Canada

Contents

Contributors

Larry S. Bourne
Department of Geography
University of Toronto

Christopher R. Bryant
Département de géographie
Université de Montréal

Trudi Bunting
Department of Geography and School of Planning
University of Waterloo

William J. Coffey
Département de géographie
Université de Montréal

Philip M. Coppack
School of Applied Geography
Ryerson Polytechnical University

Adela Cosijn
Centre for Environmental Design Research and Outreach
University of Calgary

Kim England
Department of Geography
University of Washington

Pierre Filion
School of Planning
University of Waterloo

Susan Friesen
Centre for Environmental Design Research and Outreach
University of Calgary

Gunter Gad
Department of Geography
University of Toronto

Len Gertler
Ontario Environmental Assessment Board

Jill Grant
Department of Environmental Planning
Nova Scotia College of Arts and Design

Richard S. Harris
School of Geography and Geology
McMaster University

Walter Jamieson
Faculty of Environmental Design
University of Calgary

Ken Jones
Centre for the Study of Commercial Activity
Ryerson Polytechnic University

David Ley
Department of Geography
University of British Columbia

Larry McCann
Department of Geography
University of Victoria

Lynn McDonald
Faculty of Social Work
University of Toronto

Malcolm Matthew
Department of Geography
University of Windsor

John Mercer
Department of Geography
Syracuse University

Eric J. Miller
Department of Civil Engineering
University of Toronto

John Miron
Department of Geography
University of Toronto

Clare J.A. Mitchell
Department of Geography
University of Waterloo

Robert A. Murdie
Department of Geography
York University

Sherry Olson
Department of Geography
McGill University

Tracy Peressini
Department of Sociology
University of Toronto

Brian Ray
Department of Geography
McGill University

Damaris Rose
INRS-Urbanisation
Montreal

Tod Rutherford
Department of Geography
University of Waterloo

Andrew Sancton
Department of Political Science
University of Western Ontario

Anne-Marie Séguin
INRS-Urbanisation
Montreal

Jim Simmons
Centre for the Study of Commercial Activity
Ryerson Polytechnic University

Peter J. Smith
Department of Earth and Atmospheric Science
University of Alberta

Carlos Teixeira
Department of Geography
University of Toronto at Scarborough

Mary Ellen Tyler
Faculty of Environmental Design
University of Calgary

Paul Villeneuve
Aménagement du territoire et
éveloppement régional (ATDR)
Université Laval

Chapter 1

Cities and Transition: Changing Patterns of Urban Growth and Form in Canada

Pierre Filion, Trudi Bunting, and Len Gertler

Cities are worthy of our interest because of their inherently complex and dynamic nature. As we move into the twenty-first century, major urban transitions are generated by shifts, for example, from industrial to post-industrial society, from modern to post-modern lifestyles, from social structures dominated by the middle class to an increasingly polarized society, from transportation to telecommunication, and from national to global economies. The past century witnessed profound urban change, in particular the shift from compact city form to dispersed urbanization, the adverse environmental consequences of which are increasingly felt. We obviously need to understand cities better if we want to plan them more effectively. We could list many more reasons to study cities. As the daily living environment for the vast majority of households and the locale of most production, consumption, and administrative activity, cities play a crucial role in a country's economic and social development. Urban problems such as traffic congestion and housing shortage have a deleterious impact on economic performance and residents' living conditions.

This book is about cities—how and why they work (or don't work), their appearance, evolution, distinctive patterns of change and transition, problems, and the improvements they call for. It singles out the Canadian city as a distinct entity that can be seen as situated between European and United States counterparts, although closer to the latter. Comparatively speaking, Canadian cities share strong commonalities with US cities. Yet there are differences in how cities in Canada are structured, built, managed, and planned for. There is, therefore, great

merit to an exclusive focus on Canadian cities. This should not, however, negate the need to understand the universal principles of urbanization that explain the existence of cities since their inception. This first chapter discusses basic parameters of all urban places, using them as an initial way to understand how Canadian cities are constituted and have evolved.

The discussion to follow begins with an exploration of four intrinsic properties of cities. It then describes three periods of urban development in Canada over the last 100 years, concentrating on the influence of shifting economic, cultural, demographic, and political trends on the city's evolving transportation and land-use structure. The brief discussion of twentieth-century intra-urban change highlights the concept of transition that runs throughout the volume. As understood in this volume, transition is about how urban areas generate and respond to technological, economic, and social change. The chapter then reflects on possible urban futures for Canada before closing with a brief overview of the book.

Properties of the City

Many attempts have been made to capture the urban phenomenon. For example, the urban sociologist Louis Wirth (1938: 8) defined cities as 'large, dense, relatively permanent settlements of socially heterogeneous people'. Most scholars agree that cities are places of concentrated settlement whose occupants engage in relatively specialized kinds of non-agricultural economic activities. Lewis Mumford, probably this century's most influential

North American writer on urban matters, pictured the city as the hub of civilization, where culture and values evolve in a context of intense interpersonal interaction (Mumford, 1961). In this chapter, our aim to understand the existence, respective importance, and inner structure of cities leads to the identification of four fundamental properties inherent in the very essence of the urban phenomenon: *proximity*, *production*, *capitalization* (of the built environment), and *management*. These properties are timeless —they were as influential 4,000 years ago in early Chinese and Mesopotamian settlements as they are in the contemporary Canadian city.

Proximity

Above all, individuals and activities congregate in cities to be close to each other in order to facilitate communication and minimize the cost (in time, effort, and monetary expense) of interaction. If we probed the reasons why people live in cities, most would place the need to be close to work at the top of their list of answers. This has been and still is the foremost motive for people to move from the country to the city and from city to city. Other explanations would include proximity to educational establishments, shopping opportunities, cultural activities, entertainment, family and friends, medical facilities, etc. People opt for urban living because they either interact or anticipate interacting frequently with such activities and individuals. Likewise, businesses and institutions locate in cities so they can be close to their market, labour force, and the establishments with which they maintain linkages. By concentrating activities and people and thus creating proximity, the city makes frequent interactions affordable in terms of both cost and time. In a rural setting, many recurring contacts that are routine in the city would involve prohibitive transportation times and/or costs due to long distances. A by-product of interaction is innovation. Easy interaction is one of the major reasons why cities have been catalysts for social change.

It follows that the city can be perceived as comprised of numerous overlapping markets of fre-

quently repeated exchanges. Because cities are fundamentally places of economic enterprise, daily commuting between residences and workplaces is of unparalleled importance in explaining their existence and structure. This pre-eminence is acknowledged by Statistics Canada. Like many other national census agencies, Statistics Canada bases its definition of a metropolitan region (census metropolitan area or CMA) on an urbanized core's commuter shed. Appendix A provides a detailed outline of the current method used to delineate a census metropolitan area. In essence:

> CMAs are comprised of one or more census subdivisions (CSDs, that is, municipalities) which meet at least one of the following criteria:
> (1) the CSD falls completely or partly inside the urbanized core;
> (2) at least 50 per cent of the employed labour force *living* in the CSD *work* in the urbanized core; or
> (3) at least 25 per cent of the employed labour force *working* in the CSD *live* in the urbanized core. (Statistics Canada, 1997)

But this is by no means the only urban market of frequently repeated exchanges that affects the size and spatial organization of cities. Examples of other markets of this nature include the ones that tie retail facilities to their markets and public services to their clients. Also worth mentioning are the markets that connect cultural and recreational activities to their publics—the archetypical attraction of the city's 'bright lights'.

The inherent importance of proximity has a number of highly visible consequences on urbanization. One obvious repercussion is the high cost of city relative to country land. The appeal of proximity raises demand for space in the city. This, in turn, raises land values. As a result, certain functions that consume large amounts of land, such as farming, are generally ruled out. In this same vein, high land cost prevents functions present in the city from consuming as much space as they would like. Of course, wealthier land users have less need to compromise their space consumption. High-income households can afford substantial amounts of land in the city, although far less so than in country settings, while the very poor are typically confined to small apartments or rooms, if not to hostels and street corners. This disparity is vividly expressed by social status maps (see Chapter 9). They portray the stark discrepancy between the large portion of a metropolitan region taken up by high-income groups and the relatively small share occupied by low-income households.

Proximity is conditioned by prevailing transportation systems and activity distribution patterns in a relation that will be reiterated throughout this volume. In the pre-industrial city, which depended on non-mechanized forms of transportation (primarily walking and horse-drawn transport) and where activities were centralized, this principle severely confined the expanse of urbanized territory. Things are different in the contemporary car- and truck-oriented and highly decentralized metropolis. In this case, adequate accessibility levels can be maintained over large territories and residents and activities can consume far more land than in the past. But the proximity principle remains influential even in these more dispersed circumstances, as evidenced by the enduring existence of higher densities in cities than in the countryside. Even within cities there is variation in density and other important characteristics, such as building style and land-use type around sites of heightened accessibility (junctions along transit routes, major arterials, and expressways). Today debate rages as to whether our ability to substitute telecommunication for actual movement holds the potential for an even more dispersed urban form.

Production

Another fundamental characteristic of the city stems from its need to host production activities. Economic production creates jobs and thus is the main reason for urban growth. Many economic activities, of course, are aimed at the consumption needs of a city's own residents. Catering to local demand does not in itself differentiate the city from other forms of settlement, however. For example, in a self-reliant farming situation, the land a family occupies fulfils virtually all its needs. What most sets urban settlements apart from traditional self-reliant rural economies is the historic inability of the city to satisfy all its consumption requirements and the resulting imperative for it to export goods and services in order to be able to acquire needed products from outside. The quest for proximity rules out the presence within cities of the large surfaces needed to feed their populations. A city must also reach beyond its territory to secure other products and resources essential to sustain its population and economic activity. This includes different forms of staples and energy and, often, water. Research records cities' dependency for their natural resources on a territory (or 'ecological footprint') that far exceeds the urbanized perimeter (Rees and Wackernagel, 1994; Wackernagel and Rees, 1996). In developed countries, cities have become highly specialized economically and trade far more with other cities than with non-urban areas. Cities account for the vast majority of these countries' economic activity as well as for most of their population.

For a city to exist, it must be in a position to export sufficient goods and services to counterbalance its imports. Exports need not be of a pure market nature. Capital cities, for example, export decisions and derive their monetary returns from tax revenues; in medieval times, it was usual for cities to draw taxes, often in kind, from a hinterland to which they extended military protection. Cities that fail to export decline and may disappear altogether, as illustrated by the fate of resource ghost towns whose staple has run out (see Chapters 4 and 5). Increasingly, goods originate from foreign countries and continents. Likewise, production targets international markets. This opening of national markets has resulted in economic restructuring involving a collapse of metropolitan regions' production in sectors that have become non-competitive, while activities in areas where they hold comparative advantages on world markets have flourished. Some of Canada's successful export sectors presently include the pharmaceutical, aerospace, automobile, and natural resource industries. The tendency is for developed countries to depend increasingly on knowledge-intensive activities. Establishments that broker knowledge-based services, e.g., the professions, management, and financial services, are among the fastest-growing sectors of the economy. These kinds of establishments are grouped together under the rubric 'advanced service sector'. An economic trend of the last decades has been the growing importance of services in general relative to manufactured goods in the economy. This transition has had a profound effect on urban consumption, as evidenced, for example, by the explosion of restaurants, places of entertainment, and cultural activities. But these changes are also felt, albeit with less intensity, within cities' export sphere. Among services Canadian cities export are engineering and development expertise, culture, and tourism.

Capitalization

A third fundamental property of cities derives from their concentrated nature. Because urban land is a scarce resource, it has been heavily capitalized and modified. This means that the urban built environment is not only distinctly expensive, because of the vast resources invested to accommodate agglomerations of businesses, residents, and other activities, but also highly durable and thus long lasting. Almost all urban territory is heavily engineered. This includes buildings, roads, sewers, electrical and communication systems, parks, even 'natural' areas when located in an urban context. The extended time span of built structures calls for control mechanisms to minimize the occurrence of development blunders.

Change, especially concerning modes of production or accessibility as brought about by new transportation technologies, demands adjustments of the built environment to new conditions. But a city is not easily retrofitted. This is why it remains difficult to fully accommodate high levels of automotive transportation in the central city. Equally, a future transition from the automobile to some

other, hypothetical, mode would be difficult because of the massive financial investment, both public and private, that has been sunk into cars, trucks, and different types of roads.

While financial constraints can play a critical role, they are not the only impediment to altering the urban environment. Plenty of developers are interested in redeveloping high-accessibility and amenity-rich sites. But redevelopment of built-up areas (as opposed to development on 'greenfield' sites) often clashes with residents' strong emotional attachment to home and neighbourhood. Citizen organizations have been instrumental in protecting inner-city residential areas from both commercial developments and private or public infill housing. These organizations also played a major part in ending the construction of expressways through built-up areas. Across Canada, NIMBY (Not In My Back Yard) movements carry considerable weight on the municipal scene (see Chapter 24). The sensitivity of elective representatives to such pressures explains their frequent reticence to sanction radical modifications, particularly where residential areas are concerned.

Another obstacle to urban environment adaptability is the symbiosis that emerges between patterns of behaviour and built environments. To return to our transportation example, the presence of high-capacity road systems encourages reliance on the automobile and the truck. High rates of car and truck use mean a continued demand for improved and expanded roads. Moreover, once cars and trucks have filled available road space, it becomes nearly impossible to scale down the road system even slightly. A good example is the staunch resistance encountered when attempts are made to remove as little as one metre from an arterial road to create a bicycle lane.

One implication of durability is the frequent absence of adaptation between existing built forms and prevailing economic and social conditions. The massive abandonment of inner-city industrial belts illustrates this disconnection. The urban environment has also been blamed for encouraging the persistence of lifestyles not necessarily consistent with contemporary social values and needs. In this respect, feminists have criticized suburbs on the ground that they are not suited to women's new role in the workplace and the family (Hayden, 1984; Werkerle, 1985; see also Chapter 22).

Investment in the built environment, whether economic or sentimental, and the patterns of behaviour it supports are on the whole a conservative force that assures continuity by inhibiting rapid change. This conservative aspect of the built environment contrasts with the transformative role of successive modes of production and proximity. As we point out later in the chapter, the entrenchment of low-density, auto-dependent real estate in Canadian cities presents a considerable obstacle to their environmental improvement.

Management

The final characteristic of the city we discuss here is 'management', for cities have an intrinsic need for specialized administrations to make them work. In itself the principle of proximity calls for distinct management measures. Urban planning can in fact be traced back to nineteenth-century public health interventions intended to reduce the risk of epidemics in densely built environments (Hodge, 1998: ch. 4). Proximity requires control and co-operation. The smooth functioning of cities relies on infrastructures (transportation, communication, electricity, water mains, and sewers), services (policing and garbage collection), and a battery of legal measures intended to assure orderly cohabitation for a wide variety of land uses. As suggested in the case of built environments, haphazard development decisions can plunge a city into a state of chaos. For example, without planning controls incompatible land uses such as noisy and polluting industry and high-traffic generators could locate in residential areas and new developments could proceed without heeding infrastructural capacity, thus provoking all sorts of bottlenecks. A pure *laissez-faire* approach is clearly not suited to the city.

Different types of administrations have developed over time to provide urban infrastructures, services, and controls. These administrations can be local or regional, or indeed can be lodged in senior governments, as is the case with provincial ministries of municipal affairs. They generally belong to the public sector, but some urban management responsibilities can be vested in community-based or private-sector organizations. As cities grew, as buildings became bigger and required greater infrastructure (roads, water, sewage), as reliance on mechanized forms of transportation (particularly the automobile) increased, and as the public demanded more and better services, administrations responded by becoming larger and more complex—so complex and so costly to maintain that the recent trend has been to 'downsize' governments (municipal or otherwise) and to engage in the privatization of public facilities and services.

As they provide infrastructure, services, and control mechanisms, local and regional administrations keep an eye on the capacity of their interventions to please the electorate and generate investments (and thus raise tax revenues and employment levels). These concerns assure a measure of congruence between the form urban development takes and society-wide economic and social tendencies. One should take care, however, to dispel any impression that urban management takes place in a fashion that is always fair to all economic and social interests. Research points to a tendency for governments to favour economically powerful interests with the capacity to affect tax revenues and employment levels, as well as those groups that can mobilize the electorate. It follows that businesses and wealthy and well-organized neighbourhoods receive better treatment than low-income areas. This is reflected in observed differences in the amount of green space and recreational facilities and in levels of road and park maintenance accorded to neighbourhoods of different social status. Many have also noted a tendency to concentrate locally undesirable land uses (referred to as LULUs in the planning jargon) in low-income districts (e.g., Joseph and Hall, 1985). Social divisions are in fact mirrored in the very structure of municipal administrations. In most cases, suburban municipalities host a higher-income population and enjoy a healthier assessment base (and thus lower tax rates) than central cities. This explains suburbs' vigorous resistance to any form of metropolitan administration that would entail a sharing of their tax revenues with the central city. In the Greater Toronto Area, for example, pressures from out-of-Metro suburbs (those found within the 905 telephone zone) assured their exclusion from the 1998 administrative reorganization that led to the amalgamation of Metro Toronto boroughs.

Limits of present urban management systems are highlighted by difficulties in addressing environmental issues. Some environmental achievements are undeniable. Measures have been taken to prevent soiling the urban nest and threatening residents' health and quality of life. These include emission and effluent controls and the use of zoning to minimize the impact of industries on residential districts. Without such controls, air and water quality within cities as well as urban living conditions would be much poorer than they are now. But the state of the urban environment reflects urban management's limits under present conditions. Because of their interest in maximizing economic development, municipal (as well as senior) governments refrain from imposing environmental policies that firms perceive as too rigid. Likewise, because of their residents' housing and transportation preferences, local governments have steered away from measures to reduce car use and urban sprawl.

Urban Transitions: The Land-Use Dimension

Together, proximity, production, capitalization, and management produce a specifically urban dynamic that causes cities variously to propel or to dampen emerging society-wide trends, in other words, to operate as agents of both change and continuity. Cities provide the playing field where various forces of change come into action. Throughout this volume, authors categorize the periodicity of urban change and transition in different ways, depending on the time-scale and subject-matter under consideration: changes in the Canadian urban hierarchy

(Chapters 2 and 3); phases of downtown development (Chapter 11); the urban employment effect of stages of economic development (Chapter 15); the evolution of urban planning (Chapter 19); changes in cities' political life (Chapter 24). In the present chapter, we discuss twentieth-century transitions, focusing on land use. Three distinct periods of transition can be identified: *city development*, until about the end of World War II; *metropolitan development*, which was dominant from the war to the mid-1970s; and *suburban domination*, which takes us to the present and possibly beyond.

City Development (before 1945)

'City development' refers to the period when what we today call the inner city was developed. In many older metropolitan areas, the inner city coincides roughly with the boundaries of the central city (a metropolitan region's oldest municipality, which occupies its centre). A generic outline of land-use patterns characteristic of city development is provided in Figure 1.1. Spatially, the city development area includes: the central business district (CBD); a 'zone of transition' with a mixed and changing land-use pattern (Preston and Griffin, 1966); factory belts along waterways and railways; and relatively high-density (though not high-rise) residential neighbourhoods, most of them segregated along lines of income, class, and ethnicity. Industrial production was the main impetus of urban growth over this period, though administrative activities played an important role in large centres and resource extraction supported the economy of many communities outside the Canadian heartland.

On the demand side of the 'city development' equation, modest incomes accounted for relatively low rates of home-ownership. Despite the large size of households, domestic space was limited by affordability constraints. Women generally worked unwaged in the home and this, along with limited incomes, attenuated demand for household goods and purchased services. Workers put in long hours. Time (the workweek generally included Saturday), expense, and a general reliance on transit and walk-

Figure 1.1 **City Development Land-Use Patterns (before 1945)**

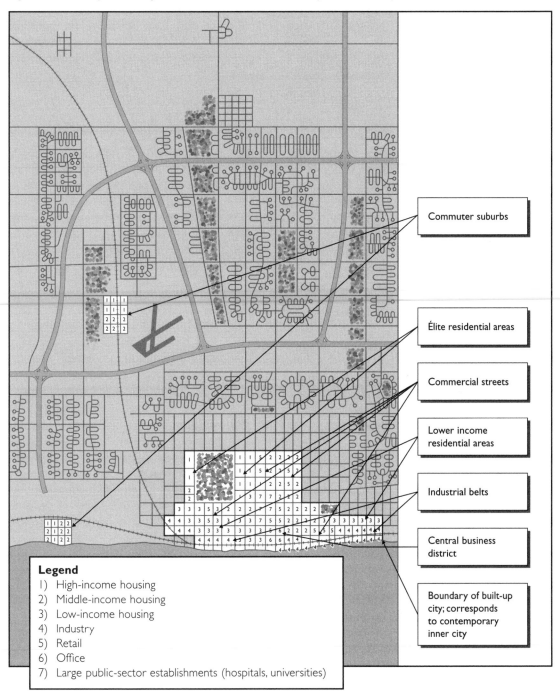

Commuter suburbs

Élite residential areas

Commercial streets

Lower income
residential areas

Industrial belts

Central business
district

Boundary of built-up
city; corresponds
to contemporary
inner city

Legend
1) High-income housing
2) Middle-income housing
3) Low-income housing
4) Industry
5) Retail
6) Office
7) Large public-sector establishments (hospitals, universities)

ing in a period when the car remained the preserve of the rich limited regular journeys to short distances. Accordingly, buildings were closely packed together, residential density was high, distance between home and work was short (except for a small contingent of well-heeled suburban commuters), and various stores for shopping were found along streets throughout the city, at walking distance from virtually every house (Adams, 1970; Colby, 1933; Jacobs, 1961). These streets catered to most shopping needs with the exception of high-order goods found in the CBD. The high density of the built environment also made it easy to walk to schools, medical services, churches, and other facilities. Transit was then composed primarily of fixed-line rail services (streetcars and, in larger cities, commuter trains). Its linearity left a profound mark on the inner city's urban structure and skewed growth outward along its lines (Adams, 1970; Hoyt, 1939; Warner, 1962). The CBD enjoyed unchallenged accessibility, with virtually all transit lines radiating from this point.

The pre-1945 city was characterized by a steep accessibility gradient that peaked at the CBD, the central activity focus, and dropped off rapidly towards transit's outer limit at the edge of the city. Accessibility gradients were mirrored by land values, a consequence of demand levels that varied primarily according to transportation costs. The expression 'distance decay' is used to describe this basic parameter of early twentieth-century urban form. Accessibility, land and real estate values, and population and building density all dropped off rapidly as a function of increased distance from the centre of the city. Accordingly, the CBD concentrated activities that could afford the most expensive land—office buildings, major institutions, and high-order retail and service outlets. These relationships are detailed in Chapter 11.

Like industry, élite residential areas stretched out along radial sectors, but these sectors were found close to amenities such as major institutions, superior transportation facilities, and large parks or attractive landscape features (e.g., water, valleys, scenic views). The neighbourhoods of North Toronto and West

Montreal are good examples. Most of these high-income sectors grew from wealthy neighbourhoods built near the edge of the city in the late-nineteenth century and the first decades of the twentieth century, when pollution and other negative externalities associated with heavy industrial growth made core-area living less desirable (see Beaudet, 1988; Goheen, 1970; Hoyt, 1939). Today many of these neighbourhoods remain the most established élite residential locations, e.g., Westmount in Montreal, Rosedale in Toronto, and Shaughnessey Heights in Vancouver. In direct contrast to high-income housing, working-class residential districts were generally located within walking distance of factories and thus were in close proximity to heavy manufacturing and other less appealing features like railway tracks. Meanwhile, increasingly between the two world wars, some middle-class households took advantage of streetcar and commuter train lines to find a better home environment in so-called 'streetcar suburbs' and commuter train suburbs.

Urban planning before 1945 was not the major force it is today. Most institutionalized planning-related activity was devoted to creating amenities (particularly large parks) under the inspiration of the City Beautiful Movement in the early years of the century (Boyer, 1983: 43–56; Hodge, 1998: 58–63). Zoning was timidly introduced in the early part of the century but its application was limited to certain areas, such as high-income neighbourhoods. Master and official plans were pretty much unknown before the 1950s. The occurrence of mixed-use districts in the older parts of the contemporary city can be traced back to this relative absence of planning. This is not to say that pre-war city development was spatially disorganized. Quite to the contrary, referring again to Figure 1.1, steep transit-induced accessibility gradients dictated clear land-use hierarchies.

Metropolitan Development (1945–1975)

Overall, the 1945–75 period was one of brisk economic and demographic growth. This 'metropolitan' period of urban development was driven by overall economic prosperity achieved through a balancing of the forces of big business, big government, and big unions underpinning heavy reliance on Keynesian policies (see Amin, 1994). This form of economic management resulted in a correspondence between rapid productivity and consumption growth. In terms of urban form, this period marks the time when the term 'metropolitan' was first used in reference to Canadian cities. In its geographic meaning, the term connotes a balance between city and suburban styles of urbanization, between a central city and rapidly growing suburban municipalities (Blumenfeld, 1967; Hitchcock and McMaster, 1985; Hoover and Vernon, 1962). Suburban areas developed over this 30-year period are now generally referred to as 'mature' or 'inner' suburbs. It is easy to distinguish areas built after 1945 from earlier ones because, as a result of the Great Depression of the 1930s and World War II, the 1929–45 period experienced little urban development. On the other hand, this 16-year lull witnessed considerable technological advancements and value changes, which were directly reflected in the composition and style of development in newly urbanized suburbs. The new growth occurred at a dramatic rate, driven by pent-up demand and spiralling population expansion (the baby boom) alongside a period of sustained prosperity.

Widespread home-ownership and increased indoor and outdoor per capita residential space consumption distinguished the suburb from the inner city (Miron, 1988; Spurr, 1976). Over this era, well-paid blue-collar and public-sector workers swelled the ranks of the middle class so that a much higher proportion of families could afford to own their homes. Meanwhile, the production of relatively large homes on relatively large lots (by comparison to earlier residential standards) generated an unprecedented demand for mass-produced goods (cars, furniture, appliances). Lifestyles, characterized as 'modern', were conformist: they were consumer-oriented and centred on the nuclear family and the single-family home (Clark, 1966; Dobriner, 1958; Florida and Feldman, 1988; Hamel, 1993; Harvey, 1989; Muller, 1981; Popenoe, 1977). Another distinctive feature of the new 'suburban' form—increased car ownership and use—was inextricably linked to the rise in residential space and single-family home-ownership. With prosperous times and a proliferation of low-density environments that made automobile travel a necessity rather than a matter of choice or indulgence, automobiles became commonplace. In turn, this abrupt change in travel mode profoundly transformed spatial arrangements, as greatly increased accessibility translated into raised space consumption for all forms of land use.

An enhanced capacity for government intervention marked a profound change in how cities were managed. In the 1950s, professionally trained planners were hired in cities throughout Canada to manage and guide urban growth (Carver, 1962; Chapin, 1965; Cullingworth, 1987; Hodge, 1998; Sewell, 1993). Comprehensive urban planning, with its main tools of zoning by-laws and master plans, configured the new suburb into a car-oriented environment where land use was highly segregated to assure the livability of residential areas. At this time, too, the territory and jurisdiction of municipal governments were reformed so as to marry the 'city' with newer outlying suburban jurisdictions. Governments intervened directly in the urban landscape by building educational establishments, hospitals, subsidized housing, and, most notably, roads and expressways (on the development of suburbs over this period, see Fishman, 1987; Rowe, 1991). The federal government played a prominent role in stimulating suburban development through a mortgage subsidy and guarantee program for new single-family homes (Dennis and Fish, 1972).

It needs to be emphasized that the predominant land use in early suburbs was residential. In fact, suburbs in their first period of development were often spoken of as 'bedroom communities' (Mackenzie and Rose, 1983; Mazy and Lee, 1983; Reisman, 1958). But with previously centralized functions relocating to newly developed areas, suburbs soon came to host a wide range of functions. Figure 1.2 identifies some of the more salient properties of suburban areas developed in the immediate postwar period. The construction of highways and high-

Figure 1.2   **Metropolitan Development Land-Use Patterns (1945–1975)**

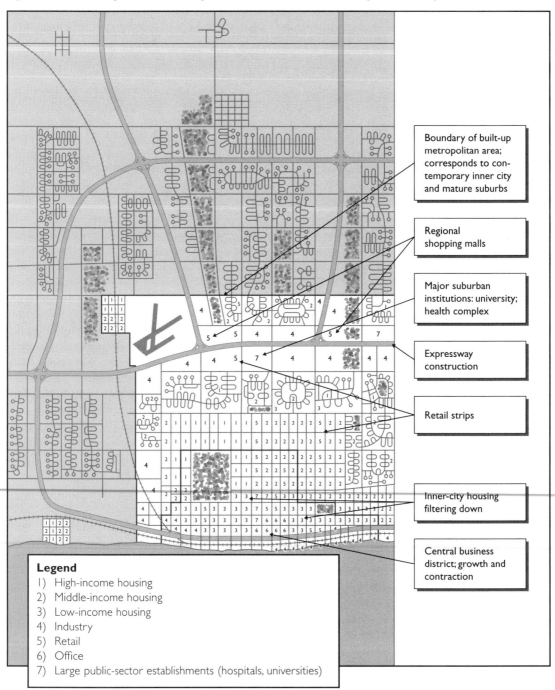

Boundary of built-up metropolitan area; corresponds to contemporary inner city and mature suburbs

Regional shopping malls

Major suburban institutions: university; health complex

Expressway construction

Retail strips

Inner-city housing filtering down

Central business district; growth and contraction

Legend
1) High-income housing
2) Middle-income housing
3) Low-income housing
4) Industry
5) Retail
6) Office
7) Large public-sector establishments (hospitals, universities)

capacity arterials, combined with rising car and truck use, greatly altered accessibility, land value, and density gradients by making them flatter and creating numerous nodes of equivalent importance.

High-accessibility nodes located at major expressway interchanges and arterial intersections became preferred sites for regional malls. Able to secure large catchment areas from such strategic locations, these malls accommodated the largest concentrations of retail establishments, with the exception of CBDs in very large metropolitan regions (Jones, 1991; Jones and Simmons, 1990). Other locations offering good accessibility along, off, or close to high-capacity roads attracted industrial and business parks, small retail malls, and self-standing retail and service establishments (fast-food outlets, car dealerships, gas stations, and so on). Chapters 15 and 17 examine the way this decentralization process was played out on the retail and employment scene. Also attracted to the periphery were space-hungry activities such as university campuses. The list of universities that opted for suburban sites in the 1950s and 1960s includes Université Laval in Quebec City, Carleton University in Ottawa, York University in Toronto, University of Waterloo, University of Calgary, and Simon Fraser University in Vancouver. Suburbs distinguished themselves from the central city in yet another manner by adopting an inwardly focused system of curvilinear streets. Ties with older parts of the city and, for that matter, with other suburban areas were maintained via a limited number of high-capacity expressways and arterial roads (see Figure 1.2).

A generalization of car use and the construction of arterial and expressway networks made it possible for households to reach activities within a greatly enhanced perimeter, thus broadening their choice. But the combination of a dispersion of activities and lower density was damaging to transit (Bottles, 1987; Cevero, 1986, 1989). When public transit was extended to the suburb, deficits soared because densities were insufficient and origins and destinations too scattered to generate the level of patronage required to support effective services (see, e.g., Pushkarev and Zupan, 1977).

Quality of life in inner-city neighbourhoods suffered considerably from efforts to improve suburban commuters' accessibility to the CBD. Most dramatic was the impact of expressway construction (Nowlan and Nowlan, 1970). Another consequence of suburban development was a dramatic fall in the CBD's share of metropolitan sales once regional malls became well established. Moreover, the exodus of much of the middle class towards the suburbs triggered a 'filtering down' of inner-city housing (that is, a decline in households' socio-economic status, conversions of single-family units into multi-family accommodation, and subsequent physical deterioration of an aging housing stock) (see Figure 1.2 and Chapter 16, Figure 16.2). Perceived decline in older housing stocks was a major incentive for urban renewal schemes that demolished existing structures to make way occasionally for public housing, but more frequently for private redevelopment (Birch, 1971; Bourne, 1967; Dennis and Fish, 1972; Hoover and Vernon, 1962; Miron, 1992; Smith, 1964). It must be stressed that the proverbial inner-city blight was more characteristic of American than Canadian cities (Chapter 3 elaborates on this point). Many Canadian inner cities were fortunate in that the period of rapid suburbanization coincided with a huge wave of immigration. This initiated a cycle of private home renovation in older inner-city neighbourhoods that would later find its fullest expression in the process of gentrification (see Chapter 12 on inner-city change).

Over the 1945–75 period, downtown redevelopment was encouraged by massive public-sector investment in widening roads and, in larger agglomerations, public transit. The erection of highly symbolic public buildings such as the new City Hall in Toronto and Place des Arts in Montreal was intended to improve the image of the core. Redevelopment was also promoted by liberal zoning regulations authorizing high-rise structures over much of the inner city (Bourne, 1967; Leo, 1994; Sewell, 1993). In the larger agglomerations, 1960–75 was a time of feverish office employment growth in the CBD, made obvious by much altered cityscapes profiled by new towers (see Chapter 11; also Code,

1983; Gad, 1991). Core-area retailing was also transformed. In virtually every Canadian downtown, malls now reproduced conditions offered by their suburban counterparts (Curtis, 1994; Frieden and Sagalyn, 1989; Paumier, 1988; Redstone, 1976). Thanks to such developments, many CBDs were able to maintain or even increase their absolute retail activity level, at least for a time. Everywhere, however, massive suburban retail developments caused a serious drop in the relative weight of downtown cores within the metropolitan-wide retail marketplace.

On the whole, the 30-year period of metropolitan development favoured the suburb over the central city. Increasingly, over the years 1945–75, a growing dependence on the car, a taste for modernism, and a drive to accumulate durable goods placed the higher-density inner city at a disadvantage relative to the spacious suburb. It is not surprising that so many middle-class households, businesses, and even major public institutions opted for suburban locations.

Suburban Domination (1975–21st Century)

The contemporary, post-1975 period is the time when the suburbs surpass the central city in terms of sheer population size, as well as in retail activity, manufacturing, and later office and public institution employment. Despite the enduring symbolic pre-eminence of the central business district in the largest cities, Canadian metropolitan areas have followed the trend set earlier in the US so that most economic activity is now based in the suburbs (Baldassare, 1986; Bourne, 1989; Bunting and Filion, 1999; Knox, 1994; Muller, 1981). In addition, dispersed styles of suburbanization over this period have resulted in a rate of outward physical expansion that far exceeds demographic growth. Even cities that saw little population increase over this period experienced considerable peripheral suburban development. The dense inner-city environment with its heavy reliance on walking and public transit has become a subsidiary urban form within an agglomeration dominated by suburban, car-ori-

ented land uses. In these circumstances, the implication that *sub*urban territory is dependent on, or in any way lesser than, the central city is inappropriate. In this sense, continued use of the term 'suburban' is a misnomer (Evenden and Walker, 1993; Kling, Olin, and Poster, 1991; Knox, 1994).

By 1975, hubs enjoying metropolitan-wide accessibility had multiplied throughout the suburbs. The transportation/land-use pattern inherited from the previous period had become the norm, enhanced in most larger metropolitan areas by an expanded expressway system. Densities in the inner zones are markedly lower than in earlier periods, though the drop tends to have stabilized after 1981. There has been infilling in many suburban areas, reflecting, among other things, the attraction of expressway-induced accessibility. Overall, the low densities of the outermost suburbs perpetuate the pattern set in the early postwar period. Today, any expressway exit constitutes a high-accessibility site, and any location within a 15-minute drive from such an exit offers adequate accessibility for housing. The lessening of accessibility constraints on location produces the complex land-use patchwork quilt that characterizes contemporary suburban areas. Specialized zones come in different sizes and are juxtaposed in apparent random fashion, which makes it more difficult to grasp the urban structure of the contemporary metropolis than that of earlier urban forms (Filion and Bunting, 1990; Filion, Bunting, and Curtis, 1996). There is a sharp contrast between the apparent standardization and repetition of the suburban landscape as seen from the street and the intricacy of this type of environment when observed from the air. Another outcome of this transportation/land-use dynamic is a further extension of access to rural hinterlands surrounding metropolitan regions. The movement of activities like employment and shopping to the outer edge of a city's built perimeter encourages residential relocation to rural areas within commuting range of the urban periphery (Coppack, Russwurm, and Bryant, 1988; Joseph, Keddie, and Smit, 1988). As discussed in Chapter 14, this growth in 'urban' rural living in turn transforms the retail and service landscape of those villages that cater to the tastes of former city dwellers as well as to those of visitors from nearby larger places (Coppack, 1988; Mitchell, 1992).

As suggested in Figure 1.3, land-use arrangements changed with the transition from 'metropolitan balance' to 'suburban domination'. A number of innovations distinguish the current period from the preceding one. With the decentralization of offices, the post-1975 period witnesses the creation of suburban business (or office) parks and, more recently, the emergence of so-called suburban downtowns that combine office and retail concentrations with civic centres, generally smaller in scale but comparable in many respects to so-called US 'edge cities' (Cevero, 1989; Garreau, 1991; Kling, Olin, and Poster, 1991; Stanback, 1991). On the retail scene, the appearance of factory outlets, 'big-box' stores, and 'power malls' perturbs the shopping centre hierarchy (local, community, regional) inherited from the previous period (Berry, 1963; Brown, 1992; Dawson and Lord, 1985; Guy, 1994; Howe and Rabiega, 1992; Jones and Simmons, 1990). These establishments achieve unprecedented size for specialized outlets and thus enjoy substantial economies of scale. They opt for relatively inexpensive but highly accessible sites, usually near one or more expressways. This locational advantage, along with their strong appeal in terms of price and merchandise variety, allows the new big-box stores and power malls to capture catchment areas that greatly exceed those of regional malls.

In contrast to substantial retailing transformations, residential communities built over the last 25 years conform generally to the pattern of the previous period. This does not prevent new residential areas from incorporating certain innovations, however. Most significant is a heightened environmental awareness that translates in some subdivisions into measures to protect water quality and to preserve natural settings along marshes, streams, ponds, lakes, and rivers (see Chapter 21). There is also a tendency to safeguard other environmentally significant areas, such as woods and other natural habitats. The outcome is more and different forms of green space than in standard forms of subdivi-

sions. Another trend is seen in the appearance of 'neo-traditional' communities. The neo-traditional movement promotes the creation of neighbourhoods that replicate positive features of pre-war forms of urbanization: a main street, less visual intrusion of the car, vernacular architectural styles, picket fences, etc. Presently, though numerous new developments borrow some elements of neo-traditionalism, there have been few attempts in Canada to create full-fledged neo-traditional neighbourhoods (examples of such projects include Mackenzietown in Calgary and, in southern Ontario, Cornell in Markham, River Oaks in Oakville, and Montgomery Village in Orangeville). Despite all the media hype, however, there is no evidence to date to support the contention that this form of development is able to induce, as intended, a marked increase in walking and transit use.

The suburbs, as a whole, have become more socially heterogeneous (Miron, 1988; Poulton, 1995). For one thing, as pointed out in Chapter 13, there is now a great amount of ethnic and racial diversity in the suburbs. The drift of social housing towards 'greenfield' sites in the 1960s and 1970s has also created distinct pockets of poverty. Some older suburbs have undergone 'filtering down' as the original occupants have been replaced over time (Conrad, 1996; Gutowski and Field, 1979; Vischer, 1987). Other suburban communities, in contrast, have experienced a new kind of filtering up as 'mega-homes' replace the original stock in some of the more desirable suburban locales.

One obvious tension inherent in the postwar suburban-dominated urban structure is the dissonance between the ongoing currency of suburban development, an urban form that is costly to build and maintain, and a slowing down of the economy after the early 1970s, which translates into reduced employment security and descending wages (Donner, 1991). Even middle-class families face increasing difficulties in juggling the purchasing and upkeep expenses of their suburban houses and their cars (often, one per adult household member), though clearly, these difficulties pale in comparison to the problems the poor encounter. For them,

Figure 1.3   **Suburban Domination Land-Use Patterns (1975–21st Century)**

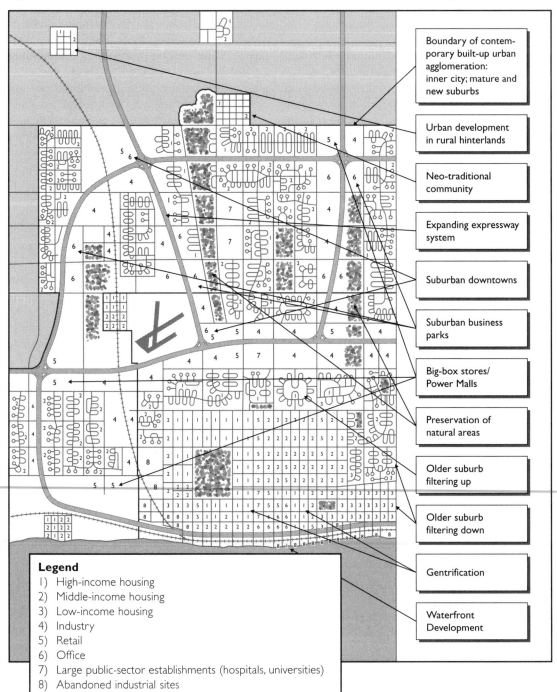

Boundary of contemporary built-up urban agglomeration: inner city; mature and new suburbs

Urban development in rural hinterlands

Neo-traditional community

Expanding expressway system

Suburban downtowns

Suburban business parks

Big-box stores/ Power Malls

Preservation of natural areas

Older suburb filtering up

Older suburb filtering down

Gentrification

Waterfront Development

Legend
1) High-income housing
2) Middle-income housing
3) Low-income housing
4) Industry
5) Retail
6) Office
7) Large public-sector establishments (hospitals, universities)
8) Abandoned industrial sites

transportation can be an unsurmountable obstacle, and insufficient affordable housing is widely reputed to result in doubling up and homelessness (see Chapter 23).

At the same time, economic stringency (and, to a lesser extent, public protest) makes it increasingly difficult for the public sector to provide the massive infrastructure called for by the dispersed suburban form. Lack of funds to build sufficient arterial roads and expressways goes a long way in explaining the relentless traffic congestion that plagues all larger metropolitan regions. Harsh government financial conditions also account for the gap between demographic growth and the provision of public services, such as schools and hospitals, in newly urbanized areas. This financial hardship equally reverberates on the inner city. Transit services in most Canadian cities have been cut back and governments are less able than in the past to compensate for the effects of urban decentralization on central areas (Frisken, 1994). To deal with these financial difficulties, whether suburban or central city in locus, governments presently explore different forms of privatization and partnership (Frieden and Sagalyn, 1989). But it remains difficult to see how such formulas would reduce substantially consumer expenses associated with the suburban model of development.

There is further incongruity between present forms of urbanization and society-wide tendencies. The suburban landscape, which now comprises the vast majority of the urbanized perimeter, does not express the diversity of lifestyles and values characteristic of contemporary life. Generally, within the suburban realm housing types and neighbourhoods are differentiated according to the income of their residents and, to a lesser extent, their life cycle, rather than according to lifestyle and values. This is why, as discussed more fully in Chapters 12 and 22, individuals espousing alternative lifestyles and values tend to opt for the inner city because they are unable to see their distinct identity reflected within the suburban realm.

Another difficulty with the suburban form of urbanization is that, despite efforts to make it more environmentally sound, it generates ever more car and truck traffic and is thus responsible for worsening emission problems, which culminate in intolerable air pollution, especially on hot sunny days. There is a paradox to this form of urbanization: while it appears to be environmentally benign by virtue of its abundant green space, it is in reality a major source of air pollution. Environmentalists maintain that this type of city is not sustainable because of the large amount of natural resources it requires for its day-to-day operation. In their view, it is only a matter of time until this urban form falls victim to either a scarcity of resources or increasingly injurious levels of pollution.

The impact of suburban domination on the inner city has been more varied than in the immediate postwar period, when decline and government-sponsored renewal were in evidence. Over the post-1975 period, there is a stark discrepancy between the ascending trajectory of attractive, prosperous inner-city sites in large metropolitan areas with well-developed public transit systems and the decline of sites that lack appealing features and/or are found in medium or small, car-dependent, metropolitan regions. Inner-city areas of less prosperous agglomerations also fare poorly. This divergence results from a growing importance of market trends relative to government intervention in a context of fiscal stringency. Many facets of the post-industrial, advanced service sector favour core area locations. Where circumstances are favourable, gentrification and luxury condominium infill predominate and public-private partnerships lead to large-scale redevelopment, as seen in many waterfront redevelopment complexes. Elsewhere, socio-economic descent endures, former industrial sites are left in a derelict state, and street-front vacancy is the order of the day on the 'main street' (e.g., in Hamilton, Kitchener, and Winnipeg). In the post-1975 market-driven inner city, some sectors win, others lose.

Across the board, the planning of cities over the most recent period tends to have been fragmented. Within the contemporary Canadian agglomeration, the attentive planning of individual subdivisions contrasts with poorly co-ordinated growth and infrastructure development at a metropolitan scale. This situation is largely due to the absence in all large Canadian metropolitan regions of agencies capable of formulating and implementing plans on a regional scale. The problem is that few municipal administrations are willing to relinquish power to a metropolitan-wide agency. Suburban administrations, which are concerned about possible limitations on their expansion and a sharing of their tax base with fiscally ailing central cities, are especially averse to any form of influential metropolitan agency.

Transition and Continuity

Table 1.1 summarizes the trends outlined above in conjunction with the urban properties that were discussed at the outset of this chapter. It provides a framework from which we can conceptualize the transitions and continuities that mark the evolution of Canadian metropolitan regions over the three periods we respectively term 'city development', 'metropolitan development', and 'suburban domination'. The table underscores the sharp transitions that distinguish the pre-1945 and 1945–75 periods of development. The nature of proximity and its influence on land use changed radically between the two periods. Before 1945 the geographic range of frequently repeated exchanges was limited by the distance one could walk or travel on public transportation, which necessitated a dense urban environment. Steep accessibility and land-use gradients focused on the CBD, which became, de facto, the uncontested agglomeration-wide activity centre. All this changed when generalized car and truck use and massive road investments extended accessibility and promoted the emergence of suburban centres of activity, which, in turn, resulted in a relative and often absolute decline of the CBD.

A second distinction between the 'city' and 'metropolitan' eras was witnessed in a profound change in the location of production. Over both periods, urban areas exported primarily manufactured products and economic (and in certain cases, political) control. However, while manufacturing was concentrated along waterways and railways before 1945, after this time such establishments depended on truck transport and opted for low-density suburban industrial parks. Also, as we progressed into the second half of the twentieth century, the role of manufacturing in the Canadian urban economy (as everywhere in developed economies) diminished relative to that of services. The expansion of the service sector manifested itself in increasing amounts of office space, shopping centres, and public institutions in the post-1945 urban landscape.

The capitalized built environment represents a third feature reflecting the deep urban transformation associated with the transition from city to metropolitan form. Prevailing transportation modes assured the enduring functionality of higher-density, mixed land-use districts over the first period. The situation changed abruptly when rapidly ascending car and truck use and a predilection for greater space consumption modified urban development norms. The new suburban environment was expensive to produce and maintain, but this did not cause major problems in the generally prosperous 1945–75 period.

Finally, from an urban management perspective, it is notable that city development required relatively little public intervention apart from the provision of basic infrastructure. Land-use control and planning were minimal by comparison to what was to follow. It is also worth noting that since most development was then occurring within the administrative boundaries of the central city (often expanded through annexation), co-ordination problems at the scale of the agglomeration were minimal. By contrast, over the second period all new development was planned. Meanwhile, however, metropolitan-wide co-ordination was jeopardized in most agglomerations by the tendency for growth to take place in independent suburban municipalities. The high infrastructure expenses associated with the postwar model of urbanization necessitated a sizeable financial involvement on the part of senior levels of government, especially in the sectors of housing, transportation, and central city redevelopment.

Table 1.1	**Evolution of Canadian Urban Form**		
Urban Properties	Pre-1945	1945–75	1975–21st Century
Proximity	Proximity determined by walking and public transportation, which results in a strong CBD, steep accessibility and land value gradients, and tight urban texture.	The accessibility range is vastly expanded by the car and new road networks. This causes flatter accessibility and land value gradients and a decentralization of activities.	The suburban land-use pattern becomes dominant. Ongoing flattening of accessibility and land value gradients. Reduced constraints on location. Congestion is compensated by a dispersion of activities.
Production	Manufacturing is a major source of employment in many cities. Reliance on waterways and railways for freight transportation. Larger agglomerations export control functions from downtown establishments.	Manufacturing relocates in suburban industrial parks. Heavy dependence on trucks. Increasing importance of the service sector translates into service centres in suburbs and office development in both the CBD and suburbs.	More flexible forms of production, intense truck-based linkage patterns. Added importance of service sector leads to more and larger suburban concentrations than over the previous period. The advanced service sector favours core area sites in large metropolitan areas.
Capitalization	Blends earlier urban forms because of sufficient compatibility.	Generalization of a new, costly form of urban development and adaptation of some older areas to emerging production and consumption standards. This urban form is consistent with the economic climate of the time.	The high cost of the suburban form of urbanization causes tensions for households and governments in a more difficult economic context.
Management	Provision of basic infrastructures but little land-use control. The central city controls most of the built-up area.	Intense infrastructure development and land-use control. Urban renewal. Co-ordination problems at the metropolitan scale.	Same approach as over previous period, but less urban renewal and difficult to maintain required levels of expenditure on urban infrastructures and services. Increased co-ordination problems at the metropolitan scale.

By contrast to the sharp transition between the two types of urbanization, continuity marks the passage from 'metropolitan development' to 'suburban domination'. Over both periods, proximity requirements are relaxed by a generalization of car and truck use. The differences characterizing the contemporary phase are: (1) a heavier reliance on cars and trucks; and (2) an advancing adaptation of the urban landscape to this transportation context. This causes a further depletion of the relative importance of the CBD and the emergence of more and larger suburban centres of activity. In the production sphere, the suburban-dominant period experiences the ongoing postwar shift from manufacturing to services, reflected in the appearance of different forms of suburban service centres ranging from business 'parks' to suburban 'downtowns'. While in the largest metropolitan agglomerations the advanced service sector exhibits locational attraction to sites in and around downtown, manufacturing maintains its suburbanization trend and further increases its dependence on the truck, which explains increasing truck traffic on urban arterials and expressways.

Overall, the suburban built environment fashioned over the previous periods remains the dominant form of urbanization. Its high production and maintenance expense is, however, a source of problems both for households and for government in a context of household income stagnation and public-sector cutbacks. This takes us to the final urban characteristic—management. While governments continue to adopt infrastructure and land-use control policies that contribute to the perpetuation of the postwar suburban model of urbanization, doubts are increasingly raised about its economic and environmental sustainability. Meanwhile, development co-ordination difficulties seem to be worsening as large metropolitan regions further expand without effective metropolitan-wide planning agencies.

In summary, we have observed a sharp transition in pre- and postwar urban form, followed by relative continuity. Changes between the 'metropolitan development' and the 'suburban domination' periods are the outcome of an ongoing expansion of the postwar realm rather than of the introduction of new urban development models. By comparison to the deep transformation that demarcated pre-war from postwar urbanization, transitions between the 'metropolitan balance' and 'suburban-dominant' periods have been subtle, resulting from an ongoing advancement of suburban-style urbanization introduced after the war. This continuity is tied to the urban dynamic that emanates from the interaction of low density, car use, and activity decentralization. The location choices and daily behaviour of individuals and organizations operating within the suburban environment perpetuate this dynamic (Isin and Tomalty, 1993; Leung, 1993; Mary McDonough Associates, 1994; Skelton et al., 1995).

Future Transitions in the Canadian City

At this vantage point—the retrospective view of a century of changing, indeed turbulent, urban development—it is possible to discern in each of the foregoing characteristics of the city an interplay of contending forces. These are particularly visible in urban Canada because our cities are truly the products of industrial and post-industrial society. Here, the impact of these relatively recent but pervasive cultures are transparent, writ large on the landscape for all to see, without the detracting charms of other eras—say, of the Renaissance in Florence or Paris.

The analysis of proximity as a factor in city development leads to the paradoxical insight that the proximity principle—the concentration of individuals and activities to optimize communication and minimize the cost of all kinds of interaction—is in strenuous contest in our cities with the dispersion principle, the outward thrust of people, activities, and land uses in search of cheaper land, transportation convenience, space amenities, or speculative opportunity (see Chapters 2 and 8). A difficulty with dispersion is its mounting costs—in time, money, energy, loss of productive farmland, and environmental degradation. The ecological footprint of a Montreal, Toronto, or Vancouver is, indeed, territorially extensive, but with growth and expansion, dependence on the life supports of land, water, and air becomes progressively more critical. Ultimately, we are bound by basics. There is no free lunch.

The end-of-century view of production leads to another dichotomy. On the one hand, the prominence of electronics and the associated industrial/service superstructure, which is the hallmark of our times, have the potential to provide unprecedented empowerment of people through information and knowledge. On the other hand, computer communications linked to aggrandizing corporate culture becomes an instrument for domination and control. Production and services are readily decentralized, while authority, decision-making, and many supporting arms of the advanced service sector are anchored in the big city head office. This phenomenon occurs at all levels: regional, national, and international. The nature and role of the city of the future may, indeed, be shaped by the interplay of these endemic forces (Gertler, 1989). The employment trend has been authoritatively charted as 'segmentation of the labour force into relatively permanent and well-paid workers and disposable low-paid employees' and 'polarization' (Chapter 15). According to Yalnizyan (1998: x–xi) three sets of data are particularly noteworthy:

The Rich are Richer: In 1973, the richest 10% of families with children under 18 made 21 times more than the poorest 10% of Canadian families. In 1996, the richest 10% of families made 314 times the poorest 10% of Canadian families.

Shrinking Middle Class: In 1973, 60% of families with children under 18 earned between $24,500 and $65,000 (in 1996 dollars). By 1996, that middle class shrunk: only 44% of families with dependent children made between $24,500 and $65,000.

Women and Work: . . . Two-thirds of mothers with children under three are in the labour force, compared to one-third a generation ago.

Alongside these shifts are distinctive changes in the Canadian labour market. First we see a shift away from regular full-time employment—in 1976, 65 per cent worked between 35 and 40 hours a week; by 1997, 54 per cent. A second trend is towards more part-time work—in the mid-1970s one in ten jobs; in 1997, one in five jobs. A third change is the increasing importance of self-employment. Of the total net new employment between 1993 and 1997, over half came from self-employment; and in the latter two years, the figures were 76 and 83 per cent (Yalnizyan, 1998). Income polarization trends are well established. What is more difficult to forecast are the social and political dynamics, and the consequences for urban life, arising from these unfolding changes.

In the field of built-environment capitalization, the emerging contest appears to be between knee-jerk responses to immediate pressures for more of the same, that is, suburbanization with all its attendant pitfalls, and knowledge-based investment sensitive to current and longer-term needs and to the great human diversity in the contemporary Canadian city: socially, culturally, ethnically. The very durability, longevity, high cost, and relative irreversibility of urban infrastructure underscore the importance of wise planning. We can anticipate that the impact of polarization on the built environment will be felt in different ways. There will be winning places, those at the periphery of metropolitan areas and beyond that host emerging economic sectors such as high-tech industries, research and development, and their workers. Moreover, corporate command and financial functions will secure the health of large metropolitan regions' CBDs and of the neighbourhoods housing their high-status workers. But by contrast, urban sectors associated with declining industries will filter down, possibly to the ultimate 'abandonment' stage, as has happened in some US cities. If it carries on unabated, polarization will thus translate into a dual city, where the wealthy will shield themselves from the poor, using distance and strategies such as 'gated' communities to do so. Yet another consequence of polarization with deleterious consequences for quality of life will be the difficulty for low-income areas to generate sufficient taxes to maintain the costly infrastructures and services needed to support dispersed urbanization. In the face of fiscal constraints, a coherent image of the city as a basis for investment and of how it must be restructured will be critical.

The challenge of management arises out of the divergent requirements of each of the aforementioned urban characteristics. With the rise of social and economic issues, as indicated in the perspectives on production and capitalization, the administration of cities, in the interest of equity and efficiency, will have to be effective over complete areas of urban settlement and their surroundings. This will be particularly important for functions related to planning—for projecting a coherent image of the city, for major infrastructure investments, and for economic development. The city's changing social structure will impinge on that administration as it struggles to fulfil its 'public interest' mandate in the face of the contrary forces of power and privilege and ordinary citizens struggling to make a living.

In coming decades, urban management will turn its attention to two components of cities that had long been taken for granted: their people (in particular, their production capacity) and the environment. The disturbing irony of the emerging Canadian social condition is that just when a knowledge-based economy dictates programs that extend opportunities for upgrading the quality of human resources, access to education is becoming more restricted. For example, partly as a result of federal government Canadian Health and Social Transfer cutbacks, average tuition fees at Ontario universities rose 60 per cent between 1995 and 1997, which was to a level in Arts and Science that is 200 per cent higher than in 1982 (Yalnizyan, 1998). In this light, sustaining a decent quality of life in our cities will supersede the management capabilities of cities alone. It will require a high degree of co-ordination, and the orchestration of policies, among all levels of governance.

Unfortunately, in this new century it is necessary to admit that most of our Canadian cities, in spite of all the sophistication of our building and planning professions and industry, are environmentally precarious. They are not sustainable. The pre-

dominance of dispersion, together with the differentiation and segregation of land uses (residential, shopping centres, industrial parks), has produced an urban form highly dependent on the automobile. And the devilish reality is that this marvellous machine, this icon of contemporary technology, which provides unprecedented mobility and supports an industry that is one of the mainstays of the Canadian economy, is also a major source of atmospheric pollution and of emissions of carbon dioxide, the dominant 'greenhouse gas' contributing to global warming and global climate change (Chapters 8 and 21). But the environmental critique goes deeper: the modern industrial city is an ecological dead end (Hahn and Simonis, 1991). It contaminates its own and surrounding environments, countering natural processes, and it does so at a high monetary cost. The problem is structural and will not yield to crisis management. Nothing less than a policy of urban ecological restructuring is called for to deal with energy, water, sewage, habitat, biodiversity, environmental gradients, soil and food production, wetlands, and watersheds, alongside the economic, social, and land-use factors involved in regional urban design (Chapter 21).

The twenty-first century transition to essential innovation in the form and management of cities will not be an easy passage. But we can take heart from the historians and philosophers of the city who have found that the very characteristics of the city here explored have been associated with most of the epiphanies—the high points—of human civilization.

Canadian Cities in Transition: A Guide to the Text

The perspective on the city offered in this volume is primarily centred on the disciplines of urban geography—because of its contribution to understanding spatial and economic structure—and urban planning—because it represents the active development or structuring arm of a city. But the study of the urban phenomenon is inherently multidisciplinary. Depending on their topics, some chapters draw heavily from such disciplines as economics (Chapters 6,

7, and 15), engineering (Chapter 8), sociology (Chapters 9, 22, and 23), political science (Chapter 18), and ecology (Chapter 21). This broad introductory discussion finds a sequel in a second scope-setting chapter, Chapter 2. Using population change and other statistical markers, Larry Bourne provides an empirically based outline of Canadian cities' growth patterns over the course of the twentieth century and suggests an agenda for the next. The remainder of the volume is organized into six sections.

Issues of change and transition at the national scale are the object of Part One, 'The Context: Urban Systems'. In Chapter 3 John Mercer and Kim England sharpen our thinking about Canadian cities by comparing patterns in urban Canada with those witnessed in American cities. Some of their arguments derive from the classic work *The Myth of the North American City* (Goldberg and Mercer, 1986) and speak to broad similarities as well as profound differences in urban development in the two countries. Chapters 4 and 5, by Larry McCann and Jim Simmons, are concerned with external city structure. These chapters chart the interrelationships that have developed among the cities that make up the Canadian urban system. Chapter 4 provides a historic overview of the evolution of the Canadian urban system. Chapter 5 elaborates on contemporary organization and change in this system. William Coffey, in Chapter 6, focuses on the restructuring economy of Canadian cities, emphasizing that cities are first and foremost economic systems. This chapter sets the scope for many of the subsequent chapters, which explore urban changes influenced by the shifting nature of urban economic development.

In the second and subsequent sections of this volume the area of interest moves to the intra-urban scale. Part Two, 'City-Wide Processes', is concerned with the forces that shape cities' internal structure. In Chapter 7, John Miron looks at how urban land takes on value and how the urban real estate market works. This chapter explains how and why land is bought and sold, developed, and redeveloped. Chapter 8 explains how the configuration of the built environment and land-use/activity patterns determine transport demand, and how the location

and quality of existing transportation facilities determine what gets built and where it gets built. In this chapter, Eric Miller introduces us to the transportation planning process. He also highlights the environmental peril associated with continued development of the low-density, auto-dependent suburban forms that are so integral to present urban society. Chapter 9, by Robert Murdie and Carlos Teixera, looks at urban social geography. This chapter enlightens us as to how change and transition in social categories (life cycle, household categories, income, and ethnicity) are reflected in changing patterns of social space. The chapter gives particular attention to the important role that immigration has played in the distinctive social geography of Canadian cities. The subject-matter for Sherry Olson in Chapter 10 is the urban physical environment—the land, the buildings and architecture, their use and abuse, distinguishing features of the natural and built environment that symbolize an individual city's image and, of course, change. This chapter also considers the environmental consequences of current built forms.

Part Three, 'The Internal Geography of the City', describes the different parts of the contemporary metropolis, which reflect distinct phases of urbanization as described in the present chapter and illustrated by Figures 1.1, 1.2, and 1.3. The section begins at the centre of the city by focusing on downtowns. Chapter 11, by Gunter Gad and Malcolm Matthew, concerns transition in the evolution of downtowns. It looks at change both in the traditional central city downtown and in its recent suburban counterparts. In Chapter 12, David Ley examines the inner city, which is seen to be 'chaotic' to the extent that it manifests the contradictions and tensions inherent in the shift to a post-industrial, post-modern urban society. In Chapter 13, on suburbs, Peter J. Smith explains the profound shift in intra-urban spatial organization that came about after World War II with widespread prosperity and automobile ownership and the advent of institutionalized planning. This chapter also highlights the functional and socio-economic diversification characteristic of Canadian suburban development over the last decades. Christopher Bryant, Philip Coppack, and Clare Mitchell discuss in Chapter 14 the zone outside the built-up city that looks rural but has a functional base that is primarily urban. It is this zone's natural environment that attracts urbanites. But these areas are undergoing severe environmental degradation because of intense development pressures that urban encroachment brings.

Part Four, 'Land Uses and Activities', is divided along functional lines. It describes three broad categories of activities inherent to cities that play a critical role in determining their size, internal structure, and evolution. The first chapter in this section, Chapter 15, by Pierre Filion and Tod Rutherford, deals with the changing nature of work and of workplace locations. It is followed by Richard Harris's chapter on housing and a chapter on retailing by Ken Jones. These chapters relate changes in these activities and land uses to broad social and economic trends and demonstrate how employment, housing, and retail establishments have contributed to urban dispersion. They are equally concerned with how we will manage the new trends facing housing, work, and retailing in the new century.

In Part Five, 'Governance and Planning', the management principle discussed in this chapter is examined in detail. Chapters in this section deal with decision-making processes pertaining to infrastructure and service provision, as well as to controls needed to assure an acceptable quality of life in the city. Andrew Sancton, in Chapter 18, explores the organization, role, and operation of local government. Sancton addresses current issues facing this level: downloading on the part of senior governments and attempts at municipal government reor-

ganization. The two following chapters concentrate on urban planning. In Chapter 19, Jill Grant provides an overview of the history of Canadian planning, including recent developments, describes the operation of contemporary planning processes, and links these with observable urban outcomes. In Chapter 20, Walter Jamieson, Adela Cosijn, and Susan Friesen address contemporary issues confronting urban planning, such as urban dispersion and car dominance, loss of sense of place, environmental damage, and ineffective public participation.

Finally, Part Six, 'Pressing Issues', considers some of the significant problems and perplexities facing Canadian cities today. Mary Ellen Tyler, in Chapter 21, reviews the state of environmental thinking and research concerning urban areas. She also offers examples of planning innovations that minimize the environmental impact of urban development. In the next chapter, Damaris Rose and Brian Ray look at gender and sexual orientation as representative of social issues that demand recognition in urban places where minority groups have traditionally been marginalized. One message to come out of this chapter is that cities must adapt to a growing variety of needs and lifestyles. Chapter 23, by Tracy Peressini and Lynn McDonald, considers the growing ranks of the underclass. This chapter deals with spaces of marginality in cities, including the spaces of the homeless. In the final chapter, Paul Villeneuve and Anne-Marie Séguin focus on the exercise of power in Canadian cities. They emphasize the uneven capacity of people, according to gender and social class, to influence policy-making, and detail the evolution of the municipal political scene over the last decades.

References

Adams, J.S. 1970. 'Residential Structure of Mid-Western Cities', *Annals, Association of American Geographers* 60: 37–62.

Amin, A., ed. 1994. *Post-Fordism: A Reader*. Oxford: Basil Blackwell.

Baldassare, M. 1986. *Trouble in Paradise: The Suburban Transformation in America*. New York: Columbia University Press.

Beaudet, P. 1988. 'Elite Residential Areas in Toronto and Buffalo: Comparative Examples from United

States and Canadian Cities', in T. Bunting and P. Filion, eds, *The Changing Canadian Inner City*. Waterloo: University of Waterloo Department of Geography Publication Series No. 31.

Berry, B.J.L. 1963. *Commercial Structure and Commercial Blight: Retail Patterns and Process.* Chicago: University of Chicago Department of Geography Research Paper No. 85.

Birch, D. 1971. 'Toward a Stage Model of Urban Growth', *Journal of the American Institute of Planners* 37: 78–87.

Blumenfeld, H. 1967. *The Modern Metropolis.* Cambridge, Mass.: MIT Press.

Bottles, S. 1987. *Los Angeles and the Automobile: The Making of a Modern City.* Berkeley: University of California Press.

Bourne, L.S. 1967. *Private Redevelopment of the Central City.* Chicago: University of Chicago Department of Geography Research Paper No. 112.

———. 1989. 'Are New Urban Forms Emerging? Empirical Tests for Canadian Urban Areas', *Canadian Geographer* 33: 312–28.

Boyer, M.C. 1983. *Dreaming the Rational City: The Myth of American City Planning.* Cambridge, Mass.: MIT Press.

Brown, S. 1992. *Retail Location: A Micro-Scale Perspective.* Aldershot: Ashgate Publishing.

Bunting, T., and P. Filion. 1999. 'Dispersed City Form in Canada: A Kitchener CMA Case Study', *Canadian Geographer* 43: 268–87.

Carver, H. 1962. *Cities in the Suburbs.* Toronto: University of Toronto Press.

Cevero, R. 1986 'Urban Transit in Canada: Integration and Innovation at its Best', *Transportation Quarterly* 40: 293–316.

———. 1989. *America's Suburban Centers: The Land-Use Transportation Link.* London: Unwin Hyman.

Chapin, S.F. 1965. *Urban Land Use Planning.* Urbana: University of Illinois Press.

Clark, S.D. 1966. *The Suburban Society.* Toronto: University of Toronto Press.

Code, W.R. 1983. 'The Strength of the Centre: Downtown Offices and Metropolitan Decentralization in Toronto', *Environment and Planning A* 15: 1361–80.

Colby, C. 1933. 'Centripetal and Centrifugal Forces in Urban Geography', *Annals, Association of American Geographers* 23: 1–20.

Conrad, S. 1996. 'Recycled Suburbs: The Case of Kitchener in a New Suburban Area', in P. Filion, T. Bunting, and K. Curtis, eds, *The Dynamics of the Dispersed City: Geography and Planning Perspectives.* Waterloo: University of Waterloo Department of Geography Publication Series No. 47.

Coppack, P. 1988. 'The Role of Amenity in the Evolution of the Urban Field', *Geografisker Annaler* 70B: 353–61.

———, L.H. Russwurm, and C.R. Bryant, eds. 1988. *Essays on Canadian Urban Process and Form III: The Urban Field.* Waterloo: University of Waterloo Department of Geography Publication Series No. 30.

Cullingworth, J.B. 1987. *Urban and Regional Planning in Canada.* New Brunswick, NJ: Transaction Books.

Curtis, K.R. 1994. 'A Comparative Analysis of CBD Planning in Kitchener and London, Ontario 1961–1991', Ph.D. dissertation, University of Waterloo.

Dawson, J., and J. Lord. 1985. *Shopping Centre Development: Policies and Prospects.* London: Croom Helm.

Dennis, M., and S. Fish. 1972. *Programs in Search of a Policy.* Toronto: Hakkert.

Dobriner, W.M., ed. 1958. *The Suburban Community.* New York: Putnams.

Donner, A. 1991. 'Recession, Recovery and Redistribution: The Three R's of Canadian State Macro-Policy in the 1980s', in D. Drache and M. Gertler, eds, *The New Era of Global Competition.* Montreal and Kingston: McGill-Queen's University Press.

Evenden, L.J., and G. Walker. 1993. 'From Periphery to Centre: The Changing Geography of the Suburbs', in L.S. Bourne and D. Ley, eds, *The Changing Social Geography of Canadian Cities.* Montreal and Kingston: McGill-Queen's University Press.

Filion, P., and T. Bunting. 1990. *Affordability of Housing.* Ottawa: Minister of Supply and Services, Statistics Canada Catalogue No. 93–130.

———, ———, and K. Curtis. 1996. *The Dynamics of the Dispersed City: Geographic and Planning Perspectives.* Waterloo: University of Waterloo, Department of Geography Publication Series No. 47.

Fishman, R. 1987. *Bourgeois Utopias: The Rise and Fall of Suburbia*. New York: Basic Books.

Florida, R.L., and M.M. Feldman. 1988. 'Housing in US Fordism', *International Journal of Urban and Regional Research* 12: 187–210.

Frieden, B.J., and L. Sagalyn. 1989. *Downtown, Inc.: How America Rebuilds Cities*. Cambridge, Mass.: MIT Press.

Frisken, F. 1994. 'Provincial Transit Policy-Making for the Toronto, Montreal and Vancouver Regions', in F. Frisken, ed., *The Changing Canadian Metropolis: A Public Policy Perspective*. Berkeley: Institute of Governmental Studies Press, University of California; Toronto: Canadian Urban Institute.

Gad, G. 1991. 'Office Location', in T. Bunting and P. Filion, eds, *Canadian Cities in Transition*. Toronto: Oxford University Press.

Garreau, J. 1991. *Edge City: Life on the New Frontier*. New York: Doubleday.

Gertler, L. 1989. 'Telecommunication and the Changing Global Context of Urban Settlements', in R.V. Knight and G. Gappert, eds, *Cities in a Global Society*. Newbury Park, Calif.: Sage.

Goheen, P. 1970. *Victorian Toronto 1850–1900: Pattern and Process of Growth*. Chicago: University of Chicago Department of Geography Research Paper No. 142.

Goldberg, M., and J. Mercer. 1986. *The Myth of the North American City*. Vancouver: University of British Columbia Press.

Gutowski, M., and T. Field. 1979. *The Graying of Suburbia*. Washington: The Urban Institute.

Guy, C. 1994. *The Retail Development Process: Location, Property and Planning*. London: Routledge.

Hahn, E., and U.E. Simonis. 1991. 'Ecological Urban Restructuring', *Ekistics* 58, 348–9: 199–209.

Hamel, P. 1993. 'Modernity and Postmodernity: The Crisis of Urban Planning', *Canadian Journal of Urban Research* 2, 1: 16–29.

Harvey, D. 1989. *The Condition of Postmodernity*. Oxford: Basil Blackwell.

Hayden, D. 1984. *Redesigning the American Dream: The Future of Housing, Work and Family Life*. New York: W.W. Norton.

Hitchcock, J., and N. McMaster, eds. 1985. *The Metropolis: Proceedings in Honour of Hans Blumenfeld*.

Toronto: University of Toronto, Department of Geography.

Hodge, G. 1998. *Planning Canadian Communities: An Introduction to the Principles, Practice, and Participants*. Toronto: ITP Nelson.

Hoover, E.M., and R. Vernon. 1962. *Anatomy of a Metropolis*. New York: Doubleday Anchor.

Howe, D., and W. Rabiega. 1992. 'Beyond Strips and Centres: The Ideal Commercial Form', *Journal of the American Planning Association* 58: 213–19.

Hoyt, H. 1939. *The Structure and Growth of Neighborhoods in American Cities*. Washington: US Federal Housing Administration.

Isin, E., and R. Tomalty. 1993. *Resettling Cities: Canadian Residential Intensification Initiatives*. Ottawa: Canada Mortgage and Housing Corporation.

Jacobs, J. 1961. *The Death and Life of Great American Cities*. New York: Random House.

Jones, K. 1991. 'The Urban Retail Landscape', in T. Bunting and P. Filion, eds, *Canadian Cities in Transition*. Toronto: Oxford University Press.

———— and J. Simmons. 1990. *The Retail Environment*. London: Routledge.

Joseph, A.E., and G.B. Hall. 1985. 'The Locational Concentration of Group Homes in Toronto', *Professional Geographer* 37: 143–55.

Joseph, A., P. Keddie, and B. Smit. 1988. 'Unraveling the Population Turnaround', *Canadian Geographer* 32: 17–31.

Kling, R., S. Olin, and M. Poster, eds. 1991. *Postsuburban America*. Berkeley: University of California Press.

Knox, P. 1994. *Urbanization: An Introduction to Urban Geography*. Englewood Cliffs, NJ: Prentice-Hall.

Leo, C. 1994. 'The Urban Economy and the Power of the Local State: The Politics of Planning in Edmonton and Vancouver', in F. Frisken, ed., *The Changing Canadian Metropolis: A Public Policy Perspective*. Berkeley: Institute of Governmental Studies Press, University of California Press; Toronto: Canadian Urban Institute.

Leung, H.-L. 1993. *Residential Density and Quality of Life*. Ottawa: Canada Mortgage and Housing Corporation.

MacKenzie, S., and D. Rose. 1983. 'Industrial Change, the Domestic Economy and Home Life', in A.S.

Duncan and R. Hudson, eds, *Redundant Spaces in Cities and Regions?* London: Academic Press.

Mary McDonough Research Associates. 1994. *Comprehensive Buyer Profile*. Toronto: Greater Toronto Home Builders Association.

Mazy, M.E., and D.R. Lee. 1983. *Her Space Her Place*. Washington: Association of American Geographers.

Mitchell, C. 1992. 'Economic Impact of the Arts: Theatre Festivals in Small Ontario Communities', *Journal of Cultural Economics* 17: 55–65.

Miron, J. 1988. *Housing in Postwar Canada: Demographic Change, Household Formation and Housing Markets*. Montreal and Kingston: McGill-Queen's University Press.

———, ed. 1992. *Housing Progress in Canada Since 1945*. Ottawa: Canada Mortgage and Housing Corporation.

Muller, P. 1981. *Contemporary Suburban America*. Englewood Cliffs, NJ: Prentice-Hall.

Mumford, L. 1961. *The City in History: Its Origins, Its Transformations, Its Prospects*. New York: Harcourt, Brace and World.

Nowlan, D., and N. Nowlan. 1970. *The Bad Trip: The Untold Story of Spadina Highway*. Toronto: Anansi Press.

Paumier, C.B. 1988. *Designing Successful Downtowns*. Washington: Urban Land Institute.

Popenoe, D. 1977. *The Suburban Environment*. Chicago: University of Chicago Press.

Poulton, M. 1995. 'Affordable Homes at an Affordable [Social] Price', in G. Fallis et al., eds, *Home Remedies: Rethinking Canadian Housing Policy*. Toronto: C.D. Howe Institute.

Preston, R.E., and D.W. Griffin. 1966. 'A Restatement of the Zone of Transition Concept', *Annals, Association of American Geographers* 56: 339–50.

Pushkarev, B.S., and J.M. Zupan. 1977. *Public Transport and Land Use Policy*. Bloomington: Indiana University Press.

Redstone, L. 1976. *The New Downtowns: Rebuilding Business Districts*. New York: McGraw-Hill.

Rees, W., and M. Wackernagel. 1994. 'Ecological Footprints and Appropriate Carrying Capacity: Measuring the Natural Capital Requirements of the Human Economy', in A.-M. Jansson, M.

Hammer, C. Folke, and R. Constanza, eds, *Investing in Natural Capital: Ecological Economics Approach to Sustainability*. Washington: Island Press.

Reisman, D. 1958. 'The Suburban Sadness', in W.M. Dobriner, ed., *The Suburban Community*. New York: Putnams.

Rowe, P.G. 1991. *Making a Middle Landscape*. Cambridge, Mass.: MIT Press.

Sewell, J. 1993. *The Shape of the City: Toronto Struggles with Modern Planning*. Toronto: University of Toronto Press.

Skelton, I., B. Moore Milroy, P. Filion, W. Fisher, and L. Autio. 1995. 'Linking Urban Development and Environmental Concerns: Constraints and Opportunities', *Canadian Journal of Urban Research* 4: 228–47.

Smith, W. 1964. *Filtering and Neighborhood Change*. Berkeley: University of California, Center for Real Estate and Urban Economics, Report No. 24.

Spurr, P. 1976. *Land and Urban Development: A Preliminary Study*. Toronto: James Lorimer.

Stanback, T.M. 1991. *The New Suburbanization: Challenge to the Central City*. Boulder, Colo.: Westview Press.

Statistics Canada. 1997. *Census of Canada 1996: A National Overview, Population and Dwelling Counts*. Ottawa: Ministry of Industry, Science and Technology, Catalogue No. 93–357.

Vischer, J.C. 1987. 'The Changing Canadian Suburb', *Plan Canada* 22: 130–40.

Wackernagel, M., and W. Rees. 1996. *Our Ecological Footprint: Reducing Human Impact on the Earth*. Gabriola Island, BC: New Society Publishers.

Warner, B.J. 1962. *Streetcar Suburbs: The Process of Growth in Boston*. Cambridge, Mass.: Harvard University Press.

Wekerle, G.R. 1985. *Creating a New Toronto Neighbourhood: The Planning Process and Residents' Experience*. Toronto: Canada Mortgage and Housing Corporation.

Wirth, L. 1938. 'Urbanism as a Way of Life', *American Journal of Sociology* 44: 1–24.

Yalnizyan, A. 1998. *The Growing Gap: A Report on Growing Inequality Between the Rich and Poor in Canada*. Toronto: Centre for Social Justice.

Chapter 2

Urban Canada in Transition to the Twenty-First Century: Trends, Issues, and Visions

Larry S. Bourne

Looking Back: Setting the Stage

For those interested in anticipating our urban future, the place to begin is with the present and the immediate past. The twentieth century, we might conclude, was indeed the 'urban' century, during which urbanization was the fundamental process of economic, social, and territorial transformation. Canada became an urban nation, at least in numerical terms, around 1920. At that time more than 50 per cent of the country's population resided in those settlements of 1,000 or more defined in the census as urban places.[1] It also became a predominantly 'metropolitan' country by the mid-1960s when over 50 per cent of the national population resided in large urban centres of over 100,000 population. By the early 1970s the nation had also become predominantly suburban in that more than half of the population lived outside the municipal boundaries of the older central cities. Although these dates are somewhat arbitrary, they do illustrate how recently, and relatively quickly, Canada became an urbanized society.

This chapter follows the broad overview of the nature of urban settlements in Chapter 1 to provide a set of signposts to the more detailed chapters to come. It begins by examining the scale of the urban transformation in Canada and offers an overview of post-1945 trends in urban growth and development and an outline of the changing context within which urban development has taken place. On this basis the chapter identifies a 'top-10' list of contemporary urban problems and issues of policy concern that flow from these trends. It then suggests how perceptions of these problems differ, how these differences are mirrored in public policy initiatives, and how these in turn are mediated through alternative—often competing and sometimes contradictory—visions of the 'new' city and new urban regions. The chapter concludes with a brief discussion of alternative urban futures and poses questions for further discussion and debate.

Initially, a brief clarification of terms and concepts is in order. In this chapter, the urbanization process is defined as that process by which a society is transformed from one organized around rural activities to one organized by urban activities. A simple measure of the outcome of that transformation is the proportion of national population living in census-defined 'urban areas' (that is, the level of urbanization). The spatial expression of that process —the growth of cities and towns—can be examined at either of two geographic scales: one scale considers the entire set of cities in the country, called the 'urban system', and undertakes to identify the changing properties of that system (e.g., the distribution of cities by size, type of economy, growth rates, quality of life); the second looks at the growth, physical form, and internal structure of individual urban areas. Although Statistics Canada recognizes as 'urban' places those with a baseline minimum population of 1,000, in most analyses the urban designation is limited to places of over 10,000 population (Bourne and Olvet, 1995) (see Chapter 5). This is the set of observations most often used in this and subsequent chapters. Figure 2.1 maps out the distribution of Census Agglomerations (CAs) (which contain typically between 10,000 and

Figure 2.1 **The Canadian Urban System 1996 CMAs and CAs**

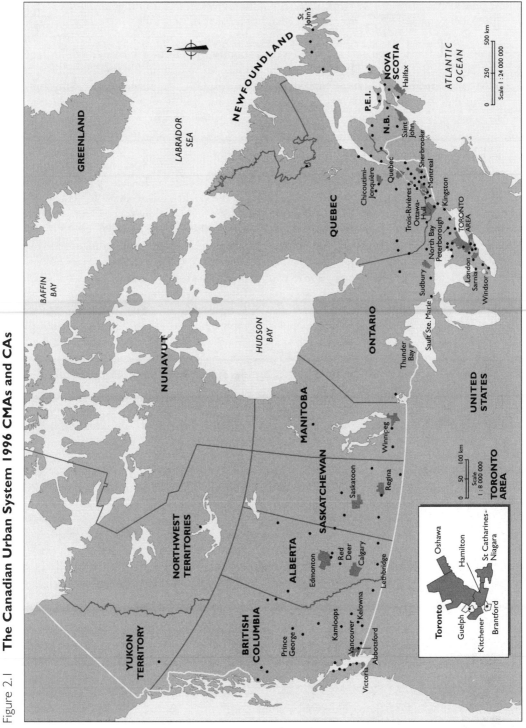

100,000 residents) and Census Metropolitan Areas (CMAs) (generally over 100,000) across the Canadian territory. Unless otherwise specified, the term 'cities' as used here refers not to political cities, such as the City of Montreal or the City of Vancouver, but to the entire metropolitan area—indeed, the entire 'urban region'—of which they are an integral part.

The Urban Transformation

The scale and rapidity of the urban transformation of Canadian society and economy in the last century have been dramatic (Table 2.1). In 1900 out of a population of about 5.4 million, just over two million or 37.5 per cent were classified as urban residents. By 1921 this percentage had reached 49.5 per cent, in 1941 it was 54.5 per cent, and by 1961, 69.6 per cent. During the same time period, the rural farm population declined from 4.4 million to just over 2 million, while the rural non-farm popula-

tion grew from 2.1 million in 1941 to 3.5 million. The urban explosion continued after 1961, although at a somewhat slower pace. While the country's population increased by 58.2 per cent, from 18.2 million in 1961 to 28.8 million in 1996, the urban population almost doubled, from 12.7 to 22.5 million. By that census date the nation was 77.9 per cent urban, and the rural farm population represented only 2.5 per cent of the total population.

These figures, however, tell us little about changes in how and where people live and work and the quality of life that they enjoy or endure. One expression of this transformation is the changing size distribution of urban places. In 1921, for example, there were only six urban areas in Canada with over 100,000 population, and no metropolitan area had more than one million. The average Canadian at that time was primarily a small-town or small-city dweller. By 1961 there were eighteen places with over 100,000 population and two with

Table 2.1   **The Urban Transformation of Canada: Rural and Urban Population Distributions, 1901–1996**

Year	Total Pop. (000s)	Rural farm (RF) (000s)	(%)	Rural non-farm* (RNF) (000s)	(%)	Urban** (000s)	(%)	Annual growth rates (%) (Tot.)	RF	RNF	Urban
1901	5,371	3,357	62.5	n.a.	n.a.	2,014	37.5	n.a.	n.a.	n.a.	n.a.
1921	8,788	4,436	50.5	n.a.	n.a.	4,352	49.5	3.2	1.6	n.a.	5.8
1941	11,507	3,113	27.1	2,123	18.4	6,271	54.5	2.5	0.9	n.a.	2.2
1961	18,232	2,073	11.4	3,465	19.0	12,700	69.6	2.9	−1.7	3.2	5.1
1981	24,343	1,040	4.3	4,867	20.0	18,436	75.7	1.7	−2.5	2.0	2.3
1991	27,296	806	3.0	5,481	20.0	21,008	77.0	1.2	−2.3	1.3	1.4
1996	28,847	713	2.5	5,673	19.7	22,461	77.9	1.1	−2.3	0.07	1.4

*Not identified separately until the census of 1931.

**Definitions of urban populations from 1901 to 1941 were not the same as those from the 1951 census to the present.

n.a. = Not available.

Source: *Census of Canada*, various years.

over one million. Since then the urban system has continued to expand in both the number and sizes of urban places. By 1996 there were 25 metropolitan areas with over 100,000, four of which had over a million, as well as nine other functional urban areas (CAs) with populations over 100,000, and a further 103 places with over 10,000 (see Figure 2.1 and Chapters 4 and 5). Over 17.8 million Canadians, 61.7 per cent of the national population, now live in the 25 metropolitan areas, and 10.4 million or 36.1 per cent live in the four largest metropolitan areas with populations over one million (Toronto, Montreal, Vancouver, Ottawa–Hull). In other words, the average Canadian now lives and works in a large metropolitan environment, a very different living experience from that of previous generations.

There is frequent confusion regarding the relationship between the definitions of metropolitan and urban populations. The two definitions are simply different. To illustrate the differences, Table 2.2 provides a cross-classification between CMA/CA populations on the one hand and urban–rural populations on the other. All CMAs and most CAs, given their spatially extensive boundaries, contain substantial rural populations (two million in 1996); and the non-CMA/CA part of the country contains substantial urban populations (those living in settlements of 1,000 to 10,000). Ironically, the proportion

of the nation's population living in CMAs and CAs (77.8 per cent), including the rural fringes of those CMAs and CAs, is almost exactly the same as that population designated as urban, including those living in rural areas and small towns as well as the urban component of metropolitan areas (77.9 per cent).[2] They are, of course, not the same people.

What this example also suggests is that given high levels of mobility and the diffusion of modern communications systems (e.g., the media, the Internet) across the country, attitudes, lifestyles, and consumption patterns have become more homogeneous over space. Thus, the traditional contrasts drawn between rural and urban areas, and the living experiences of their residents, may now have lost much of their meaning. In the twenty-first century, almost everywhere and everyone may be considered 'urban'.

The Components of Urban Growth

Why has this transformation from a rural and small-town to a metropolitan environment taken place? And why has the concentration of population, wealth, and production activity in metropolitan areas continued to increase? Cities are the spatial manifestation of two sets of forces: first, are those forces emanating from changes in the economic, social, and technological contexts—both national

Table 2.2	**Urban and Rural Populations, by Size Category, Canada, 1996 (000s)**			
	Urban	Rural	Totals	%
CMAs	16,707.2	1,157.4	17,864.6	61.9
CAs	3,703.6	881.5	4,585.1	15.9
Subtotal	20,410.8	2,038.9	22,449.7	77.8
Small town and rural	2,050.3	4,346.6	6,396.9	22.2
Totals	22,461.1	6,385.5	28,846.6	100
%	77.9	22.1	100	

CMAs = Census Metropolitan Areas (≥ 100,000) n = 25
CAs = Census Agglomerations (≥ 10,000) n = 112
Source: Statistics Canada, author's calculations.

and global—in which cities function; and second, are the local processes shaping development (e.g., the urban land and property market) that operate within urban areas. Both sets of forces are related; the first represents the principal determinants of variations in levels of urbanization, rates of urban growth, and metropolitan concentration, while the second defines the internal organization, dynamics, and living environments of cities.

Transitions in five different domains have shaped the processes of urbanization and urban development in Canada, as in other market economies: (1) the evolution of the macroeconomic system, including the effects of globalization; (2) the ongoing demographic transition; (3) the changing roles of the public sector and the political system; (4) continuing technological innovations; and (5) changes in lifestyles, preferences, and choices of living arrangement. The first domain of interest is the economic system; that is, the changing nature of the production system, employment, and occupational structures. There is little doubt that the 'work' performed by, and in, cities has continued to evolve (Sassen, 1994). The complexity of urban economic change, and the impacts of globalization, have called forth varied explanations (Clarke and Gaile, 1998; Cohen et al., 1996; Wilson, 1997). As these kinds of structural changes are covered in considerable detail by William Coffey in Chapter 6, it will suffice here to note only general trends. The Canadian economy has shifted over the postwar period from one dominated by primary (resource exploitation) and secondary (manufacturing) sectors to a service-based economy (Britton, 1996) (see also Chapter 15). By 1996, for example, 77 per cent of all jobs were in the service sector, 17 per cent in manufacturing and construction, with only 6 per cent in agriculture and the resource industries. Service jobs, in turn, are largely urban-based jobs, and the more highly specialized services (e.g., financial services) are overwhelmingly concentrated in the largest metropolitan areas. A table of economic change by sectors is also a map of change in the urban system.

The second domain of interest is the country's changing demographic system. Canada has under-gone a profound demographic transition since 1946. The war was followed initially by a period of high fertility (the baby boom) and increased marriage rates (the marriage boom), combined with high levels of immigration, that extended to the mid-1960s. This was followed by a period of rapidly declining birth rates (the baby bust), later marriage, reduced immigration, and higher divorce rates (Dumas and Bélanger, 1997; Foot and Stoffman, 1996). The size of the baby-boom population, combined with the effects of immigration, was proportionally much larger in Canada than in either the US or Western Europe. As the huge baby-boom population moves through the life cycle and has children (the echo), it alters the demands for housing, jobs, private goods, and public services (e.g., schools), and shifts the locations where those demands are expressed. Given continuing lower fertility rates through the 1980s and 1990s, the population is also starting to age, a process that will accelerate after 2011, with considerable consequences for all aspects of urban life and public policy.

As fertility levels declined, migration and immigration became the prominent determinants of variations in urban growth rates and of the changing character of individual cities (see Chapter 5). Every five years, nearly 50 per cent of the population (11.5 million people between 1991 and 1996) change their place of residence, and half of these migrate across municipal and provincial boundaries (Bourne and Flowers, 1999). Why and where those migrants actually move are difficult to predict, but in most cases people move for obvious reasons: job opportunities; higher wages; schooling; family ties; improved housing; retirement; and the search for a better quality of life (Clark and Dieleman, 1996). The point to keep in mind is that it is through these relocations that the country's demographic system (and its labour force) adjusts to changes in the economic system, and vice versa.

Immigration adds a further degree of uncertainty to the chemistry of urban growth. Canada has always been a nation of immigrants, although the number of arrivals has varied widely over time in response to changes in government policies and economic conditions at home and abroad (Beaujot, 1991). Since 1961 Canada has admitted over 5.3 million immigrants, an increasing proportion of whom have gone to the larger cities, and to Toronto, Montreal, and Vancouver in particular. Since 1991, when the number increased to over 220,000 annually, the Toronto area has received 43 per cent of these immigrants, Vancouver 18 per cent, and Montreal 13 per cent. During the 1990s over 50 per cent of national population growth is attributable to immigration. These flows have also contributed substantially to metropolitan concentration and urban social change. The sources of the immigrants have also shifted: before 1961, 92 per cent came from traditional sources (Europe, US); after 1981, over 80 per cent have come from non-traditional sources (East and South Asia, Africa, the Caribbean). Not only have these flows added to metropolitan population growth, they have augmented social pluralism and ethnocultural diversity, while enriching cultural and economic life in the receiving cities. Coping with such diversity, however, raises real challenges for both governments and service-providers (see Chapter 9). The fact that immigrant flows are increasingly focused on only a few metropolitan areas also means that these cities are becoming more distinct socially from the rest of the country.

The three other domains of change are included here to illustrate that cities mirror their contexts—in this case the structures of government, the technologies, and the social attitudes and preferences of the larger society. Cities are not simply products of the private market. They are in considerable part cultural constructs and public-sector creations (Hall, 1998; Lemon, 1996; Zukin, 1995). The public city is constructed through the provision of infrastructure (e.g., sewers, water, roads) and other public goods and services (e.g., schools, parks, welfare), and through the state's varied roles as regulator of private development and as negotiator when conflicts arise between competing interest groups. Moreover, the organization of urban government, whether it is centralized (e.g., unicity, megacity) or fragmented into numerous small municipalities, also leaves a visible imprint on the urban landscape (Frisken et al., 1997) (see Chapter 18). Technology has an equally important impact, as is evident from the introductory chapter, for example, in the contrast between the form of cities built around public transit and those built primarily on the basis of automobile accessibility (Brotchie et al., 1995; Office of Technology Assessment, 1996).

Finally, changing attitudes with respect to where and how Canadians will live, and with whom, shapes the demand for most consumer goods, as well as for public services, and the locations at which those demands are expressed. One obvious example is housing, where the steady decline in average household size (from 3.7 persons in 1961 to 2.7 in 1996), and changes in household composition (e.g., more single-person households, single parents), have fuelled an unprecedented increase in the demand for alternative forms of housing, especially for non-family housing, just as the previous baby-boom cohort stimulated the demand for new family housing in the suburbs.

Postwar Phases in Urban Development: An Overview

Most observers of urban growth and development over the longer term try to capture the myriad of transitions that have taken place—made more complex because they often occur simultaneously and at different geographical scales—through the introduction of some type of simple 'periodization'. In this vein, Table 2.3 provides one interpretation of the principal directions of evolution in urban Canada from the end of the war. Allowing for oversimplification, three distinct periods or phases are suggested, based principally on three criteria: demographic change, sector shifts in the economy, and business cycle effects. These three periods, 1946–64, 1965–82, and 1983 to the present, closely complement the two-stage model put forward in Chapter 1 to characterize major transitions in urban land-use patterning across the entire country. For each period the dominant directions of change are identified in the table within five spatial scales: the nation (the national urban system); the urban-rural balance;

Table 2.3   Major Phases of Urban Growth and Development: Canada, 1946–Present

	Early postwar 1946–1964 (Urban Boom and Metro Concentration)	Later postwar 1965–1982 (Deconcentration and Decline)	Recent 1983–Present (Concentration, Recession, and Renewal)
National urban system	Rapid population growth; high fertility (baby boom) and high immigration; economy booming	Declining rate of growth; lower fertility and immigration; intense economic restructuring, service-led growth and manufacturing decline	Slower population growth; stable natural increase; aging population; immigration picks up in 1990s; service economy dominates growth
Level of urbanization and urban-rural balance	Rapid increase in % of urban population; rural farm decline	Stabilizing level of urbanization (%); rural farm population decline; rapid non-farm growth	Stable level (78%); rapid rural farm decline; slower non-farm rural growth
Regional variations	Rapid growth in industrial heartland and selected resource locations; some growth almost everywhere	Slower growth in heartland; rapid growth in the West and many resource regions; decline in the East	Renewed growth in heartland; slower growth in the prairies and resource periphery; small-town decline widespread; retirement/leisure regions boom
Urban size hierarchy	Massive concentration in metropolitan areas and larger cities; relative decline of small towns	Slower metropolitan growth; middle-size cities growing rapidly; selective growth of small towns and rural areas (counter-urbanization?)	Modest metropolitan revival; city size influences growth; small towns decline, except in metro commuting fields and in retirement/leisure areas
Intra-urban form and development	Highest growth in suburban areas; inner cities declining; slow growth on rural-urban fringe; densities declining	Rapid decentralization; outer suburbs and exurbs growing rapidly; jobs spreading to suburbs; core jobs increase, but population declines (despite revitalization)	Continued rapid decentralization; outer suburbs and rural-urban fringe booming; downtown office growth slows; central-area population stable or growing slowly (reurbanization)

regional variations (e.g., heartland vs periphery); the urban size hierarchy; and intra-urban form and development.

The first phase, roughly from 1946 to 1964, may be characterized as a period of rapid growth in population and jobs almost everywhere. Nearly all regions and city size-groups grew, floating, as it were, on a sea of high levels of fertility and immigration, in combination with widespread economic prosperity and rising real incomes. The traditional heartland region of southern Ontario and Quebec grew rapidly as the manufacturing sector expanded, as did those urban areas located in the periphery with economies based on resources that were in high demand in international markets. Metropolitan concentration continued apace, as employment growth in the service sector accelerated. In contrast, small towns in agricultural areas, and places with a declining resource base, suffered significant losses of jobs, functions, income, and population. The urban size hierarchy was slowly being redefined. Toronto asserted national primacy in an increasing number of economic and cultural sectors, while Montreal's role was reduced. Vancouver emerged as a prominent regional and international centre, linked to the Pacific rim (Hutton, 1998), while Calgary and Edmonton captured a large part of Winnipeg's service area in the prairies. At the local scale, the rapid growth of population, particularly of young families with children (the initial baby-boom cohort), again combined with rising real incomes and the spread of automobile ownership, led to massive suburbanization of population and retailing, and often to declining populations in the inner cities.

The second phase, through the late 1960s and the 1970s, produced a rather different geography. The national population growth rate slowed, as fertility levels declined sharply (the baby bust) and high postwar immigration rates abated. Regional differences in growth widened as prices of commodities (e.g., such resources as oil) increased, and the manufacturing sector suffered from obsolescence, intensified international competition, the shift of production off-shore and technological change. The overall pattern of growth—in terms of migration, jobs, and capital investment—shifted from the Ontario-Quebec industrial belt to the West, and especially to cities in Alberta and BC. Declining places became more common in the Atlantic and central regions, and in the North, while most places (including small towns and medium-sized cities) grew in the West. As a result, there was a significant redistribution of population, jobs, and wealth from east and central regions to the West, and a marked 'deconcentration' of population within the urban size hierarchy. During this period, over 50 per cent of all growth took place in Alberta and BC. Also, for the first time since the Depression, large metropolitan areas experienced a net migration loss in the exchange with non-metropolitan areas. This was the first period, however brief, when Canada demonstrated a trend to 'counter-urbanization' (or de-urbanization), a process that received widespread attention in other countries (Berry, 1976; Champion, 1989; Hart, 1991) (see also Chapter 14).

This phase of urban growth was brought to a rather abrupt end by the severe recession of the early 1980s. When the country came out of that recession, yet another geography of urban growth and development ensued. The pendulum of uneven growth, reflecting shifts in the economic sectors undergoing expansion or contraction, swung back to the industrial heartland and to a few selected metropolitan areas. The service economy continued to expand (notably in business and financial services), and even manufacturing enjoyed a modest revival. The Toronto region, with a diverse economy based on manufacturing, government, and service industries, boomed, and so did Vancouver and (to a lesser extent) Montreal. Metropolitan concentration returned with renewed vigour. In contrast, as resource prices declined, smaller urban areas in the North and the agricultural periphery suffered once again. The only small urban places that were growing were those with economies based on retirement and recreation functions, often located in environmentally attractive areas, and those within extended commuting range of the larger metropolises.

In fact, the recent period, from 1983 to the present, might well be subdivided into two distinct sub-phases, separated by two recessions. By 1989 the boom in the core region, and particularly in Toronto, had ended. The subsequent recession, largely a 'made-at-home' recession, but combined with intense international competition, hit the industrial heartland especially hard. While the rest of the country, especially the West, but particularly Calgary and Vancouver, emerged from the recession relatively quickly, Toronto and southern Ontario did not fully recover until after 1994. Despite continuing economic difficulties, however, levels of immigration increased significantly in the early 1990s, most of it focused on Toronto and Vancouver.

There is a question of whether the later part of this period represents a continuation of the 1980s or a new phase carrying us into the new century. This question has yet to be answered. What is clear is that the effects of business cycles and regional sectoral changes in the economy are firmly imprinted in the geography and the time path taken by the urbanization process in Canada.

Evolving Urban Forms: Recent Trends in Urban Development

Changes in the context of urbanization are most visible in the changing form and character of urban development and in more subtle changes in the nature of everyday life at the local scale. The most obvious change in the form of cities over this period is that of increased size: most of our metropolitan areas at the end of the 1990s are quantitatively different entities from those in the 1950s. With increased size invariably comes greater social diversity and functional complexity. Consider the Toronto example. In 1951 the greater Toronto area (the GTA) had 1.5 million residents; by 1996 it had over 4.6 million, a massive threefold increase. Yet, over the same period, the physical size of the urban region grew by a staggering six to seven times, as population densities declined and almost all urban activities consumed more space. The principal contributor to this increase in land consumption per

capita, and the dominant physical expression of postwar urban development, has been the suburbanization process—a process driven by increases in income and by the changing space requirements of the production system.

In addition to growth there have been other substantial changes in the form of Canadian cities, as the last row in Table 2.3 suggests, but these have been largely evolutionary rather than revolutionary. Cities, and neighbourhoods, reflect the socio-economic, political, and technological conditions prevailing at the time they were built. Most of our urban areas, as a result, are physically layered. Each layer or ring of new suburban development and each node of redevelopment, are added to and selectively modify the built environment and institutions inherited from previous periods. In most cities the keen observer is able to identify distinct breaks in the urban built environment, for example, between the pre-Depression (1929), pre-automobile era and the post-1945 auto-dominated landscapes; and then between the bungalow suburbs of the 1950s and 1960s and the more diverse eclectic 'burbs' of the 1980s and 1990s. The fabric of older urban areas typically consists of higher-density housing on small lots, with a mix of commercial and industrial uses, and with major industries oriented towards the railways for goods transportation. More recent suburban landscapes have been built at much lower densities (in part because family size has declined), with a wider variety of house types, new clusters of workplaces, sprawling regional shopping centres and 'big-box' stores, interspersed with new industrial and office parks, all based on the widespread use of automobiles and trucks and oriented to a suburban expressway system.

Despite extensive rebuilding of downtown business cores, which itself has transformed the skylines of all but the smallest urban centres during the 1960s and 1970s, the dominant trend has continued to be the decentralization of population, local services, and jobs to the suburbs. Most of this postwar development, as noted, has occurred at lower densities, largely as the result of three principal factors: (1) the desire for more living space (larger, perhaps newer, and less expensive housing), particularly on the part of young families, and facilitated during the 1950s and 1960s by substantial increases in real household income; (2) a massive increase in the land required to accommodate our machines—the assembly line, automobiles, and trucks (e.g., for parking, roads, storage); and (3) the overzealous imposition of 'exclusionary' zoning that separated activities into large blocks of homogeneous land use, and in particular separated employment lands (that is, jobs) from residential areas (that is, labour). The latter separation, in turn, increased commuting volumes and trip lengths, necessitating the construction of extensive road and expressway networks. This further reduced densities and made efficient transit provision almost impossible.

The form of new suburban landscapes also changed as the nature of the property development industry itself changed. Residential subdivisions became larger and, until very recently, more homogeneous in social composition and building style. This was the combined result of tighter subdivision controls and the emergence in the 1960s of an integrated property development industry. Large corporate developers tended to design and build complete subdivisions or even entire new communities—often called 'corporate suburbs'. Starting with Don Mills, Bramalea, and Erin Mills in Toronto in the 1950s and 1960s, almost all large metropolitan areas in Canada have now become the home of planned suburban new towns. These 'modernist' designs attempted to achieve, among other goals, a more equal balance of housing and local jobs as a way of reducing long-distance commuting while encouraging more community involvement and an increased sense of place.

Most such corporate suburbs have not, however, functioned as initially planned, largely because they were overwhelmed by trends they were intended to avoid; for example, by changes in household living arrangements (e.g., two-worker households) and by more diverse links between households and job markets, as well as by new expressways and the continued dispersion of employment opportunities throughout the metropolitan region. As the inte-

grated land development industry began to collapse, through the accumulation of debt, during the 1970s and 1980s, and zoning regulations became more flexible, suburban forms began to diversify.

The immense geographical scale of recent development, combined with lower densities overall, and rising standards and expectations, have increased the cost of providing the basic physical infrastructure (e.g., sewers, water, roads), social services (e.g., schools, recreation facilities) and community health facilities (e.g., clinics, hospitals), necessary to support that development. It is instructive to compare a typical new suburban street in the 1950s with a similar street today. In the 1950s many (but not all) residential developments were built without sewers, sidewalks, paved streets, recreation spaces, street lighting, or even schools. Those services all came later. Now, all of these services, plus many others (e.g., underground wiring, community centres), must be in place before housing is built and occupied. The result is that the costs of these services are paid for 'up front', as part of the initial cost to consumers. Thus, while the quantity and quality (that is, the 'standards') of suburban development have increased substantially over time, so, too, have the costs of serviced land and housing. Moreover, in those urban areas where there are many small independent political jurisdictions—the classic 'fragmented' metropolis—these services may be difficult to finance and thus may be unevenly distributed over the entire urban region.

The second dominant spatial process shaping the character of Canadian cities is the redevelopment process. Redevelopment—defined here as the replacement, rebuilding, or adaptive reuse of built environments—has been a part of the city-building process since urbanization began (Ford, 1994). Yet, and despite the presence of severe barriers to the reuse of urban land (Bourne, 1996a), the pace of change since the 1960s has been staggering. With the exceptions of a limited number of special heritage districts and listed buildings, and a few decaying industrial, port, and warehousing areas, much of the pre-war building stock in the downtown commercial cores has been demolished. Most of this outdated stock has been replaced by new offices (often high-rises), condominiums, in-town shopping centres, cultural facilities, public buildings, sports and amusement facilities, and, of course, parking. Our images of cities are defined by the skylines and streetscapes created by these constructions.

The process through which redevelopment has taken place itself provides insight into the changing nature and politicization of the urban growth process. Many of the gleaming downtown edifices were built by large development corporations, financed by the major banks, and represent the outcome of a complex process of 'negotiation' among landowners, investors, developers, prospective tenants, community groups, and local governments. Almost without exception, such projects create conflicts, as well as winners and losers. All required rezoning, itself a time-consuming and costly set of procedures, and usually involving complex trade-offs (e.g., with respect to density bonuses, land-use mix) among the various stakeholders. Our downtown landscapes then mirror the resolution of these conflicts and the specific trade-offs involved, as well as the changing corporate organization of the property development industry.

Between the new suburban fringe and the redeveloped commercial core lie the older city neighbourhoods and the vast expanse of older postwar suburbs. Here, too, change has been widespread, but in somewhat different forms and in more discontinuous patterns. Change in the built environment has taken place in three principal forms: (1) through localized demolition and redevelopment, often around transit stations, at the intersections of major arterial roads, or adjacent to parks and other local amenities; (2) through infill development (intensification); and (3) through rehabilitation of the older stock. In these cases the tension between the desire to preserve and maintain an older building fabric and familiar neighbourhood environments, and the pressures to reuse or replace that fabric, have been intense and highly visible. Resolving such conflicts is one of the principal concerns of local governments, the source of intense political debates on the need for both sta-

bility and renewal, as well as the primary reason for the rise of neighbourhood and community organizations and the proliferation of NIMBY ('Not In My Back Yard') attitudes. But the issue of balancing stability with change in cities is real, and highly political (Caulfield and Peake, 1996; Lemon, 1985). How do we manage growth and change so as to preserve neighbourhoods, while allowing for new development that may better meet the needs and aspirations of the next generation with respect to housing, living space, and jobs?

The organization, daily activities, and ambience of Canadian cities have changed in numerous other and often more subtle ways, as the following chapters demonstrate. Our urban areas have obviously become much more complex as economic, political, and social systems. Traditional postwar land use patterns have given way to new combinations of different kinds of uses, as in multi-use buildings. At the same time highly specialized clusters of commercial uses and employment have emerged. The latter are especially evident in the new suburbs in 'high-tech' industrial corridors, in clusters of insurance, software, and pharmaceutical firms (e.g., Pill Hill), in factory-outlet shopping malls, planned suburban downtowns, and the like. There is far more diversity here than implied in Garreau's (1991) misleading 'edge city' concept.

The social character of urban areas has also changed, perhaps even more dramatically. The demographic transition outlined above has affected every city and every neighbourhood, reducing densities and altering the demands for everything from housing, schools, and daycare to shoes. The earlier baby boom led to more and larger families, thus spawning suburbanization; the later baby bust produced more non-family, and smaller, households. The latter, in turn, generated a strong demand for apartments and in some circumstances, among a rapidly expanding professional class, a renewed demand for inner-city housing. Nevertheless, in most older established neighbourhoods, the decline in average family size has meant a sharp drop in population—an average of 15 to 25 per cent—even within the same set of dwelling units.

In parallel, a substantial number of individuals and households—often those with few or no children—chose not to live in traditional suburban housing. Many preferred the convenience of apartment living, thus generating a boom in rental housing (in the 1960s and 1970s) and then subsequently in condominiums. A majority of these condominiums are in the form of townhouses or high-rise buildings, many located in central areas in close proximity to amenities, workplaces, and entertainment. This construction boom reversed the decline in population in many inner-city neighbourhoods. Other multiple-unit structures are located in the suburbs. Indeed, one of the striking features of the landscapes of Canadian cities, especially of the larger metropolises, in comparison to most American cities, is the presence of high-rise (largely private rental) apartments and social housing in the older suburbs, and the appearance of high-rise condos almost everywhere—including the new suburbs. Our textbook images of both cities and suburbs need to be rewritten.

From the 1970s onward, some members of the expanding professional class sought housing in older inner-city neighbourhoods, a process known as revitalization or gentrification (Ley, 1996) (see Chapter 12). Members of this movement purchased and then rehabilitated housing formerly occupied by lower-income tenants and owner-occupiers. This has produced considerable economic benefits for local governments, realtors, and merchants, but at the same time displaced the former residents to places largely undocumented. To some observers the process of gentrification is seen as one of the principal mechanisms transforming the landscapes of older neighbourhoods, but there are other processes of at least equal or greater significance operating on those landscapes.

One of those processes, as described above, is immigration. Most cities have always had immigrant neighbourhoods, some more distinctive, colourful, and restrictive than others. Waves of new postwar immigrants, however, have added further dimensions of ethnocultural diversification and challenged our collective sense of social identity. With the changing ethnic origins of immigrants has come a different social mix, including new racial and language mixes, and a much richer and more vibrant urban environment. Yet this transformation has not been without tensions, and heightened feelings of uncertainty and alienation on the part of both newcomers and older residents. With immigrant destinations in recent years concentrated within a few metropolitan areas, visitors from small-town Canada are amazed at the extent of the transformation of these areas.

Today, most new immigrants go not to the traditional 'reception' areas in the inner city, but directly to the suburbs where housing and jobs are more readily available, and the social environment may be more accommodating (Lo and Wang, 1997). At the risk of overgeneralization, it appears that many lower-income immigrants end up in the older suburbs (some in subsidized housing), while higher-income families tend to locate in the newer suburbs. The combination of a shift in the ethnocultural backgrounds of new Canadians and the differential shift in the flows to the suburbs has changed the social character of suburban Canada, again calling for a revision of older conventional perceptions and the public policies that were conditioned by those images.

What kinds of urban landscapes remain within the older central districts? In the shadow of the downtown is a landscape of immense complexity. In some sectors that landscape is one of decay, an often ugly and chaotic mix of old, underused buildings, vacant industrial premises, parking lots, and other transitional properties. In other sectors are the formal public spaces of government offices, cultural facilities, and well-tended parks; in still others, the revitalized night-life districts that are alive with restaurants, clubs, and theatres. Nearby are the up-scale élite and gentrified neighbourhoods, areas of privilege and wealth, that stand in stark opposition to the down-scale neighbourhoods of the poor and marginalized that border the older industrial and commercial districts. This diversity makes for varied landscapes and perhaps a renewed sense of urbanity; but it also implies conflicts and contradictions—landscapes and living spaces increasingly polarized between wealth and poverty, and partitioned into distinctly different spaces for different social classes. Whether these landscapes are called 'modernist' or 'post-modernist' is less important than understanding the processes that are reshaping our cities and their consequences for different social groups.

Changing Places: A Note on the Fluidity of Urban Areas

Even when changes in the built environment are not that obvious, it is worth reiterating how much movement actually goes on within those environments. Remember that cities are continually reconstituting themselves socially, particularly through household changes and population movements, and functionally, through changes in the nature of work and workplace relations. Consider the experience of the Toronto CMA in terms of population transitions over the decade 1986–96, an experience replicated on a smaller scale in many other cities. During that single decade 389,700 people migrated to Toronto from elsewhere in the country; while 592,000 left. Total in-and-out movements, therefore, involved almost a million people (981,700). During the same decade net foreign immigrants totalled 573,000. Natural population increase added roughly 255,000 new residents (the difference between 570,000 births and 315,000 deaths). In other words, of the 4.3 million residents of the Toronto CMA in 1996, over 1.5 million are 'new arrivals' since 1986, and over 900,000 have departed. That is to say, more than one-half the metropolitan population is different. To further complicate the picture, fully 35 per cent of the resident population, or 1.1 million people, changed their place of residence within the metropolitan area during that decade. The sheer volume of this turnover suggests the potential for rapid social change.

Despite all of this movement, cities may not in fact change all that much either in total population or in social composition, if the in-migrants are similar in both numbers and attributes to the out-migrants. We know, however, that this is often not the case. In effect, the overall rate of urban growth

and the degree of social reconstitution within an urban area and its constituent neighbourhoods are directly related to differences in the attributes of in- and out-migrants—their ages, genders, family situations, ethnicities, occupations, and incomes. If the differences are large, neighbourhoods can change their character dramatically in a very short time period. Over the 1986–96 decade, Toronto had a net loss of 205,000 residents to other parts of the country, while gaining 573,000 residents from outside the country. The impacts of these kinds of differential population exchanges are evident in every street, neighbourhood, and workplace.

Contemporary Urban Concerns and Policy Issues

Canadian cities, on the whole, provide reasonably high-quality, safe and comfortable settings in which to carry out daily life, at least for most people. But there are conflicts, tensions, and real problems, some that are relatively new, others that have persisted for some time. Each reader will have her or his own list of problems that arise from the trends outlined briefly above. In this section, for purposes of stimulating interest and posing questions for further discussion, I propose to summarize my own 'top-10' list of contemporary urban concerns and policy issues, most of which are then addressed in more detail in subsequent chapters.

1. Economic Restructuring, Technological Change, and Urban Competitiveness

At the top of almost everyone's list of urban concerns, especially since the recession of the early 1990s, has been persistent unemployment and the fragile state of local economies. Even in growing regions the last two recessions left a mark on the productive fabric and labour force of most communities, as well as on social and physical landscapes, and on the local tax base. Plant closings, job losses, vacant buildings, cancelled construction projects, and declining real estate values became more common. Most of the blame has been placed on global competition, free trade, weak productivity, the introduction of new technologies, or the inhibiting effects of high tax rates and bureaucratic red tape. Whatever the argument, however, the pressures have mounted for government action, including action by local governments. In response, almost all municipalities now have economic development agencies and strategies in place to encourage inward capital investment and stimulate local entrepreneurship. The standard slogan in urban planning and public policy has become 'improving the economic competitiveness' of cities (Rondinelli et al., 1998).[3] With it have come efforts to reduce taxes and red tape (e.g., more flexible zoning), to channel public investment into new infrastructure and to solicit public-private partnerships for major improvements in community facilities. Whether these strategies are feasible, or even appropriate, given the limited resources and jurisdiction of local, and even regional governments, remains to be seen. Urban regions may indeed be the engines of economic growth, but their governments are not the agencies that formulate the major policies having an impact on the economy. Nor can economic development initiatives be detached from the support of social services and the quality of urban life they provide.

2. Those Left Behind: Poverty, the Disadvantaged, and Marginalized Groups

Part of the challenge posed by economic restructuring and social change is our ability to respond to the needs of those left behind in the competition for living space and a larger slice of the urban economic pie. There is a continuing debate as to whether or not Canadian society has become more unequal in terms of income distributions (Beach and Slotsve, 1996; Yalnizyan, 1998). Within cities, on the other hand, there is considerable evidence that levels of income polarization and poverty have indeed increased (Bourne, 1997; Murdie, 1997). While there have always been poor and disadvantaged populations in Canadian cities, there is little evidence of the emergence of a permanent 'underclass' in Canada. But there is a general feeling that new and different marginalized groups have appeared during the 1990s. Perhaps the most visible of these groups are the homeless and street people, the mentally ill, and transient unemployed youth. But there are others 'at risk' of falling into poverty—those on fixed or marginal incomes, those living under severe housing pressures, some recent refugees, young single mothers, the frail elderly—for whom conditions have worsened during the 1990s. Caught in the vice-grip of rising living costs, especially in the larger metropolitan areas, and reduced job opportunities, such groups bear a disproportionate share of the social costs of urban economic growth and restructuring. Recent reductions in levels of social assistance, and restrictions on social housing, have added to the severity of these pressures. How can the social costs of economic progress be shared more broadly? Can cities be made more humane and equitable?

3. Urban Sprawl and Inner-City Decline

To some observers the dominant problem facing urban planning, at least physical planning, is the seemingly unending spread of urban development into the rural countryside. This process is invariably associated with the loss of population, jobs, and tax revenue in the older inner cities. Sprawl, however it is defined, has become a rallying cry for environmental groups concerned with the loss of farmland, natural sites, and recreational space. These concerns, in turn, have generated a range of recent policy initiatives intended to encourage more 'compact' urban forms, for example, through growth management schemes (e.g., imposing urban growth limits or boundaries), higher densities (e.g., intensification), and the resettlement or 'reurbanization' of underused sites in older inner cities (Bourne, 1996b; Isin and Tomalty, 1993; Sewell, 1993; Tomalty, 1997). There is, however, a continuing debate on what sprawl is and where it is a problem, and specifically on whether low-density, dispersed urban forms are more costly to service (e.g., for infrastructure), and on the costs (e.g., higher housing prices) often associated with restrictions on growth (Breheny, Gent, and Lock, 1993; Downs, 1994; Katz, 1994; Office of Technology Assessment, 1996). There is also little agreement on whether valuable agricultural land is lost in the process or through other factors. Nor is it clear that tighter controls on development would reduce servicing costs. What is more obvious is that appropriate pricing practices for new infrastructure in the suburbs might abate sprawl without at the same time reducing accessibility to the new housing that people seem to want.

4. Stuck in Virtual Space: Transportation, Technology, and Congestion

The trend toward more dispersed urban forms, and specifically the increasing separation of jobs and housing, combined with the growth of two-worker households, have undoubtedly increased the demand for transportation at a faster rate than new facilities can be provided (Downs, 1994; Hodge, 1996). Even with the boom in new telecommunication systems and the Internet, and the rise in telework and work-at-home, congestion on the roads and transit systems, as the media often tells us, seems to be getting worse. But is it? It would appear that a 'frictionless' landscape, promised by the electronic highway and the 'wired' city, have not, at least as yet, annihilated the importance of place or distance, or even reduced traffic. As with the earlier telephone revolution, people seem to be consuming more of both—travel and communication provided through the Internet. The challenge for policy-makers is to find the appropriate balance between the need for new infrastructure investment and the desire to 'manage' the growing demand for travel and communications. Can we, for example, rearrange land uses so as to minimize the need for new roads and expressways while encouraging transit use? Are mixed-use developments (e.g., residential-commercial; live-work spaces) the answer? Or is full-cost road pricing (e.g., toll roads) the answer? If so, who should pay for new facilities? What is the role of the private sector? What becomes of those who are left off the information superhighway?

5. Coping with Sociocultural Diversity: Tensions and Opportunities

All Canadian cities, even those receiving few immigrants, accommodate a much more diverse population than in the past, and this diversity is likely to increase in the future. In the larger metropolitan areas in particular, a bewildering array of changes in working conditions, demography, lifestyle, ethnicity, culture, income distributions, and living arrangements (e.g., single-person households, single parents, the elderly)[4] have swept over the urban landscape, altering almost everything in their path. How should planners, as well as the providers of public goods and services, regulatory agencies, and governments, respond to such changes? Greater social pluralism suggests the need for more flexible policies, and more carefully targeted and just-in-time service provision. But how is this to be achieved in a period of fiscal restraint, lean-and-mean governments, and strong interest-group politics? The challenges posed by social diversity are considerable, but the opportunities for social progress are even greater.

6. Access to Housing, NIMBYism, and Community Empowerment

Issues of poverty, marginalization, and economic well-being are invariably tied to housing conditions and costs. While urban Canadians on the whole are very well housed, those who live on the edge of the housing market have seen their situation deteriorate during the 1990s in light of the cessation of new social housing programs and private rental construction. The problem is especially acute in those areas with rising housing costs and welfare cutbacks. In large and rapidly growing cities housing is invariably in short supply, and thus expensive. Land speculation, overly rigid zoning, high servicing standards, inadequate transportation facilities, and neighbourhood resistence to change (notably to infill and social housing) have all contributed to higher costs and affordability problems. Even in slow-growth areas where jobs are in short supply, increases in housing costs have exceeded income growth. Demand also plays a major role; the reduction in average household size has substantially increased the demand for housing, even when population growth rates have been declining. There appear to be no easy solutions to such problems, and most levels of government do little more than pay lip service to increasing the supply of reasonably priced housing, in part because local revenue flows depend on assessed values. Many suburban municipalities, in fact, through the imposition of minimum lot sizes on new residential building, and development levies,[5] do exactly the opposite. How do we balance the desire for local community autonomy (and empowerment) with the need for new and affordable housing? Who is responsible for housing provision?

7. Providing Public Goods and Services: Who Benefits, Who Pays, Who Delivers?

The levels of urban public goods (e.g., schools, parks) and services (e.g., education, health, policing) in Canadian cities are relatively high by any standard. Yet we still hear complaints that the quality of those services has declined in recent years. Justified or not, the perception of declining public goods is widespread and must be addressed. Some blame the apparent decline on the fiscal problems facing local governments, the downloading of social costs from federal and provincial governments, or pressures from new and increasing demands. Others cite the trend to cutting taxes, still others the tendency for expectations to rise. Whatever the cause, the pressures for change are mounting, and the long-standing debate on the merits of alternative models of service delivery has taken on renewed vigour (Ford and Zussman, 1997; Hobson and St Hilaire, 1997). Should the users actually pay for certain goods and services? Should everyone receive the same level of services? What services should be in the public domain? Or should some services be privatized, as in a number of other countries (e.g., waste disposal, water, electricity), and if so, who should then regulate their provision and cost?

8. Environmental Quality and Urban Sustainability: The Price of a Clean Environment

There is little doubt that urbanization imposes severe strains on the natural environment (Roseland, 1992). The media provide us with daily horror stories of polluted air, leaking waste dumps, toxic spills, contaminated soils and water, and a host of other ecological problems. Despite the rhetoric, these are real concerns that warrant careful analysis and collective action. How do we reconcile the need for continued urban expansion—to provide jobs, housing, and social spaces for a growing population—and the negative impacts of such expansion on local ecosystems? Can cities be made more environmentally 'sustainable'? The challenge is to find ways and means of managing urban development that contain, limit, and indeed repair the environmental damage, without unduly raising the costs of living and of production. Can the natural environment be priced? If so, who should pay? In one sense cities can never be totally environmentally sustainable, at least in terms of being in balance with their local environments. Cities, by definition, are 'heterotrophic'; that is, they draw resources (e.g., water, food, energy) from an increasingly wide geographical area, and in exchange they send goods, services, income, and waste back to those areas. Ironically, a further concentration of population and production activities in large metropolitan areas may help in finding solutions since the environmental impacts of urban growth are concentrated and thus—potentially—easier to deal with. Without a renewed commitment to addressing environmental concerns, however, large Canadian metropolises—as surely as those in much of the developing world—can also turn out to be downstream ecological disasters.

9. Social Segregation and Polarization: Alienation and Crime

Almost all Western societies and their major cities have become more heterogeneous, more socially polarized, and spatially differentiated (or segre-grated) by class and ethnicity (Bourne, 1997; Murdie, 1997; O'Loughlin and Friedrichs, 1996). Although the latter form of differentiation—if vol-untary—is not necessarily a bad situation, a polar-ized society almost invariably produces feelings of alienation and isolation, and often higher levels of antisocial behaviour. Cities are also widely misrep-resented in the media as unsafe, as places to be feared, as somehow wicked. Nevertheless, and despite the fact that rates of violent crime have been decreasing, there is real and justifiable concern that crime levels are still far too high, that some urban spaces are frightening, and that some groups (e.g., the poor, the frail elderly, and women) are especially vulnerable. While it is only in small part a matter of planning and urban design (e.g., better street light-ing), most solutions to the question of how to deal with crime require that we address the conditions that lead to crime and to feelings of social isola-tion—notably the quality of public services and the inequitable distribution of income and opportunity in our society.

10. Governance and the Management of Growth and Change

The pace and complexity of change in our cities—especially in the larger metropolitan areas—and the very uneven distribution of growth and change also raise fundamental questions about how we plan and manage those cities. What forms of institutions and governing structures are most appropriate (Frisken, 1994)? Is it even possible to govern, let alone plan, such huge agglomerations? If so, who should do it? Should we strive for more efficient urban forms, or more socially equitable forms, or both? If so, how? How do we compensate for the impacts of uneven urban growth rates in which rapid growth is juxta-posed with decline?

About all that is clear is that the structures of local governance have been overwhelmed—because of their restricted geographical size and limited capacity to respond—by the physical expansion and functional complexity of our cities. Indeed, as Table

2.4 suggests, we are no longer talking about stan-dard metropolitan areas but of new—and in some cases gigantic—'city-regions' (Greater Toronto Area Task Force, 1996). In Canada we have tried a range of alternative means of adapting local political struc-tures to these economic and social realities (see Chapter 18). These have varied from the imposition of two-tier regional governments (e.g., Ottawa-Carleton), to special purpose regional service dis-tricts (e.g., GVRD Vancouver and the Greater Toronto Services Board),[6] to direct regulation by provincial governments (e.g., in the Montreal region), to annexation (e.g., Calgary) and outright amalgama-tion (e.g., the former Metro Toronto). None has proven to be entirely satisfactory. In other words, in the face of continued urban growth, we must go back to the drawing board and rethink our current government organization, as well as our service delivery systems, and the building and planning reg-ulations that shape our urban environments.

The issue of governance raises other questions of fundamental importance for the quality of urban life. One of the most critical is the question of polit-ical fragmentation—that is, the presence of numer-ous local governments within a metropolitan area—and the relationship of that fragmentation to the uneven distribution of public goods and serv-ices, and tax rates, among those municipalities. Although the existence of many local municipali-ties does not inevitably mean that services will vary in quality, this is usually the case. One reason that urban areas in Canada have, on balance, continued to be pleasant places to live is that public services are generally of high standard and are more-or-less uniform across the city, at least relative to conditions in comparable metropolitan areas in the US (Barnett, 1995; Rusk, 1995). This uniformity of services, with schools as a prime example, is attrib-utable to the strong intervention of provincial gov-ernments, the presence of regional authorities, and the ability of both regional and provincial govern-ments to redistribute revenues (e.g., taxes) and resources (e.g., school budgets) to areas of need. This redistributive function, operating between the older central city and new suburbs, and among high- and

Table 2.4   **Canada's Emerging Metropolitan Regions, 1991–1996**

Rank	Urban Region	Population (000s) 1991	1996	% Change 1991–1996
1.	Toronto region	4,857.8	5,303.4	9.1
	Toronto CMA	3,893.9	4,263.8	9.4
	Oshawa CMA	240.1	268.8	11.9
	Barrie CA	97.2	118.7	22.2
	Cobourg/Pt Hope	26.6	27.7	4.1
	Hamilton CMA	600.0	624.4	4.1
2.	Montreal region	3,461.4	3,581.5	3.5
	Montreal CMA	3,298.9	3,326.5	3.7
	Lachute, Joliette, Sorel, Saint Hyacinthe, Saint Jean sur Richelieu, Salaberry de Valleyfield CAs	252.5	255.0	0.1
3.	Vancouver-Fraser Valley	1,771.2	2,034.5	14.9
	Vancouver CMA	1,602.6	1,831.7	14.3
	Abbotsford CA	113.6	136.5	20.2
	Chilliwack CA	55.0	66.3	20.5
4.	Ottawa-Hull region/CMA	941.8	1,010.5	7.3
5.	Edmonton region	865.4	887.3	2.5
	Edmonton CMA	841.3	862.6	2.6
	Camrose CA	13.4	13.7	2.3
	Wetaskiwin CA	10.7	11.0	2.8
6.	Calgary region/CMA	754.0	821.6	9.0
7.	Winnipeg region	681.4	687.6	0.9
	Winnipeg CMA	660.4	667.2	1.0
	Portage La Prairie CA	21.0	20.4	2.9
8.	Quebec region/CMA	645.5	671.9	4.1
9.	Grand River region	578.9	617.5	6.7
	Kitchener CMA	356.4	382.9	7.4
	Brantford CA	97.1	100.2	3.2
	Guelph CA	97.7	105.4	7.9
10.	London region	434.1	455.4	4.9
	London CMA	381.5	398.2	4.5
	Strathroy CA	10.5	11.9	12.2
	Tillsonburg CA	12.0	13.2	9.9
	Woodstock CA	30.1	32.1	6.7

(continued)

Table 2.4   **(continued)**

Rank	Urban Region	Population (000s) 1991	Population (000s) 1996	% Change 1991–1996
11.	St Catharines region/CMA	364.5	372.4	2.2
12.	Vancouver Island South	318.8	340.1	6.7
	Victoria CMA	287.9	304.3	5.7
	Duncan CA	30.9	35.8	15.8
13.	Halifax region/CMA	320.5	332.5	3.7
14.	Windsor region	299.5	319.4	6.6
	Windsor CMA	262.1	278.7	6.3
	Leamington CA	37.4	40.7	8.9
15.	Okanagan region	195.9	233.2	19.0
	Kelowna CA	111.9	136.5	22.1
	Penticton CA	35.8	41.3	15.2
	Vernon CA	48.2	55.4	15.0

CMA = census metropolitan area n = 25

CA = census agglomeration n = 112

Note: The regional populations include only the CMA and those CAs within commuting distance of the CMA. They do not include rural and small-town populations outside of CMA and CA boundaries.

Source: Census of Canada; author's calculations.

low-income neighbourhoods, has helped to prevent the emergence of sharp differences in the quality of private and public life in urban Canada (Frisken et al., 1997). Unfortunately, recent trends in government funding, and the absence of new initiatives in establishing institutions of regional governance that would facilitate the redistribution of resources, suggest that these differentials may well increase in the future. The challenge is to find means of allowing for the local autonomy that some observers feel comes with small local governments, while at the same time meeting the need to provide services that are best delivered at the regional rather than local scale (e.g., transit, waste management, environmental planning), and also maintaining the redistributive component that has characterized Canadian urban areas for much of the postwar period.

Perceptions, Policies, and Visions of the New City

Public policies introduced to shape and improve the quality of urban life, as subsequent chapters demonstrate, do not arise in a vacuum. The choices of policies and policy instruments reflect, among other things, the perceptions of urban problems held by politicians, professionals, the business community, and the media—in other words, the élite. These perceptions, in turn, give rise to images, or what Downs (1994) and others (Bourne, 1996b; Isin, 1996) have called 'visions' of the kind of urban area that would best address these problems. To illustrate, Table 2.5 takes the top-10 problem list described above and assigns to each problem area the types of urban visions that are often proposed as solutions.

Table 2.5   Problems and Policies: Visions for a New City

Urban Problem	The Vision	Policy Responses
1. Economic decline	Entrepreneurial city	Encouraging competitiveness Reducing institutional bottlenecks Encouraging local innovation networks Public-private partnerships Investment in infrastructure, training
2. Poverty and social polarization	Equitable city	New social housing provision Extending public services and grants Encouraging socially mixed housing Rent review/security of tenure
3. Sprawl and inner-city decline	Compact city	Controls on suburban growth Neo-traditional communities Multinucleated urban forms Intensification/reurbanization policies
4. Congestion	Energy-efficient city/ Wired city	Encouraging mixed use, new nodes Demand management, user pricing New toll roads Telecommunications innovations
5. Social diversity	Humane city	Community empowerment Healthy-city initiatives Supporting cultural diversity Encouraging institution building Anti-discrimination measures
6. Housing costs and homelessness	Affordable city	Shorten approval process Legalize accessory apartments Increase affordable housing in the suburbs Housing allowances and shelters
7. Environmental deterioration	Sustainable city/ Green city	Sustainable development practices Bioregional/ecosystem planning Agricultural land preservation Green-land strategies
8. Governance and public goods	Empowered and privatized city	Reduce overlapping jurisdictions Downsizing public institutions Encouraging inter-agency co-operation Restoring fiscal balance/equity Privatizing public goods and services

(continued)

Table 2.5   **(continued)**

Urban Problem	The Vision	Policy Responses
9. Crime and violence	Safe city	More community police patrols Law-and-order legislation Improved street lighting Youth services Neighbourhood watch
10. Managing growth and change	Efficient city	New forms of governance Revising planning acts Full-cost pricing for infrastructure Flexible regulations

Such visions vary from economically efficient (entrepreneurial, competitive) cities to environmentally sustainable 'green' cities, from the wired cities and virtual communities of the Internet age to compact cities, and to cities variously defined as safe, humane, empowered, and equitable. Each of these visions, in themselves representing laudable objectives, solicits certain kinds of policy responses. The point here is to illustrate where our policy initiatives come from, and the variety of different ideas or models proposed with respect to creating new— and we assume—better cities that shape our policy agenda and planning practice.

Consider the continuing debate on the question of urban sprawl. For those who see the spread of urban development into surrounding rural areas as a problem, particularly if it takes place in a haphazard, low-density form on valuable agricultural land, the solution is for more 'compact cities'. To achieve that objective, conventional policy initiatives tend to include introducing tight controls on suburban growth (e.g., growth management), creating higher-density suburban downtowns and employment nodes (e.g., a multinucleated urban form) linked to transit, encouraging a different mix of housing styles (especially higher-density), more closely integrating job locations with housing, as we see attempted in so-called neo-traditional community design (Katz,

1994), and a host of other policies intended to encourage more intensive use of land and revitalization (or reurbanization) of older urban areas. All, or most, of these initiatives are (presumably) appropriate, depending on local circumstances. The question is whose visions are they? And, what are the trade-offs involved, for example, in terms of whether or not controls on suburban development increase housing and land costs and reduce choice? How does one reconcile the different priorities that underlie these competing visions and the envelope of policies that surround them? These are questions for further discussion and debate.

Looking Ahead: Alternative Urban Futures

The purpose of this chapter, indeed of the entire book, is to better situate us to understand, anticipate, and, when and where appropriate, modify future trends, rather than to provide concrete forecasts. Nonetheless, it is appropriate here to speculate briefly on where the urban transformation may take us in the future and what kinds of urban environments may be the result. Chapter 1 commented on the properties of cities that guide and structure future change. Here the focus is more specifically on the Canadian agenda. As we enter the twenty-first century all that seems clear is that population growth and economic development will be as volatile as in the past. With slower overall population growth anticipated, the processes acting to redistribute population, wealth, and economic activity will assume even greater importance. Our uncertainty reflects the increasing impacts of globalization, trade liberalization, capital mobility, and rapid technological change, the effects of an aging population combined with the volatility of immigration, the uncertain future of the welfare system and the social safety net, as well as changes in lifestyles and choices of living arrangement. The effects of all of these changes will work their way through the urban system in ways that are difficult to predict.

Nevertheless, we can probably assume that most of the trends outlined above will continue over the next decade or two. The concentration of population and economic power in a small number of metropolitan areas will likely increase. Toronto, Vancouver, and Calgary will increasingly dominate the urban system at both regional and national scales. The Canadian urban system will also become more closely integrated with cities in the adjacent US urban system, notably in BC and southern Ontario (Courchene and Telmer, 1998). The sectoral shift to high-order services and the net effects of new information technologies (leading to both dispersion and concentration) will continue to favour concentration in the larger metropolitan areas, in their suburbs, and in a few smaller places in amenity-rich locations (Office of Technology Assessment, 1996). Most growth, as a result, will be 'telescoped' on a few urban regions; while almost all other areas of the country will witness only modest, if any, expansion. Urban decline will become more common. Thus, the contrasts between those cities that are winners and those that are losers in the national growth sweepstakes will become even more pronounced. The challenge for senior governments is to respond to the increasing variability of growth and change; but first they must recognize that the problem exists.

Within metropolitan areas, the processes of suburbanization and dispersal will be difficult, if not impossible, to reverse—even should we wish to do

so. We have built new suburban structures that depend almost entirely on the automobile and the truck, oriented around expressways, malls, and parking lots. These structures render alternative urban forms in the future highly unlikely (Sewell, 1993). Although average population densities are higher in Canadian metropolitan areas than in the US, they are still too low to permit widespread introduction of transit, rapid or otherwise. And densities are still falling. Part of the problem, as noted, is the widening geographical separation of residential areas from employment areas, recreation, and shopping in the new suburbs, and the obvious lack of co-ordination in planning these complementary uses—and between these activities and public transit—at the macro-scale. Although we have done a reasonable job of micro-level site and subdivision design, the lack of regional co-ordination in the newer suburbs may be one of the principal failures of urban planning in Canada in the late-twentieth century. Part of the problem, of course, is the increasingly varied demand for urban travel and the proliferation of work locations. Canadian cities have a higher proportion, on average and in comparison to US metropolitan areas, of total metropolitan employment located in the CBD, which is most easily served by transit. But this proportion is now relatively small, and declining. Dispersed work locations are especially difficult to service with transit, and new information technologies will make it easier to substitute electronic exchanges for certain kinds of travel.

At the same time we can assume that the level of social, ethnic, and lifestyle diversity in Canadian cities will increase. Generally this transition will occur in positive ways, but not without tensions and struggles over the use of space and access to resources. The population will continue to age as the baby-boom generation grows older, and immigration—one obvious form of globalization—will continue to provide new sources of diversity. It is also likely that social diversity, and the fragmentation of households into ever smaller units, will be linked to deepening poverty, especially among children, thus increasing social polarization as income distributions within cities become more skewed.

Table 2.6   **Contrasting Directions for Future Urban Forms**

Attributes	Scenario 1	Scenario 2
Spatial organization	Decentralized, dispersed	Decentralized, multi-nodal
Population density	Low and declining (sprawl)	Stable (increasing in selected locations—reurbanization)
Land-use segmentation	Highly segmented, homogeneous zones	Mixed uses, heterogeneous zones
Social structure	Increasingly polarized, homogeneous social areas	Increasingly diverse, mixed communities
Production spaces	Dispersed throughout urban area	Decentralized, but reconcentrating in new suburban nodes
Local labour markets	Disintegrating, dispersed	Reintegrating, balanced and diverse
Public goods and services	Increasingly unequal, largely privatized	Uniform, equitable, largely state-provided
Transportation mix	Exclusively auto-oriented and expressway biased	Auto-transit balanced
Governance	Fragmented, numerous local governments, highly competitive	Regionally co-operative, with local empowerment
Sense of community	Strong, but locally focused and exclusionary	Strong, but with a broader region-wide commitment

It is still possible, nonetheless, to sketch out alternative scenarios for future urban forms. As one example, Table 2.6 offers contrasting directions or trajectories of change in urban development using a number of conventional attributes as strategic indicators. These attributes incorporate 'polarities'—or contradictory directions—of change, for example, in densities, land-use mix, production spaces, labour markets, public goods, transportation, governance, and our sense of community and collective responsibility. While most of these indicators are self-explanatory, given the earlier discussion, it is useful to illustrate briefly how they might be interpreted. One scenario, the first listed in Table 2.6, suggests that urban areas will become even more decentralized, with widely dispersed activities and populations. An alternative scenario, the second, accepts that decentralization will be the dominant process in the future, but that new development (and redevelopment) will become more focused on and concentrated in a number of higher-density nodes. In this case, and in terms of all of the indicators used, it is important to remember that the tendencies outlined in both scenarios are currently present in our urban areas. Our urban future depends on a balancing of these forces. We do have real choices to make.

This is not a forecast of impending urban nightmares, but a recognition that serious challenges await governments, planners, and social service agencies in the next few decades. Many of the same challenges face decision-makers in other parts of the developed and developing worlds (United Nations, 1996). How well we as a society meet these challenges will determine whether or not Canadian cities retain their existing living environments and their overall quality of life.

Notes

1. The census definition of 'urban' is the population living in incorporated settlements of 1,000 or more people and with a density of at least 400 persons per square kilometre.
2. An alternative definition of the urban population is to sum the entire populations of all CMAs and CAs and those of all other places with over 1,000 population. That exercise shows the urban population to be 84.5 per cent of the national total.
3. The increasing emphasis on competitiveness and urban economic development in public policy is clearly evident in both the mandate and the final report of the Task Force on the Future of the Greater Toronto Area (the Golden Report) (Greater Toronto Area Task Force, 1996).
4. For example, between 1991 and 1996 the number of one-person households in Canada increased by 15 per cent to 2.6 million—almost one-quarter of all households. In some inner cities the proportion is over 50 per cent.
5. Development levies, widely used in the Toronto region, are fees imposed by local and regional governments (and in some cases by school boards and electricity commissions) on all lots for new housing in order to pay for the costs of municipal services such as sewers, roads, schools, and libraries. These levies can amount to as much as 30 per cent of the cost of serviced residential land.
6. GVRD refers to the Greater Vancouver Regional District, a co-operative organization of municipalities in the Fraser River valley designed to deliver region-wide services (Hutton, 1998). The Greater Toronto Services Board (GTSB), the follow-up to the original Metro Toronto regional government, was formally established in January 1999 to co-ordinate services across the entire GTA. At present it has only one major responsibility—managing GO Transit.

References

Barnett, J. 1995. *The Fractured Metropolis*. New York: Harper Collins.

Beach, C., and G. Slotsve. 1996. *Are We Becoming Two Societies? Income Polarization and the Myth of the Declining Middle Class*. Toronto: C.D. Howe Institute.

Beaujot, R. 1991. *Population Change in Canada: The Challenges of Policy Adaptation*. Toronto: Oxford University Press.

Berry, B.J.L., ed. 1976. *Urbanization and Counter-urbanization*. Beverly Hills, Calif.: Sage.

Bourne, L.S. 1996a. 'Reurbanization, Uneven Urban Development and the Debate on New Urban Forms', *Urban Geography* 17: 690–713.

———. 1996b. 'Normative Urban Geographies: Recent Trends, Competing Visions and New Cultures of Regulation', *Canadian Geographer* 40, 2–16.

———. 1997. 'Social Inequalities, Polarization and the Redistribution of Income in Canadian Cities', in B. Badcock and M. Browett, eds, *Developing Small Area Indicators for Policy Research*. Adelaide, Australia: University of Adelaide, Monograph Series No. 2.

——— and M. Flowers. 1999. *Changing Urban Places: Mobility, Migration and Immigration in Urban Canada*. Toronto: Centre for Urban and Community Studies, University of Toronto, Research Paper 195.

_____ and A. Olvet. 1995. *New Urban and Regional Geographies in Canada: 1986–91 and Beyond.* Toronto: Centre for Urban and Community Studies, University of Toronto, Major Report 33.

Breheny, M., T. Gent, and D. Lock. 1993. *Alternative Development Patterns: New Settlements.* London: HMSO.

Britton, J.N.H., ed. 1996. *Canada and the World Economy.* Montreal and Kingston: McGill-Queen's University Press.

Brotchie, J., et al., eds. 1995. *Cities in Competition: Productive and Sustainable Cities for the 21st Century.* Melbourne: Longman.

Caulfield J., and L. Peake, eds. 1996. *City Lives and City Forms.* Toronto: University of Toronto Press.

Champion, A. 1989. *Counterurbanization.* London: Edward Arnold.

Clark, W.A.V., and F. Dieleman. 1996. *Households and Housing: Choices and Outcomes in the Housing Market.* New Brunswick, NJ: Rutgers University Press.

Clarke, S., and G. Gaile. 1998. *The Work of Cities.* Minneapolis: University of Minnesota Press.

Cohen, M., et al., eds. 1996. *Preparing for the Urban Future: Global Pressures and Local Forces.* Washington: Woodrow Wilson Center Press.

Courchene, T., and C. Telmer. 1997. *From Heartland to North American Region State.* Toronto: University of Toronto Press.

Downs, A. 1994. *New Visions for Metropolitan America.* Washington: Brookings Institution.

Dumas, J., and A. Bélanger. 1997. *Report of the Demographic Situation in Canada.* Ottawa: Statistics Canada, Catalogue 91–209.

Foot, D., and D. Stoffman. 1996. *Boom, Bust and Echo.* Toronto: Macfarlane Walter and Ross.

Ford, L. 1994. *Cities and Buildings: Skyscrapers, Skid Row and the Suburbs.* Baltimore: Johns Hopkins University Press.

Ford, R., and D. Zussman, eds. 1997. *Alternative Service Delivery: Sharing Governance in Canada.* Toronto: Institute of Public Administration.

Frisken, F., ed. 1994. *The Changing Canadian Metropolis: A Public Policy Perspective.* Berkeley: University of California Press.

_____ et al. 1997. *Governance and Social Well-being in the Toronto Area: Past Achievements and Future Challenges.* Toronto: Centre for Urban and Community Studies, University of Toronto, Research Paper 192.

Garreau, J. 1991. *Edge City: Life on the New Frontier.* New York: Doubleday.

Greater Toronto Area Task Force. 1996. *Greater Toronto: Report of the GTA Task Force.* Toronto: Queen's Printer.

Hall, P. 1998. *Cities in Civilization: Culture, Innovation and Urban Order.* London: Weidenfeld and Nicolson.

Hart, J.F., ed. 1991. *Our Changing Cities.* Baltimore: Johns Hopkins University Press.

Hobson, P., and F. St Hilaire, eds. 1997. *Urban Governance and Finance: A Question of Who Does What.* Montreal: Institute for Research on Public Policy.

Hodge, D.C. 1996. 'Urban Congestion: Reshaping Urban Life', *Urban Geography* 13: 577–88.

Hutton, T.A. 1998. *The Transformation of Canada's Pacific Metropolis: A Study of Vancouver.* Montreal: Institute for Research on Public Policy.

Isin, E. 1996. 'Metropolis Unbound: Legislators and Interpreters of Urban Form', in J. Caulfield and L. Peake, eds, *City Life and City Forms.* Toronto: University of Toronto Press.

Katz, P. 1994. *The New Urbanism: Toward an Architecture of Community.* New York: McGraw-Hill.

Lemon, J. 1985. *Toronto Since 1918: An Illustrated History.* Toronto: James Lorimer.

———. 1996. *Liberal Dreams and Nature's Limits: Great Cities of North America since 1600.* Toronto: Oxford University Press.

Ley, D. 1996. *The New Middle Class and the Remaking of the Central City.* Oxford: Oxford University Press.

Lo, L., and S. Wang. 1997. 'Settlement Patterns of Toronto's Chinese Immigrants: Convergence or Divergence?', *Canadian Journal of Regional Science* 20, 1–2: 49–72.

Murdie, R.A. 1997. 'The Welfare State, Economic Restructuring and Immigrant Flows: Impacts on Socio-spatial Segregation in Greater Toronto', in S. Musterd and W. Ostendorf, eds, *Segregation and Social Exclusion in Western Metropolitan Areas.* London: Routledge.

Office of Technology Assessment (OTA), US Congress. 1996. *The Technological Reshaping of Metropolitan America.* Washington: OTA.

O'Loughlin, J., and J. Friedrichs, eds. 1996. *Social Polarization in Post-Industrial Metropolises*. New York: W. de Gruyter.

Rondinelli, D.A., et al. 1998. 'The Changing Forces of Urban Economic Development: Globalization and City Competitiveness in the 21st Century', *Cityscape: A Journal of Policy Development and Research* 3, 3: 71–106.

Roseland, M. 1992. *Toward Sustainable Communities*. Toronto: Alger Press.

Rusk, D. 1995. *Cities without Suburbs*, 2nd edn. Washington: Woodrow Wilson Center.

Sassen, S. 1994. *Cities in the World Economy*. Thousand Oaks, Calif.: Pine Forge Press.

Sewell, J. 1993. *The Shape of the City: Toronto Struggles with Modern Planning*. Toronto: University of Toronto Press.

Tomalty, R. 1997. *Compact Cities: Growth Management and Intensification in Vancouver, Toronto and Montreal*. Toronto: ICURR.

——— and E. Isin. 1993. *Resettling Cities*. Ottawa: Canada Mortgage and Housing Corporation.

United Nations Centre for Human Settlements. 1996. *An Urbanizing World: Global Report on Human Settlements*. New York: Oxford University Press.

Wilson, D., ed. 1997. 'Globalization and the Changing American City', *Annals of the American Academy of Political and Social Science* 551 (Special Issue).

Yalnizyan, A. 1998. *The Growing Gap: A Report on the Growing Inequality between Rich and Poor in Canada*. Toronto: Centre for Social Justice.

Zukin, S. 1995. *The Culture of Cities*. New York: Blackwell.

Part One

The Context: Urban Systems

The following four chapters provide important information about the Canadian 'system of cities', the entire set of cities in the country viewed at the national level. These chapters are concerned with how cities perform from a regional, national, and international perspective, and with the interrelationships that have evolved between the different cities that make up the system. This area of interest is referred to as the study of external city structure.

Because the Canadian urban system is relatively small, and because it shares many features with its US counterpart, Canadian cities have often been lumped together with American cities in the study of the 'North American city'. This approach was most popular when the study of cities was dominated by positivist methodologies that relied heavily on quantifiable empirical data and rigorous statistical analysis. In the 1970s other approaches to understanding cities gained credence. Foremost among these was the structuralist position, the premise of which is that empirical patterning must first be seen as an expression of underlying structures observable only through their effect on different aspects of social life. These structures constitute the complex and abiding rules that guide all facets of society. Structuralists argue that cities cannot be fully explained outside of their distinctive historical and geographic context. In Chapter 3, John Mercer and Kim England discuss the issue of a continental urban geography. Because their chapter is based on a cross-sectional or comparative case study, it provides a concrete introduction to the 'unseen hand' that structures patterns of urban development in Canada. In particular, the authors are able to identify social, political,

and economic forces as the root cause of distinctly different styles of urbanization in Canada and the US.

Historical trends from the distant or recent past are a central subject of the other chapters here. Because they focus on change, these, too, afford us insight into the broad structural parameters that govern urban growth. Economic and technological change in particular are widely recognized as having engendered distinct cycles of urbanization. While scholars quibble as to the exact periodicity of these cycles or transitions, the historic record itself is proof of a shifting evolutionary sequence.

According to Larry McCann and Jim Simmons in Chapter 4, features specific to the Canadian urban system include the fact that Canadian urban growth was delayed by a lengthy 'mercantile' period. Confederation and its attendant cross-country transportation network and protective tariffs brought industrialization to cities, which incurred high growth rates. Government intervention in general, particularly a strong federal presence, has had an important impact on the development of the Canadian urban system, especially so in contrast to the US. In the aftermath of Confederation, the Canadian government played an important role in opening up and uniting the country 'from shore to shore', at the same time, largely through import tariffs, fostering the concentration of urban growth and economic prosperity in the core, or industrial heartland, running from Windsor to Quebec City.

The 'boom' period that followed World War II brought high rates of urban growth spurred on by the interrelated forces of a late Fordist economic regime, a population explosion, and a Keynesian political agenda that leaned towards the welfare state. In Chapter 5, Simmons and McCann explain how the postwar boom cemented the strength of the core urban heartland and augmented the dominance of the largest metropolitan cities. After 1975, Canada, along with other developed nations, entered what William Coffey, in Chapter 6, refers to as the non- or post-industrial revolution. In this period, growth shifted significantly to the West and factors of growth and change became more variable. In terms of trends over time and into the future, all the authors here represented agree that the Canadian urban system has become one of greater complexity and uncertainty over time. Mercer and England also suggest that it may be moving closer to the US pattern. The table below provides an outline of some of the more important structural shifts that have produced the Canadian system of cities.

Table 1.1   **Canadian Society and Urban Evolution**

Period	Pre-1900	1900–1945	1945–1975	1975–2000+
Regime	Mercantile	'Great Transformation', early industrial capitalism, establishment of urban industrial society	Postwar boom, advanced corporate capitalism	Post-industrial shift, globalization
Prevailing technology	Sail, horse cart, water and early steam power	Steel, rail, early auto, telephone, telegraph	Auto, air, television	Expressway, telecommunications
Urban system	Small number of port cities act as entrepôts, hierarchy of service centres develops as agriculture expands	Industrial core (Windsor to Quebec City), resources-based periphery, incipient decline in eastern provinces	Metropolitan dominance	Toronto gains primacy, shift to the West, Quebec system becomes more autonomous, some centres decline
Urban economy	Staples based	Early corporate capitalism, Fordism	Advanced corporate capitalism, late Fordism	Deindustrialization, shift to service economy
Urban demographics	Immigration (primarily European) is major input to population growth	Urbanization, growth slowed by WWI, Great Depression, and WWII	Baby boom, high rates of postwar immigration	Baby bust, population growth becomes a function of immigration
Political agenda	From colonies to Confederation	Nationalism: transportation, protective tariffs, regional support	Keynesian policies, federal transfers, regional economic development	Federalism under siege, NAFTA, multiculturalism, retrenchment of welfare agenda
Canadian distinction	Colonialism	Staples base	Welfare state	Multiculturalism

Chapter 3

Canadian Cities in Continental Context: Global and Continental Perspectives on Canadian Urban Development

John Mercer and Kim England

Contemporary cities are the product of the interaction of large-scale processes with local urban forms, mediated through institutions that have a distinctively national character. So the cities of Canada can be differentiated from those in other major world regions, such as Europe, Latin America, and East Asia, in terms of prevailing urban forms, political geographies, and socio-economic characteristics. However, from a global perspective Canadian cities are commonly seen as being more similar to US cities, giving rise to the concept of the North American City (Yeates, 1998). And, from an international perspective, this concept has real utility and a certain coherence for both teaching and research. Indeed, given the global prominence of American social science and theorizing about the city, it is not surprising that 'the North American city' concept has considerable intellectual purchase and is widely accepted. Yet, there is great value in geographers' claims that place matters, that local and regional contexts do make a difference—a difference not merely evident in urban landscapes but important in the everyday lives of ordinary Canadians.

In this chapter we challenge the singular concept of 'the North American city'. We reflect on differences and similarities between Canadian and US cities and how they have persisted or changed over approximately the last 25 years.[1] At the outset we want to make it clear that during this period cities on both sides of the border have become more variable and complex at both the intra-urban and inter-urban scale, making it increasingly difficult to make broad generalizations about differences between the US city and the Canadian city (hence the plural

'cities' in our title). In our chapter we attempt to draw out the nature of several Canadian-US differences with respect to the nature of the urban form, including housing and transportation, and urban processes that shape cities in both countries. It is essential that Canadians understand the global processes that directly produce change in their cities, and that there be an appreciation that these changes are not necessarily experienced in a similar way in different places. Of course, some urban areas are relatively untouched by certain global processes (international immigration, for example). But the key is that cities are open systems in an era marked by increasing economic globalization and restructuring, rapid transformations in telecommunications, massive increases in international travel for business, administration, and tourism, and new dynamics in international migration and settlement. A wide range of such large-scale processes markedly affects cities in Canada. Subsequent chapters in this volume will provide much greater detail on specific features of Canada's metropolitan and urban centres with respect to the interplay between these processes and local structures, and how this interaction is manifested in the various geographies of Canadian cities.

Urban Canada in Context

In common with other economically advanced countries, including the US, a high proportion of Canadians live in urban places. Of greater importance is the fact that the vast majority of Canadians live in metropolitan areas. Just under two-thirds of Canadians (and almost four-fifths of Americans) reside in these key locations. In terms of metropolitanization, the twentieth century witnessed vast transformations. At its dawn just over 1 million Canadians lived in the principal metropolitan regions, but by its close almost 18 million did so. The scale of these metropolitan areas has also increased such that at the end of the century, there were four 'million plus' metropolitan areas in Canada (and 40 in the US, a roughly equivalent number keeping in mind that the US population is larger than Canada's by a factor of approximately 10). There are two particularly notable cross-national differences in the two contemporary metropolitan systems. First, the Canadian system has grown faster in the most recent decade for which data are available (1985/6 to 1995/6), at 16.8 per cent compared to 11.8 per cent in the US. Second, geographic concentration is more marked in the smaller Canadian urban system with just under one-third of the national population living in the three largest CMAs, whereas only about 17 per cent of Americans live in the three largest Metropolitan Standard Areas (MSAs)—New York, Los Angeles, and Chicago. Thus, Toronto, Montreal, and Vancouver continue to dominate the Canadian urban system in both perceptual and practical terms, and with the national capital region (Ottawa-Hull) recently joining the 'million plus' club, the principal economic and political Canadian players are well represented at the top of the urban hierarchy. However, no Canadian city is among the top rank in the various orders of 'global cities', which includes New York and Los Angeles. In the growing literature on 'world cities' Toronto is generally given a second-tier ranking, as are several major US centres (Friedmann, 1986; Sassen, 1991).

As the absolute size of the metropolitan population grew over the twentieth century there has also been an important geographical redistribution throughout North America. First, there is a strong relationship between metropolitan growth and economic performance of the regional hinterland, and increasingly (at least for certain favoured metropol-

itan areas) their growth is linked to their performance in the international economic system. Thus, we find in both the Canadian and US urban systems considerable variation in terms of population and household change depending on their location within their respective national space economies. In general terms, metropolitan areas in western Canada, especially in Alberta and British Columbia, and those in southern Ontario have prospered and grown, while CMAs in Atlantic Canada and Quebec have done less well. To characterize the US experience is more challenging because of the greater variation within that system. However, particularly dramatic growth is evident in the metropolitan areas in the Pacific states, and in Arizona, Texas, Florida, Georgia, and North Carolina, while the places of slower growth, stagnation, or decline are concentrated in the old industrial heartland states.

The second major redistribution has occurred within the metropolitan complexes themselves. As a consequence of burgeoning suburban growth and decentralization of economic activity, some observers argue that a demonstrably different urban form has been created, as captured in Deyan Sudjic's provocative yet prophetic title, *The 100 Mile City* (1992). In the last decade of the twentieth century, almost half of all Americans live in suburbs (46 per cent) and within metropolitan areas those residing in the outer city outnumber those in the central city by roughly three to two. In Canada, metropolitan suburbanites account for just over one-third of the national population and the ratio of outer to central city population is 1.3 to 1. Thus, while suburbanization is common in both countries, these data suggest that suburbs remain more dominant in the US than in Canada. This is more than a mere geographical curiosity. The predominantly white American suburbanites are a major political force whose allegiance is hotly contested in national and statewide elections. Likewise, while suburbanites are of lesser demographic significance in the Canadian context, their votes in the electoral districts surrounding the principal metropolitan areas, especially Toronto and Montreal, are pivotal in provincial and national elections.

Canadian and US Cities: Differences and Similarities in Urban Form

Conventionally, Canadian cities are characterized as having more vital central cities, and as being more compact and less dispersed than their US counterparts. In this section we compare and contrast the urban form of Canadian and US cities along a series of dimensions that previous research indicates are a useful basis for cross-national comparisons. These are population and household change, urban transportation systems, urban housing stock, and the planning process and geopolitical structure at the metropolitan level.

Population and Household Change

The dynamics of population and household shifts within metropolitan areas are useful indicators of structural changes in urban form. To summarize population shifts in the two urban systems we developed a five-type classification based on population change in metropolitan areas and their central cities. Note that central cities usually approximate, but are not synonymous with, the 'inner city' as defined in the literature and treated at length in this volume in Chapter 12. The central city is the incorporated political unit around which outlying units have grown. It is usually the largest and oldest of the municipalities that make up a metropolitan region, statistically defined as census metropolitan area (CMA) by Statistics Canada (see Appendix A).

The classification presented in Figures 3.1 and 3.2 provides revealing cross-national comparisons. For the 1981–91 decade (see Figure 3.1), there are no Canadian cases where both the central city and the overall metropolitan region lost population (Type 1), and hence there are no places in serious difficulty by this criterion. There are not even many CMAs (four out of 25—fewer than a fifth, examples being Windsor and Saint John) that fall into Type 2, what we call the classic type of population change in urban areas: central city decline within overall

metropolitan growth. The majority of the CMAs (76 per cent) are to be found in the two classes that capture either a stagnating central city with metropolitan growth (Type 3), or a solidly growing central city along with metropolitan growth (Type 4). Examples from Type 3 are Montreal, Hamilton, and Halifax, and from Type 4, London, Calgary, and Vancouver. So, although only two CMAs (Kitchener and Saskatoon) exhibit what we term booming central city and metropolitan growth (Type 5), the vast majority of Canada's CMAs did not suffer from central city population decline in this decade. In stark contrast, the US system has 39 cases (out of 230—almost one-fifth) where the entire metropolitan area, as well as its central city, lost population (Type 1) and another 54 areas classified as experiencing the classic type of population change (Type 2). In the Type 1 group we find places such as Buffalo, Detroit, New Orleans, Flint, and Akron to name but a few, and in Type 2 examples include Philadelphia, Denver, Memphis, Syracuse, and Mobile. However, perhaps the most striking aspect of the US evidence is its diversity. Although Figure 3.1 shows that there are 93 MSAs with central city population decline (Types 1 and 2), it also indicates that there are 37 areas classified as Type 5, where central city growth exceeded 20 per cent, combined with overall metropolitan growth. This diversity is not new. Findings here echo the results of Goldberg and Mercer (1986) based on the 1970/1 to 1975/6 period.

Central cities can lose population because of absolute loss resulting from out-migration, or because households locating in the central city, where smaller households have traditionally been found, are becoming even smaller. While population loss tends to distress politicians and the media, a more profound loss for a local jurisdiction is that of households. The loss of households' effective demand for goods and services, including housing, has a cumulatively negative effect on a city's quality of life. The US experience is more threatening in this regard as some 60 central cities experienced a loss in households (over 20 per cent of the nation's central cities with populations larger than 50,000) in the 1980–90 period. Such a loss is common in

Figure 3.1   **Metropolitan Population Change: Distribution of Metropolitan Areas by Type of Change, Canada and the US, 1980/1–1990/1**

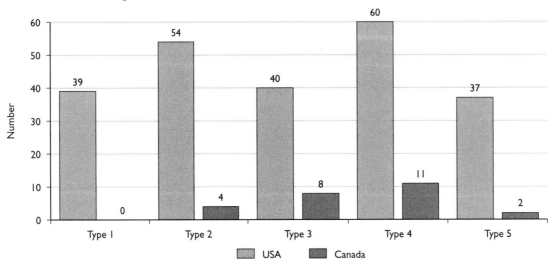

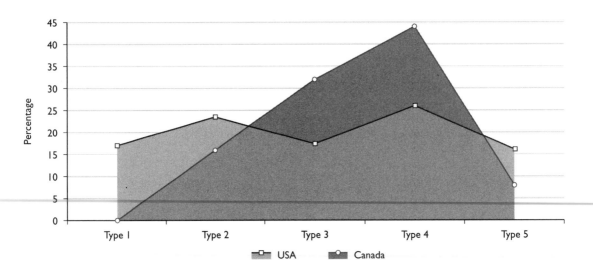

Legend
Type 1: central city decline allied to metropolitan decline
Type 2: central city decline and metropolitan growth
Type 3: central city stagnation (equal to or less than 5% over five years*) and metropolitan growth
Type 4: solid central city growth (in the 5.1 to 19.9% range) and metropolitan growth
Type 5: booming central city growth (20% and over) and metropolitan growth

*Numbers are rates of population change over a decade.

the Types 1 and 2 in our classification: 28 of the 39 grouped into Type 1 and 25 of the 54 in Type 2 suffered this potentially devastating loss. It was most pronounced in some of the largest metropolitan areas, thus posing a longer-term danger to many major places if this decline cannot be reversed. Furthermore, the weakest central cities are spatially clustered in America's industrial core encompassing such states as Pennsylvania, New York, New Jersey, Ohio, Indiana, and Illinois. In contrast, only four Canadian CMAs are of the two types that suffered population loss, and none of them experienced household loss. The Canadian–US difference seems clear. It points to the continued overall vitality of Canadian central cities compared to US cities. Households in the central cities of both countries are generally more varied than those of the suburbs in terms of measures such as household size, family structure, and marital status. But an important difference between Canada and the US, and one that explains some of the patterns described here, is that households in Canadian central cities are much more likely to house families with children.[2]

More recent population data for the first half of the 1990s (using estimates for the US, since there is no mid-decade census as in Canada) do indicate some convergence between Canadian and US metropolitan regions for this period (Figure 3.2). In proportional terms, the Canadian system now has a higher percentage of CMAs in Types 1 and 2 than does the US and there are no Canadian areas in the most rapidly growing group (Type 5), whereas a fifth of US cases are in this 'booming' category. This shift (compared to Figure 3.1) may suggest that there is need for concern. However, it is also likely that it reflects the depth of recession in Canada in the early 1990s and the current strength of the US economy.

Urban Transportation

In a global context, North American cities demonstrate an enormous dependence on autos and trucks in terms of daily personal mobility and the movement of goods. While this affords great individual mobility and flexibility for road users, there are massive environmental and infrastructure costs, or 'externalities', to be borne collectively (see Chapter 21). Nevertheless, the commitment to the car is particularly strong. While Canadians have been greater users of public transportation than Americans, negotiating the low-density suburbs and urban fringe makes the automobile particularly attractive and mass transit particularly costly (and hence in need of substantial subsidy) in both countries.

The size, density, and form of an urban area tend to dictate the modes of urban transportation that can be effectively provided, but once in place transportation systems have an important triggering and location effect on private, speculative development that characterizes capitalist cities like those in North America (for more details on urban transportation in Canada, see Chapter 8). Previous research shows that Canadian commuters were significantly less likely to use automobiles in the daily commute (about two-thirds compared to 85 per cent for Americans). Although it has narrowed, that difference persists into the 1990s, with 77 per cent of Canadians using autos compared to 88 per cent for US metropolitan commuters (see Table 3.1). The rates in both countries are lower for women and certain 'racialized' groups. Canadians are also far less reliant upon expressway systems as there is much less expressway capacity in metropolitan Canada than in metropolitan America (for more details, see Goldberg and Mercer, 1986). There is a striking public transit difference. In a ranking of North American metropolitan areas using 1993–5 per capita public transit trips (thereby standardizing for city size), Canadian CMAs occupied eight of the first 10 ranks and 12 of the top 20. In fact, it is noteworthy that medium-sized Canadian CMAs (under 500,000) have per capita transit patronage values equivalent to large US agglomerations in the several millions, a fact that is revealing given a well-established positive relationship in urban North America and elsewhere in the world between city size and modal split (Urban Transport Fact Book, 1997). Table 3.1 shows that the proportion of transit users amongst commuters in metropolitan America

Figure 3.2   **Metropolitan Population Change: Distribution of Metropolitan Areas by Type of Change, Canada and the US, 1990/1–1996**

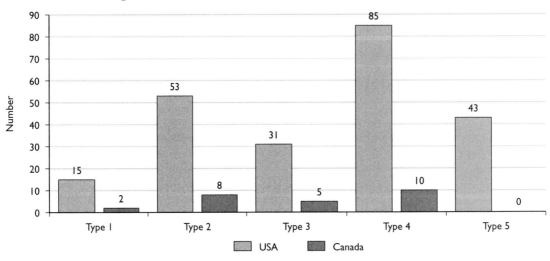

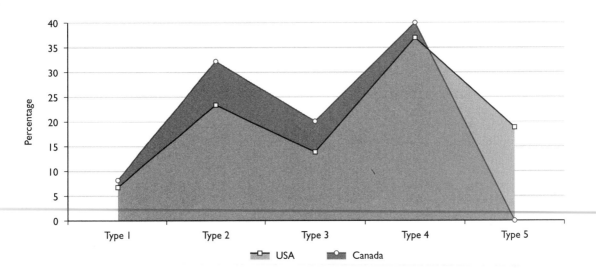

Legend
Type 1: central city decline allied to metropolitan decline
Type 2: central city decline and metropolitan growth
Type 3: central city stagnation (equal to or less than 5% over five years*) and metropolitan growth
Type 4: solid central city growth (in the 5.1 to 19.9% range) and metropolitan growth
Type 5: booming central city growth (20% and over) and metropolitan growth

*Numbers are rates of population change over the period 1990/1–1996.

Table 3.1   **Modal Choice and the Journey to Work: Metropolitan Areas in Canada and the US (per cent)**

	United States (1989/1991/1993)	Canada (1996)
Driving self	76.2	70.5
Carpool	11.5	7.0
Mass transit	5.7	14.8
Walking	3.1	5.8
All other	3.5	2.2

Note: Mass transit refers to bus, streetcar, subway, elevated railroad, and railroad; carpool includes those who are passengers in cars, trucks, or vans driven by others. These are the modes used by workers in the week prior to the survey or census.
Sources: Statistics Canada, 1998; Supplement to the American Housing Survey for the US, various years.

is a low 5.7 per cent. Note, however, that some places exceed this considerably (such as New York, Chicago, San Francisco, and Washington), by factors ranging roughly from eight to two. Given the costs of mass transit provision in lower-density suburban settings, one would expect that transit use would be higher in central cities. It is, but for central cities alone the US national proportion of paid workers using transit reaches only 12 per cent, and this percentage is exceeded only in 26 out of about 270 or so central cities across the US.

It is clear that a striking cross-national difference persists in urban public transportation. There are, however, some worrying signs for Canadian transit operators and their riders. Perl and Pucher (1995) compared ridership trends from 1950 to 1990 and found that following massive postwar declines in both countries, there was strong recovery in ridership on Canadian transit systems in the 1970s and 1980s, but only modest gains in the US. However, Perl and Pucher also report that recently

(1990–4) ridership has steadily declined and at a faster rate in Canada than in the US. Increased employment opportunities in dispersed suburban locations, growing numbers of women combining paid employment with family responsibilities (child-care centres are often in different locations from workplaces, both of which are often located away from retail nodes), fewer transit-dependent youth, auto price competition, and fiscal austerity in the public sector are all factors eroding the effectiveness and patronage of Canadian transit systems. Perl and Pucher argue that without appropriate policy interventions there will be a decline in transit and an obvious increase in auto dependency from which it will be difficult to recover. Such a scenario would inevitably increase demand for more expressway construction. If this should occur, movement towards a more American pattern of land use and transportation is highly likely in Canadian cities.

Housing

The housing stock of a city is one of its most durable features. Of course, until recently many suburbs have been the domain of the single-family detached dwelling unit (mostly in an owner-occupied tenure). Indeed, a common and accurate enough perception of North American cities is that their stock is dominated by owner-occupied, single detached housing units, although there are a number of large central cities in both countries where other forms of housing, such as row housing or apartment structures, predominate—a partial listing of the latter includes Montreal, Quebec City, St John's, and Toronto, and Baltimore, Philadelphia, San Francisco, and New York. In both countries, the level of home-ownership is broadly similar, typically in the 60–65 per cent range of all units. Levels of home-ownership in both countries vary across such social groups as 'race'/ethnicity, age, and gender; for instance, rates are much higher for women with male partners than they are for single women or sole-support mothers (Novac, 1995). However, Canadians do not have access to the various tax advantages provided to Americans to promote home-ownership, widely seen as an essential under-pinning of capitalist democracy and a fine repre-sentation of US individualism and the commitment to private property.

Even if the dominant tenure is essentially sim-ilar across the two countries, the form of housing is clearly not. The generally lower proportion of sin-gle-family units in Canadian metropolitan housing stocks, together with urban transportation differ-ences, suggest a more compact and less dispersed form in Canadian cities—a goal sought by their his-torically more effective local planning and regula-tory systems. Although the single detached unit is the majority of all units in both sets of metropoli-tan areas, a clear cross-national difference exists. For 1990/1, the single detached unit accounts for 61 per cent of all housing units in metropolitan America and 55 per cent in Canadian areas. The typically higher percentages for the US are also found in cen-tral cities (52 per cent in the US and 45 per cent in Canada). There is, however, a striking reversal in the outer city, where the US average is 68 per cent and for Canada 74 per cent. The strong demand for housing in the outer suburbs of US cities, compared to soft demand in the central cities, has driven up land values in recent decades. Land costs, changing household structures in the suburbs, and environ-mental regulations reducing land supply have all contributed to a greater production of multiple forms of housing. These factors are likely also at work in the outer parts of Canadian metropolitan areas but their aggregate impact seems reduced, probably because in Canada the inner parts of the central city have remained a bastion of higher-den-sity multiple-family dwellings, especially of late, high-rise condominiums. Falling numbers of pop-ulation and households, vacant housing, abandon-ment, and eventually clearance have reduced the aging single-family stock in many central cities in the US, compared to two decades ago.

In the US, the gated community or defended suburb is seen as a clear expression of the American ideology of individualism and a withdrawal from the larger metropolitan community (including an abdication of any responsibility for its social condi-tion) (Blakely and Snyder, 1997; Davis, 1990;

Mackenzie, 1994). Gated communities can also be perceived as a reflection of the extraordinary con-cern of Americans over violent crime. Of course, relatively few folk live in gated communities com-pared to the millions of ordinary suburbanites; nev-ertheless, many suburbanites will feel that they, too, have achieved an acceptable level of security in their homes, schools, and parks by moving from the cen-tral city to outer-city locations and investing in some form of personal security system. While there has been increased concern about crime in Canadian metropolitan regions, even in their suburban parts, defended or gated communities are far less com-mon. Still, exclusive suburbs that afford high levels of privacy, comfort, and a sense of personal well-being and security certainly exist.[3]

The suburbs of US and Canadian cities are infi-nitely more diverse than ever before and have shucked off the perception of being residential 'bedroom' communities, with visual uniformity arising from the mass production of so-called 'little boxes' and social uniformity based on their gener-ally middle-class appeal and affordability (see Chapter 13). Historically, suburbs have been associ-ated with women engaged in (unpaid) domestic labour and the reproduction of the family unit in the home. As such, suburbs have come to play con-trasting roles in national discourses and symbolic representations in different countries. Strong-Boag and her collaborators argued that suburban life in the US stands close to the core of the national vision but that suburbs in Canada and Britain do not embody the nation in the same way (Strong-Boag et al., 1998). The small town of America's republican heritage has been re-created in the sprawling realms of the suburbs. Thus, while US and Canadian suburban form may be similar, their lived realities and symbolic meanings can differ. For example, schools in the cities and suburbs of North America may not differ greatly in appearance and have a common function. But the names chosen for US schools invoke republican heroes and icons, American literary figures, and the like, whereas in Canada different political traditions and cultural icons are celebrated—as exemplified by Sir John A. Macdonald and Georges P. Vanier. The tone of the urban landscape is thus different, requiring a different reading; it can only be understood in terms of contrasting cultural contexts. At one level, this is perhaps superficial in terms of functionality, but such namings, public statuary, holiday observances, and other civic rituals combine to convey cumulatively a different sense of place and identity.

Planning and Local Government Fragmentation

Evidence on population and household change, urban transportation, and housing structure has been employed to argue for a generally more compact urban form in Canada. This pattern may be weakening somewhat over time, although we suggest that the newer evidence is mixed; decentralization and spread may be more common in dynamic metropolitan areas, such as Toronto, Vancouver, Kitchener–Waterloo–Cambridge, Oshawa, and Ottawa–Hull, but is less likely to occur elsewhere in Canada where pressures for growth, development, and space are not so evident. Another factor that has contributed to the compactness and livability of Canadian cities has been greater regulation and governance. Over a decade ago a respected planning scholar observed that 'Canadian urban and regional planning has a more wide-ranging and acceptable role than is the case in the United States' (Cullingworth, 1987: 462). More recently, planning systems encompassing 10 large US and Canadian metropolitan areas were studied in five paired comparisons (Rothblatt, 1994). Researchers concluded that the metropolitan management system in Canadian areas was more developed, possessing more fiscal power and authority, than the US counterparts. But they also observe that a global process of decentralization is undermining the historically stronger metropolitan systems because most of the explosive outer city growth occurs outside metropolitan jurisdictions. (Sancton's comments on the restructuring of metropolitan Toronto in Chapter 18 provide an illustrative case in point.) Despite the expectation of increased provincial/state involvement to shape more effective institutions to address metropolitan development,

Rothblatt and associates believe (but do not yet demonstrate) that a cross-national convergence is occurring and will accelerate.

Planning systems in Canada and the United States are generally seen as weaker and ineffective compared to most European equivalents. In the US, where local governments are supported and preserved by the strength of the local autonomy concept, weaker planning systems are exacerbated by highly fragmented local government systems. One striking difference between Canadian and US cities is the extent of local government fragmentation. While fragmentation occurs in numerous Canadian urban areas, those in Quebec being typically more fragmented than most, the Canadian level remains much lower than the US level. Within fragmented metropolitan regions, the central city is commonly portrayed as the loser in the struggle for investment, taxable property, residents (the more affluent the better), and higher government fiscal transfers. While this is much more a characteristic US urban problem, in Canada's few largest metropolitan areas this scenario is becoming increasingly fitting.

Some 20 years ago, one measure of municipal fragmentation in metropolitan areas yielded a statistic approximately 2.5 times higher in metropolitan US than in Canada (Goldberg and Mercer, 1986: 214). Little has changed since then. In fact, the number of local governments per US metropolitan area increased in the 1977–87 decade, from 93 to 113, contributing to even greater fragmentation (Rothblatt, 1994). There is a Canadian predilection for unilateral local government reform through provincial action and legislation, completely disregarding local autonomy in a way that borders on the unthinkable in the US. This trend continues apace in Canada. In the 1996–8 period, there were significant reductions in the numbers of municipal governments with the intent of achieving greater efficiencies and reducing expenditures. In the Halifax urban region, the Nova Scotia government created a new metropolitan-wide municipal government, thereby eliminating the cities of Halifax and Dartmouth as well as smaller suburbs, and amalgamating this urbanized core with a huge rural territory. The most recent restructuring of the

Greater Toronto Area (GTA) was, given this metropolitan region's pre-eminence and size, an extremely important local government reform. The provincial government created a new and much larger City of Toronto by integrating the existing city with the five suburban boroughs that had made up the Municipality of Metropolitan Toronto. The population for the new City of Toronto totals just over 2.25 million, making it by far the largest municipality in Canada and the fourth largest in North America, behind New York, Los Angeles, and Chicago. At one fell swoop, six local governments were replaced by one, markedly reducing fragmentation in a metropolitan area already less fragmented than most.[4]

Canada and US Cities: Differences and Similarities in Urban Processes

A whole host of large-scale or global processes influence Canadian and US cities. Large-scale processes of particular importance to Canadian cities include economic restructuring and the changing nature of immigration. These processes have also affected US cities, but the manner of their working out both locally and cross-nationally suggests a degree of distinctiveness that challenges the concept of 'the North American city' and highlights the significance of comparing Canadian and US cities to uncover what is similar and what is different, and why. In this section, we address a series of large-scale processes—economic restructuring; immigration, race and ethnicity; and inequality and poverty—in order to investigate how the Canadian or US context makes a difference.

Economic Restructuring and Urban Economic Geographies

Given the economic transformation of the last two decades or so, the manufacturing basis for much of the past metropolitan growth has been severely eroded and replaced by a service-based economy (see Chapters 5 and 6). The magnitude of the change is reflected in the use of such terms as the informational city, the post-industrial city, deindustrialization, and the like. Whatever it is called, rapid economic change should be evident in the form and spatial organization of North American urban areas because both Canadian and US economies are open to a common global system and are increasingly integrated under free trade agreements. Thus, we might not expect outstanding cross-national urban differences in this regard. However, the mediating role of the government at all levels (federal, provincial/state, and municipal) is important. The historically greater role in Canada of the public sector in economic development and the stronger commitment to social support systems continue to make a meaningful difference, even if currently weakening under the whips of deregulation and balanced budgets.

Given recent rhetoric, one might expect the landscapes of North American cities to be littered with signs of industrial decay. Many indeed are, but industrial growth and even boom cannot be overlooked. Manufacturing industries, though reshaped, have not vanished, and they remain important in numerous metropolitan areas in both countries. Nonetheless, manufacturing-based metropolitan areas generally have done poorly in terms of growth in recent decades (Bourne, 1999); examples include Detroit, Pittsburgh, Youngstown–Warren, Flint, Erie, and in Canada Chicoutimi–Jonquière, Montreal, and Winnipeg. Conversely, metropolitan areas with diverse economies and new industrial sectors have prospered: examples include Calgary and Vancouver; and Los Angeles, Phoenix, Raleigh–Durham, San Jose, and Atlanta. While the growth impulses are not especially different across the two countries, it is striking that the Canadian core region has retained its share of national manufacturing employment, more so than its US counterpart. As of 1995, three-quarters of manufacturing employment was still located in Ontario and Quebec, chiefly in the Windsor-Quebec City corridor where the Toronto and Montreal CMAs contain just under 40 per cent of national manufacturing employment. The Greater Toronto Area is the dominant industrial region, a position now occupied by the Los Angeles agglomeration in the US, a newer centre outside the traditional industrial heartland of the Northeast. It is clear, however, that at the national level in Canada as in the US, manufacturing employment declined both absolutely and proportionately in the 1985–95 decade, and plant closures also increased steadily from 1986 onwards (MacLachlan, 1996).

A pattern of manufacturing decline in the central city and inner suburbs and expansion in outer-city locations is evident in cities on both sides of the border, as exemplified in studies of Detroit and Toronto (Norcliffe, 1996; Pollard and Storper, 1996). In US medium-sized metropolitan areas where manufacturing employment has steadily declined, the geographic pattern is now that of suburban closure and job loss—central city locations having been abandoned decades ago when alternative suburban sites opened up (for example, Akron, Ohio, and Syracuse, NY). Moreover, the loss of manufacturing employment in US central cities combines with racialized residential patterns to create spatial mismatch whereby inner-city minority (especially male) workers are disconnected from growing job opportunities in the outer city. With industrial decline comes rising poverty and, as Kodras (1997) shows for Detroit, the burden falls disproportionately on Blacks, whose poverty rate is 35 per cent compared to 22 per cent for Whites (1990 data); another chilling indicator is that half of the city's Black children are living in poverty. Although the 'race' dimension is much less salient, similar industrial decline in Montreal has exacerbated poverty in many neighbourhoods. Norcliffe's (1996) Toronto evidence also reveals inner-city streetscapes of industrial decay and a spatial mismatch between unemployed city workers and suburban jobs. But the devastation wrought on America's inner cities by industrial decline, population loss, and housing abandonment as documented in Vergara's (1995) photographic record of urban decay and clearance, where prairie grasses are shown waving on entire empty city blocks in Detroit and elsewhere, is not yet being experienced on a similar scale in Canadian cities.

Economic transformations have also produced changes in the form and landscapes of North American cities in terms of the explosive growth of service-related employment. The downtown office tower and the suburban office park have replaced the factory as emblematic of the age. Moreover, the rise of the service sector has come in tandem with increased female labour force participation since the 1970s. The widely observed decline in US CBDs has been arrested in certain instances, such as Philadelphia, Cleveland, and St Louis. In the cities that house key command and control functions in the continental and global economy, massive reinvestment has occurred in the CBD, producing new office complexes (and dramatic skylines) to house information-rich activities that are part of these functions. Core-area workers seeking inner-city residences (especially two-income couples) have stimulated demand for housing that has been met by condominium redevelopment and gentrification. But as is detailed in Chapter 11, even when there has been absolute increase in central area office floor space, rapid office growth in outer-city locations means that the core has less proportional importance in the overall metropolis.

Further down the urban size hierarchy, it has been difficult to revive the downtown because investment has been harder to come by, given the lesser importance of offices for command and control functions in small cities. Most CBDs in cities in this size range have also lost major retail functions to the suburban malls, with only specialty or niche retailing surviving, possibly linked to downtown entertainment sites. There is ample documentary evidence to show that in the immediate postwar decades, Canadian city cores did not on the whole decline to the extent noted generally for the US (Jones and Simmons, 1993; Goldberg and Mercer, 1986). More recently, however, there has been some convergence with the revival of core areas in many US locations. Places such as Phoenix, Orlando, Boston, Chicago, Seattle, and San Diego, to name but a few, have likely attracted more core-area investment than, say, Winnipeg or Saint John. In both countries, the transformation of the cities at the upper levels of the urban hierarchy means that they are becoming more similar in certain respects as participants in a global economic network, whereas less well-situated or connected places further down the hierarchy are passed by. Research comparing Toronto, Vancouver, and Calgary, for example, with Winnipeg, Hamilton, Kitchener, and Sudbury would be instructive and would probably reveal similar outcomes to comparing Boston, Atlanta, and Denver with Buffalo, Memphis, and Omaha.

We cannot provide a detailed comparison of mall development in urban North America (but see Jones and Simmons, 1993; see also Chapter 17 in this volume). This form of retailing, now with several additional functions (such as entertainment, libraries, and the like) and a sense of a quasi-public space for community use—but carefully controlled by mall managers, is common throughout North American cities. However, as Simmons (1991) notes, there are three important differences between Canada and the US. First, in the US there are significantly more malls per million persons and more floor area per person in malls. Second, US regional malls are more likely to be surrounded by other retail and commercial facilities, benefiting from the consumer flow to the regional centre (the obvious Canadian exception being the West Edmonton Mall). A third and distinctive feature of Canadian regional mall development is the success of city governments in persuading or enabling developers to create this type of mall in downtown cores (almost 10 per cent of all regional malls compared to less than 1 per cent in the US), which helps to bolster the vitality of inner cities. There are also extensive networks of underground shopping in central Toronto and Montreal that provide a controlled, quasi-mall setting in the CBD (other Canadian cities have these, too, but they are most extensive in Toronto and Montreal).

Prior commentary suggests that it is in the outer city that US and Canadian cities are most alike (Goldberg and Mercer, 1986; Harris, 1996), though

even here Goldberg and Mercer were able to show important differences. Some of the most notable features of the contemporary outer city are 'edge cities', regional and super-regional malls, and defended or gated residential communities. Edge cities, although identified earlier as mini-CBDs by Muller (1981), became nationally prominent with the publication of the book of the same name by Joel Garreau (1991). Characterized by several million square feet of office space, between one-half and one million square feet of retailing in a mall-type environment, adjacent residential developments at higher density than typical suburban subdivisions, and an almost total reliance on automobiles as the means of travel, these massive complexes have been produced across the US by private-sector initiatives. Such new forms are rarer in Canadian cities but outer cores, or town centres, have been actively promoted in Toronto and Vancouver (see Chapter 11; see also Relph's [1991] discussion of Toronto's suburban downtowns). The major cross-national difference is the public planning ideology that generated high-intensity suburban centres in the Canadian context, although private development largely occupies the sites. These planned centres were intended to reduce pressure on core CBDs and related inner districts and at the same time to contribute towards 'intensification' of suburbs. The rationale was that long and energy-wasting commutes into the core could be reduced to some degree by facilitating employment clusters within walking distance of medium-density suburban residential clusters and integrating them into suburban transit systems. Given that private capital actually develops these (though civic and cultural institutions are also located there), the outcome may be broadly similar to the edge city form; but the smaller size of Canadian centres (see Hartshorn's [1992] comparison of Scarborough, Ontario, with a typical US suburban core) and much higher-density housing and transit links serve to differentiate them from their US equivalents. Even in the case of Toronto, arguably Canada's most decentralized metropolis and the closest to Sudjic's '100 Mile City', the US edge city model is not yet completely appropriate, either descriptively or in explanatory terms.

Immigration, 'Race', and Ethnicity[5]

Both countries have a common immigrant heritage and, indigenous peoples aside, are nations of immigrants—social, historical, and geographic facts of profound importance. Bearing in mind the factor of 10 in regard to population size, Canada has been admitting immigrants at twice the rate of the US since 1960: 4.1 million entering Canada and 18.2 million the US (or 1.82 when adjusted for the size difference) (Bourne, 1999). In association with global economic change, there have been important shifts in the source countries of the immigrants coming to North America. The proportion of European immigrants has declined—a fact of particular importance in Canada, where this shift in source countries has reduced the significance of the cultural links to Britain. However, while immigration from non-European sources has shot up, there are some key cross-national differences that are important demographically, culturally, and politically. Broadly, the Americas, especially Mexico and other Central American states, as well as various Caribbean countries are the most important source for the US, followed by Asia and Africa. In Canada, the dominant Asian regions (Eastern, Southeastern, and South) alone accounted for just under half of all immigrants (46 per cent) in the 1988–91 period, with the Caribbean/Bermuda and Africa also contributing notable flows (another 13.5 per cent jointly). More recently, for those arriving in 1991–6, the Asian origin proportion increased to 49 per cent while that for Africa and the Caribbean/Bermuda declined slightly to 12.8 per cent. Even within the broad category 'Asian', there are differences that reflect Canada's membership in the Commonwealth (formerly the British Empire) and the US geopolitical involvement in Pacific Asia. Thus, people from India and Hong Kong are proportionately more numerous in Canada, whereas people from Korea, the Philippines, and Taiwan and an array of refugees from the Vietnamese conflict are more significant in

the US context (for Canada, see Badets, 1993; for the US, see US Bureau of the Census, 1997). The impact, culturally and in ethnicized/racialized terms, on the cities to which the immigrants have migrated has been major, not only in terms of social relations but also in terms of labour and housing markets, as well as service provision, with education being particularly emotionally charged.

One thing that Canadian and US cities do share is what could be termed the 'gateway model' of settlement. New international immigrants settle disproportionately in just a very few urban regions, the leading destinations in Canada being Toronto and Vancouver, which attracted a remarkable 60 per cent or so of all immigrants who arrived in the late 1980s, as well as in the 1991–6 period. Montreal, although numerically an important immigration destination, now attracts proportionately fewer given its size (16 per cent in the 1988–91 period, and 13 per cent for 1991–6), a product of the joint effects of perceived language barriers and more limited economic growth prospects (Mercer, 1995). Gateways also dominate in the US, but the concentration is in a larger set of cities than in the Canadian case. The vast metropolitan complexes centred on Los Angeles and New York are the principal US destinations (in the 1985–95 period, as ranked by Frey, 1996); in addition, the Bay Area (San Francisco and Oakland), southern Florida (chiefly Miami), and Chicago, along with the first two, are the five preeminent places for settlement, although Washington and Boston are other noteworthy gateways.

Outward population shifts in US cities are not new and have long been associated with the changing racial composition of cities. The depth of racial aversion and geographic separation in urban America is made clearly evident in works such as *American Apartheid* (Massey and Denton, 1993). Although racialized minorities have increased significantly in numerous Canadian cities, especially the gateway ones, as a consequence of immigration, there is no counterpart to the way in which 'race' marks the US city. Until the 1996 census, one could only impute the numbers of racialized peoples in Canadian cities using data from variables such as place of birth, ethnicity, and mother tongue (Mercer, 1995). Despite the volatile politics of 'race', mounting frustration led to Statistics Canada asking a question in the 1996 census that enabled the agency to establish the numbers and proportions of 'visible minorities'.[6] Accordingly, we now know that only six CMAs, Toronto, Vancouver, Calgary, Edmonton, Montreal, and Ottawa-Hull, have proportional shares greater than the national proportion of 11.2 per cent (Table 3.2). In no CMA does the proportion of visible minorities exceed a third and only in Toronto and Vancouver, the principal gateways, does it exceed one-quarter. For the central cities of Vancouver and Toronto, the visible minority proportion is 44 per cent and 28 per cent, respectively, indicating that in the former this population is somewhat more concentrated in the central city but that in Toronto there is not much difference from the overall CMA proportion. The six CMAs listed in Table 3.2 account for the vast majority of all the visible minorities in the country, but again a marked concentration (a consequence of immigration and settlement in the gateways) is evident in that about 60 per cent of the total reside in the Toronto and Vancouver metropolitan areas. Not surprisingly, then, in the local governments and neighbourhoods of these CMAs racial issues have been most prominent on the public agenda. Many urban Canadians do not experience social and cultural issues that relate to immigration and its racialized consequences, especially controversial and divisive ones, except through the media. This places considerable moral responsibility on media owners and workers and there is continued debate about representations of issues related to racialized groups and immigrants (for a discussion of race relations, crime, and policing in Toronto, see Jackson, 1993).

While 'race', as represented in the black–white duality, has been enormously significant in many if not most US cities, intergroup relations have been complicated by the growth of Asian origin and Latino communities, especially in the rapidly growing metropolitan areas of California, Texas, Arizona, and Florida, as well as in New York, Washington, and Chicago. However, this more recent demographic transformation, with its distinctive geographical patterns, overlies a historic concentration of racialized minorities in America's central cities. In 1990, there were 17 US cities where blacks (mostly African Americans) were in the majority (Detroit, 76 per cent, and Washington, 66 per cent, had the largest proportions) and fully one-fifth of all central cities had proportions greater than one-third, including such major cities as St Louis, Cleveland, Chicago, and Philadelphia (recall that in Canada only in one central city, Vancouver, was the 'visible minority' population greater than one-third). It is highly likely that many of these American cities will be majority black in a few decades. The conditions under which most of these central-city minorities live are, simply put, challenging and often devastating, as William Julius Wilson (1987) illustrates in his book with the poignant title, *The Truly Disadvantaged*.

Massey and Denton (1993: 109) conclude that in America's cities, 'residential segregation continues unabated in the nation's largest black communities, and this spatial isolation cannot be attributed to class ... [and that] ... discrimination against blacks is widespread and continues at very high levels in urban

Table 3.2	**Leading Metropolitan Areas in Terms of Visible Minorities, 1996**
CMA	% Visible Minority
Toronto	31.6
Vancouver	31.1
Calgary	15.6
Edmonton	13.5
Montreal	12.2
Ottawa–Hull	11.5
Canada	11.2

Note: Given that these data are based on a census sample, it is possible that the Winnipeg CMA, with 11.1 per cent, may also exceed the national proportion, allowing for measurement error and rounding.
Source: Statistics Canada, 1998.

housing markets.' While black Americans have participated increasingly in suburbanization, there, too, they face highly segregated communities. There is nothing comparable in scale in a Canadian urban context. For example, the principal destinations of the Jamaican immigrant population in Toronto are distributed across the metropolitan area, although there is clustering in several locations, some in suburban districts with concentrations of social housing (Ray, 1998). And although the central city of Vancouver attracts many Asian-origin immigrants who add to Canadian-born descendants of Asian peoples, only in a few small areas, such as those around Chinatown, is the level of concentration of racialized minorities similar to that in the extensive black ghettos of many US cities. Indeed, a thorough comparative analysis by Fong (1996) concludes that blacks in Canada experience minimal residential segregation, even accounting for the lower proportions they represent in cities, compared to the extreme segregation for urban blacks in the United States. Furthermore, the prospects for dismantling the US ghetto are bleak, suggesting that this urban fact will continue to be an important cross-national difference. Again, while there is greater ethnic and racial diversity than ever before in Canadian cities, nothing compares to the rapidly expanding Latino population in certain US urban regions; Latinos are now a majority in 10 US central cities and represent a significant 25 per cent or more in 34 others. While their residential segregation from the white population is not as pronounced as that for the black–white separation, it is significant and expresses the avoidance behaviour of whites, housing market discrimination against Latinos, and relative poverty.

Inequality and Poverty

Socio-spatial polarization has been well documented, especially in relation to economic restructuring (see Sassen, 1991, for example). The debate over the extent of increasing inequality in industrial countries is complex, reflecting in part problems of data comparability and the interpretation of statistics from various data sources. However, evidence points to a clear Canadian–US difference on inequality. Hanratty (1992) indicates that family poverty rates in the mid-1980s were at 12 per cent nationally in the US but 7 per cent in Canada. However, this masks important differences among family types. The gap is greatest and continues to grow between two-earner couples and sole-support mothers. Hanratty reports a cross-national difference in the poverty rate of single-parent families (of whom over 80 per cent are mothers): just over 40 per cent in the US and a little over 25 per cent in Canada. The difference is based on a more generous and effective social assistance system in Canada. Over the most recent decade, attempts to balance public budgets have placed increased fiscal pressure on the welfare systems in both countries, eroding or eliminating long-established support programs. One might thus expect more convergence in inequality. But the work of social economists Gottschalk and Smeeding (1997) indicates that whereas there has been a significant rise in income inequality in the US from the mid-1970s to the mid-1990s, there was actually a modest decrease in Canada from the mid-1970s to the mid-1980s, and no change through to the mid-1990s (their study is based on a summary of national studies of 24 countries).

Using 1970s data, Goldberg and Mercer (1986: Table 7.12) employed a ratio measure to show that the income disparity between the central city and the metropolitan area as a whole was higher in the US than in Canada. They also found a difference in the distribution of this ratio within the two urban systems, with more acute disparities clearly evident for almost one-third of the US cases but for no Canadian cases. We repeated this analysis for 1990/1 data and found that the cross-national difference persists; the ratios (for household income) are higher for the Canadian cases. At the same time important distributional differences also continue.[7] In studying the geography of income in Canadian cities (although Toronto as a case study within the broader context predominates), Bourne rightly argues for going beyond the rather arbitrary central city-suburban distinction in urban studies. He finds that parts of the Canadian central city reveal continued, even deepening impoverishment; pronounced accumulation of wealth and expansion of élite districts; and a remarkable degree of persistence in both the location and composition of well-established high- and middle-income districts. This characterization does not fit the inner parts of most US urban areas (although some individual cities undoubtedly are a better fit—possibly Seattle, Houston, Dallas, and Minneapolis–St Paul). Bourne (1993: 1313) concludes that the ecology of income 'is significantly more complex' than is suggested by the simple model of affluent suburbs surrounding a poorer central city. An important factor in producing this complexity is the widespread construction of luxury and moderately priced condominiums in Canada's central cities (as well as in the suburbs in such locales as Vancouver and Victoria, which have large retiree populations). Such construction results in the demolition of cheaper, often rental housing, displacing its residents—but with a declining or static social housing sector being unable to house such folk, homelessness and living in shelters is on the increase, likely intensifying the view that Canadian cities are becoming more like US ones.

The city-versus-suburbs dichotomy can distort underlying urban realities that do not respect local government boundaries and tends to homogenize the suburbs at great analytical cost. Yet it is hard to see it disappearing from public discourse. It frames community debate over fiscal health and equity issues concerning taxation and the financing of services. In the US context in particular, 'city' has too often become an emotional signifier for White suburbanites in relation to a heavily racialized 'other' they seek to avoid engaging with or from which they have consciously moved away and outward. Even as Americans now receive more news from television than print media, a steady diet of nightly local TV news paints a depressing picture of the city: no longer the home to the majority in the metropolitan area but a 'left-behind place', replete with arson and violent crime, much of it related to drug use and trafficking; complaints over inadequate or ineffective city services (policing, education, parks, street conditions, housing code enforcement, and trash removal ... the litany goes on); and beset

with fiscal problems (see Beauregard, 1993, for more details on 'voices of decline').

Conclusion

Students of North American cities have to grapple with increasing variability and complexity within the metropolitan areas where the vast majority of North Americans reside. In addition, those who research, and teach about, these places need to work at a finer grain and be more geographically sensitive to the local. Simple, some might say elegant, urban models and broad generalizations will be of less heuristic and practical value. But as long as capitalism persists as the mode of production, North American cities will have a common heritage of considerable social and economic inequalities.

Increasing variability and complexity are principally the result of enormous economic transformations and social changes that are global in nature and that impinge directly on open metropolitan systems. Some of the most fundamental changes are the decreasing significance of manufacturing as the principal economic foundation for urban growth, its replacement with a service-based metropolitan economy with information as a key commodity, the dramatic shift in immigration source regions from Europe to other world regions leading to complex social changes in both inner cities and suburban districts where immigrants now also settle, and a greater array of household structures whose demands for housing provoke change in urban housing markets. Given the large scale of these transformations, the changes they produce are being more or less equally felt in the urban places of Canada and the United States. This could result in greater similarities between the two sets of cities, a direction supported by some of the empirical evidence reviewed here— in short, a convergence thesis.

But a second theme in our essay is that of persistent cross-national differences between Canadian and US cities. Over time, these have arisen as one society and its people made different choices from the other. The United States experienced colonialism and then gained nationhood via revolutionary independence, whereas Canada exemplifies a gradual and still contested nationhood after a much longer colonial dependence. In terms of economic development, Canada became more of a resource-based economy tied to the prosperity of external markets, initially in Britain and then the US itself, while the United States grew into a significant industrial power, eventually a global power. Both expanded their territories—sometimes in conflict with each other—and both experienced massive inward population movements, some forcible in nature (indentured servants and slaves), but with different social consequences in terms of composition and subsequent social histories (French and English, as against Black and White). These strategic choices, and the distinctive urban places that resulted, occurred then in the context of common and widely experienced processes (such as colonialism and industrialization). Canadians continue to desire to differentiate themselves from their huge neighbour despite increased and closer economic integration. It is undeniable that the US now serves as the primary reference and point of comparison—Canada's other. But inherited urban forms, the social mores that shape interpersonal and intergroup relations, and the political culture and institutional structures, including metropolitan and local governance, planning systems, and intergovernmental relations, have all demonstrated effective resistance to continental homogenization. Thus, significant cross-national urban differences persist.

These differences are not simply the result of a greater role for the state in the life of Canadians, although this singular feature of Canadian society was recognized early (Clark, 1968). Today, however, the lessening of public-sector influence and the growth of market dictates may well contribute towards a degree of convergence such that Canadian and US cities will become more alike. With just under half of Canada's 25 CMAs in Ontario, the actions of this single province are absolutely key in this regard. But if urban differences are reflective of a fundamental divergence in values between Canadians and Americans, albeit within a common set of social relations attendant on a shared capital-

ism, then differences will indeed persist, because, to paraphrase Card and Freeman (1993), even small differences do matter.

Thus, it is our considered judgement that the distinctiveness of Canadian cities can still be conveyed by asserting that Canadian cities are more public in their nature and US ones are more private (Warner, 1968). But rather than these being sharply drawn polarities, the concepts need to be seen as having both a range and overlap on a public-private continuum anchored by ideal types (Figure 3.3). In proposing this continuum, we attempt to capture a series of characteristics that include: (1) the strong national commitment in the US to individualism and individual freedoms; (2) the protection of private property rights under the US Constitution; (3) the reliance on private mechanisms and individual user fees in the provision of infrastructures, as well as certain public goods and services; (4) the emphasis on home-ownership, especially of the single detached residence as the ideal type; and (5) the power of the concept of local autonomy in government, the still increasing profusion of special-purpose districts and small municipalities being seen as extensions and expressions of relatively homogeneous social groupings. In a privatized society, problems are solved in a highly personalized manner. The conditions of daily life in many US central cities and certain metropolitan areas have led to withdrawal of population and activity to the perceived safer ground of suburban and exurban places. This listing is partial but conveys something of the essence of the notion of the privatized city.

The public city is more attuned to Canadian values, ideologies, and practices. It expresses a strong commitment to a greater emphasis on collectivities over individuals, though this has weakened with the

Figure 3.3   **The Public-Private Continuum**

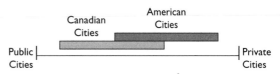

emphasis on individual rights and freedoms of the Canadian Charter of Rights and Freedoms (an emphasis that Lipset [1990] sees as quintessentially American in nature and likely to have important social and political consequences for Canadians and their institutions); to the maintenance of social order and effective public practices over individual pursuits; to a greater trust and belief in the competence of governments and their bureaucracies, though this has clearly diminished in recent decades as the effectiveness of the public sector has been widely and relentlessly attacked by ideologues in Canada and elsewhere; to the idea of active intervention in the chiefly private process of city-making by city and suburban planners, some working for innovative forms of metropolitan government. Public cities are also places where there is a higher quality of urban development consistent with high servicing standards set by local authorities, a well-developed and high-quality public transportation system, an extensive network of community and recreation centres with quality parks and open spaces, all publicly provided, and a school system that is not seen as having virtually collapsed in central cities. In public cities central city-suburban disparities in income and educational terms are lesser than in the private city, although they do exist.

The distinction between the private US city and the public Canadian city owes much to the nature of state intervention rather than the degree of intervention, for considerable state intervention certainly does occur in the former. But governments in the US have been extremely active in support of private consumption and in facilitating private (corporate) gain (although we do acknowledge that the latter is and has been common in Canada as well). This is well illustrated by the vast expenditures on urban freeways that encourage private auto and truck use. By contrast, governments in Canada have adopted a more balanced approach to urban transportation, although this may now be tilting away from the public transit sector in an effort to reduce public expenditures. The willingness of provincial governments to reorganize the administration of metropolitan areas to achieve

regionally integrated forms means a more uniform distribution of municipal services and a more uniform planning process. With US state governments being more sensitive to 'home rule' arguments voiced by those opposed to metropolitan ('big, inefficient, remote') government and being unwilling in most cases to take the lead, sharp variations persist in service standards and property tax levels within metropolitan regions.

Over two decades ago, the question was put: 'Is there a distinctive Canadian city?' (Kerr, 1977). While we avoid the use of the singular 'city' in favour of 'cities' which allows for the inherent variability across the country, we answer confidently 'Yes, but ...', for there is an important qualifier. While distinctive within their continental context, the North American character of Canadian cities needs also to be acknowledged, for they are inevitably open to continental and global interaction and influences.

Notes

1. To some degree we revisit certain findings of Goldberg and Mercer (1986) regarding North American comparisons in their book, *The Myth of the North American City*, which offers a fuller analysis than we can provide here.

2. In addition, a large literature drawing on examples from both Canada and the US develops the idea of family and women-friendly cities. The argument is that multi-purpose, mixed-use, compact neighbourhoods mean greater proximity to services (and perhaps less reliance on cars), while higher densities provide sufficient concentrations of users to support a greater diversity and choice of services within a smaller geographic area (see Eichler, 1995, on Canadian cities, and Weisman, 1994, on US cities).

3. However, the perception of safe suburbs is increasingly being challenged. For example, Ley, Hiebert, and Pratt (1992) found an increase in crimes against property and violent crime in Vancouver's suburbs since the late 1970s.

4. On a 1971 fragmentation index, the Toronto CMA score of 0.009 was well below the

Canadian average of 0.031 and far below US areas paired with it for comparison (Goldberg and Mercer, 1986, Tables 8.1, 8.2).

5. Throughout this chapter we use 'race' consistent with the position that the division of people into separate, distinct 'races' is a social and political construction, not a biological truism. Racialized and ethnicized identities are highly contested and socially significant (for example, inclusion within named categories can have important effects in terms of counting for national censuses), and consequently are important electorally and fiscally. Furthermore, in keeping with the constructed character of 'race' (and also ethnicity), the naming of particular groups changes over time and space (for example, 'Black' and 'African American' in American discourse, and 'Aboriginal', 'Indian', 'Native', and 'Indigenous Peoples' in Canadian discourse).

6. Statistics Canada asked this question in the 1996 census (Question 19): 'Is this person: White; Chinese; South Asian (e.g., East Indian, Pakistani, Punjabi, or Sri Lankan); Black (e.g., African, Haitian, Jamaican, Somali); Arab; West Asian (e.g., Armenian, Egyptian, Iranian, Lebanese, Moroccan); Filipino; Southeast Asian (e.g., Cambodian, Indonesian, Laotian, Vietnamese); Latin American; Japanese; Korean; or other (specify).' While there has been public debate over the appropriateness of descriptive categories (e.g., Latin American, West Asian) to capture racialized identities, the results arguably convey the numbers of people whom most Canadians would consider as belonging to racially distinctive groups.

7. Analysing the 1990/1 median household income for the central city as against that for the metropolitan area yielded consistently higher ratio values for the Canadian urban areas (Canadian mean and median were 90 and 92, whereas for the US cases they were 86 and 87, where 100 indicates that the central city income is equal to that for the entire metropolitan area). Distributional differences also are evident. Over half the Canadian areas have ratio values in the 90–9 range, with only 16 per cent less than 80 and none under 70. By contrast, over a quarter of US metropolitan areas have values less than 80, about 10 per cent are under 70, and the modal category is the 80–9 range (with one-third of all areas). Lastly, there are 32 areas in the US where the ratio value exceeds 100 but only one such case in Canada. In sum, there is much more variability in the US system, as was true in the original 1970/1 analysis.

References

Badets, J. 1993. 'Canada's Immigrants: Recent Trends', *Canadian Social Trends* 29: 8–11.

Beauregard, R.A. 1993. *Voices of Decline: The Postwar Fate of US Cities*. Cambridge, Mass.: Blackwell.

Blakely, E., and M.G. Snyder. 1997. *Fortress America*. Washington: Brookings Institution.

Bourne, L.S. 1993. 'Close Together and Worlds Apart: An Analysis of Changes in the Ecology of Income in Canadian Cities', *Urban Studies* 30: 1293–1317.

———. 1999. 'The North American Urban System: The Macro-Geography of Uneven Development', in F.W. Boal and S.W. Royle, eds, *North America: Environment and Society*. London: Edward Arnold.

Card, D., and C.B. Freeman. 1993. *Small Differences That Matter: Labor Markets and Income Maintenance in Canada and the United States*. Chicago: University of Chicago Press.

Clark, S.D., ed. 1968. *The Developing Canadian Community*. Toronto: University of Toronto Press.

Cullingworth, J.B. 1987. *Urban and Regional Planning in Canada*. New Brunswick, NJ: Transaction Books.

Davis, M. 1990. *City of Quartz: Excavating the Future in Los Angeles*. New York: Verso.

Eichler, M., ed. 1995. *Change of Plans: Towards a Non-Sexist Sustainable City*. Toronto: Garamond Press.

Frey, W.H. 1996. 'Immigration, Domestic Migration, and Demographic Balkanization in America: New Evidence for the 1990s', *Population and Development Review* 22: 741–63.

Fong, E. 1996. 'A Comparative Perspective on Racial Residential Segregation: American and Canadian Experiences', *Sociological Quarterly* 37: 199–226.

Friedmann, J. 1986. 'The World City Hypothesis', *Development and Change* 17, 1: 69–84.

Garreau, J. 1991. *Edge Cities: Life on the Frontier*. New York: Doubleday.

Goldberg, M., and J. Mercer. 1986. *The Myth of the North American City*. Vancouver: University of British Columbia Press.

Gottschalk, P., and T. Smeeding. 1997. 'Cross-National Comparisons of Earnings and Income Inequality', *Journal of Economic Literature* 35: 633–87.

Hanratty, M. 1992. 'Why Canada Has Less Poverty', *Social Policy* 23: 32–7.

Harris, R. 1996. *Unplanned Suburbs: Toronto's American Tragedy, 1900 to 1950*. Baltimore: Johns Hopkins University Press.

Hartshorn, T.A. 1992. *Interpreting the City: An Urban Geography*. New York: John Wiley and Sons.

Jackson, P. 1993. 'Policing Difference: "Race" and Crime in Metropolitan Toronto', in Jackson and J. Penrose, eds, *Constructions of Race, Place and Nation*. Minneapolis: University of Minnesota Press.

Jones, K.G., and J.W. Simmons. 1993. *Location, Location, Location: Analyzing the Retail Environment*. Scarborough, Ont.: Nelson Canada.

Kerr, D. 1977. 'Review of George A. Nader, Cities of Canada Vols. 1 and 2', *Annals, Association of American Geographers* 61: 163–5.

Kodras, J. 1997. 'The Changing Map of American Poverty in an Era of Economic Restructuring and Political Realignment', *Economic Geography* 73: 67–93.

Ley, D., D. Hiebert, and G. Pratt. 1992. 'Time to Grow Up? From Urban Village to World City, 1966–91', in G. Wynn and T. Oke, eds, *Vancouver and Its Region*. Vancouver: University of British Columbia Press.

Lipset, S.M. 1990. *Continental Divide*. New York: Routledge.

Mackenzie, E. 1994. *Privatopia: Homeowner Associations and the Rise of Residential Private Government*. New Haven: Yale University Press.

Maclachlan, I. 1996. 'Organizational Restructuring of U.S.-Based Manufacturing Subsidiaries and Plant Closure', in J.N.H. Britton, ed., *Canada and the Global Economy: The Geography of Structural and Technological Change*. Montreal and Kingston: McGill-Queen's University Press.

Massey, D., and N. Denton. 1993. *American Apartheid: Segregation and the Making of the Underclass*. Cambridge, Mass.: Harvard University Press.

Mercer, J. 1995. 'Canadian Cities and Their Immigrants: New Realities', *Annals, American Academy of Political and Social Science* 538: 169–84.

Muller, P.O. 1981. *Contemporary Suburban America*. Englewood Cliffs, NJ: Prentice-Hall.

Norcliffe, G. 1996. 'Mapping Deindustrialization: Brian Kipping's Landscapes of Toronto', *Canadian Geographer* 41: 266–72.

Novac, S. 1995. 'Seeking Shelter: Feminist Home Truths', in M. Eichler, ed., *Change of Plans: Towards a Non-Sexist Sustainable City*. Toronto: Garamond Press.

Perl, A., and J. Pucher. 1995. 'Transit in Trouble? The Policy Challenge Posed by Canada's Changing Urban Mobility', *Canadian Public Policy* 21: 261–83.

Pollard, J., and M. Storper. 1996. 'A Tale of Twelve Cities: Metropolitan Employment Change in Dynamic Industries in the 1980s', *Economic Geography* 72: 1–22.

Ray, B.K. 1998. *A Comparative Study of Immigrant Housing, Neighbourhoods and Social Networks in Toronto and Montreal*. Ottawa: Canada Mortgage and Housing Corporation.

Relph, E. 1991. 'Suburban Downtowns of the Greater Toronto Area', *Canadian Geographer* 35: 421–5.

Rothblatt, D.N. 1994. 'North American Metropolitan Planning: Canadian and U.S. Perspectives', *Journal of the American Planning Association* 60: 501–20.

Sassen, S. 1991. *The Global City*. Princeton, NJ: Princeton University Press.

Simmons, J. 1991. 'The Regional Mall in Canada', *Canadian Geographer* 35: 232–40.

Strong-Boag, V., I. Dyck, K. England, and L. Johnson. 1998. 'What Women's Spaces?: Women in Australian, British, Canadian and US Suburbs', in R. Harris and P.J. Larkham, eds, *Changing Suburbs: Foundation, Form and Function*. London: Chapman and Hall.

Sudjic, D. 1993. *The 100 Mile City*. New York: Harcourt Brace & Company.

Urban Transport Fact Book. 1997. *Canadian and US Public Transport Ridership by Metropolitan Area*. Available at: <http://www.publicpurpose.com/ut–uscnp.htm>, retrieved Sept. 1998.

US Bureau of the Census. 1997. *Statistical Abstract of the United States*, 117th edn. Washington: US Government Printing Office.

Vergara, C.J. 1995. *The New American Ghetto*. New Brunswick, NJ: Rutgers University Press.

Warner, S.B. 1968. *The Private City*. Philadelphia: University of Pennsylvania Press.

Weisman, L. 1994. *Discrimination by Design: A Feminist Critique of the Man-Made Environment*. Urbana: University of Illinois Press.

Wilson, W.J. 1987. *The Truly Disadvantaged: The Inner City, the Underclass, and Public Policy*. Chicago: University of Chicago Press.

Yeates, M. 1998. *The North American City*. New York: Addison-Wesley Longman.

Chapter 4

The Core-Periphery Structure
of Canada's Urban System

Larry D. McCann and Jim Simmons

No city today functions free of the unprecedented forces currently restructuring the world system. As the organizational units of the world economy, all cities are interconnected through an intricate geography of core and periphery shaped by various economic, demographic, and political processes. Traditionally, urban centres relied on nearby rural areas for food, water, sources of energy, and sometimes capital, but as the twenty-first century approaches in countries like Canada, the interplay between city and hinterland is far more complex. Food now enters our supermarkets from around the world. As a nation, we debate the possibility of selling fresh water abroad. Vancouver's housing industry and import-export trade recoil from declining Asian investment. An oil embargo in the Middle East would affect manufacturing production in Ontario communities, lessening that province's exports to the United States. The people of Canadian cities, like their counterparts elsewhere, daily experience and consider the influence of incessant global change, including the widening reach and tightening control of transnational corporations based in world cities—in particular New York, Tokyo, and London. In fact, every Canadian community, even rural places like a small Newfoundland outport or a Canadian Shield logging camp, functions within a global urban system of ever-changing and metropolitan-dominated networks of capital flows, commodity markets, and immigration (Sassen, 1991).

At the century's end, transition again marks the geography of Canada's urban system, but it does so in rather paradoxical fashion. The first transition in the country's core-periphery geography occurred when several British North American colonies experienced the unifying and centralizing forces of confederation and industrialization during the Great Transformation (c. 1867–1929), conferring on central Canada the status of industrial heartland, and on regions like the Maritimes, western Canada, and the Canadian Shield the role of resource periphery. Today, in our so-called post-industrial age when the tertiary, quaternary, and quinary sectors grow proportionally more important, cities of heartland and hinterland continue to compete by offering economic incentives to high-tech and producer-service firms while promising the amenities of the good life to domestic migrants and immigrants alike. But in reality, only a few centres—in partiular Toronto, and to a lesser extent Vancouver, Calgary, Edmonton, and Ottawa—have mounted a challenge to the once-dominant economic leadership of Montreal. Unquestionably, the space economy of Canada's urban system, like the world system itself, is far from static. The traditional core in southern Ontario and Quebec is more divided today, not just culturally but also economically, and regional core-periphery patterns in western Canada show greater metropolitan strength. This release of power westward to Toronto and the West's leading metropolitan centres is highly significant, indicating a fundamental transition in Canada's space economy. Paradoxically, though, the core-periphery structure of the country remains intact as the fundamental spatial context in which urban development takes place—despite geographical shifts in power and control. Indeed, core and periphery persist everywhere as the fundamental spatial structure of the world economy.

This chapter introduces the spatial and temporal character of Canada's urban system. We first consider some basic conceptual, geographical, and structural properties of Canada's core-periphery urban system by addressing several questions: What are the functions and sizes of cities found in heartland and hinterland regions? What location factors influence these patterns? What are the basic components or subsystems of a national urban system? And how do cities grow in a core-periphery system? We then explore economic, demographic, and political aspects of the urbanization process, emphasizing selected examples of Canada's urban past that illustrate the historical development and transitional nature of the urban system. The subsequent chapter, Chapter 5, goes on to examine transition in the contemporary urban system during the most recent period of global change, building on concepts and themes introduced here.

Canada's Urban System: A Framework for Analysis

For students of city structure, the urban system remains the context—the backdrop—against which any interpretation of the changing landscape of Canadian cities must be made. Industrial landscapes of hinterland resource towns (e.g., mine, mill, or fish plant) differ substantially from heartland manufacturing centres (e.g., integrated steel fabrication, automobile and parts complexes). Similarly, provincial capitals support more office space than regional transportation cities, and the business cores of financial centres have more office buildings than do tourism towns. The transitional nature of the urban landscape today—as regards any of a number of major issues such as immigration, industrial abandonment, gentrification, renewal of the urban core—is influenced by global change and restructuring (Ley, 1997; Sassen, 1991). As the economic and social structures of cities change continuously in many different ways, so do their landscapes.

Defining the Urban System

The all-embracing term 'urban system'—called by some 'system of cities'—includes many relationships and forces that affect the evolution, functioning, and landscape of a particular city. A central feature of the urban system approach requires that each city be viewed within the context of other cities. When an urban system is described in aggregate, the resulting structural characteristics are more or less the same for any developed country like Canada, including uneven spatial patterns. Whatever pairing of terms is used to describe the system's major spatial feature—core and periphery, heartland and hinterland, metropolis and hinterland, developed or underdeveloped, or centre and margin—geographers and other social scientists usually agree with Fernand Braudel that 'geographical space as a source of explanation affects all historical realities, all spatially-defined phenomena' (Braudel, 1984: 21; Krugman, 1996; Landes, 1998).

Within the core-periphery paradigm, core regions are the more dominant spaces. Core areas are always accessible to markets and usually possess favourable physical qualities. They display a diversified profile of secondary, tertiary, and quaternary industries as well as a full division of labour; they are well advanced along the development path and possess the capacity for innovative change; they are characterized by a highly urbanized and concentrated population forming a well-integrated regional urban system; and they are able to influence and usually control—through the power of metropolitan centres—economic, social, and political decisions of national importance. Peripheral areas are distinguished by the opposite qualities: an emphasis on primary resource production; a more dispersed population; limited innovative capacity; restricted political power; and narrowly based urban economies and weakly integrated urban systems (McCann, 1998). The core and periphery tensions within global, national, or regional urban systems critically affect the urban process in a variety of ways, acting upon cities within the context of particular economic, demographic, and political sub-systems or networks (Simmons, 1986).

The Size and Function of Cities

Just over three-quarters of Canada's increasingly multicultural society now live in urban places—defined here, and in the next chapter, as cities with a population greater than 10,000.[1] In 1996, Statistics Canada identified 137 such places. Although these communities occupy very little space, they house most of the country's economic, social, cultural, and political strength.

The CMAs and CAs that comprise Canada's urban system are mapped in Figure 2.1 (in Chapter 2), revealing regional variation in their distribution within the Canadian ecumene. The term 'ecumene' refers to areas settled and exploited (or worked) by a country's labour force (Gajda, 1960). The nation-wide city distribution pattern shows a dominant core area (that is, the Windsor–Quebec City corri-

dor); the resource ecumene (e.g., the Canadian Shield and eastern and most of western Canada); and the largely uninhabited zones or non-ecumene (that is, the Far North). The urban character of these generalized zones is summarized in Table 4.1. The most intense concentration is found in the industrial heartland, or Windsor–Quebec City corridor, that envelops the country's two largest urban nodes: Toronto and Montreal. Most of the country's manufacturing and post-industrial activity occurs in this zone, where the population density exceeds 100 people per square km. The 50 cities in the corridor include more than 60 per cent of Canada's urban population. Cities here compete as production centres—of both manufactured goods and financial and producer services—by attracting investment to create new jobs (Yeates, 1991). The resource ecumene is a broad sweep of territory extending east, north, and west from the Great Lakes–St Lawrence Lowlands. Population density in this zone is roughly one-twentieth that of the industrial heartland.

Table 4.1 **Regions of Urbanization: Canada, 1996**

Region	Area (sq.km.)	Population (000s)	Population Density (/sq.km.)	Number of Cities	Urban Population (000s)	Percentage Urban
Windsor-Quebec City corridor	147,600	15,665	106.10	50	13,648	87.1
Remainder of ecumene	2,301,800	12,579	5.46	76	8,476	67.4
Total ecumene	2,449,400	28,244	11.53	126	22,291	78.3
Non-ecumene	6,753,800	603	.09	11	328	54.4
Total Canada	9,203,200	28,847	3.13	137	22,452	77.8
United States context*	2,973,244	129,343	43.35	99	98,731	76.3

*The United States context is defined as those states located within 500 km of Canada: Washington, Oregon, Idaho, Montana, North Dakota, South Dakota, Minnesota, Wisconsin, Illinois, Indiana, Michigan, Ohio, Pennyslvania, New Jersey, New York, Maryland, Connecticut, Massachusetts, Rhode Island, Vermont, New Hampshire, and Maine (but not Alaska). Note that only those cities over 100,000 population are included.

Sources: Statistics Canada, *Census of Canada 1996* (Ottawa); United States Bureau of the Census, *Statistical Handbook of the United States* (Washington: Government Printing Office).

Smaller core areas here, including southwestern British Columbia's Georgia Strait region and the Edmonton–Calgary corridor, organize the population and economic activities of surrounding resource hinterlands. Although these outlying cores are gaining national prominence in economic activity and metropolitan power, they still rank well below those of the central Canadian heartland. Many cities in the resource ecumene remain focused on basic service functions or the processing of primary commodities. They typically compete against each other to serve a resource hinterland, their pull on people and investment increasing or decreasing as the demands for

resources rise or fall. But the economies of some—especially Calgary, Edmonton and Vancouver—are finally maturing to the point where they offer financial and other producer services to expanding global markets. The area beyond the resource ecumene—the non-ecumene—includes very little urbanization. Settlements are small and widely dispersed in the Far North. Functionally, they serve mainly the local community and some remote and distant customers.

The core-periphery distinctiveness of Canada's urban system is further illustrated by differentiating cities that serve the primary sector from those that produce manufactured goods (Figure 4.1). Urban-

Figure 4.1   **Economic Specialization of Canadian Cities in 1996**

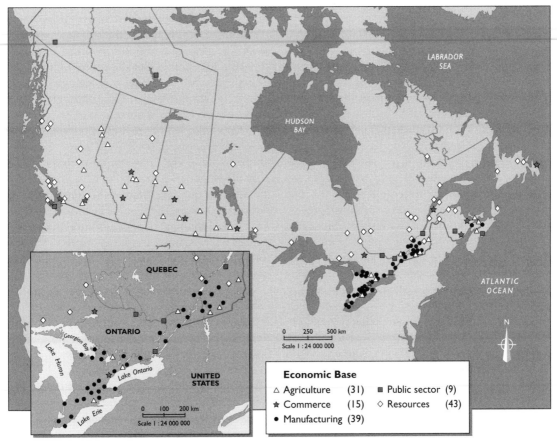

centred regions in the Windsor–Quebec City corridor have traditionally produced goods and services for the entire Canadian market, taking advantage of external (urbanization and localization) economies and the savings associated with transfer economies and relative market accessibility. The manufacture of producer and consumer goods for the domestic market was aided historically by protective tariffs, but this situation is now in transition. Following the free trade agreements of the late 1980s and early 1990s, central Canadian cities are becoming increasingly linked to manufacturing centres in adjacent parts of the United States, jointly serving North American customers. By comparison, most towns and cities of the periphery remain distant from major Canadian markets, a significant factor serving to explain their continuing emphasis on primary production (e.g., lumber, pulp and paper, natural gas) for export to the United States, Asia, or Europe.

Networks of Connection

Interdependence among places is the central feature of any urban system, shaping the geographic patterns of core and periphery. Further, variations in city size and location generate uneven flows of migrants and information among cities, and economic specialization or diversification requires adjusting flows of goods and services to satisfy consumers. Interpreting the patterns of interaction and integration reveals, in fact, the essential geographic features of the Canadian urban system. This can be analysed by considering the example of inter-city migration. Within Canada's system of some 137 cities of 10,000 or more people, many of the thousands of potential migration links are non-existent, but others are extremely large. Cities have their strongest connections with other cities that are, first and foremost, large and located nearby. Thus, Victoria connects with Vancouver, Edmonton with Calgary, Hamilton with Toronto, and Quebec City with Montreal. But the pull of the dominant metropolis cannot be denied. Halifax, Saint John, Winnipeg, Calgary, Vancouver, and other leading provincial centres are linked strongly with Toronto.

This hierarchical pattern of inter-city migration is widely observed in most industrial countries, with minor variations shaped by the relative importance of city size and distance.[2]

Three subsystems or networks of connections—economic, demographic, and political—capture most of the linkages that shape Canada's core-periphery structure and growth patterns in the urban system (Table 4.2). Interaction within the economic subsystem measures production and consumption processes, such as the movement of raw materials from the periphery to international markets or the flow of manufactured goods and producer services from the corridor to consumers across the nation. The economic subsystem is the most open to external influences, the most rapidly changing, and the most variable in growth rates over space. Change in any one place is transmitted to other cities, whether located nearby or far away, according to the strength of their linkages with this place. The economic component can be vulnerable to wild fluctuations. Over the course of a year, for example, the number of jobs or aggregate income can change from −10 to +30 per cent annually in small, resource-based communities.

The demographic subsystem measures flows of people and information. Though sensitive to economic impulses, the demographic network usually responds slowly to economic change. Local demographic structures are always struggling to keep up with such changes. There might be too many workers or not enough, or workers may possess the wrong skills. Raising a child to enter the labour force takes at least a generation; downsizing a community's population by 10 per cent through out-migration may take many years. While, in general, changes in economic conditions—especially jobs—determine the location of urban population growth, there is usually a fairly long response time to the downward restructuring of the urban system. True, in resource-based regions there might well be a sudden exodus of workers from a declining town, especially a single-enterprise resource community that abruptly closes its only mine or mill, but this is the exception, not the rule (Bradbury, 1984). The slow

Table 4.2   **Types of Urban System Linkages**

Type of Subsystem	Examples	Characteristic Patterns
Economic	Commodities, manufacturing products, consumer goods, financial services	High volume of continuing flows reflect overall activity Roughly symmetrical Specialized flows of commodities
Demographic	Migration, information flows, telephone calls, airline passengers	Proportional to city size and distance Reduced flows across national and linguistic boundaries Depending on context, larger centres attract more flows (e.g., migration) or generate more flows (e.g., information)
Political	Taxes, provincial and municipal transfers, pensions, welfare, employment insurance, health and education, government wages	Roughly 50 per cent of GNP Spatial variability shaped by the different responsibilities of each level of government Net flows from larger, richer places to smaller and poorer regions

demographic reactivity to economic descent is exemplified by the perseverance of long-declining manufacturing towns in the Maritimes—places like Sydney (steel), Amherst (railway cars), and New Glasgow–Trenton (metal products). As a consequence, abandonment marks their gritty industrial landscape in tell-tale fashion (DeBenedetti and Price, 1987).

The network of political connections refers to the movement of money and political influence both within and among political jurisdictions, as tax revenues flow to governments from firms and individuals, and transfer payments and services flow in other directions (Davis, 1996; Simmons, 1984). Thus, the political subsystem is more closed than open, with connections largely moving downward from the federal or provincial capitals to other places in the urban system, but seldom internationally. Different levels of government (especially federal and provincial) redistribute funds in an attempt to mediate tensions between the rapidly changing space economy and the resistant demographic

structure. Traditionally, this has been accomplished largely through public policies that support declining regions by taxing areas of growth. From one point of view (Courchene, 1984), these measures actually slow down the response to economic innovation and prevent the economy from achieving its full potential. After all, politicians represent the current distribution of voters, not the ones who might relocate. From another, more liberal, viewpoint (DeBenedetti and Lamarche, 1994; Savoie, 1992), these programs are the necessary support systems for people suffering the effects of unpredictable economic changes through no fault of their own, and represent countershifts that might benefit both regional and national economies (Kent, 1997).

Urban Interaction and Integration

Regional differences in the Canadian space economy shape complex flows of capital, labour, and goods between cities. The amount and degree of interaction among cities are important features of an urban system. Within the Windsor–Quebec City corridor, many cities are closely interconnected. Manufacturing inputs and outputs move frequently and readily from place to place or to nearby American cities, facilitated by a dense network of highways, railroads, and water routes. The manufacture of automobiles and their parts exemplifies these basic features of the urban system. Steel and plastics from Hamilton and Sarnia are fabricated into various car parts—e.g., bodies, axles, engines, dashboards, bumpers, distributor caps—in a number of Ontario and Quebec cities and then shipped to assembly plants in Oakville, Oshawa, and Windsor or across the border into Michigan or Ohio. Despite the transitional nature of the global economy and recent North American free trade agreements, this pattern, enshrined since the 1960s by the Auto Pact between Canada and the United States, continues to hold firm in support of the country's most important industrial sector. In the new century, after a period of uncertainty and difficult adjustment, manufacturing continues to grow, led by both new and renewed sectors—e.g., pharmaceuticals and telecommunication products (Britton, 1996). Beyond this resurgence, the most significant economic growth today is fuelled by specialized producer-service industries (like scientific research), global financial services, and cultural and educational activities. Most of the new jobs associated with post-industrial sectors are concentrating in southern Ontario cities, notably Toronto.

Elsewhere, in the periphery, staple products continue to support regional specialization, e.g., offshore oil in Newfoundland; minerals and pulp and paper in the Maritimes and the Canadian Shield; wheat, livestock, and natural gas across the prairie provinces; and lumber and pulp and paper in coastal and interior British Columbia. This output remains overwhelmingly destined for American and other international markets; the network connections are therefore external, not internal. Because bulky primary products usually move out of the country by the most direct route to minimize transportation costs, urban integration within the resource hinterland is quite limited. Conversely, the control and management of resource production remains highly centralized in a few core centres. Within Canada, these include Toronto, Montreal, Calgary, and Vancouver. Externally, global cities like New York, London, and Tokyo are the all-important control points (Semple, 1996).

Boundaries and the Urban System

Discussion of the networks of flows among urban places and of the degree of openness suggests that boundaries are an integral part of an urban system. In the Canadian situation, why do we perceive ourselves as a nation of cities rather than a region—or continent—of cities? There are very obvious and practical reasons when writing a textbook chapter designed for Canadian students and based on Canadian data. But, as suggested in Chapter 3, this question is not so readily answered. The spatial scale of any urban system should, in fact, be determined by the actual extent of linkages among cities at any point in time. One tries to choose a boundary for the system that maximizes flows *within* a group of cities and minimizes flows *across* boundaries.

The significance of boundaries has changed over time. To understand the history of Canadian urban development, at least until the early-twentieth century, it has made more sense to study cities within a regional context (McCann and Smith, 1991). But in the future, if contemporary changes in the world economy persist, it might be necessary to take a continental or even global, rather than a national, approach. To be sure, the economy operates increasingly at an international scale, with corporate, financial, and production systems connecting many countries. But the demographic (e.g., migration) and political (e.g., federal laws and taxes) components of the Canadian urban system are still primarily national in scope. Studies of air travel links, for example, suggest that flows across the border to the United States are only one-tenth the magnitude of flows to comparable locations in Canada. International migration is still less frequent than interprovincial movements. And almost all activities of the political system stop at the border.

The properties of the national border—e.g., its permeability to various flows of information, money, people, and goods—are of enormous importance to the operation and evolution of the urban system. Defining and maintaining a boundary can be considered one of the most important actions carried out by the federal government. Without the national border, the Canadian urban system would likely disappear as a distinct entity and blend into a larger North American system. For now, a national perspective prevails.

Regardless of this reality, or of nationalist feelings about continental integration, the United States is an immense presence that cannot be ignored. Information presented in Figure 4.2 and earlier in Table 4.1 emphasizes the contextual importance of the Canada–United States relationship by drawing attention to the size and market influence of the neighbouring regions of the United States (Bourne and Olvet, 1995; Mercer, 1991). This economic territory is rather arbitrarily cut off at approximately 500 km south of the border, but even so, it includes a population of 130 million and 100 cities with over 100,000 population. Adjusting for the higher income level in this part of the United States, the northern tier of states comprises more than one-half of the

Figure 4.2   **Urban Places in Canada and the Northern United States**

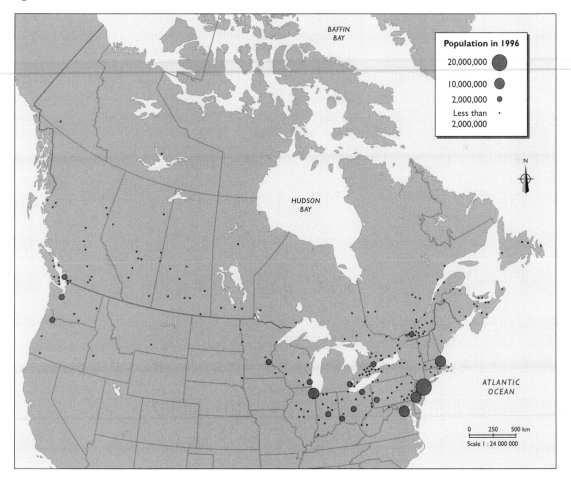

United States market. More to the point, as defined here this American presence is more than four times the size of the Canadian population or economy. These American cities provide markets for industrial goods (e.g., auto parts and newsprint) and act as sources of information (TV, radio, and newspaper), finance, and recreation for the people and businesses of the Canadian urban system. Without these connections to American cities, the Canadian urban system would be profoundly different. As it is, the landscape of Canadian cities is heavy with American branch businesses of all types, including department stores, fast-food outlets, auto dealerships, gas stations, movie chains, major banks, and brokerage houses.

Urban Population Growth

The population growth of any city takes place within the context of the system's urban hierarchy. The Canadian urban system comprises a majority of small cities, with only a few large cities. This hierar-

chical pattern of city size variation can be interpreted in terms of competition among cities for urban activities and trade areas. Small places compete with nearby small places over lower order goods and services; but as cities seek higher positions in the urban hierarchy, the spatial scale of competition increases, involving larger and more distant centres. This hierarchical city size distribution is an almost universal feature in all countries across time, even when urban systems are in transition (Berry, 1973).

Population size is a significant feature that differentiates cities. To illustrate this, the population growth rates of Canadian cities over 10,000 population since 1991 are plotted along the Y-axis of Figure 4.3. The range is from −8.1 per cent (Labrador City) to over +23 per cent (Courtney, BC), revealing two clear regularities. First, the variation in growth rates tends to be much greater for small places. Small cities are much more vulnerable to shocks of sudden growth or decline than are large cities, which are more likely to grow at about the

Figure 4.3   **City Size and Growth Rate, 1991–1996**

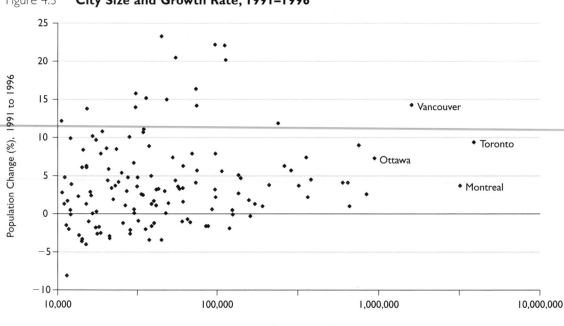

average rate for the urban system as a whole. Second, on average, all cities grow at about the same rate. There is no necessary growth advantage to urban size, but an early start or initial advantage within the urban system is an asset for any city. The largest cities, in fact, are those that have been able to grow for a long period of time and through a variety of economic situations (e.g., the transition from mercantile to industrial capitalism, from one economic staple to another, or from industrialism to post-industrialism). This view of the urban system suggests that a set of cities has overall structural characteristics and growth regularities, such that each individual city fits within a national hierarchical pattern.

Urban Growth in a Core-Periphery Space Economy

When a city such as Saskatoon or Halifax is studied in isolation by a local resident, government official, or historian, urban growth is usually attributed to specific events. Factors like winning a new railway connection or a package of development incentives are cited as the cause of the boom period. The problem with this approach is the illusion it creates that any urban centre can grow given the right political leadership or the innovation capacity of a successful entrepreneur. Or, for that matter, that growth follows from attracting industries or transportation facilities. By contrast, the value of the urban system approach is its ability to set local events within a larger framework of spatial competition. Saskatchewan or Labrador will never attract automobile factories, nor will Ontario's northern hinterland develop a commercial centre to challenge Toronto. A city's size and economic role are shaped by its location and by competing cities. During particular phases of economic growth, some kinds of activities can occur at almost any location, but others cannot. During the rise of nineteenth-century industrialization, for example, many cities were able to offer manufacturing jobs to rural migrants and thus grow appreciably in size. Later, when real income per capita doubled during the

1950s, every town or city generated service jobs that attracted migrants from rural areas. In the recent transition to a post-industrial regime, however, the spatial destinations of immigrants have proven to be limited, favouring large metropolitan centres and restricting, accordingly, this type of growth in smaller places.

A Model of City Growth

How, then, do cities actually grow over time? What is the process of growth that explains why certain cities in an urban system become larger than others, attracting more economic activities and people than competing places? To answer these questions, we can examine the growth possibilities offered by a core-periphery space economy (Figure 4.4). In short, cities function as intermediaries, their economic character and specialized roles stemming from their handling of the factors of production (e.g., labour, capital, staple products) as these are channelled between core and periphery. For example, staples are transported abroad; consumer goods are imported; raw materials are converted to consumer durables; loans are made; advertisements are sold; and inventions are patented, attracting overseas investment. Interaction, therefore, creates cities whose livelihood depends on some combination of transportation, wholesale-trading, manufacturing, financial, and business activities. One or more of these basic activities trigger a circular and cumulative growth process that is sustained by the strength of the multiplier effect (the increased demand for services and, hence, for more service workers that is engendered by the entry of more employees into the economy) and the threshold size of critical markets.[3] In an industrial economy, manufacturing was the all-important stimulant of growth. In the transition to post-industrialism, the producer service industries generated in the tertiary, quaternary, and quinary sectors—whether by small firms or giant transnational corporations—are now the leading stimuli of growth.

Cities will differ in their response to the growth opportunities offered by economies that are

Figure 4.4 **The Process of Urban Growth in a Heartland-Hinterland Space Economy**

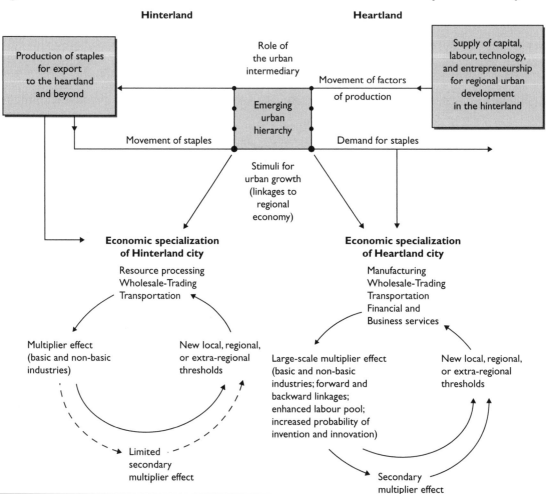

local, regional, national, or international in scale, and by their location within either a core or periphery area. The degree of specialization and the composition of economic sectors will vary, therefore, in each situation. For example, it is unlikely that the economy of a hinterland city will be fully diversified. Depending on the type and distribution of natural resources, settlements in the periphery will function chiefly as resource towns, central places, break-in-bulk or transshipment points. In most heartland cities, on the other hand, manufacturing, financial, and business services play a more vital role because the core area's advantages of historical inertia, accessibility to national markets, and external economies create a wider range of economic possibilities.

Within a national or regional urban system, usually one city—a metropolis of considerable size and power—gains prominence in commerce, transportation, manufacturing, and finance. Within a developing urban system, the metropolis greatly influences different aspects of a country because of its concentration of people, wealth, and innovating power. Metropolitanism is the historical and geographical process that accounts for the growth of a dominant city (or dominant cities) that leads the national urban hierarchy, and so controls the geographical structure of core and periphery. Once achieved, this dominant status overshadows that of all other towns and cities. Montreal and Toronto long ago won control over vast hinterlands; today, Vancouver, Calgary, and Edmonton are increasingly demonstrating this ability.

The Impact of Urban Growth

The growth of any one city depends on its relationships with other cities in other parts of the urban system, or even outside of it—as markets, as suppliers of goods and services, or as competitors. Consider the case of a resource-based, hinterland city. In a national and open spatial system, in which most cities of the periphery depend on the economic fortunes of one or two sectors, the potential for growth is largely determined outside of Canada by the expansion of world commodity markets and by the relative effectiveness of competing sources of natural resources. Sometimes, violent shocks in commodity prices dramatically change the level of economic activity in the community. The urban system must respond to the fact that certain cities and regions will inevitably grow faster than others, leading ultimately to reorganization through the creation of new spatial linkages. For example, in the prairie region, as the Alberta economy grew increasingly stronger after World War II because of changing patterns of world energy production and consumption, Calgary and Edmonton overtook Winnipeg in population size by eventually capturing many of Winnipeg's commercial, transportation, and financial services. As a result, Winnipeg's growth over the past several decades has been very modest.

Growth impulses within the Canadian urban system are often felt in predictable ways. Big cities attract more growth than small ones. Nearby cities have more impact than more distant ones. Some economic sectors are more localized than others, in the sense that inputs and outputs affect places located nearby. In most cases, the key linkages affecting growth and competition accrue to the national metropolis, regional commercial centres, several major product destinations, and the provincial capital. This process can be illustrated by considering how the development of a mine somewhere in the Canadian Shield might affect growth throughout the urban system, imparting forward, backward, and final-demand linkages on various Canadian cities. Consider, for example, a Vancouver geologist who works with Ontario government officials in Sudbury to register a claim. Development capital is raised by selling stocks on the Toronto Stock Exchange. Road and rail infrastructure is put in place mostly by government investment, using asphalt from Sarnia and steel from Sault Ste Marie. Mining equipment is purchased from firms in Montreal and the ore is processed locally and then shipped through a Pacific coast port. With income earned, mine workers purchase consumer goods shipped to stores in the resource community from key distribution centres across the country. Insurance policies are bought from Kitchener–Waterloo, London, or Montreal companies; money is deposited in Toronto banks. In sum, each purchase or transaction transmits growth impulses throughout the urban system; because goods and services are typically purchased from a variety of sources, the impact of the single mine is diffused across the space economy. In the same way, when the mine eventually runs out of ore and closes, a series of negative growth impulses will retrace a similar spatial path. When any town experiences an economic downturn or complete misfortune, the impact is felt by other places in the urban system. Thus cities often rise or decline because of events occurring far away, even far beyond their own culture. For larger cities, the growth impulses average out, producing predictable patterns of change. For smaller, more specialized centres, it is never clear how long the boom will last, or whether it will ever come, as in the case of Voisey's Bay in Labrador.

Urbanization and the Canadian Urban System

Urbanization can be defined from several perspectives: structurally or economically—by the growth of cities, the emerging settlement hierarchy, and the changing economic relationships between urban places; demographically—with a region becoming more urban, increasing its proportion of people residing in urban places relative to the total population of the region; and behaviourally—as a way of life, as urbanism (Stelter, 1990). Implicit in each perspective is the notion of spatial and historical change casting and reshaping the character of the urban system. Although a country's system of cities maintains fundamental characteristics in the course of its development—e.g., core and periphery, a distinctive hierarchical structure, the power of the metropolis—the urbanization process is often shaped by major transitions at critical moments that leave a distinctive mark on individual regions, as well as on the system as a whole. These transitions are associated with the subsystems or key components of the larger system, that is, the economic, the demographic, and the political. Here we will discuss a select few of a broad series of such transitions that have shaped urban Canada. The three illustrative examples considered are: the basic economic and system-defining impact of staple production; the demographic force of immigration on turn-of-the-century settlement and urban growth in the prairie provinces; and the political effect of Canada's National Policy of incentives and tariff protection on the nineteenth-century industrialization of central Canada and the subsequent deindustrialization of the Maritimes. Like the contemporary period of globalization and post-industrial growth, each of these examples was responsible for bringing about a major spatial transition within the Canadian urban system.

Urbanization in Time and Space

Today, the urbanization level in Canada stands at nearly 80 per cent. The 50 per cent mark was passed just after World War I; at Confederation, the proportion had not quite reached 20 per cent. As the overall population of the country increased, the urban population grew even more rapidly, and the population of the very largest cities grew the fastest. Also, the process of urbanization has been more or less constant over time, although two periods of rapid change and transition stand out. First, urbanization accelerated dramatically early in the twentieth century when the West was settled and the industrial heartland consolidated its hold over the space economy. Second, after World War II, new or expanded staples production (e.g., oil, hydroelectric power, pulp and paper, mining) provoked urban growth in peripheral regions, and rising incomes stimulated manufacturing, financial, and government sectors in such places as Montreal, Toronto, and Ottawa, consolidating their leading role in the urban system.

Urbanization in all its dimensions underlies the basic restructuring of Canada's core-periphery system of cities, and has done so over four centuries of growth and change. Canadian urbanization is rooted in the seventeenth century. Substantial Native settlements were noted by the first European explorers—the emissaries of mercantile capitalism. Some of these were taken over as the sites of future cities, e.g., Quebec City. Much of the French and British settlement sequence that followed began at coastal and inland waterway sites, which became the trading posts, garrisons, ports, and administrative centres of the old colonial system. Settlers moved outward from these places to areas of agricultural potential across the Canadian frontier, but they remained dependent on their point of origin for supplies. Even in areas not suitable for farming, the network of trading posts created a kind of urban system, with a hierarchy of settlements of varying sizes linked ultimately by a water-based transportation system to a European metropolitan core (Meinig, 1986; Vance, 1970). In fact, many city locations and external relationships that mark Canada's urban system today were first established in this way. Key places emerged early to dominate and direct the established regional and still embryonic national urban systems—cities such as St John's, Halifax, Saint John, Montreal, Kingston, Toronto, Winnipeg, Edmonton, and Vancouver.

Fuelled by factors like the staples trades, immigration, and political decisions to protect domestic manufacturing, Canadian urbanization has progressed through various phases of economic growth. These include early mercantile and nineteenth-century commercial trade; the urban-industrial take-off during the Great Transformation (c. 1867–1929); sustained industrialization; and most recently, the stimulating effect of producer services on post-industrial growth. The regional sequence of settlement and urban system development—hence the founding periods of cities—has proceeded roughly from east to west, beginning in Quebec (seventeenth century), followed by the Maritimes (mid-eighteenth century), southern Ontario (early nineteenth century), and more recently western Canada (late nineteenth century). A scattering of mining and pulp and paper towns emerged across the southern edge of the Canadian Shield in the late nineteenth and early twentieth centuries. The newest urban frontier is sometimes referred to by the term 'counter-urbanization', that is, the tendency for people to flee cities and take up residence in rural areas or small towns, even though they will usually commute daily to workplaces in a large and nearby city. In advanced economies, large cities tend to experience certain diseconomies, sometimes forcing people to seek residence elsewhere. This type of migration is one of the reasons why Canada's urbanization level has stabilized at the 80 per cent mark. The strength of the metropolitan economy is not diminished, but counter-urbanization does change the patterns of social integration around large cities.[4]

Staples and Economic Networks

The sequence of discovering and developing various staple commodities over long periods of time—the early cod fishery, coal and hard-rock mining, wheat, pulp and paper, natural gas, and oil—have indelibly and forever shaped the geographic character of Canadian urbanization. Strongly affected, for example, are distinctive settlement patterns, the size and specialized functions of towns and cities, the necessity of export-oriented transportation systems, and the degree of regional well-being.[5] Take the case of the Atlantic region's cod fishery, which for the past four centuries has been geared to export markets located mainly in the West Indies, southern Europe, and other fish-eating regions. The nature of the staple is such that it creates some backward linkages but few linkages of a forward or final-demand nature. As a result, fishing settlements across Atlantic Canada are scattered along the coast in relation to inshore and offshore fishing grounds, and have always been quite small and poorly integrated within the urban system. Their viability has always been subject to fluctuating incomes as the catch shifts and markets for fish ebb and flow, but the recent collapse of cod stocks has brought a virtual halt to fishing and threatens the very foundation of these communities (Muise et al., 1993).

Coal and base-metal production gained momentum through the nineteenth century in response to changing mining technologies, increased accessibility aided by railroad construction, and, of course, rising national and even continental and world demand. Similar forces pushed the lumber, pulp and paper, oil, and natural gas industries to the forefront of Canadian economic development in early twentieth-century British Columbia and the Canadian Shield region. Coalmining settlements in the Maritimes, Alberta, and British Columbia, and their hard-rock counterparts across the Canadian Shield, were fixed in space by the location of the mineral resource. Clusters of specialized company towns developed at pit heads and built railroads across their coalfields. Similar events unfolded at the turn of the twentieth century in the silver and lead-zinc regions of the Canadian Shield and the Kootenays in British Columbia. However, the depletion of the mineral base could mean the collapse of the resource-town economy. This has been much less likely to happen in lumber and pulp and paper towns because forests are a renewable resource, although the efficiencies achieved from technological change can mean a smaller workforce or even the closing down of an obsolete plant. Forest communities are also small in size—few total more than 10,000 people—but are much more scattered across Canada, whether fronting British Columbia tidewater sites on the Pacific Ocean, stretching across the boreal forest in the prairie provinces and Ontario and Quebec, or seeking Atlantic Canada's coastal fall zone. They continue functioning today wherever forests provide the raw material of production, their locational pattern also determined by rivers supplying access and power, and by the size of wood harvesting allotments (Marchak, 1995). Even Alberta, Saskatchewan, and British Columbia gas and oil towns of the mid-twentieth century share the standard settlement features of staples production: small in size, orientation to mineral deposits (that is, oil and gas fields), an export focus, and often transience in the town's social order (Pratt and Richards, 1979).

Each staple network, therefore, shapes its own distinctive settlement pattern within Canada's hinterland regions. As part of the larger urban system, staple-based towns and cities share common ground: control by external and often foreign corporations; low position in the urban hierarchy; volatile growth through periods of boom and bust; and dependency on export markets. The planned landscapes of many resource towns have been engineered by multinational corporations to ensure a stable labour force (McCann, 1980). When functioning at full production, the staple-based industries yield good wages that assure family well-being, causing few to worry about the precise nature of control and decision-making, which is based almost always in distant metropolitan centres. But resource towns are the least stable of Canada's urban communities. Across the staple-producing regions, abandoned settlements record the difficulties faced by these communities—e.g., resource depletion, shifts in consumer preferences, and falling commodity prices. Nonetheless, they stand as one of the most distinctive features of the Canadian urban system. Collectively, they affect the growth patterns of the regional centres that supply them and are, in turn, shaped by the decision-making power of metropolitan-based corporations.

Demographic Networks and Western Settlement

The mobility of labour, such as the movement of immigrants or migrants to a newly opened resource frontier or to industrializing cities, is a powerful demographic agent of urbanization. Depending on the resources or industries that initially attract settlement, immigration will shape the demographic network in particular and significant ways. Canada's urban development was profoundly influenced historically by the movement of hundreds of thousands of Western and Eastern European immigrants to the prairie region at the close of the nineteenth century (approximately from 1896–1913). Shaped by the federal government's decision to encourage agricultural settlement, particularly the growing of such cereal crops as wheat, this immigration quickly spurred explosive economic growth. Prompting the so-called 'wheat boom', it also triggered the highest rate of urbanization in Canadian history and impacted a number of cities closely connected to the development of the western agricultural hinterland.

Winnipeg was the gateway city for the expanding prairie hinterland (Burghardt, 1971). Through it passed most of the immigrants, capital, and goods and materials destined for the developing West, as well as many of the agricultural products bound for European export markets. The actual volume and movement of immigrants through the city and onto prairie homesteads were directed by the federal government in Ottawa. Winnipeg's banking, wholesaling, and transportation sectors were connected primarily to financial, distribution, and industrial corporations based in Montreal and Toronto. Farm machinery and building supplies came chiefly from the Hamilton area and Vancouver, respectively. Connections with other central Canadian cities were actually quite limited (McCann and Smith, 1991). The size and spacing of settlements in the urban system that subsequently developed in the West were influenced by the federal government's township survey system, by the space-extensive form of agriculture (e.g., grains, cattle), and by the location of railway stations serving export-oriented agricultural production. In cities and towns across the prairies, the services of central places prevailed over manufacturing activities, even flour milling and meat-packing (Kerr, Holdsworth, and Laskin, 1990).

As a unique episode in Canadian history, the opening of the West stands as one of the more remarkable historical examples of how the urban system was shaped by political and demographic processes (Artibise, 1981; Voisey, 1975). Although dependent on political and corporate decision-making in central Canadian cities and even in places abroad (e.g., London, New York, Chicago, Minneapolis), the major cities of the West experienced phenomenal growth. Between 1901 and the close of the 1920s, for instance, Winnipeg climbed from 42,000 to 219,000 people; Edmonton and Calgary from 4,000 each to 79,000 and 84,000, respectively; and Vancouver—which shared in the growth of the prairie region by supplying goods and exporting grain—rose from 26,000 to nearly 250,000 (Table 4.3). Canada's urban system was extended from coast to coast, and its spatial form became indelibly structured during this transformation. A host of factors—external demand for staple products, immigration, technological change, transport innovations, government policies—lay at the root of this transformation.

Heartland Growth, Hinterland Decline: The National Policy, Industrialization, and Deindustrialization

The political subsystem, it will be recalled, involves the interaction among cities and the resulting spatial impact of government policies and financial flows (e.g., transfer payments). In keeping with the broad concept of 'public' cities put forward in Chapter 3, the federal government has, at crucial stages in Canada's urban-industrial development, established policies that have directly shaped the spatial character of growth in the urban system. A number of these actions were taken in the years immediately after Confederation, including policies that encouraged province building, established the

Table 4.3   **Changing Population of Canada's Largest Urban Places, 1871–1996**

	Population (000s)				
	1871	1901	1931	1961	1996
Toronto	59	208	631	1,824	4,264
Montreal	115	268	819	2,110	2,921
Vancouver	—	26	297	790	1,832
Ottawa	24	60	127	930	1,010
Edmonton	—	4	79	338	863
Calgary	—	4	84	250	822
Quebec City	60	69	131	358	672
Winnipeg	—	42	219	265	667
Hamilton	27	53	156	395	557
London	18	38	71	181	399
Kitchener	3	10	31	155	383
St Catharines	8	10	25	84	372
Halifax	30	41	59	93	333
Victoria	3	21	39	154	304
Windsor	4	12	63	193	278
Oshawa	3	4	23	62	269
Saskatoon	—	—	43	96	219
Regina	—	2	53	112	194
St John's	23	29	39	91	174
Sudbury	—	2	19	111	160
Chicoutimi–Jonquière	1	4	12	32	160
Sherbrooke	1	12	29	67	147
Trois-Rivières	8	10	35	53	140
Saint John	41	41	98	64	126

Source: Statistics Canada, *Census of Canada*, various years.

Canadian Pacific Railway, set the regulations for the Canadian branch banking system, and specified the National Policy of industrial incentives and tariffs to foster and protect Canadian manufacturing. The National Policy had long-standing impacts, affecting the organization of the urban system for over a century until the recent North American Free Trade Agreement (Williams, 1994). The tariffs created a metaphorical wall around the country, designed to encourage domestic production and discourage reliance on imports. By defining a captive domestic market (particularly in the periphery), these measures supported a Canadian manufacturing region, the Industrial Heartland, and a transportation and distribution system to serve it. To be sure, investment in infrastructure, such as railways, generated economic development in the periphery, but in doing so it also increased the demand for high-value goods, further spurring the growth of central Canadian manufacturers, wholesalers, and transportation companies. By adopting the policies of a free market system but within a closed market supported by generous subsidies, these government actions favoured the continued concentration of urban growth at the core of the space economy.

Industrialization lay at the heart of late-nineteenth-century and subsequent twentieth-century urbanization in the central provinces. Towns and cities began to specialize in certain products. Steel came from Hamilton; automobiles from Windsor, Oshawa, and Oakville; rubber from Kitchener; plastics from Sarnia; textiles from Sherbrooke. Urban-industrial development was aided and abetted by many other economic and geographic factors operating within the context of the National Policy, including: agglomeration economies that encouraged linked activities; a skilled labour force; access to regional markets that reduced production costs and in turn made long-distance shipping across Canada more bearable; proximity to the United States manufacturing belt, which encouraged the proliferation of American branch plants; availability of raw materials and producer goods; and cheap hydroelectric power and later natural gas. By the close of World War II, the consolidation of urban-industrial strength in the Windsor–Quebec City corridor was an unmistakable and established fact (Kerr, 1998; Semple and Smith, 1981; Yeates, 1998).

But consolidation and concentration at the core carried a price: the deindustrialization and subsequent prolonged impoverishment of the Maritimes, now Canada's least urbanized region. Yet, the Maritimes showed strong promise of urban development through the late-nineteenth century when the various National Policy incentives fostered considerable growth (Acheson, 1972). Since the mid-nineteenth century, coal from Cape Breton and Pictou County fuelled industry in the St Lawrence region, and by 1882 Canada's steel industry was established in Nova Scotia. Small towns like New Glasgow, Amherst, Moncton, and Marysville made the transition from mercantile to industrial capitalism. For a brief span, their steel mills, railway car plants, and textile factories were prominent on the national stage. But the urban system was fragmented, poorly integrated, and weakly led by its regional centres. Halifax and Saint John battled strenuously with each other, not as major industrial or financial centres, but as national ports competing for the products of distant markets. The region's urban-industrial base collapsed with devastating effects in the 1920s. The cumulative disadvantages of earlier business take-overs by Montreal corporations, the new Toronto outreach of branch businesses, a peripheral location and marginal resource base, regressive government policies (e.g., severe cuts in rail and industrial incentives), and hesitant investors, among other factors, caused industries to close and many towns to lose population (McCann, 1994). Rather than move into towns and cities, many Maritimers chose to retain a small farm and work a seasonal round of rural (and sometimes urban) activities to earn a livelihood. Such pluralistic patterns of work and residence help to explain the limited urbanization of the region even today. Against this trend, Halifax, Saint John, Moncton, and a few other cities attracted the region's young and footloose, but few immigrants. No urban centre controlled the regional economy. Only in the 1970s and 1980s did Halifax emerge as a place of singular importance, although dependent still on external metropolitan centres.

The Metropolitan Factor

Within the emerging urban system, a few cities—particularly Montreal and Toronto—grew as power centres in the late-nineteenth and early-twentieth centuries to control hinterland markets, to attract the majority of urban-bound immigrants, and to use the political process to their decided advantage. Montreal occupied the top position in the urban hierarchy well into the twentieth century, growing rapidly from 268,000 in 1901 to over 819,000 in 1931 (Table 4.3). As Canada's metropolis, it dominated the transportation, manufacturing, trade, and financial sectors of the country. Its entrepreneurs organized these sectors through branch businesses to control much of the Maritimes, the West, and even parts of Ontario (McCann and Smith, 1991). Montreal possessed many locational advantages, including the initial advantage and accessibility to markets and materials offered by the Great Lakes–St Lawrence system, an efficient and low-wage labour force, access to capital markets, and strong connections to the political subsystem of subsidies and industrial incentives.

Montreal's competition came mainly from Toronto, particularly after World War I when the Ontario city reorganized its stock market to tackle industrial development in many new manufacturing sectors. It also took advantage of new business strategies associated with the rise of managerial capitalism. For example, access to the American manufacturing belt helped Toronto attract American branch manufacturing plants. As the twentieth century progressed, Toronto's Canadian corporations also reached deep into the hinterland regions, becoming a crucial force in the distribution and retail sectors, organizing resource development across the Canadian Shield, and expanding financial and banking networks to compete successfully with Montreal (McCann and Smith, 1991).

Toronto and Montreal are Canada's largest cities. They have long set the pace for many features of the metropolitan lifestyle that give character to the social and cultural patterns of the country. While local traits are important, giving regional distinctiveness to peripheral cities, there can be little doubt that Toronto and Montreal have established patterns of consumption in such areas as business strategies, publishing ventures, architectural styles, and radio and television programming that have been widely adopted—albeit sometimes begrudgingly—throughout the country. Of course, it must be remembered that even Toronto and Montreal remain under the larger orbit of economic and cultural influence stemming from first-order global cities—like New York and London. But internally, just as Toronto has surpassed Montreal to dominate the Canadian urban system, increasingly Vancouver, Calgary, Edmonton, and other regional centres are joining in the organization of vast resource hinterlands, formulating distinctive cultures, and tapping more and more directly into the new global economy. In Canada, as in any urban system, power centres at the top of the hierarchy control national economic development.

Conclusion

Each of the historical examples considered above had dramatic impacts on the development of the urban system, leaving reminders of the growth processes still visible a century or more afterward. The urban landscape of Winnipeg's ethnic neighbourhoods, Montreal's shifting financial district, and Hamilton's manufacturing zones record the impact of these processes. But equally dramatic shifts have occurred in more recent times—e.g., the massive population movement from rural areas to cities in the 1950s; the postwar baby boom and the shift from central city neighbourhoods to suburban communities; the migration of Anglophones from Montreal to Toronto over the last two decades; and Alberta's energy boom in the 1980s (Bourne and Olvet, 1995; Simmons and Bourne, 1989). The future may hold equally important transitions. Globalization could continue opening the borders of the Canadian urban system, further reversing the protective measures of the now abandoned National Policy. Declining birth rates and high immigration levels might well exacerbate the volatility of urban growth rates, even in the largest, traditionally more stable metropolitan centres where most of these immigrants have recently taken up residence. Clearly, urban systems are dynamic and ever susceptible to change, even unpredictable change. But the sheer weight of the existing urban system means that most anticipated future change and transition can be reasonably predicted. The recent past with a view to the future is the theme of the next chapter.

Notes

1. The various maps and graphs that accompany this chapter and Chapter 5 are based on analyses of CMAs and CAs only. At other times, when we discuss in a descriptive way the overall urban pattern of Canada, we include settlements of 1,000 or more people, which Statistics Canada defines as the minimum population threshold of any urban place in Canada. Over 700 such places meet this population criterion.

2. Readers who would like to examine the map of migration patterns on which the comments in this paragraph are based are encouraged to refer to the most recent (5th) edition of *The National Atlas of Canada*. It consists of dozens of individual map sheets, released over an eight-year period. Each plate or map sheet shows the national pattern, and a number of the economic and social plates provide useful sources for the study of urban systems. In the demographic section there are maps of the overall population distribution (Map 14.3) and of provincial and net migration rates (Map 17.1). A series of urban economic plates provides essential material that complements the arguments of this chapter. These include the urban system (Map 39.1), income per capita (Map 37.1), and employment variability (Map 36.2). Map 39.2 shows the basic central place patterns of the country. The economic series includes maps of mineral commodity flows (Map 27.2); manufacturing (Map 29.1); manufacturing productivity (Map 29.2); and transportation routes (Map 31.5).

3. A 'multiplier' is a measure of the effect on the total economy of a change in one of its components. According to the economic base model, from which this perspective on growth is broadly derived, goods and services produced within a locality but exported outside its territory generate revenues that circulate within the local economy and in the process stimulate economic sectors catering to local consumption (Tiebout, 1962). Thus, in this understanding, the multiplier effect concerns the capacity of export revenues to fuel growth within different sectors of a local economy.

4. Canada's period of most rapid counter-urbanization took place in the late 1960s and early 1970s. Some argue that it abated with the energy crisis of the 1970s. Stricter planning controls—for example, regional government restrictions on the severance of agricultural land—also contributed to a slowing down of counter-urbanization. As well, because the outer portions of CMAs and CAs have since 1971 been defined in terms of commuter sheds, many erstwhile rural townships are classified as a part of urban agglomerations as defined by Statistics Canada. Chapter 14 of the present volume discusses counter-urbanization at greater length.

5. Each of Canada's major staples-based industries, as well as all varieties of economic, demographic, and political processes, are well illustrated by maps in the three volumes of the *Historical Atlas of Canada*.

References

Acheson, W. 1972. 'The National Policy and Industrialization of the Maritimes, 1880–1910', *Acadiensis* 1: 2–34.

Artibise, A.F.J. 1981. *Prairie Urban Development, 1870–1930*. Ottawa: Canadian Historical Association, Historical Booklet No. 34.

Berry, B.J.L. 1973. *The Human Consequences of Urbanization*. London: Macmillan.

Borchert, J. 1991. 'Future of American Cities', in J.F. Hart, ed., *Our Changing Cities*. Baltimore: Johns Hopkins University Press.

Bourne, L.S.. and A.E. Olvet. 1995. *The Canadian Urban System Revisited: A Statistical Analysis*. Toronto: University of Toronto, Centre for Urban and Community Studies, Research Paper No. 192.

Bradbury, J. 1984. 'Industrial Cycles and the Mining Sector in Canada', *International Journal of Urban and Regional Research* 8: 311–31.

Braudel, F. 1984. 'The Perspective of the World', in Braudel, *Civilization and Capitalism 15th–18th Century*, vol. 3. New York: Harper and Row.

Britton, J., ed. 1996. *Canada and the Global Economy: The Geography of Structural and Technological Change*. Montreal and Kingston: McGill-Queen's University Press.

Burghardt, A.F. 1971. 'A Hypothesis About Gateway Cities', *Annals, Association of American Geographers* 61: 269–85.

Courchene, T.J. 1984. *Social Canada in the Millennium*. Toronto: C.D. Howe Research Institute.

———. 1998. *From Heartland to North American Region State: The Social, Fiscal and Federal Evolution of Ontario*. Toronto: University of Toronto, Centre for Public Management.

Davis, J.T. 1996. 'Canada's Public Space Economy', in Britton, ed., *Canada and the Global Economy*.

DeBenedetti, G., and R. Lamarche, eds. 1994. *Shock Waves: The Maritime Urban System in the New Economy*. Moncton, NB: Canadian Institute for Research on Regional Development.

——— and R. Price. 1987. 'Population Growth and the Industrial Structure of Maritime Small Towns, 1971–1981', in L.D. McCann, ed., *People and Place: Studies of Small Town Life in the Maritimes*. Fredericton, NB: Acadiensis Press.

Gajda, R.T. 1960. 'The Canadian Ecumene—Inhabited and Uninhabited Areas', *Geographical Bulletin* 15: 5–18.

Kent, T., ed. 1997. *In Pursuit of the Public Good*. Montreal and Kingston: McGill-Queen's University Press.

Kerr, D. 1998. 'The Emergence of the Industrial Heartland, c. 1760–1960', in L.D. McCann and A. Gunn, eds, *Heartland and Hinterland: A Geography of Canada*, 3rd edn. Scarborough, Ont.: Prentice-Hall Canada.

———, D. Holdsworth, and S. Laskin, eds. 1991. 'Addressing the Twentieth Century', in *Historical Atlas of Canada*, vol. 3. Toronto: University of Toronto Press.

Krugman, P. 1996. *Pop Internationalism*. Cambridge, Mass.: MIT Press.

Landes, D.S. 1998. *The Wealth and Poverty of Nations*. New York: Norton.

Ley, D. 1997. *The New Middle Class and the Remaking of the Central City*. New York: Oxford University Press.

McCann, L.D. 1980. 'Canadian Resource Towns: A Heartland-Hinterland Perspective', in R.E. Preston and L. Russwurm, eds, *Essays on Canadian Urban Process and Form II*. Waterloo, Ont.: University of Waterloo, Department of Geography.

———. 1994. 'Shock Waves in the Old Economy: Maritime Cities and the Great Transformation, c. 1867–1939', in DeBenedetti and Lamarche, eds, *Shock Waves: The Maritime Urban System in the New Economy*.

———. 1998. 'Interpreting Canada's Heartland and Hinterland', in McCann and A. Gunn, eds, *Heartland and Hinterland: A Geography of Canada*, 3rd edn. Scarborough, Ont.: Prentice-Hall Canada.

——— and A. Gunn, eds. 1998. *Heartland and Hinterland: A Geography of Canada*, 3rd edn. Scarborough, Ont.: Prentice-Hall Canada.

———— and P.J. Smith. 1991. 'Canada Becomes Urban: Cities and Urbanization in Historical Perspective', in T. Bunting and P. Filion, eds, *The Canadian City in Transition*. Toronto: Oxford University Press.

Marchak, P. 1995. *Logging the Globe*. Montreal and Kingston: McGill-Queen's University Press.

Meinig, D. 1986. *Atlantic America, 1492–1800*. New Haven: Yale University Press.

Mercer, J. 1991. 'The Canadian City in Continental Context: Global and Continental Perspectives on Canadian Urban Development', in T. Bunting and P. Filion, eds, *The Canadian City in Transition*. Toronto: Oxford University Press.

Muise, D., et al. 1993. *Urban and Community Development in Atlantic Canada, 1867–1991*. Ottawa: Canadian Museum of Civilization, Mercury Series Paper No. 44.

Pratt, L. and J. Richards. 1979. *Prairie Capitalism: Power and Influence in the New West*. Toronto: McClelland & Stewart.

Sassen, S. 1991. *The Global City: New York, London, Tokyo*. Princeton, NJ: Princeton University Press.

Savoie, D. 1992. *Regional Economic Development: Canada's Search for Solutions*. Toronto: University of Toronto Press.

Semple, R.K. 1996. 'Quarternary Places in Canada', in Britton, ed., *Canada and the Global Economy*.

———— and R. Smith. 1981. 'Metropolitan Dominance and Foreign Ownership in the Canadian Urban System', *Canadian Geographer* 25: 4–26.

Simmons, J.W. 1984. 'Government and the Canadian Urban System: Income Tax, Transfer Payments, and Employment', *Canadian Geographer* 28: 18–45.

————. 1986. 'The Impact of the Public Sector on the Canadian Urban System', in G.A. Stelter and A.F.J. Artibise, eds, *Power and Place: Canadian Urban Development in the North American Context*. Vancouver: University of British Columbia Press.

———— and L.S. Bourne. 1989. *Urban Growth Trends in Canada, 1981–86: A New Geography of Change*. Toronto: University of Toronto, Centre for Urban and Community Studies, Major Report No. 25.

Stelter, G. 1990. 'Introduction', in Stelter, ed., *Cities and Urbanization: Canadian Historical Perspectives*. Toronto: Copp Clark Pitman.

Vance, J. 1970. *The Merchants's World: The Geography of Wholesaling*. New York: Prentice-Hall.

Voisey, P. 1975. 'The Urbanization of the Canadian Prairies, 1871–1916', *Histoire sociale/Social History* 15: 77–101.

Williams, G. 1994. *Not For Export: The International Competitiveness of Canadian Manufacturing*, 3rd edn. Toronto: McClelland & Stewart.

Yeates, M. 1991. 'The Windsor–Quebec Corridor', in T. Bunting and P. Filion, eds, *Canadian Cities in Transition*. Toronto: Oxford University Press.

————. 1998. 'The Heartland Today: Its Changing Role and Internal Structure', in L.D. McCann and A. Gunn, eds, *Heartland and Hinterland: A Geography of Canada*, 3rd edn. Scarborough, Ont.: Prentice-Hall Canada.

Chapter 5

Growth and Transition in the Canadian Urban System

Jim Simmons and Larry McCann

Throughout its evolution, certain structural features of the Canadian urban system have remained firmly in place. These include a core-periphery space economy, a dominant metropolis, and an integrated hierarchy of cities. Recently, under this shroud of apparent stability, other features of the urban system have been in transition. The economic base of many cities is changing markedly as the country adjusts to the post-industrial forces of a restructured world economy. For many cities in Canada, specialized producer-service industries have taken on heightened relevance, creating an expanded global network of new and diversified economic connections that signal a major change in trading relationships beyond traditional resource and manufactured products. The demographic dimension is also experiencing profound transition. Canada is no longer the Anglophone/Francophone *deux nations*. A new wave of immigration—people from Asia, the Caribbean, the Middle East, and South America—has created a multicultural population concentrated overwhelmingly in just a few of the largest cities. Even the political network is in transition. International financial forces have pressured the federal government to reconsider its once all-pervasive role by reducing funding, for example, in key health, education, and transportation areas, passing over to the provinces and the private sector many of its responsibilities.

These economic, demographic, and political processes are reshaping the geography of the urban system, most notably in the rising prominence of a few metropolitan centres to anchor regional patterns. For some writers, core and periphery are taking on a new meaning: the 'city states' of Toronto, Montreal, and Vancouver are becoming all-important in the lives of Canadians; they represent the new multicultural, post-industrial, and 'post-modern' Canada (Gwyn, 1995). The periphery, by contrast, is more like the 'old Canada' of a few decades ago, bypassed by the new immigrants, still producing staples for export, and supposedly the repository of traditional culture. In this chapter, we examine the contemporary Canadian urban system at the dawn of the twenty-first century, focusing on the growth processes that are shaping and reshaping the economic and demographic character and the landscape of Canada's cities. We also attempt to project current trends into the future by developing estimates of urban growth and by speculating about the impact of broad trends in the global economy on the Canadian urban system.

Structural Features of the Urban System in 1996

Even in an era of notable change, the most important factors differentiating Canadian cities are population size and location. Canada's most recent census in 1996 revealed that 77 per cent (22.5 million) of Canadians resided within 137 census metropolitan areas (CMAs) and census agglomeration areas (CAs) (Table 5.1). Almost half of this urban population—some 35 per cent of all Canadians—now live in the nation's four, 'million plus' metropolitan centres: Toronto, Montreal, Vancouver and Ottawa–Hull. In Table 5.1, the city size classes extend over three orders of magnitude, from 10,000

Table 5.1   **Urbanization by Region and City Size, 1996**

City Size	British Columbia	Prairie Provinces*	Ontario	Quebec	Atlantic Provinces	Canada
Number of Cities						
>1,000,000	1	—	2	1	—	4
300,000–1,000,000	1	3	4	1	1	10
100,000–299,999	2	2	9	3	4	20
30,000–99,999	10	9	13	14	4	50
10,000–29,999	9	11	14	10	9	53
Total Urban	23	25	42	29	18	137
Population of Cities (000s)						
>1,000,000	1,832	—	5,274	3,327	—	10,433
300,000–1,000,000	304	2,351	2,047	672	333	5,707
100,000–299,999	273	413	1,133	448	531	2,798
30,000–99,999	573	399	722	650	218	2,563
10,000–29,999	166	182	231	195	177	951
Total Urban	3,148	3,346	9,408	5,291	1,258	22,452
Percentage Urban	84.5	68.3	87.5	74.1	53.9	77.8

*Includes Yukon and the Northwest Territories.
Source: Statistics Canada, *Census of Canada*, 1996.

to 4,000,000 people. The metropolis Toronto is more than 400 times larger than the smallest census agglomeration, Labrador City. Distances across the urban system range as great as 8,000 kilometres. Nearly all Canadian cities are located within 200 km of the United States border; only two are found north of 60°N latitude.

The number of cities in each size category is inversely related to city size, with 50 or more cities in each of the two smallest categories and only four with populations over 1,000,000. The largest city size category includes almost half the urban population. Ontario and Quebec—the provincial com-

ponents of the Windsor–Quebec City corridor—dominate in both number of cities and aggregate urban population. Together they hold 52 per cent of Canada's cities and 65 per cent of the urban population. The two western regions are rapidly increasing their proportion, which comprised 35 per cent of the cities and 29 per cent of the urban population in 1996. With 87 per cent of its population living in cities, Ontario not surprisingly has the highest urbanization level. Right behind is British Columbia, with just over 84 per cent. Unlike Ontario, Quebec, and British Columbia, provinces in the Atlantic and Prairie regions (with the exception of Alberta) lack cities in the larger categories. Thus, not only is Canada an urban nation that has grown around core-periphery patterns, but it is also a nation of increasing metropolitan prominence.

Table 5.2 introduces another significant urban characteristic, average income per capita, which is closely related to city size, region, and core-periphery location. Two features stand out. First, there is a regular and notable increase in the level of income as city size increases. Incomes in big cities are often higher than elsewhere because the principles of economies of scale offered by large-scale urbanization make workers more efficient and firms more profitable, encouraging higher wages. Even more important, big cities have higher proportions of their population in the workforce, especially women and older people. This obviously generates more income per household. Second, regional variations partly reflect the differences in city size distribution, but they also show the effects of long-term growth patterns within the urban system. On the periphery, the slow-growth Atlantic and Quebec regions have not generated sufficient jobs to retain or attract population. Unemployment is high, participation in the workforce is low, and many young people move

away (Bourne and Flowers, 1996; Bourne and Olvet, 1995).[1]

The Transitional Character of Urban Growth

The number of CMAs and CAs identified by Statistics Canada has now begun to decline, from 140 in 1991 to 137 in 1996. Some simple accounting provides a numerical explanation. The number of new nodes with the necessary threshold size of 10,000 population (+2) is not keeping up with the decline in size of previously defined nodes (−3) and the coalescence of existing nodes into larger metropolitan regions (−2). As Canada's largest CMAs have expanded outwards—especially Vancouver, Toronto, and Montreal—they have annexed surrounding communities.

Figure 5.1 and Table 5.3 record the most recent patterns of regional urban growth. It is a truism that every new Canadian census reveals a different situation. Urban growth is a complex process involving many different economic sectors and social trends, which together can sometimes lead to rather unpredictable shifts in city size and regional demographic

Table 5.2   **Income Levels by Region and City Size, 1996 (Average income per capita in $000s)**

City Size	British Columbia	Prairie Provinces*	Ontario	Quebec	Atlantic Provinces	Canada
>1,000,000	20.6	—	21.2	18.1	—	20.1
300,000–1,000,000	21.5	19.3	19.7	18.2	18.6	19.4
100,000–299,999	17.6	18.2	19.6	16.1	16.5	17.4
30,000–99,999	18.1	17.8	18.0	16.1	16.5	17.4
10,000–29,999	18.6	18.5	17.5	15.5	15.3	17.1
Total Urban	19.9	19.0	20.4	17.6	16.7	19.2

*Includes Yukon and the Northwest Territories.
Source: Statistics Canada, *Census of Canada*, 1996.

Figure 5.1   **Growth Distribution in the Canadian Urban System**

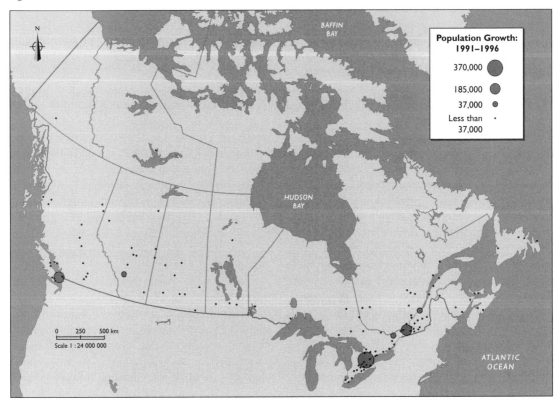

Source: Statistics Canada, *Census of Canada*, 1991, 1996.

structure. Nonetheless, several distinctive trends have marked the character of urban growth during the past several decades, and they continued apace during the most recent census period. Overall, Canadian cities grew by 6.2 per cent between 1991 and 1996, compared to 5.7 per cent for the country as a whole, or, more significantly, to 3.9 per cent for the non-urban population. The aggregate growth rates calculated for the various city-size and regional combinations indicate that the largest cities were most favoured, while the smallest cities grew more slowly than non-urban places. To a certain extent, the slower growth of smaller places holds true across all regions (Table 5.3). But the regional differences, which support the core-periphery character of

regional urban systems, are quite striking: British Columbia's growth rates were almost twice as high as Ontario's, which were twice as fast as the Prairie region, where Alberta nevertheless stood well ahead of Manitoba and Saskatchewan. Continuing a 20-year trend, growth in Quebec and the Atlantic provinces progressed slowly. In fact, despite claims of a 'Silver Horseshoe' stretching from Saint John through Moncton and on to Halifax, a dominant core region has yet to emerge in the still largely fragmented Maritimes (Wynn, 1998).

At this point, we consider the locational importance of these differences in the amount and concentration of growth. Population increase, of course, is closely linked to job creation, which stimulates

Table 5.3   **Urban Growth by Region and City Size, 1991–1996**

City Size	British Columbia	Prairie Provinces*	Ontario	Quebec	Atlantic Provinces	Canada
Aggregate Growth Rate (Per cent)						
>1,000,000	14.3	—	9.0	3.7	—	8.1
300,000–1,000,000	5.7	4.2	4.5	4.1	3.7	4.3
100,000–299,999	21.1	2.5	6.9	2.3	1.1	5.7
30,000–99,999	15.2	2.8	1.3	2.0	3.6	4.7
10,000–29,999	5.1	2.6	4.2	1.3	− .3	2.6
Total Urban	13.6	3.8	7.0	3.3	2.0	6.2
Non-Urban	12.9	4.2	3.9	4.2	− 1.1	3.9
*Growth Rate Variations (Coefficient of variation in per cent**)*						
>1,000,000	—	—	—	—	—	.47
300,000–1,000,000	—	.80	.42	—	—	.53
100,000–299,999	—	—	.92	.91	2.55	1.27
30,000–99,999	.27	1.43	3.08	1.31	.78	1.36
10,000–29,999	.88	2.15	1.10	2.31	—	1.85
Total Urban	.51	1.21	.70	.82	1.85	.95

*Includes Yukon and the Northwest Territories.
**The coefficient of variation is defined as the standard deviation/mean.
Source: Statistics Canada, *Census of Canada,* 1996.

investment in housing, schools, shopping centres, utilities, and other elements of urban infrastructure, all of which leave their distinctive mark on the landscape. There was much to record between 1991 and 1996, as Canada added some 1.5 million persons— 85 per cent of them urbanites. Ontario and British Columbia absorbed 64 per cent of this advance. More than half took up residence in Canada's four largest CMAs. In fact, Toronto and Vancouver together absorbed 38 per cent of the population increase. Despite immigration and the return of the middle class into older inner-city neighbourhoods, most growth in Toronto and Vancouver was focussed in a half-dozen suburban municipalities like Markham and Vaughan (Toronto) and Surrey and Delta (Vancouver). In both CMAs, Asian investment and immigration, from Hong Kong, Taiwan, Vietnam, and India in particular, accounted strongly for the transitional and multicultural character of suburban growth in these communities, including both commercial and residential development.

The lower half of Table 5.3 records the pattern of growth rate variability within each region-size category. This is measured by the coefficient of variation, which is the ratio of the standard deviation to the average value for the set of cities in each cell of the table. The previous chapter argued that variability should be associated with two types of regional and city size effects. First, cities of the corridor in Ontario and Quebec should show lower values or less variability than cities of the periphery. As the analysis confirms, this relationship is largely supported. The prairies and the Atlantic region both displayed greater variation than the corridor. The exception was British Columbia, where the average growth rate was so large that it obscures the high value of the standard deviation. The second pattern, that of higher variability in small cities, is also strongly supported (Table 5.3). The coefficients of variation for the three smallest city size categories are more than twice the level of the larger places.[2]

Growth and Transition

While change in the Canadian urban system has generally occurred as expected, the question remains about what actually determines growth at a particular place during a period of transitional urban development. Cities do not grow in isolation. The myriad of linkages of various kinds to other cities is instrumental in attracting growth from elsewhere and, in turn, in transmitting growth to other cities. The growth pattern of urban systems, then, is not only determined by economic, demographic, and political events, but also by the spatial context of the city at any one of several geographical scales, whether regional, national, or international.

Economic Processes and Transition in the Urban System

Although urban system features such as political boundaries and transportation infrastructure can play an enabling role in urban growth, most of the variation in urban population growth is driven by economic processes. Urban economic growth can be measured, for example, in terms of investment, income, or production, but the salient factor driv-

ing an increase in population is job creation. This is an important distinction because in Canada there are many instances of growth in economic output or investment occurring without any job creation. The level of income in farming communities, for example, often varies widely from year to year, causing little impact on the farm job market. Farmers might not invest in new machinery, but will almost certainly still farm this year and the next. The decision to delay investments, though, can ripple through various sectors of the economy, affecting not only the farm machinery sector but also fertilizer sales, railway and port activity, and other linked businesses. By contrast, the mining and petroleum industries in recent years have been able to increase production enormously by investing heavily in labour-saving technology. Much of the employment impact of the petroleum industry, in fact, comes by way of the public sector from royalties paid to governments, which in turn provide expanded educational and health care facilities—and hence new jobs (Davies and Donoghue, 1993).

Understanding the location of urban growth has become more difficult, particularly as economic activity becomes more footloose. The reason to choose Toronto over Vancouver or Montreal—even over Chicago or New York—is not always apparent (Coffey, 1994). Part of the uncertainty comes from the nature of the contemporary world-system, for example: the revolution in the exchange of information and the speed of communication; the forceful emergence of Asian production and markets; the demise of communism; the rapid spread of global capitalism; and the growing integration of global economic activity via transnational corporations. In Canada's case, production and distribution sectors are now dominated by a half dozen major firms in each sector. Over time they expand, contract, acquire, and merge; all the while their production and distribution networks become more complex. To understand the location of any one plant in Canada requires a knowledge of the firm's product mix, markets, and competition, as well as the historical record of its acquisitions. Increasingly, the study of economic geography and its links to the global urban system has become the study of the geography of the transnational corporation.

Keeping in mind caveats like these, Figure 5.2 tracks Canada's sectoral and regional employment growth since 1976, capturing key aspects of the transition to post-industrialism. The number of jobs increased by more than 40 per cent, with marked cyclical peaks in 1980, 1988, and 1995. The most striking image in Figure 5.2a is the overwhelming concentration of newly created jobs—over 90 per cent—in the service industries. The service economy is central to our understanding of post-industrial growth in Canada's largest cities during the past few decades. Many of the new producer service jobs are in the financial, management, legal, computing, and other specialized service sectors. They have become mainly concentrated in the largest commercial centres of the country. Expansion in the manufacturing and transportation-utility-construction sectors was much slower, standing at just over ten per cent, while the primary sectors grew even more slowly, at less than 10 per cent. The small, especially peripheral communities of the resource ecumene (see definition in Chapter 4), whose economic base remains in primary production, face new challenges. Growth now comes indirectly from the productivity and increased profits of an industry that enables it to support or invest in public and private sector services. Unfortunately, these linked services enjoy more locational freedom than loggers, miners, or fishers. The final result of new job creation was a marked regional redistribution of economic activity. The big winner since 1976, with an 80 per cent growth rate, was British Columbia, followed in order by Ontario, the Prairies (mostly Alberta), Atlantic Canada, and Quebec (Figure 5.2b). Quebec created only 650,000 jobs, about one-sixth of the national total, for a growth rate of 25 per cent. The differences in cyclical fluctuations among regions are also interesting. Alberta and British Columbia continued to grow during the recession-like conditions of the early 1990s, while Ontario declined sharply.[3]

During the past decade, Canada's sectoral and regional patterns of job creation have remained quite strong, but at any time in the future growth could be offset by demographic forces and public-sector programs that resist adjustment. In boom times, jobs are created almost everywhere. In the first phase of growth, a backlog of unemployed workers or workers currently not in the labour force will quickly fill the jobs. But as the leading sectors of the national economy continue to surge ahead, thousands of jobs are created in a small number of industries and locations (where wages rise), attracting migrants to these growth points. These notions are supported by recent data. During 1997, for instance, the Canadian economy added 265,000 new jobs, of which 55 per cent were in Ontario and Alberta and 80 per cent were in the two sectors of manufacturing and private-sector services (Table 5.4). One-third of all new jobs were generated in the Toronto CMA alone. These are the sort of economic signals that lure young people to migrate to different cities and regions, leading to changes in the structure of the urban system. This is the time to move, as it was before in 1979 and 1980, when rapid job creation in Alberta's 'oil patch' and British Columbia's service sector attracted thousands of migrants from across the country. The net inter-provincial migration in one year alone—1980—totalled almost 90,000, testing the ability of the urban system in the target regions to adjust housing markets, to provide health and educational facilities, and to meet other essential needs and services. Five years later, the boom was over and another migration peak marked the return flow of many workers to Ontario. Still, the enormous movement of people in the 1970s and 1980s has contributed to a westward shift that signals a permanent reorganization of the urban system (Simmons and Bourne, 1989).

The geography of job creation and migration at a particular time reflects the spatial organization of the economic subsystem. An overview pattern of the economic subsystem, derived from the flow of air passengers among cities, is presented in Figure 5.3. The majority of people flying are on business; airports and flights are designed to serve them. Note the intense concentration of flows within the

Figure 5.2   **Employment Change**

a) The Sectors
(employment relative to 1976 = 1.00)

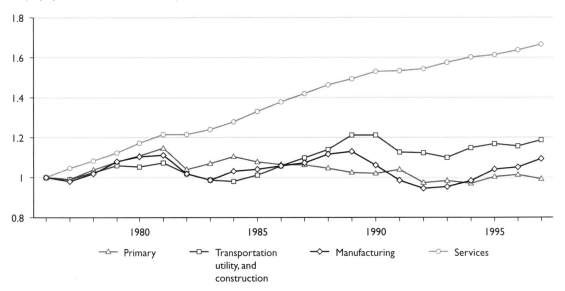

b) The Regions
(employment relative to 1976 = 1.00)

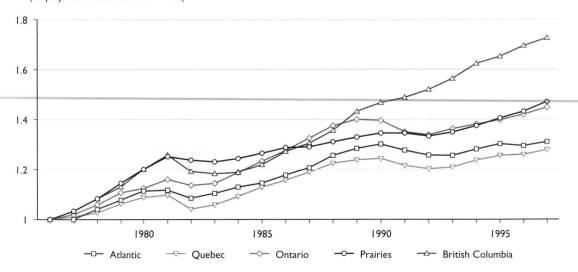

Source: Statistics Canada, *Historical Labour Force Statistics,* Catalogue No. 71–201.

Table 5.4   **Employment Growth in Canada, 1996–1997 (000s of jobs)**

	1996	1997	Change
Sector			
Agriculture	453	423	−30
Other primary sectors	280	292	12
Manufacturing	2,083	2,167	84
Construction	719	747	28
Transport, utilities, and communications	1,020	1,037	17
Trade	2,361	2,386	25
Finance	800	795	−5
Community services	2,355	2,387	32
Business and personal services	2,786	2,916	130
Public administration	820	791	−29
Region			
Atlantic provinces	947	961	14
Quebec	3,213	3,260	47
Ontario	5,311	5,413	102
Prairie provinces*	2,399	2,469	70
British Columbia	1,806	1,838	32
Canada	13,676	13,941	265
Major CMAs			
Toronto	2,159	2,247	88
Montreal	1,558	1,591	23
Vancouver	933	941	8
Ottawa	525	532	7
Edmonton	454	476	22
Calgary	450	469	19
Quebec City	325	319	−6
Winnipeg	346	353	7
Hamilton	309	315	6
Halifax	168	170	2

*Includes Yukon and the Northwest Territories.
Source: Statistics Canada, *Historical Labour Force Statistics*, Catalogue No. 71–201.

Figure 5.3   **Air Passenger Flows, 1995**

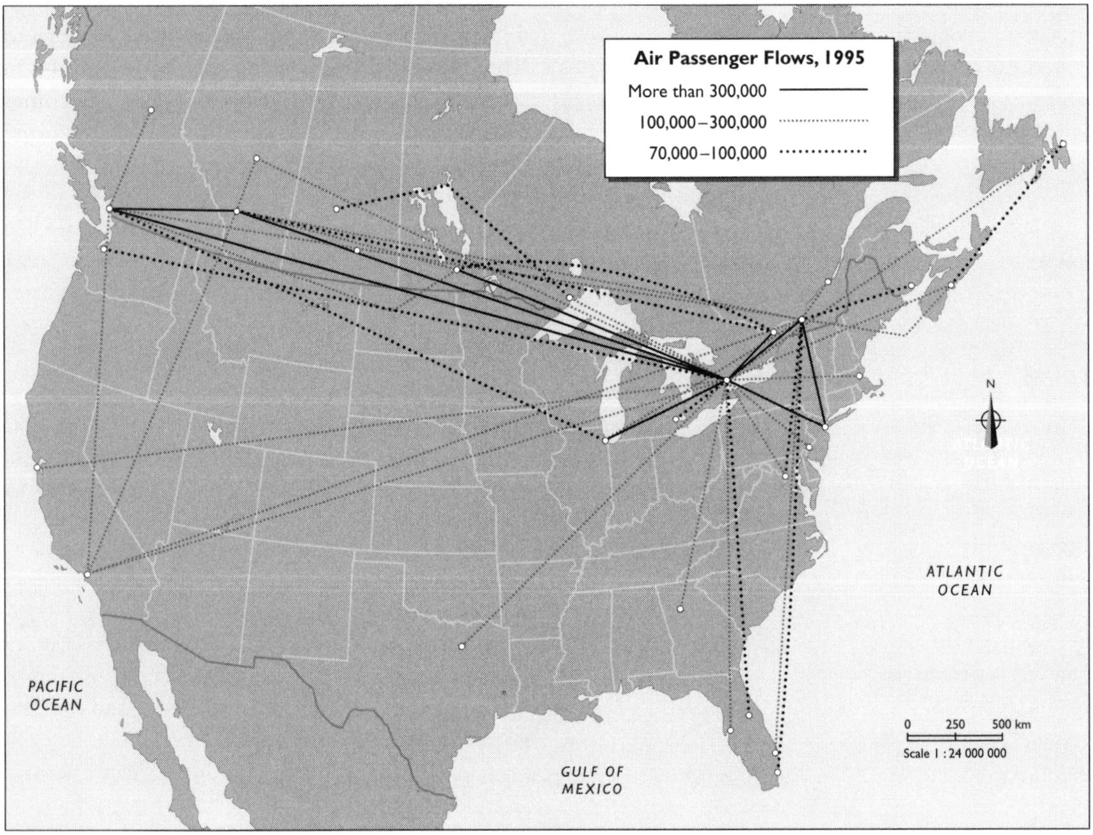

Source: Statistics Canada, 'Air Passenger Origins and Destinations', Catalogue Nos. 51–204 and 51–205.

Windsor–Quebec City corridor, even though trains and cars offer alternative means for making short trips. The most popular route is Toronto–Montreal. Toronto–Vancouver is next, followed by Toronto–Ottawa. All of our economic linkage evidence emphasizes the intensity of contacts in the corridor, as inputs and outputs flow readily among sectors and locations. Job creation in one firm affects all the firms that produce inputs for the firm, or process its product output. Eventually, the expansion of local employment will increase the sales of consumer goods and services as well. Toronto and Montreal anchor seven of the 10 largest air passenger routes in the national urban system. Beyond the corridor,

the main ties are spatially defined through linkages between a regional centre and other places (e.g., Vancouver–Kelowna, Halifax–Sydney); and through each regional centre—Halifax, Winnipeg, Calgary, Edmonton, and Vancouver—to the country's major metropolitan centre, Toronto. Regional cities also interact with each other. The Calgary–Vancouver link is fourth largest in the system. Regional centres benefit from growth within the hinterland areas they serve: through administrative functions, growth in trade, added tax revenues, or selling services. Ultimately, of course, benefits flow back to the corridor cities, which house corporate headquarters (Semple, 1996). Thus, higher prices or increased

production in farming, mining, or oil and gas production generate growth in central Canada by
means of linkages or added tax revenues. These benefits do not necessarily flow in the opposite direction though, except through the public sector.

The most fascinating linkages in Canada's
periphery, even in this phase of post-industrial transition, are those that track the economic fortunes of
resource communities. Each specialized town or
city obviously connects externally with regional,
corridor, or global production centres that manufacture resource-processing equipment or purchase
staple products. In most phases of economic growth,
we can observe either the rise or decline of well-
being in Canada's resource towns: growth in pulp
and paper employment across the Canadian Shield
after the war spurred by foreign demand and new
technologies; decline in Newfoundland fishing
communities in the 1990s associated with the collapse of the cod fishery. When staple commodities
fluctuate in supply, demand, or price, the impact is
felt in many different places, from peripheral wood
and fish harvesting areas to Toronto's Bay Street
financial district (Watkins, 1997).

Demographic Change and Transition in the Urban System

Whether an urban system is changing gradually or
is in rapid transition, the sources of population growth
remain the same: natural increase (the surplus of
births over deaths); net migration (the surplus of in-
migrants over out-migrants to other parts of Canada);
and net immigration (the surplus of immigrants over
emigrants). In the urban system's current phase, international and inter-metropolitan migrations are
having a marked impact on the system's core-
periphery structure. What fascinates students of
urban systems is that these demographic processes
have quite different spatial and temporal characteristics, some of which are outlined in Table 5.5.[4]

Demographic events are linked directly to the
age structure of the population. Economist David
Foot (1996), in *Boom, Bust, and Echo*, argues that
almost everything from crime rates and housing

costs to the television programs we watch depends
on demographics. Forecasters certainly rely on the
regularities of natural increase: children are born to
women mostly between the ages of 14 and 44, in
predictable patterns; death, of course, becomes
increasingly likely as we age. What is less recognized
is that migration and immigration are also strongly
related to age. On average, about 20 per cent of the
population moves each year, but for young people
aged 18 to 33, the rate can rise to 50 per cent, after
which the frequency of moves declines regularly
with age, to less than 10 per cent. Immigration and
emigration rates follow a similar pattern. So, given
the age structure of a city, we can make pretty good
estimates of births, deaths, out-migrants (within
Canada), and emigrants. More difficult to anticipate
are immigrant flows to specific destinations—e.g.,
from Pacific Rim countries to Vancouver, from
South America to Toronto—which is now the most
important demographic process changing the urban
system.

Figure 5.4 illustrates the major factors driving
David Foot's arguments. Note that these graphs
show actual numbers: if they were modified to show
rates of natural increase, the changes would be even
more marked. Still, the extraordinary historical variation in the sources of population growth in Canada
has so distorted the country's age structure that each
year the proportion of people in various age groups
has changed significantly. For instance, the high level
of post-war immigration in the 1950s and 1960s
(bringing many women of child-bearing age to
Canada) was followed by the reduced immigration
of the 1970s. Thus, a decline in the fertility rate was
especially rapid in Canada during the 1970s, and
continues firmly. Without immigration, which is
currently quite strong, zero population growth
would likely have occurred early in the twenty-first
century. Thus, the combined effect of increased
immigration and reduced natural increase in recent
years has left net immigration as the major source
of population growth. Immigration to Canada, of
course, is determined jointly by conditions in the
source country and those throughout Canada's
urban system. Recent increases in immigration to a

Table 5.5   **Elements of the Demographic Subsystem**

Event	Magnitude (annual)	Spatial Pattern	Causal Factors
Births	375,000	Universal, but higher in growing cities with younger population	Females, age 15–44 years
Deaths	210,000	Universal, but higher in slow-growth cities with older population	Proportional to age of population
Out-Migrants*	325,000	Universal, especially young adults	Young adults, age 15–35, and retirees
In-Migrants*	325,000	Concentrated in cities that are creating jobs and/or are high in amenities	Job opportunities and lifestyle choices for young adults and retirees
Immigrants	225,000	Highly concentrated in a small number of cities with both jobs and ethnic institutions	Young adults seeking jobs; international 'push' factors
Emigrants	50,000	Universal, but also related to previous immigration patterns	Young adults: travel, study, job transfer; return migration

*Interprovincial only. About five million Canadians move each year within the same province, mainly to adjust housing.
Source: Estimated from Statistics Canada, *Census of Canada*, 1986, 1991, 1996.

few large cities like Vancouver and Toronto reflect socio-economic conditions in Asia, policies set in Canada (such as those that favour immigrants with substantial investment capital), and the changing post-industrial economies of Canada's largest metropolitan centres. To the extent that the geographies of natural increase and net immigration are different, urban population growth patterns will change in the future. Regions like Quebec, which once depended on natural increase for growth, are no longer able to grow without attracting immigration. Regions like Ontario and British Columbia with a strong immigrant base and, as a result, large numbers of households in child-bearing age will continue to grow more rapidly.

From an urban perspective, what are the spatial patterns of Canada's demographic growth components? Births and deaths, the components of natural increase, are directly related to the population characteristics that do not differ greatly from place to place. A few retirement centres, such as Victoria, have a sufficiently high proportion of the elderly to produce an excess of deaths over births. This may also be true of smaller centres in Quebec and the Atlantic provinces, where years of out-migration have left behind an aging population. For the most part, however, the spatial variation in natural increase is relatively small. During periods of high rates of natural increase, such as the baby boom in the 1950s, all parts of the urban system grew rapidly. The average annual contribution of natural increase, at present, is about 0.5 per cent.

With few exceptions, the rates of out-migration (to places within Canada) and emigration

Figure 5.4   **Population Changes in Canada**

a) Sources of Canada's Growth
(000s per year)

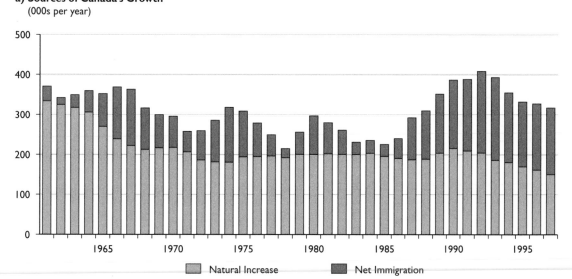

b) Interprovincial Migration
(000s per year)

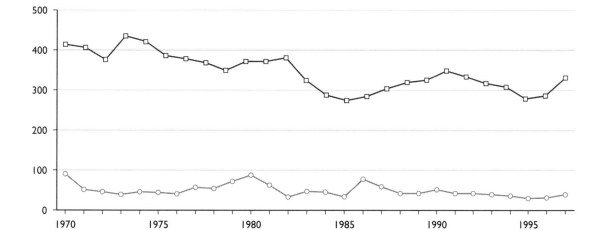

Source: Statistics Canada, *Annual Demographic Statistics,* Catalogue No. 91–213.

(abroad) are also relatively uniform in space (Table 5.6). Like life and death processes, migration rates are directly determined by age structure; by social processes such as seeking an education, job, or partner; or by simply looking for adventure. Because big cities (e.g., Toronto and Montreal) have a wider range of opportunities, the rates of out-migration from these places tend to be lower than for smaller communities. A significant regional variation does occur in the lower levels of out-migration (as well as in-migration and immigration) that characterize Atlantic Canada and Quebec. Despite lower incomes and higher unemployment levels in these regions, people are less likely to leave the cities.[5] Two explanations have been put forward. Sociologists argue that these regions enjoy a more traditional society in which family, ethnic identity, and lifestyle are especially important (McVey and Kalbach, 1995). Some geographers might argue that the differences in behaviour stem from the relative lack of migration opportunities within the region because it has no rapidly growing urban centres with substantial employment opportunities. At the same time, reflecting long-standing cultural patterns, many non-farm workers living in rural areas seek temporary work in the cities, migrating seasonally or commuting daily, either way keeping urbanization rates down (McCann, 1988). Whatever the reasons, the contrast with the migration system observed in Ontario and western Canada is striking. Here, people move back and forth easily among cities, responding to surges of job creation or job loss. Most cities west of Quebec have high levels of both in- and out-migration (Table 5.6). A specific exception to the overall migration pattern is the continuing flow of Anglophones from Montreal to Toronto. This flow began in earnest during the FLQ political crisis in 1970, and has since continued. In this instance, the political subsystem has directly affected the demographic pattern.

The most spatially variable components in the demographic subsystem are the in-migrants (within Canada) and immigrants. Although each group deals with a limited set of alternatives, both will obviously be attracted to cities that either provide jobs or offer pleasing lifestyles. Migrants within Canada are generally restricted in choice of destination by their geographic origins: the longer the distance, the less likely the move. In the same way that every city generates migrants because of its demographic characteristics, each city will also attract a certain number of in-movers—those who live in nearby centres, young people returning from college, workers transferred from other towns or cities, and so on. The distinguishing trait of in-migration is greater concentration within certain places, leading to negative net migration in some cities and population gain in others (Table 5.6). Because of lower levels of out-migration in the eastern regions, cities in Quebec and Atlantic Canada will have a lower level of in-migration as well. But because of low job creation and high unemployment, there will also be a net loss of population in most cities in eastern regions.[6] In Quebec, language is also a very powerful barrier to migration. With the exception of the Montreal Anglophones noted above, relatively few people move across the linguistic boundary marking French- and English-speaking Canada. In a practical sense, Canada consists of two separate labour markets, with different rates of growth and unemployment, one for each language group. Most pronounced in Quebec, the Francophone labour market also includes part of New Brunswick. The political subsystem must respond to each labour market.

In theory, immigrants are the least spatially-constrained element in the Canadian demographic subsystem, but they are nonetheless the most spatially concentrated. This fact is a major force in reshaping Canada's urban system. Since they arrive from outside the urban system, immigrants should have no a priori preferences, but in reality they favour locations with a history of previous immigration, supportive institutions, and employment and money-making opportunities. In fact, of all movers, immigrants (mostly young adults) are by far the most job-oriented. Canada has depended for decades on immigrants to settle the frontiers, both westward and northward. But immigrants now flock mainly to the growing big cities, especially

Table 5.6   **Migration Rates for Census Metropolitan Areas, 1991–1996**

| CMA | Migration Rates (per cent)* | | | |
	In-Migrants	Out-Migrants	Net Migration	Immigration
Toronto	4.2	6.2	−2.0	7.9
Montreal	4.1	5.5	−1.4	3.6
Vancouver	8.6	7.9	0.7	9.9
Ottawa–Hull	9.0	8.9	0.1	3.7
Edmonton	12.7	11.8	0.9	2.9
Calgary	12.4	11.3	1.1	4.1
Quebec City	7.6	7.3	0.3	1.1
Winnipeg	6.8	9.4	−2.5	2.4
Hamilton	8.1	8.0	0.1	2.5
St Catharines	6.6	6.6	0.0	1.5
London	10.3	11.1	−0.8	2.4
Kitchener	10.8	10.5	0.3	3.1
Halifax	11.6	12.8	−1.1	1.8
Victoria	15.9	12.8	3.2	2.8
Windsor	6.8	6.3	0.5	3.2
Oshawa	15.5	10.7	4.8	1.1
Saskatoon	13.8	15.6	−1.8	1.9
Regina	11.4	13.7	−2.3	1.7
St John's	8.4	10.6	−1.2	0.9
Sudbury	8.6	10.1	−2.9	0.8
Chicoutimi	6.3	8.8	−2.5	0.6
Sherbrooke	10.9	11.8	−0.9	1.6
Trois-Rivières	9.5	9.0	0.5	0.5
Saint John	6.7	7.9	−1.2	0.3
Thunder Bay	7.3	10.1	−2.9	0.8

*Migration rate = migrants, 1991–6/population of CMAs, 1996
Source: Statistics Canada, *Census of Canada*, 1996.

Toronto and Vancouver. The slow-growth regions—Atlantic Canada and Quebec—attract very few newcomers. The extraordinary concentration of immigrants in Toronto and Vancouver, and to a lesser extent in Calgary, is now one of our country's distinguishing features.

We can only speculate about the interaction of the two processes of immigration and migration in Canada. For the most part, the effects of net internal migration are small (from −2.9 per cent in Thunder Bay to +3.2 per cent in Victoria between 1991 and 1996), but immigration levels are as high as 9.9 per cent (see Table 5.6). The causal factors are apparently different. From 1991 to 1996, Toronto CMA lost 87,000 net migrants mostly to neighbouring areas, but gained 340,000 immigrants. Vancouver gained 10,000 net migrants, as well as 180,000 immigrants. Chicoutimi regularly loses net migrants but attracts very few immigrants. The graph of interprovincial migration (Figure 5.4b) suggests that while immigration has increased, the mobility of Canadians at this spatial scale has declined over the years from about 400,000 per year (when the population was younger) to between 300,000 and 350,000 at present. Because the impact of many migrants is offset by return movers, net migration—or the effective change in the urban system—is much more restricted, always less than 100,000 per year. Think of this as an upper limit to demographic adjustments in the urban system, unless there is immigration. As the immigration level increases, the potential for rapid demographic adjustments increases proportionately. The national urban system clearly responds to demographic events outside the country.

Demographic processes are obviously central to any explanation of the evolution of the urban system, as well as of the changing landscapes that characterize the contemporary Canadian city. Regional variations in the demographic subsystem distinguish the social make-up of Canadian cities in powerful ways, highlighting differences in the timing of settlement and immigration. Demographic processes also help to explain why some places are more or less likely to grow in the future, and why certain

population characteristics like age and ethnicity vary from place to place. Such processes form the backdrop or context for understanding the recent emergence of new and distinctive cultural landscapes (e.g., immigrant residential and shopping areas) in our largest metropolitan centres. And in recent years they surely provide a partial explanation for the growing dominance of the urban system by a few large metropolitan centres. Ultimately, the demographic subsystem influences the rate of population growth and change in any city, which in turn affects the extent of landscape change.

The Public Sector

The Canadian urban system, with its divergent patterns and processes of growth in economic activity and population, presents many problems that governments must attempt to solve. Each locality—whether province, city, or neighbourhood—has different needs and points of view to be represented. Each competes with nearby localities for government attention. The spatial allocation of political power is therefore of fundamental importance—in cabinet, Parliament, Senate, Legislative Assembly, or municipal council. It should also be noted that each political party has a spatial base and increasingly tends to represent a region rather than an ideology; and that spatial representation tends to look backward, not forward. Seats are allocated according to population distributions that are at least five and sometimes 15 years out of date. Rural areas and regions tend to be over-represented, at the expense of the growing suburbs. People who move frequently, such as young people or immigrants, tend to be disenfranchised. Smaller and peripheral provinces or regions feel alienated from the process by the continued domination of parties and politicians representing the core regions.

While the public sector accounts for only 18 per cent of the gross domestic product (GDP)—roughly its share of employment—the various levels of government spend the equivalent of over 40 per cent of GDP each year. Much is in transfer payments that redistribute large sums of money from firms and individuals in some locations to firms and individuals in other places.

Virtually every action of government modifies the geography of Canada in some fashion. Simmons (1986) has identified four main areas in which the public sector affects the development of the urban system. The first is bounding, the process of negotiating and controlling the flows of goods and individuals across the national boundary. We can open or close the boundaries to trade and immigration, creating growth in certain locations and decline in others. Connecting describes the traditional role of governments in Canada in linking places together by various transportation modes, either by direct investment (e.g., highways), subsidy (e.g., railways), or regulation (e.g,. airlines, pipelines, television). Each network of transportation or communications makes some places central and others peripheral. Development programs attempt to modify the regional patterns of economic activity. Historically, governments have encouraged the settlement of the West and the exploitation of the North. More recently, there have been subsidies for manufacturing firms in the Atlantic provinces and investment in oil exploration in the Arctic and Newfoundland. By far the largest expenditures at present are the various aspects of stabilization, by which tax revenues from the rapidly growing, high-income, and big city locations are expended in slow-growth, low-income, and small city or rural locations. The overall effect is to smooth out the rate of economic growth over time and space, the magnitude of which can be considerable, especially in times of economic and population transition.

Government programs are seldom static. The magnitude and patterns of their spatial impacts are affected by changes in scope and eventual termination. The federal government's Department of Regional Economic Expansion, which offered, for example, grants-in-aid for manufacturing development in the Maritimes and elsewhere, no longer exists. Some specialized programs have emerged at times of emergency, such as TAGS (The Atlantic Groundfish Strategy) for the east coast fishery, but they were not designed to last forever. Figure 5.5 shows how the ratio of all government expenditures to GDP has evolved since 1961. The initial ratio was only 28 per cent, but as (un)employment insurance

Figure 5.5   **Expenditures by Level of Government as Proportion of GDP, 1961–1996**

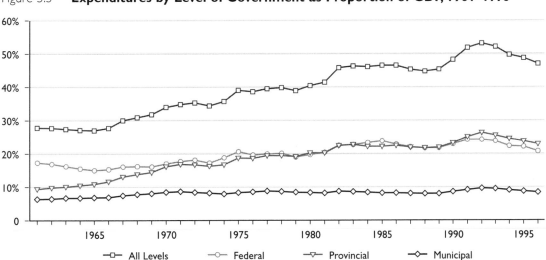

Source: Statistics Canada, *Provincial Economic Accounts*, Catalogue No. 13–213.

took on added significance, as pension plans increased, and as the health care system expanded, the ratio increased to a maximum of 53 per cent in 1992. The ratio is presently declining as the federal and provincial governments restructure their role within the Canadian political system, but whether this trend is cyclical or permanent remains unclear. Traditionally, government expenditures tend to be counter-cyclical—increasing in recessions, declining during booms—but in recent years, expenditures have diminished regardless of cyclical position.

One of the strengths of government is its ability to assist in the management of the economy, particularly to overcome spatial disparities by making various expenditures. This ability to redistribute income spatially, of course, depends on the level of government. Using income and sales taxes, provinces make expenditures principally on health care and education. While income disparities still exist within provinces, the differences are greatest between them. If the federal government transfers money, it does so at a national scale, from the wealthiest areas (e.g., Toronto, Ottawa, Calgary) to the poorest (e.g., rural Newfoundland or inner-city Montreal). If each province were to control its own programs, as Quebec and Alberta might prefer, redistribution would stop at the provincial boundary. Alberta money, for example, would stay in Alberta. If this happened, St John's would do its best to help rural Newfoundland, but would certainly not do as well without the assistance of federal transfer payments gathered from all provinces. Figure 5.5 shows that the federal role has been fairly stable over the past three decades, rising from 17 per cent of GDP to a maximum of 24 per cent, and then back to 21 per cent. (Note that total government expenditures are less than the sum of the totals because of double-counting: the federal government gives to the provinces, which in turn give to local governments.) Provincial expenditures showed their most rapid growth in the 1960s when health and education needs came to the fore, growing from 9 to 26 per cent of GDP from 1961 to 1992, but declining somewhat thereafter. Local governments have changed the least, from 6.5 to 9 per cent, and then back to 8 per cent.

The logic of spatial redistribution as a policy of stabilization in a period of global transition is illustrated for Saskatchewan, where wheat, oil, and potash have always been highly dependent upon global markets (Figure 5.6). The values above the straight mid-line refer to the private sector; those below are measures of government activity. Taking the private sector first, the direct effects of the primary sector are recorded as fluctuations in farm income, which is highly erratic in Saskatchewan. The more indirect effects are shown as private income after taxes. That part of private income that pays for government is shown as taxes imposed upon private income. Taxes tend to be counter-cyclical, smoothing out income variations. Two indicators of government activity are plotted below the line: government expenditures and transfers to individuals. The former includes government wages and health care; the latter pensions, welfare, and employment insurance. The lesson from this evidence is that government expenditures are very steady over time; and that private sector activity varies widely from year to year, and from place to place. Left to itself, the private sector typically creates a series of economic crises. Put another way, the needs of Saskatchewan's population remain generally the same from year to year, while the ability of the private sector to meet these needs is variable. Government thus intervenes to prevent hardship, rather like a giant insurance scheme. The larger the public sector, the more this is possible. The difficult task is to judge just how much government intervention is sufficient. If intervention is too great, it tends to suppress the economic signals that tell people to change jobs, to sell the farm, or even to move away—in short, to create complacency or at worst dependency on government (Courchene, 1994).

The great constitutional debates in Canada that affect the distribution of powers and responsibilities between the federal government and the provinces, as well as the year-to-year debates about programs and expenditures, have profound implications for patterns of growth and change within the urban system, especially for small places. This is why government policies at all levels are so bitterly con-

Figure 5.6   **Income Variability in Saskatchewan, 1961–1994 (millions of 1986$)**

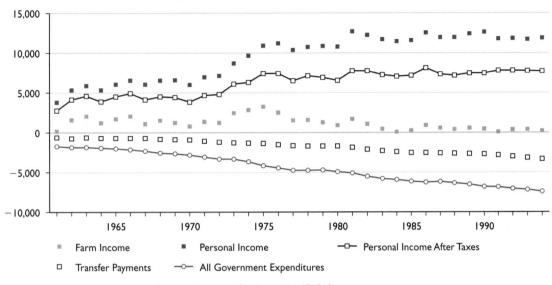

Source: Statistics Canada, *Provincial Economic Accounts*, Catalogue No. 13–213.

tested. Political power translates into economic programs, and ultimately into the population growth of cities—hence economic opportunities for local people. Countering the strength of countries, one of the more recent and interesting outcomes of globalization has been the shift of political power from the nation state to international agents, including transnational corporations (TNCs) and the International Monetary Fund (IMF). As headquarters for most Canadian TNCs, Canada's chief metropolitan centres—Toronto, Montreal, Vancouver, Ottawa–Hull, and Calgary—have assumed greater strength as important economic decision-making centres. While certainly not possessing status as first-rank global cities like New York, London, or Tokyo, they are, nevertheless, operating more and more at a global scale (Semple, 1996). The continuation of this process could well result in the increased fragmentation of the Canadian urban system. By this measure, the cities and regions of Canada would focus more on external rather than internal connections, breaking down the national urban system in favour of stronger global integration.

Looking to the Future in a Period of Transition

It is always useful to consider the future, if only as a check against our understanding of the present, and in anticipation of problems yet to come. While prediction is difficult in any period of transitional growth, one way to do this is to offer evidence derived from Statistics Canada's projections for Canada and the provinces for 2001 to 2016. We will also offer a more speculative perspective about the potential impact of further globalization on the urban system.

Forecasting Urban Growth

After each census, Statistics Canada examines the nation's population patterns, tracks the growth over the previous two decades, and extrapolates into the future the likely population characteristics of Canada and the provinces. These are rather simple, 'more-of-the-same' projections, based solely on the demographic system. They use age-structure data to predict natural increase, and apply recent trends in immigration and internal migration to project growth instigated through migration.

Some predictions are easy, others difficult. Canada's population is relatively easy to predict. It will total about 37 million in 2016, certainly less than 40 million but more than 33 million. It might rise to 45 million by the year 2050, but it will likely decline thereafter. Forecasting provincial and urban growth is much more difficult because immigration and migration within Canada can change rapidly and in unpredictable ways, depending upon development in the economy. Table 5.7 simply allocates the projected growth of each province among the existing urban areas. Based as they are on the results of the last two censuses (1991 and 1996), the projections suggest 'more of the same'. Still, even this is revealing. Very little urban growth will occur in

the Atlantic region, although Halifax might add 45,000 people by 2016 to total 375,000. Montreal (+650,000) is the magnet within Quebec, less so Quebec City (+145,000). Most of the urban expansion is projected for Ontario, where Toronto will add another 2.4 million to reach 6.6 million in 2016. Ottawa will also grow, adding 440,000 to reach the 1.45 million mark. Urban growth projections for western Canada vary widely. Winnipeg, Regina, and Saskatoon should grow modestly, but Calgary could add almost 400,000 people to become Canada's fifth largest city (c. 1,200,000). Edmonton will likely grow more slowly. Vancouver's projected growth stands at 2.7 million in 2016, achieving growth second only to Toronto by adding 900,000 people.

How accurate are these forecasts? Historically, such projections have seldom predicted the precise amount of population growth in any particular city,

Table 5.7   Projections of Population Growth: Canada and Regions, 1996–2016 (000s)

Region	1996	2016	Change	Urban Growth	Major Cities: Growth Projection	
Atlantic provinces	2,334	2,425	91	91	Halifax	+45 → 375
Quebec	7,139	8,491	1,352	942	Montreal:	+658 → 3,867
					Quebec:	+145 → 817
Ontario	10,754	15,107	4,353	4,027	Toronto:	+2,375 → 6,639
					Ottawa:	+443 → 1,453
Prairie provinces	4,896	5,926	1,030	678	Calgary:	+381 → 1,203
					Edmonton:	+123 → 986
					Winnipeg:	+39 → 706
British Columbia	3,725	5,171	1,446	1,232	Vancouver:	+878 → 2,710
Canada	28,847	37,120	8,272	6,970		

Note: Estimates of urban growth assume that 1991–6 urban shares are maintained in the future.
Source: Statistics Canada, *Projections of Population Growth: Canada and Regions, 1996–2016.*

but they have correctly highlighted the probable impact of current trends that exist within the urban system. The projections in the past have told us, for example, that St John's and Charlottetown would never threaten Halifax, let alone Montreal. In the most recent forecast, Calgary is projected to become the most important city in the expanse between Toronto and Vancouver, which will continue to be the most rapidly growing census metropolitan areas. Current trends of national decentralization and increased metropolitanization and polarization in the western provinces are likely to continue well into the twenty-first century.

Globalization and Its Changes

While recent growth trends and an operational knowledge of the urban system help us make projections for five- or ten-year periods, the more fundamental organization of the system, such as the original settlement of the West or the shaping of the core-periphery dichotomy, require analysis at a different spatial scale. It can be argued that left to itself, without the influence of external events, the Canadian urban system would be self-maintaining (Simmons, 1992). It would grow only slowly, without really changing its spatial distribution within the country. The economic and political relationships that are already in place would reinforce each other and resist change. Real change to the urban system, that is, alterations in the linkages among places and the ways in which growth processes operate, must come from outside the country (Courchene, 1995). In Canada's past, these external forces have included the threat of American economic expansion, the influx of immigrants and major shifts in world commodity prices. Currently, Canada is undergoing a period of accelerated change due to the combined effects of new and different globalization processes, bringing much greater interdependence on a world scale. As the country becomes more open to such trends, the rate of spatial redistribution within the urban system will likely accelerate. Among the global processes reshaping Canada are the following:

- Innovations in computers and telecommunications (symbolized by the Internet) permit instantaneous transfers of data and money among countries and cities.
- There have been explosive increases in the international flow of capital and business information.
- Deregulation of financial activities has intensified international investment flows.
- Transnational firms have grown to integrate production and distribution across international boundaries.
- International barriers to trade and investment have been reduced, e.g., through the North American Free Trade Agreement (NAFTA) and the World Trade Organization (WTO).
- International trade has increased, with the rate of world trade growing almost twice as fast as production.
- Significant new sources for international exchanges in finance (e.g., Japan) and manufactured goods (e.g., Japan, Korea, China, countries in Southeast Asia) have emerged.
- As the national and provincial governments compete for international investment, public sector activities have been privatized and the regulatory role of government reduced.
- Tensions in the world political system increasingly influence economic decision-making.
- Many First World countries, including Canada, have found that their rapid decline in fertility rates has left them with an aging population that cannot reproduce itself, suggesting that a greater share of population growth must take place by means of immigration.

Impact on Urban Systems

These globalization processes impact national urban systems in substantial ways, in part because of shifts in the spatial scale of relevant linkages and of increased competition at the international rather than national level; and in part because globalization alters the relationships among the economic, demographic, and political subsystems within the country. Among these impacts are the following:

- The national economy will become more specialized, pursuing a smaller number of production sectors while withdrawing from others, in accordance with Canada's comparative advantages relative to its trading partners. Successful specialized sectors are determined externally, but within Canada, they will inevitably benefit some regions to the detriment of others. For example, through negotiated access to the American market in the mid-1960s, Canada has developed unexpected strength in manufacturing automobiles and parts in Ontario. Within the free trade agreement, many agricultural activities, such as dairy production in Quebec, are threatened by elimination of market monopolies.

- Economic specialization for export means that the growth of an economic sector (and region) is no longer tied to the expansion of the national economy, but can expand or contract with world export markets. At the same time, Canadian firms compete with all foreign producers. While Canada's resource periphery has always been part of the 'boom and bust' world commodity market, the industrial corridor (especially its auto industry) has been reoriented to international markets. Many manufacturing firms are now in a position to expand in Canada, or migrate to Mexico.

- As the national market assumes less and less significance, the locational advantage of access to the Canadian market enjoyed by the Windsor–Quebec City corridor will decline. Export-oriented manufacturing and service activities may prefer to locate somewhere in the periphery, closer to their world markets. The initial stages of globalization in the 1970s and early 1980s were marked by a worldwide redistribution of economic activity away from national core regions (even in the United States) towards peripheral locations—part of the so-called 'counter-urbanization' process.

- 'Gateway' regions and cities will gain in importance. In North America, the explosion of world production and markets in East Asia has benefited west coast cities and hurt eastern ports.

- At the same time, technological advances in production favour big cities with well-developed financial and business service facilities over cities oriented to goods production.

- Higher levels of disposable income within upper socio-economic categories favour places of consumption (distribution centres and recreation and retirement cities) over places of production. Production sites located in attractive venues will be doubly advantaged.

- Globalization affects the economic subsystem directly. There is usually no immediate change in the demographic subsystem, except for the need to respond more quickly to economic change. In theory, the gradual convergence of world income levels will discourage immigration, but if this ever materializes, it will take a long time.

- As immigration contributes a higher proportion of population growth, the variation in urban growth rates within the Canadian urban system will likely increase. Some cities (e.g., Vancouver) are attractive to immigrants because of the local culture (influenced by previous immigration), access to the country of origin, and economic growth opportunities. Other places, such as Moncton, Moose Jaw, and Quebec City, are less appealing to immigrants because of the absence of such attractions.

- The role of the political subsystem in managing urban growth will become increasingly circumscribed as international agreements replace many of the traditional government programs with market mechanisms. Unlike political unions (e.g., the European Union), economic globalization does not involve a system of transfer payments among its participants. In fact, it essentially eliminates tariffs, subsidies, and preferential purchasing. The enormous pressure of trade competition restricts the range of a country's public programs, taxes, and environmental protection. Privatization will reduce the scale of the public sector. In all likelihood, the relative importance of provincial and national capital cities will decline.

- Within the cities, globalization will have a direct impact on particular landscapes, e.g., the 'grey' areas of deindustrialization in the transition zone, the skyscraper headquarters of transnational corporations in the CBD, and the massive malls on the suburban periphery (e.g., commercial and institutional centres).

Conclusion

In the new economic environment, the Canadian political system will find it more and more difficult to protect lagging regions, by either sectoral or regional aid, or by income redistribution. After decades of convergence in regional income per capita, we can expect to see greater variation in the future. Core and periphery patterns will persist, but gathering strength in western Canada will allow urban parts of this region to stand on their own, increasingly independent of the industrial heartland. There is every expectation at the same time of continued growth in income for the system as a whole, but disparities between centre (or centres) and margin could well increase once again. The problem for policy-makers is to think about cities and regions in Canada as part of a continental or global economy, instead of a national urban system. It may also be necessary to re-evaluate demographic policies to be more responsive to labour requirements that are highly variable in time and space. Governments at all levels will have to acknowledge their reduced capacity to alleviate the spatial inequities of the economy.

The urban system is an important way of introducing the geography of Canada as a context for studying particular cities. It is a geography that takes explicit note of the extraordinary concentrations of human activity on the Canadian landscape, and of the way that urban nodes channel and organize the spatial structure of surrounding areas. The urban system has become by far the most important context for interpreting the characteristics and development of individual cities. It affects the amount and timing of growth, and especially the economic, demographic, and political processes that, either separately or intertwined, shape and reshape the landscapes of cities.

Notes

1. Readers are encouraged to explore the rich collection of maps in the *National Atlas of Canada*, 5th edn (Canada, n.d.), that enhance the spatial dimensions of arguments like these. For example, the map of income per capita (Map 37.1) shows the same pattern in greater detail, highlighting in particular the rural-urban differences. The map uses 1981 data, suggesting that regional urban and city size patterns are long-standing in Canada. The maps in the *National Atlas of Canada* examine a wide range of economic, social, and political conditions.

2. These patterns also characterize the period 1983–8 as revealed in Map 36.1 of the *National Atlas of Canada*, which shows the variability in employment growth across the urban system.

3. See also Map 36.2 of the *National Atlas of Canada* for more details on employment growth from 1971–86.

4. See also the patterns of migration in Map 17.1, *National Atlas of Canada*.

5. See also Map 17.1 of the *National Atlas of Canada*.

6. See Map 17.1, *National Atlas of Canada*.

References

Bourne, L.S. and M. Flowers. 1996. *The Canadian Urban System Revisited: A Statistical Analysis.* Toronto: University of Toronto, Centre for Urban and Community Studies, Research Report No. 192.

——— and A.E. Olvet. 1995. *New Urban and Regional Geographies in Canada: 1986-1991.* Toronto: University of Toronto, Centre for Urban and Community Studies, Major Report No. 33.

Canada, Energy, Mines and Resources, Surveys and Mapping Branch. n.d. *National Atlas of Canada*, 5th edn. Ottawa: Geographical Services Division.

Coffey, W. 1994. *The Evolution of Canada's Metropolitan Economies*. Montreal: Institute for Research on Public Policy.

Courchene, T.J. 1994. *Social Canada in the Millennium*. Montreal: C.D. Howe Institute.

———. 1995. 'Globalization: The Regional/International Interface', *Canadian Journal of Regional Science* 18: 1–20.

Davies, W.K.D., and D.P. Donoghue. 1993. 'Economic Diversification and Group Stability in an Urban System: Canada, 1951–1986', *Urban Studies* 30: 1165–86.

Foot, D.K., and D. Stoffman. 1996. *Boom, Bust, and Echo: How to Profit from the Coming Demographic Shift*. Toronto: McFarlane Walter and Ross.

Gwyn, R. 1995. *Nationalism Without Walls: The Unbearable Lightness of Being Canadian*. Toronto: McClelland & Stewart.

McCann, L.D. 1988. '"Living a Double Life": Town and Country in the Industrialization of the Maritimes', in D. Day, ed., *Geographical Perspectives on the Maritime Provinces*. Halifax: St Mary's University Press.

McVey, W.W., and W.E. Kalbach. 1995. *Canadian Population*. Toronto: Nelson.

Semple, R.K. 1996. 'Quaternary Places in Canada', in J.N.H. Britton, ed., *Canada and the Global Economy*. Montreal and Kingston: McGill-Queen's University Press.

Simmons, J.W. 1986. 'The Impact of the Public Sector on the Canadian Urban System', in A.F.J. Artibise and G. Stelter, eds, *Power and Place: Canadian Urban Development in the North American Context*. Vancouver: University of British Columbia Press.

———. 1992. *The Reorganization of Urban Systems: The Role and Impacts of External Events*. Toronto: University of Toronto, Centre for Urban and Community Studies, Research Report No. 186.

——— and L.S. Bourne. 1989. *Urban Growth Trends in Canada, 1986-1991: A New Geography of Change*. Toronto: University of Toronto, Centre for Urban and Community Studies, Major Report No. 25.

Watkins, M. 1997. 'Canadian Capitalism in Transition', in Wallace Clement, ed., *Understanding Canada: Building on the New Canadian Political Economy*. Montreal and Kingston: McGill-Queen's University Press.

Wynn, G. 1998. 'Places at the Margin: The Atlantic Provinces', in L.D. McCann and A. Gunn, eds, *Heartland and Hinterland: A Geography of Canada*, 3rd edn. Scarborough, Ont.: Prentice-Hall Canada.

Chapter 6

Canadian Cities and Shifting Fortunes of Economic Development

William J. Coffey

As Canada enters a new century, the nation, like other developed countries, is in the midst of a series of major economic transformations—a 'Non-Industrial Revolution', many would say—that may well rival the earlier Industrial Revolution in terms of its impacts on society. The changing economic structure and performance of Canada's urban areas, particularly its larger metropolitan areas, may be regarded as both a cause and an effect of this transformation. On the one hand, the economic performance of individual urban areas contributes to national trends; on the other hand, national and international trends have specific impacts on the economic performance of individual urban areas. A major aspect of this period of transformation is that patterns of economic growth, decline, and restructuring have been highly uneven across space; depending on the specific period, economic growth has occurred in some urban areas but not in others. Such uneven economic development obviously has important impacts on all aspects of urban life: access to jobs; housing quality; family and household income levels; and even social and health conditions, which have been demonstrated to decline in economically troubled areas.

This chapter examines the changing economic structure and performance of Canadian urban areas. What have been the major elements of this economic transformation? In what urban areas have growth or decline occurred? And why has this been so? After identifying the major economic changes that have recently occurred in Canada and other developed nations, this chapter traces the principal dimensions of economic growth and structural

change in Canada's urban economies over the period 1971–91. The latter portion of the chapter then considers a number of explanations for the observed patterns of urban economic growth.

The Nature of Economic Transformation

The economic transformation that is currently being experienced by urban areas in Canada and in other developed countries consists of seven major and interrelated elements. First, urban economies are becoming increasingly *tertiarized*. One of the major phenomena that has marked the economies of developed countries in the latter half of the twentieth century has been the growth of service industries. The provision of services has replaced the production of goods as the principal form of economic activity in these countries. In Canada in 1991, service activities accounted for 73.5 per cent of total employment and 66.4 per cent of the GDP; for 1961 the respective percentages were 57.8 and 60.4. These figures are indicative of a long-term structural transformation that is fundamentally modifying the production systems of advanced economies. Presently, with the US, Canada is the world's most tertiarized nation.

Second, urban economies are becoming increasingly *professionalized*. The concept of occupation refers to the kind of work performed (that is, the duties and tasks carried out) by a person, irrespective of the kind of business (and thus the economic sector) in which this work is accomplished. In Canada, as in other developed nations, the workforce has become progressively more professionalized, with a higher proportion of workers now found in white-collar occupations (e.g., managers and administrators, social and physical scientists, engineers, teachers, and doctors) and a correspondingly lower proportion in blue-collar occupations (e.g., materials handlers, machine and equipment operators, fabricators and assemblers, and construction workers). Over the period 1961–91, for example, the proportion of white-collar workers approximately doubled, attaining 28 per cent in 1991.

Third, urban economies are increasingly composed of *non-standard forms of employment*, that is, forms that differ from the traditional model of a permanent full-time job within a firm. Among these new forms are: (1) part-time employment (defined by Statistics Canada as involving less than 30 hours of work per week); (2) contractual employment (work that may be full-time, but that has a fixed duration of less than six months); and (3) self-employment. In sum, the recent period has been marked by a shift towards less stable, more marginal forms of employment. While these non-standard forms of employment may be seen in all sectors of the economy, they are most prevalent in those that have traditionally been characterized by low levels of qualifications and remuneration. These changes have important implications for the employment security, remuneration, and social benefits of workers (see Chapter 15).

Fourth, urban economies are experiencing changes in the *manner in which work is performed*. To begin with, even in the case of manufactured goods, manual labour is increasingly being replaced by inputs of capital equipment and technology. In addition, across all economic sectors and across all occupational categories, the tasks performed are becoming more technical and sophisticated. Further, even in the case of the production of manufactured goods, the 'raw material' of the production process increasingly involves information rather than physical material. Thus, 'production' workers on the shop floor are now often called on to use computers and computer-assisted machine tools rather than their own muscles. Even in the

case of traditionally 'contact-intensive' high-order services such as management consulting, more and more capital and technology inputs are employed. In sum, there has been an up-skilling of the labour force and firms now require workers who are better trained, better educated, and who are characterized by a higher level of social skills.

Fifth, from the viewpoint of the firms themselves, the *production process is being organized in innovative ways*. Much has been written recently concerning the adoption of new flexible methods of production. Often cited are approaches involving the use of computer-controlled machine tools and other new technologies that allow smaller runs of more diversified products, and involving dense networks of interconnected independent firms linked by just-in-time deliveries of inputs. In addition, however, many strategies for achieving flexibility involve methods of deploying the labour force: functional flexibility (the use of the same worker for a variety of tasks), numerical flexibility (the ability of a firm to adjust the aggregate quantity of labour in response to fluctuations in the demand for individual products), temporal flexibility (the use of labour on a part-time or overtime basis), and tenurial flexibility (the use of temporary workers or of subcontracts to independent workers). Further, in the new era of 'lean and mean' organizations, there is a marked tendency for firms to externalize (that is, to contract out) tasks not directly related to the production of their principal product. Thus, a new social division of labour is often created between large firms and small firms.

Sixth, important changes have been occurring in the *location of economic activity*. On the one hand, the trends identified above mean that Canadians are now doing more work in offices than in factories or on construction sites. On the other hand, however, given the nature of the activities that have experienced the most rapid growth, work is increasingly taking place in urban areas, particularly in those at the upper end of the urban hierarchy. In addition, recent advances in computer and telecommunications technologies ('telematics') have begun to alter the traditional models of where both production and consumption actually take place; 'tele-working' and 'teleshopping' (that is, work and shop-ping carried out in locations other than the 'normal' ones; in the home, for example, rather than in the office or in the shopping mall) have become inte-gral parts of the vocabulary of modern urban and economic geography. 'Teleworkers' include not only those who work at home on one or more days per week, but also those 'mobile workers' such as con-sultants whose 'normal' place of work is at their clients' facilities, whether the latter be within the same metropolitan area or in a foreign country, rather than on the premises of their own company.

Finally, all levels of the urban hierarchy are becoming increasingly *integrated into the newly emerg-ing global economy*. In the present era, where both goods and services are often the products of a 'global assembly line', local patterns of production and consumption are subject to the influence of worldwide trends and market conditions. This global integration of urban economies operates through the importation and exportation of both goods and, increasingly, services; through the spatial deployment strategies of transnational corporations; and through the new international division of labour. Although all levels of the urban hierarchy are generally involved in the globalization phenome-non, larger urban areas often have a particular role to play—that of 'gateway cities' that serve as relay points that link their region or their nation to the larger global economy. A small number of cities at the top of the global urban hierarchy aspire to the status of 'world city'—a centre of command and control on the world economic and cultural scene. Toronto, Montreal, and Vancouver clearly have such ambitions, but none of them has yet come to rival places like Tokyo, New York, or London (UK). Further, subject to worldwide trends, certain cities can see their economic importance decline within their national urban system (e.g., historically indus-trial cities such as Windsor or Hamilton), while oth-ers can see their role increase (e.g., service-oriented cities such as London, Ontario, or Quebec City).

Overlaying these 'global shifts' that have left their imprint on all developed economies are a number of 'home-grown' Canadian trends: the boom-and-bust cycle of western resource exploita-tion; an increasing focus on economic relations with the Pacific Rim countries; the widening gap between Toronto and Montreal at the head of Canada's urban hierarchy; and, last but not least, an increas-ing incertitude concerning the role of Quebec within Confederation. These national trends, too, have left their mark on the structure of Canada's economy and, more specifically, on the economic geography of its urban system.

The discussion to follow begins with an over-view of economic change across the entire system, by sector and by occupational classification of workers. The next section treats employment dynamics through an examination of the fastest- and slowest-growing places. Attention then turns to the location of economic activity as assessed by location quotients and an index of specialization. These empirically based sections of the chapter are followed by a discussion of growth and change that is guided by six hypothesized relationships believed to embrace major parameters of growth in urban systems across developed economies. Finally, this chapter returns to empirical analysis, with a multi-variate statistical model designed to assess each of the six hypothesized features of urban growth. In general terms, it finds that growth has become more complex and variable over time. The conclu-sion considers the implication of economic transi-tion as regards local economic development issues and policy.

Overview of Urban System Sectoral and Occupational Change, 1971–1991

As employed in the present chapter, the term 'urban system' refers to 152 urban units—census metro-politan areas, census agglomerations, and munici-palities—having more than 10,000 inhabitants; in 1991, the urban system contained 77.4 per cent of the national population.[1] In any analysis of eco-nomic growth and development it is important to consider both the sectoral and the occupational dimensions of change. While most studies concentrate on the sectoral dimension, such an approach actually leads to an underestimation of the extent of service *functions* within an economy. For example, the head office of Alcan, located in downtown Montreal, is classed, along with the rest of the firm, as a part of the manufacturing sector. From an occupational perspective, however, it is clear that this establishment primarily fulfils service functions; it is staffed by managers, engineers, computer analysts, lawyers, accountants, clerks, and secretaries. There are no smokestacks and virtually no blue-collar workers at the Sherbrooke Street headquarters. The situation is similar for the vast majority of primary-sector employment located within urban areas.

Sectoral Transformation

Table 6.1 summarizes the transformation of sectoral structure within the urban system over the period 1971–91, indicating (1) the percentage distribution of employment across sectors, (2) growth rates, and (3) the corresponding numbers of employed workers involved in (1) and (2). Perhaps the most striking feature of this period is the *relative shift* of employment out of goods production (a decline of 8.9 points, from 32.2 per cent of the employed labour force in 1971 to 23.3 per cent in 1991) into services. In fact, given that the primary sector actually saw its share of total employment increase slightly from 2.8 to 2.9 per cent, and given that construction underwent a decline of only 0.6 points, it would be more correct to speak specifically of a relative decline of *manufacturing* employment. The latter sector underwent a decline of 8.4 points, from 23 per cent in 1971 to 14.6 per cent in 1991. In the decade 1981–91, the relative decline of manufacturing also involved an absolute decline, with 203,300 jobs lost. Due to its performance during the preceding decade (an increase of 335,600 jobs), however, the manufacturing sector finished the study period with an *absolute increase* of 132,300 jobs, yielding a growth rate of only 10 per cent, well below the figure of 72.7 per cent obtained for all

sectors taken together. The primary and construction sectors registered growth rates of 75.8 per cent and 55.2 per cent, respectively, over the two decades.

The service industries increased their relative share of employment from 67.8 to 76.7 per cent of total employment between 1971 and 1991; thus, more than three-quarters of all employed persons in the urban system now work in a service sector. This expansion involved a growth rate of 95.4 per cent and an absolute increase of 3,743,700 jobs. The behaviour of the service industries was not uniform, however. While business services (277.8 per cent), other producer services (267 per cent), accommodation and food services (166.1 per cent), health and social services (127.2 per cent), finance, insurance, and real estate (or FIRE, 114.9 per cent), and consumer services (103.9 per cent) all experienced growth rates significantly above the urban system average of 72.7 per cent, certain other sectors performed more poorly than average: transport and communications (48 per cent), wholesale trade (64.2 per cent), public administration (64.9 per cent), education (65.5 per cent), and public utilities (68.9 per cent). The growth rates of individual sub-sectors within the business services group are particularly impressive: 2,068 per cent for computer services and 724 per cent for management and business consultants. (In addition to computer services and management and business consultants, the business services group also includes accounting services, advertising services, architectural services, engineering and scientific services, and legal services.) In terms of absolute growth, employment increases in retail trade (567,300) and in health and social services (533,700) were individually superior to the whole goods-producing sector. Absolute growth levels in accommodation and food services (386,400), business services (366,100), FIRE (357,800), consumer services (334,600), and public administration (328,700) were all quite high. At the other extreme, public utilities added only 46,100 jobs over the 20-year period. Overall, the goods-producing sectors accounted for only 11 per cent (that is 460,700 of 4,204,300 jobs) of net new job creation between 1971 and 1991, with services contributing the remaining 89 per cent.

Table 6.1 **Sectoral Structure, Canadian Urban System, 1971–1991**

Sector	1971 (000)	1971 %	1981 (000)	1981 %	1991 (000)	1991 %	1971–1981 absolute growth (000)	1971–1981 growth rate %	1981–1991 absolute growth (000)	1981–1991 growth rate %	1971–1991 absolute growth (000)	1971–1991 growth rate %
Primary	163.5	2.8	266.3	3.1	287.4	2.9	102.8	62.9	21.2	7.9	123.9	75.8
Manufacturing	1,330.0	23.0	1,665.6	19.6	1,462.3	14.6	335.6	25.2	−203.3	−12.2	132.3	10.0
Construction	370.3	6.4	513.0	6.0	574.7	5.8	142.7	38.5	61.7	12.0	204.4	55.2
Subtotal: goods production	1,863.8	32.2	2,444.9	28.8	2,324.4	23.3	581.1	31.2	−120.5	−4.9	460.7	24.7
Transport & communications	448.9	7.8	623.8	7.4	664.4	6.6	174.9	39.0	40.6	6.5	215.5	48.0
Public utilities	66.8	1.2	97.7	1.2	112.9	1.1	30.8	46.1	15.2	15.6	46.1	68.9
Wholesale trade	283.5	4.9	444.7	5.2	465.5	4.7	161.2	56.9	20.8	4.7	182.0	64.2
Retail trade	707.2	12.2	1,054.0	12.4	1,274.5	12.8	346.8	49.0	220.5	20.9	567.3	80.2
Consumer services	321.9	5.6	472.8	5.6	656.5	6.6	150.9	46.9	183.7	38.9	334.6	103.9
Accommodation & food serv.	232.6	4.0	459.6	5.4	618.9	6.2	227.0	97.6	159.4	34.7	386.4	166.1
Finance, insurance, real estate	311.3	5.4	530.3	6.3	669.2	6.7	219.0	70.3	138.9	26.2	357.8	114.9
Business services	131.8	2.3	293.9	3.5	497.9	5.0	162.1	123.0	204.0	69.4	366.1	277.8
Other producer services	50.8	0.9	120.8	1.4	186.4	1.9	70.0	137.9	65.6	54.2	135.6	267.0
Education	442.3	7.6	587.1	6.9	732.2	7.3	144.8	32.7	145.1	24.7	289.9	65.5
Health & social services	419.5	7.2	667.9	7.9	953.2	9.5	248.4	59.2	285.3	42.7	533.7	127.2
Public administration	506.4	8.8	686.4	8.1	835.1	8.4	180.0	35.5	148.8	21.7	328.7	64.9
Subtotal: services	3,923.0	67.8	6,038.9	71.2	7,666.7	76.7	2,115.9	53.9	1,627.8	27.0	3,743.7	95.4
Total	5,786.8	100.0	8,483.8	100.0	9,991.2	100.0	2,697.0	46.6	1,507.3	17.8	4,204.3	72.7

Source: Calculated by author from special data tabulations of *Census of Canada*, 1971, 1981, 1991.

A final point of note in Table 6.1 concerns the variation of growth rates by decade. Without exception, all sectors experienced higher growth rates during the period 1971-81 than during the period 1981–91. For all economic activities together, the growth rate in the former period was 46.6 per cent, while that in the latter period was only 17.8 per cent (a value of only 38 per cent that of the 1971–81 value). Even in business services and other producer services, the two most rapidly growing sectors, the differences were enormous: 123.0 and 137.9 per cent, respectively, during the 1970s versus 69.4 and 54.2 per cent during the 1980s. These figures reflect the difficulties faced by Canadian job-seekers during that decade.

Occupational Transformation

Table 6.2 presents a similar overview of changes in the occupational structure of the Canadian urban system over the period 1971-91.[2] The major feature of this table is the *relative* (but not absolute) shift of employment out of blue-collar occupations (e.g., farming, fishing, trapping; processing and machining; fabricating and assembling; construction, materials handling, and equipment operating)—a decline of nine percentage points, from 33.6 per cent of the employed labour force in 1971 to 24.6 per cent in 1991—into white-collar occupations (managerial and administrative jobs, those in the natural and social sciences and engineering, and those in education and health), an increase of 8.2 percentage points, from 21.5 to 29.7. The grey- (and pink-) collar category (e.g., clerical jobs and those in sales and service functions), in contrast, remained relatively stable, increasing by 0.9 percentage points. Among the white-collar occupations, those of a managerial and administrative nature experienced the largest relative increase (3.5 points), followed by science and engineering occupations (2.8 points) and education and health-related occupations (1.9 points). Among the grey-collar occupations there is a difference between the performance of the clerical and related occupations, whose share declined by 0.2 points, and sales and service occupations, whose share increased by 1.1 points.

In 1991, almost one-half (45.7 per cent) of all employed persons in the urban system were involved in a grey-collar occupation, as opposed to only 29.7 per cent involved in white-collar occupations. Over the period 1971–91, however, the growth rate of white-collar occupations (135.7 per cent) was almost double that of the grey-collar occupations (73.9 per cent) which, in turn, grew only slightly more rapidly than total employment (70.6 per cent). Note, too, that the growth rates for both managerial and administrative (174.4 per cent) and science and engineering (172.1 per cent) occupations are considerably higher than the overall white-collar figure. Among the grey-collar occupations, there is a gap of approximately ten points between the clerical (68.8) and sales and service (78.1) growth rates. Finally, the blue-collar occupations, due to an absolute decline of employment in the 1980s, registered a two-decade growth rate of only 24.6 per cent—almost three times less than that of total employment and almost six times less than that of white-collar employment. As in the case of sectoral employment, growth rates for all occupational categories were significantly lower in the 1980s than in the 1970s. Note, however, that the most rapidly expanding white-collar category during the 1970s, managerial and administrative occupations, declined into the third position, behind science and engineering and education and health, in the 1980s. A similar reversal may be observed within the grey-collar occupations, where sales and service occupations grew more rapidly than clerical occupations in the 1980s.

In terms of absolute growth between 1971 and 1991, the sales and service (1,070,100 jobs) and clerical (794,000) categories head the list, followed by education and health (619,200) and managerial and administrative (563,700); blue-collar occupations (465,600), due to a loss of over 180,000 jobs in the 1980s, finished the two decades only slightly ahead of science and engineering (461,600). Overall, blue-collar occupations accounted for only 11.7 per cent (that is, 465,600 of 3,974,200) of new job creation between 1971 and 1991, with grey-collar (46.9 per cent) and white-collar (41.4 per cent) occupations having a much more significant impact.

Table 6.2   **Occupational Structure, Canadian Urban System, 1971–1991**

Occupation	1971		1981		1991		1971–1981		1981–1991		1971–1991	
	(000)	%	(000)	%	(000)	%	absolute growth (000)	growth rate %	absolute growth (000)	growth rate %	absolute growth (000)	growth rate %
Managerial & administrative	323.3	5.7	695.3	8.3	887.0	9.2	372.0	115.1	191.7	27.6	563.7	174.4
Science & engineering	268.3	4.8	496.1	5.9	729.8	7.6	227.8	84.9	233.7	47.1	461.6	172.1
Education & health	620.2	11.0	942.2	11.3	1,239.4	12.9	322.1	51.9	297.2	31.5	619.2	99.8
Subtotal: white-collar	1,211.7	21.5	2,133.6	25.5	2,856.2	29.7	921.9	76.1	722.6	33.9	1,644.5	135.7
Clerical & related	1,153.5	20.5	1,774.0	21.2	1,947.5	20.3	620.4	53.8	173.6	9.8	794.0	68.8
Sales & service	1,370.1	24.3	1,926.0	23.0	2,440.2	25.4	555.9	40.6	514.2	26.7	1,070.1	78.1
Subtotal: grey-collar	2,523.6	44.8	3,700.0	44.2	4,387.7	45.7	1,176.3	46.6	687.8	18.6	1,864.1	73.9
Blue-collar	1,892.0	33.6	2,539.1	30.3	2,357.5	24.6	647.1	34.2	–181.6	–7.2	465.6	24.6
Total	5,627.3	100.0	8,372.7	100.0	9,601.5	100.0	2,745.3	48.8	1,228.8	14.7	3,974.2	70.6

Source: Calculated by author from special data tabulations of *Census of Canada*, 1971, 1981, 1991.

Although an occupational analysis provides a useful perspective on economic development, the remainder of the chapter will focus exclusively on sectoral trends.

Urban System Employment Dynamics

This section explores changes in economic development by examining several aspects of the dynamics of urban system employment change: growth rate patterns, the role of the manufacturing and business service sectors in employment growth and decline, and sectoral diversity, specialization, and concentration.

Patterns of Growth and Decline

Table 6.3 indicates the 10 urban areas that experienced the most rapid rates of total employment growth during each decade and over the entire study period; the 10 slowest-growing spatial units are also indicated. Several general observations may be made concerning this table. First, relatively few metropolitan areas emerge as either fast-growth or slow-growth units; the exceptions are Calgary (fast), and Sudbury and Windsor (slow) in the 1970s, and Ottawa-Hull and Oshawa (fast) in the 1980s. Indeed, the majority (28 out of 40) of urban areas listed have populations below 30,000 in 1991; the absolute numbers of employment growth or decline tend, therefore, to be relatively modest in spite of growth rates that are very high in certain cases. Second, during the 1970s, the growth rates of the rapid growth areas are extremely high, while those of the slow growth areas tend to be positive (with the exception of Thompson and Kirkland Lake). During the 1980s, however, the growth rates of the most rapidly growing places are significantly lower, while those of the slow-growth areas are uniformly negative. In fact, a total of 24 urban areas had negative rates in the 1980s.

Third, in the 1971–81 period, with the exception of Elliot Lake, Ontario, all of the most rapidly growing urban areas are resource-based communities located in western Canada (Alberta, British Columbia, and the Northwest Territories, having five, three, and one urban areas, respectively). On the other hand, seven of the slow-growth areas are located in Ontario, two in the Maritime provinces (Summerside and Sydney), and one in Manitoba (Thompson). Thus, a portrait of slow job growth in the East and more rapid growth in the West emerges. From a sectoral perspective, during the 1970s, the largest absolute employment increases in the rapid-growth urban areas came in 'goods-related' sectors (construction, manufacturing, primary sector) and transportation. Interestingly, however, in what appears to be a classic example of induced job growth, the retail sector is the only service activity to appear among the three sectors that experienced the largest absolute employment increases in each of the 10 rapid-growth urban areas. Where the slow-growth urban areas are concerned, the sectors involved in employment decline also mainly include manufacturing and the primary sector.

Fourth, the period 1981–91 presents eight new high-growth areas (only Yellowknife and Matsqui remain from the previous period), and nine new slow-growth areas (Kirkland Lake remains). Elliot Lake, a rapid-growth area in the 1970s, now appears as the most rapidly declining area. In the 1980s, the rapid-growth and slow-growth urban areas both tend to be located in the East, and are much less distinguished along sectoral dimensions than they were in the previous period. Among the rapid-growth centres, seven are now found in Ontario and Quebec (three are in the West), and their economic specializations are relatively diverse (manufacturing, construction, primary, public utilities). The slow-growth areas are also primarily in the East (five in Ontario, one in each of Quebec, Newfoundland, and New Brunswick); they tend to be identified mainly as primary (e.g., Elliot Lake, Kirkland Lake, Port Alberni, Labrador City, Gaspé) and manufacturing (e.g., Kitimat, Kapuskasing, Hawkesbury) centres. During this decade, among the rapid-growth areas, the greatest absolute changes in employment are spread over a number of sectors: retail (six of the 10 areas), health and social services (five areas), public administration (four), construction (four), manufacturing (three),

Table 6.3   **Total Employment: Rapid-Growth and Slow-Growth Urban Areas, Canada, 1971–1991**

Rapid-Growth Urban Areas			Slow-Growth Urban Areas		
1971–1981					
Urban Area	Growth Rate (%)	Number (000s)	Urban Area	Growth Rate (%)	Number (000s)
Fort McMurray	323	14.8	Thompson	−11	−0.9
Grand Prairie	141	7.0	Kirkland Lake	−3	−0.2
Matsqui	138	17.5	Sudbury	11	6.3
Elliot Lake	135	4.3	Pembroke	14	1.2
Lloydminster	132	4.1	Windsor	14	12.0
Fort St John	130	3.5	Summerside	16	0.8
Calgary	126	188.3	Dunnville	16	0.6
Red Deer	126	12.6	Port Hope	17	0.6
Kelowna	123	19.4	Woodstock	17	1.8
Yellowknife	113	2.8	Sydney	19	6.1

			1981–1991		
Urban Area	Growth Rate (%)	Number (000s)	Urban Area	Growth Rate (%)	Number (000s)
Yellowknife	67	3.6	Elliot Lake	−28	−2.1
Barrie	61	17.0	Kitimat	−21	−1.4
Matsqui	58	17.5	Kapuskasing	−19	−1.0
Huntsville	43	2.0	Kirkland Lake	−16	−0.8
Ste-Marie	39	1.4	Port Alberni	−10	−1.2
St-Georges	37	2.6	Labrador City	−10	−0.5
Oshawa	37	31.3	Campbellton	−7	−0.4
Bracebridge	36	1.4	Kenora	−7	−0.5
Grand Centre	33	3.0	Hawkesbury	−6	−0.3
Ottawa-Hull	33	116.6	Gaspé	−6	−0.4

(continued)

Table 6.3   **(continued)**

	Rapid-Growth Urban Areas			Slow-Growth Urban Areas	
			1971-1991		
Urban Area	Growth Rate (%)	Number (000s)	Urban Area	Growth Rate (%)	Number (000s)
Fort McMurray	414	18.9	Kirkland Lake	−18	−0.9
Matsqui	276	35.0	Thompson	−3	−0.3
Yellowknife	254	6.4	Kitimat	6	0.3
Kelowna	195	30.6	Port Alberni	8	0.8
Grand Prairie	190	9.4	Campbellton	10	0.5
Barrie	187	29.2	Kapuskasing	11	0.4
Red Deer	185	18.6	Sydney	13	4.3
Calgary	164	245.3	Pembroke	14	1.2
Lloydminster	162	5.0	Dunnville	14	0.6
Fort St John	153	4.2	Kenora	18	1.0

Source: Calculated by author from special data tabulations of *Census of Canada*, 1971, 1981, 1991.

and accommodations and food (three). For slow-growth areas, there is a similar diversity of sectors, although most are related to the production or handling of goods: manufacturing (eight of the 10 areas), primary sector (five), construction (four), transportation (four), wholesaling (three).

Manufacturing and Business Services

We saw in Table 6.1 that manufacturing and business services represent the two extremes of employment change in the Canadian urban system between 1971 and 1991; while employment in the former grew by only 10 per cent (compared to a growth rate of 72.7 per cent for all sectors taken together), employment in the latter grew by 277.8 per cent. During the decade 1981–91, manufacturing employment actually declined by 12.2 per cent.

In the previous section, manufacturing was frequently identified as among the sectors that experienced the greatest absolute employment change (both positive and negative). The business services sector, however, was conspicuous by its absence; only in the case of Ottawa–Hull, the tenth most rapidly growing urban area over the period 1981–91, do business services appear among the three sectors that experienced the largest absolute employment changes. Where, then, is business services growth occurring? In order to answer this question, this section shifts its focus from growth rates to *absolute levels of employment change*. More precisely, our approach is to examine the places that experienced the highest and the lowest absolute levels of total employment change, and to look at the specific performance of the two 'bellwether' sectors—manufacturing and business services.

Table 6.4 lists the 15 fastest-growing and 15 slowest-growing urban areas—in terms of total employment—in each of the two decades, indicating levels of absolute change and growth rates for total employment, manufacturing, and business services. It comes as no surprise that the places experiencing the greatest absolute change in total employment are the largest census metropolitan areas (CMAs).[3] A number of important points emerge from an examination of this table.

In the 1970s, although the growth rates of employment in business services are uniformly higher than those for manufacturing across the set of 15 urban areas, absolute growth in manufacturing is actually superior to that of business services in the case of 11 CMAs, indicating that at the beginning of the decade manufacturing employment generally represented a larger share of total employment in these urban areas. In addition, in the case of seven of these 11 CMAs, the absolute change in manufacturing employment exceeds that in business services by a factor of at least two, as in the case of Toronto (85,200 vs 42,200) and Montreal (44,200 vs 19,500). Further, the level of absolute change in both manufacturing and business services is generally proportional to the level of change in total employment, with Toronto heading the list in both sectors. Absolute change in manufacturing employment as a percentage of absolute change in total employment ranges between 26.2 per cent in Kitchener and 2.8 per cent in Victoria. Hamilton (19.2 per cent), Toronto (17.1), London (16.7), and St Catharines (15.3) also have high percentages. For business services, the range is much narrower: 9.2 per cent of total employment growth in Calgary and 3.9 per cent in Quebec City. Calgary (93.8 per cent) and Edmonton (70.3) clearly lead in manufacturing growth rates, while Edmonton (302.8) and Ottawa-Hull (266.7) stand out in business services.

In the 1980s, business-service growth rates were significantly higher than those in manufacturing across all of the 15 CMAs. Indeed, in the case of 11 of the 15 CMAs the growth rate for manufacturing employment was actually negative. Further, unlike in the previous decade, absolute employment

change in business services exceeded that in manufacturing in all 15 CMAs. In nine of the CMAs the decline (or the slow growth) of manufacturing employment was more than compensated for by the performance of business services. In Toronto, the difference between manufacturing job loss and business-service job creation is approximately 110,000 jobs; in Montreal, the difference is approximately 75,000 jobs. Once again, the level of absolute change in business services is generally proportional to the level of change in total employment. Absolute change in manufacturing employment as a percentage of absolute change in total employment now ranges between a high of 3.2 per cent in Quebec and a low of −62.3 per cent in Hamilton. On the other hand, in the case of business services, the percentages are substantially higher, ranging from a low of 6.1 in Saskatoon to a high of 20.4 in Montreal. Toronto (19.3), Hamilton (16.5), and Ottawa-Hull (15.0) also have very high percentages. In terms of growth rates, Ottawa-Hull (12.7) and Halifax (8.5)—two CMAs that are not at all known for their manufacturing activity—head up the modest performance of CMAs in manufacturing; on the other hand, Oshawa (174.7) and Kitchener (122.7)—two industrial CMAs—and Ottawa-Hull (115.5) are at the head of the list in business services.

In sum, where the 15 CMAs experiencing the highest levels of total employment growth are concerned, the decade of the 1970s is substantially different from that of the 1980s. In the 1970s, changes in total employment within each CMA depend much more on manufacturing job creation than on that in business services. In the 1980s, the reverse is true; in order to achieve high absolute levels of total employment growth a dynamic business service sector (which is often called upon to compensate for manufacturing job losses) is a *sine qua non*.

Turning to those urban areas that experienced the lowest levels of absolute employment change, the most striking aspect of Table 6.4 is that, in 1971–81 and 1981–91 alike, business service employment remained virtually stable, increasing or decreasing by less than one hundred workers in most instances. In

Table 6.4   **Manufacturing and Business Service Change in Urban Areas Experiencing Highest and Lowest Absolute Total Employment Growth, Canada, 1971–1991**

Urban Area	Total Employment		Manufacturing			Business Services		
	Change (000s)	Gr. Rate (%)	Change (000s)	Gr. Rate (%)	Ch. as % of tot. emp. ch.	Change (000s)	Gr. Rate (%)	Ch. as % of tot. emp. ch.
High Absolute Total Employment Growth 1971–1981								
Toronto	499.3	44.8	85.2	28.4	17.1	42.2	121.2	8.5
Montreal	336.3	36.7	44.2	17.4	13.1	19.5	77.1	5.8
Vancouver	210.4	51.9	17.1	23.7	8.1	16.9	124.9	8.0
Calgary	188.3	125.8	15.9	93.8	8.5	17.4	302.8	9.2
Edmonton	177.2	88.9	17.2	70.3	9.7	11.4	266.7	6.5
Ottawa–Hull	116.1	48.1	4.9	24.0	4.2	9.8	185.1	8.5
Quebec	83.4	52.5	4.0	18.8	4.8	3.2	101.1	3.9
Winnipeg	67.2	30.7	5.9	13.9	8.8	3.4	83.5	5.0
Hamilton	64.3	34.2	12.3	17.7	19.2	3.1	101.2	4.7
Kitchener	41.5	42.0	10.9	26.7	26.2	1.9	167.2	4.7
London	41.0	35.5	6.9	25.3	16.7	1.9	86.1	4.5
Victoria	37.4	52.4	1.1	16.0	2.8	2.1	169.5	5.6
Halifax	36.6	39.5	1.5	17.3	4.0	2.0	113.1	5.4
St. Catharines	33.4	29.0	5.1	12.6	15.3	1.7	85.8	5.0
Saskatoon	33.2	66.9	2.4	46.5	7.3	1.9	199.5	5.6
High Absolute Total Employment Growth 1981–1991								
Toronto	333.8	20.7	−46.7	−12.1	−14.0	64.5	23.8	19.3
Vancouver	170.4	27.0	−1.5	−1.6	−0.9	19.4	63.7	11.4
Montreal	157.9	12.6	−42.7	−14.3	−27.1	32.2	71.8	20.4
Ottawa–Hull	116.6	32.6	3.2	12.7	2.8	17.4	115.5	15.0
Quebec	61.3	25.3	2.0	7.7	3.2	6.3	97.7	10.3
Calgary	56.9	16.8	−0.2	−0.5	−0.3	6.6	28.7	11.6
Edmonton	45.1	12.0	−4.5	−10.8	−9.9	2.9	18.7	6.5
Kitchener	36.4	25.9	−5.7	−11.1	−15.8	3.8	122.7	10.5
Oshawa	31.3	36.7	−1.2	−3.9	−3.8	2.9	174.7	9.4
Hamilton	31.0	12.3	−19.3	−23.6	−62.3	5.1	84.4	16.5
London	30.8	19.6	−4.4	−13.0	−14.4	3.0	74.5	9.7
Halifax	29.5	22.8	0.9	8.5	2.9	2.7	71.0	9.0
Winnipeg	27.7	9.7	−7.0	−14.4	−25.1	2.8	37.4	9.9
Victoria	26.0	23.9	−0.8	−10.8	−3.2	3.3	97.6	12.6
Saskatoon	17.7	21.4	0.4	4.9	2.1	1.1	38.4	6.1

Table 6.4   **(continued)**

Urban Area	Total Employment		Manufacturing			Business Services		
	Change (000s)	Gr. Rate (%)	Change (000s)	Gr. Rate (%)	Ch. as % of tot. emp. ch.	Change (000s)	Gr. Rate (%)	Ch. as % of tot. emp. ch.
Low Absolute Total Employment Growth 1971–1981								
Thompson	−0.9	−11.4	−0.1	−16.8	14.5	0.0	42.9	1.7
Kirkland Lake	−0.2	−3.0	0.1	17.1	−43.3	0.0	9.1	3.3
Port Hope	0.6	16.9	0.3	24.9	54.1	0.0	0.0	0.0
Dunnville	0.6	15.5	0.0	0.7	1.6	0.0	11.1	0.8
Lachute	0.7	20.1	−0.0	−1.7	−2.9	−0.0	−8.3	−0.7
Montmagny	0.8	22.0	0.1	10.6	14.3	0.0	72.7	5.0
Summerside	0.8	16.1	0.0	7.3	4.9	0.0	22.2	1.2
Cobourg	0.9	20.0	0.4	24.3	44.0	0.0	61.5	4.3
Campbellton	1.0	19.1	0.1	14.2	8.4	0.0	55.6	2.6
La Tuque	1.0	23.4	0.2	13.8	22.9	0.0	200.0	3.1
Haileybury	1.0	19.4	0.1	19.5	11.5	0.1	72.2	6.8
Selkirk	1.0	30.0	0.0	3.8	3.1	0.0	66.7	2.1
Estevan	1.0	28.8	0.1	52.5	10.7	0.0	75.0	4.6
Wallaceburg	1.1	27.8	0.5	25.8	47.9	−0.0	−12.5	−0.5
Dawson Creek	1.1	29.7	−0.1	−38.8	−8.5	0.1	120.0	8.0
Low Absolute Total Employment Growth 1981–1991								
Sault Ste Marie	−2.2	−5.7	−5.6	−43.6	257.1	0.2	28.4	10.0
Elliot Lake	−2.1	−28.4	0.1	135.7	−4.4	−0.0	−47.1	1.9
Sydney	−1.8	−4.6	−2.5	−44.5	142.1	0.1	32.2	7.9
Kitimat	−1.4	−21.5	−0.9	−25.8	64.0	0.1	266.7	5.8
Port Alberni	−1.2	−10.2	−1.6	−37.8	132.2	0.1	50.0	4.1
Kapuskasing	−1.0	−18.5	−0.7	−37.6	72.3	−0.0	−40.0	1.0
Shawinigan	−0.9	−4.2	−2.1	−29.5	227.3	0.1	60.4	15.8
Kirkland Lake	−0.8	−15.8	−0.3	−68.5	40.4	0.1	216.7	17.2
Thetford Mines	−0.7	−5.6	−0.2	−10.8	23.2	−0.1	−23.4	7.7
Labrador City	−0.5	−9.6	−0.0	−33.3	4.7	−0.0	−71.4	4.7
Kenora	−0.5	−6.8	−0.4	−32.3	74.7	0.0	28.1	9.1
Powell River	−0.5	−6.0	−0.9	−35.1	201.1	0.1	110.0	11.7
Campbellton	−0.4	−7.4	−0.2	−31.0	45.5	−0.0	−42.9	6.8
Gaspé	−0.4	−6.2	−0.6	−55.2	164.0	0.0	12.5	1.3
Hawkesbury	−0.3	−6.4	−0.7	−32.1	238.3	0.0	11.8	3.3

Source: Calculated by author from special data tabulations of *Census of Canada* 1971, 1981, 1991.

general, however, business service employment tended to increase, if only in very modest amounts. On the other hand, manufacturing employment was slightly more volatile, especially in the 1980s. While any changes registered in manufacturing employment tended to be positive in the 1970s, they tended to be negative in the 1980s (with the sole exception of Elliot Lake, which added about 100 jobs). Sault Ste Marie (−5,600), Sydney (−2,500), Shawinigan (−2,100), and Port Alberni (−1,600) were the only urban areas to experience any appreciable change in manufacturing employment in the period 1981–91. Thus, as a general rule, 'stagnation' appears to be the appropriate description for the set of low absolute growth urban areas, at least where manufacturing and business service employment are concerned. Our 'bellwether' sectors therefore appear to be more useful indicators in the case of those urban areas that experienced the highest positive levels of employment change.

Sectoral Diversity, Specialization, and Concentration

In this section, we turn our attention from issues of growth to those more specifically concerning the location of economic activity, both across the urban system and in individual urban areas. In this analysis, we employ two common measures: the index of specialization and the location quotient.

The *index of specialization* is a measure of the extent to which the economic structure of a given urban area (or, more generally, any spatial unit) is relatively specialized in a few types of activities or, rather, relatively diversified across a wider range of activities. Table 6.5 presents the urban areas that were the most specialized and the most diversified (that is, the least specialized) sectorally in 1991. Calgary, with a value of 21.0, was characterized by the most diversified economic structure. Note that out of the 15 most diversified urban areas listed, 13 are located in the four western provinces; the only eastern urban areas to appear in the list are Rouyn–Noranda and Sept-Iles, both located in Quebec. At the other extreme, Labrador City, with a value of

71.1 in 1991, is the most specialized urban area. Twelve of the 15 most specialized urban areas are located in the East; Kitimat, Grand Centre, and Ft McMurray are the exceptions. Note, further, that the index value for all 30 urban areas shown decreased over the period 1971–91, indicating that among the most specialized and the most diversified urban areas alike, there was a general tendency towards increasing diversification. In fact, only 12 of the 152 urban areas became more specialized over the period; most of these changes were relatively small in magnitude (e.g., St John's, 0.3 points; Rimouski, 0.7). Finally, as a benchmark, the average index values for all 152 urban areas are presented. The average fell from 49.0 to 41.4 over the period 1971–91.

A second useful and frequently employed indicator of specialization is the *location quotient* (LQ). In contrast to the index of specialization, which provides a general measure of the extent to which a given urban area is characterized by a relatively specialized or relatively diversified economic structure, the location quotient compares the spatial concentration of employment *in a given sector* in a given spatial unit (here, each of the individual elements of the Canadian urban system) to that sector's level of concentration in a 'benchmark' spatial unit—in this case the entire Canadian economy. Thus, a sector having the same level of concentration in a given urban unit as in the national economy will have a value of 100. Values below 100 indicate a lower degree of specialization than in the national system, while those above 100 indicate a higher degree of specialization.

The use of the location quotient enables us to determine, for example, that Labrador City is hyper-specialized in the primary sector (where a location quotient of 850 indicates that this urban unit is seven and one-half times more specialized than the national system in primary sector activities), but is significantly under-specialized in virtually all other sectors. Toronto is characterized by very high levels of specialization in high-order service activities: FIRE (161), business services (168), and other producer services (174); its manufacturing

Table 6.5   **Sectoral Specialization Index: Most Specialized and Least Specialized Urban Areas, 1991**

	1971	1981	1991	Change		
				1971–81	1981–91	1971–91
Least Specialized, 1991						
Calgary	27.4	26.1	21.0	−1.3	−5.1	−6.4
Edmonton	35.1	29.3	26.4	−5.9	−2.9	−8.7
Vancouver	36.3	31.1	27.1	−5.1	−4.0	−9.1
Regina	38.0	32.7	28.4	−5.3	−4.3	−9.6
Saskatoon	35.3	27.9	28.6	−7.4	0.7	−6.7
Grand Prairie	35.0	29.3	29.1	−5.7	−0.1	−5.9
Rouyn–Noranda	42.3	34.9	31.0	−7.4	−3.9	−11.3
Nanaimo	38.7	36.3	31.1	−2.4	−5.1	−7.6
Sept-Iles	47.0	41.7	31.4	−5.3	−10.3	−15.6
Kelowna	36.9	35.0	32.3	−1.9	−2.7	−4.6
Kamloops	39.9	31.9	32.6	−8.0	0.7	−7.3
Matsqui	41.7	37.1	32.6	−4.6	−4.6	−9.1
Swift Current	35.3	33.7	33.0	−1.6	−0.7	−2.3
Terrace	45.0	39.9	33.1	−5.1	−6.7	−11.9
Fort St John	41.4	35.9	33.1	−5.6	−2.7	−8.3
Most Specialized, 1991						
Ste-Marie, Que.	62.7	54.3	51.6	−8.4	−2.7	−11.1
La Tuque	59.4	58.3	52.3	−1.1	−6.0	−7.1
Stratford	59.1	56.4	53.0	−2.7	−3.4	−6.1
Corner Brook	62.0	55.6	53.3	−6.4	−2.3	−8.7
Cowansville	66.1	60.6	53.4	−5.6	−7.1	−12.7
Ft McMurray	58.1	51.6	54.0	−6.6	2.4	−4.1
Magog	65.0	61.4	54.1	−3.6	−7.3	−10.9
Kapuskasing	62.6	58.1	54.9	−4.4	−3.3	−7.7
Grand Centre	68.9	55.9	56.6	−13.0	0.7	−12.3
Roberval, Que.	57.4	53.9	56.7	−3.6	2.9	−0.7
Hawkesbury	61.9	68.1	58.4	6.3	−9.7	−3.4
Elliot Lake	69.6	69.9	60.1	0.3	−9.7	−9.4
Wallaceburg	68.1	67.3	60.9	−0.9	−6.4	−7.3
Kitimat	72.6	67.1	64.3	−5.4	−2.9	−8.3
Labrador City	77.4	74.1	71.1	−3.3	−3.0	−6.3
Average over 152 urban areas	49.0	45.2	41.4	−3.8	−3.8	−7.6

Note: Values can range between 0 (least specialized) and 100 (most specialized).

Source: Calculated by author from special data tabulations of *Census of Canada*, 1971, 1981, 1991.

sector (120) is also characterized by a high level of specialization relative to the national average. An analysis of system-wide location quotients enables one to identify certain general trends: the manufacturing specialization of many urban units in Quebec and Ontario, and the low degree of specialization in this sector by urban units in the Atlantic and prairie provinces; the primary-sector specialization of the prairie provinces and British Columbia; the very small number of urban areas with a high level of specialization in high-order service activities (FIRE, business services, other producer services); the specialization of urban areas in Quebec, Manitoba, and Saskatchewan in health and social services; and a relatively small number of places with very high levels of specialization in public administration.

Similarly, changes in location quotients over the period 1971–91 for each sector in each urban unit may be examined. Once again, certain broad trends are visible: some major decreases in primary-sector specialization in Quebec, Ontario, Manitoba, British Columbia, and the Territories, but significant increases in Saskatchewan and Alberta; and the relative stability of specialization in the retail, consumer services, and FIRE sectors.

Table 6.6 identifies the urban areas that are the most specialized and the least specialized in the two 'bellwether' sectors—business services and manufacturing. Seven urban areas have business service sectors that are more than 20 per cent more specialized than the national system; only two of these, Pembroke (adjoining the Canadian Forces base at Petawawa) and Fredericton (the capital of New Brunswick), are not among the set of Canada's largest metropolitan areas. Ottawa–Hull (an increase of 47 points) significantly reinforced its level of specialization over 1971–91, as did Toronto (an increase of 10 points) and Fredericton (+12 points), although to a much lesser degree. The four other urban areas have seen their business services location quotients decline; the decline of Pembroke's location quotient (−252 points) is particularly impressive, and corresponds to a decrease in demand caused by a reduction of activity at Petawawa. On the other hand,

seven smaller, resource-based urban areas display business-service location quotients that are less than or equal to 25 (that is, their level of specialization is more than four times less than the national average); with the exception of Thompson, whose LQ remained stable, all suffered declines.

In the case of manufacturing, eight urban areas are characterized by levels of specialization that exceed the national average by more than 100 per cent. Seven of the eight urban areas (that is, with the exception of Kitimat) are located in the Quebec–Ontario 'industrial heartland'; with the exception of Magog, whose LQ suffered a modest decline, all of these manufacturing centres became more specialized over the period. Finally, a set of eight resource-based and public administration centres display manufacturing LQs below 25.

Table 6.7 presents evidence concerning the high degree of *spatial concentration* of high-order services. In 1991, the 10 largest Canadian CMAs contained 49 per cent of the national population, up from 45 per cent in 1971. Thus, the population of Canada is becoming more concentrated in the ten largest CMAs. All CMAs have not experienced the same level of performance, however. Montreal's share of the national population has declined from 12.7 per cent in 1971 to 11.5 per cent in 1991, while the shares of Winnipeg, Quebec, Hamilton, and London have been relatively stable. On the other hand, Toronto, Vancouver, Ottawa–Hull, Edmonton, and Calgary have seen their relative shares improve considerably.

While employment across all economic sectors is more highly concentrated than the population, the difference is not enormous; the cumulative percentage of total employment is generally several points in advance of the cumulative percentage of total population for the entire set of 10 CMAs. In fact, the gap between population and total employment declined considerably between 1971 and 1991: from a difference of 6 points (51.3 to 45.3) to one of 3.2 points. Using 50 per cent as a benchmark figure, we see that total employment is becoming slightly more concentrated over time; while 49.7 per cent of all employment was con-

Table 6.6   **Most Specialized and Least Specialized Urban Areas: Business Services and Manufacturing, Canadian Urban System, 1991**

Urban Area	Location Quotient 1991	Change 1971–1991	Urban Area	Location Quotient 1991	Change 1971–1991
Business services					
Most specialized: LQ ≥ 120			*Least specialized: LQ ≤ 25*		
Calgary	174	−20	Labrador City	5	−52
Pembroke	172	−252	Kapuskasing	8	−12
Toronto	168	10	Campbellton	17	−29
Ottawa–Hull	158	47	Gaspé	18	−28
Vancouver	146	−23	Elliot Lake	19	−5
Montreal	126	−14	Thompson	24	0
Fredericton	125	12	Sorel	25	−13
Manufacturing					
Most specialized: LQ ≥ 120			*Least specialized: LQ ≤ 25*		
Kitimat	348	86	Corner Brook	7	−3
Wallaceburg	309	73	Labrador City	7	0
Hawkesbury	239	45	Yellowknife	13	3
Granby	227	28	Ft McMurray	14	−2
Cowansville	224	6	Whitehorse	16	7
Ste-Marie	224	22	Grand Centre	19	12
Stratford	209	23	Elliot Lake	21	15
Magog	206	−6	Kirkland Lake	24	−11

Source: Calculated by author from special data tabulations of *Census of Canada,* 1971, 1991.

centrated in the nine largest CMAs in 1971, this figure rose to 50.8 per cent in 1991. Once again, there are variations in the performance of individual CMAs during the period, with Montreal, Winnipeg, Hamilton, and London losing ground while the six other CMAs increased their shares.

Service employment, in general, is even more highly concentrated than total employment. While 50 per cent of all Canadian service employment is contained in the eight largest CMAs in both 1971 and 1991, nine CMAs are required to achieve this benchmark figure in the case of total employment. Service employment has been relatively stable over time, becoming slightly more concentrated; the 10 largest CMAs contained 54.4 per cent of all service employment in 1971 and 55.6 per cent in 1991.

Table 6.7   Metropolitan Concentration of Population and Employment, Canada, 1971–1991

	Population		All Sectors		All Services		FIRE Services		Business Services		Other Producer Services		Retail Services	
	% Canada	cumul. %	% Canada	cumul. %	% Canada	cumul. %	% Canada	cumul. %	% Canada	cumul. %	% Canada	cumul. %	% Canada	cumul. %
1971														
Toronto	12.2	12.2	15.4	15.4	15.5	15.5	24.0	24.0	24.4	24.4	28.0	28.0	15.5	15.5
Montreal	12.7	24.9	12.7	28.1	13.0	28.4	17.1	41.2	17.7	42.1	17.9	45.9	11.9	27.4
Vancouver	5.0	29.9	5.6	33.7	6.2	34.7	7.8	49.0	9.5	51.5	7.8	53.7	6.1	33.5
Ottawa–Hull	2.8	32.7	3.3	37.0	4.3	39.0	3.3	52.3	3.7	55.3	5.0	58.7	2.9	36.4
Edmonton	2.3	35.0	2.8	39.8	3.2	42.1	2.8	55.0	3.0	58.3	2.9	61.6	3.0	39.4
Calgary	1.9	36.9	2.1	41.8	2.3	44.4	2.7	57.7	4.0	62.3	3.2	64.8	2.1	41.5
Winnipeg	2.5	39.4	3.0	44.9	3.4	47.9	3.6	61.4	2.8	65.1	3.2	68.0	3.4	44.9
Quebec	2.2	41.6	2.2	47.1	2.6	50.5	2.2	63.6	2.2	67.3	2.3	70.4	2.2	47.1
Hamilton	2.3	43.9	2.6	49.7	2.2	52.7	2.3	65.9	2.1	69.4	2.4	72.7	2.6	49.7
London	1.3	45.3	1.6	51.3	1.7	54.4	2.3	68.2	1.5	70.9	1.6	74.3	1.6	51.3
1991														
Toronto	14.3	14.3	15.6	15.6	16.2	16.2	25.2	25.2	26.2	26.2	27.3	27.3	14.9	14.9
Montreal	11.5	25.7	11.3	27.0	11.7	27.9	13.2	38.4	14.2	40.4	14.4	41.7	11.2	26.2
Vancouver	5.9	31.6	6.3	33.3	6.9	34.8	8.3	46.7	9.2	49.7	8.4	50.2	6.3	32.4
Ottawa–Hull	3.4	34.9	3.8	37.1	4.5	39.3	3.2	50.0	6.0	55.7	5.1	55.2	3.3	35.7
Edmonton	3.1	38.0	3.4	40.4	3.7	43.0	3.1	53.1	3.5	59.1	3.6	58.8	3.4	39.2
Calgary	2.8	40.8	3.2	43.6	3.3	46.3	3.7	56.7	5.5	64.6	4.4	63.2	3.0	42.1
Winnipeg	2.4	43.2	2.5	46.1	2.8	49.0	2.9	59.6	1.9	66.5	2.8	66.1	2.5	44.6
Quebec	2.4	45.5	2.4	48.6	2.8	51.8	3.0	62.6	2.4	68.9	2.0	68.1	2.5	47.1
Hamilton	2.2	47.7	2.3	50.8	2.2	54.0	2.4	65.0	2.1	70.9	2.4	70.5	2.4	49.5
London	1.4	49.1	1.5	52.3	1.6	55.6	1.9	66.9	1.3	72.2	1.6	72.1	1.6	51.1

Source: Calculated by author from special data tabulations of *Census of Canada*, 1971, 1991.

Employment in the three high-order service sectors—finance, insurance, and real estate (FIRE) services; business services; and other producer services—is significantly more concentrated than total service employment. Approximately one-half of total Canadian employment in the FIRE sector is contained within the four largest CMAs; the 10 largest CMAs consistently account for over two-thirds of all FIRE employment in Canada, although there appears to be a deconcentration over time: the 10 largest CMAs contained 68.2 per cent of all FIRE employment in 1971, but only 66.9 per cent in 1991. Employment in business services and other producer services is even more highly concentrated, with the three largest CMAs accounting for 50 per cent of employment, and the 10 largest accounting for over 70 per cent of all Canadian employment in these sectors. Note, however, that while business service employment has become slightly more concentrated within the ten largest CMAs over the period (72.2 per cent in 1991 vs 70.9 per cent in 1971), employment in other producer services has moved in the opposite direction (72.1 per cent in 1991 vs 74.3 per cent in 1971).

Finally, as a counterpoint to the high-order services, Table 6.7 also indicates the relative level of concentration of retail services. As may be seen, employment in this sector is less concentrated than for all services, more closely approximating the distribution of total employment across all sectors.

Factors of Growth and Change

What are the factors underlying the patterns of economic growth and decline that have been explored in the previous sections? A detailed exploration of why certain urban areas have undergone growth or decline at certain periods is well beyond the scope of the present chapter. In general, however, conceptual frameworks for explaining urban economic performance tend to be divided into demand-oriented and supply-oriented approaches. Demand-oriented approaches focus on a city's links with other places. The best known of these approaches is the economic-base model (Tiebout, 1962), which posits

that the principal impetus for economic growth in a city is the export of goods and services beyond the boundaries of the local economy; when exports occur, the local economy receives payments from the exterior (injections of money, in economic jargon) which, through the multiplier mechanism and the circular flow of income, stimulate all local economic activities. On the other hand, supply-oriented approaches emphasize the social and economic characteristics of an urban area, and the manner in which these contribute to economic growth. Traditionally, supply-oriented approaches have focused on the nature and use of an urban area's factors of production—labour (human resources), capital, technology, and physical resources. More recently, however, an increasing emphasis has been placed on the social and organizational context: innovative milieux, networks of firms, entrepreneurial spirit, and local development initiatives (Dicken, 1998; Coffey and Polèse, 1985; Porter, 1990).

The literature on urban economic development poses a number of hypotheses concerning variations in the relative level of employment growth among cities. Guided by these hypotheses, the remainder of this section undertakes an empirical analysis of the factors and correlates of employment change in the Canadian urban system over the period 1971–91.

Growth Hypotheses

In this section, we identify a set of widely used hypotheses concerning economic growth, describing their underlying logic, and identifying the variables used to test them empirically. These hypotheses reflect both supply-oriented and geographic frameworks for explaining urban economic performance.

Region

The 'regional factor' often exerts an important influence upon job creation (Landis, 1987). Certain regions may be characterized by a higher proportion of rapid-growth activities, while others may be principally involved in slowly growing 'traditional' activities. In the Canadian context, it has long been accepted as an integral part of the national identity that, from a regional economic development perspective, the Atlantic provinces generally perform well below the national average, while the performance of Ontario (certain temporary downturns notwithstanding) is generally well above average; Quebec and the western provinces, except in the context of the latter's oil booms, have tended to situate themselves between the two extremes. Does a similar (or alternative) logic hold in the case of the performance of the individual elements of the urban system? To answer this question, our analysis considers the variation of urban employment growth rates across Canada's five traditional major administrative regions: Atlantic provinces, Quebec, Ontario, prairie provinces, and British Columbia.

Population Size

Another recurrent theme in the urban economics literature is that the population size of an urban area can exert an important influence on economic performance. The basic argument is that a large population size confers certain advantages upon an urban area—advantages that manifest themselves on both the supply side and the demand side of economic activity and that are usually referred to in terms of economies of scale and agglomeration economies. (The full argument goes on to state that the advantages of size can become disadvantages once a certain size threshold is passed, that is, that diseconomies of scale and of agglomeration can eventually emerge. In the Canadian context, however, where even the largest census metropolitan areas are quite modest in size, we would not expect diseconomies to be an issue.) Here, we examine the influence of urban size on employment growth rates using six size categories: million+; 300,000–million; 100,000–300,000; 50,000–100,000; 25,000–50,000; 10,000–25,000. We have chosen to employ these six categories, rather than considering urban size as a continuous variable, since our previous research (Coffey and Shearmur, 1996) has indicated that the relationship between size and employment growth is not a linear one.

Metropolitan Proximity

In previous studies (Coffey, Fullum, and Polèse, 1989; Coffey and McRae, 1989; Coffey and Polèse, 1988), we have found that urban size alone is not sufficient to understand patterns of economic performance. According to the reasoning advanced in these studies, major metropolitan areas (defined here as those having populations of 300,000 or more inhabitants) may be viewed as economic centres surrounded by functionally dependent urban fields. Within the urban field of a given large CMA there may exist an 'urban shadow effect' that can inhibit individual smaller urban areas from developing certain types of activities (e.g., specific high-order functions may be acquired directly at the nearby CMA) or, conversely, that can stimulate the level of economic activity found in these smaller places (e.g., the nearby presence of a major market may increase the quantity and the range of the goods and services that would normally be produced). Using the criterion of a 100-kilometre radius around each major CMA (the distance corresponding to an automobile trip of approximately one hour's duration—a critical threshold according to the market research literature—and approximating the extent of the urban field), urban areas with less than 300,000 inhabitants are classified as 'central' or 'peripheral' according to whether or not they are located within 100 kilometres of a large (300,000–million or million+) CMA. Thus, our analysis is based on three classes of urban areas: major metropolitan areas (that is, CMAs having a population above 300,000 in 1991), central units, and peripheral units, as defined above.

Firm Size Structure

The hypothesis that an economy composed of a large number of small firms will grow more rapidly than one composed of a small number of large firms was originally proposed by Jane Jacobs (1969, 1984). Jacobs's argument that the existence of many firms within a given sector will foster competition and thus create an environment that is more conducive to growth, although never tested empirically by the author herself, has been subsequently reinforced by the work of Porter (1990) and Glaeser et al. (1991). In addition, the path-breaking (if now somewhat tainted) work by David Birch (1987) on the role of job creation by small firms, has placed considerable emphasis upon the relative size distribution of firms within an urban economy as a factor of employment growth.[4] As an indicator of firm size structure, we employ a 'competition index' (Glaeser et al. 1991): the number of firms in a given sector divided by the number of workers in that sector; this indicator measures the extent to which inter-firm competition reigns within an individual sector, within an individual city. Higher index values indicate that, in a given urban area and a given sector, employment is distributed across a larger number of firms. (Due to the unavailability of firm size data for the 1971–81 period, the competition index is not used as a variable in the analyses of this period.)

Diversity of Economic Structure

Once again, it was Jane Jacobs (1969, 1984) who originally suggested that the most dynamic urban economies are those that are diversified, rather than specialized, in structure. Jacobs's argument is that the prime engine of economic growth is the externalities associated with knowledge transfers. Since the most significant knowledge transfers have historically been those of an intersectoral (rather than intrasectoral) nature, she reasoned, more diversified urban economies will have a higher likelihood of developing growth-inducing spillovers. Jacobs's hypothesis has received empirical support from the work of Glaeser et al. (1991) in the context of the US metropolitan system. We examine the influence of urban structural diversity on patterns of employment growth and change using the index of specialization (see the discussion of Table 6.5 above).

Socio-economic Attributes

A final approach to identifying the correlates of growth and change involves an analysis of the socio-economic attributes that characterize the individual elements of the urban system. Stated in other terms, this approach reflects the characteristics of local labour markets. The underlying logic here is that job

creation will be highest in those areas where the most suitable labour force for rapid-growth activities (generally, high-order services and high value-added manufacturing) is to be found. From over 500 specific socio-economic characteristics available in urban area census data, we chose to focus our attention on a set of 46 variables that logically might be expected to have some sort of relationship to an urban area's level of economic performance (that is, as cause or effect of the latter, or simply as co-variate). Variables concerning religion, mother tongue, and marital status, for example, are considered irrelevant in the present context. A preliminary analysis of the data indicated that certain groups of variables tend to assume values that are interrelated in a predictable manner across the urban system (e.g., total population, total male population, male population 15 years and over, male population 25 to 54 years, total female population). In these cases, the behaviour of the entire group of variables can be effectively represented by the use of one single variable (e.g., total population in the preceding example). Therefore, we reduced the total number of variables to 27 by performing a regression analysis. Among this latter set, the variable most strongly and significantly related to the growth rate of total employment is the percentage of the population with a university degree.

Multivariate Analysis

Are the attributes identified above significantly related to the employment growth rates observed in the Canadian urban system over the periods 1971–81 and 1981–91? To answer this question we have performed a multivariate analysis of the variables identified above using a general linear models approach. Due to space constraints, we are unable to present results pertaining to each of the groups of activities identified in Table 6.1. Rather, our results will be limited to eight groups: total employment and subtotals for goods-producing and service-producing sectors, as well as five individual key economic sectors: manufacturing, wholesale trade, the FIRE sector (finance, insurance, and real estate), business services, and other producer services.

Table 6.8 enables us to determine which of the variables associated with the above hypotheses are most strongly related to the employment growth of individual urban areas. For the period 1971–81, when the five attributes (recall that available data do not permit the calculation of a competition index for this period) are considered individually ('individual variables' columns), region emerges as the most consistently significant variable, for all eight groups. This variable yields the highest individual R^2 value in six of the eight cases; significance levels are above 90 per cent in all eight cases, and above 99 per cent in six of the eight. The specialization index also proves to be significant for five groups, and provides an R^2 value that is higher than that of region in two cases: manufacturing and business services. Again, significance levels are very high. Among the other variables, the percentage of university degree-holders proves significant for two groups, and size for one group; the R^2 values of these latter two variables are very small, however. Metropolitan proximity is not significant for any group. Where the full model is considered ('full model' columns), region and the specialization index are again the most consistently significant variables, being so in the case of seven and five groups, respectively; region drops below the 90 per cent significance level in the case of business services. Size and university degree are each significant in two cases, and metropolitan proximity in none. All models are significant, with seven of the eight exceeding the 99 per cent level.

For 1981–91, the results are less clear-cut. In particular, the influence of region is manifestly less important than it was in the preceding period. When the variables are considered individually, region is significant in six of the eight cases, but its R^2 value is generally lower, except in the case of business services, where it is now twice as high (0.30). The specialization index is significant in six cases, while size, proximity, and university degree are significant in five cases each, and the competition index in four cases. Note, however, that region displays the highest R^2 value for three of the eight groups; each of the five remaining variables presents

the highest value for an individual group. Thus, it is clear that a wider range of factors comes into play in the later decade. This observation is reinforced when the full models are considered; even taking into consideration the fact that six variables are being employed rather than five, the number of significant variables appearing in the models has increased substantially in the case of seven of the eight groups; in one case it has remained the same. For the period 1981–91, the R^2 values of the full models remain the same as in the preceding period for three groups, decrease in the case of two groups, and increase for three groups. The largest change in the R^2 value occurs in the case of business services, where it increases from 0.29 to 0.54.

The signs of the three continuous variables are also instructive. The sign of the university degree variable is consistently positive (except for manufacturing in 1971–81), indicating that higher employment growth is associated with a higher proportion of university degree-holders. Similarly, the sign of the specialization index is generally negative (except for wholesale trade and business services in 1981–91), indicating that highest growth rates are found in urban areas that are less specialized (that is, more diversified) at the beginning of a period. Finally, the sign of the competition index variable is consistently negative (with an exception: the goods-producing group), indicating that high growth rates tend to be found where employment is more concentrated among a smaller number of firms. While the first two relationships accord well with conventional wisdom, the latter result is contrary to the hypothesis advanced by Jane Jacobs (1969, 1984), and to the empirical verification of this hypothesis by Glaeser et al. (1991). Further, this finding represents another refutation of the 'small firms as engines of job growth' school of thought initiated by Birch (1987).

Discussion

The region in which an individual urban area is located appears to exert a statistically significant influence on the latter's employment growth rates. The nature of this influence is not constant from one

Table 6.8   **Factors and Correlates of Employment Growth Rates, Canadian Urban System, 1971–1991***

| | 1971–1981 | | | | 1981–1991 | | | |
| | Individual Variables | | Full Model | | Individual Variables | | Full Model | |
	R^2	Signif.	R^2	Signif.	R^2	Signif.	R^2	Signif.
A. Total employment								
Region	0.30	0.99		0.99	0.01			0.95
Size	0.01				0.09	0.99		
Proximity	0.01				0.06	0.95		0.99
Competition	n.a	n.a.	n.a.	n.a.	(−) 0.01		(−)	
Specialization	(−) 0.11	0.99	(−)	0.95	(−) 0.10	0.99	(−)	0.99
University	(+) 0.02		(+)		(+) 0.13	0.99	(+)	0.99
Full Model			0.33	0.99			0.36	0.99
B. Subtotal: goods producing								
Region	0.33	0.99		0.99	0.05			0.99
Size	0.01				0.01			
Proximity	0.02				0.01			
Competition	n.a	n.a.	n.a.	n.a.	(+) 0.00		(+)	
Specialization	(−) 0.13	0.99	(−)	0.95	(−) 0.10	0.99	(−)	0.95
University	(+) 0.02	0.90	(+)		(+) 0.07	0.99	(+)	0.99
Full Model			0.37	0.99			0.26	0.99
C. Subtotal: services								
Region	0.29	0.99		0.99	0.10	0.99		0.95
Size	0.02				0.10	0.99		0.95
Proximity	0.01				0.16	0.99		0.99
Competition	n.a	n.a.	n.a.	n.a.	(−) 0.03	0.95	(−)	
Specialization	(−) 0.01		(−)		(−) 0.00		(−)	0.90
University	(+) 0.00		(+)	0.95	(+) 0.08	0.99	(+)	
Full Model			0.33	0.99			0.33	0.99

(continued)

Table 6.8   **(continued)**

| | 1971–1981 | | | | 1981–1991 | | | |
| | Individual Variables | | Full Model | | Individual Variables | | Full Model | |
	R²	Signif.	R²	Signif.	R²	Signif.	R²	Signif.
D. Manufacturing								
Region	0.13	0.99		0.99	0.13	0.99		0.99
Size	0.01			0.90	0.03			
Proximity	0.00				0.01			0.90
Competition	n.a	n.a.	n.a.	n.a.	(−) 0.01		(−)	
Specialization	(−) 0.18	0.99	(−)	0.99	(−) 0.07	0.99	(−)	0.99
University	(−) 0.00		(−)	0.95	(+) 0.04	0.95	(+)	0.95
Full Model			0.31	0.99			0.31	0.99
E. Wholesale trade								
Region	0.19	0.99		0.99	0.06	0.90		
Size	0.05	0.90		0.95	0.06	0.90		
Proximity	0.00				0.16	0.99		0.99
Competition	n.a.	n.a.	n.a.	n.a.	(−) 0.21	0.99	(−)	0.99
Specialization	(−) 0.00		(−)		(+) 0.03	0.95	(+)	0.95
University	(+) 0.00		(+)		(+) 0.01		(+)	0.90
Full Model			0.25	0.99			0.38	0.99
F. Finance, insurance, real estate								
Region	0.22	0.99		0.99	0.14	0.99		0.99
Size	0.00				0.03			
Proximity	0.01				0.08	0.99		0.99
Competition	n.a	n.a.	n.a.	n.a.	(−) 0.00		(−)	
Specialization	(−) 0.05	0.95	(−)		(−) 0.03	0.95	(−)	
University	(+) 0.00		(+)		(+) 0.00		(+)	
Full Model			0.23	0.99			0.23	0.99

Table 6.8   **(continued)**

| | 1971–1981 | | | | 1981–1991 | | | |
| | Individual Variables | | Full Model | | Individual Variables | | Full Model | |
	R²	Signif.	R²	Signif.	R²	Signif.	R²	Signif.
G. Business services								
Region	0.16	0.95			0.30	0.99		0.90
Size	0.06				0.12	0.99		
Proximity	0.03				0.11	0.99		0.90
Competition	n.a	n.a.	n.a.	n.a.	(−) 0.24	0.99	(−)	0.99
Specialization	(−) 0.21	0.99	(−)	0.95	(+) 0.15	0.99	(+)	0.99
University	(+) 0.06	0.95	(+)		(+) 0.04	0.95	(+)	0.99
Full Model			0.29	0.99			0.54	0.99
H. Other producer services								
Region	0.24	0.90		0.90	0.11	0.90		
Size	0.01				0.17	0.99		0.90
Proximity	0.02				0.01			0.95
Competition	n.a	n.a.	n.a.	n.a.	(−) 0.15	0.99	(−)	
Specialization	(−) 0.00		(−)	0.90	(−) 0.02		(−)	0.90
University	(+) 0.01		(+)		(+) 0.03		(+)	
Full Model			0.40	0.90			0.34	0.99

*Note: Only significance levels of 90% or more are indicated in the Signif(icance) column.

Source: Calculated by author from special data tabulations of *Census of Canada*, 1971, 1981, 1991.

decade to another, however, the relationship being less strong in the 1980s. In addition, the influence of region is not constant across all sectoral groups. In general, these results reinforce the notion that the economic performance of an individual urban area is intimately related to the performance of the broader regional economy in which it is situated. The most vivid example of this relationship is the performance of urban areas in the prairie provinces during the regional resource boom of the 1970s, characterized by the highest growth rates in the nation, and their subsequent 'reversal of fortune' during the 'bust' of the 1980s, characterized by the lowest growth rates. Thus, being located in one of Canada's regions rather than in another confers no absolute and enduring advantage on an urban area.

Much depends on the economic performance of the region (province, multiprovincial zone, or even sub-provincial zone) to which an urban area has its most important functional linkages. Thus, the growth prospects of an urban area must always be considered within a larger regional (and even national) context.

The population size of individual urban areas, too, appears to exert some degree of influence on employment growth rates. This influence does not, however, conform to the simple linear relationship (diseconomies of scale and of agglomeration notwithstanding) posited by the urban economics literature, since widely differing size categories have relatively similar growth rates (e.g., the largest places and the smallest places have comparable growth rates). In general, we note that: (1) the influence of size on growth rates is much less clear than the influence of region; and (2) there is an appreciable difference between decades, with the relationship between size and growth rates being stronger in the 1980s. The differences between the two decades are very likely related (at least in part) to the fact that the 1970s were marked especially by the growth of activities often situated in smaller places (e.g., goods-producing functions), while the 1980s were characterized more by the growth of activities that tend to be disproportionately located in larger places (e.g., business services).

Employment growth rates vary significantly across the three categories of metropolitan proximity, although the relationships are both stronger and more significant in the 1980s. In the 1970s, the growth rate for total employment is highest in the major metropolitan areas and lowest in the central urban areas. This order is not necessarily preserved across the individual economic sectors, where considerable variability exists. In the 1980s, the total employment growth rate is highest in the central units and lowest in the peripheral units. Across the individual sectors of activity, however, the relative ordering of growth rates more directly follows that of total employment. Thus, in the 1970s a location in the 'urban shadow' of a major metropolitan area is associated with growth rates that are lower than in the other two classes, while in the 1980s a simi-lar geographic position is associated with growth rates that are higher than for the other two classes.

Firm size structure also proved to be significant over the 1981–91 period in the case of the services subtotal and of three individual sectoral groups. The nature of the relationship indicates, however, that contrary to conventional wisdom, growth is more rapid when employment is distributed among a smaller number of larger firms. This finding complements our previous results (Coffey and Shearmur, 1996) that show that high rates of employment growth are associated with the presence of firms in the middle size range (that is, 100–199 employees, in particular); a high percentage of firms either above or below this range is generally associated with lower growth rates. Together, these results reinforce the 'post-Birch' studies that have shown that small firms are not necessarily the engines of growth they once were considered to be.

The relationships between the sectoral specialization index and employment growth rates are generally significant, and are in the direction hypothesized by Jacobs: higher growth rates are found in more diversified urban economies. The diversity/specialization variable is second only to region in its performance in the models. Finally, using a supply-side perspective on local labour markets, the relationship between employment growth and university education is both widespread and significant, although its strength is lower than in the case of region and the specialization index. The nature of the relationship is positive, reinforcing the conventional wisdom concerning the role of education in economic growth.

Conclusion

Economic change within urban Canada evokes a number of key themes: economic transformation, impacts of transformation, and policy issues.

Economic transformation

Over a period of 20 years, from 1971 to 1991, the economic structure of Canada's urban areas has become both more *tertiarized*, from the viewpoint of sectors of activity, and more *professionalized*, from the viewpoint of occupations. At the root of these changes is a broader transformation occurring within the national and world economies, one involving fundamental modifications in what is produced, in how the production of goods and services is organized and carried out, in the nature of work, and in the demand for labour. A number of factors have contributed to these modifications: the opening of national and world markets; increasing competition from newly industrializing countries; improvements in transportation and communications methods; and increases in purchasing power. Perhaps even more important, however, has been the rapid progress of new information-processing technologies.

For over two decades, our urban areas have been participants in the rise of a 'new service economy' that, as both cause and effect of these transformations, has wrought fundamental modifications in the nature of work. Blue-collar factory employment has declined while 'orientation' functions—design, planning, control, and managerial tasks—have risen in importance both within manufacturing firms and, more broadly, across all sectors of the economy. The increasing importance of high-order service *functions*, many of which are found in non-service sectors, has created a host of new employment opportunities for white-collar workers. These changes, in turn, have increased the need for a range of other managerial, professional, and (in absolute, if not relative, terms) sales and clerical personnel.

Impacts of Transformation

Uneven development
From a spatial perspective, perhaps the most striking aspect of economic trends within the Canadian urban system is the geographic concentration of high-order service employment in a small number of large urban areas. As we have seen, in 1991 one-half of all Canadian employment in the business service sector was contained in the three largest CMAs—Toronto, Montreal, and Vancouver; these

three CMAs contained only 31.6 per cent of the national population. The level of concentration was similar for the 'other producer services' and FIRE sectors. In fact, the level of concentration of business-service employment increased within the 10 largest CMAs from 70.9 per cent of all Canadian employment in the sector in 1971 to 72.2 per cent in 1991. Uneven development is thus a major element of Canada's space-economy, as it is in virtually all developed countries.

Socio-economic impacts
From the perspective of both society and individual urban areas, the trends reviewed here also have far-reaching consequences. First, the slow economic growth of the 1980s and early 1990s has limited the fiscal capacity of individual municipalities, thereby reducing their ability to provide essential services to their population. Second, the recent decline in the level of job creation has reduced the ability of individuals, families, and households to acquire the goods and services that they need in order to maintain a reasonable quality of life. Third, economic transformation has created an expanding demand for a new type of labour: workers who are better-educated, better-trained, and more skilled in terms of social interactions. Thus, in the new economy, increased employability is directly related to higher educational and skill levels. Those with low levels of educational attainment or those lacking 'modern' (e.g., information technology) skills—be they young high-school dropouts or laid-off middle-aged factory workers—are finding that their possibilities for employment are becoming increasingly restricted. There is a strong possibility not only that a major portion of the labour force will be severely disadvantaged by the continuing 'Non-Industrial Revolution', but also that the labour market will become further dichotomized into two categories: 'good jobs'—those that are full-time, well remunerated, and satisfying—and 'bad jobs'— those that involve unstable, poorly paid, and devalourizing employment opportunities (Economic Council of Canada, 1990). A major problem that society must face, then, is that of integrating into the economic system those persons

who do not possess the educational and skill attributes to allow them access to suitable employment. The major public policy challenge is, therefore, to find new and more effective methods of developing our society's human resources.

Policy Issues

Policy initiatives

Faced with increasing economic difficulties, local governments have sought to stimulate growth by means of various policy initiatives. Individual urban areas have formulated policies that specifically emphasize: the development of one or more individual sectors (e.g., Vancouver's emphasis on business and financial services; Laval's creation of a 'technopole' involving a range of high-technology manufacturing sectors); human resource development and training; support to entrepreneurs and small and medium-sized enterprises; local development corporations; infrastructure projects, including transport networks; the attraction of external investment; the promotion of a 'world city' image; and so forth. In addition, urban areas are increasingly adopting the point of view that they must act as collectivities (that is, as metropolitan areas or 'city regions'), rather than as individual municipalities. In spite of considerable experimentation, however, the magic solution to urban economic development problems has not yet been discovered. The discussion of growth-stimulation measures often involves the following two more philosophical issues: the nature of an urban area's economic base, and the overall efficacy of local-level economic development policy.

Economic base

The issue of what constitutes the principal economic base of an urban area has, both implicitly and explicitly, been the object of considerable debate by researchers and, especially, policy-makers in recent years. The respective roles played by manufacturing and services activities lie at the heart of this debate.

In general, one can identify two diametrically opposed schools of thought concerning the 'real'

economic base of urban economies. The first, based on what many would now consider an antiquated view of the nature of production systems, holds that the production of *goods* is the driving force of a local (or regional or national) economy. This view has its origins in the writings of Adam Smith in the eighteenth century and in those of Karl Marx in the nineteenth century and has been reinforced by the pre-World War II Fisher-Clark typology of economic activity, with its explicit relegation of all services to the category of 'non-productive' activity. The second school of thought, often termed a 'post-industrial' perspective, takes an inverse view, stressing the declining significance of manufacturing in most urban economies and the rising importance of services, particularly of high-order, knowledge-related services.

Of the two schools of thought, the view that manufacturing is solid and genuine, whereas service industries are parasitic and ephemeral, is the most firmly entrenched, particularly in local-level (that is, urban and metropolitan) policy-making circles. That services cannot thrive without a strong manufacturing base is a claim that is rarely challenged. The opposite argument, that manufacturing needs services, is rarely advanced; the notion that services, rather than manufacturing, may indeed constitute the economic base of many modern urban areas has only recently begun to gain acceptance. Commenting on this debate, the prestigious economic review, *The Economist*, observes that the notion of the pre-eminence of manufacturing is based on a series of long-standing 'myths' (*The Economist*, 1993).

In light of the information presented in this chapter, it is indeed difficult to support the notion that services do *not* represent an important element of the economic base of modern urban areas. Implicitly accepting this antiquated view, however, many local policy-makers have invested huge amounts of energy and money in attempting to prevent the erosion of their local manufacturing base, to the exclusion of other possible initiatives. These efforts have been particularly desperate and fruitless in the case of the central cities of metropolitan areas, which have seen their manufacturing base migrate not only towards other regions or nations but also towards suburban municipalities (see Chapter 15). Gradually, however, the strategic role played by high-order services, in particular, in economic development has been acknowledged. This new consciousness has been aided by an awareness that the share of manufacturing employment has dwindled to approximately 20 per cent in many local economies, while the share of service employment has risen to over 70 per cent. In response, some Canadian local governments have begun to establish economic development policies that explicitly target service industries, but there are leaders and there are laggards. Development policies need to become more comprehensive, reflecting the role of all economic sectors and the interrelations between them.

Efficacy of urban economic development policy

More fundamentally, the role and the impact of *explicit* economic development policy at the local level remain open to debate. On the one hand, local-level policy often remains subordinate to forces operating in the larger sociopolitical context. At the international scale, in the current era of economic globalization and integration, the level of demand for an urban area's products and services may well be determined on the other side of the world. At the national and subnational scale, internal social, cultural, and political factors may be exceedingly important. For example, in spite of a complex set of local-level policies, an organization that promotes the metropolitan area as a 'world city', and the specific intervention of a provincial-level ministry devoted to stimulating its economic development, Montreal's economy has remained moribund since the mid-1970s, in large measure due to the political instability associated with Quebec and its role in the Canadian confederation. On the other hand, national-level sectoral policies (e.g., in the energy, automobile, biotechnology, and aerospace sectors), with their *implicit* impacts on different regions and different levels of the urban hierarchy, often have a far more important effect on local-level economic development, as in the case of

the growth of the prairie provinces' urban areas in the 1970s. Urban areas in different regions, of different sizes, and characterized by different economic structures, for example, have reacted differently to the opportunities and constraints presented by these trends. The issue of differential levels of employment growth among urban areas is a complex one, and analyses of this phenomenon must take into account the multiple factors and influences that are at work.

Notes

1. The reader will note that the basis of observation in this chapter is slightly different from that used in the previous chapter. Here the urban system is defined as including all urban places with a population of 10,000 or more. There are 152 places so defined in 1991. In the previous chapter, Simmons and McCann defined the urban system in terms of CMAs and CAs only (see Appendix A for complete definitions), which in 1991 produced a system comprising 140 urban places.

2. In the case of both sectors and occupations, workers falling in the 'unspecified' or 'undefined' category have been eliminated from the analysis. Since the number of 'unspecified' or 'undefined' workers differs according to whether sectors or occupations form the basis of the analysis, the total number of workers in the urban system, and in each of its elements, will also differ according to the concept used. For example, in 1991 the urban system contained 9,991,200 workers who were classed in an identifiable economic sector, but only 9,601,500 who were classed in a specific occupational category. Thus, in Tables 6.1 and 6.2, total employment by *sector* is slightly larger (by approximately 390,000) than in the case of total employment by *occupation*.

3. For the period 1981–91, St Catharines–Niagara, the eleventh largest CMA in 1991, and Windsor, the fifteenth largest, are absent from the list of rapid growth urban areas, having been replaced by Oshawa and Saskatoon, the sixteenth and

seventeenth largest CMAs, respectively. For the period 1971–81, Windsor is absent from the list, having been replaced by Saskatoon.

4. Subsequent research has demonstrated that Birch's approach was methodologically flawed and that the importance of small firms is not nearly as clear-cut as Birch argued. See Davis and Haltiwanger (1990) and Davis, Haltiwanger, and Schuh (1994), for example, who show that the growth of small firms is not more rapid than that of large firms when one accounts for the higher failure rates of the former.

References

Birch, D. 1987. *Job Creation in America: How Our Smallest Companies Put the Most People to Work*. New York: Free Press.

Coffey, W.J., with the collaboration of R. Shearmur. 1996. *Employment Growth and Change in the Canadian Urban System, 1971–1994*. Ottawa: Canadian Policy Research Network.

———, R. Fullum, and M. Polèse. 1989. *La restructuration de l'économie canadienne, 1971–1981: une nouvelle dynamique régionale?* Moncton, NB: Institut canadien de recherche sur le développement régional.

——— and J.J. McRae. 1989. *Service Industries in Regional Development*. Montreal: Institute for Research on Public Policy.

——— and M. Polèse. 1985. 'Local Development: Conceptual Bases and Policy Implications', *Regional Studies* 19: 85–93.

——— and M. Polèse. 1988. 'Locational Shifts in Canadian Employment, 1971–1981: Decentralization versus Decongestion', *Canadian Geographer* 32: 248–56.

Davis, S.J., and J. Haltiwanger. 1990. *Gross Job Creation, Gross Job Destruction, and Employment Reallocation*. Chicago: University of Chicago Press.

———, ———, and S. Schuh. 1994. 'Small Business and Job Creation: Dissecting the Myth and Reassessing the Facts', *Business Economics* 29: 13—21.

Dicken, P. 1998. *Global Shift*. New York: Guilford Press.

Economic Council of Canada. 1990. *Good Jobs, Bad Jobs*. Ottawa: Minister of Supply and Services.

Economist, The. 1993. 'Wealth in Services', 20 Feb., 15–16.

Glaeser, E.L., H.D. Kallal, J.A. Scheinkman, and A. Shleifer. 1991. *Growth in Cities*. Cambridge, Mass.: National Bureau of Economic Research.

Landis, D.J. 1987. 'An Empirical Basis for National Urban Policy', *Urban Studies* 24: 518–33.

Jacobs, J. 1969. *The Economy of Cities*. New York: Vintage Books.

———. 1984. *Cities and the Wealth of Nations*. New York: Vintage Books.

Porter, M.E. 1990. *The Competitive Advantage of Nations*. New York: Free Press.

Tiebout, C. 1962. *The Community Economic Base Study*. New York: Committee for Economic Development.

Part Two

City-Wide Processes

Here we are concerned with commonalities of internal composition among cities. At an earlier point in time, before World War II, the research literature featured several unified or 'generic' models of city structure, referred to as land-use models. These models simplified the patterns observable on the ground. They also claimed to be generalizable from one place to another. Today, it would be virtually impossible to produce a simple representation of the internal structure of contemporary Canadian cities. Since the middle of the twentieth century, cities have grown much more complex. We have come to understand that many different processes are at work in cities and that the effects of interaction among them can be expected to vary considerably from one place to another. However, while it may be truly impossible to put forward one single model that captures *the* urban pattern, strong regularities do exist within the different processes that structure the development of cities. The first three chapters here introduce the reader to the most important of these city-wide structural processes, which can be generalized because they operate much the same way in all cities: the land market; the land-use/transportation nexus; and socio-spatial processes. A fourth chapter introduces morphology as an idiosyncratic component that produces a good portion of the specificities that distinguish cities from each other. Figure II.1 suggests how these separate parameters collectively contribute to the real world setting.

Urban development begins as a real estate process. In Chapter 7, John Miron introduces us to the fundamental principles of the real estate market. He demands that we look behind the immediate juxtaposition of buildings and activities to examine the underlying process of buying, selling, and developing or redeveloping land. A primary relationship in real estate models is that between land value, capitalization (or intensity of development), and accessibility. As suggested in Chapter 1, in the early part of the twentieth century when most intra-urban person movement was on foot or by public transit, this relationship took the form of a distance decay surface outwards from the CBD. Population density, building height, and property value dropped off rapidly with distance from the centre. Today, things seem different because some of the most highly capitalized real estate in cities is found in 'suburban downtowns'. But the underlying relationship with accessibility still holds, since these new suburban downtowns are located at transportation interchanges that provide sites of very high metropolitan-wide accessibility.

Transportation represents the skeletal frame holding the urban entity together. As a result, land value and use are both closely linked to transportation availability. Thus, if we know the characteristics of land use in one part of a city, we can predict what its transportation generation will be. Alternatively, if we know an area's transportation flow, we can generally arrive at a good estimate of its land-use configuration. In Chapter 8, Eric Miller introduces us to how transportation structures land use. The accuracy of statistical models that exist in this field and that are widely used for transportation planning and forecasting attests to the strong link between transportation and land use. Miller further illustrates this point when discussing the apparent inseparable

Figure II.1   **City-Wide Processes**

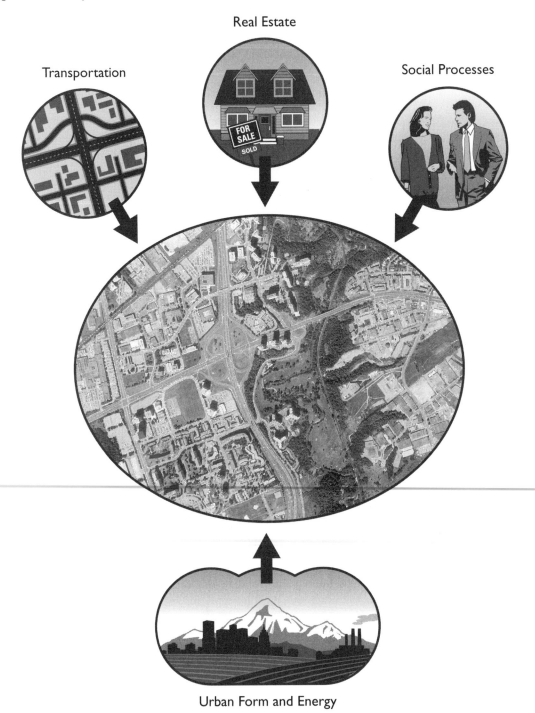

Real Estate

Transportation

Social Processes

Urban Form and Energy

interrelationship between low-density suburban form and near-universal automobile use. This latter entrenchment introduces concern about the impact of low-density, automobile-oriented suburban form on the environment—a point taken up further by Sherry Olson in Chapter 10.

Social processes as discussed by Robert Murdie and Carlos Teixeira in Chapter 9—who prefers which kind of accommodation, who can afford what, who wants to live near whom and in what kind of urban setting—contribute another dimension, generally referred to as a city's socio-spatial structure. Neighbourhood and community social status can be seen to be all pervasive because, in addition to residences being the primary use of urban land, residential areas are closely linked to other activities—shopping, schools, community services, recreational facilities, even employment. The quality of housing and related social status of neighbourhoods and communities have a direct influence on real estate values. They also tend to correlate with the volumes and types of trips that are generated.

Olson, in Chapter 10, considers two main themes: the distinctiveness of individual cities and cities' 'metabolism' or energy flows into and out of the natural environment that supports urban living. Olson begins by making the point that each city possesses unique geographic features. These features influence the real estate market and the transportation network as well as where different subgroups choose to live. Along with distinctive history and architecture, they also create the compelling sense of place that residents and visitors alike come to associate with one particular city's 'image'. From a theoretical perspective, what is perhaps most important about the unique characteristics of individual cities is that they blur the regularities produced by major city-wide processes. This is one reason why the search for a generic pattern of urban form has been so elusive. Olson's other theme, urban metabolism, returns to a more generalizable realm as regards processes shared by all urban places: the negative externalities of urban growth and form, the fouling of the urban nest as it were. Olson introduces us to this fundamental life-sustaining/life-threatening quality of cities everywhere. In Chapter 21, as part of this volume's concluding focus on pressing concerns, this issue is revisited with a look at the emerging field of urban ecology.

Chapter 7

Cities as Real Estate

John Miron

Imagine a city, any city. What is the first scene that comes to mind? If you think like most Hollywood movie directors, at least four scales are possible. First, viewed from high above, the city might be a jumble of indistinguishable structures. Second, viewed from ground level, the city might appear as a massing of office and apartment towers jutting skyward. Alternatively, you might want to view a city at closer range. That view might be of a 'brown site' with dilapidated buildings on abandoned properties or a 'science park' with shiny new buildings in a lush and quiet setting. It might be a cluster of 'monster homes' or neotraditional housing. Viewed at an even closer range, you might focus on one particular building or a unique grouping of buildings that signifies that city: Toronto's City Hall, Quebec City's Château Frontenac, Ottawa's Parliament Hill. What do these images of a city have in common? They each focus on the city as real estate, that is, buildings assembled in close proximity, on sites improved to make the property more usable, and linked by roads, utilities, and communications lines.

To understand cities is, in part, to know how land and buildings acquire monetary value and how this value influences what gets built, where, and why. The motivations of individuals, firms and governments are central to this understanding. For their part, firms behave as they do because of the profits to be made, and the risks involved, in real estate investment. To firms, cities embody institutions that may help increase the profit and mitigate the risk in real estate investment. Risk and profit are central to understanding both why cities exist and how real estate development has evolved in recent decades.

There are two kinds of risk here. One is the risk involved when market conditions change unexpectedly in the future. An example would be the advances in road and rail transportation technology in the late-nineteenth and early-twentieth centuries that reduced the advantage of water transportation and therefore access to a port. As addressed elsewhere in this volume, transitions brought about by unanticipated technological change have been frequent, making this risk ubiquitous. The consequences of this first type of risk pervade contemporary urban landscapes: from abandoned warehousing and industry, to blight along 'main streets', to noticeable vacancies in shopping malls. The second kind of risk arises from illiquidity. Put simply, liquidity is the ease with which an owner can find a willing buyer for an asset at a fair price within a reasonable time. Alternatively, in an illiquid market, there are few buyers relative to the number of sellers. An important tool for assuring liquid markets is standardization. In real estate investment, risk mitigation has spurred standardization in design of buildings, planning approvals, the methods of financing of new construction, the quality and kinds of construction materials, and the fittings and equipment these buildings incorporate. Planned suburban communities and their individual components—from homes to shopping malls and business parks—reflect the importance of standardization in today's real estate market. As emphasized in Chapter 1, this quality creates a consistency and stability in the urban landscape over time. In fact, risk aversion in real estate investment and the appeal of standardization are major reasons why planners and urban designers find it so difficult to impose radical change in the way cities develop, no matter how well they argue its need.

One way of looking at the risk factor in real estate is through market structures. We can characterize markets in an advanced market economy as of two kinds: familiar and unfamiliar. In the first, the markets for accommodation, food, clothing, household furnishings, transportation services, and entertainment are familiar to consumers. The second kind, which includes the markets for such 'products' and services as mutual funds or mortgage insurance to insure lenders against default by the borrower, is less familiar. Often, these less familiar markets spread the risks of uncertainty, on the presumption that no one person or firm wants to take a big risk but most are willing to take a small risk. Any market is thought to be efficient if it provides a good or service in the quantity demanded in the market and at a price that is as low as possible. By spreading risks, these less familiar markets help to reduce the cost of providing goods or services (e.g., accommodation) in familiar markets.

A second way to categorize real estate markets is between where properties are bought and sold versus where the use of property (consumption) is allocated. Purchasers and vendors exchange land and built structures in the property market. In the market for rental accommodation, landlords use property, buildings, and improvements to produce shelter services for occupants. Consumption in this second type of market (rents paid, structures occupied, and vacancy rates) drives the demand for real estate assets in the first type of market. Households purchasing single-family homes buy an exchangeable asset but are also investing in the consumption of daily shelter, a roof over their heads, and whatever else is housed under that roof. Cities are useful vehicles for efficient investment in real estate because they constitute agglomerations of buyers and sellers of real estate assets and shelter services. More market participants means greater liquidity and less risk. Suppose, for example, that you want to sell a property that only one prospective buyer in 100 might like to purchase. In a small market—say, one with only 10 prospective buyers looking at

your property each week—you must typically wait longer to find a willing buyer than in a market where 100 prospective purchasers pass through weekly. Another point of note is that in cities, real estate development can be regulated more efficiently for example, through building codes, zoning by-laws, and property maintenance standards. The cost of administering regulation is smaller per property in large urban areas because the fixed costs (e.g., management and computerization of administrative records) can be spread over more properties in total. Such regulation tends to sustain property values and at the same time serves to protect or enhance liquidity.

This chapter considers the following questions in sequence. First, just how large is the real estate sector overall, and real estate investment in particular, in the Canadian economy? How are land values linked to accessibility within cities? How does raw land get transformed into the 'developed' stock of real estate within cities? How might we best characterize the 'markets' for real estate? What motivates investment in real estate? How have the methods of financing real estate changed in recent decades? What is the role of government in real estate investment? The approach taken to answer these questions is positive rather than normative, and the focus is on agency rather than structure. This chapter describes the motivations and choices of economic actors (households, firms, or governments) rather than the political-economy structures within which such choices are exercised. As a result, this chapter does not consider the work by neo-Marxists among others who write on capitalism, capital-labour conflict, and power relations.

Real Estate in the Canadian Economy

Real estate is a major component in the Canadian economy. One way to think about this is in terms of the number of persons employed. While there are few published data in this area, the real estate sector clearly accounts for much employment in Canada. Included here would be jobs in the following categories: realtors and developers; surveyors and civil engineers; planners and architects; marketing and advertising professionals; financiers and accountants; contractors and the construction trades; manufacturers and distributors of building materials and fittings; manufacturers and distributors of home furnishings, equipment, and major appliances; landlords and property managers; superintendents and cleaning staff; building repair and maintenance trades; manufacturers and distributors of repair and renovation materials. In addition, one might also include the time spent by households on unpaid housework and do-it-yourself maintenance and repairs. A second way to measure the importance of the real estate sector is in terms of dollar magnitudes. There are several ways to quantify this.

Component of National Wealth

The National Balance Sheet (NBS), prepared by Statistics Canada, gives an accounting of assets, liabilities, and net worth in Canada, whether these are held by individuals, firms, or governments. According to the NBS, the total value of all land assets (excluding built structures) in Canada in 1997 was $710 billion, up from $684 billion in 1996. The value of land assets increases over time partly because of inflation: the same parcel of land sells for more this year than last. It also increases because land is improved (e.g., drainage, levelling and landscaping, subdivision or assembly, and paving and other servicing). On top of this, we may add the value of structures (all buildings, whether residential or non-residential) on that land; in 1997, these amounted to $1.57 trillion. Altogether, then, real estate assets (land plus structures) in Canada in 1997 totalled $2.28 trillion. All assets in Canada (which range from property to savings accounts to equity stocks) amounted to $8.16 trillion in the same year; therefore, real estate in 1997 was 28 per cent of all assets in Canada.

Component of National Income

Gross investment in the form of construction of new buildings and additions and repairs and reno-vations of existent buildings amounted to $85 billion in 1997, fully 10 per cent of Canada's total gross domestic product in that year. In comparison to the $1.57 trillion total in stock, the $85 billion of gross new investment in structures in 1997 is a small amount. And, even this is before netting out the effect of depreciation, abandonment, destruction, and obsolescence. On net, the value of real estate assets grows only slowly over time; that these assets have reached $1.57 trillion by 1997 indicates the durability of buildings and other improvements to property. The end-use of real estate investment, however, changes more rapidly. As of 1997, structure assets in the residential sector of real estate (including owner-occupied, tenant-occupied, and vacant dwellings) account for $804 billion; assets in the non-residential sector account for the remaining $766 billion. However, the mix of new investment differs from year to year because of the boom-and-bust cycle of real estate investment (see Figure 7.1). New construction tends to occur in concentrated bursts as investors anticipate profits to be made in a particular kind of real estate venture. Later, investors pull out as overbuilding erases profit, leaving real estate in a slump. One year, residential investment is hot; the next year, a particular form of non-residential investment might be preferred (e.g., shopping centres, offices, or industrial parks); the following year, it might be none of the above. Figure 7.2 shows the fluctuating level of new housing construction in Canada over the years.

How much of these assets are to be found in urban areas? Here, there are few published data. However, the 1996 census reports that 56 per cent of Canada's population lived in urban areas of 250,000 people or more. Much of the improvement to land is found there. In the 1991 census, residents of the three largest CMAs (Toronto, Montreal, and Vancouver) make up 31 per cent of all households and account for 44 per cent of the value of residential real estate. As well, much of business and public-sector investment in non-residential buildings is to be found in cities. Therefore, it is safe to assume that cities account for much of the real estate assets in Canada. Cities also reflect the chang-

Figure 7.1   **Annual Total Investment in Building in Canada (current billions of dollars), 1981–1997**

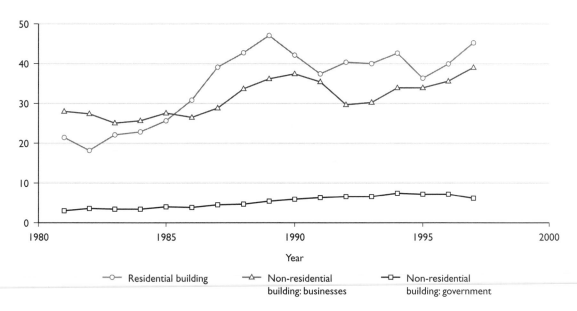

Source: Statistics Canada, CANSIM Series D16213, D16250, and D16237.

Figure 7.2   **Housing Starts in Canada, 1948–1997**

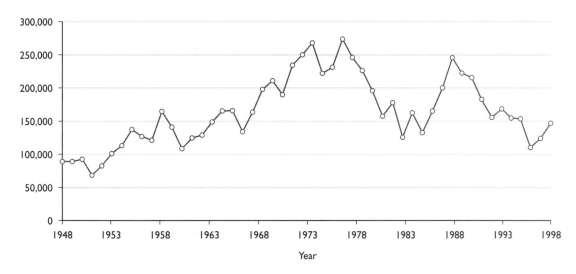

Source: Statistics Canada, CANSIM Series G2717.

ing nature of investment in real estate. Before the mid-1950s, much real estate development was undertaken at a small scale. Factories, office buildings, and retail shops were typically 'one-off' projects (that is, not part of an industrial park, office complex, or shopping centre) and often of a small size by today's standards. As is pointed out in Chapter 10, some larger office and professional buildings, especially those in and around the CBD, and a few apartment buildings were constructed by life insurance companies and other large investors of the day. However, much of this was built on the account of one or just a few small investors. This situation was even more pronounced among builders of homes; they often erected only a few houses at any one time (Harris, 1996).

The scale of real estate development increased sharply in Canada after the mid-1950s for several reasons. On the finance side, deregulation of the banking sector and mortgage interest rates helped to increase substantially the amount of capital available to fund real estate development. On the demand side, rapid population growth (the baby boom and high rates of postwar immigration) created a need for much new residential, commercial, and industrial space. As well, consumers began to show a willingness to pay for the 'corporate suburb': large-scale planned developments in which housing, neighbourhood amenities, commercial activities, and educational facilities are developed and sold as a bundle. In the office and commercial sector, too, real estate developers found that firms would pay for site amenities (e.g., an atrium, expansive parking, and mixed-use developments) that could be provided cost-effectively only in relatively large developments. Important, too, were changes in construction technology that favoured large-scale developments: from new concrete-forming techniques in high-rise construction through modularization of kitchen, bathroom, and other fittings in residential construction. Finally, another important innovation on the supply side was the advance in computer technology (e.g., computerized control of furnace and air-conditioning systems) that made it relatively easier to maintain and operate large structures efficiently.

Land Value and Access in Cities

In any real property market, some parcels of land attract a premium price because of a feature unique to the site. Among residential sites, for example, those prized might be on the waterfront or a mountainside, at the edge of a ravine, on a quiet street, or in an old forest or a historic district. Such valued characteristics are often referred to as factors of place or 'amenity' rent that contribute to selling price. Traditionally, however, the urban economics literature has been less concerned with 'site' features, focusing more on features of 'situation' or access that, in the simplest case, are calibrated as space costs in terms of distance from downtown. Because of situation, land at the centre of almost any large city is extraordinarily costly. Developed land (that is, land serviced by a paved road and with municipal water and sewage connections) that might sell for $200 per square metre in a conventional suburban setting would garner 10 times that amount or more in a desirable downtown location. And, of course, the larger the city the bigger the premium for a downtown site. Why so? There are three distinct theoretical models that help us to understand the process.

The Wingo Effect

The first model is termed the Wingo effect in recognition of the urban economist who first wrote about it. Wingo (1961) formalized a model wherein households bid up the price of land for a more central location because such a location brings them closer to a job site, shopping, concert halls, or other amenities of downtown. Suppose, for example, that someone commutes to work downtown 250 days a year and that the trip costs $0.30 per kilometre each way. Suppose that this person moves one kilometre closer to work, from site A to an identical home at B. At B, the person saves two kilometres a day in commuting back and forth for an annual total of ($0.30 × 2 × 250) = $150. If the same amount is saved each succeeding year, the present value of these savings (at a discount rate of, say, 5 per cent calculated over perpetuity) would be ($150/0.05) = $3,000. In other words, as long as the home purchased at site B is less than $3,000 more than the house at A (ignoring the costs of moving), the purchaser is better off at B. Now imagine that suburban site A is 10 kilometres away from the job site and is priced at $100,000. If another site, C, is adjacent to the job site, the above argument suggests that the person will pay up to ($100,000 + $3,000(10)) = $130,000 to live at C (see Figure 7.3). Note, however, that the price at C in this example is only 30 per cent higher than A—a far cry from the tenfold increase suggested above. Therefore, the Wingo effect by itself is too small typically to account for dramatic differences in property values between downtown and suburb.

The Alonso Effect

Households are generally willing to pay a bigger premium for a central location than is suggested by the Wingo effect alone. The reason is that households substitute between consumption of land and other goods in choosing a dwelling. In a remote suburb at distance t, say, an exurban country estate, land is relatively inexpensive and the homeowner typically purchases a larger lot. With the larger lot, the homeowner might build a large one-storey home with a generous front yard, and perhaps a pond, an orchard, or large garden out back. There might even be enough room to put in an extra building, for example, a barn, workshed, or cabana. Now consider a second location, t', closer to downtown where land is more expensive. Here, the homeowner typically forgoes large yards and their amenities. The homeowner may also now choose to occupy a two-storey home with a smaller building 'footprint' to save further on land costs. Now consider a third location, t'', even closer to downtown where land is so expensive that the homeowner now lives in a condominium tower where perhaps 20 or more dwellings occupy the land area that in a suburban site would be thought fit for just one dwelling. Figure 7.4 presents an indifference curve analysis for a consumer residing at each of the distances, earning the same income (Y) and paying the same annual commuting cost of k dollars per kilometre. At each distance, we can calculate the income net of commuting—e.g., Y-kt for the consumer at distance t. This gives us the budget lines for the three consumers: a1a2, b1b2, and c1c2 respectively. If the annual rents for land at the three dis-

Figure 7.3   **Property Price: The Wingo Effect**

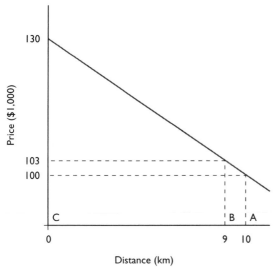

Figure 7.4   **Indifference Curves at Different Distances from Downtown**

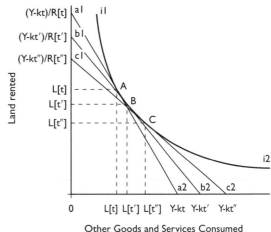

tances—R[t], R[t'] and R[t″]—are such as to make each consumer indifferent as to location, they must allow all three consumers to reach the same level of utility (shown as indifference curve i1i2). The consumer at the remote location t will therefore consume L[t] units of land and Z[t] units of other goods and services, that is, combination A. The residents at t' and t″ will consume less land but more other goods and services: combinations B and C respectively.

Alonso (1964) first articulated the argument that land prices increase faster than the Wingo effect would suggest as one moves closer to downtown because households increasingly substitute (that is, give up) increasingly costly land in favour of consumption of other kinds of goods and services. Because, in proximity to the CBD, consumers are willing to live at much higher densities, the 'rent' returns to the property owner will be substantially higher than in locations further out. Figure 7.5

Figure 7.5   **Property Price: The Alonso Effect**

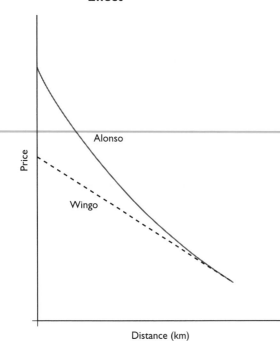

illustrates the Alonso effect; note that property rents rise faster than predicted by Wingo as one moves towards the downtown.

The Envelope Effect

Households, however, are not all identical, nor are they the only users competing for urban land. An urban landlord might be approached by industrial land users, shopping centre developers, office builders, and others who are also interested in acquiring land in the urban area. Suppose that each of these potential purchasers bids for the land and that the landlord accepts the highest offer. In this case, the price accepted (that is, the market price) is said to be the envelope of (that is, the highest among) the bid prices. Consider Figure 7.6. Let the bid price of residential users be the curve 'Bid 1', drawn here as convex with respect to the origin to reflect the Alonso effect. Now suppose there are two other bidders at each site, with bid curves shown as 'Bid 2' and 'Bid 3' respectively in Figure 7.6. Starting from the downtown, the market rent traces out the highest bid prices: first Bid 3, then Bid 2, and finally Bid 1. Therefore, users of type 3 get all the land out to distance d3, users of type 2 get land from d3 to d2, and residential users in this example get the land beyond d2. Note now that the market rent rises much faster than does Bid 1 as we move downtown from inside the radius d2. This model helps us to understand why some households (e.g., nuclear families with children and others who want large properties and/or privacy) find it economically advantageous to locate in the outer suburbs. It also explains why developers and property owners are eager to build at high densities and why land close to the CBD is so heavily capitalized. For further discussion of the envelope effects, see Turnbull (1995) and DiPasquale and Wheaton (1996).

Let us now distinguish among three related concepts: market rent, bid rent, and Ricardian rent. Ricardian rent is an above-normal ('excess') profit that arises because of monopoly power attributable to a factor of production. In the example above, some properties are closer to downtown than oth-

Figure 7.6   **Property Price: The Envelope Effect**

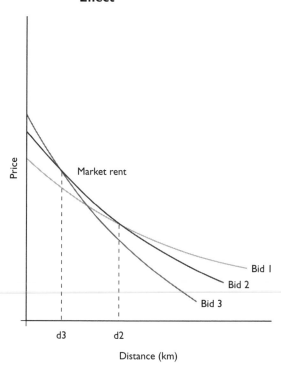

ers, and such proximity allows firms to earn above-normal profits. If we assume a large number of identical firms each bidding for a site where production is most profitable, then the bid of each firm is eventually driven up to the Ricardian rent. We have already seen that the market rent is the maximum of the bid rents and so is therefore equal to the largest Ricardian rent that any one kind of firm can earn at that site. Now, what about residential land users? Households are consumers; they are interested in utility rather than profits. What determines how much they will bid for land? Households would be happiest if they could bid nothing for land and get it. However, Figure 7.6 suggests that low bidders risk getting nothing. On the other hand, if residential users bid high, they will get land but may end up with a low utility because they have little income left to purchase the other necessities of life. Expressed

this way, we can imagine that each consumer has an array of non-intersecting bid rent curves (each curve corresponding to a given level of utility); some of these curves (higher utility) lie below Bid 1 in Figure 7.6, others (lower utility) lie above Bid 1. Which bid rent curve (and its attendant level of utility) is selected by households? Here, there are two possible versions of an answer. In the 'open version', households in-migrate into (or out-migrate from) a city if the level of utility there differs from the utility level possible elsewhere. As data presented in Chapter 2 suggest, this effect may explain the negative net internal migration rates that occurred in the Toronto CMA in the 1990s. Here the bid rent curve used is that which corresponds to the exogenous level of utility. In the 'closed version', the number of households is assumed fixed, and utility (and bid rent) adjusts upward or downward until the requisite number of households is accommodated. Here, the bid rent curve used is that which generates enough land to accommodate the given population.

These ideas about how property values vary across a city are built on the idea that the city contains many landlords who face many tenants (whether households or businesses) competing for available sites. Further, these ideas emphasize the role of the market in allocating land to the highest bidder. For a market to work well, however, there must be good information available to both landlord and prospective tenant and an appropriate set of institutions to make the market work efficiently. This is why an advanced market economy is necessary to make property markets work efficiently. But there is much more to this story. To this point, I have considered property essentially as a parcel of land. As we well know, real estate investment typically involves erecting and maintaining buildings and other structures on that parcel of land. In what follows, attention is focused on the decision to invest in real estate.

Real Estate Development and Planning

In practice, how does raw land make its way into the real estate of a city? Imagine for the moment a fifty-hectare farm that an investor intends to develop. First, the developer typically must subdivide the land, that is, partition the site into small parcels or 'lots', each to be sold to an individual property owner, plus rights-of-way to allow owners access to their sites. The rights-of-way will accommodate roads and sidewalks, pipes for water, sewer, and natural gas, and lines for electricity, cable television, and telephones. In the absence of rights-of-way, the lot buyer would have to be given an 'easement', a legal clause typically included in the deed to the property, that allows him or her the right of passage over the vendor's property to reach his or her own. Usually, subdivision also requires grading of the land, for example, to render developable lots level or to facilitate drainage and run-off. If such development is unregulated, the problem for the developer, put simply, is to design the layout of lots to maximize the profit from subdivision. (A summarized outline of the land development process is found in Figure 16.1, Chapter 16.)

In practice, land subdivision is generally regulated by provinces and territories in Canada. Sometimes, they in turn authorize regional or municipal governments to approve land subdivision by means of enabling legislation. In Ontario, for example, such authority is given to regional governments through the Planning Act (RSO 1990, ss. 50–1). Although there are exceptions in the case where a property is being subdivided into only a few lots, in general, the developer must submit a draft plan of subdivision for approval by government. In considering whether to approve the subdivision, planners typically look at such factors as conformity to the local Official Plan and zoning by-laws, environmental impacts, access to municipal infrastructure (from roads to pipes to schools), adequacy of the proposed rights-of-way, and the suitability of the sites for the proposed land uses. Planners may require that the developer agree to construct roads and do other improvements to particular standards (see Chapter 19 for additional information on the planning process). Where the subdivision occurs within a local jurisdiction, the local government typically 'assumes' ownership of the right-of-way after the developer has installed roads and other public utilities that conform to municipal standards. The government also typically will require that the developer set aside land within the subdivision (usually called a 'dedication') for parks, schools, or other municipal uses. Governments now also typically require developers to pay a fee (sometimes called a 'lot levy' or 'development charge') to compensate them for the additional costs of building new schools, libraries, fire stations, and other facilities needed to accommodate the new residents of the subdivision. Since the 1970s, the trend in Canadian cities has been for municipalities to pass more and more costs on to the developer. This has become a factor contributing to the escalating costs of home ownership in cities across the country. It also helps to explain the recent trend to reduce residential lot size. Finally, developers sometimes want to put certain legal restrictions (often called 'deed restrictions' or 'restrictive covenants') on the title of every lot sold in the subdivision. Such restrictions are used to ensure that lot owners preserve a certain vision of how the subdivision ought to look or operate—e.g., permissible exterior colour schemes, or the possibility of outdoor clothes-lines or rooftop antennae. In the past, restrictive covenants were applied mainly to up-market developments, but their use is spreading. In a sense, restrictive covenants are simply another kind of standard used to ensure the preservation of real estate value over time.

Once subdivision has been approved, the developer is free to sell the individual lots. Usually, this is done in conjunction with the construction of buildings. The developer may undertake the construction himself or herself, or may enter into agreements with one or more builders to do the work. Often the developer will build part of a site, selling some portion to other smaller construction companies. Typically, three more sets of approvals need to be obtained. First, the plans for construction on each lot must satisfy any zoning requirements that local governments may have imposed on that area of town. Second, a building permit must be obtained to allow construction to commence. Third, the requirements of the provincial building code (and any complementary regulations of municipalities and utilities) in construction must be met.

An increasing proportion of real estate investment today takes the form of redevelopment in older parts of a city. Sometimes, this investment takes place property by property, as in renovation. Sometimes, it takes the form of demolition and rebuilding. Because it is costly to acquire built-up sites and demolish existing structures (and, in the case of former industrial sites, to carry out the necessary environmental remediation), the redevelopment process almost always leads to intensification, sometimes to 'higher use' (see the discussion in Chapter 11 of downtown growth). Either way, there will be higher capitalization of buildings constructed on the original site, and, in the case of residential use, higher densities. On larger properties, there may be subdivision or some other rearrangement of property boundaries. Sometimes redevelopment takes the form of large new developments, often condominium or other kinds of common-interest developments, that may require land assembly. Compared to land subdivision, land assembly is relatively unregulated. As a result, planners have to rely more on zoning regulation to control this form of redevelopment.

The Markets for Real Estate

A market can be defined as the locus where buyers and sellers interact to exchange goods or services. This definition presumes a set of potential actors (individuals and firms possibly interested in purchasing or selling a product or asset). In a simple version of a market, each unit of the product or asset transacted is the same as every other unit. The actors share the same information (e.g., they know what was paid recently for each unit). As a result, there is a single equilibrium price (at which the quantity offered by sellers equals the demand by purchasers). Of course, no market for real estate actually looks like this simplified representation. After all, as real estate agents often say, every real estate property is unique. Various factors influence selling price: the structure itself (e.g., age of structure, floor area, state of repair); the plot of land (e.g., land area, drainage, road access, and zoning); and neighbourhood characteristics (e.g., traffic volumes on nearby streets, 'prestige' of the area, amenities nearby, accessibility to the rest of the city).

How, then, might we think of a real estate market for Winnipeg, say, if in fact all the properties being transacted are different? The counter-argument made by real estate economists is that, although price does indeed differ from one property to the next, it does so in a regular and predictable fashion. Suppose dwellings with two bathrooms typically sell for $5,000 more than dwellings with only one bathroom. We can still imagine a single market for housing wherein, whatever the market prices for the two types of dwelling, the difference between them will be $5,000. Note that, with this convenience, we switch from a separate market for each property, in which there are presumably few actors, to one market with many properties and hence many actors. For this idea to make sense, each property has to be sufficiently standardized so that the distinction between any two properties (in the case above, an additional bathroom) is readily discerned and priced.

Complementary to this is the notion that we can partition a real estate market into two or more submarkets. It is common to think of a city's real estate market in terms of submarkets by type of property: e.g., one submarket for residences, another for commercial, and still another for industrial. We differentiate these submarkets in part because their bids for land respond to different site amenities (e.g., proximity to an expressway exit versus a ravine or mountain slope) and in part because the demand is driven by different factors (e.g., locations of customers versus locations of employers). Other times, we might think of tenure submarkets for housing, for example, owner-occupied versus rental accommodation. At still other times, we can imagine submarkets defined by neighbourhood—that is, we might argue that the price gap between two neighbourhoods will grow or shrink for some reason. We might readily argue that one submarket is linked to the next because price effects can reasonably be expected to 'spill over'. If rents go up substantially in the residential rental submarket, for instance, we might expect some tenants to switch tenure, thus leading to more demand, and hence higher prices, in the homeowner submarket. Nonetheless, submarket partitioning makes sense because prices offered or demanded may well be different depending on the submarket targeted. In other words, the price for property in two submarkets will respond to different factors (especially in the short run), even though real estate prices in general are affected by much the same market forces and tend to move similarly over the longer run. Empirical research of this type is mainly focused on the US, and includes Blackley and Follain (1987), Heikkila et al. (1989), and Waddell et al. (1993).

What Motivates Investment in Real Estate?

This chapter argues that cities are vehicles for the efficient production of valuable real estate. The concepts of risk management and liquidity help us to understand what motivates investment. Let us consider two illustrative examples of a real estate investment problem. In the first case, property is developed initially for purposes of accommodation; in the second, for purposes of asset acquisition or investment.

Firm Builds Factory for Own Use

In the first example, a manufacturing firm invests in a new factory in the year 2000. The following costs are incurred:

- *Asset acquisition.* The firm buys a site with road frontage that is serviced with utilities. The firm improves the site by levelling, installing drainage, and building loading and parking facilities. It then builds a factory to manufacture its product. It purchases and installs the machinery necessary for production. Each of these is a once-only cost incurred in the year 2000.
- *Operating expense.* The firm then undertakes production there at a fixed annual cost (inflation is ignored here, but normal expenses on maintenance and improvements are included).

Suppose that the manufacturer considers several sites. For each site, the firm can calculate the present cost of construction and operation. Presumably, the manufacturer will choose that site where present cost is lowest. Suppose, for example, that two sites are possible: A and B. At site A, the one-time-only asset acquisition cost in year 2000 is $30 million and the annual operating expenditure is $2 million thereafter. If the discount rate is 5 per cent, the present value of this stream of operating expense into the infinite future is $2 million/0.05 = $40 million.[1] Together, asset acquisition and operating expense amount to $70 million. At site B, suppose that the acquisition cost is higher ($35 million), but this is offset by a lower annual operating expense ($1.5 million annually). This lower cost could be the result of lower taxes or wage rates, or increased productivity because of access to a superior labour force; most often, transport costs figure heavily in an industry's operating costs. At the same discount rate, the present value of asset acquisition cost and operating expense at B is $35 + 1.5/0.05 = $65 million. Therefore, site B is chosen because it has the lower present cost (even though, at $35 million, it is more expensive to build).

The manufacturer's decision is only slightly more complicated if the firm plans to keep this factory for only a finite length of time. Suppose, for example, that the firm plans to produce at the chosen site from 2001 through 2020 inclusive and then sell the property (including building and equipment). The firm believes that it can resell site A for $27 million, but that site B can be resold for only $23.6 million. Table 7.1 shows outlays (negative for resale price since it offsets earlier expenditures). Outlay (o_t) in year t is discounted back to year 2000 using the expression $o_t/(1+r)^t$ where $r = 0.05$ is the discount rate. The totals shown at the bottom of the table sum these discounted outlays to give the present value of the net outlays in year 2000. Using this table, our hypothetical manufacturer would be indifferent between the two sites. In this case, the advantage of site B, because of lower operating expense, is fully offset by the prospect of a poor resale price in 2021.

Table 7.1   **Outlays for Sites A and B**

Year	Outlay (millions of current dollars)		Present value of outlay (millions of dollars discounted to year 2000)	
	Site A	Site B	Site A	Site B
Asset acquisition				
2000	30.0	35.0	30.0	35.0
Operating expense				
2001	2.0	1.5	1.9	1.4
2002	2.0	1.5	1.8	1.4
2003	2.0	1.5	1.7	1.3
2004	2.0	1.5	1.6	1.2
2005	2.0	1.5	1.6	1.2
2006	2.0	1.5	1.5	1.1
2007	2.0	1.5	1.4	1.1
2008	2.0	1.5	1.4	1.0
2009	2.0	1.5	1.3	1.0
2010	2.0	1.5	1.2	0.9
2011	2.0	1.5	1.2	0.9
2012	2.0	1.5	1.1	0.8
2013	2.0	1.5	1.1	0.8
2014	2.0	1.5	1.0	0.8
2015	2.0	1.5	1.0	0.7
2016	2.0	1.5	0.9	0.7
2017	2.0	1.5	0.9	0.7
2018	2.0	1.5	0.8	0.6
2019	2.0	1.5	0.8	0.6
2020	2.0	1.5	0.8	0.6
Resale value				
2021	−27.0	−23.6	−9.7	−8.5
Total (Present value of outlay net of resale)			45.2	45.2

Unfortunately for our manufacturer, the choice of site is not so simple once we consider four risks that confront the firm. One risk is that the asset acquisition cost and/or operating expense might not be what had been expected. If, for example, the firm is sufficiently uncertain about the relative savings in future operating expense at site B, it might prefer to build at A. At least that way the firm saves the $5 million in asset acquisition costs. A second risk is that changes in production technology or in customer demand could make the plant obsolete after just a few years. In the example above, the advantage of site B is the saving in operating expense downstream; if that saving is curtailed by obsolescence, site A starts to look more attractive. A third risk concerns the expected resale price of the property. In Table 7.1, given the resale price at A, the firm prefers site B if its resale price exceeds $23.6 million and prefers site A if the resale price at B is less than that amount. Whichever site the firm chooses, it must bear the risk in 2021 of having made the wrong choice.

The fourth risk concerns liquidity of the asset at resale. In a worst-case situation, the manufacturer has to salvage machinery and fittings and then abandon the structure; in this case, the real estate investment is illiquid. (This may sound extreme but it is in fact close to what has happened to former central city industrial lands across North America. The case of Detroit, cited in Chapter 3, epitomizes the problem.) In a best-case situation, the firm resells the property (including installed machinery) quickly and at the anticipated price. In such a situation, the firm's real estate investment is liquid. These are two polar cases; in fact, properties may range from more to less liquid. In Table 7.1 (where the firm is indifferent—i.e., does not have a preference—at the expected resale prices), the firm would then choose site A on the basis of liquidity.

The risk associated with liquidity has three important implications. First, the quest for improved liquidity will attract firms to town sites over non-urban locations, and to cities over towns. The larger the local property market, the more liquid the investment. A second implication is that if firms prefer to invest in real estate that is more liquid, their demands will cause the present-day price of property to rise in preferred locations. The firm looking for a liquid site in a town or city will find that it is correspondingly more expensive. The third implication has to do with risk aversion. Since some people are gamblers by nature while others are cautious, we might expect firms to mirror these various attitudes to risk. For example, suppose the firm manufactures colour pigments to sell to paint and wallpaper makers. Usually, pigment factories are difficult to convert into some other use. They contain large tanks for storing liquid chemicals, an extensive network of pipes to feed these chemicals to mixers, and a tiered layout to accommodate efficiently the accompanying furnaces (to dry precipitates) and blenders (to grind and mix the resulting granules). Because of these specialized needs, the pigment manufacturer appears to be more risk-averse than is a firm that needs only a one-floor factory site of standard size. Put differently, the pigment manufacturer would be willing to pay a premium for a site that has more liquidity. The implication here is that, all other things being equal, firms especially sensitive to risk will migrate to the larger cities despite higher property values; the firms that are less sensitive to risk will migrate to smaller cities and towns.

What can a manufacturer do to mitigate the four risks listed above? Some of the possible actions need not have any effect on real estate investment or property prices. One action that directly affects property price and real estate investment is that the firm keeps these risks in mind as it makes decisions about maintenance, renovations, and additions to the property. In each case, the firm will consider how these actions affect the resale price. Second, unless intending to remain at the site for a long time, the firm will be cautious about major investments in structure that, while improving the efficiency of production, make it difficult to resell the property later on. Third, the firm might participate in public deliberations about zoning, building codes, and provision of municipal infrastructure (e.g., road improvements) as these affect its own property price both directly and indirectly (through

their effect on properties nearby). A fourth action is that the firm joins a business improvement association or other voluntary business organization that lobbies government and takes other initiatives to improve business and/or property values in the area. A fifth action is that the firm purchases a site in a designated industrial park. In this case, the developer generally sells properties with restrictive covenants in the deed that prevent firms in the industrial park from taking actions that undermine property values for fellow owners.

Up to this point, we have assumed that the firm purchases property and builds its own plant. In many circumstances, however, the firm will choose instead to lease its factory premises from a landlord. In part, a decision to lease is a question of financial capital; the firm may simply not have enough capital to buy a building as well as cover the equipment, inventory, and other demands. In part, the firm rents space because it wants to focus on what it does best. It may be very efficient at producing, distributing, and marketing its product, but not very good at managing real estate. The decision to lease also represents an attempt by the firm to spread the risks associated with the real estate market. Leasing a production site usually involves less cost or risk downstream should the firm have to quit that site. This presumes, of course, that other investors (commercial landlords) are willing to take part of these risks because they have expertise in the property management business.[2]

Landlord and Rental Residential Building

Suppose that an investor plans to construct and operate a rental apartment building as a profit-making enterprise. Let us assume that the investor puts in some equity as a downpayment on the building and finances the rest with a bank mortgage. Once the building is completed, the landlord provides accommodation to tenants in the form of floor space, fittings and equipment, heat, and other amenities and services in return for a monthly rent. In some respects, this example looks like the first example except that here the landlord is providing accommodation services to tenants; in the first example, the manufacturer was its own 'tenant'.

The landlord behaves like the manufacturer; he or she, too, will seek a property where profits are maximized after taking risk into account. There are similarities in the risks borne as well. The landlord faces risks of changes in prices and profitability, and also has concerns about liquidity. In some markets, acceptable new tenants are plentiful, apartment vacancy rates are low, and rents keep up with or exceed inflation because the market for accommodation services is liquid. In other markets, new tenants are scarce, vacancies are high, and rents sag; the accommodation market is illiquid. Other things being equal, a landlord would prefer to invest in an apartment building in an area where the market for accommodation services is liquid. In this sense, the market for accommodation services and the market for real estate assets are linked.[3]

A landlord's problem is complicated by matters of property maintenance. Suppose that the landlord knows that the obtainable market rent for an apartment is directly related to his/her expenditure on maintenance, renovation, and upkeep. Suppose that a landlord considers spending $1,000 more today on upkeep. Presumably, this will generate more rent revenue both this year and in the future, and possibly a higher resale value for the property downstream. After discounting future revenue gains back to today to take into account interest rates, suppose that gain amounts to $1,500. Such an investment would therefore be attractive to the landlord. At the same time, we might expect diminishing marginal returns; that is, tenants are willing to pay more rent for better upkeep, but their willingness to pay declines at the margin as the level of upkeep improves. Therefore, a landlord will put money into maintenance up to the point where a marginal dollar expended is rewarded with a dollar increase in discounted future gains (in rent for the accommodation and in resale price for the property).

What makes this example different from the first is the nature of the contractual relationship between landlord and tenant. The landlord's stream of profits to be earned over the ensuing years depends on the market rents to be paid by the tenant. Suppose that the landlord has a 35-year fixed-rate mortgage on the building. The interest rate on that mortgage presumably takes into account the expected inflation over the period.[4] A landlord might therefore wish to rent the apartments on a 35-year lease with an annual 1 per cent rent escalation clause to match. If, instead, the landlord leases apartments for periods of from one to three years only, he or she must bear the risk that rents in the future may not keep up with the inflation anticipated in the mortgage interest rate. A tenant who is willing to take a 35-year lease (that is, one that matches the landlord's mortgage) assumes the inflation risk in lieu of the landlord, but few tenants in the North American context find a long-term lease attractive, presumably because with a 35-year lease the price to a tenant starts to look much like the price of home-ownership itself. Therefore, consumers do not choose between short- and long-term leases so much as they choose between (short-term) leases and (long-term) home-ownership.

This example also differs from the first in that tenancies usually are guided by a lease agreement. A lease is a contract between landlord and tenant that details the occupancy arrangement and specifies the rights and responsibilities of each party. Tenancies are also subject to the provisions of 'landlord and tenant' legislation in each province, other legislation that takes precedence (e.g., the Charter of Rights), and to precedents in English common law or Quebec's civil code. A lease is a device by which landlord and tenant agree to allocate the foreseeable risks associated with their mutual endeavour. The tenant typically lacks information about the landlord. The tenant presumably wants quiet enjoyment of the property and intends that the lease require that of this landlord or any successor. The landlord similarly lacks much information about the tenant. The landlord wants to be assured that the tenant will not (1) waste heat, electricity, or other utilities that are to be paid by the landlord, (2) be noisy, disruptive, unruly, dangerous, or unsanitary, (3) be tardy in payment of rent, or (4) vandalize or cause undue wear and tear to the property. The lease typically sets out the length of the contract, options for renewal, security deposit, a schedule of rents, performance standards to be met by the landlord and tenant, penalties for failure to perform, and conditions for termination. In part, also, a lease reduces the risk of the 'moral hazard' in renting—the possibility that tenants may use or abuse the property in ways that they would not if they themselves owned it.

What risks does the landlord face in making this investment decision? As with the manufacturer, the landlord runs the risk that the asset acquisition cost or operating expense might not be what had been expected. In part, this is because of the risk of inflation. In addition, costs also vary because tenants differ in terms of usage, for example, heat and utilities, wear and tear, and vandalism. Part of the landlord's job is to differentiate among prospective tenants, to find the least costly tenant to serve at the given market rent. A second risk concerns the expected resale price of the property. Resale price is partly tied to the value of the rental building as a going concern. It is also tied to the potential for conversion to some other use. The third risk, as mentioned above, concerns liquidity of the asset at resale. These risks vary substantially with location. In general, the risks are lower in large cities than in smaller towns and non-urban areas.

A final risk is that rent revenue will be less than what was expected at the outset. This can occur because vacancy rates turn out to be higher than expected or because of overbuilding. If many landlords decide to invest in new buildings at the same time, rents will be depressed. This is not uncommon because new buildings may take a couple of years to construct.

What can an investor do to mitigate the risks involved in rental housing markets? There are several mechanisms by which an investor can spread the risks involved. We have already seen how the landlord uses a lease to share risks with tenants. Other investors reduce risks by owning rental properties in several different markets, perhaps different cities or different submarkets within the same city.

Others use various contracting mechanisms to spread risks among various owners, partners, and/or shareholders.

- The investor can incorporate as a limited-liability firm. Here, the investor caps his/her loss at the initial equity contribution. If the business becomes unprofitable and the firm is forced into bankruptcy, the investor's loss is limited to this initial equity. In this way, other lenders, notably the mortgage holder, bear more of the risk involved.

- The investor can focus on just one aspect of rental housing investment (say, new construction). The investor constructs the new rental building and then immediately sells it to a second investor who will operate the building. In this way, the risks are shared between them. This method is workable only if there is a second investor—the buyer—with sufficient capital, management skill, and the willingness to take on the risk of purchasing and maintaining the building as a rental property. Another variant of this is the investor who constructs the building, passes title to a partnership, and then syndicates the project (that is, sells partnership units) to potential investors. Usually, this scheme also requires a property manager to take care of the building operation on a day-to-day basis. This scheme is used when investors each have only a small amount of capital or are more risk-averse.

- The investor can create a limited partnership. Here, one person becomes the general partner, taking most of the risk and most of the profit; other investors earn smaller profits in return for limited liability (that is, less risk).

- Another variant is condominium syndication. Here the builder registers the property as a condominium, sells units to investors, and a property manager then rents out units in the building to tenants on behalf of the unit owners. This is like a partnership except that here each investor owns legal title to a dwelling (as opposed to simply a partnership interest).[5]

- Still another variant is the head lease, whereby an investor as landlord gives a head lease on the entire building to a property manager who then rents out individual units to tenants, collects rents, and earns a profit based on the difference.
- As well, the investor can mitigate risks by taking actions that improve the liquidity of the property. Standardization is the key here.

Innovations in Financing

In the last half-century, there have been several innovations in the method of financing real estate. Much of this innovation has occurred in the housing sector. Perhaps the most important of these was the mortgage insurance scheme first introduced by the federal government in 1954. This scheme, operated under the National Housing Act and popularly known as NHA insurance, insures institutional lenders against loss through default by the borrower household (see also Chapter 16). Suppose, for example, that a household purchases a home for $150,000 and puts $30,000 of its own money down. The remaining $120,000 is mortgaged. The household, as 'policyholder', pays a single lump-sum insurance premium (say $3,000) at the time a first mortgage is negotiated; this is usually added to the mortgage principal (now $123,000).[6] Because a lender would otherwise charge a higher interest rate to cover default loss, mortgage insurance lowers the applicable interest rate by spreading the risk of default across all participating borrowers. Whether an individual household is made better or worse off depends on whether the savings in interest expense are sufficient to offset the insurance premium.

A second important innovation in financing real estate has been the emergence of secondary mortgage markets. The 'primary' mortgage market is the familiar retail market in which mortgage loans are originated. There, a borrower (the property owner) might go to a mortgage originator (e.g., bank, trust company, or mortgage broker) to obtain that mortgage. Prior to the advent of the second-ary mortgage market, the mortgage originator would use the moneys of depositors to fund these mortgages. The secondary mortgage market is less familiar. It is the market where mortgage originators sell their mortgages. A bank might, for example, bundle together 1,000 mortgages and sell them to a pension fund. In this way, the bank can focus on the parts of mortgage lending where it has strength, that is, in the retailing and servicing of mortgages. For its part, the secondary market purchaser (the pension plan) earns interest on its investment and assumes risks, for example, the risks of default, early prepayment, and inflation. Another related mortgage security facility is the mortgage-backed security (MBS).[7]

A third innovation has been the development of the real estate investment trust (REIT). Typically, a REIT is formed by a developer. The developer constructs buildings for the rental market; these might be apartment buildings, offices, hotels, shopping centres, or industrial parks. The developer then sells these buildings to a REIT. Generally, a REIT includes properties drawn from different cities and different regions across the country. The REIT then issues a security, called a 'unit', which can be bought or sold by investors. Each unit entitles the owner to a proportion of the net annual revenue from the REIT properties: revenue here may include both the rents paid by tenants and the moneys received from resale of a property. In a sense, a REIT is like a real estate corporation, and units in a REIT are like shares in a corporation. The principal difference is that a REIT is primarily a means for flowing income back to the small investor, whereas a real estate corporation might well choose to retain its earnings and use them to build up the corporation. For further discussion, see Schulkin (1970), Windish (1991), Han and Liang (1995), and Nelson and Owens (1996).

Real Estate and Local Government

Much has to be done to create and protect valuable real estate. Until now, I have focused on the contributions and decisions made by the property owner. However, local governments also play an important role in shaping the value of real estate. In general, real estate development is heavily regulated: from building codes, to zoning by-laws, to property maintenance standards. Such regulations can sometimes be seen simply as 'red tape', that is, as unnecessary and indeed inefficient. At the same time, much regulation is an outcome in part of the desire by owners to protect or enhance property values. Regulation affects property values. Local governments also play a role through decisions in regard to spending and taxation. The value of real estate is also heavily influenced by public spending on hard services in the vicinity: roads and sidewalks, water and sewer lines, parks and recreation centres. Also important is spending across the community for soft services: fire-fighters and police, social services, public transit. All of these expenditures can help to make a community more attractive to residents and/or businesses. At the same time, these hard and soft services have to be financed through taxation and other charges. If local taxation is onerous (that is, if the benefits provided by public services pale in comparison to the taxes that fund them), businesses and households will not want to locate in that city and the real estate market will be correspondingly depressed. This explains why, for example, taxation rates have been a major item on the agenda of the new City of Toronto, which has very real concerns that its high property tax relative to the outlying suburbs, the so-called '905' area, depresses growth.

An implication here has to do with the level of government at which regulation occurs. If regulation varies locally, real estate investors must learn the intricacies in each new municipality where they choose to invest. On the other hand, if the regulation is standardized at the provincial or national level, then investors do not have to relearn the intricacies as they move from municipality to municipality. The Canadian approach to building codes reflects this idea. Before the 1970s, construction standards for the most part were a local matter. If you were a real estate investor in Toronto, you would have to learn the city's building code to know what you were permitted to build. If you decided instead to build in Mississauga, there would

have been a different code. In the 1970s, the provincial governments gradually took over the regulation of construction, so that now, for example, the province of Ontario has a single building code. Further, as each of the provincial codes is based on the model building code of the National Research Council, there are many similarities to construction standards across Canada. These serve to reduce the risk of real estate investment for investors who are new to a municipality but who have had experience in investing in other communities.

A related argument about regulation is that it improves the liquidity of property. Suppose that you are considering purchasing an older apartment building for the purposes of renting it out. You will carry out the usual investigations, researching current market rents and vacancy rates, checking for necessary repairs and overdue maintenance, and looking for outstanding work orders or liens on the building. Also important are the quality of construction of the building and the quality of repairs and renovations that have been done over the years. The advantage of having a building code, with attendant building inspections, is that when such work is done it must meet the minimum standards set in the code. Such regulation helps to assure the new investor that substandard practices were not used. Put differently, regulation helps to reduce the risk to the purchaser of real estate.

When viewed from the perspective of risk, the tools available to local government include more than just regulation, taxation, and spending. One important tool is a decision-making process that is responsive and, at the same time, stable and well defined. Mayors quickly learn the importance that investors attach to local governments that are not capricious—that is, that do not suddenly change policy or direction. Investors know that property values are sensitive to decisions that municipal councils make about changing regulations, taxation, and spending. To avoid unnecessary risk, investors prefer municipalities where governments 'stay the course'. If governments are going to change course, investors prefer that this happens in well-defined and predictable ways so that real estate developments can be planned accordingly. Important here is the structure of municipal decision-making. Players in this structure include the committees, boards, and commissions that deliberate and consider facets of a policy issue before making a decision, the professional administrative staff that advises them, and local non-governmental organizations (the Chamber of Commerce, service clubs, neighbourhood associations) that consult and are consulted. Put differently, investors are reassured by municipalities where civic-mindedness is widespread, that have a capacity to build a consensus, and that can remain focused on long-run goals.

Here, then, is another rationale for the emergence of cities, that is, the management property that was discussed at some length in the introductory chapter to this volume. Any size of community can be civic-minded and, depending on its leadership, have the ability to remain focused on long-term goals. The problem for small communities, however, is to have the range of committees, boards, and commissions, and the professional administrative staff, to make good decisions. In larger cities it is easier to find the range of people with talent and experience necessary to make good government.

Conclusion

A city is just real estate. On the one hand, such a statement is trivially true. To know that a city is made up of buildings would not seem to tell us much in answer to basic questions such as why cities exist, how they operate, and why and how they change over time. However, this chapter has argued that the essential point is that investment in real estate creates risks and that cities are mechanisms for reducing these risks. In part, this is because cities are agglomerations of buyers and sellers of property and thus provide a strong market for the purchase and sale of property assets. In part, it is because city governments can provide the stable decision-making environment for public policy that helps to reduce the risk of real estate investment.

Notes

1. Put differently, $40 million is the present value because that amount invested at 5 per cent would generate $2 million annually in perpetuity: just enough to cover the recurring annual operating expense.

2. For example, in terms of minimizing construction and operation costs, making maintenance and renovation decisions wisely, finding new tenants for the property downstream, and predicting resale prices and conversion opportunities. Also, commercial landlords may be sufficiently diversified to avoid the risks of a downturn in the local property market. By holding property in several different cities or in different kinds of property markets within the same city, commercial landlords in effect ensure themselves against adverse conditions in any one market.

3. Of course, there are parallels to each of these arguments in the example of the manufacturer above. What is novel in this second example is an emphasis on the role of landlord as financier and risk-taker. The manufacturer takes risks in that he or she 'borrows long' (invests equity in plant and equipment) to 'lend short' (sell to consumers amounts at a time that are a small fraction of lifetime production at the factory). The landlord, too, borrows long (that is, takes a long-term mortgage from the bank) in order to lend short (that is, rent floor space out month-to-month).

4. For example, a bank that expects 1 per cent annual inflation in consumer prices would insist on a mortgage rate in excess of that amount to allow for a 'real' return on its investment.

5. Other factors may also make condominium syndication more attractive to investors. In Ontario, for example, property tax assessments (and therefore property taxes) are usually higher for apartments in rental buildings than for otherwise similar condominium units or other owner-occupied homes.

6. In the event that the household defaults in its mortgage payments, the institutional lender is expected to seize the property and to recoup its loan from the sale proceeds. If the lender is still owed $118,000 at the time of foreclosure and the property nets only $105,000 upon resale, the lender (as beneficiary) is insured against loss.

7. In an MBS scheme, an agent called a 'securitizer' (often a bank or other large financial institution) takes a large pool of mortgages and sells a security that distributes the monthly mortgage payments (principal plus interest) to investors. Suppose, for example, that a bank has a bundle of new five-year mortgages, with an aggregate present value of $1 billion, against which it issues 20 million units in an MBS at $50 per unit. Each unit holder gets a proportional monthly flow of interest and principal repayment, and the risk that any one mortgager defaults is spread across all unit holders. In this way, small investors can purchase units and participate with less risk than in the conventional mortgage market.

References

Alonso, W. 1964. *Location and Land Use: Toward a General Theory of Land Rent.* Cambridge, Mass.: Harvard University Press.

Blackley, D.M., and J.R. Follain. 1987. 'Tests of Locational Equilibrium in the Standard Urban Model', *Land Economics* 63: 46–61.

DiPasquale, D., and W.C. Wheaton. 1996. *Urban Economics and Real Estate Markets.* Englewood Cliffs, NJ: Prentice-Hall.

Han, J., and Y. Liang. 1995. 'The Historical Performance of Real Estate Investment Trusts', *Journal of Real Estate Research* 10, 3: 235–62.

Harris, R. 1996. *Unplanned Suburbs: Toronto's American Tragedy, 1900 to 1950.* Baltimore: Johns Hopkins University Press.

Heikkila, E., et al. 1989. 'What Happened to the CBD-Distance Gradient? Land Values in a Polycentric City', *Environment and Planning A* 21, 2: 221–32.

Nelson, W.A., and R.W. Owens. 1996. 'Rockefeller Center Properties, Inc.: A REIT Case Study', *Journal of Real Estate Literature* 4, 1: 65–70.

Schulkin, P.A. 1970. 'Real Estate Investment Trusts: A New Financial Intermediary', *New England Economic Review:* 2–14.

Turnbull, G.K. 1995. *Urban Consumer Theory.* Washington: Urban Institute Press.

Waddell, P., et al. 1993. 'Residential Property Values in a Multinodal Urban Area: New Evidence on the Implicit Price of Location', *Journal of Real Estate Finance and Economics* 7, 2: 117–41.

Windish, D.F. 1991. *Real Estate Taxation: A Practitioner's Guide.* Chicago: Commerce Clearing House.

Wingo, L. 1961. *Transportation and Urban Land.* Washington: Resources for the Future.

Chapter 8

Transportation and Communication

Eric J. Miller

Over the past 50 years urban planning has given priority to accommodating the car. We are increasingly confronted with problems resulting from this strategy: traffic congestion, high urban development expenses, and, most seriously, pollution. Transportation planning, along with land-use planning, has contributed to low urban density and high levels of land-use segregation, that is, to the postwar urban form that is still replicated today.

This chapter discusses the urban transportation system and the planning process associated with the design and evolution of this system. A primary focus is on the interaction between transportation and urban form, as well as the three-way interconnections among transportation, communications, and urban form. Key transportation policy issues are discussed, as are the range of alternatives available for addressing these issues. Important attributes of both the demand and supply sides of the transportation system are described, as are the analytical methods used to forecast travel behaviour.

Transportation and Urban Form

The role of the urban transportation system is to provide the means by which people and goods can move from point to point within an urban area to participate in the broad range of activities (economic, social, recreational, etc.) that define urban life. In so doing, the transportation system provides 'operational spatial definition' to an urban area. That is, the distance between two points, *per se*, is not of primary importance in the determination of the

level of interaction between these points. Rather, it is the relative ease of travel (as defined by travel time and cost, frequency and reliability of service, etc.) that will affect where, when, and how often people will travel for various purposes.

Figure 8.1a provides a simplified representation of the interaction between the *transportation system* and the *urban activity system*. As defined in this figure, the urban activity system consists of:

- the spatial distribution of *land uses* (buildings of different types, purposes and densities, etc.), which are determined through the land development and redevelopment process;
- the spatial distribution of the *location* of people (i.e., where they live) and activities (jobs, stores, schools, etc.), which are determined through the location choices of households, firms, etc.;
- the spatial and temporal distribution of the *activity patterns* in which people engage daily.

The transportation system, in turn, consists of:

- the *network* (streets, expressways, rail lines, etc.), other physical infrastructure (stations, control systems, etc.), and *services* (transit, taxi, etc.) that collectively provide the potential for travel within the urban area (that is, the *supply* of transportation services);
- the extent to which people have *access to automobiles* for their personal use;
- the spatial and temporal distributions of *flows* of people and vehicles over the transportation network resulting from people's participation

Figure 8.1   **Transportation-Activity System Interactions**

a) The Urban Activity and Transportation Systems

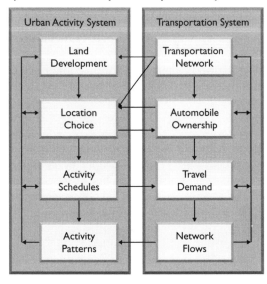

b) System Interactions

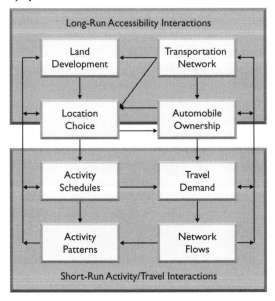

Source: Adapted from Meyer and Miller (1984).

in activities that are distributed in both time and space.[1]

As is highlighted in Figure 8.1a, both the activity system and the transportation system can be viewed as semi-independent, each being evolutionary and dynamic in nature. The activity system evolves over time (new land is developed and previously developed land is redeveloped for new uses; households and firms move in and out of the urban area as well as relocate within this area; activity schedules and patterns change) in response to a wide variety of stimuli, some endogenous to the system (e.g., new land-use patterns may emerge in response to changing activity patterns) and some exogenous to the system *per se* (e.g., zoning, interest rates, macroeconomic trends). The transportation system, similarly, has its own 'internal logic' by which both the supply of and demand for transportation services will respond over time to en-

dogenous factors such as roadway congestion levels and exogenous factors such as government subsidies, the price of gasoline, etc.

As depicted in Figure 8.1b, however, the two (urban activity and transportation) systems are also interconnected in several significant ways, with these interconnections running in both directions and occurring in both the short and the long run. As has already been briefly discussed, the transportation system defines the *accessibility* of each point in space to every other point in space and thereby influences long-run (year by year, decade by decade) decisions concerning both land development and location choice. In the short run (daily, weekly), the activity participation and travel demand processes are inextricably linked, given that participation in out-of-home activities requires travel and that the location, timing, and duration of these activities may well be influenced by the availability, cost, etc. of the travel options available to the participant.

Decisions of auto ownership might be qualified as 'medium-run' in that they occur more frequently than most location choices but much less frequently than most activity/travel decisions. Auto ownership, however, interacts with both the longer-run location decisions (choice of both residential and employment locations may well affect decisions concerning auto ownership and/or be constrained in turn by feasible ownership levels) and the short-run activity/travel decisions (which will be conditional on current auto availability constraints, but might over time influence changes in auto ownership so as to better match this level with household activity/travel needs and aspirations).

Over the very long run, the historical influence of transportation on urban form has been profound and readily apparent. Prior to the mid-nineteenth century, walking and horse-drawn vehicles were the primary means of transportation, resulting in small, dense cities that were often circular or semi-circular in shape to maximize pedestrian accessibility. The inner cores of many Maritime cities display characteristics of the 'horse-cart-pedestrian city' (Yeates and Garner, 1980), while the old town portion of Quebec City provides a classic example of this urban form.

The Industrial Revolution and associated technological innovations in transportation generated dramatic changes in urban form in the second half of the nineteenth century and early-twentieth century. Industries depended heavily on rail transportation for the movement of raw materials into their factories and finished products out.[2] The result was high-density industrial areas stretching along the rail lines passing through the city. Given that the railway was the primary means of intercity person travel, these lines invariably penetrated directly to the centre of the city (the point of maximum access to the resident population and business community).

Industrialization created considerable new demand for labour, attracting many workers and their families to the city. The poorer among these workers settled in high-density housing located within walking distance of the factories where they worked, both because they could not afford to live elsewhere and because higher-income households avoided these areas due to the high pollution levels typical of nineteenth-century industrial areas.

Given the need for face-to-face contact, direct access to clients, and the still relatively rudimentary state of communications and transportation, retail and commercial activity remained concentrated in the city centre (the central business district or CBD). This concentration was further encouraged by advances in building technology (that is, the emergence of high-rise buildings), which permitted significant increases in the density of commercial activities. Unlike factory workers, however, the white-collar employees of CBD businesses were not tied to housing within walking distance of their places of employment. Rather, new modes of transit—principally street railways (first horse-drawn but then much more effective electric-powered streetcars) and longer-distance commuter railways (first steam, later electric or diesel)[3]—permitted middle-class and upper-middle-class households to move out of the city centre to new homes located on larger lots in lower-density 'streetcar suburbs' (Warner, 1962).

Although densities along these rail lines were lower than in the CBD, the need to be within convenient walking distance of the streetcar line or commuter rail station ensured that densities in most cases remained at least moderately high. Further, local stores and restaurants serving the streetcar suburb tended to concentrate with relatively high density along the streetcar line (or at the commuter rail station) so as to be within walking distance or a short streetcar ride of the resident population.

The result of these various trends was, by the beginning of the twentieth century, much larger cities (in terms of space, population, and economic activity) than could possibly have existed a century before. While the detailed arrangements of these cities were dictated by local geography and historical evolution, their overall structure tended to be quite similar: a dense central area containing most major commercial activities, well-defined industrial areas with associated low-income worker housing stretching along intercity rail corridors penetrating the city, and middle-class and upper-middle-class white-collar residential neighbourhoods of moderate to high density stretching along streetcar and commuter rail lines radiating from the CBD. All major Canadian cities of the time (Montreal, Toronto, Vancouver, Winnipeg) displayed this general structure, which survives to this day in these metropolitan regions' older portions.

The automobile first emerged as a cost-effective means of transportation for many people with Henry Ford's mass-produced Model T in 1908. Although the impact of the auto on travel patterns (e.g., declining transit ridership per capita) could be discerned in the United States as early as the mid-1920s (Jones, 1985), only since World War II have the full impacts of the automobile on lifestyles, travel, and urban form been felt. The postwar period was one of considerable economic and demographic growth throughout Canada, creating an unprecedented demand for new housing. Most of this new housing was provided on newly developed land on the urban fringe in low-density suburban housing tracts. The almost ubiquitous availability of the automobile both facilitated and encouraged this low-density, dispersed suburban design. Indeed, the postwar low-density suburb requires universal access to the automobile, since almost no 'trip ends' (stores, jobs, etc.) are within walking distance of the suburban home and conventional transit cannot cost-effectively serve the dispersed travel patterns generated by such low-density developments.

Retail and other population-serving activities quickly followed their markets to the suburbs. Generally, they first located in unplanned strip developments along major arterials. Calgary's Ventura Boulevard is a classic example of this type of location, although similar examples can be found in all Canadian urban areas (Boal and Johnson, 1965). But it is now more typical for such activities to opt for large, planned shopping malls located at points of transportation advantage such as expressway intersections. In the last 20 years or so manufacturing and office activities have also suburbanized to a considerable extent, reflecting changes in transportation (shifts from rail to trucking for shipping goods), communications (advanced communications systems reduce the need to be tied to CBD locations), production methods, land values, and taxes, among other factors.

Associated with the suburbanization of people and activities is the trend to segregate land uses. In both the pre-industrial and the nineteenth-century cities land uses tended to be interspersed and integrated (i.e., stores were beside houses, which were themselves beside offices, etc.) so as to maximize pedestrian-based accessibility and the use of scarce land within a dense urban structure. Partially as a result of the automobile, which eliminates the perceived need for diverse activities to be in close proximity (let alone walking distance), and partially as a result of modernist planning principles, traditional suburban land uses are almost invariably segregated into planned single-use areas: industrial parks, shopping centres, and residential developments differentiated by type and cost of housing. This leads to a considerable increase in the amount of travel required to accomplish given sets of tasks and to a total dependence on the automobile (postwar urbanization patterns are discussed from different perspectives in Chapters 1, 13, 15, and 17).

The net result of these trends in the second half of the twentieth century is, again, a dramatic increase in urban area size (with respect to population, economic activity, and, most dramatically, spatial area) and a radically different aggregate urban form. This new form involves dispersed, low-density distributions of residential, commercial, industrial, and retail areas, often in planned, segregated developments. Travel patterns are no longer concentrated within a few radial corridors. Rather, they consist of dispersed flows from many origins to many destinations. Although this dispersion results in a tremendous amount of daily travel and often considerable congestion at various points in the road network, the 'many-to-many' nature of the flows does not generate sufficient density of travel along any one corridor or route to make transit cost-effective. In addition, distance between trip ends has become too long for walking to be an option for the vast majority of trips. As a result, the automobile represents the only viable means of transportation.

Such postwar suburban/urban forms have been labelled 'nonplace city' by Webber (1964). More recently, Garreau (1991) has described them as 'edge cities'. Many US metropolitan regions are almost completely dominated by the edge city form, with the traditional central city downtown being virtually irrelevant for most purposes. Most Canadian agglomerations display a more complex pattern in that they have maintained a strong (and usually still growing), relatively dense central city, combined with dispersed, low-density growth of both population and economic activity on the urban fringe. The transportation system and associated travel flows for Canadian metropolitan regions are similarly complex, involving both heavy radial flows into/out of central cities (which are generally well served by a competitive transit system) and more dispersed many-to-many flows throughout the suburban periphery (which is fully auto-oriented).

This thumbnail sketch of the historical evolution of Canadian urban form illustrates the two-way nature of the transportation interaction described in Figure 8.1. We have seen that major shifts in transportation technology fundamentally redefined accessibility within urban areas, giving rise to new urban forms. In particular, technological advances have tended to extend the 'reach' of travellers, allowing them to travel at higher speeds and so travel further within a given amount of time. This has resulted in an expansion in the amount of land covered by urban areas (with associated reductions in average densities) as people take advantage of this extended reach to consume more land for their activities (residential or commercial). This trend towards using increased transportation speed to consume more land has been at work for the better part of two centuries now, is a worldwide phenomenon as automobile ownership and usage continue to increase, and shows little sign of abating.

At the same time, once a given land-use pattern is in place it reinforces the need for, or suitability of, a given type of transportation system.

High-density, mixed-use, radial development patterns encourage and support cost-effective rail transit systems. Walking is also a viable alternative in such areas. The low density and segregated use of edge city patterns can only support auto-based travel: trip distances are too long to walk and flow densities too low to support cost-effective transit. Thus, a positive feedback loop connects a given transportation technology to a given form of urban development and vice versa.

This observation underscores the importance of an integrated approach to transportation and land-use (that is, urban) planning if we are to achieve integrated goals. Unfortunately, this rarely occurs effectively in practice. As is implied in Figure 8.1a, the two 'systems' are typically dealt with in virtual isolation from each other. This largely reflects institutional and professional divisions. Different government agencies are typically responsible for transportation and land-use planning, and they tend to be staffed with people possessing different professional backgrounds and world-views. The result of this division is myopic decision-making in which transportation planners take land-use plans as given and plan the transportation system around these, while land-use planners do the reverse (if they consider the transportation system at all). Such an approach severs the dynamic feedbacks of Figure 8.1, replacing them with static inputs from the other side of the flowchart (an example of this approach is provided in the conventional travel demand modelling process shown in Figure 8.6 and discussed belo v). Loss of the dynamic interaction between transportation and land use is responsible for serious flaws in the planning process.

Separating transportation from land use may well cause us to look in fundamentally wrong ways at our urban problems and their possible solutions. Congestion is generally viewed as a chronic and worsening transportation problem in most Canadian cities. Since it is defined as a 'transportation problem' we seek 'transportation solutions': increases in roadway capacity, real-time traffic control, congestion pricing, etc. A more comprehensive, integrated view of the 'problem', however, might well gener-

Figure 8.2   **Population Base Trends and Planning Goals, Vancouver Long-Range Plan**

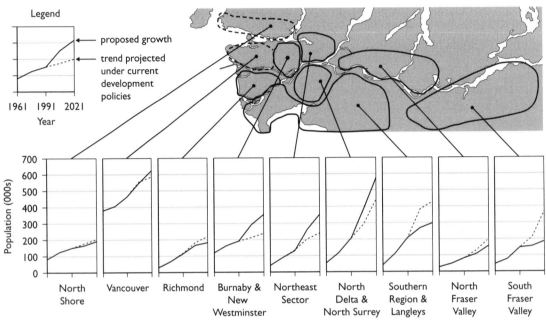

GVRD Liveable Region Strategy Proposals, 1993
(proposed population growth compared with trend)

Source: Transport 2021 (1993a).

ate quite a different diagnosis: perhaps much of our congestion arises from a land-use pattern that places too heavy a burden on the road system. An alternative land use, which could make better use of higher-capacity transit lines and encourage shorter and/or fewer trips, might well provide a more lasting solution.

Recently, the Greater Vancouver Regional District (GVRD) developed both a medium-range and a long-range transportation plan that intentionally adopted an integrated approach to land use and transportation planning. The plans take the view that current land use and transportation trends (increasing sprawl and auto orientation) are inconsistent with Vancouver's planning objectives and recommend alternative forms of development. Various combinations of land use and transportation

design are investigated. The result is a plan that calls for a departure from current development patterns, with inner suburbs designated to receive more growth and outer areas less than projected by current trends, and for central areas generally to maintain current trends (see Figure 8.2). Combined with these land-use controls are a range of medium- and long-range transportation proposals (involving both demand management and infrastructure investment) designed to support and promote the desired land-use structure. The Vancouver plan is also of interest in that it deals both with 'macro' urban form issues (that is, the overall distribution of population and employment within the urban region) and the role that 'micro' neighbourhood design plays in influencing travel behaviour (Transport 2021, 1993a, 1993b).[4]

Transportation and Communications

Communications represents the second major way we interact over space; as such, it is a potential substitute for travel. One can argue that travel is simply one more way for people who are spatially separated to communicate with one another. Historically, communications and transportation have had strong complementary effects: improved communications stimulates interactions among more people over greater distances, which in turn stimulates the demand for more travel. The net result is that increased usage of both transportation and communications has tended to go hand-in-hand with economic and demographic growth.

Communications can have direct substitution and complementary (generation) impacts on travel, as briefly discussed above. In addition, it can have indirect effects, either through secondary and tertiary impacts on people's activity/travel schedules or by altering household and firm location choices, which, in turn, will alter activity/travel patterns. The key question of interest to urban transportation planners is which of these effects will dominate the impact on travel behaviour as current and emerging information systems (fax, e-mail, Internet, conventional telephones, mobile phones, etc.) continue to play increasingly important roles in homes and businesses. Three communications-based activities that are much discussed in terms of their potential to replace their travel-based counterparts are:

- *telecommuting*, in which a person works at home rather than travels to the office;
- *teleshopping*, in which a person orders goods to be delivered to the home, either over the telephone or via computer; and
- *teleconferencing*, in which groups of people 'meet' via conference telephone calls or videoconferencing without having to travel to a common site.

As demonstrated by Mokhtarian and Salomon (1997), empirical evidence concerning the impact of telecommunications on travel is far from definitive, but, on balance, this evidence suggests that it is much smaller than forecast. There are at least three reasons for this lesser effect. First, work possesses social as well as utilitarian dimensions, and shopping is a form of recreation/entertainment for many people. It is far from certain that most people want to stay home, interacting with the world only via telephone and computer. People enjoy the stimulation of location change and social encounter. Thus, to date, market penetration of telecommunications has been less than expected due to these factors. Second, new travel can be induced that at least partially offsets trips forgone. For example, more home-based non-work travel may replace commuting to work, or more delivery van trips replace shopping trips. Third, in addition to this directly induced travel, indirect latent demand can materialize in response to system capacity that has been freed by telecommunications-related travel reductions.[5] For example, the non-worker in the household mentioned above now has access to a car. Similarly, if large numbers of former commuters work at home each day, this will reduce congestion on roadways, thereby encouraging other people to take advantage of this extra supply, either by switching from transit to auto or by making additional trips.

Even less clear is the long-run effect that modern telecommunications may have on urban form (and, hence, travel). To the extent that telecommuting means that one can live anywhere and dial into work, and that teleshopping means that physical access to stores loses importance, telecommuting is further loosening bonds between the home (and, for that matter, the firm) and activity locations and so further encourages the dispersed, low-density urban form discussed above. While anecdotal evidence exists to support this hypothesis, again, little hard data exist to indicate the extent of this impact. The travel implications of such a trend are similarly murky, although it is reasonable to speculate that while they might imply fewer traditional trips to work, shopping, etc., the trips that will be made will almost certainly be by car and may well be significantly longer on average.

Transportation Impacts: The Policy Challenge

Virtually every resident is directly affected on a daily basis by the transportation system, as is virtually every economic activity. Ideally, we would all like to travel wherever we want, when we want, at modest cost, and with minimal delay. In reality, travel is obtained at significant cost (especially if the full personal cost of auto ownership is factored in), varying degrees of schedule convenience, and, depending on the time of day and the urban area in question, considerable delay and frustration due to roadway congestion.

In addition to the direct impacts that the transportation system has on the daily activities of people and firms (that is, the *users* of the system) and its longer-run impacts on urban form, this system generates significant indirect social and environmental impacts on urban residents, users and non-users alike. These impacts are labelled 'indirect' because they are unintended consequences of transportation system operations. They include:

- *Consumption of land.* As was briefly noted above, the transportation network—in particular the road network—is a significant land use in its own right. Construction of roads and other physical transportation facilities obviously displaces previous land uses, natural or man-made.
- *Neighbourhood intrusion.* Over and above the physical displacement of other land uses and activities, the physical presence of a major transportation facility can have adverse impacts on adjoining neighbourhoods. Depending on the facility, these can include physical unsightliness, physical barriers within neighbourhoods, noise, and reduced safety on local streets (when these streets experience increased traffic due to the facility).
- *Safety.* The road system is a major cause of death, personal injury, and property damage. Despite having the fifth best safety record in OECD countries, 3,347 Canadians were killed in 1995 in traffic-related accidents, while 241,800

were injured in 166,950 collisions involving injury. In total, over 1.2 million vehicles were involved in collisions in 1995 in Canada (Transport Canada, 1997). One is hard-pressed to think of *any* other technology that inflicts such a predictable and significant toll and whose clear dangers are so willingly accepted.[6]

- *Security.* In transportation 'safety' usually refers to the level of risk due to accidents. 'Security', in turn, generally refers to the risk people feel when interacting with others within the transportation system. Growing concerns within many cities (especially larger cities) about issues such as crime on the transit system and incidents associated with 'road rage' exemplify potential security impacts.
- *Atmospheric pollution.* Fossil fuel-based vehicles are a source of many damaging atmospheric pollutants. Of particular concern are the various precursors of low-level ozone—carbon monoxide (CO), various nitrix-oxide compounds (generically referred to as NOX), different uncombusted hydrocarbons (HC, also referred to as volatile organic compounds or VOC), as well as particulate matters of varying sizes (Miller and Hassounah, 1993). In the United States, federal law (particularly the Clean Air Act Amendments of 1990) mandates maximum acceptable levels for most of these pollutants. Urban areas that are neither in compliance with these mandates nor actively moving towards such compliance are subject to serious financial penalties (e.g., loss of federal funds) and risk lawsuits from environmental groups.[7] In Canada, comparable legislation does not exist at the federal or provincial level despite concern over high air pollution levels in many Canadian metropolitan regions.
- *Other pollutants.* Other pollutants can be generated by transportation operations. Perhaps most notable is the pollution of soils and groundwater due to run-off from roadways that carries contaminants such as salt and oil.
- *Greenhouse gas emissions.* Carbon dioxide (CO_2) is one of the primary emissions from fossil fuel

combustion in road vehicles. While not a pollutant *per se* (because not directly harmful to human health), it is the dominant greenhouse gas contributing to global warming and climate change (Miller and Hassounah, 1993). The recent Kyoto Protocol agreement commits Canada to a 6 per cent reduction in CO_2 emissions relative to 1990 levels by 2012 at the latest. If this very ambitious objective is to be met, significant reductions in CO_2 emissions from the transportation sector will have to be achieved.

The policy challenge facing transportation planners and decision-makers is how best to provide the level and mix of transportation services that maximize the direct benefits derived from these services, at the same time minimizing/mitigating their adverse impacts. Central to responding to this challenge are a number of key questions:

- How best to maintain and improve the transportation system given the fiscal constraints facing all levels of government. Associated with this issue are questions concerning who pays for transportation services, the extent/nature of subsidies, how to price transportation services, etc.
- The appropriate balance between public and private provision of services, construction of infrastructure, etc. The opening in 1997 of the privately built and operated electronic toll road, Highway 407, running east–west just north of Toronto, provides a new model for highway construction and operation. Similarly, transit industry deregulation and/or privatization has occurred in recent years in many countries, most notably the United Kingdom.
- The role of transit. It is almost routinely assumed by planners that transit represents a significant part of the solution with respect to increasing urban transportation sustainability. How this can occur in the face of the urban form trends discussed above (which are both driven by and promote auto usage) is not entirely clear.
- The role of the auto. To what extent should we build more roads to meet demand? To what extent should we curtail auto usage in the name of urban sustainability?

Dimensions of Travel Behaviour

The key dimensions characterizing travel demand include space (from where to where are trips made?), time (when is the trip made, and how long does the trip take to execute?), mode (what combination of technology/service is used to undertake the trip?), and purpose. The spatial, two-dimensional nature of travel demand complicates the analysis due to the difficulty involved in visualizing travel flows over space and in dealing with the very large and complex data sets required to describe these flows. Modern geographic information systems (GIS) are of considerable assistance in this task. Still, the data and computational requirements associated with the analysis of travel demand in cities are formidable, even given modern computing capabilities.

Typical trip purposes used in travel demand analyses include: work, school, shopping, social and recreational, personal business, work-related (trips to visit clients, etc.), and the ubiquitous catch-all 'other'. Trips are often further categorized as being *home-based*, if either the origin or destination of the trip is the home, or *non-home-based* if neither 'trip end' is the home.

Clearly, the choice of travel mode is of central concern to transportation planners. Modes usually considered in planning analyses are: auto driver; auto passenger; transit; walk; and (when numbers warrant) bicycle. Auto passengers are typically separated from drivers, since their characteristics and behaviour tend to be quite different (auto passengers are more similar in their attributes to transit riders than to auto drivers), as is their impact on the transportation system. An auto driver, by definition, generates a vehicle trip with its attendant pollution and contribution to roadway congestion, while an auto passenger, *per se*, does not. Alternatively, auto drivers and passengers can be 'repackaged' into a drive-alone mode (often referred to as a 'single-occupant vehicle' or SOV trip) and a shared-ride mode (car pool, 'high-occupancy vehicle' or HOV trip). In addition, in larger metropolitan regions with complex multi-modal transit systems, such as Montreal and Toronto, the transit mode might be further divided by sub-mode (e.g., local transit versus commuter rail). In such cases, mixed modes of travel, such as trips involving the use of the car to access a commuter rail or subway line, may also be of interest.

Table 8.1 tabulates daily person trips for Edmonton in 1994, categorized by trip purpose and mode. As shown in the table, nearly three-quarters

Table 8.1   **Daily Person Trips by Trip Purpose and Mode, Edmonton CMA, 1994**

(a) Modal Split by Trip Purpose (%)

Trip Purpose	Auto Drive	Auto Passenger	Transit	Walk	Other	Total
Home-based work	78.1	7.7	8.6	4.4	1.3	100.0
Home-based post-secondary	37.4	8.8	38.1	13.2	2.5	100.0
Home-based school	2.7	34.3	12.3	32.5	18.2	100.0
Home-based shopping	64.3	21.6	6.2	7.2	0.6	100.0
Home-based social/recreation	50.0	37.1	2.5	9.2	1.3	100.0
Home-based other	61.0	28.5	3.3	6.1	1.1	100.0
Home-based subtotal	**54.1**	**24.2**	**7.4**	**10.6**	**3.8**	**100.0**
Non-home-based work	71.5	8.6	5.8	12.8	1.2	100.0
Non-home-based other	58.4	26.8	4.4	8.8	1.6	100.0
Non-home-based subtotal	**60.1**	**24.4**	**4.6**	**9.3**	**1.5**	**100.0**
Total trips by mode	**55.6**	**24.3**	**6.7**	**10.2**	**3.2**	**100.0**

(b) Distribution of Trip Purposes by Mode (%)

Trip Purpose	Auto Drive	Auto Passenger	Transit	Walk	Other	Total avg. (%)
Home-based work	23.2	5.3	21.3	7.1	6.7	16.5
Home-based post-secondary	1.7	0.9	14.9	3.3	2.1	2.6
Home-based school	0.6	16.1	21.0	36.1	64.7	11.4
Home-based shopping	11.7	9.0	9.4	7.1	2.0	10.1
Home-based social/recreation	8.6	14.6	3.6	8.6	3.9	9.6
Home-based other	26.5	28.4	12.1	14.5	8.2	24.2
Home-based subtotal	**72.3**	**74.3**	**82.2**	**76.7**	**87.7**	**74.4**
Non-home-based work	4.3	1.2	2.9	4.2	1.3	3.4
Non-home-based other	23.3	24.5	14.8	19.1	11.0	22.2
Non-home-based subtotal	**27.7**	**25.7**	**17.8**	**23.3**	**12.3**	**25.6**
Total trips	**100.0**	**100.0**	**100.0**	**100.0**	**100.0**	**100.0**

Source: AMCL (1995).

(74.4 per cent) of all trips in Edmonton are home-based, with 30.5 per cent of all trips being home-based work- or school-related.[8] Auto travel dominates, with nearly 80 per cent of all trips being made in a car, either as driver or passenger. Seventy-eight per cent of all workers drive, while 60 per cent or more of trips for almost all purposes except school are accomplished by driving a car. Although only 8.6 per cent of home-based work trips are made by transit, these represent a significant proportion of transit ridership (21.3 per cent), second only to school-related travel (35.9 per cent in total).

Figure 8.3 and Table 8.2 present additional information concerning work trip mode splits in Canadian CMAs, as reported in the 1996 census. As shown in Figure 8.3, auto-drive is the dominant work trip mode throughout the country, with the variation in auto-drive mode split correlating roughly with city size (that is, the larger the CMA, the lower the proportion of people who drive to work). Table 8.2 provides a more complete breakdown of work trip mode choice for the seven CMAs exhibiting the lowest auto-drive usage. In Toronto and Montreal, with their extensive, multi-modal transit systems,

Figure 8.3   **Work Trip Auto-Drive Mode Split, Canadian CMAs, 1996**

Employed labour force driving to work,
census metropolitan areas, 1996

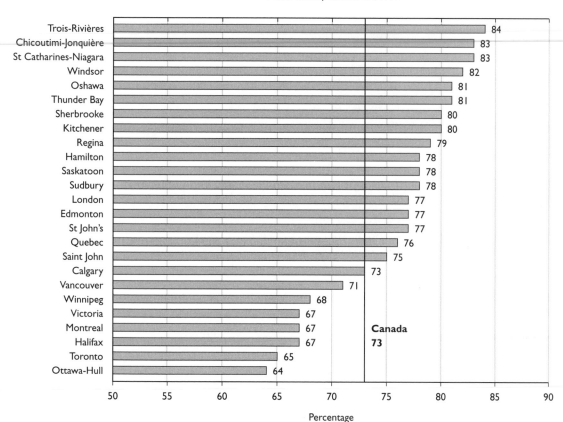

Percentage

Source: Statistics Canada.

Table 8.2   **Work Trip Mode Splits, 1996, Selected CMAs**

CMA	Auto Drive	Car, Truck or Van as Passenger	Public Transit	Walk	Bicycle	Other
Ottawa-Hull	64.3	8.8	17.1	7.0	2.1	0.8
Toronto	65.3	6.7	22.0	4.6	0.8	0.7
Halifax	66.6	10.4	10.9	9.9	1.0	1.2
Montréal	66.6	5.5	20.3	5.9	1.0	0.6
Victoria	67.1	6.8	9.9	9.8	4.9	1.5
Winnipeg	68.1	9.0	14.4	6.2	1.4	0.9
Vancouver	70.6	6.6	14.3	5.8	1.7	1.0

Source: 1996 Census, Statistics Canada.

transit is the major alternative to driving. In smaller cities walk and auto-passenger modes (e.g., Halifax) or walk and bicycle modes (e.g., Victoria) provide significant competition to auto-drive and are equal to or even greater in importance than public transit.

Given the importance of work and school trips in urban travel, combined with the relatively fixed schedules associated with these activities, it is to be expected that typical urban weekday travel will exhibit strong morning and afternoon peaks. Figure 8.4a illustrates this phenomenon, showing 1996 trip start times for all trips generated by residents of the Regional Municipality of Hamilton–Wentworth. Figure 8.4b breaks trip start-time distribution down by trip purpose, demonstrating the not surprising fact that different trip purposes (e.g., shopping versus work or school) display quite different temporal patterns.

Mode choice also varies dramatically by location within a given urban area. Figure 8.5 presents morning peak-period mode-choice data for the City of Toronto (formerly Metropolitan Toronto)

categorized by destination and trip purpose. Three destination zones are used: 'central' refers to Planning District 1, the expanded CBD; 'inner' refers to the relatively dense urban areas immediately surrounding the central area; and 'outer' refers to the more suburban remaining areas of the city. This figure demonstrates the extent to which transit usage drops off as one moves away from the CBD, regardless of trip purpose.

It is well known that travel behaviour (especially mode choice) varies with several key socio-economic variables, such as auto ownership, age, gender, occupation, and income. Table 8.3 offers a profile of transit riders in Quebec City by gender, age, and employment status. As is typical of Canadian transit properties, a majority of Quebec City transit riders are female, young, and workers or students. Students are disproportionately represented among transit users. Table 8.4 presents a somewhat more detailed breakdown of transit use for Hamilton by household auto ownership level, possession of a driver's licence, occupation, and gender. This table

Figure 8.4   **Trip Start Times, Regional Municipality of Hamilton-Wentworth, 1996**

a) Trip Start Times, All Trips

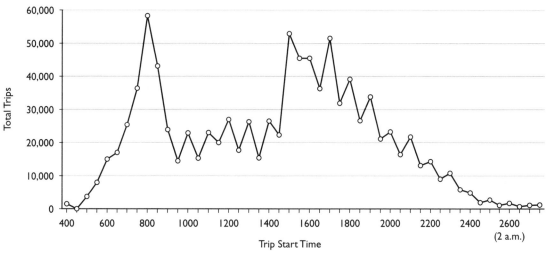

b) Trip Start Times by Trip Purpose

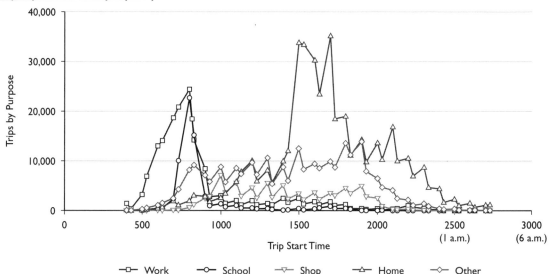

Source: 1996 Transportation Tomorrow Survey. Toronto: University of Toronto Joint Program in Transportation.

shows that the likelihood of using transit declines with levels of auto ownership and driver's licence possession. Men are generally somewhat less likely to take transit, even when occupation and possession of a driver's licence are accounted for. The effect of occupation is somewhat mixed in this table, but in general white-collar workers are more likely than blue-collar workers to take transit.

Figure 8.5   **Transit Mode Splits by Destination and Trip Purpose, Toronto, 1996**

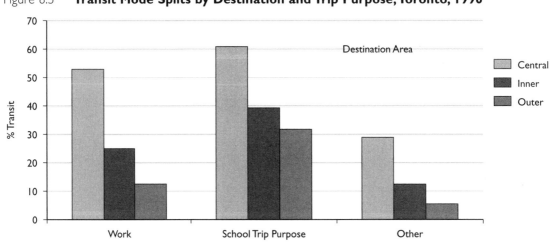

Source: 1996 Transportation Tomorrow Survey. Toronto: University of Toronto Joint Program in Transportation.

Table 8.3   **Transit User Profile, Quebec City, 1991**

Employment Status	%	Gender	%	Age	%
Worker	36.6	Female	60.3	6–18	22.9
Student	46.6	Male	39.7	18–24	24.2
Homemaker	3.8			25–44	29.5
Retired	10			45–59	10.6
Other	3			60+	12.8

Source: Unpublished data, 1991 Origin-Destination Survey, Quebec City.

Conventional Travel Demand Modelling System

Mathematical, computer-based models are used by transportation planners as one means of assessing the likely impacts of alternative transportation (and land-use) policies on: the demand for travel (by mode, purpose, time of day, etc.); the performance of the transportation system (congestion levels, level of service, etc.); and the various environmental and social impacts associated with urban transportation systems. Given the complex nature of travel behaviour, it is not surprising that these models are themselves complex, as well as costly and difficult to construct and use.[9]

A standard approach to urban travel demand modelling is employed throughout the world, wherever resources permit and need dictates its use. This approach was first developed in pioneering comprehensive transportation planning studies in Detroit and Chicago in the mid- to late 1950s. It quickly spread to other US and Canadian cities, as well as outside North America, through the 1960s, during which time the process and procedures we use today were developed. Since the 1960s, improvements have been made in individual sub-models, in the data sets used in the models, and in the computer hardware and software that serve to run the models. But the overall model paradigm has changed surprisingly little over the last 30 years.

Figure 8.6 presents the basic urban travel demand modelling system (UTMS), which is most often simply referred to as the four-stage or four-

Table 8.4   **Public Transit Use by Socio-economic Factors, Hamilton–Wentworth, 1996**

Gender	Driver's Licence	No. of Vehicles	Office/ Clerical	Blue Collar	Prof./ Manager	Sales/ Service	Total
Female	No	0	46.7	38.9	64.7	51.9	52.4
		1	27.8	30.2	27.3	29.2	28.7
		2+	26.2	19.1	31.6	23.0	23.7
	Yes	0	50.5	36.2	46.0	42.2	44.9
		1	6.0	3.5	3.1	7.7	5.2
		2+	2.1	0.9	1.8	2.2	1.9
Male	No	0	35.0	40.3	33.5	46.8	40.2
		1	24.0	25.2	19.8	45.7	31.0
		2+	0.0	18.7	8.3	13.3	14.4
	Yes	0	15.5	40.0	32.0	38.5	35.3
		1	8.7	1.2	2.5	3.5	2.5
		2+	1.3	0.3	1.5	1.4	1.0

Source: Unpublished data, 1996 Transportation Tomorrow Survey, Toronto: University of Toronto Joint Program in Transportation <http//www.jpint.utoronto.ca>.

step process. Primary inputs to this model are estimates of population and employment for each zone in the urban area for the forecast year, as well as a detailed computerized representation of the forecast-year road and transit networks. Primary outputs from the process are person and vehicle flows by mode on both origin-destination (O-D) and network link bases, as well as travel times and costs (again at both O-D and link levels). From these primary outputs additional measures of system performance (volume-to-capacity ratios, transit boardings by station, etc.) and impacts (emissions, energy use, accidents, etc.) can subsequently be estimated. As shown in Figure 8.6, travel demand is estimated in four sequential steps, consisting of:

- *trip generation*, in which the total number of trips originating from each zone and destined to each zone are estimated;

- *trip distribution*, in which the 'trip ends' estimated by the trip generation model are linked together to provide estimates of the total 'O-D flow' of trips (also referred to as the 'trip interchanges') between origins and destinations for all O-D pairs in the urban area;

- *modal split*, in which the total O-D flows are 'split' or allocated among the various modes (auto, transit, walk, etc.) available for use between any given O-D pair;[10]

- *trip assignment*, in which the paths or routes taken by auto users on the road network and transit users on the transit network are determined, and the road and transit O-D flows are assigned to these paths.

Trip generation actually involves two models for each trip purpose: one to predict trip origins by zone and one to predict trip destinations by zone.[11]

Figure 8.6   **The Urban Transportation Modelling System**

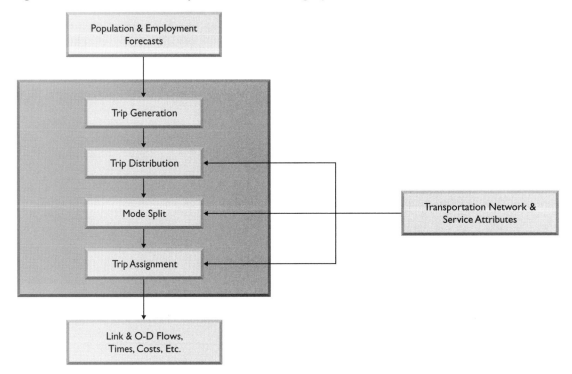

As shown in Figure 8.6, the fundamental inputs to these models are population and employment totals for each zone in the urban area, as well as, perhaps, additional information concerning these people and jobs (auto ownership, household size, type of employment, etc.).

As is also indicated in this figure, it is usually assumed that the transportation system does *not* affect trip generation. That is, the total number of trips made in an urban area is assumed to be independent of the level of service provided. This greatly simplifies the analysis, but, as has been discussed above, can potentially introduce significant bias into the analysis and is an incorrect assumption in most applications.

The methods used to perform trip generation analysis are typically quite simple, and primarily fall into two categories: linear regression models and cross-classification analysis. Linear regression simply assumes that a linear relationship exists between the number of trips generated (e.g., the number of morning peak-period home-to-work trips originating in a given zone) and one or more explanatory variables. Advantages of the linear regression approach include: ease of development and use; modest data requirements; ability to handle many explanatory variables; and transparency of the model procedure and results to users.

The assumption of a linear relationship between the number of trips made and the explanatory variables is easy to make but can be misleading. To dispel this assumption, cross-classification analysis is often used. In this approach persons or households are gathered into homogeneous groups based on a small number of variables or attributes, and average trip rates are computed from observed data for each group. Table 8.5 provides an example of this approach

| Table 8.5 | **Cross-Classification Trip Generation Model, Edmonton, 1994** |

Daily Person Trips Per Household Size

No. of Vehicles	1	2	3	4	5+	Total
0	2.82	6.17	9.73	n/a	n/a	4.19
1	4.03	6.55	9.46	13.47	17.39	6.81
2	4.61	7.59	11.24	15.13	20.17	11.69
3	4.93	7.86	11.12	15.03	19.95	12.71
4	n/a	n/a	12.42	17.38	17.08	14.11
5+	n/a	n/a	n/a	n/a	n/a	12.01
Total	3.77	7.12	10.69	14.83	19.3	9.17

Source: AMCL (1995).

for Edmonton. In this model, households have been grouped based on the number of vehicles and the number of people in the household, and average trip rates for each group have been computed. Thus, for example, the average number of daily person trips generated by three-person households owning one car is 9.46. Note the non-linear relationship exhibited in this table between trip rates and both explanatory variables (that is, auto ownership and household size), as well as the existence of interactions between the two variables. For example, moving from one to two vehicles in the household increases daily person trips by 1.04 trip per day for two-person households (from 6.55 to 7.59 trips per day), while it only results in a 0.58 trip per day increase for one-person households—a sensible result, since two people can clearly take better advantage of a second car than a single person can. Cross-classification models, however, generally require more data both for their development and application than linear regression models do.

While alternative methods exist, by far the most common approach to trip distribution mod-

elling is to use a *gravity* or *entropy* model. Such a model provides the most likely (or least biased) estimates of the O-D flow pattern, given the known information concerning these flows. This information is expressed in terms of a set of constraints on feasible values of the O-D flows. At a minimum, these constraints usually include:

$$\sum_{j=1}^{N} T_{ij} = O_i \quad \text{for each origin zone i,} \quad [8.1]$$
$$i=1,\dots,N$$

$$\sum_{i=1}^{N} T_{ij} = D_j \quad \text{for each destination} \quad [8.2]$$
$$\text{zone j, j}=1,\dots,N$$

$$\frac{\sum_{i=1}^{N} \sum_{j=1}^{N} T_{ij} t_{ij} = t_{avg}}{\sum_{i=1}^{N} \sum_{j=1}^{N} T_{ij}} \quad [8.3]$$

where:

T_{ij} = predicted number of trips from origin zone i to destination zone j

O_i = the number of trip origins in zone i (as determined by the trip generation model)

D_j = the number of trip destinations for zone j (as determined by the trip generation model)

t_{ij} = travel time from zone i to zone j

t_{avg} = average observed travel time for trips in the urban area

In words, equations [8.1] and [8.2] require that the predicted O-D flows be such that they add up to the known (that is, previously determined) trip origins and destinations for each zone. Equation [8.3] states that O-D flows be chosen so that the average travel time predicted by the model (the left-hand side of the equation) equals the known, observed average travel time (t_{avg}). Other constraints representing other known information can be added to this system of equations, as available data and need dictate.

Given these three constraints, it can be shown[12] that the most likely, least biased set of O-D flows to satisfy these equations are given by:

$$T_{ij} = A_i B_j O_i D_j e^{-\beta t_{ij}} \qquad [8.4]$$

where β is a parameter calibrated for a given urban area from observed data and A_i and B_j are 'balancing factors' ensuring that constraints [8.1] and [8.2] are satisfied by equation [8.3] for all zones i and j. They are iteratively defined as functions of one another as follows:

$$A_i = 1/\sum_{j=1}^{N} B_j D_j e^{-\beta t_{ij}} \qquad [8.5]$$

$$B_j = 1/\sum_{i=1}^{N} A_i O_i e^{-\beta t_{ij}} \qquad [8.6]$$

The O-D flows predicted by the trip distribution model are next 'split' among the various modes available for travel between each O-D pair. This is usually done using some form of *logit model*, derived from *random utility theory*.[13] A logit model expresses the probability P_{mt} that a person t will choose mode m from a set of feasible alternatives C_t as a function of the 'utility' of mode m for person t, V_{mt}, relative to the utilities of all competing modes, $V_{m't}$, $m' \neq m$:

$$P_{mt} = \frac{\exp(V_{mt})}{\displaystyle\sum_{m' \in C_t} \exp(V_{m't})} \qquad [8.7]$$

where exp() is the exponential function. The 'utility' of mode m for person t is, in turn, usually assumed to be a linear function of a set of attributes of mode m (travel time, travel cost, etc.) and person t (age, income, sex, etc.); that is:

$$V_{mt} = \beta_1 X_{mt1} + \beta_2 X_{mt2} + \dots + \beta_k X_{mtk} \qquad [8.8]$$

where X_{mtk} is the kth variable in the mode m utility function for person t and β_k is the parameter value (or utility function weight) associated with this variable. For example, the following equations describe the utility functions for a three-mode (auto-drive, auto-passenger, transit) morning peak-period work-trip mode-choice model for the Ottawa–Carleton region (Delcan, 1993):

$$V_d = -0.5472 - 0.5691 \star COST_d \\ -0.0161 \star IVTT_d \\ +0.7520 \star NVEH \qquad [8.9.1]$$

$$V_p = -2.282 - 0.5691 \star COST_p \\ -0.0161 \star IVTT_p \\ -0.0261 \star OVTT_p \\ +0.4529 \star NVEH \qquad [8.9.2]$$

$$V_t = -0.5691 \star COST_t \\ -0.0161 \star IVTT_t \\ -0.0261 \star OVTT_t \\ +1.0746 \star TWY \\ -0.9784 \star REGION \qquad [8.9.3]$$

where:

V_m	= utility for mode m (m = d, drive; p, passenger; t, transit)
$COST_m$	= out-of-pocket travel cost ($) for mode m
$IVTT_m$	= in-vehicle travel time for mode m (min.)
$OVTT_m$	= out-of-vehicle travel time for mode m (min.)
NVEH	= average number of vehicles per household in the home zone
TWY	= 1 if employment zone is located within the catchment area of a Transitway station outside the CBD; = 0 otherwise
REGION	= 1 if the home zone is located in the Outaouais; = 0 otherwise

Table 8.6 illustrates the use of this model to predict the mode-choice probabilities for a hypothetical origin-destination pair. In this case, given the travel times and costs and other data for the O-D pair, the model estimates that 46.6 per cent of the trips would be auto-drive, 3.7 per cent would be auto-passenger, and the remaining 49.7 per cent would use transit. These percentages would then be multiplied by the total number of trips predicted by the trip distribution model for this O-D pair to compute the number of trips by mode.

Table 8.6   **Logit Mode Choice Model, Example Calculations**

Mode	COST	IVTT	OVTT	NVEH	TWY	REGION	Vm	exp(Vm)	Pm
Drive	$2.60	15		1.4			−1.2156	0.2965	42.6
Pass	$0.80	15	5	1.4			−2.4752	0.0841	1.2
Transit	$1.00	20	10		0	0	−1.1521	0.3160	45.4
							SUM =	0.6967	

COST   = Out-of-pocket travel cost ($) for mode m
IVTT   = In-vehicle travel time (min.) for mode m
OVTT   = Out-of-vehicle (walk + wait) travel time (min.) for mode m
NVEH   = Average number of vehicles per household in the home zone
TWY   = 1 if employment zone is located within the catchment area of a Transitway station outside the CBD; = 0 otherwise
REGION = 1 if the home zone is located in the Outaouais; = 0 otherwise
Vm is computed using equations [8.9] and the data provided above.
Pm   = exp(Vm)/SUM

Once the number of auto–drive (and hence vehicle) trips and the number of transit trips have been computed for all O-D pairs, these trips can be *assigned* to specific paths through the road and transit networks, respectively. Various transit assignment algorithms exist to determine likely paths used as a function of transit service headways, in–vehicle travel times, number of transfers required, etc.[14]

Road network assignment is usually performed using the concept of *deterministic user equilibrium*. The user equilibrium assumption is that drivers individually choose routes so as to minimize their own personal travel times. Equilibrium is achieved when no one driver can unilaterally change routes and improve his/her travel time. Figure 8.7 illustrates the user equilibrium concept for a single O-D pair with only two feasible routes, each of which consists of a single link. If V_{ab} is the flow between origin A and destination B, then the flows on links (routes) 1 and 2, V_1 and V_2, must satisfy the constraint:

$$V_{ab} = V_1 + V_2 \qquad [8.10]$$

Each link in a road network will have a *volume-delay curve* (the supply or performance functions discussed

above) that determines the travel time along the link as a function of the volume of traffic using the link (Figure 8.7a). Drivers are free to choose either link (route) so as to minimize their individual travel times. As shown in Figure 8.7b, equilibrium occurs when the travel times are the same on the two routes (that is, $t_1 = t_2 = t^\star$, which occurs when the volume flow on link 1 is $V_1^\star$ and the flow on link 2 is $V_2^\star$), since otherwise some of the drivers on the slower link can and will switch to the faster link.

Although Figure 8.7 is extremely simplified, its results can be shown to generalize to networks of any size and complexity. For example, the network model for the Greater Toronto Area has over 1,400 traffic zones (approximately two million O-D pairs), tens of thousands of links, and thousands of feasible paths for any given O-D pair. User equilibrium assignments are routinely made to this network using commercially available software.[15]

Emerging Modelling Methods

The research state of the art has progressed considerably beyond the conventional modelling state of

Figure 8.7   **Deterministic User Equilibrium Example**

a) Volume-Delay Curves for the Two Routes

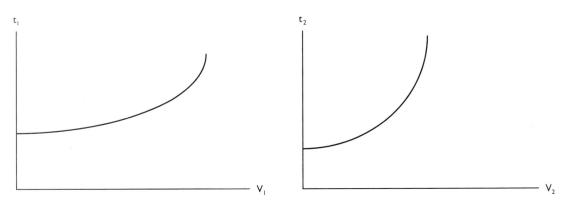

b) User Equilibrium Solution, Two Route Case

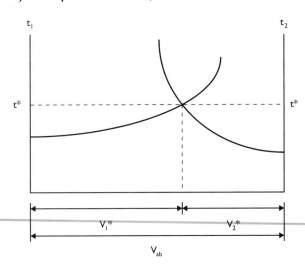

practice described above, to the point that it is very likely we are on the verge of a 'paradigm shift' to a fundamentally different approach to urban transportation demand and network performance modelling (Pas, 1990). The need for such a paradigm shift is driven by the long-standing recognition that the conventional methods described above simply are not adequate for addressing the complex range of transportation issues and policies facing contemporary urban areas (Deakin and Harvey, 1993; Miller and Hassounah, 1993; Stopher, 1993). The capability to undertake this paradigm shift is provided by a significant improvement over the past 30 years in: travel behaviour and transportation system performance theory; considerably improved databases and data collection methods to support improved model development (Stopher, 1995); and vastly enhanced computational capabilities.

While a detailed discussion of these emerging modelling methods is well beyond the scope of this chapter, key elements of the 'next generation models' include the following (Spear, 1994):

- The new travel demand models are explicitly *activity-based* in nature; that is, they take seriously the notion (shown in Figure 8.1) of travel as a demand derived from the need to participate in activities, many of which are dispersed in time and space and hence require travel. Thus, the first three stages of the four-stage process of generation, distribution, and mode choice are replaced with a modelling system in which people schedule their activities over the course of a day (in terms of what activities they are going to engage in, when, for how long, at what location). Travel (including decisions regarding mode choice) arises out of the execution of this activity schedule (Ettema and Timmermans, 1997). Region-wide, comprehensive activity-based models that can fully replace the regional four-stage models are not yet fully operational. More focused, special-purpose models, however, are in use. For example, a model called AMOS has been developed to analyse the short-run impacts of transportation demand management (TDM) measures intended to reduce total demand or divert demand from less desirable modes (RDC, 1995). In addition, 'tour-based' modelling systems are being implemented as an intermediate step between the conventional trip-based models described above and a 'full' activity-based modelling system (Bowman and Ben-Akiva, 1997; Pas, 1997).
- Static user-equilibrium network assignment models are being replaced by dynamic (often probabilistic) models of network performance and route choice. These dynamic network assignment models provide much more reliable representations of vehicle performance and traveller route choices within the road network

(e.g., effects of queueing, more realistic vehicle speeds and acceleration/deceleration profiles, more realistic assumptions concerning driver decision-making), and so provide a much better basis for estimating vehicular emissions and energy use, and the impact of real-time control and other strategies related to intelligent transportation systems (ITSs) (Golledge, 1997).
- Both the activity/travel models and the network performance/assignment models require a much more detailed, disaggregated representation of trip-makers and the transportation network. That is, the aggregate, zone-based representations of the conventional four-stage model simply cannot support the new models. *Microsimulation* is a fast-evolving method for implementing disaggregate behavioural models in which individual actors (households, trip-makers, vehicles, etc.) are explicitly modelled within a dynamic simulation framework (Goulias and Kitamura, 1992; Miller, 1996; Miller and Salvini, 1997).
- Integrated models that simultaneously model land use and transportation processes (that is, all of Figure 8.1) have existed for over 30 years but have not received widespread application, in large part due to their complexity (Lee, 1973). In recent years, interest in developing and applying integrated urban systems models has increased considerably, as have the operational capabilities of these models. Given the growing recognition that the land-use–transportation interaction must be taken seriously if sustainable urban systems are to be achieved, it is expected that integrated models will play an increasingly important role in the planning process (Miller, Kriger, and Hunt, 1998; Southworth, 1995; Wegener, 1994).

Canadian Urban Transportation in the Twenty-First Century

The long-run sustainability (in economic, social, and environmental terms) of our urban transportation systems is almost certainly the key issue facing planners as we enter the twenty-first century. As documented above, current land-use trends and travel behaviour preferences are not conducive to improving sustainability, since these universally encourage automobile usage at the expense of transit and non-motorized modes of travel, such as walking and bicycling. Many policy-makers implicitly assume that technological fixes, such as ITSs, cleaner cars, and advanced telecommunications, will solve this problem. While these technologies can and will have a positive impact, they will not, in and of themselves, ensure sustainability. This is particularly the case in regard to greenhouse gas emissions, which will continue to be generated in considerable amounts by road vehicles as long as they burn carbon-based fuels, no matter how 'clean' these vehicles are otherwise.

Of the many policy questions pertaining to urban transportation planning, none is more central to 'the urban transportation problem' than that concerning the role of the automobile. For at least 40 years, planners, economists, engineers, and social scientists (among others) have wrestled with this issue.[16] Far from resolving the debate, this rich literature simply serves to illustrate the fundamental nature of this question for urban areas, as well as its endurance. We are no closer as a society to answering this question than we were 20, 30, or 40 years ago. One can plausibly argue that no other single piece of technology has affected twentieth-century life more than the automobile, computers and nuclear weapons notwithstanding. It provides us with levels of mobility unprecedented in human history. It is central to our personal lifestyles. It is fundamental to the modern economy (both as a medium through which the economy operates and as a major industry in its own right). But at the same time these enormous benefits come at a very high cost. The automobile kills and maims thousands of people every year. It consumes enormous amounts of land, both directly for roads and indirectly in terms of the urban forms it facilitates and promotes. It pollutes our air and contributes significantly to global climate change. How we as a society deal with these huge trade-offs in benefits and disbene-

fits will go a long way towards determining the nature of our twenty-first-century cities.

Notes

1. Figure 8.1 and its associated discussion focus on the activity system and transportation supply and demand from the point of view of people and their personal participation in activity and travel. With only minor reworking, this discussion applies equally to the economic activity processes of firms and the associated issues of transportation supply and demand for the movement of goods within (and into/out of) the urban area. Similar comments apply to the role the truck has had on the location and nature of economic activities and their interactions, largely displacing rail as the primary mover of goods, except in specialized markets (e.g., long-distance haul of bulk goods). It should also be noted that the diesel bus has largely replaced the electric streetcar as the primary transit vehicle in most cities. For simplicity of discussion, this chapter focuses on the personal activity system and personal travel. Goods movement, however, is clearly an equally important part of the transportation system, complete with its own behavioural relationships, policy issues, etc.

2. Although in many cases, water transportation still played a major role, such as in the location of the steel industry in Hamilton and the export of grain from ports such as Thunder Bay.

3. In the United States and many European cities, subways (underground heavy rail lines) were added to the mix of transit technologies in the early-twentieth century. These subways further accentuated the land-use trends generated by the street railways. No subway, however, was operated in Canada until the Yonge Street line opened in Toronto in 1954, replacing a very successful surface streetcar line. This was followed by the opening of the first Montreal Metro lines in 1966.

4. For reviews of the role of 'micro' urban design on travel behaviour, see, for example, PBQD (1996) and Badoe and Miller (1997).

5. This distinction between induced and latent demand comes from Mokhtarian and Salomon (1997).

6. It is the case, however, that our roads are becoming safer over time. Road accident deaths and injuries in 1995 were down 23 per cent and 7 per cent respectively relative to 1985 totals, despite increases in registered vehicles and licensed drivers over the same 10-year period of 15 per cent and 21 per cent (Transport Canada, 1997).

7. Major lawsuits have occurred in San Francisco (Garrett and Wachs, 1996) and, more recently, in Chicago. These lawsuits attempt to prevent a highway from being built (in Chicago) or operated (in San Francisco).

8. In this discussion 'school' includes both home-based school and home-based post-secondary trips.

9. For a complete discussion of urban travel demand modelling methods, see, among other works, Ortuzar and Willumsen (1990).

10. In some versions of the four-stage process, modal splits are performed prior to trip distribution rather than after, as shown here. Such models are called *trip-end modal split* models, since it is the trip origins and destinations that must be allocated to the various modes. Separate trip distribution models must then be used to link origins to destinations for each mode. Trip-end modal split models are rarely applied in larger urban areas, since they generally are not sensitive to modal-level service changes. For further discussion of this type of model, see, for example, Hutchinson (1974) or Steuart (1977).

11. Transportation planners often speak in terms of trip *productions* and *attractions*, rather than in terms of origins and destinations. A trip production is defined as the home end of a home-based trip (regardless of whether it is the origin or destination of the trip) and the origin of a non-home-based trip. A trip attraction is the non-home end of a home-based trip or the destination of a non-home-based trip. The production-attraction terminology has some utility if one is modelling 24-hour trips, otherwise the loss of information concerning origins versus destinations of home-based trips can be problematic. For this and other reasons, most models today are based on an origin-destination framework.

12. See, for example, Wilson (1967) and Webber (1977).

13. For a detailed, rigorous, but accessible presentation of random utility choice models and their application to travel demand modelling, see Ben-Akiva and Lerman (1985).

14. Two well-known Canadian procedures for transit assignment are implemented within MADITUC (Chapleau, 1986) and EMME/2 (Inro Consultants, 1996).

15. For a detailed discussion of user equilibrium assignment methods, see Sheffi (1985).

16. Classics in this literature not cited elsewhere in this chapter include Buchanan (1963), Meyer, Kain, and Wohl (1965), Mumford (1960), and Owen (1966, 1972). Also of relevance is the more recent work by Pucher and Lefèvre (1996).

References

AMCL (Applications Management Consulting Limited). 1995. *Transportation Master Plan Household Travel Survey Project Report*. Edmonton: Applications Management Consulting Ltd, prepared for the City of Edmonton Transportation Department.

Badoe, D.A., and E.J. Miller. 1997. *The Transportation–Land-Use Interaction: Empirical Findings and Implications for Modelling*. Toronto: University of Toronto Joint Program in Transportation, Technical Memorandum No. 2, Transit Cooperative Research Project H–12 'Integrated Urban Models for Simulation of Transit and Land-Use Policies'.

Ben-Akiva, M.E., and S.R. Lerman. 1985. *Discrete Choice Analysis: Theory and Application to Travel Demand*. Cambridge, Mass.: MIT Press.

Boal, F.W., and D.B. Johnson. 1965. 'The Functions of Retail and Service Establishments on Commercial Ribbons', *Canadian Geographer* 9: 154–69.

Bowman, J.L., and M.E. Ben-Akiva. 1997. 'Activity-Based Forecasting', in *Travel Model Improvement Program Activity-Based Travel Forecasting Conference, June 2–5, 1996, Summary, Recommendations and Compendium of Papers*. Washington: US Department of Transportation, DOT–T–97–17.

Buchanan, C. 1963. *Traffic in Towns: A Study of the Long Term Problems of Traffic in Urban Areas*. London: Her Majesty's Stationery Office.

Chapleau, R. 1986. 'Transit Network Analysis and Evaluation with a Totally Disaggregate Approach', in *Proceedings of the World Conference on Transport Research, Vancouver, May 1986* 1: 1427–42.

Deakin, E., and G. Harvey. 1993. *A Manual of Regional Transportation Modeling Practice for Air Quality Analysis*. Washington: National Association of Regional Councils.

Delcan. 1993. *TRANS EMME/2 Transportation Model Development Study Technical Report*. Ottawa: Delcan Corporation.

Ettema, D.F., and H.J.P. Timmermans. 1997. *Activity-Based Approaches to Travel Analysis*. Amsterdam: Pergamon.

Garreau, J. 1991. *Edge City, Life on the New Frontier*. New York: Doubleday.

Garrett, M., and M. Wachs. 1996. *Transportation Planning on Trial: The Clean Air Act and Travel Forecasting*. Thousand Oaks, Calif.: Sage Publications.

Golledge, R.G. 1997. 'Dynamics and ITS: Behavioral Responses to Information Available from ATIS', conference resource paper, 8th Meeting of the International Association for Travel Behavior Research, Austin, Texas, 21–5 Sept.

Goulias, K., and R. Kitamura. 1992. 'Travel Demand Forecasting with Dynamic Microsimulation', *Transportation Research Record* 1357: 8–17.

Hutchinson, B.G. 1974. *Principles of Urban Transportation Planning*. New York: McGraw-Hill.

Inro Consultants. 1996. *EMME/2 User's Manual Release 8*. Montreal: Inro Consultants Inc.

Jones, D. 1985. *Urban Transit Policy: An Economic and Political History*. Englewood Cliffs, NJ: Prentice-Hall.

Lee, D.B. 1973. 'Requiem for Large Scale Models', *Journal of the American Institute of Planners* 39, 3: 163–78.

Meyer, J.R., J.F. Kain, and M. Wohl. 1965. *The Urban Transportation Problem*. Cambridge, Mass.: Harvard University Press.

Meyer, M.D., and E.J. Miller. 1984. *Urban Transportation Planning: A Decision-Oriented Approach*. New York: McGraw-Hill.

Miller, E.J. 1996. 'Microsimulation and Activity-Based Forecasting', in *Travel Model Improvement Program Activity-Based Travel Forecasting Conference, June 2–5, 1996, Summary, Recommendations and Compendium of Papers*. Washington: US Department of Transportation, DOT–T–97–17.

——— and M.I. Hassounah. 1993. *Quantitative Analysis of Urban Transportation Energy Use and Emissions: Phase I Final Report*. Toronto: University of Toronto Joint Program in Transportation.

———, D.S. Kriger, and J.D. Hunt. 1998. 'Integrated Urban Model Research Needs', presented at the American Society of Civil Engineers Conference on Transportation, Land Use and Air Quality, Portland, Oreg., 17–20 May.

——— and P.A. Salvini. 1997. 'Microsimulation of Travel Activities in Networks', conference resource paper, 8th Meeting of the International Association for Travel Behavior Research, Austin, Texas, 21–5 Sept.

Mokhtarian, P.L., and I. Salomon. 1997. 'Emerging Travel Patterns: Do Telecommunications Make a Difference', conference resource paper, 8th Meeting of the International Association for Travel Behavior Research, Austin, Texas, 21–5 Sept.

Mumford, L. 1961. *The City in History: Its Origins, Its Transformations and Its Prospects.* New York: Harcourt, Brace & World.

Ortuzar, J.D., and L.G. Willumsen. 1990. *Modelling Transport.* New York: John Wiley and Sons.

Owen, W. 1966. *The Metropolitan Transportation Problem.* Washington: Brookings Institution.

———. 1972. *The Accessible City.* Washington: Brookings Institution.

Pas, E.I. 1990. 'Is Travel Demand Analysis and Modelling in the Doldrums?', in P. Jones, ed., *Developments in Dynamic and Activity-Based Approaches to Travel Analysis.* Aldershot, UK: Gower.

———. 1997. 'Recent Advances in Activity-Based Travel Demand Modeling', in *Travel Model Improvement Program Activity-Based Travel Forecasting Conference, June 2–5, 1996, Summary, Recommendations and Compendium of Papers.* Washington: US Department of Transportation, DOT–T–97–17.

PBQD (Parsons, Brinkerhoff, Quade, and Douglas Inc.). 1996. *Influence of Land Use Mix and Neighborhood Design on Transit Demand.* Washington: Parsons, Brinkerhoff, Quade, and Douglas Inc., report prepared for the Transportation Co-operative Research Program, US Transportation Research Board.

Pucher, J.R., and C. Lefèvre. 1996, *The Urban Transport Crisis in Europe and North America.* London: Macmillan.

RDC (Resource Decision Consultants). 1995. *Activity-Based Modeling System for Travel Demand Forecasting.* Washington: US Department of Transportation, DOT–T–96–02.

Sheffi, Y. 1985. *Urban Transportation Networks: Equilibrium Analysis with Mathematical Programming Methods.* Englewood Cliffs, NJ: Prentice-Hall.

Southworth, F. 1995. *A Technical Review of Urban Land Use–Transportation Models as Tools for Evaluating Vehicle Travel Reduction Strategies.* Knoxville, Tenn.: Oak Ridge National Laboratory, ORNL–6881.

Spear, B. 1994. *New Approaches to Travel Forecasting Models: A Synthesis of Four Research Proposals.* Washington: US Department of Transportation, DOT–T–94–15.

Steuart, G.N., ed. 1977. *Urban Transportation Planning Guide.* Toronto: University of Toronto Press.

Stopher, P.R. 1993. 'Deficiencies of Travel-Forecasting Methods Relative to Mobile Emissions', *Journal of Transportation Engineering* 119, 5: 723–41.

———, ed. 1995. *Household Travel Surveys: New Concepts and Research Needs.* Washington: Transportation Research Board, Transportation Research Board Conference Proceedings 10.

Transport 2021. 1993a. *A Long-Range Transportation Plan for Greater Vancouver.* Vancouver: Transport 2021.

———. 1993b. *A Medium-Range Transportation Plan for Greater Vancouver.* Vancouver: Transport 2021.

Transport Canada. 1997. *Transportation in Canada 1996, Annual Report.* Ottawa: Minister of Public Works and Government Services.

Warner, B. 1962. *Streetcar Suburbs: The Process of Growth in Boston.* Cambridge, Mass.: Harvard University Press.

Webber, M. 1977. 'Pedagogy Again: What is Entropy', *Annals of the Association of the American Geographers* 67: 254–66.

Webber, M.M. 1964. 'The Urban Place and the Nonplace Urban Form', in M.M. Webber et al., eds, *Explorations into Urban Structure.* Philadelphia: University of Pennsylvania Press.

Wegener, M. 1994. 'Operational Urban Models: State of the Art', *Journal of the American Planning Association* 60: 17–28.

Wilson, A.G. 1967. 'A Statistical Theory of Spatial Distribution Models', *Transportation Research* 1: 253–69.

Yeates, M., and B. Garner. 1980. *The North American City*, 3rd rev. edn. New York: Harper and Row.

Chapter 9

The City as Social Space

Robert A. Murdie and Carlos Teixeira

This chapter concerns the city as social space. We focus particularly on the emerging social mosaic of Canadian cities and examine the changing patterns of residential differentiation and the processes that have created these patterns. We are concerned with both the diverse social landscapes within Canadian cities and the variations between cities. Many of the empirical examples are drawn from Canada's three largest metropolitan centres, Toronto, Montreal, and Vancouver. This emphasis is not intended to diminish the importance of smaller urban areas. Rather, it reflects the reality that most research concerning the social mosaic of Canadian cities has focused on the three largest centres.

Two spatial scales of analysis are considered—national and urban. First, at the national level, it is important to view the social mosaic of the city as a reflection of the society within which it is located as well as the changing nature of that society. Trends in economic restructuring, age and family structure, and immigration, alongside declining support for the welfare state, are particularly significant in understanding the changing social geography of Canadian cities. In some cases, these trends are the outcome of globalization processes that impact at the national level but over which local governments have relatively little control.

The second, or urban, level of analysis considers the general patterns of social differentiation within cities and how these patterns have changed over time. Much of our understanding of the Canadian urban mosaic is based on an interpretation of the spatial distribution of social groups, relying primarily on census tract data and the statistical manipulation of these data. These spatial patterns are the outcome of decisions made by numerous individual households seeking a residence within the constraints of household income, the existing built form of the city, and the actions of various gatekeepers who filter information about housing opportunities. It is important, therefore, to seek further understanding of inter- and intra-group variations in residential behaviour and in the constraints that some individuals and groups face when seeking a suitable residence in the city.

The underlying theme of the chapter is transitional shifts in the social geography of Canadian metropolitan areas and the processes responsible for these newly emerging patterns of social space. These shifts in social geography reflect more general changes from a modern to a post-modern society, including increased societal fragmentation and the creation of an increasingly complex urban social mosaic. They also cast doubt on the adequacy of spatial models from the first half of the twentieth century to represent completely the intricate nature of the emerging socio-spatial complexity of many Canadian metropolitan centres.

The remainder of the chapter is divided into four sections. We begin with a brief overview of important societal trends that potentially impact on intra-urban social space. This is followed by a discussion of the emerging social mosaic, focusing particularly on the nature and spatial distribution of social groups in Canadian metropolitan areas. The third and fourth sections offer more detailed examinations of two major and highly visible shifts in the social make-up of Canadian cities. In the third section, we examine the dynamics of income polarization and explore the possible existence of an underclass in Canada's three largest metropolitan areas. In the fourth section we deal at length with the changing geography of ethnicity, including implications of the increased 'internationalization' of Canada's immigrant population for cities and neighbourhoods within cities.

Post-World War II Societal Trends and Their Impacts on the Socio-Spatial Dimensions of Canadian Metropolitan Areas

Since the end of World War II, Canadian metropolitan areas have been impacted by four important societal trends. The first three—economic restructuring, changes in age structure and living arrangements, and immigration—relate closely to the three major divisions of society identified in the 1950s as a primary basis for the residential differentiation and spatial organization of modern North American cities. These divisions include economic status, family status, and ethnic status. The fourth, declining support for the welfare state, cuts across these societal divisions and affects the life chances of a variety of the most vulnerable groups in society, including the unemployed, female-headed single-parent families, and refugees.

Economic Restructuring

The first trend, economic restructuring, concerns the relative decline in manufacturing and increase in service jobs, a phenomenon that characterizes most post-industrial cities (e.g., Fainstein and Harloe, 1992; Sassen, 1991, 1994). In Canada these trends have been accentuated by trade liberalization agreements such as the North American Free Trade Agreement (NAFTA) and the recession of the late 1980s and early 1990s, resulting in plant closures and lay-offs throughout the country, but especially in the industrial heartland of Ontario and Quebec (Rutherford, 1996).

Overall, employment in manufacturing (including construction) declined from 30.6 per cent of the Canadian labour force in 1951 to 19.3 per cent in 1996, while service employment (including trade, transportation, and communication) increased from 48.5 per cent to 75.3 per cent during the same period (Bourne and Olvet, 1995: 8; Statistics Canada, 1998).[1] Much of this growth was in the financial services and community, business, and personal services sectors. For example, employment in these sectors increased by 23.7 per cent between 1986 and 1996 compared to an increase of only 13.5 per cent in the labour force as a whole. While many of these new service-sector jobs are well paid, others are not. Of the latter, many are part-time and increasingly held by women and young people under the age of 25. As a result, the potential for enhanced social and spatial inequalities within cities has increased. There has also been an increased spatial redistribution of employment within cities, especially a decentralization of manufacturing and routine office functions to the outer suburbs and a concentration of financial firms and business services in the core. For many employees, especially females, the result is an increased spatial mismatch between home and work. In Toronto, for example, many of the lower-paid jobs are increasingly found in the inner and outer suburbs, while lower-income households are still concentrated in parts of the central city and the inner suburbs (Frisken et al., 1997: 31). (For further discussions of employment, see Chapters 6 and 15.)

Changes in Age Structure and Family and Household Formation

The second major societal trend concerns changes in age structure and family and household formation. Canada's age structure has been characterized by a decline in the number and proportion of children and youth and a rapid increase in the elderly population. The proportion of Canada's population under 15 years of age declined from a post-war peak of 33.5 per cent in 1961 to 20.5 per cent in 1996, while the proportion of the population aged 65 and over increased from 7.6 per cent to 12.2 per cent during the same period. These general trends are related to well-documented changes in birth and death rates. First, the baby boom from the late 1940s to the mid-1960s was followed by the baby bust from the late 1960s to the end of the 1970s and a slight baby-boom echo thereafter. Second, the period following the war has been characterized by increasingly lower mortality rates for the older population (Beaujot, 1991: 208; Foot and Stoffman, 1996). City-specific differences, on the other hand, relate to variations in the age structure of migration streams—for example, elderly persons moving to the retirement centre of Victoria and younger persons in the childbearing years seeking employment opportunities in Calgary. By 1996, 17.9 per cent of Victoria's population was 65 years of age or older compared to 8.7 per cent for Calgary. In contrast, 37 per cent of Calgary's population was in the 25–44 age category compared to 31.3 per cent for Victoria. The result is considerably different population pyramids for the two cities—a comparative bulge at the top end of the pyramid in Victoria and a relative protrusion in the childbearing years and the younger age groups in Calgary. These differences are shown in Figure 9.1, where Calgary is contrasted with Victoria, and as a benchmark comparison, similar figures are shown for the combined set of all 25 Canadian census metropolitan areas (CMAs). The general pattern of the diagram indicates that Victoria has a considerably older population structure than both Calgary and the entire set of metropolitan areas, whereas Calgary has a younger population structure than either Victoria or all metropolitan areas combined. For almost all age groups, the bars for Victoria and Calgary lie on opposite sides of the benchmark comparison.

This postwar demographic transition is also reflected in the emerging social geography of the city. For example, the aging of older central city neighbourhoods and the rapid growth of suburban bedroom communities in the 1950s and 1960s were dampened in the 1970s and 1980s by the move by baby boomers to the gentrifying inner-city areas of Toronto, Montreal, Vancouver, Ottawa–Hull, Edmonton, and Halifax and the reduced demand by the baby-bust generation for family dwellings in the suburbs. During the 1980s and 1990s, with the increased cost of inner-city housing in centres such as Toronto and Vancouver, the demand for new suburban housing accelerated, although it is unclear whether this demand will be sustained into the early part of the twenty-first century (Bourne and Olvet, 1995: 9; Foot and Stoffman, 1996: 132–3).

Canada's family and household structure also changed dramatically during the postwar period. A major trend has been decline in household size. The relative number of one-person households, for example, increased from 7.4 per cent in 1951 to 24.2 per cent in 1996, while the proportion of households with six or more persons dropped from 19.7 per cent in 1951 to 3.3 per cent in 1996. In some central cities the proportion of single-person households is as high as 30–40 per cent (Bourne and Olvet, 1995: 9). Many of the latter are older women. At the same time, family structure has become increasingly diversified. The proportion of single-parent families increased dramatically from 2.3 per cent in 1951 to 17.1 per cent in 1996. Of the latter, 83 per cent are headed by women, often with low incomes. Another major trend, especially beginning in the 1970s, has been the tendency for a larger proportion of young adults to move out of the family home. Between 1971 and 1981, the proportion of 20 to 24-year-olds still living at home dropped from 78 per cent to 64 per cent (Miron, 1993: 81). This general trend has continued, although the percentage fluctuates according to housing market and economic conditions. In high-priced markets such as Toronto and Vancouver, the trend of living at home may be increasing again. The outcome of these trends has been a fragmentation of living arrangements that has important implications at the individual level for the intersection of life-cycle stage and housing careers, and at the aggregate level for the social geography of the city.

Increased 'Internationalization'

The third major trend is the increased 'internationalization' of Canada's population (e.g., Hiebert,

Figure 9.1   **Age Distribution: Calgary, Victoria, and All CMAs, 1996**

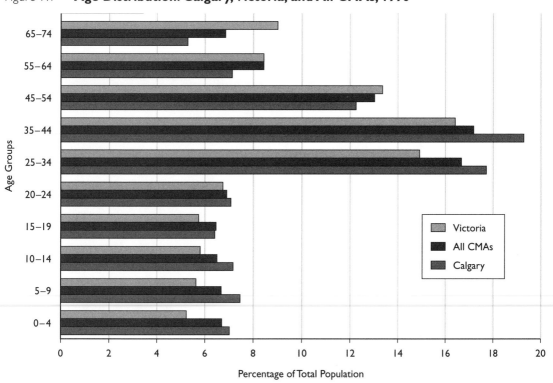

Source: Statistics Canada, *Census of Canada,* 1996.

1994). In this respect, Canada is not much different from many other highly developed countries (Castles and Miller, 1998: ch. 4). The trends for Canada are evident in Table 9.1, which shows the 10 leading source countries of immigrants for 1951, 1968, 1984, and 1996. During the period from 1945 until the early 1970s immigrants were needed to provide labour for the rapidly developing Canadian economy. Preference was given to 'white' immigrants from other Commonwealth countries, continental Europe, and the United States. In 1951, the 10 leading source countries for Canadian immigrants were located in these parts of the world, while in 1968 Hong Kong was the only point of origin outside of these areas. Beginning in the early 1970s, economic

restructuring reduced the need for manual workers in manufacturing. Instead there was a demand for both high- and low-skilled employees in the newly emerging service industries. Canada's immigration policies also changed during this period and a point system was introduced allowing people from other parts of the world to apply for entry into Canada. The objective was to remove the discriminatory policies of earlier immigration legislation. The result was a sharp decline in European immigration and a substantial increase in immigration from Asia, Africa, the Middle East, the Caribbean, and Latin America. By 1996, seven of the 10 leading source countries of Canadian immigrants were Asian, and another, Iran, was Middle Eastern. Indeed, the 1996

| Table 9.1 | **Ten Leading Countries of Immigrant Origin: Canada, 1951, 1968, 1984, 1996** | | |
1951	1968	1984	1996
Britain	Britain	Vietnam	Hong Kong
Germany	United States	Hong Kong	India
Italy	Italy	United States	China
Netherlands	Germany	India	Taiwan
Poland	Hong Kong	Britain	Philippines
France	France	Poland	Pakistan
United States	Austria	Philippines	Sri Lanka
Belgium	Greece	El Salvador	United States
Yugoslavia	Portugal	Jamaica	Iran
Denmark	Yugoslavia	China	Britain

Sources: McVey and Kalbach (1995); Citizenship and Immigration Canada Web page: <http://cicnet.ci.gc.ca//>.

census revealed that for the first time in Canada's history more than half of the country's immigrants were born in non-European countries. These recent immigrants also represent a wide spectrum of economic groups, including refugees admitted on humanitarian grounds, those joining family members already in Canada, business people with money to invest, and independent immigrants admitted on the basis of educational achievement, labour market skills, and language proficiency.

These shifts in immigrant source countries have meant a dramatic change in the ethnocultural mosaic of Canadian metropolitan areas, especially Toronto and Vancouver, the cities that have received the largest and most diverse groups of recent immigrants. The most obvious change in spatial patterning has been the development of new suburban immigrant reception areas in these cities. In Toronto, for example, the shift in source countries and the changing geography of ethnicity has resulted in a bifurcated form of immigrant settlement in the suburbs, with business immigrants from various Asian countries moving directly into relatively

high-priced single-detached dwellings, while refugees, with limited choice of housing, are forced into lower-rent private-sector apartment dwellings, often of low quality.

Retrenchment of the Welfare State

The fourth major change, especially in the last decade, has been the retrenchment of the welfare state and the potential impact of these cutbacks for the development of a Canadian underclass. The life chances of low-income immigrants and refugees, as well as the Canadian-born, are determined to a considerable degree by various policies of the welfare state. Although Canada's social welfare policy has traditionally been closer to the United States than Western Europe, Canada, unlike the US, has a universal health-care system and somewhat more generous social service programs, such as employment insurance. Until the 1980s, Canada's two major political parties generally followed a pragmatic and centrist approach to social welfare provision. More recently, however, governments at both the federal and provincial levels have implemented changes in social welfare provision in order to control the deficit. Low-income people in Canada's largest cities have been particularly affected by the suspension of new social housing construction, the dramatic reduction in welfare payments (especially in Alberta and Ontario), and cancellation of employment training programs and job creation initiatives.

The Emerging Social Mosaic: The Nature and Distribution of Social Groups in Canadian Cities

Traditional Models of the Social Mosaic and Their Application to Canadian Metropolitan Areas

In the early 1950s, sociologists such as Shevky and Bell (1955) hypothesized that the social mosaic of the modern (industrial) city could be summarized by three major divisions of society: class structure or income, age or stage in the life cycle, and cultural differences reflected in ethnicity, race, and language. More generally, these were known as economic status, family status, and ethnic status (Figure 9.2). Each of these societal divisions derived from a broad theory of social change and each was operationalized using a set of census variables for sub-areas within cities, usually census tracts.[2] It was assumed that each structure summarized a separate dimension or component of social variation and that all three were needed to capture the social complexity of modern cities.

Subsequently, the empirical validity of Shevky and Bell's social area model was tested using factorial ecology, a statistical method designed to tease out the interrelationships between census variables. The result from this analysis is a set of factors or dimensions summarizing the interrelationships among census variables. Each factor identifies a set of variables with similar patterns of spatial variation. When evaluated using a limited number of variables, Shevky and Bell's hypothesis of three major social dimensions was confirmed. But as additional variables were added to the analysis the factor structures became more complex. For example, analyses of Toronto and Montreal between the early 1960s and early 1980s resulted in six major dimensions of social variation reflecting a more complex social mosaic than the three-factor model hypothesized by Shevky and Bell (Foggin and Polèse, 1977; LeBourdais and Beaudry, 1988; Murdie, 1969). Rather than denying the validity of the Shevky and

Figure 9.2   **Societal Divisions and the Social Mosaic of the City: From the Modern (Industrial) City to the Post-Modern (Post-Industrial) City**

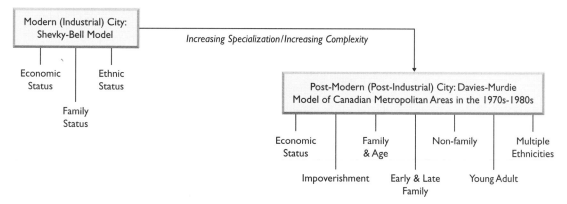

Source: Adapted from Herbert and Thomas (1997).

Bell hypothesis, the inclusion of more variables in the analysis tended to add reality to the model by revealing additional societal and city-specific details of the three major social dimensions.

In addition to evaluating the validity of the Shevky and Bell hypothesis, factorial ecology researchers calculated scores for each census tract on each major dimension of social variation and mapped these scores to determine the spatial form of the social mosaic and to identify possible links with the classic spatial models of urban form: Burgess's concentric zones, Hoyt's sectors, and Harris and Ullman's multiple nuclei (Burgess, 1925; Hoyt, 1939; Harris and Ullman, 1945). These three models were developed primarily as summaries of the residential change taking place in North American industrial cities during the interwar period (Figure 9.3). Using Chicago as a laboratory, Burgess and his colleagues argued that low-income migrants and immigrants first settled in older housing near the central business district, and upon improving their economic position moved outward through a series of increasingly higher-status concentric zones towards the periphery. The process is best described as invasion and succession, with one group invading and succeeding the residential space occupied by another. In contrast, Hoyt based his sectoral model on preferences by higher-income groups for amenity-rich locations, such as elevated areas with a view and proximity to commuter transport lines and the homes of community leaders. Although the basic geometry of the model was characterized by alternating sectors of high- and low-income groups, Hoyt also allowed for variations within sectors. The underlying process was identified as filtering, with older houses being passed down to lower-income households as new housing was built at the periphery. Harris and Ullman's multiple nuclei model is the most recent of the three and takes into account the increased spatial complexity of the North American metropolis in the early 1940s. In particular, it was hypoth-

Figure 9.3   **Traditional Spatial Models of Urban Form: Burgess (Concentric Zone), Hoyt (Sectoral), Harris and Ullman (Multiple Nuclei)**

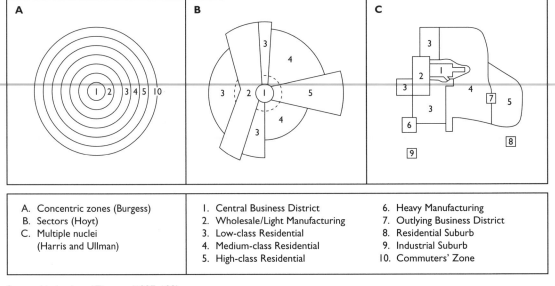

A. Concentric zones (Burgess)	1. Central Business District	6. Heavy Manufacturing
B. Sectors (Hoyt)	2. Wholesale/Light Manufacturing	7. Outlying Business District
C. Multiple nuclei (Harris and Ullman)	3. Low-class Residential	8. Residential Suburb
	4. Medium-class Residential	9. Industrial Suburb
	5. High-class Residential	10. Commuters' Zone

Source: Herbert and Thomas (1997: 199).

esized that individual land uses, including various types of residential areas, tend to be organized around relatively discrete nuclei.

When scores from the factorial ecology studies were mapped, the results showed that the three models were complementary rather than competitive. For example, using census data from the 1950s and 1960s for Toronto, Murdie (1969) determined that economic status was linked to alternating sectors of high and low economic status, family status to the concentric model, and ethnic status to various clusters or nuclei (Figure 9.4). These results have been generally confirmed for other Canadian metropolitan areas, such as Winnipeg (Nicholson and Yeates, 1969), Hamilton (Taylor, 1987), and Kitchener (Filion and Bunting, 1996), but with variations based on the physiography, land-use structure, and historical development of each city (the physical space of the city in Figure 9.4).

Economic status takes on a sectoral form because high-status residents are attracted to desirable features such as lakefronts or ravine lands and, given a choice, stay clear of noxious uses such as railroads and industries, as well as of persons who are considered to be socially undesirable. Family status tends to be concentric because of the presumed preference of families with young children for a suburban environment, the attraction of households without children to the amenities of the central city, and the aging in place of households in the inner suburbs. This spatial form is based on locational decisions made by households during various stages of the life cycle and links closely to models of urban residential mobility and housing careers (Clark and Dieleman, 1996). Ethnic status tends to be nucleated because of the tendency for many ethnic groups to cluster together for mutual support and cultural preservation or, in some cases, to avoid discrimination by members of the receiving society. These spatial forms, especially sectors and concentric zones, are based on the traditional monocentric city in which the central business district predominates over all other areas of the city. Recently, Filion and Bunting (1996) have argued that in Canada's increasingly dispersed urban agglomera-

Figure 9.4   **Idealized Spatial Model of the Modern (Industrial) City Based on Shevky-Bell and Murdie**

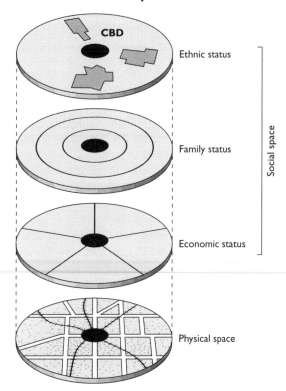

Source: Murdie (1969: 8).

tions more localized place-based features are likely to take on increased significance in structuring social space as the traditional monocentric city becomes a less predominant urban form.

The Social Complexity of Canadian Metropolitan Areas in the 1970s and 1980s

Most studies of the social mosaic of Canadian metropolitan areas have been carried out for individual cities and none have used comparable data sets. A series of studies undertaken by Davies and Murdie

(1991, 1993, 1994) for various census years from 1971 to 1991 extended these single-city analyses by identifying the social dimensionality of all Canadian metropolitan areas and the differences between centres using a common set of variables. The variables were selected to reflect the hypothesized Shevky and Bell dimensions, the results from previous factorial ecology studies of individual Canadian cities, and speculation about recent changes in the structure of post-industrial society (Davies, 1984: 311–12; Knox, 1995: 51). Each of the 15 hypothesized sources of variation was indexed by two to four census variables. Particular importance was given to family variables in recognition of the increased importance of changes in the living arrangements of Canadian households, as noted above (Miron, 1993). In contrast, ethnicity was measured as a more general source of variation and only French ethnic origin, ethnic origins other than British or French, and immigrants were included in the analysis. Individual ethnic origins were not incorporated because of the increased complexity and city-specific nature of ethnicity in many Canadian census metropolitan areas.

The studies were based on the analysis of a joint data set whereby all of the census tracts from all of the census metropolitan areas were incorporated in a single analysis. An important feature of the joint analysis approach is the ability to compare census tracts across metropolitan areas on a single social dimension or factor. From the results of this analysis it is possible to view the social complexity of Canadian metropolitan areas in three separate but complementary ways. The first concerns the number of factors needed to summarize the social complexity of Canadian metropolitan areas and the relationship between these factors and the classic Shevky-Bell social area model. The second is intercity variation in social structure or the extent to which metropolitan areas include more than their expected share of high-scoring census tracts on each factor. The third is the spatial variation of individual factors and their relationship to the concentric, sectoral, and multiple nuclei models of residential differentiation within cities. Brief consideration is

given to each of these perspectives in the remaining part of this section.

1. *The Social Structure*

The results from the Davies and Murdie analyses indicate that the social dimensionality of Canadian metropolitan areas in the 1970s and 1980s was much more complex than the three-factor model hypothesized by Shevky and Bell. This complexity was characterized by two notable distinctions (Figure 9.2). The first was the presence of two separate economic status factors, one providing the familiar contrast between areas occupied by high-income managerial workers and lower-income blue-collar workers, and the other identifying areas of impoverishment originating outside the formal employment sector and characterized by low-income female-parent families and high levels of unemployment. This additional economic factor links closely to changes taking place at the national level, especially the increased number of low-paid employees in the rapidly expanding service sector.

The second departure from the classic threefold social area model was the emergence of not one but four family status dimensions (Figure 9.2). In the Davies and Murdie study these dimensions were identified as family and age, early and late family, non-family, and young adult. This increased fragmentation of the family status factor relates closely to changes in family and household structure noted earlier at the national level. The family and age factor most closely approximates the unidimensional family status concept hypothesized by Shevky and Bell. Areas containing relatively large two-parent families contrasted with those dominated by the elderly and an absence of children. The early-and-late family factor clearly contrasts areas characterized by adults in the early childbearing years with those occupied by older children and middle-aged adults. The non-family and young adult factors identify individual areas in the city characterized by non-family and divorced people, on the one hand, and single young adults, on the other. These two factors reflect the splintering of the family status dimension based on societal trends such as increased divorce rates and young adults leaving home at an earlier age. The opportunity for these groups to occupy separate areas of the city has been facilitated by the construction of new private rental apartments in the central core areas of many Canadian metropolitan areas, especially in the 1960s and 1970s.

Because ethnicity was measured as a general source of variation (British, French, and immigrant), only one ethnic status dimension emerged from the analysis. If individual origins of the various immigrant groups that have come to Canada in the postwar period had been included, the result would have likely been a multiplicity of ethnic dimensions, reflecting the continued spatial segregation of many of these groups in Canadian metropolitan areas. This point is considered further later in this chapter. In the meantime, multiple ethnicities have been added to Figure 9.2 to capture the reality of ethnic differentiation in many of Canada's largest postmodern (post-industrial) cities.

2. *Inter-City Variations in Social Structure*

Inter-city variations on the individual factors are closely related to the political, economic, and regional differentiation of Canada's metropolitan areas (on this, see Chapters 5 and 6). For example, the largest proportions of high-status census tracts on the traditional economic status factor (falling in the top quintile of all census tracts for all metropolitan areas) occur in the capitals and economic centres of the country (e.g., Ottawa, Toronto, Calgary, Halifax, Regina, Vancouver, Quebec City). In contrast, the largest percentages of low-status tracts (falling in the lowest quintile) are associated with blue-collar manufacturing and mining centres (e.g., Trois Rivières, St Catharines, Sudbury, Windsor, Saint John). Census tracts scoring high on the impoverishment factor are particularly concentrated in Saint John and four Quebec centres (Montreal, Trois-Rivières, Sherbrooke, and Quebec City). In contrast, the fast-growing manufacturing and financial service centres in southern Ontario, such as Oshawa, Kitchener, St Catharines, and London, have a relatively low proportion of tracts with high scores on this dimension.

Between-city variations in the incidence of tracts scoring high on the family status dimensions illustrate two major regional contrasts. One is the high proportion of tracts on the early side of the family factor in prairie cities such as Calgary, Saskatoon, and Edmonton. This is easily accounted for by the rapid growth and extensive development of family-oriented suburbs in these centres, especially in the 1970s. The other is the high proportion of tracts on the young adult factor in the prairie cities, as well as in capitals elsewhere, such as Ottawa, Halifax, and St John's, and centres in southern Ontario, such as London and Kitchener. All of these cities provide educational opportunities for young people as well as employment in government offices and/or rapidly growing high-technology industries.

3. *Intra-City Variations in Social Structure*

It is impossible to show all the maps for the entire set of Canadian metropolitan areas. Therefore, a composite illustration of the general spatial form of each major economic and family status factor has been developed (Figure 9.5). These are discussed below with reference to specific cities where appropriate.

The traditional economic status factor revealed the continued presence of Hoyt-like sectors with high-status sectors connected to amenity-rich areas of the city, such as environmentally attractive shorelines and ravine lands, and low-status sectors juxtaposed with long-established industrial areas and rail corridors (Davies and Murdie, 1993: 61). Three major types of high-status areas can be recognized: older inner-city areas that have retained their traditional status (e.g., Rosedale and Forest Hill in Toronto, Westmount in Montreal, Shaughnessy in Vancouver); new suburbs that have often developed around a recreation complex such as a golf course; and newly gentrified and redeveloped neighbourhoods (e.g., Don Vale and Harbour Square in Toronto, Fairview Slopes and Kitsilano in Vancouver).

The spatial distribution of high-impoverishment areas revealed the concentrated areas of poverty in cities such as Quebec City and Winnipeg —'Le croissant de pauvreté' in Quebec City and the

Figure 9.5   **Composite Spatial Model of the Post-Modern (Post-Industrial) City Based on Davies-Murdie Model of Canadian Metropolitan Areas in the 1970s-1980s**

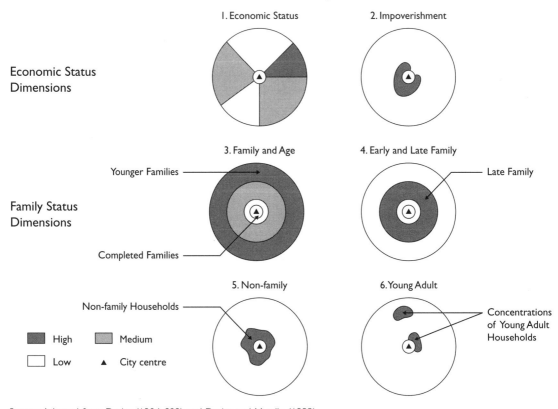

Source: Adapted from Davies (1984: 323) and Davies and Murdie (1993).

North Main Street area in Winnipeg—that have existed for most of this century (ibid., 64–5). Elsewhere, isolated examples of highly impoverished tracts are associated with large public housing estates (e.g., Regent Park in downtown Toronto, the Jane-Finch corridor in Toronto's inner suburbs, and Jeanne-Mance in Montreal) built in the early postwar era. For Toronto, in particular, poverty has become as much a phenomenon of the inner suburbs as the central city.

The family status dimensions revealed less consistent spatial patterns than the economic status factors (ibid., 66–9). Nevertheless, using Calgary as an example, the family and age scores showed the hypothesized concentric ring pattern with middle-aged persons and completed families in the older central area of the city (developed prior to 1960) and younger families in the suburban periphery. The early-and-late family factor was also distributed concentrically but in a more complicated fashion than the family and age dimension—the youngest families in particular parts of the new suburbs, older families in the mature suburbs developed in the 1960s, and some younger families in the central city. The mapped pattern of the non-family dimension shows a tightly defined cluster of extreme scores in the central city and nearby areas of apartment complexes. Finally, tracts scoring high on the young adult factor were located close to downtown but also in the vicinity of major educational and medical institutions in the northwestern part of Calgary.

The Dynamics of Social-Spatial Polarization: An Emerging Canadian Underclass?

In contrast to the previous discussion, this section focuses more specifically on the dynamics of social-spatial polarization in Canadian cities. Given the deepening and broadening of underclass areas in many major US cities, several issues have been at the forefront of academic and policy-relevant discussions in Canada. These include the nature and changing distribution of income inequalities in Canadian cities and the possible emergence of a Canadian underclass, similar in nature to the impoverishment factor identified in the joint analysis of all metropolitan areas in the previous section (e.g., Bourne, 1996; Ley and Smith, 1997; Murdie, 1998). The nature and existence of an underclass have been subject to considerable debate during the past decade, especially among scholars in the United States (e.g., Wilson, 1987, 1996). Without going into the various arguments, the important point for this discussion is that the underclass includes multiple forms of deprivation in addition to low income. Examples include unemployment and the presence of single-parent families and racial or ethnic minorities.

Income Inequalities

Societal trends such as the decline in well-paid manufacturing jobs and the increase in both high- and low-paid service jobs, the retrenchment of the welfare state, and the increased economic differentiation between business-class immigrants and refugees have led a number of researchers to speculate about increased income inequalities in Canadian metropolitan areas. Income inequalities are difficult to measure for individual metropolitan areas. It is possible, however, to say something about the central city-suburban income gap. This is par-

ticularly important from a policy perspective given the extreme differentials in socio-economic status between suburbs and central cities in many US metropolitan areas. For Canada, results show that between 1960 and 1990 central city incomes as a percentage of census metropolitan area incomes declined for all Canadian metropolitan areas except Toronto, where the ratios remained constant.[3] The average percentage for all census metropolitan areas in 1960 was 87.2 compared to 81.1 in 1990 (Bourne, 1996: 139). Although not as low as average percentages of 50–60 in US cities, the decline is surprising given the amount of gentrification and luxury condominium development from the 1970s onward in many Canadian central cities (e.g., Ley, 1996; Preston, Murdie, and Northrup, 1993).

By 1996 this decline had been arrested for several of Canada's largest metropolitan areas (e.g., Vancouver, Ottawa–Hull). Indeed, in Toronto the ratio increased to 104.2 from 91.3 in 1991, indicating that average household income in the central city was slightly higher than in the metropolitan area as a whole. This upward shift in the ratio reflects a number of changes occurring in the central city. From the housing supply perspective these include extensive revitalization of existing stock and the construction of new, relatively high-priced condominiums. On the demand side, this change reflects an increase in high-income earners, especially in the rapidly expanding financial and business service sectors of the economy. Many of these jobs are located in the core area of the city and, in many instances, are filled by people who prefer to live near their place of work. Thus, census tracts in the West Annex and North Riverdale, on the perimeter of Toronto's central business district, experienced some of the most rapid increases in household income between 1991 and 1996.

Two other trends in income distribution are noteworthy. Both can be illustrated using data for Toronto. The first concerns the increased polarization between rich and poor areas in the inner city (the central business district and surrounding residential area). Using average household income for census enumeration areas in Toronto's inner city, the range between the bottom and top deciles in 1990 dollars increased from $31,000 in 1970 to $60,000 in 1990.[4] Put another way, the ratio between the top and bottom deciles increased from 2.8 in 1970 to 4.1 in 1990 (Murdie, 1998). Areas in the lowest decile are primarily public housing developments, while those in the top decile tend to be areas occupied by new luxury condominiums. The second trend concerns the declining fortunes of the inner suburbs—areas of the city developed primarily between the end of the war and the 1970s. For Toronto, Bourne (1996: 139) has shown that these areas experienced the fastest relative decline in incomes between 1970 and 1990, while Murdie (1998), for the 1980s, has demonstrated substantial relative increases in low-income households, low educational achievement, and high unemployment rates in Toronto's inner suburbs. These changes in Toronto's social geography are the result of two major factors—the increased number of refugees who have found accommodation in pockets of low-rent private apartments in the inner suburbs and the increased social residualization of public housing developments, many of which were built on greenfield sites in the inner suburbs in the 1960s and 1970s (Murdie, 1994).

The Emergence of a Canadian Underclass?

These trends raise a more general issue about the extent of the Canadian underclass, its change over time, and the relationship between the underclass and immigration. Using four census variables (lack of a high school diploma, male unemployment, female lone-parent families, and government transfer payments), Ley and Smith (1997) concluded that areas of relative deprivation in Toronto, Montreal, and Vancouver are much less extensive than in most large US cities. Indeed, the extent of social deprivation in the largest Canadian metropolitan areas was much more like that of smaller American agglomerations such as Birmingham, Memphis, New Orleans, and Seattle than large ones such as New York, Detroit, and Chicago. Given this evidence, Ley and Smith question whether an underclass ghetto, in the

American usage of the term, exists in Canadian metropolitan areas. On the other hand, there were differences between the three largest Canadian metropolitan areas. In Vancouver, the census tracts indicating social deprivation were concentrated in the inner city. In Toronto, areas with similar characteristics were located both in the inner city and in isolated suburban neighbourhoods. Over time, between 1971 and 1991, the Vancouver map showed little change in the location of deprived tracts but in Toronto the pattern changed dramatically. In 1971, Toronto exhibited the same inner-city pattern of disadvantaged tracts as Vancouver, but by 1991 the inner-city underclass area had become much more fragmented, and, as noted, pockets of underclass areas began to appear in the inner suburbs. The final issue concerns the relationship between the underclass and immigration. In the US, underclass areas are closely aligned with Black poverty whereas in Europe the underclass is associated with immigrant status. Preliminary analysis of similar relationships in the three Canadian metropolitan areas suggests that there has been little association between immigrants as a whole and underclass status. Recent immigrants from 'new' source regions, however, are much more likely to reside in deprived census tracts in all three cities. This raises important questions about the residential location, housing careers, and economic mobility of immigrant groups in Canadian cities. We consider a number of these issues in the following section of the chapter.

The Changing Geography of Ethnicity: 'EthniCities' and 'Ethnoburbs'

The postwar era has been termed 'the age of migration' by scholars who perceive its defining characteristics as the 'globalization' of urban populations, particularly in North American cities where transnational migration has led to an unprecedented degree of ethnic diversity and the creation, in effect, of 'EthniCities' (Castles and Miller, 1998; Roseman, Laux, and Thieme, 1996). Canadian cities such as

Montreal, Toronto, and Vancouver have become mosaics of ethnic neighbourhoods, marked by complex patterns of socio-spatial stratification. Although many of the initial postwar immigrants to Canadian metropolitan areas first settled in inner-city 'ports of entry', more recent groups, of both high- and low-income status, have bypassed the traditional immigrant reception areas and settled directly in suburban ethnic clusters or what Li (1998), in her study of recent Chinese settlement in Los Angeles, has called 'Ethnoburbs'.

Although ethnicity is a highly complex and contested concept it remains an important aspect of self-identity for most Canadians. Ethnic groups are characterized by shared cultural characteristics, such as origin, language, religion, and cultural values, that not only differentiate them from other ethnic groups but in many instances lead to residential segregation and the development of unique ethnic enclaves within cities. As noted in Table 9.1, one of the most important changes in Canadian society during the postwar period has been a shift in the origins of immigrants from Europe primarily to various countries in Asia. This shift has had a dramatic impact on the social space of Canada's largest metropolitan areas, the places within Canada where most recent immigrants reside. Indeed, an understanding of the social mosaic of Canada's largest metropolitan areas would be incomplete without considering the transformation of these centres from predominantly British or French cities to their present multi-ethnic complexity.

The Spatial Segregation of Ethnic Groups

The settlement experiences and residential patterns of ethnic groups in most Canadian metropolitan areas are so varied that they cannot be easily captured by the more generalized dimensions and spatial models introduced above. Some groups concentrate spatially and form ethnic enclaves, initially in immigrant reception areas close to downtown and more recently by either resegregating in the suburbs or immigrating directly to suburban concentrations. Others tend to disperse spatially after acquiring a working knowledge of English or French and improving their socio-economic position. Still others assimilate quickly into Canadian society from the outset and do not experience spatial segregation. The factors responsible for these various settlement patterns are varied and complex. They include factors internal to the group, such as the retention of cultural traditions and the use of culturally biased information sources in the search for a new place to live, and external factors, such as discriminatory practices by the receiving society that impose constraints on the residential location of new immigrant groups.

One way of illustrating differences in the spatial segregation of ethnic groups is by means of an index of dissimilarity. A summary of average dissimilarity indexes for selected Canadian census metropolitan areas (CMAs) and ethnic groups in 1991 is given in Figures 9.6 and 9.7. The indexes are ranked from highest to lowest by CMA and ethnic group. The dissimilarity index can take on values ranging from zero to 100, with an index value of 100 indicating complete spatial separation between a specific ethnic group and the British group (French in Montreal), and a value of zero indicating no spatial separation between the two groups.[5]

For metropolitan areas, trends indicate that older CMAs in central Canada (e.g., Montreal, Toronto, St Catharines, and Hamilton), which have been important destinations for immigrant groups throughout the twentieth century, have higher segregation levels than their counterparts in western Canada (e.g., Edmonton, Victoria, and Calgary). While there are some differences among central Canadian CMAs, the differences are not noteworthy except for Montreal. Most ethnic groups show their highest levels of segregation for the Montreal CMA. This is due primarily to the sharp spatial divisions between French (Francophone) and English (Anglophone) Montreal and the tendency for some non-English- or non-French-speaking ethnic groups (Allophones) to reside in English Montreal, mainly for cultural and language reasons (Figure 9.8). This spatial patterning has the effect of reinforcing their high level of segregation from the French majority population.

Figure 9.6   **Average Dissimilarity Index by Selected Ethnic Origin Groups for Selected Metropolitan Areas, 1991**

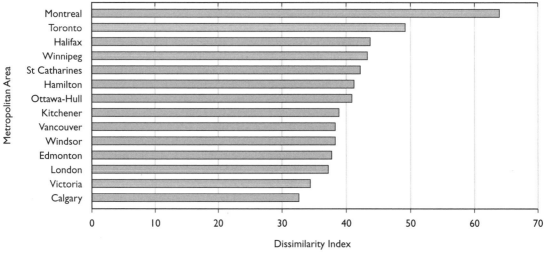

Source: Adapted from Balakrishnan and Hou (1995).

Among ethnic minority groups, Jews are the most segregated overall. Their concentration is more likely due to voluntary factors, such as the retention of cultural and religious traditions, than to discriminatory practices by the receiving population (Hiebert, 1993; Olson and Kobayashi, 1993). Visible minority groups, comprised largely of South Asians, Blacks, and Chinese, most of whom arrived in Canada since the 1960s, also show high average levels of segregation. Both voluntary factors, such as

Figure 9.7   **Average Dissimilarity Index by Selected Metropolitan Areas for Selected Ethnic Origin Groups, 1991**

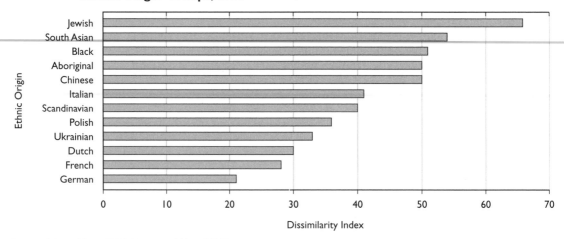

Source: Adapted from Balakrishnan and Hou (1995).

Figure 9.8   **The Geography of Language in Montreal, 1991**

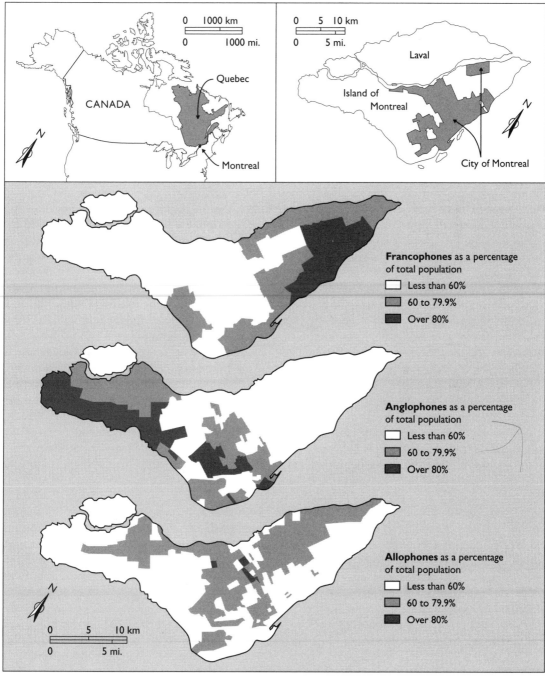

Source: Lo and Teixeira (1998: 487).

retention of cultural traditions, and involuntary characteristics, such as barriers in housing and labour markets, have been identified as contributing factors to the relatively high level of segregation of these groups. The Aboriginal population, despite its status as native-born Canadians, is also highly segregated. The continued spatial segregation of this group, often in the poorest areas of the city, is indicative of its continuing struggle with poverty and discrimination (Balakrishnan and Hou, 1995).

White European groups (Dutch, Germans, Italians, Polish, Scandinavians, and Ukrainians) display lower segregation indexes than the Jews and visible minorities. There are some variations, however, between the European groups. These variations are primarily associated with period of arrival, size of the group, religious and cultural background, and physical appearance. For example, the Ukrainians, Dutch, and Germans, who immigrated to Canada before the 1960s, show lower levels of segregation than do the Italians, who arrived in large numbers primarily during the 1960s. The lower indexes for most of the European groups are not surprising given their earlier arrival in Canada and their lack of visible minority status. Europeans face fewer constraints on residential location based on discriminatory practices than visible minorities do (Balakrishnan and Hou, 1995; Richmond, 1972).

Although the index of dissimilarity is an effective measure of the spatial separation between immigrant groups and the receiving population, the variety of immigrant experiences can be best illustrated by more detailed analysis of a sample of groups that settled in metropolitan Canada under different circumstances in the twentieth century. We do so by considering three separate periods or 'transitions' in Canada's immigrant history: the pre-World War II period, the post-World War II European immigrant experience, and the increased 'internationalization' of immigration following the 1960s.

Pre-War Immigration

Although most immigrant groups prior to World War II settled in agricultural areas of western Canada, two groups—the Jews and Chinese—located primarily in urban areas. They did so under different circumstances, however. The Jews, as noted earlier, are highly segregated in Canadian cities. This segregated pattern is largely the result of cultural traditions, employment opportunities, and proximity to synagogues. In the early-twentieth century, Jewish immigrants to Toronto and Montreal settled in downtown immigrant reception areas or 'ports of entry'. In both cities the Jews formed distinctive enclaves where institutional completeness and ethnic segregation converged, often around employment opportunities in the garment trades (Dennis, 1997: 389; Hiebert, 1993; Robinson and Butovski, 1995: 18). Beginning in the early 1950s, most Jews left their initial areas of settlement and moved in a sectoral, and highly segregated, fashion towards the suburbs. The Chinese, in contrast, experienced much greater overt discrimination and often concentrated in ethnic enclaves for defensive reasons. Chinatowns served as 'ports of entry' and safe havens where Chinese immigrants could live and carry on their business free of discrimination. Before the 1940s it was not easy for Chinese to move into better residential areas (Anderson, 1991; Lai, 1988: 85). Thus, while it has been argued that Chinatowns were created by Chinese for self-protection, from an 'outsider perspective' they may also be seen as a physical manifestation of racial discrimination (Olson and Kobayashi, 1993).

Postwar European Immigration

In contrast to the first half of the twentieth century, when a majority of immigrants to Canada settled initially in rural areas in the West, immigrants in post-World War II Canada went primarily to metropolitan centres. By 1996, 85 per cent of Canada's immigrants and 93 per cent of immigrants who arrived between 1991 and 1996 lived in census metropolitan areas. More than three-quarters of these recent immigrants resided in Toronto, Montreal, and Vancouver.

The complexities of ethnic residential settlement patterns have increased in the post-World War II era compared to the period preceding the war. Until the

1970s, most of Canada's immigrant population came from Britain and other European countries, initially Western Europe and then Southern Europe, especially Italy, Greece, and Portugal. During the 1960s and 1970s, Southern Europeans were among the largest immigrant groups to arrive in Toronto and Montreal. The arrival of entire extended families by means of 'chain migration' encouraged the establishment of distinctive residential neighbourhoods with ethnic businesses and cultural and religious institutions (Anderson and Higgs, 1976; Sturino, 1990: 182). These groups also tended to attach considerable importance to home-ownership and home improvements (Dansereau, 1993: 307; Richmond, 1972). Several strategies were used to achieve security through home-ownership. Private sources of finance (particularly second mortgages) facilitated undercapitalized purchases (Lavigne, 1987; Murdie, 1991). As well, many families occupied part of the house and rented the remainder for extra income (Richmond, 1972: 47). During the postwar economic boom, many new immigrants achieved upward economic mobility through employment in the construction industry and relied on their construction skills to renovate their own homes. Home-ownership itself also became a vehicle for economic mobility and provided capital through resale of the house for a move to a larger and more modern home in the suburbs.

By investing in housing (both home-ownership and housing renovation), Southern European groups have contributed substantially to maintaining the vitality of older inner-city neighbourhoods in Montreal, Toronto, and Vancouver (Germain, 1997: 3; Lavigne, 1987; Ley, 1993: 328). The renewal that took place in these working-class neighbourhoods was successful, partially because of the tendency of these ethnic groups to rely extensively on strong social networks, including friends, relatives, and community ties, for help, advice, and labour participation. In many instances, Southern Europeans have continued this practice of urban rejuvenation in their move to older suburban areas (Ley, 1993: 328; Holdsworth, 1993: 50).

The Portuguese, who settled in large numbers in Montreal and Toronto, are typical of the Southern Europeans. In the 1950s and 1960s, Portuguese immigrants bought relatively inexpensive houses in the downtown immigrant reception areas of Toronto (Kensington Market) and Montreal (St Louis neighbourhood), where they settled in large numbers. Extensive renovations were often done by the new owners, and mutual help and co-operation among Portuguese immigrants became a key factor in the rejuvenation of older working-class neighbourhoods (Krohn, Fleming, and Manzer, 1977; Lavigne, 1987; Teixeira, 1996: 186).

During the past two decades, the Portuguese in Montreal and Toronto have undergone important changes in residential location, at the same time retaining the original core of the community. First, in each city the Portuguese expanded from the immigrant reception area towards the suburbs, following the Italians who earlier moved in the same sectoral direction. The second pattern, as illustrated for Toronto in Figure 9.9, is a resegregation or transplantation of the Portuguese to suburban Mississauga in the Toronto CMA and Laval in the Montreal CMA (Teixeira and Murdie, 1997). Some of these families live within, or in close proximity to, existing pockets or nuclei of Portuguese concentration, while others are more dispersed. Thus, distinct and separate Portuguese communities seem to be forming in these suburbs. In part, resegregation occurs because of obstacles to corridor expansion (that is, decentralization along an axis) resulting from the presence of earlier immigrant groups, such as the Italians. Resegregation is also made possible because relatively efficient transportation networks allow suburbanized minorities such as the Portuguese to return to their original ethnic neighbourhood to shop for special ethnic goods and participate in the institutional life of their community.

Recent Changes in Immigration: Towards a Multicultural Canada?

As indicated in Table 9.1, the source countries of immigrants settling in Canada's metropolitan areas have changed dramatically since the early 1970s—primarily from European to Asian origins. In 1996,

Figure 9.9   **Portuguese Population by Mother Tongue in the City of Toronto and Mississauga, 1971 and 1991**

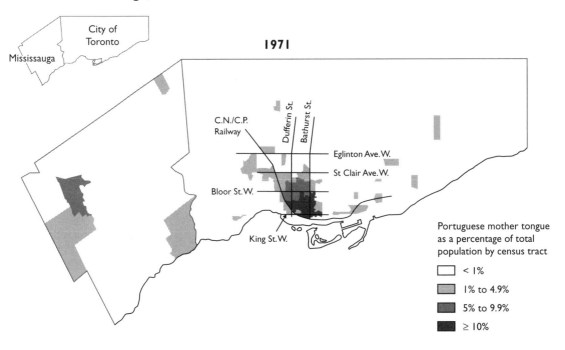

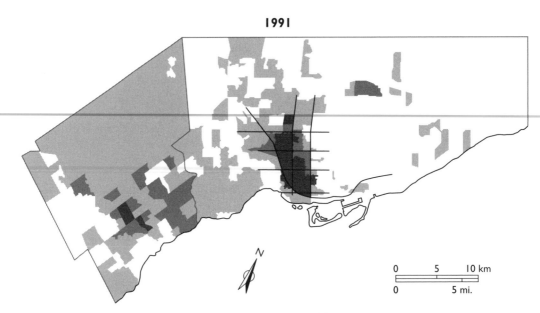

Source: Statistics Canada (1974, 1993), from Teixeira and Murdie (1997: 503).

the top five countries (in rank order) for residents of Toronto who immigrated before 1961 were Italy, Britain, Germany, Poland, and Greece. For Vancouver, the comparable list included Britain, Germany, Italy, the Netherlands, and China. In contrast, the top five source countries of Toronto's recent immigrants (1991–6) were Hong Kong, Sri Lanka, China, the Philippines, and India, and for Vancouver the top five were Hong Kong, China, Taiwan, India, and the Philippines. By 1996, 32 per cent of Toronto's population and 31 per cent of Vancouver's were members of visible minority groups. By 2011 it is estimated that visible minorities will comprise about 20 per cent of Canada's population, an increase from 11 per cent in 1996 (Kettle, 1998). The countries of origin of recent immigrants to Montreal differ from Toronto and Vancouver, partially reflecting the Francophone character of that city. The top five source countries for immigrants arriving between 1991 and 1996 were Haiti, Lebanon, France, China, and Romania. As noted earlier, recent immigrants to Canada, and especially to the major metropolitan centres, belong to a wide spectrum of economic groups. Here, we contrast immigrants and refugees at two ends of the spectrum—relatively wealthy Chinese business immigrants and lower-income immigrants from the Caribbean and Africa.

While the pre-World War II Chinese community was ghettoized and mistrusted, recent Chinese business immigrants have been welcomed for their financial resources, their education, and their occupational skills. These immigrants are often professionals and business people who have the economic resources to start small businesses and buy expensive housing in the suburbs of Vancouver (e.g., Shaughnessy Heights, Richmond, Kerrisdale, Oakridge) and Toronto (e.g., Scarborough, Markham, Mississauga). The direct movement of many wealthy Chinese and other Asian groups to suburbs in Vancouver and Toronto and the physical changes they have brought to existing neighbourhoods by building so-called 'monster homes' and Asian theme malls have led to some racial tensions (Brosseau et al., 1996; Mitchell, 1997; Ray, Halseth, and Johnson, 1997; Smart and Smart, 1996).

Another major wave of newcomers includes immigrants and refugees from the Caribbean, Latin America, and Africa. For most of these groups there were no pre-existing ethnic enclaves to assist their integration into Canadian society (Balakrishnan and Hou, 1995: 33; McNicoll, 1993: 198). For example, black migration to Canada is relatively recent, with a large proportion, particularly those of Caribbean origin, arriving in the last three decades (Anderson, 1993; Henry, 1994). Upon arrival, some of these new immigrants and refugees settled not only in the inner city but also in suburban communities. Pockets of concentration of Caribbean immigrants (often in public housing) have been identified in both the inner city and the suburbs of Montreal and Toronto (Ley and Smith, 1997: 25; McNicoll, 1993; Murdie, 1994, 1996). In part, the increased number of blacks in public housing is due to low household income compounded by supply, cost, and discriminatory constraints in Toronto's private rental market (Murdie, 1996: 228). However, it is important to reiterate that none of these areas of concentration can be described as a ghetto, since they do not resemble the large-scale ghettos that characterize many US cities (Henry, 1994: 230; Ley and Smith, 1997). Like many Afro-Caribbeans, recently arrived African immigrants from countries such as Somalia and Ghana live in high-rise apartments in the inner suburbs (Figure 9.10). In the case of the Ghanaians, the suburban emphasis and the tendency to concentrate in a relatively few high-rise apartment buildings result from the availability of relatively low-cost housing in these large-scale apartment areas, the highly structured social networks within this group, and opportunities for employment in manufacturing firms that are increasingly located in Toronto's suburbs (Owusu, 1999).

Conclusion

In the second half of the twentieth century, Canada's cities have been transformed by a number of societal forces, including economic restructuring, an aging population and new approaches to family

Figure 9.10   **The Ghanaian Population in the City of Toronto and Region of Peel (by Census Tract), 1994**

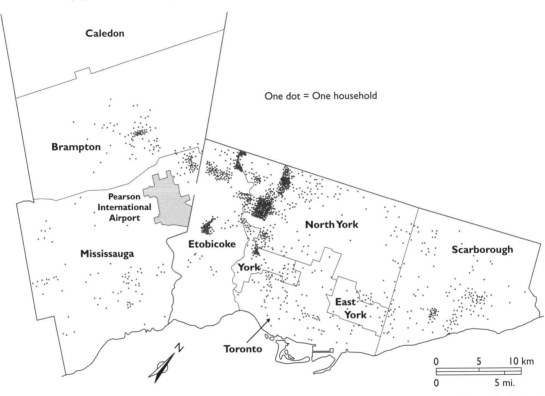

Source: Owusu (1999). Used by permission of Carfax Publishing, Taylor & Francis Ltd, P.O. Box 25, Abington, Oxfordshire, OX14 3UE, UK.

organization, changes in immigration patterns, and a rethinking of the traditional welfare state. Within this broad national-level context, the diversity and the complexity of the socio-spatial structure of Canadian metropolitan areas have increased.

Of all the characteristics discussed here, perhaps ethnicity has most visibly transformed the social space of Canadian cities. In the second half of the twentieth century, Canada has become a culturally and racially heterogeneous society and its immigrant groups have been major factors in the social differentiation of large Canadian cities. Canadian cities vary dramatically, not only with respect to the ethnic composition of their populations—with some cities being more culturally heterogeneous than others—but also with respect to the tendency of certain minorities to concentrate spatially. The settlement experiences of immigrant groups have taken different forms—from pockets of ethnic concentration marked by a rich and distinctive cultural identity to dispersed populations lacking any defining features that distinguish them within the metropolis. Some immigrant communities, particularly recently arrived refugee groups, are highly marginalized with respect to the quality of housing and kinds of neighbourhoods within which they live. Improvement of the life chances of these groups is a major challenge for Canadian policymakers, especially in the context of a sharp retrenchment of the welfare state.

Finally, what about the future? In general terms, it is likely that the social structure of Canadian metropolitan areas will be impacted by continued changes in the four major societal forces mentioned earlier (economic change, age and family structure, immigration, and the curtailment of the welfare state). Accelerated globalization and economic restructuring, combined with the uncertain development prospects of many emerging economies, suggest an extended period of economic slowdown in Canada and a further decline in manufacturing employment accompanied by an increase in both high- and low-valued service jobs. The general sectoral pattern of economic status that has been in place for several decades will remain for many cities, but the potential for increased social and spatial inequalities will continue apace.

As for age structure, cities will be forced to adapt to the aging of the baby-boom generation and the smaller numbers in younger generations. This will have a major impact on the housing stock of Canadian urban areas, particularly those where younger generations are not supplemented with newcomers. In these circumstances, the demand for diverse forms of retirement dwellings will increase, while the demand for other forms of housing will stagnate.

The flow of immigrants into major Canadian cities and the make-up of the immigrant population depend on policies established by the Canadian and Quebec governments as well as on global economic and political circumstances.[6] There is some evidence, for example, that with the economic downturn in Asia, business people have less money to invest and therefore their capacity to come to Canada as business-class immigrants has diminished. If this trend continues, it will have a considerable impact on the further development of Asian enclaves in suburban Toronto and Vancouver. At the same time, however, there is no shortage of political refugees attempting to gain admission to Canada. More generally, it is likely that immigrant groups will continue to suburbanize, either resegregating in the suburbs following initial settlement near the downtown core of the city or, as is increasingly likely, immigrating directly to the inner suburbs of

major metropolitan centres. The segregation levels between some immigrant groups and the rest of the population will remain high and the spatial outcome will be an increasingly fragmented and economically differentiated pattern of ethnic enclaves in almost all parts of the city.

Finally, an accelerated dismantling of the Canadian welfare state remains a very real possibility as governments continue to emphasize the reduction of public debt. It is unlikely that social housing programs will be reinstated in the near future or that welfare payments and public funding for agencies serving immigrants and refugees will be increased to previous levels. Consequently, a deepening and widening of underclass areas, especially in those cities that attract disproportionate numbers of society's most vulnerable groups—the chronically unemployed, single-parent families, refugees, and psychiatric out-patients—is a strong likelihood.

This is the general outline. The social dimensions will be more complex than portrayed here and the spatial patterns will depend on the physical space of individual cities, expressed as both the natural and built environment. The patterns will also depend on how social structures interact with physical space. The fortunes of disadvantaged groups and their integration with broader society will be determined to a considerable extent by the attitudes and generosity of individual Canadians as well as the willingness of politicians at the national, provincial, and local levels of government to place higher priority on the needs of the most vulnerable in Canadian society.

Notes

1. When not cited, Statistics Canada census data originate from the Statistics Canada Web page, <www.statcan.ca>, or other forms of electronic dissemination. At writing, only a limited number of 1996 census bulletins had been published.

2. Census tracts are small neighbourhood-like areas into which metropolitan areas have been divided by Statistics Canada for data reporting

and analysis purposes. The population of a census tract ranges between 2,500 and 8,000, with a preferred average of 4,000.

3. Although the census was taken in June 1961 and June 1991, incomes are for the calendar years 1960 and 1990, respectively.

4. An enumeration area is the geographic area canvassed by one census enumerator. These are the smallest geographic areas for which census data are available and generally contain a maximum of 375 dwellings.

5. The index of dissimilarity is the percentage of one population that would have to relocate in order to equal the spatial distribution of the population with which it is being compared (Duncan and Duncan, 1955). The indexes are usually computed using census tract data.

6. Quebec has had the right to select its own independent-class immigrants since 1978 and has had jurisdiction over integration and settlement programs for immigrants and refugees since 1991.

References

Anderson, G., and D. Higgs. 1976. *A Future to Inherit: The Portuguese Communities of Canada*. Toronto: McClelland & Stewart.

Anderson, K. 1991. *Vancouver's Chinatown: Racial Discourse in Canada, 1875–1980*. Montreal and Kingston: McGill-Queen's University Press.

Anderson, W.W. 1993. *Caribbean Immigrants: A Socio-Demographic Profile*. Toronto: Canadian Scholars' Press.

Balakrishnan, T.R., and F. Hou. 1995. *The Changing Patterns of Spatial Concentration and Residential Segregation of Ethnic Groups in Canada's Major Metropolitan Areas 1981–1991*. London, Ont.: University of Western Ontario, Population Studies Centre, Discussion Paper No. 95–2.

Beaujot, R.J. 1991. *Population Change in Canada: The Challenges of Policy Adaptation*. Toronto: Oxford University Press.

Bourne, L.S. 1996. 'Social Polarization and Spatial Segregation: Changing Income Inequalities in Canadian Cities', in R.J. Davies, ed., *Contemporary City Structuring: International Geographical Insights*. Wits, South Africa: Society of South African Geographers.

———— and A.E. Olvet. 1995. *New Urban and Regional Geographies in Canada: 1986-91 and Beyond*. Toronto: Centre for Urban and Community Studies, University of Toronto, Major Report 33.

Brosseau, M., P. Garvie, L. Chen, and A. Langlois. 1996. 'Les méga-maisons de Kerrisdale, Vancouver: Chronique d'un quartier en transformation', *Canadian Geographer* 40: 164–72.

Burgess, E.W. 1925. 'The Growth of the City', in R.E. Park, Burgess, and R.D. McKenzie, eds, *The City*. Chicago: University of Chicago Press.

Castles, S., and M.J. Miller. 1998. *The Age of Migration: International Population Movements in the Modern World*, 2nd edn. New York: Guilford Press.

Clark, W.A.V., and F.M. Dieleman. 1996. *Households and Housing: Choice and Outcomes in the Housing Market*. New Brunswick, NJ: Centre for Urban Policy Research, Rutgers University.

Dansereau, F. 1993. 'Neighbourhood Differentiation and Social Change', in J.R. Miron, ed., *House, Home and Community: Progress in Housing Canadians, 1945–1986*. Ottawa: Canada Mortgage and Housing Corporation.

Davies, W.K.D. 1984. *Factorial Ecology*. Aldershot, England: Gower.

———— and R.A. Murdie. 1991. 'Changes in the Intraurban Social Dimensionality of Canadian CMAs: 1981–1986', *Canadian Journal of Regional Science* 14: 207–32.

———— and ————. 1993 'Measuring the Social Ecology of Cities', in L.S. Bourne and D.F. Ley, eds, *The Changing Social Geography of Canadian Cities*. Montreal and Kingston: McGill-Queen's University Press.

———— and ————. 1994. 'The Social Complexity of Canadian Metropolitan Areas in 1986: A Multivariate Analysis of Census Data', in F. Frisken, ed., *The Changing Canadian Metropolis: A Public Policy Perspective*, vol. 1. Berkeley, Calif. and Toronto: Institute of Governmental Studies Press and The Canadian Urban Institute.

Dennis, R. 1997. 'Property and Propriety: Jewish Landlords in Early Twentieth-Century Toronto', *Transactions of the Institute of British Geographers* 22: 377–97.

Duncan, O.D., and B. Duncan. 1955. 'A Methodological Analysis of Segregation Indices', *American Sociological Review* 20: 210–17.

Fainstein, S.S., and M. Harloe. 1992. 'Introduction: London and New York in the Contemporary World', in Fainstein, I. Gordon, and Harloe, eds, *Divided Cities: New York and London in the Contemporary World*. Oxford: Basil Blackwell.

Filion, P., and T. Bunting. 1996. 'Space and Place: The Social Geography of the Dispersed City', in Filion, Bunting, and K. Curtis, eds, *The Dynamics of the Dispersed City: Geographic and Planning Perspectives on Waterloo Region*. Waterloo: Department of Geography Publication Series No. 47, University of Waterloo.

Foggin, P., and M. Polèse. 1977. *The Social Geography of Montreal in 1971*. Toronto: Centre for Urban and Community Studies, University of Toronto, Research Paper 88.

Foot, D.K., and D. Stoffman. 1996. *Boom, Bust, and Echo: How to Profit from the Coming Demographic Shift*. Toronto: Macfarlane Walter and Ross.

Frisken, F., L.S. Bourne., G. Gad, and R.A. Murdie. 1997. *Governance and Social Well-being in the Toronto Area: Past Achievements and Future Challenges*. Toronto: Centre for Urban and Community Studies, University of Toronto, Research Paper 193.

Germain, A. 1997. 'Case Studies of Research and Policy on Migrants in Cities—Montreal', paper presented at the Second International Metropolis Conference, Copenhagen, 25–8 Sept.

Harris, C.D., and E.L. Ullman. 1945. 'The Nature of Cities', *Annals, American Academy of Political and Social Science* 242: 7–17.

Henry, F. 1994. *The Caribbean Diaspora in Toronto: Learning to Live with Racism*. Toronto: University of Toronto Press.

Herbert, D.T., and C.J. Thomas. 1997. *Cities in Space: City as Space*. New York: John Wiley & Sons; London: David Fulton Publishers.

Hiebert, D. 1993. 'Integrating Production and Consumption: Industry, Class, Ethnicity, and the Jews of Toronto', in L.S. Bourne and D.E. Ley, eds, *The Changing Social Geography of Canadian Cities*. Montreal and Kingston: McGill-Queen's University Press.

———. 1994. 'Canadian Immigration: Policy, Politics, Geography', *Canadian Geographer* 38: 254–8.

Holdsworth, D.W. 1993. 'Evolving Urban Landscapes', in L.S. Bourne and D.E. Ley, eds, *The Changing Social Geography of Canadian Cities*. Montreal and Kingston: McGill-Queen's University Press.

Hoyt, H. 1939. *The Structure and Growth of Residential Neighbourhoods in American Cities*. Washington: Federal Housing Administration.

Kettle, J. 1998. 'Canada Takes a New Look', *Globe and Mail*, 21 May, B11.

Knox, P. 1995. *Urban Social Geography: An Introduction*, 3rd edn. Essex, England: Longman.

Krohn, R.G., B. Fleming, and M. Manzer. 1977. *The Other Economy: The Internal Logic of Local Rental Housing*. Toronto: Peter Martin Associates.

Lai, D.C. 1988. *Chinatowns: Towns Within Cities in Canada*. Vancouver: University of British Columbia Press.

Lavigne, G. 1987. *Les ethniques et la ville: L'aventure urbaine des immigrants Portugais à Montréal*. Montréal: Le Préambule.

LeBourdais, C., and M. Beaudry. 1988. 'The Changing Residential Structure of Montreal: 1971–1981', *Canadian Geographer* 32: 98–113.

Ley, D.F. 1993. 'Past Elites and Present Gentry: Neighbourhoods of Privilege in the Inner City', in L.S. Bourne and D.E. Ley, eds, *The Changing Social Geography of Canadian Cities*. Montreal and Kingston: McGill-Queen's University Press.

———. 1996. 'The New Middle Class in Canadian Central Cities', in J. Caulfield and L. Peake, eds, *City Lives and City Forms: Critical Research and Canadian Urbanism*. Toronto: University of Toronto Press.

——— and H. Smith. 1997. *Is There an Immigrant "Underclass" in Canadian Cities?* Vancouver: Vancouver Centre of Excellence, Research on

Immigration and Integration in the Metropolis, Working Paper Series 97–08.

Li, W. 1998. 'Anatomy of a New Ethnic Settlement: The Chinese "Ethnoburb" in Los Angeles', *Urban Studies* 35: 479–501.

Lo, L., and C. Teixeira. 1998. 'If Quebec Goes ... The "Exodus" Impact?', *Professional Geographer* 50: 481–98.

McNicoll, C. 1993. *Montréal: Une société multiculturelle.* Paris: Belin.

McVey, W.W., and W.E. Kalbach. 1995. *Canadian Population.* Toronto: Nelson.

Miron, J.R. 1993. 'Demography, Living Arrangement and Residential Geography', in L.S. Bourne and D.F. Ley, eds, *The Changing Social Geography of Canadian Cities.* Montreal and Kingston: McGill-Queen's University Press.

Mitchell, K. 1997. 'Conflicting Geographies of Democracy and the Public Sphere in Vancouver BC', *Transactions of the Institute of British Geographers* 22: 162–79.

Murdie, R.A. 1969. *Factorial Ecology of Metropolitan Toronto, 1951–1961.* Chicago: University of Chicago, Research Paper No. 116.

———. 1991. 'Local Strategies in Resale Home Financing in the Toronto Housing Market', *Urban Studies* 28: 465–83.

———. 1994. 'Social Polarisation and Public Housing in Canada: A Case Study of the Metropolitan Toronto Housing Authority', in F. Frisken, ed., *The Changing Canadian Metropolis: A Public Policy Perspective,* vol. 1. Berkeley, Calif. and Toronto: Institute of Governmental Studies Press and The Canadian Urban Insitute.

———. 1996. 'Economic Restructuring and Social Polarization in Toronto', in J. O'Loughlin and J. Friedrichs, eds, *Social Polarization in Post-Industrial Metropolises.* Berlin and New York: Walter de Gruyter.

———. 1998. 'The Welfare State, Economic Restructuring and Immigrant Flows: Impacts on Socio-spatial Segregation in Greater Toronto', in S. Musterd and W. Ostendorf, eds, *Urban Segregation and the Welfare State: Inequality and Exclusion in Western Cities.* London: Routledge.

Nicholson, T.G., and M.H. Yeates. 1969. 'The Ecological and Spatial Structure of the Socio-economic Characteristics of Winnipeg, 1961', *Canadian Review of Sociology and Anthropology* 6: 162–78.

Olson, S.H., and A.L. Kobayashi. 1993. 'The Emerging Ethnocultural Mosaic', in L.S. Bourne and D.E. Ley, eds, *The Changing Social Geography of Canadian Cities.* Montreal and Kingston: McGill-Queen's University Press.

Owusu, T. 1999. 'Residential Patterns and Housing Choices of New Immigrants in Canada: The Case of the Ghanaians in Toronto', *Housing Studies* 14, 1: 77–97.

Preston, V., R.A. Murdie, and D. Northrup. 1993. 'Condominiums: An Investment Decision or Life-style Choice? A Comparative Study of Resident and Nonresident Condominium Owners in the City of Toronto', *Netherlands Journal of Housing and the Built Environment* 8: 281–300.

Ray, B.K., G. Halseth, and B. Johnson. 1997. 'The Changing "Face" of the Suburbs: Issues of Ethnicity and Residential Change in Suburban Vancouver', *International Journal of Urban and Regional Research* 21: 75–99.

Richmond, A.H. 1972. *Ethnic Residential Segregation in Metropolitan Toronto.* Toronto: Institute for Behavioural Research, York University.

Robinson, I., and M. Butovsky. 1995. 'Introduction', in Robinson and Butovsky, eds, *Renewing Our Days: Montreal Jews in the Twentieth Century.* Montreal: Véhicule Press.

Roseman, C., H.D. Laux, and G. Thieme. 1996. *EthniCity: Geographic Perspectives on Ethnic Change in Modern Cities.* Lanham, Md.: Rowman and Littlefield.

Rutherford, T. 1996. 'Socio-spatial Restructuring of Canadian Labour Markets', in J.N.H. Britton, ed., *Canada and the Global Economy: The Geography of Structural and Technological Change.* Montreal and Kingston: McGill-Queen's University Press.

Sassen, S. 1991. *The Global City.* Princeton, NJ: Princeton University Press.

———. 1994. *Cities in a World Economy.* Thousand Oaks, Calif.: Pine Forge Press.

Shevky, E., and W. Bell. 1955. *Social Area Analysis.* Stanford, Calif.: Stanford University Press.

Smart, A., and J. Smart. 1996. 'Monster Homes: Hong Kong Immigration to Canada, Urban Conflicts, and Contested Representations of Space', in J. Caulfield and L. Peake, eds, *City Lives & City Forms: Critical Research & Canadian Urbanism*. Toronto: University of Toronto Press.

Statistics Canada. 1974. *Population and Housing Characteristics by Census Tract—Series B*. Ottawa: Minister of Industry, Trade and Commerce, Catalogue 95–751.

————. 1993. *Profile of Census Tracts: Toronto—Part A*. Ottawa: Minister of Industry, Science and Technology, Catalogue 95–353.

————. 1998. *Historical Labour Force Statistics 1997*. Ottawa: Minister of Industry, Catalogue 71–201XPB.

Sturino, F. 1990. *Forging the Chain: Italian Migration to North America, 1880–1930*. Toronto: Multicultural History Society of Ontario.

Taylor, S.M. 1987. 'Social Change in Hamilton, 1961–1981', in M.J. Dear, J.J. Drake, and L.G. Reeds, eds, *Steel City: Hamilton and Region*. Toronto: University of Toronto Press.

Teixeira, C. 1996. 'The Suburbanization of Portuguese Communities in Toronto and Montreal: From Isolation to Residential Integration?', in A. Laperièrre, V. Lindstrom, and T.P. Seiler, eds, *Immigration and Ethnicity in Canada*. Montreal: Association for Canadian Studies.

———— and R.A. Murdie. 1997. 'The Role of Ethnic Real Estate Agents in the Residential Relocation Process: A Case Study of the Portuguese Home-buyers in Suburban Toronto', *Urban Geography* 18: 497–520.

Wilson, W.J. 1987. *The Truly Disadvantaged: The Inner City, the Underclass and Public Policy*. Chicago: University of Chicago Press.

————. 1996. *When Work Disappears: The World of the New Urban Poor*. New York: Alfred A. Knopf.

Chapter 10

Form and Energy in the Urban Built Environment

Sherry Olson

The form of an object can be understood as a product of forces, for instance, the energies applied to clay by the potter, or by wind and water to a sand beach. The form of a city, or urban morphology, is an expression of forces exerted on it during the years of its existence. As D'Arcy Thompson expressed it with reference to shells and skeletons, 'The form of an object is a diagram of forces', and 'from it [the form] we can judge of or deduce the forces that are acting or have acted upon it' (Thompson, 1961 [1917]: 11). In this essay, after some thoughts about the meaning of form as it applies to urban identity, we consider first the physical landscape on which the metropolis develops, then look at the structures we have built, examine the whole 'built landscape' as a product of flows of investment, and finally turn to the problems generated by massive flows of energy through our urban landscape. We shall see that the form of a city sets limits on our lifestyles and creates problems that may mean life or death for urban residents.

Identity and Form

Canadian cities share some formal properties because they were all shaped by the history of the nation and by the same suite of ideals and fads, but each city also has features of its own. Images of St-Hyacinthe, Quebec, and Winnipeg from about 1880 and Saint John in 1944 (Figures 10.1 to 10.3) present urban forms characteristic of particular places and moments in history. St-Hyacinthe grew from a village and was already well established by 1880, while Winnipeg was laid out in a gridiron pattern,

new, expansive, and brash. The artists who drafted the two bird's-eye views shared certain ideas of the 1880s: an admiration for the riverfront site, an appreciation of the surrounding 'breadbasket', and a perception of smokestacks as an expression of a town's ambition of industrial power. The 1944 artist erased the smoke instead of exaggerating it, and the improvements conceived for Saint John are present in other North American plans of the 1940s: a viaduct, a school set in a park, curving streets for single-family developments, and slab walk-ups for rental by low-income families.

A generation later, when Expo 67 turned the spotlight on Montreal, local architectural critics pointed to the powerful verticals of the new city centre. Slabs and point-blocks rising to 47 storeys expressed corporate ambitions. Melvin Charney referred to 'a mound fixation' and the pioneering underground city, while Norbert Schoenauer (1967) criticized the insular character of the buildings and the failure to take full advantage of the topography. The same problems of insular design are often identified in Toronto and Vancouver, and 20 years later Roger Kemble described Winnipeg's main intersection, Portage and Main, as a 'noisy, busy, hard, cold corner' and Olympic Plaza in Calgary as 'hard to read as an urban space'. Kemble argued that these two examples, along with counterparts in other Canadian cities, reflect a splintering of what was once a shared vision of urban space (1989: 20, 70).

To generalize about the common properties of our cities, or to enjoy their individuality, we observe volumes and spaces, colours and reflections. We examine a city from a distance, from close up, and

Figure 10.1

VUE A VOL D'OISEAU DE
ST. HYACINTHE, P.Q.
1881.

Bird's-eye view of St-Hyacinthe, Quebec, in 1881. The artist sought to make every commercial building identifiable, used curling smoke and rippling water to make the industrial base more prominent, and at the same time gave detail and stature to monumental buildings, curving paths, and planned green spaces. Reproduced from a copy in the National Archives of Canada (NMC 8876), original at the Séminaire de Saint-Hyacinthe.

from inside. We take clues from its sensory, even sensual, properties: visual, tactile, and kinetic—rough or smooth, hard or soft, challenging the muscles for walking uphill or downhill.

Because the form of a city expresses our various aspirations, observing the landscape we have created around us informs us about our society. It provides cues as to how, from generation to generation, our social relations have changed. Urban form offers a better appraisal of the balance of social forces at work than any other analysis. As an example, in Montreal the restored vestiges of the eighteenth-century hospital of the Grey Nuns adjoin rows of handsome warehouses that replaced the hospital—an urban renewal project of the 1870s. A second round of renewal in the 1970s converted the warehouses into condominium dwellings and offices. Dating from the same era as the warehouses are ornate banks in the central business district (CBD), bulky tobacco factories and breweries on the east and west, and superb stone mansions of the tobacco manufacturers and brewers overlooking miles of working-class row houses. Steeples of 1870s vintage are still focal points of dozens of neighbourhoods. In Point St Charles, two stone churches, cheek by jowl, St Charles and St Gabriel, still shelter Irish and French-Canadian neighbours at worship. Those remnants of earlier forms continue to provoke questions about our values and identities, past and present.

Landscape patterns reveal relationships. A landscape is an assemblage of objects in a space large enough for social interaction: a stage set. If we blow up a microphotograph of an intestinal wall or a computer chip, we perceive it as a landscape the moment we recognize that we can, in imagination, move in and out of it, bump into it, or inhabit it. Our conception of landscape therefore provides a scale and a perspective. We shift back and forth between the standpoint of observer and participant, distancing ourselves or becoming involved.

Walking down a hill in the country, we would see changes of slope and an adapted catena or chain of soils and plants. As we walk down Mountain Street in Montreal or Wentworth Street in Hamilton, we observe a similar chain of house types and household types. The sizes and heights of houses indicate a social chain of command, from which we can infer the meaning of social class. For larger regions, Humboldt (a grandfather of modern geography) used the heights of vegetation—grassland, scrub, or forest—as indicators of climate and relief. Landscape has integrating power because people have the capacity to handle fabulous amounts of information in visual form. In the city we infer hierarchical relationships from the overlay of patterns at several scales. Urban forms fit together into a whole. The Aldred Building, built in 1928 on Place d'Armes, belongs to the Montreal skyline and situates us in a 'central business district', a feature we expect to find in any big city.

Just as we are situated within the city's spatial frame, we are also situated inside its time frame. Churches, war memorials, and shade trees have longer lives than our own, and the city testifies to a long sequence of human choices, to the exercise of power and a succession of creative and destructive impulses. Even a small city like St-Hyacinthe (Figure 10.1) has the capacity to outlast us, overwhelm us, and still belong to us.

Modern geographical theories have failed to develop the full significance of urban morphology. Despite talk of 'space' and 'place' as defining concepts in geography, there has been little theorizing about scale in human geography,[1] and too little attention has been paid to form and classification of forms.[2] Urban spatial analyses of the 1960s were generally simplified to a two-dimensional geometry, and models were static rather than dynamic, snapshots rather than moving pictures.[3]

To develop more dynamic models, we are now able to employ tools such as film media, dynamic geometry, satellite imagery of terrain, and computer-assisted modelling and to look at urban forms as evidence of social processes.[4] Even landscapes of repose, like those pictured in Figures 10.1 to 10.3, are products of dynamic circulations. As was stressed in Chapter 1, the city's boxes of wood, brick, and glass represent the accumulation of masses of capital, and the moving traffic and flashing signals inform us about flows of energy in the system, which are the basis of accumulation, reproduction, and depreciation of that capital. As D'Arcy Thompson explained, 'Morphology is not only a study of material things and of the forms of material things, but has its dynamical aspect, under which we deal with the interpretation, in terms of force, of the operations of Energy' (Thompson, 1961 [1917]: 14).

The Lay of the Land

The individuality of our cities is founded on the lay of the land, which is peculiar to each place. Urban morphology therefore begins with geomorphology: the study of land-forms. A surprising number of Canadian cities have as much as 100-metre variations in their relief and therefore offer spectacular views. Their topography shapes the circulation of air, water, and energy, and the topography is itself reshaped by the work of wind and water, as well as by bulldozers and pile-drivers.

In classic descriptions of Canadian cities, the physical underpinnings have been discussed chiefly as economic assets or as initial reasons for the choice of a site. All writers attest to the historic importance of deep harbours at Halifax and Vancouver, the defensive promontory of Quebec 100 metres above the St Lawrence River, Montreal's origin at the head of navigation, and Ottawa's access to the water power available at the falls in the Ottawa River. Disadvantages are occasionally admitted, and even the most attractive sites have inconveniences such as the risk of floods in Winnipeg and Fredericton, the need for dredging the approaches to Saint John, poor drainage in Regina, earthquake risk in Chicoutimi, and a high water-table in Calgary.

The lay of the land influences the layout of our cities, sometimes constraining their design, sometimes provoking engineering ingenuity, sometimes creating problems for generations to come. Most cities, because of cost advantages for hauling, were founded at sea level and have tended to grow uphill, over rougher terrain and greater gaps. Nader (1976) notes the high cost of developing land around Halifax and Saint John because of bogs and out-croppings of rock. The cities of the Maritimes therefore developed narrow ribbons of settlement in the valleys, causing traffic bottlenecks. In St John's, Newfoundland, rows of houses climb a 100-metre ridge, and some of the older streets are simply flights of stairs. In Calgary, the decision to thread a railroad along the Bow River determined where industry would locate. The technological challenge of bridging the St Lawrence River delayed suburban expansion of Quebec, Trois-Rivières, and Montreal, and the costs of overcoming strong relief features long postponed residential expansion of Toronto across the Don Valley and of Hamilton onto the escarpment 100 metres above Lake Ontario.

As swamps were filled and hills levelled, some land-forms disappeared under the buildings. Riverfront, lakefront, and oceanfront have become the least 'natural' features of our cities, since the ease of filling and dredging made it possible to crochet a more elaborate edging at the commercial interface between land and water (McIlwraith, 1991). The 1986 Expo site in Vancouver was created on fill, and Hamilton has been greatly extended this way, as have the Toronto Islands. The Ontario Place development in Toronto was laid out on 2.5 million cubic metres of rubble from the excavation of subway tunnels and foundations for the new high-rise Toronto. With a new generation of tall buildings, Halifax is obliterating the harbour view from Citadel Hill, while Toronto and Calgary have put up artificial observation towers. A few major topographic features remain as landmarks—magical identifiers such as Mount Royal, the Niagara escarpment, and the 'reversing falls' at Saint John, where eight-metre tides reverse the flow in the gorge. Because the ravines of Toronto and Edmonton and the gorges and falls near Hamilton were costly to build upon, their character was preserved, and they gradually became valued parts of stream valley park systems.

Climatic conditions, too, affect the shapes of cities. As a result of their northerly situation, most Canadian cities face long, cold winters and heavy snowfalls. Each city is distinguished by its regional climate and vegetation: the wind in the prairie cities, Calgary's milder winter, Victoria's gardens, Vancouver's combination of ski slopes and beaches, the brilliant fall colours of the Maritime cities. Oceans or lakes modify the impact of the seasons, and a sharp break in relief, like the Niagara escarpment, can be noticed in local pockets of frost and fog. In Hamilton, McCann (1987) gives a fine example of the way the contrast of lake and land generates breezes in the course of the day. The influence of Lake Ontario produces comparable variations of micro-climate in St Catharine's and Toronto and unforgettable sunrises in Kingston.[5]

As more land is paved and roofed for urban activities, the impermeable surfaces prevent infiltration, and storms produce more rapid run-off and flash floods. Materials like asphalt tend to store heat, and concrete canyons trap solar radiation and create a rough surface modifying the winds, so that a 'heat dome' is centred on the downtown (Oke, 1987). Hamilton, under certain conditions, shows the curious variant of two warm cells, one centred over the downtown area and the other over the steel mills. Local topography fosters situations in spring and fall when cold air (at lake level) is overlain by warmer air (at the level of the escarpment); under this stable situation of temperature inversion pollutants build up, trapped in the urban area (Rouse and Burghardt, 1987).

Because local topography conveys natural and symbolic advantages and drawbacks, it indirectly affects the selection of sites for residential development, particularly the high-status areas occupied by people who can afford to choose. Every metropolis displays an example: Rosedale in the Toronto area, or the Mount Royal neighbourhood of Calgary, laid out in the 1920s to follow the contours of the land. We see comparable 'contour plowing' in Shaughnessy Heights and Point Grey (Vancouver). Most of these areas used socially restrictive covenants in their deeds, and even now provide great contrast with older working-class habitats such as low-lying 'Cork Town', 'Little Ireland', 'Cabbagetown', or 'The Ward', subject to flood, damp, and accumulation of pollutants. Quebec City had its 'Upper Town' and 'Lower Town', Montreal

its 'City Below the Hill' (Ames, 1972 [1902]). If asymmetry is an indicator of power relationships (Raffestin, 1980), the topographic situation of those neighbourhoods illustrates the power of social class.

A Succession of Built Forms

What we have built upon the land conveys a social interpretation of order and disorder. What we choose to conserve expresses the old order, or a certain conception of it, and what is proposed (as in Figure 10.3) is a conception of a new social order. In Ottawa, for instance, the elaborate rules for heights of buildings, public and private, formulate ambitions of national unity and deference for central institutions. The layout of Shawinigan, with Maple and Hemlock Streets curving up the hill and orderly rows of small lots on the flats, projects distinctions of social status and ethnicity that characterized the corporate structure of 1900.[6]

The morphology of everyday housing has everywhere been limited to a small range of basic building blocks. Early decisions about street grids, the sizes and shapes of building lots, and housing models created a cultural legacy of restraint on what could be done in the next generation. Regularity of layout and a symbolic centre recall notions of cosmic and social order (Wheatley, 1971), but the choice of a plat (a model for laying out streets and lots) was often a crude speculative option. The gridiron of Winnipeg, evident in Figure 10.2, was a quick solution for surveying the town site and offered developers as much buildable area as possible at the expense of less public space. Ease of application and profitability for developers explain why the gridiron pattern became the norm in North America. With a two-dimensional parcelling of lots in place, the range was narrowed for planning three-dimensional shapes.

A powerful determinant of townscapes was the density of settlement, a product of economic forces. Eighteenth-century cities were built up with one- and two-storey dwellings, built one at a time, with gables, shingles, and chimneys. Narrow streets were laid with cobbles, and lanes were of dirt. Halifax

Figure 10.2

Bird's-eye view of Winnipeg, Manitoba, in 1880. The artist, T.M. Fowler, displayed the ambitions of the city by projecting population from 6,000 to 10,000, exaggerating steamboat smoke, extending the geometry of streets, and rendering a railway bridge that was completed a year later. Source: National Archives of Canada (NMC 15026).

blocks, for example, were small (120 feet by 320 feet), with streets 55 feet wide. In St John's, where colonial authorities sought to discourage residence and exercised no building regulations, frame shacks persisted. In small towns of western and northern Canada, a low-density 'western-style' pattern has continued into the twentieth century, with a grid plan, streets as wide as the surveyor's chain (66 feet), and low buildings of wood. The features shown for Winnipeg in 1880 (Figure 10.2) can still be seen at Rouyn–Noranda. St John's retains a frame architecture, and the prairie cities, as well as suburbs of all Canadian cities, have retained wood as a material. Small towns and suburbs in Quebec still skimp on sidewalks, and Vancouver houses exhibit not simply a 'west coast style', associated with a milder climate, but a 'twentieth-century style' (Holdsworth, 1966).

As an urban population grew and a city spread out, competition grew more intense for space within walking distance of the centre. Until the 1890s most people walked to work and, since they worked long hours, tried to live close to their workplaces. The pressure to stack homes and businesses higher is therefore best seen in cities that had grown large by the turn of the century.[7] Under the constraint of the journey to work, the larger cities, over the second half of the nineteenth century, increased their residential densities to a spectacular degree. Urban growth was accommodated by filling and squeezing and piling higher. In Montreal, for example, population doubled between 1847 and 1861, tripled in the next 20 years, and doubled again between 1881 and 1901, and the surges of growth were accommodated by changes in urban form. Back lanes were built in already crowded areas, and dwellings were opened in rear lots. In the 1860s and 1870s builders shifted from two-storey to three-storey designs and from gabled to mansard roofs, providing more interior space on the top floor. In the booms of the 1880s and the early-twentieth century they adopted larger lots and larger blocks, and new construction took the form of the triple-decker—three flats on three and a half floors, with an L-shape to let light into more rooms (Legault, 1989). Tens of thousands of such triplex dwellings

built between 1900 and 1940 have contributed to the urban identity of Montreal. Their neighbourly balconies and their twisting outside stairways, which squeeze more usable space out of the building lot, are as distinctive a trademark as the 250-metre mountain park.

A Trajectory of Capital

Chapter 1 elaborates on capitalization as a fundamental property of cities while Chapter 7 examines the subject of urban real estate. The present chapter is more concerned with the landscape produced by cyclical shifts in capitalization. David Harvey (1972, 1978) has taught us to think of cities as built capital, including the streets, rails, and sewers as well as houses and factories. Harvey's conception of real estate in cities, derived from Marx's logic, reminds us that all the built environment was created from human labour, frozen into place for a century or more. The forms of the city reflect, therefore, the decisions of people who controlled property and deployed the labour of other people, with the object of raising the values of their private property. At every street corner or construction site we are led to wonder: Whose capital is invested? How has energy been deployed? At whose design? To whose benefit? At what human cost?

A powerful feature of built capital is its cyclical rhythm of accumulation.[8] Every 20 years or so, another boom produces another ring of suburban construction and another reconstruction of the centre. In each generation, the buildings, like ships and engines, are larger, taller, deeper, reflecting a new engineering design and taste. For all Canadian cities the waves of city-building are synchronized, but some cities can be seen to have been more successful than others over the period of a particular wave. As capital moved westward, successive financial hubs were generated: at Halifax, Montreal, Toronto, and Calgary. Economic booms and city building are synchronized with immigration. Immigrants followed economic activity and concentrated in cities, and waves of social change rippled outward from their centres. In Montreal the chunky lofts of garment factories marched north along the Main (St Laurent Boulevard), parallel with the homes and shops and places of worship of successive populations of immigrant workers, the produce markets and cheap entertainments. New populations succeeded one another in the old structures like new wine in old casks.

In each surge of construction, larger building-blocks were employed. Gad and Holdsworth (1988) have described the office blocks of King Street, Toronto, as expressions of the increasing resources capitalists could amass. The streetscape reflected their ambitions, but as the human walking-scale was exceeded, the streetscape lost its diversity and vitality. Like the office blocks, the sizes and shapes of Canadian factories trace out a North American sequence of technological opportunities. In Montreal in the 1850s, Dow's brewery, Redpath's sugar mill, and Molson's bank were little larger than the mansions of their owners, but by 1900 you could put a dozen such mansions inside any one of the top 10 enterprises. Among the largest spaces were railway stations, department stores, gasholders, and cold-storage warehouses. Large firms like Sun Life and Bell Canada created the cement wedding cakes of Montreal in the 1920s and in the 1980s the glass ice-cubes of Toronto.

Nationwide corporate institutions also placed their signatures on Canadian cities. Central post offices designated downtown itself. Eaton's stores were scaled to the size of each central place, and the fashions in their windows were adapted to different living standards and mores, distinguishing the big city from the small town. The Canadian Pacific Railway fitted its stations to the pecking order of towns, but each was unmistakably 'CP', and its turreted hotels became landmarks in every metropolis. One of the dramas of the 1970s was the sudden failure of this city-defining role on the part of chain enterprises. Crown corporations like Canada Post and Via Rail, as well as fashion chains, oil companies, and fast-food restaurants, abandoned their identification with a central site or a 'main street'. Since the 1970s, the strategy of each is to blare a little louder than the others, and television drama-

tizes their placeless symbols and colours coast to coast.[9]

Virtually all cities have an identifiable centre in which taller, more closely packed buildings reflect higher land values and a greater competition of users (see Chapters 7 and 11). Alonso (1964), more firmly than anyone else, established the importance of the land-value gradient to the centred pattern of land uses and the CBD, which is its kernel. Specialized and impressive buildings, such as railway stations and office towers, were erected in high-priced central sites. Even buildings with non-profit functions, like cathedrals and city halls, conscious of the competition of symbols, captured central sites. As we move away from the centre, we generally observe that the bulk and density of built forms diminish. Thus, the basic distance–decay gradient of land values forms the basis for building types and functions, and determines the evolution of urban form.

As cities expanded, differences of land value became more extreme. Higher land values stimulated investment in underground transit and made yet higher buildings profitable. Growth of the city as a whole produced an ever more powerful centrality and an ever greater differentiation of parts. In the central and oldest part of Montreal, for instance, residential population dwindled to nothing by 1860, but taxable commercial space continued to increase, tenfold in 20 years. The Banque du Peuple, built three storeys high in 1872, had six more storeys added in 1892. The Sun Life building reached six storeys in 1914, 10 in 1924, and 26 in 1934. Place Ville-Marie, headquarters for Alcan and the Royal Bank, in 1959 reached 42 storeys and dug its roots six storeys below street level. Establishment of underground mass transit in 1966 was associated with investment in tall buildings above many downtown stations, so that today the underground network can be inferred from the urban profile.

Public works, more particularly transportation facilities, are another important form of built capital. Continental decisions about canals, railroads, and pipelines have had exceptional importance for Canadian cities. As powerful speculative operations, they created a sense of opportunity and an indecent haste in the promotion of urban sites (Nader, 1976). Decisions about highways fostered strip development in building booms of the 1920s, 1940s, and 1960s. Stretches of the Trans-Canada highway in the 1960s bypassed city centres and undermined the economic vitality of the older strips and 'Main Streets' of small and large towns, drawing enterprises to a rim (Holdsworth, 1985). Comparable readjustments occurred in port facilities, as larger ships required larger docks and back-up spaces. Their need for specialized facilities, 24-hour access, and tight security brought shipping into conflict with other city land uses and produced radical changes in waterfront management (McCalla, 1988).

The great corridors of public works also give character to the landscape by creating paths through which we experience the city: rail lines along the waterfront; the expressway trench; the sodium glare of a highway; the lift of a bridge at Trois-Rivières. They provide visual edges for neighbourhoods and reinforce social separations (Lynch, 1960). In the 1880s, the CP embankment separated Montreal's areas of rich and poor, Westmount and Saint-Henri; in the 1970s that gulf was reinforced by construction of a parallel highway.

Changes of form in the 1980s and 1990s reflect a continued obsession with scale and continuous flow. In the shift from 'producer capitalism' to 'consumer capitalism', those strategies of industrial capital were applied to the consumer realm, notably 'big-box' shopping and entertainment complexes like West Edmonton Mall, with a sequence of 'simulated environments'. Even 'authentic' re-creations such as Quebec City's Place Royale have nourished an ambiguity between artifice and reality, and small towns compete for the tourist dollar by packaging out-of-place attractions like the African safari at Hemmingford, Quebec, or the Austrian village at Whistler, BC. The extreme case, where the flow of money is itself the fascination, are the 24-hour casinos that blaze in the night sky of Montreal and Windsor. Municipal and non-profit institutions license advertising on all public surfaces—subway walls, the glass walls of bus shelters, university urinals, and the risers of the escalator. As corporate logos and graffiti compete for dizzying ledges, ground-level shopkeepers have taken defensive measures to invite amateurs to cartoon their walls with media monsters. Post-modern pastiche, amplified to the larger-than-life scale of urban architecture, contributes to a sense of disorientation.

The City Spreads Out

The swift growth of the nineteenth-century metropolis produced monstrous problems. As we shall see, the concentration of built capital, and the haste to accumulate more, threatened health on an unprecedented scale. Concern about these hazards led to new ideas, and by the turn of the century reformers had blueprints ready for a revolution in urban form. They saw congestion as the problem, and envisioned cheaper, faster transportation as the solution. Greater mobility would permit a more generous use of space, so that city-dwellers could 'breathe' again. It took nearly a century to achieve those objectives and for later reformers to discover the drawbacks of the new spread-out city.

The great nineteenth-century threats in urban centres were fire and contagious disease. The high densities and cheap materials of Canadian cities permitted these threats to expand into massive conflagrations and epidemics. As the costs of such disasters became intolerable, cities were re-engineered to bring both threats under control through changes in shape and layout.[10] Under pressure of fire insurance costs, public water supplies were developed. While burned-out districts were usually rebuilt in haste, each episode spurred fire-conscious regulations that contributed to shifts of local building styles: brick cladding for the frame houses of Montreal, fire escapes for theatres, dikes around fuel storage tanks, the choice of reinforced concrete for the skyscrapers of the 1920s.

As a response to the scourge of tuberculosis, more attention was paid to air quality and the provision of open space. Playgrounds and parks were conceived as 'lungs' for the city, porch-front dwellings became popular, zoning laws were written to separate homes from factories, and legislation

Figure 10.3

Bird's-eye sketch of central Saint John, New Brunswick, showing Master Plan proposals of 1944. Smoke and traffic are minimized; trees are reduced to a symbolic minimum. Clean lines and curves are reinforced, and all types of urban activity are packed in neat boxes. Source: Saint John Town Planning Commission (1946, p. 83).

required setbacks for skyscrapers and ventilation for factories.

Also of epidemic proportions were the intestinal diseases (cholera, typhoid fever, and infant diarrhea) transmitted by the contamination of drinking water by human wastes. Pumps from shallow wells and outhouses that drained to septic beds were imports from rural landscapes, and at urban densities they failed. Intestinal diseases, deadliest in summer, were brought under some control by public water management. By 1900 water towers were town landmarks, and large cities had public baths and drinking fountains. With the gradual acceptance of germ theory, water was piped from more distant sources (for example, water was sent into Winnipeg from 95 miles away), and human wastes were drained to points outside the city, downstream, or into the lake or ocean. The strategy proved effective, but it meant that the city was depending on benefits captured from an environment outside its own territory.

About 1891, when cable-cars and electric tramways were introduced, cities began to spread rapidly. The higher speed and lower cost of mass transit made it possible for employees to live farther from work, and the central business district came to serve an area of larger radius. Vancouver, for example, in the 1890s occupied two square miles (the peninsula between Burrard Inlet and False Creek); by 1912, it was spread over 30 square miles (MacDonald, 1966). A hundred miles of street railway were built, the long ribbon of Kingsway was developed, and the downtown of three- and four-storey buildings was replaced by office blocks, hotels, and banks eight to 14 storeys high.

Introduction of automobiles reinforced the tendency of cities to spread. Suburbs like Westdale (in Hamilton) and Town of Mount Royal (Montreal) were laid out on a large scale to make generous use of cheaper land. Schools, as well as factories and warehouses, adopted one-storey layouts. North American theories of city planning crystallized around a conception of generous low-density lifestyles, with homes segregated from industry and business, and further segregated by levels of 'afford-ability'. To slow automobile traffic in the new suburban areas yet accelerate its flow through the metropolis as a whole, planners experimented with parkways, curves, and a 'street hierarchy'. In Montreal, engineering concern with traffic flow was supported by lobbies like the Canadian Good Roads Association and the Automobile Club of Canada, and one of the consequences was massive street widening in the late 1920s and again in the 1950s and 1970s. In the Montreal Town Planning Convention of 1921, progressive municipal engineers were already proposing integration of railways and highways, intermodal terminals and bridges, with Beaux Arts style and a rhetoric of reform.[11]

By the 1940s, 'master plans' like the one for Saint John (Figure 10.3) expressed these principles and identified 'blighted' areas where the standards had not yet been achieved. The average densities of cities were substantially reduced, and planners were beginning to congratulate themselves on having eradicated typhus, tuberculosis, and conflagration. Incinerator stacks and the trickling filters of sewage-works and water treatment plants had become major urban features visible from the air. They represented a new strategy of taking advantage of such natural processes as gravity flow and microbial digestion. They also forced cities to internalize some of the costs of their metabolism. Those costs, as we shall now see, are very high.

The Costs of the Low-Density Metropolis

Metabolism is the rate at which a system uses energy. Extension of the city at lower densities implies changes in its metabolism because continuous inputs of energy are required to cover the greater distances. Calgary is a good example, a success story of prosperity and effective urban planning, characterized by a golden triangle of oil-company skyscrapers, high levels of car ownership, superb highways, a preponderance of single-family detached housing, elaborately segregated residential neighbourhoods, and a green belt five miles wide. But these features mean that Calgary draws more kilowatts, guzzles more gasoline, and spews out more nitrogen oxides than in the past. Hamilton is an ecosystem with a still higher metabolism since its industries are exceptionally energy-intensive. The steel industry accounts for half the city's exports but consumes three-quarters of its energy inputs (Lonergan, 1987: 111).

Like Calgary, all cities now encounter threats to people's health due to air pollution and new costs arising from their high rates of metabolism. A city's energy consumption arises from daily demands for heat, industrial production, and mobility, as well as the actual process of its own construction. Of all types of landscapes, urban land is the most radically transformed, as brick, glass, and concrete have large quantities of fossil fuels baked into them (Dansereau, 1985). Hough (1984: 16-18) reports energy flow through a city as 100 times that through a natural ecosystem: 'Thus cities place enormous stresses on natural systems, depending on them for resource inputs and for the disposal of unwanted products', such as waste heat, cooling water, sewage, solid wastes (two to three cubic metres per person per year), and methane from their decomposition.

Canada has the highest per capita use of energy in the world. The heavy demand for fuels is attributable not so much to the cold climate as to the form of Canadian cities—the way they spread over the landscape. Between 1946 and 1985 the Canadian fleet of motor vehicles grew elevenfold. Federal (Canadian Mortgage and Housing Corporation—CMHC) financing for suburban detached housing fostered a dramatic reduction in residential densities, and highway improvements aggravated the problem, allowing people to move onto larger, cheaper, and more distant pieces of land without a penalty on their time.[12] Toronto 'stopped Spadina', a proposed expressway, in 1971, but because of the inertia built into the suburban habitats, the fleet of cars in that metropolitan region is still growing by 5 per cent a year, car-owners are making more trips, and half the energy consumed by the average urban household is used for driving cars. Sweden, with a comparable living standard, uses only three-fifths as much energy per person.

High fossil fuel consumption made people feel independent of place and season: 'Bulldozers made all sites equivalent, and oversized heating and cooling systems made every house a blob of paradise' (City of Hamilton, 1982: 21). The high metabolism also made city dwellers vulnerable to changes in the energy supply system, evident in 1973 when the world price of petroleum increased sixfold, and in the 1998 ice-storm that isolated Montreal and a 'triangle' of small towns from one another and from the continental power grid (see Figure 10.4).

Associated with higher demand for energy was a higher throughput of other materials and a higher excretion of waste substances, many of them uncommon in nature. Voracious cities forced massive environmental changes upon the entire Canadian landscape. Ontario cities depend for half their electricity on nuclear plants that continuously add to a stockpile of dangerous wastes—wastes that will have to be safeguarded for many generations, although after 30 years of design we still do not know how or where to do this. In Alberta, exploitation of the tar sands remains 'an expensive and environmentally suspect technology' (Sanderson and Wolfe, 1978: 7). In the North, power-related proposals such as further extension of pipelines in the Northwest Territories and hydroelectric developments in northern Quebec could cause oil spills, the melting of permafrost, and disruption of the ways of life of hunting peoples.

Waste products from central Canada, including lead, PCBs, and hydrocarbons, are carried by prevailing winds and end up in groundwater, wetlands, or the marine food web. Oxides of nitrogen from automobile emissions nearly tripled in the 1970s. Construction of tall stacks in the 1960s seemed to clean up towns like Sudbury, but instead exported sulphur and nitrogen components of acid rain to a larger area; the cloud of pollutants from Inco's 387-metre superstack arrives in Toronto, 400 kilometres away, about 18 hours later, or, depending on wind direction, reaches as far as the sensitive ecosystems in the Maritimes.[13] Thirty years ago it still seemed progressive to clean up the St Charles River in Quebec City by piping sewage and industrial wastes directly

Figure 10.4

A crumpled pylon in the outskirts of Montreal, one of thousands that collapsed under the weight of ice in January 1998, became a symbol of urban vulnerability.

into the St Lawrence River and building a 10-metre dam to prevent their backing up into the St Charles at high tide (Nader, 1976). We now recognize that such diversions, like the taller stacks, merely export the problem a little farther from its source.

In Saint John, as pictured in Figure 10.3, 75 outfalls were dumping raw sewage into the harbour. In Montreal, the St Lawrence River, in particular the wider, more tranquil reach of Lac Saint-Pierre, has become the sump of heavy metals. Industrial pollutants have accumulated over years in urban soils, in groundwater, and at the bottoms of the rivers. Every city in Canada has dis-covered dangerous dumps, and the spoils from dredging harbours are highly contaminated. As a result of steel industry pollution in the Hamilton area, genetic deformities are reported for one-tenth of the worms at the base of the food chain. Divers identified in the St Clair River near Windsor a 'blob' of the most contaminated mate-rial ever found in the Great Lakes (Sanderson, 1988), and downstream, at Quebec City, the num-ber of species of fish in the St Lawrence River has diminished (from 48 to 30 since 1940), and the bel-uga whales at its mouth are threatened with extinc-tion (Béland, 1996).

Cities have become more hospitable to a few species, notably rats, squirrels, starlings, pigeons, and roaches, and less hospitable to a great diversity of songbirds, butterflies, and small mammals. The effects of pollutants on human health are becoming apparent. One example is the gradual concentration of lead in urban environments: in the paint on old buildings, in dusts and residues from gasoline, in battery-disposal and recycling plants. Lead poisoning now affects the health of renovation workers, tunnel guards, and children of entire neighbourhoods (Olson, 1997). Allergies and physiological responses to chemical residues and 'building disease' are complicated by smoking habits. City dwellers are subject to progressive deafness from noise and to the violence of spills, explosions, and collisions, which result from the magnification of human error in the handling of powerful, energy-driven machines.

The Revolution Required

Problems associated with energy use, waste disposal, and environmental hazards will be solved by joint efforts of all members of society or not at all. To bring urban metabolism under control calls for a reconcentration of urban activities, that is, another revolution in urban form. In some parts of cities, trends can already be observed towards higher densities and a greater integration of activities, but the built landscape is so long-lived that its adaptation will take more than a generation. It will require a double process: control of new development and the retrofitting of existing habitats.

Some techniques for retrofitting have already been identified. A small example of the way individual households adapt a landscape for energy conservation is the clothes-line. These lines festooned lanes, alleys, and porches of the 1890s, but with the advent of washing-machines and laundromats they were relegated to rural settings; élite subdivisions outlawed them as unsightly. California cities have now rewritten the rules to require that new developments include a clothes-drying pole for every dwelling. At a more substantial level, a Saskatchewan study showed that energy-conscious site develop-

ment and landscaping, combined with energy-efficient construction techniques, could reduce fuel consumption for space heating by 85 per cent compared with conventional suburban forms of development. Hamilton planners asserted in 1982 that by the end of the century houses with near-zero fuel bills would be developed in southern Ontario. And indeed they were. Known as passive solar, such dwellings are built of conventional materials but designed to capture winter sunshine and provide shade in summer. Home heating bills are reduced by planting deciduous trees or vines on the south side of a house and coniferous trees for shelter on the north side.

Other techniques are effective when they are applied at the scale of an entire community. Shading parking lots, for example, reduces the urban heat load and the rate of precipitation run-off. As early as the 1970s, the design of Fermont, a mining town in subarctic Quebec, offered pointers towards energy conservation: its tallest buildings are situated to shelter the community from wind, and energy for steam heat is recovered from sewage and garbage. In 1979 Brampton, Ontario, was one of the first Canadian towns to establish a policy of securing 'access to sun' for all new buildings, by favouring the east-west orientation of streets and the north-south orientation of houses, controlling heights and setbacks to avoid winter shadows, and permitting ingenuity of layout.[14]

Technological options for energy economy have improved even beyond the prediction of 1982. A 'green and healthy' office building in Kitchener–Waterloo uses only one-sixth as much energy as the usual, and an experimental home in Calgary, by taking advantage of thermal storage, uses only 6 per cent of the average suburban energy requirement. The designer's next step is to disconnect from water and sewer lines and actually export energy to the power grid.[15] Energy-conscious plans favour cottage industries, narrower streets, bicycle paths and walkways, and greater social diversity of neighbourhoods. Some gains can be achieved by changes of lifestyles within existing urban habitats, as in north Toronto where neighbours have undertaken 'co-housing' in which they share tools, child care, and vegetable gardens in an evolving, step-by-step attempt to acknowledge mutual interdependence.[16]

Cities spend energy as well as money trying to maintain the ecosystem in an unchanging and unnatural state. Harbours and channels are continually dredged. Reservoirs fill with silt from the erosion of soil from suburban construction sites. It costs many millions each year to keep grass trimmed on the boulevards of Winnipeg (Hough, 1984: 21) and to clear 'each last snowflake' from the streets of Montreal (Sanderson and Wolfe, 1978). Instead, by taking advantage of natural processes, a city can be made more comfortable and more manageable. Winnipeg, faced with the projected high cost of extending storm sewers on low-lying land to detain rainfall, instead created lakes and ponds. The University of Alberta, to accommodate twice as many students, increased the building coverage of its Edmonton campus (from 15 per cent to 34 per cent) and at the same time made the campus more hospitable by disposing buildings so as to cut the wind and capture winter sunshine (Hough, 1984: 98). The same tactics were applied to Ontario Place on the Toronto lakefront: winter recreation areas are encircled by buildings and conifers.

The concept of retrofitting extends to cleaning up damaged urban habitats. Economies of energy have produced marked improvements in air quality, as well as savings to industry. The emerging challenge is the correction of contaminated sites such as municipal dumps and, in Ontario, aging nuclear plants. In the largest and oldest Canadian cities, *brownfield* zones abandoned by industry amount to a large bank of under-utilized land in attractive locations, situated on rail, waterfront, and highways, and already serviced with water and sewers. But redevelopers are concerned about *liability*.[17] So long as potential investors feel uncertain about the extent of contamination, the cost of remedy, or whether they may be held responsible, they will prefer 'greenfield' sites. They therefore continue to move deeper into the rural fringe and aggravate the urban sprawl.

Among the best-known Canadian cases of brownfield remediation are Port Credit (a former Imperial Oil refinery); the Cooksville quarry in Mississauga, contaminated from brick-making and disposal of Ontario Hydro fly ash; and Vancouver's Pacific Place. The last, after a century of contamination from harbour, railways, sawmills, and coal gas manufacture, was adopted as the site of Expo 86 and then redeveloped on a spectacular scale for condos, parks, parking, and roads. Its waterfront views, as well as the climate of growth in the region, made the site attractive for investment, and governments adopted strategies to speed environmental review, limit liability for investors, and find ways to tolerate toxic residues on the site by installing 'barriers' to keep toxics out of 'pathways' to human lungs and digestive systems. Such barriers include cement lids, plastic liners, layers of soil, and systems for venting and recycling methane. Through the consciousness-raising experience with Pacific Place, British Columbia alone, of all the provinces, has a credible inventory of its brownfields and a somewhat coherent set of policies for redevelopment.[18]

Metropolitan areas are just beginning to face the real costs of their metabolism. The public debt of municipalities, or even the combined debt of all levels of government—which has dominated public debate for a decade—is small relative to the *environmental debt* that has been contracted. As citizens become reluctant to accept or reprocess wastes of other regions in their 'back yards', each metropolis is forced to internalize the costs of its metabolism and search for controls it can impose at source and for changes it can make in lifestyles. The City of Montreal, after outlawing open burning and acquiring a huge quarry in which it could bury its garbage, announced its intention to close the dump by 1992. In the absence of any alternative (and in the teeth of a neighbourhood exasperated by dust, odours, truck noise, and scavenging seagulls), the dump still operates. Even after the dump is closed and re-landscaped, the site will have to be monitored, all storm drainage treated, and methane recovered for 30 years to come.

Because retrofitting takes time and money, it is a fitful process, and we seem everywhere to advance two steps forward and one step back, with a good many political sidesteps. The costs are not shared equally. Retrofitting of inner-city areas has been accompanied by 'gentrification', and the gentrifiers have purchased exurban 'second homes', while low-income families, excluded from these neighbourhoods, tend to live in the suburbs of the 1960s and 1970s, where they bear the brunt of rising energy costs. Lower-income households have been reported to be spending more than one-quarter of the family budget on energy (Sanderson and Wolfe, 1978).

A revolutionary imagination is vigorous, as are consciousness-raising efforts such as the bike choir 'song cycles' on the streets of Toronto, eco-museums, eco-parks, recycling centres, composting workshops, and home assessments by power companies. While citizens show greater sensitivity to environmental concerns, a decade of budget-cutting has had counter-revolutionary effects. The federal program for inventory and clean-up of contaminated sites has been discontinued, and policy has shifted towards reliance on corporate 'self-policing' and 'voluntary pollution prevention' by associations of industries (Van Nijnatten, 1998). In Quebec and Ontario, enforcement personnel in environmental agencies have been slashed by nearly half, and subsidies to mass transit have been withdrawn, increasing the fares and reducing ridership.[19]

Municipalities are buffeted by such shifts in federal and provincial policies that it is especially difficult to balance the command mode of enforcement (by regulation) with incentives to co-operation. A steady and predictable public policy is required, as well as a firm negotiating position, but in fact Canadian governments at all levels seem to lurch forward unpredictably and then balk.[20] None of the major political parties has yet internalized a strong environmental sensitivity. Critical in tipping the balance one way or the other will be the interpretation of the rising generation, groups such as LifeCycles in Victoria and public interest research groups in the universities,[21] and their determination to harness media as diverse as mapping, geographic information systems (GIS), storytelling, and caricature to empower people to articulate the values they attach to *place*.[22]

A century from now, the wasteful and isolating habitats typical of our modern suburbs will evoke the horror we feel when we look back at the teeming, contagious, fire-trap cities of the Victorian era: 'The style and manner in which land has been developed for residential use in the past can hardly be justified in a time of escalating costs and a diminishing supply of non-renewable sources of energy. The challenge lies in modifying the urban form' (City of Hamilton, 1982: 2).

Retrofitting of cities implies that all elements of built capital must become more a part of their natural landscape. As there is little hint of a change in the capitalist process itself, retrofitting will be obstructed by powerful forces, undermined by opportunities for profit, and delayed by disputes over who will cover the costs. The need to re-form cities will challenge the acquired 'rights' of high-income people to protect their privileged lifestyles and separate themselves from the habitats of others. 'Re-form' of the physical city will once again require social reform.

Conclusion

In this chapter we have seen that the form of the metropolis displays the effects of political, social, and economic forces. Canadian cities were laid out, each in its own topographic setting, and developed as a succession of 'built forms', changing their shapes with every surge of investment. New designs provided protection and enjoyment for those who could afford the new, but generated unexpected costs and spillovers.

Over generations, the development process stimulated massive flows of energy through the urban landscape. In the course of the nineteenth century, cities were built to ever higher densities, creating risk of fire and contagion. In response to those problems, cities were, in the course of the twentieth century, re-engineered into new patterns at much lower densities.

Today's sprawling metropolis, wasteful of energy, is vulnerable to the accumulation of its own waste products, so that once again, in response to rising costs and risks, we are beginning to conceive of a revolution of metropolitan form. The future Canadian metropolis will have to be more compact, more self-contained, more aware of its metabolism, and more conscious of the costs.

The city is always unfinished. At each construction site, the thud of the pile-driver and the whine of the cement-saw give insistence to the questions: How is energy being deployed? How is capital being deployed? To whose benefit? At what human cost? Are we building, as Brand (1994: 209) put it, 'in a future-responsible way'? I explore again the field of forces. To deflect the trend and nudge forward the fragile coalition, where shall I apply my own energy and my particle of power?

Notes

I am grateful for the help of McGill colleagues Jeanne Wolfe, Gordon Ewing, Raphael Fischler, and Brian Ray.

1. The remarkable exception is the extensive work of Hans Blumenfeld (1967).
2. Exceptions here are the fine work of German and Austrian geographers, and in Britain, of Whitehand (1981) and Conzen. The new journal *Urban Morphology* reports creative work in France and Italy, the basis for dissertation research (in progress) of Pierre Gauthier on Quebec City.
3. Challenging exceptions are the advances of 'adaptive architecture' by Brand (1994) and the analysis of changes of form and occupancy in Shawinigan by Bellavance and Guérard (1993).
4. See, for example, work of Hillier (1996) using graph theory for analysis of the configurations of dwellings, neighbourhoods, and whole cities.
5. Geographers who recognized the importance of climate and topography in urban identity were Griffith Taylor (1949) and Kerr and Spelt (1965). The importance of urban climate has again been raised over the past decade as an important area of urban ecological research (see Chapter 21).

6. See Brouillette (1990) and Bellavance and Guérard (1993). Application of 'garden city' models to design of Canadian company towns by industrial corporations is well-illustrated for Shawinigan, Arvida, Temiscaming, and Grand-Mère, in Fortier (1996).
7. West of Montreal, cities did not reach that critical size until after the introduction of tramways, so that the predominant housing type remained the free-standing frame dwelling, and even the poor, confined to small, poorly insulated spaces, lived in houses rather than flats, or built shacks outside the city limits (Harris, 1996).
8. On geographical properties of the Kuznets cycle of urban construction, which has a duration of 15 to 25 years, see Olson (1982).
9. An absurd example, at 359 St James Street, Montreal, is the blue and yellow plastic logo of the Royal Bank, mounted inside the elegant and well-preserved banking hall, all red and gold, of Italian Renaissance design.
10. Fire destroyed an entire downtown or a large share of the housing stock in Quebec City in 1845 and 1866, St John's in 1846 and 1892, Toronto in 1849 and 1904, Montreal in 1852, Halifax in 1859, Saint John in 1784, 1837, and 1877, and Ottawa–Hull in 1900.
11. On railways, see Hanna in Gournay and Vanlaethem (1998). The town planning movement, influenced by engineers and architects like H.A. Terreault, Percy Nobbs, and Frederick Todd, together with lobbies like the City Improvement League and art and women's associations, led to topographic mapping, zoning laws, and, with a lag of 40 years, a master plan. See 1920s issues of *Revue Municipale, Canadian Engineer, Revue Trimestrielle Canadienne,* and *Journal of the Town Planning Institute of Canada.*
12. Macdonald (1996) reports the dynamic interplay of lobbies, corporate interests, and public agencies in Ontario debates over taxation of 'gas-guzzlers' and beer cans. Ewing and Sarigöllü (1998) show how economic instruments (taxes and subsidies) might affect the individual's willingness to choose an 'environment-friendly' electric vehicle.

13. Maritime provinces are sensitive as a result of regional bedrock type, which has little alkalinity. Lakes and rivers have low buffering capacity. Salmon and phytoplanktons are subjected to a spring shock of nitrates, and acidic water mobilizes or dissolves metals such as aluminum from soils and sediments (Ricketts, 1988).

14. Zoning conventions had to be rewritten to permit the slanting and staggering of lots along streets oriented in another direction, and keyed or chevron layouts. The clustering of houses permitted densities of 50 to 75 dwellings per hectare and reduced areas for road, sewer, water, and electrical networks. Leaders were the California State Energy Code of 1976, the Solar Rights Act and Solar Shade Control Act of 1978, the cities of Davis and Burbank, California, and Denver, Colorado. Among the earliest and most thoughtful plans for Canadian cities were from the City of Hamilton, the Saskatchewan Department of Mineral Resources, and the Province of Prince Edward Island, 1981–2. On social diversity and competition for urban open space, see Dansereau, Germain, and Éveillard (1997).

15. Experiments such as these can be followed in *Alternatives Journal* 23, 1 (Winter 1997): 5–6 (Scott Meyer); 22, 4 (Oct./Nov. 1996): 5–6 (Garry Checora).

16. Russell Mawby in *Alternatives Journal* 22, 2 (Apr./May 1996): 4–5.

17. Similar problems of contamination and liability for clean-up apply also to a large part of the urban rental housing stock where lead paint was used (Olson, 1997) and to public buildings in which asbestos compounds were used.

18. The attempt to manage rather than remove contaminants is part of a strategy known as 'risk assessment/risk management', and is, of course, much cheaper. For 'best practices' (not, in fact, common practice anywhere in the country), see CMHC Backgrounder publications of the National Round Table on the Environment and the Economy (1997), in particular *Removing Barriers: Redeveloping Contaminated Sites for Housing*, 40–54.

19. Since 1990 the cost of public transit has nearly doubled and ridership has diminished (Ewing and Sarigöllü, 1998).

20. Fletcher (1998) compares the interplay between layers of government in the United States and Canada in selection of sites for disposal of hazardous waste in the Niagara Peninsula and the Sarnia region.

21. *Alternatives Journal* 24, 3 (Summer 1998) contains a guide to youth environmental groups. See also Web pages of Environment Canada, British Columbia Environmental Protection Agency, and Ville de Montréal.

22. On mapping, see Aberley (1993) and Wood (1992); for a helpful example of local place-consciousness, see Bowerbank (1997).

References

Aberley, D. 1993. *Boundaries of Home: Mapping for Local Empowerment*. Gabriola Island, BC: New Society Publications.

Alonso, W. 1964. 'The Historical and Structural Theories of Urban Form', *Land Economics* 40: 227–31.

Ames, H.B. 1972. [1902]. *The City Below the Hill*. Toronto: University of Toronto Press.

Béland, P. 1996. *Beluga: A Farewell to Whales*. New York: Lyons and Burford.

Bellavance, C., and F. Guérard. 1993. 'Ségrégation résidentielle et morphologie urbaine, le cas de Shawinigan, 1925–1947', *Revue d'histoire de l'Amérique française* 46, 4: 577–605.

Blumenfeld, H. 1967. *The Modern Metropolis*. Cambridge, Mass.: MIT Press.

Bowerbank, S. 1997. 'Telling Stories About Places', *Alternatives Journal* 23, 1: 28–33.

Brand, S. 1994. *How Buildings Learn*. New York: Viking.

Brouillette, N. 1990. 'Le rôle de la Shawinigan Water and Power dans la structuration de l'espace urbain shawiniganais, 1898–1921', *Cahiers de Géographie du Quebec* 34, 92: 197–208.

City of Hamilton. 1982. *Design Criteria for Energy Efficient Neighbourhood Planning*. Hamilton: City of Hamilton, prepared by the Planning and Development Department of the Regional Municipality of Hamilton–Wentworth.

Dansereau, F., A. Germain, and C. Éveillard. 1997. 'Social Mix: Old Utopias, Contemporary Experience and Challenges', *Canadian Journal of Urban Research* 6: 1–20.

Dansereau, P. 1985. 'Essai de classification et de cartographie écologique des espaces', *Études Écologiques* 10.

Ewing, G.O., and E. Sarigöllü, E. 1998. 'Car Fuel-Type Choice Under Travel Demand Management and Economic Incentives', *Transportation Research C* 5: 1–16.

Fletcher, T.H. 1998. *Environmental Justice and Hazardous Waste: A View from the Canada–United States Border*, Ph.D. thesis, McGill University.

Fortier, R., ed. 1996. *Villes industrielles planifiées*. Montreal: Canadian Centre for Architecture and Boréal.

Gad, G., and D.W. Holdsworth. 1988. 'Streetscape and Society: The Changing Built Environment of King Street, Toronto', in R. Hall et al., eds, *Patterns of the Past: Interpreting Ontario's History*. Toronto: Dundurn Press.

Gournay, I., and F. Vanlaethem. 1998. *Montréal Métropole, 1880–1930*. Montreal: Boréal.

Harris, R. 1996. *Unplanned Suburbs: Toronto's American Tragedy, 1900 to 1950*. Baltimore: Johns Hopkins University Press.

Harvey, D. 1972. *Society, the City and the Space-Economy of Urbanism*. Commission on College Geography, Resource Paper 18.

———. 1978. 'The Urban Process Under Capitalism: A Framework for Analysis', *International Journal of Urban and Regional Research* 2: 101–31.

Hillier, B. 1996. *Space is the Machine*. Cambridge: Cambridge University Press.

Holdsworth, D. 1966. 'House and Home in Vancouver: Images of West Coast Urbanism, 1886–1929', in G.F. Stelter and A.F.J. Artibise, eds, *The Canadian City, Essays in Urban History*. Ottawa: Carleton Library No. 109; Macmillan reprint 1979.

———. 1985. *Reviving Main Street*. Toronto: University of Toronto Press.

Hough, M. 1984. *City Form and Natural Process*. New York: Van Nostrand Reinhold.

Kemble, R. 1989. *The Canadian City St. John's to Victoria: A Critical Commentary*. Montreal: Harvest House.

Kerr, D., and J. Spelt. 1965. *The Changing Face of Toronto—A Study in Urban Geography*. Ottawa: Department of Energy, Mines and Resources, Geographical Branch, Memoir 11.

Legault, R. 1989. 'Architecture et forme urbaine: L'exemple du triplex à Montréal 1870–1914', *Urban History Review* 18: 1–10.

Lonergan, S.C. 1987. 'Energy Flows and the City of Hamilton', in M.J. Dear, J.J. Drake, and L.G. Reeds, eds, *Steel City: Hamilton and Region*. Toronto: University of Toronto Press.

Lynch, K. 1960. *Image of the City*. Cambridge, Mass.: MIT Press.

MacDonald, D. 1996. 'Beer Cans, Gas Guzzlers and Green Taxes', *Alternatives Journal* 22, 3: 12–19.

MacDonald, N. 1966. 'A Critical Growth Cycle for Vancouver, 1900–1914', in G.F. Stelter and A.F.J. Artibise, eds, *The Canadian City: Essays in Urban History*. Ottawa: Carleton Library No. 109; Macmillan reprint 1979.

McCalla, R.J. 1988. 'Land Use Development in Cityport Waterfronts: A Model', in D. Day, ed., *Geographical Perspectives on the Maritime Provinces*. Halifax: St Mary's University.

McCann, S.B. 1987. 'Physical Landscape of the Hamilton Region', in M.J. Dear, J.J. Drake, and L.G. Reeds, eds, *Steel City: Hamilton and Region*. Toronto: University of Toronto Press.

McIlwraith, T. 1991. 'Digging Out and Filling In: Making Land on the Toronto Waterfront in the 1850s', *Urban History Review* 20: 15–33.

Nader, G.A. 1976. *Cities of Canada: Profiles of Fifteen Metropolitan Centres*. Toronto: Macmillan.

Oke, T.R. 1987. *Boundary Layer Climatology*. London: Methuen.

Olson, S. 1982. 'Urban Metabolism and Morphogenesis', *Urban Geography* 3: 87–109.

———. 1997. 'Wind and Water, 1970–1996', in *Baltimore: Building an American City*, 2nd edn. Baltimore: Johns Hopkins University Press.

Raffestin, C. 1980. *Pour une géographie du pouvoir*. Paris: LITEC.

Ricketts, P.J. 1988. 'Shoreline Changes and Associated Coastal Management Issues in the Maritime Provinces', in D. Day, ed., *Geographical Perspectives on the Maritime Provinces*. Halifax: Geography Department, St Mary's University.

Rouse, W.R., and A.F. Burghardt. 1987. 'Climate, Weather and Society', in M.J. Dear, J.J. Drake, and L.G. Reeds, eds, *Steel City: Hamilton and Region*. Toronto: University of Toronto Press.

Sanderson, C., and J.M. Wolfe. 1978. 'The Energy Crisis and Urban Planning: A Canadian Perspective', paper presented at Canadian Institute of Planners annual meeting, 30 July–3 Aug. 1978. McGill University School of Urban Planning.

Sanderson, M. 1988. 'The Blob', *Canadian Geographer* 30: 315.

Schoenauer, N. 1967. 'The New City Centre', *Architectural Design* 37: 311–24.

Taylor, G. 1949. *Urban Geography*. London: Methuen.

Thompson, D.W. 1961 [1917]. *On Growth and Form*. Cambridge: Cambridge University Press.

Van Nijnatten, D.L. 1998. 'The Day the NGOs Walked Out', *Alternatives Journal* 24, 2: 10–19.

Wheatley, P. 1971. *The Pivot of the Four Quarters*. Chicago: Aldine.

Whitehand, J.W.R., ed. 1981. *The Urban Landscape: Historical Development and Management, Papers by M.R.G. Conzen*. London: Academic Press, Institute of British Geographers Special Publication, No. 13.

Wood, Denis. 1992. *The Power of Maps*. London: Routledge.

Part Three

Internal Geography of the City

In Part Three we begin at the centre of the city and work our way out in simple geographic progression, from the central business district (CBD) to the inner city, to the suburbs, and to the city's countryside. At one level the relationships between the zones can be thought of as simply ones of spatial juxtaposition and the zones themselves can be treated independently, as they largely are in each of the four subsequent chapters. The four zones dealt with here can also be treated as 'formal' geographic regions. Each has a distinctive history, architecture, land-use composition, and travel/activity patterning. The downtown is the place where business use has traditionally been concentrated, hence its oft-used appellation as the 'central business district'. Located at the centre of the city where transportation costs are theoretically lowest, this nodal zone usually includes some of the city's oldest buildings and streets. As it is described by Gunter Gad and Malcolm Matthew in Chapter 11, it has the highest intensity of use, and, as Chapter 7 has led us to expect, some of the city's highest-value real estate. The CBD is easily demarcated from the inner city because it is predominantly business-centred and of high density.

The inner city has more housing and lower-intensity commercial use. It generally looks 'old' because many of its original structures are still intact; redevelopment has been more subdued here than in the CBD. This is the zone where, along the city's main rail lines, heavy industry once predominated. Because at the time of its development most people travelled on foot, there is a mix of land use. Where internally homogeneous zones such as residential neighbourhoods do exist, they tend to be

small in scale. Commercial activity takes on a linear pattern because it has been laid out along the city's major transit routes, which are generally fixed-line in nature. In Chapter 12, David Ley shows that the contemporary inner city, because of its age and proximity to the CBD, is wrought by many disparate or 'chaotic' forces.

As was suggested in Chapter 1, we can also find a clear break in all Canadian cities between older zones—downtown and the inner city—and the more recently developed postwar suburbs. As Peter Smith points out in Chapter 13, there are many variants, both spatial and temporal, within the suburban zone, but these pale in contrast to the zone's overall semblance of homogeneity. This zone has been 'planned' from day one by professionals in municipal planning departments. Another factor of homogeneity is the need for all suburban places to be fully accommodating to the car. To date, the architectural form of the suburbs is predominantly 'modern' and low-rise, though the last decade or so has seen the introduction of variety with the arrival of developments previously associated with the central city (e.g., suburban downtowns). Lower densities, large monofunctional zones, and heavy reliance on the car distinguish the suburb from the inner city.

The outlying zone of the metropolitan area, which looks agricultural but functions as a part of the city, is also easy to delimit. The predominant land use is agricultural, but in terms of daily population movement and establishment types, the area is overwhelmingly linked to the city. This zone has come to host virtually all the different types of activity that coexist within the city proper. In Canada, as in the

Figure III.1   **Internal Geography of the City**

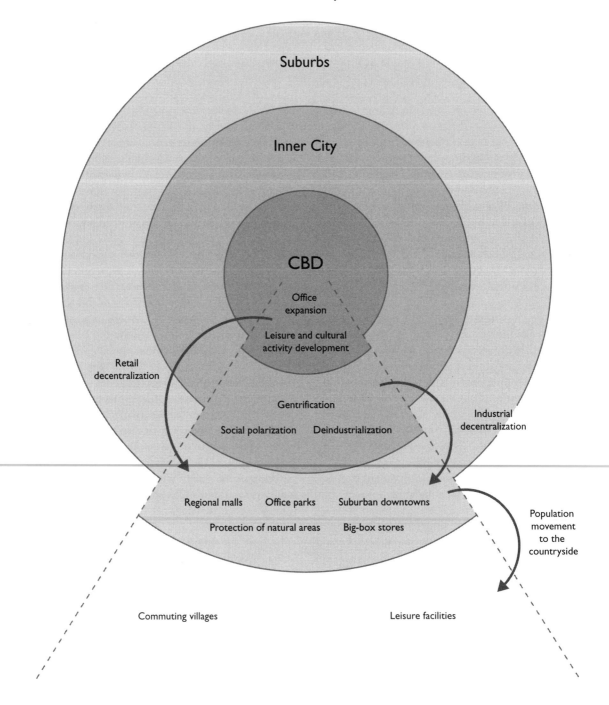

US, because the appeal of rural-like landscape settings and privacy is strong and automobile ownership widespread, this zone has come under intense pressure for residential development.

Each of the city's internal geographic zones represents a distinctive stage or transition in urban development. But development in one place does not occur independently of other places. What happens in any one zone at any one point in time will have at least an indirect, and often a direct, impact on the status of other zones, as illustrated in Figure III.1. Because of space limitations, most of the work presented in the following chapters features only one geographic zone. The obvious exception is Chapter 11, where new suburban downtowns are compared to the traditional, central city downtown and the conceptual and interactive links between the two are carefully examined. But, in Chapter 12, Ley, too, discusses what happens in parts of the inner city—i.e., gentrification—in relation to CBD change. Likewise, Christopher Bryant, Philip Coppack, and Clare Mitchell, in Chapter 14, explain growth in the rural-urban fringe as an extension of suburban lifestyles and preferences. Several other examples can be found in the pages that follow, but many remain to be forged by each individual reader.

Chapter 11

Central and Suburban Downtowns

Gunter Gad and Malcolm Matthew

Official planning documents released by urban governments in Canada include a variety of labels related to the centre of the city or to concentrations of commercial land uses at important transportation nodes at some distance from the core of the urban region. For instance, City of Vancouver planning documents (Vancouver, 1993: 2) show a central area, and within this central area is a much smaller central business district (Figure 11.1). The City of Toronto, too, declares a central area and within it a so-called central core area. Documents from Montreal show a relatively small 'centre des affaires', which most English translations equate with central business district, in a much larger area declared as 'centre-ville'. Plans for the entire urban area, rather than the 'city proper' or central city, mention other kinds of centres: documents of the Greater Vancouver Regional District show a number of regional town centres, while the official plans of the City of Toronto (formerly the Municipality of Metropolitan Toronto) include a number of 'major centres' in such metropolitan suburbs as North York, Scarborough, and Etobicoke. These suburban nodes, along with counterparts in cities across North America, are often referred to as 'suburban downtowns' (Hartshorne and Muller, 1989; Relph, 1991).

There have been attempts by social scientists to define exactly what belongs to downtown and how to delimit it. Geographers Raymond Murphy and James Vance (1954: 189) put forward a narrow definition: 'The Central Business District ... is the heart of the American city. Here one finds the greatest concentration of offices and retail stores reflected in the city's highest land values and its tallest buildings. Here, too, is the chief focus of pedestrian and automobile traffic.'

There were elaborations on this view of the CBD. Murphy and Vance investigated the changes in CBD land uses and suggested that expansion was uneven: on one side, CBD uses moved out and left behind a 'zone of discard', where 'skid row' would begin to occupy old business premises; on the other side, CBD use infiltrated new areas, especially high-status residential areas, which they termed the 'zone of assimilation' (Murphy et al., 1955). Others argued that the CBD as defined by Murphy and Vance should include a somewhat larger area comprising land uses strongly related to the CBD, such as railway and bus terminals, warehouses, automobile and furniture dealers, or medical services and government offices. This view of the CBD, then, included a CBD core (retail and offices) and a CBD frame (Horwood and Boyce, 1959).

The Murphy-Vance definition of the 'central business district' implies two notions that are important to understanding downtowns. One of them is the notion of high-order goods and services, the other is the notion of centrality. High-order goods and services can be electronic entertainment equipment, a corporate lawyer's advice, a city council meeting, or a free public lecture by a Nobel laureate. All of these have a 'high threshold', that is, they require a large clientele or audience who buy these goods and services or who take part in these events infrequently. Centrality is a spatial notion. Given a uniform plain with unrestricted mobility in all directions and an evenly distributed population, there will

Figure 11.1   **Vancouver: Central Area and Sub-Areas, including the 'Established CBD'
and 'CBD Fringe', 1993**

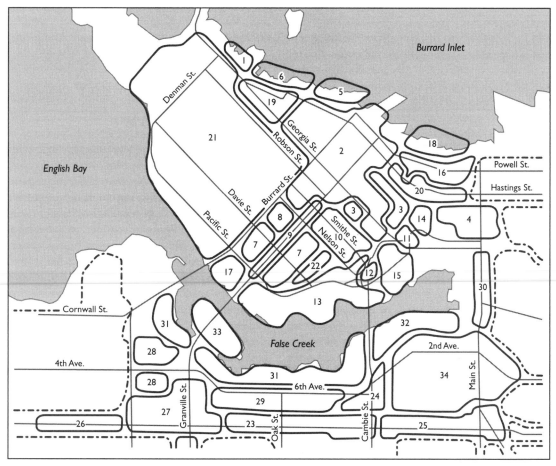

Downtown Peninsula

1. Bayshore
2. Established (CBD)
3. (CBD): Fringe
4. Chinatown
5. Coal Harbour East
6. Coal Harbour West
7. Downtown South
8. Downtown South:
    Burrard-Granville
9. Downtown South: Granville Street
10. Downtown South:
    Northeast Quadrant
11. False Creek North: Apex
12. False Creek North: Cambie Bridge

13. False Creek North:
    Granville-Cambie
14. False Creek North:
    International Village
15. False Creek North: Stadium
16. Gastown
17. Granville Slopes
18. Port Lands
19. Triangle West
20. Victoria Square
21. West End
22. Yaletown

Outside Downtown Peninsula

23. Broadway: Centre
24. Broadway: Cambie Bridge South
25. Broadway: East
26. Broadway: West
27. Burrard Slopes:
    Broadway-Burrard-Granville (C–3A)
28. Burrard Slopes:
    South of Granville Island
29. Fairview Slopes
30. False Creek East
31. False Creek South
32. False Creek Southeast
33. Granville Island
34. Mt Pleasant Industrial

Source: City of Vancouver, Planning Department, Central Area Division.

be one point of maximum accessibility. Of course, the idea of a uniform plain does not make much sense, least of all in cities where transportation networks are the result of political negotiation and provide a higher degree of accessibility at some points but not at others. Albeit more complex, the concept of centrality is still relevant. Within our larger urban agglomerations, the principal downtowns, and what we now refer to as suburban downtowns, have been very small areas with concentrations of businesses and institutions offering high-order goods and services in highly accessible places.

Another concept in portraying downtowns is that of 'agglomeration economies', first used by Alfred Weber (1909) to explain the spatial clustering of factories. Since the 1920s, urban economists and urban geographers have implicitly and explicitly employed principles of agglomeration economies to explain the dependency of downtown businesses on each other. Various firms, and especially those in office buildings, use each others' inputs and outputs; they are held together through chains of production linkages. They acquire these inputs and 'ship' the outputs over various communication channels, including direct personal contacts or so-called 'face-to-face linkages'. The concepts of agglomeration economies and face-to-face linkages are used in many studies of downtown business complexes, starting with Haig's (1926) analysis of downtown Manhattan ('transportation of intelligence') and including Robbins and Terleckyj's (1960) study of Wall Street ('knowledge in a hurry') and the major studies of office location and linkages of the 1970s (Gad, 1979; Goddard, 1973). Recently, Saskia Sassen's outline of the 'producer services complex', which is at the core of 'global cities', has also relied on the notion of agglomeration economies and face-to-face linkages (Sassen, 1991: 90–125; 1994: 65–9).

The concept of agglomeration economies can be divided into two kinds: 'external economies of scale' and 'urbanization economies' (Dicken and Lloyd, 1990: 207–15). In the case of the former, savings could be achieved because some inputs become cheaper when they are obtained from a highly specialized firm. For instance, instead of having an expensive and potentially underemployed legal department in-house, a corporation could acquire legal services from a specialized business, a law firm, that achieves economies of scale by serving a number of customers. When these are needed frequently and/or involve sudden meetings, clustering is advantageous. 'Urban economies' involve what are now termed 'untraded interdependencies', such as certain free municipal services and urban advantages, including libraries or archives, free (or under-priced) lunchtime lectures, the sheer presence of meeting places, chance encounters in streets, and informal networks.

To understand the spatial clustering of businesses and institutions of various kinds downtown rather than elsewhere, accessibility advantages must be considered. Downtown businesses and institutions are very labour-intensive and thus require excellent accessibility to a large labour pool (Hoover and Vernon, 1959: 98; Scott, 1982). The central downtown area has traditionally been the point of maximum accessibility within the metropolis. Central downtown districts have evolved through a process of circular and cumulative causation: some initial transportation or political advantage attracted businesses; improved transportation facilities were put in place; and more businesses and institutions took advantage of better transportation facilities, a larger customer base, and proximity to suppliers of input services. These circular and cumulative processes can go on uninterrupted for a long time, leading to the relatively permanent large central downtown areas of Toronto, Montreal, and Vancouver. But centrality and agglomeration are not entirely resistant to change. This chapter documents some of the important changes that have given rise to the central downtowns of the larger Canadian cities and some of the changes associated with the waning monopoly of metropolitan-wide centrality once enjoyed by the earlier downtowns.

The downtowns of Canadian cities are hard to understand without looking at their history. Rounds of cumulative change or transitions, including several waves of redevelopment (see Figure 11.2), are an important part of the story. This history is

Figure 11.2   **Development/Redevelopment Sequence at King and Bay, Toronto**

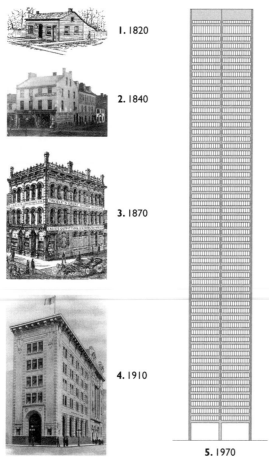

1. Wooden frame building, built 1820. Jordon Post house, clockmaker's shop and residence. From J.R. Robertson, *Robertson's Landmarks of Toronto*, vol. 2 (Toronto, 1896), 673, and vol. 5 (Toronto, 1908), 394.

2. 'Red brick warehouse', built 1840. Initially occupied by furniture company. Showrooms and warehouse. From J.R. Robertson, *Robertson's Landmarks of Toronto*, vol. 5 (Toronto, 1908), 394. Photo of c. 1870: Metropolitan Toronto Library.

3. Stone and Brick (?) commercial building, Built c. 1877–8. Retail, manufacturing, billiard parlour. From *Canadian Illustrated News*, Supplement, 28 May 1881. National Archives of Canada.

4. Steel frame, stone and terra cotta, built 1910–11. Union Bank chambers, banking hall on ground and mezzanine floors; also bank offices on one of the upper four floors, several other occupants. Height of building: 95 feet. From *Construction* 5, 2 (1912): 62–3. Photo: Royal Bank of Canada, Archives.

5. Steel and glass skyscraper, built c. 1970–2. Commerce Court, multi-building complex developed by Canadian Imperial Bank of Commerce. Houses head office of bank and many other occupants. Height: 784 feet, 57 floors. Based on architect's drawing. Canadian Imperial Bank of Commerce, Development Corporation.

briefly related here. Its narration is very crude, however, because each one of the large Canadian cities has unique features of age, size, economic function, and regional setting. The picture is also coarse because research, including our own, has been very uneven in terms of cities, periods, and topics covered. The first portion of the discussion that follows looks at the traditional downtown located in the central city. This discussion is divided into three sections that consider distinctive periods of growth and change in the central downtown area in much the same way as Chapter 1 dealt with the broader context of transition and change across the cityscape at large. The next portion turns to the suburbs and introduces the more recent form of development, the so-called suburban downtown. The two cities that show the most advanced spread of suburban downtowns, Vancouver and Toronto, are discussed here. There is an emphasis on offices in both sections of the chapter because, despite common stereotypes of 'downtown' as places for shopping and entertainment, throughout the twentieth century the main source of growth has come from office development and jobs based in offices. The concluding pages of this chapter consider how downtown might change in the twenty-first century.

The Growth and Expansion of Central Downtowns, 1900–1950

By 1900, there were districts without residential populations at the core of the older Canadian cities. These core areas housed a variety of functions or land uses, including a large proportion of the public and private high-order functions and, most likely, a large proportion of a city's jobs. The building fabric and spatial organization of the central areas of Canadian cities were profoundly reshaped between 1900 and the beginning of yet another phase around 1950. Development and building activity, like economic performance, were highly uneven during the 1900–50 period. Overall, however, the growth of the Canadian population and economy was impressive in absolute terms. While it is impossible to picture the many economic and social changes that occurred, we highlight those changes with direct implications for the development of the downtown areas. First, the organization of capitalist enterprise changed from family-based entrepreneurial firms to large 'public' (joint-stock or share-based) corporations. The economy as a whole changed from industrial to corporate capitalism. This was accompanied by mergers in all branches of the economy. Mergers in banking reduced the number of chartered banks from 38 in 1891 to 10 in 1931 and the number of Canadian cities housing a bank head office from 18 to just two, Montreal and Toronto. Newly formed large corporations needed office space, and a whole range of new offices related to corporate capitalism appeared on the scene. Other changes in the economy combined with social evolution to bring women into factories and shops, and especially into offices. Business conditions changed: US firms set up branches in Canada and scientific management brought many white-collar experts into businesses and government offices (Gad and Holdsworth, 1984: 294–8).

Vertical Expansion

Most noticeable in the central areas was the advent of tall office buildings. By the late 1920s, the Bank of Commerce Building in Toronto reached 34 floors, a Canadian record until around 1960. Floorspace also increased dramatically. Business growth caused rents to rise, and rising rents triggered a building boom. At least in Toronto, several of the high-rise office buildings built between 1900 and 1940 were associated with banks. The banks, however, shared these buildings with many tenants. Newspaper publishers were also important developers in several cities and office towers were also erected by insurance companies and a variety of other types of corporations. Many if not most tall and large office buildings, however, were speculative ventures owned by development companies.

Why the skyscraper? Beyond the fact that it was made possible by the invention of the elevator and structural steel, there is no simple answer. Traditional models of land rent tell us that demand was highest for downtown sites because they offered city-wide access, hence land values were bid up and high rates of capitalization were needed to ensure profit levels sufficiently high to defray initial pre-development land costs (see Chapter 7). Presumably, offices found it worthwhile to pay high rents in order to be close to each other and to be in a central location. Some of the large banks and insurance companies also thought they might need room to expand. Many companies, especially financial businesses, used building imagery, in particular bulk and height, to impress (Gad and Holdsworth, 1987).

During the boom periods of 1900–13 and the 1920s small office districts formed at the core of the central areas. These were centred around the bank head offices or the principal branches (also referred to as regional head offices) and were typically about 400 to 500 metres long. In Montreal it was St James Street between Place d'Armes and McGill Street; in Toronto, King Street from just east of Yonge to west of Bay; in Vancouver, West Hastings between Victory Square/Cambie and Granville. Although these early office clusters were general office districts, including a wide range of offices, they became symbols of financial power. St James Street in Montreal became the 'Wall Street of Canada' (Beauregard, 1981). The only kinds of offices absent from these general office districts were the larger government offices.

The formation of office districts occurred parallel to the move of retail stores to new locations and the move of offices out of the older wholesale districts, which became 'sectors of discard' (e.g., for Montreal, see Nader, 1976: 148). Retailing surged. Dry goods retailers like Eaton's and Simpsons became large department stores in the 1890s; the general stores of the Hudson's Bay Company turned into huge department stores in the larger cities of western Canada. These department stores formed the nuclei of new retail clusters. In all major cities the new retail clusters also became the locations of the newly emerging mass entertainment facilities— vaudeville theatres and, later, cinemas. The retail and entertainment clusters were thronged by the large numbers of young single people who arrived from almost everywhere to meet the labour demand of rapidly expanding urban economies in the boom periods (Strange, 1995).

The relatively small office and retail districts together with the government offices and the older wholesale and transportation-oriented areas (railway stations, customs houses, hotels), formed a dense inner part, or core, of the central areas. However, as early as the 1920s, many of the high-order functions of urban economy and society, including legislative buildings and a variety of offices, hotels, hospitals, universities, and museums, had started to scatter over a much larger area beyond this small downtown core.

The Modernization of Downtown, 1945-1975

The three decades after World War II constituted another boom period in Canada. Population and jobs in cities grew at a phenomenal rate (Lemon, 1996: 243–50). Many of the policies concerning the downtown area were shaped by concerns about the inner-city 'slum problem'. There were other agendas related to the inner city dating back to the time before World War II, and these were largely those of municipal governments: alleviating congestion by

improving access to the city centre and beautifying downtown. Thus, a large number of old plans were reactivated. Many projects were launched in the 1940s and 1950s, including, for example, the Yonge Street subway in Toronto, the widening of Dorchester Boulevard in Montreal (Nader, 1976: 149), and in Vancouver, both the Public Library on Burrard Street (1956–7) and the Queen Elizabeth Theatre. However, development and job growth were generally slow. Rapid suburbanization began to affect downtown. This was especially felt in the form of relatively low growth rates of retail sales and, around 1960, declining manufacturing employment in the inner cities. City governments became concerned about the 'loss of vitality' of the urban core. The rapid decline of inner-city areas of many US cities was perceived as an example of what could happen in Canada.

The Office Boom of the 1960s and Early 1970s

The 1940s and early 1950s already had seen a small office boom fuelled by the demands of government. The Great Depression years set in motion many innovations in government, e.g., unemployment insurance, the (central) Bank of Canada, and the Canadian Broadcasting Corporation. Beginning in the late 1950s, many if not most of the large Canadian cities attempted to orchestrate a downtown development boom. Since there was little hope of substantially increasing retail and manufacturing activity, municipal governments focused on office development, which was encouraged in every conceivable way. The Scotia Square development in Halifax (Nader: 1976: 46–9; Pacey, 1979) and the Civic Square project in Hamilton (Freeman, 1976) used 'slum clearance' moneys from the National Housing Act's urban renewal program to make room for new development. In both cases property was expropriated and sold to private developers so that they could build a mixture of shopping malls, high-rise offices, hotels and apartments, and some public facilities like libraries or theatres. By the 1970s, convention centres also became part of the package.

Other help, provided by municipalities, included liberal if not excessive zoning provisions (with densities in Toronto going as high as a floor-space index (FSI) of 12—a ratio of building floorspace that is 12 times lot size), street and lane closings, hard infrastructure improvements, and 'soft' design and planning advice. Municipal governments also engaged in symbolic investments, such as the decision to build a showpiece city hall in Toronto, which was planned in the 1950s and opened in 1965.

A great deal of office development took on forms unknown in pre-war Canada. The attention-getting office projects were 'modernist' in plan, elevation, and organization of uses (Collier, 1975). This meant the segregation of functions: a ceremonial ground floor with plazas and entrance halls, stacked offices above, and shops and services underground. Also, architects and planners strove to separate cars and pedestrians, allowing for underground car storage, below-ground pedestrian circulation, and moving cars on the streets. To allow for air and light access to buildings, the footprint had to be small and the number of floors large. Tall, slim towers rose up. These projects, exemplified by Montreal's Place Ville-Marie and the Toronto-Dominion Centre in Toronto, were not just buildings but complexes consisting of several buildings. The new towers reached 54 floors in the 1960s and peaked at 72 with the completion of the First Canadian tower in Toronto in 1975.

As in previous rounds of strong growth, the use of space was intensified yet again in the core section of downtown. The general office district that had emerged in the first half of the twentieth century was partially redeveloped. Building densities increased. It has been calculated that the average floor-space density of commercial and government offices in Toronto's 'inner core area' had increased from an FSI of 3.8 in 1962 to an FSI of 5.2 in 1973 (Toronto, 1974: 408). The redevelopment of the downtown core was uneven: some older parts, such as King Street East in Toronto and the area east of Seymour Street in Vancouver, received little office development. In other parts of the old CBD, offices displaced wholesale and manufacturing activities.

More frequently, office development, as in Toronto, occurred in sectors of the inner city where upper-class and upper-middle-class residential areas converged on the Yonge Street subway line (Bourne, 1967: 112).

While some of these developments can be seen as contiguous lateral expansions of the pre-World War II general office district, other developments consisted in a 'filling out' or densifying of the central area. This is particularly obvious in Toronto and Vancouver. In Vancouver a great deal of 1960s and early 1970s office development occurred in the Broadway corridor, that is, outside the 'downtown' Burrard peninsula but in an area where high-order functions such as the Vancouver City Hall and the Vancouver General Hospital located before 1945. In Toronto, offices not only dotted University Avenue, but by the 1970s they formed a continuous wall from Front Street north to the complex of hospitals near Queen's Park (see Figure 11.3). Also, Bay Street north of Queen Street all the way to Bloor Street saw many medium-size new office buildings replacing nineteenth-century houses and shops. Offices formed an almost continuous street wall along Bloor Street between the Royal Ontario Museum in the west and Sherborne Street in the east. Offices also spread north of Bloor along the Yonge Street subway, which was opened in 1954.[1] Considerable spatial differentiation occurred. This was much more visible in the larger cities than in the smaller ones. In Toronto a 'financial district' emerged between the 1950s and 1980s (Gad, 1991). At the same time, it must be noted, a whole range of offices had gradually left the old general office districts, where they found rents too high, parking too expensive, and huge buildings too impersonal.

Beyond the Downtown Office Boom

The office boom in the central areas was accompanied by a host of other changes. In the face of suburban competition, downtown retail facilities were modernized through copying the layout of the suburban shopping mall. The Pacific Centre in Vancouver, Scotia Square in Halifax, Jackson Square in Hamilton, and the Eaton Centre in Toronto are part of this, as are many smaller downtown 'malls'. Office complexes began to be equipped with underground malls after the construction of Montreal's Place Ville-Marie with an extensive underground shopping concourse in the early 1960s (Beauregard, 1972: 174–5). Specialty shopping streets or whole districts sprung up, catering to locals and tourists alike, such as Robson Street and Gastown in Vancouver, Bloor Street West and Yorkville in Toronto, and the boutique and café-lined Crescent, de la Montagne, and St-Denis streets in Montreal. New high-rise hotels catered to tourists and business travellers. The addition or expansion of hospitals, universities, museums, art galleries, theatres, concert halls, and other kinds of entertainment or 'edutainment' facilities was even more spectacular.

In retreat in the central areas were land uses (and employment) associated with manufacturing, wholesaling, and some forms of transportation (especially water-related and railway transportation). The conventional story, told by planners and academics alike, is that many factories and transportation facilities were technically outdated and something had to be done to 'revive' or to 'revitalize' blighted areas. While this was certainly the case in some instances, at the advancing edge of the financial district of Toronto hundreds of manufacturers were driven out by rising land values. In Toronto, even the big newspapers moved editorial offices and large printing plants to make way for the offices of First Canadian Place.

The changes that happened between the 1940s and 1970s can be documented by evidence, albeit fragmentary, from municipal planning departments. Table 11.1 focuses on trends in Toronto as an example. Available data show that employment in the central areas of Toronto and Vancouver increased in the 1960s and 1970s, mostly due to office employment growth. And it is likely that in most Canadian downtowns rising employment was a result of an expanding white-collar labour force. In comparison to this burgeoning office activity, retailing stagnated. Montreal, Toronto, and Edmonton data point to a stability in the land area occupied by retailing and an absence of increase in floor space after the early 1960s. By the 1960s, office floor space was becoming much larger than retail space. Toronto and Halifax data also show the increasing 'suburbanization' of office space and office-based activities. As early as 1964, 30 per cent of the office floor space in Halifax was located outside the CBD. In Toronto the central district's share of office space decreased from 97 per cent in 1953 to 90 per cent in the mid-sixties and 79 per cent in the mid-seventies.[2]

Redevelopment Meets Barriers

By the late 1960s, a variety of protests against downtown modernization began to surface. Some groups formed to oppose the demolition of historic buildings, others to oppose the destruction of amenities such as the view of mountains in Vancouver, the view of the harbour and islands in Halifax (Pacey, 1979), or the visibility of the Parliament Buildings in Ottawa. Next to high-rise buildings, the impact of the car on the central area and the ring of residential areas surrounding it was the issue that received most attention. Protesters galvanized a wide range of people and formed coalitions on municipal councils; they were labelled 'reformers' in their opposition to the 'old guard', the traditional political élite. This élite was 'pro-development' or 'pro-growth' and found support across a wide political spectrum, from business-based groups to construction workers' trade unions.

Another voice in the 'stop-growth' chorus came from university-based researchers. In the 1960s, economists and geographers built on the agglomeration economies approach by carefully studying the character of face-to-face linkages and other relationships between different kinds of firms located in CBDs. Did all branches of the economy rely on the same intensity of face-to-face contacts? Were there clusters of activities that were not strongly related to other clusters and that might therefore appropriately be encouraged to decentralize?[3] Already in the 1960s the federal government in Ottawa, and then in the 1970s Toronto and

Figure 11.3   **Land-Use Change in Downtown Toronto, 1955–1974**

Downtown 1955

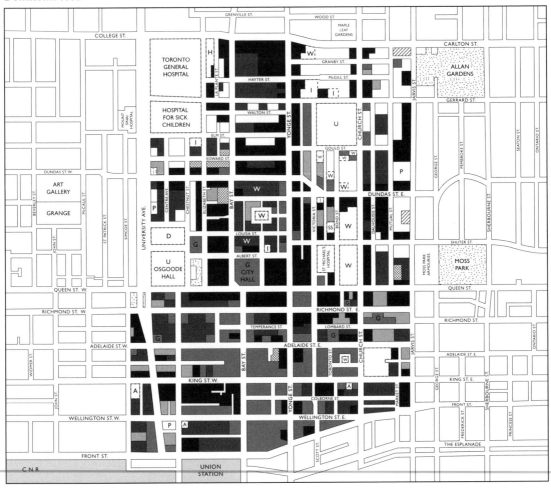

Residential
☐ Low Density Residential
▨ High Density Residential

Commercial
■ Retail and Services
S Auto Services and Sales
▦ Private Offices
G Government Offices

Industry
▨ Industry
W Indoor Warehousing
☐ Outdoor Storage

Institutions
PS Public School
HS High School (Public)
SS Separate School
PrS Private School
U University and Colleges
A Places of Amusement
L Library
W Places of Worship

Institutions
H Hospitals
I Other Institutions
D Defence Establishments

Utilities
▨ Public Utilities

Open Space
▨ Public Parks
▨ Private and Other

Parking
P Parking

Transportation
▨ Transportation
TTC TTC Subway

Vacant Lands
V Vacant
U/C Under Construction and Demolition

Figure 11.3 **(continued)**

Downtown 1974

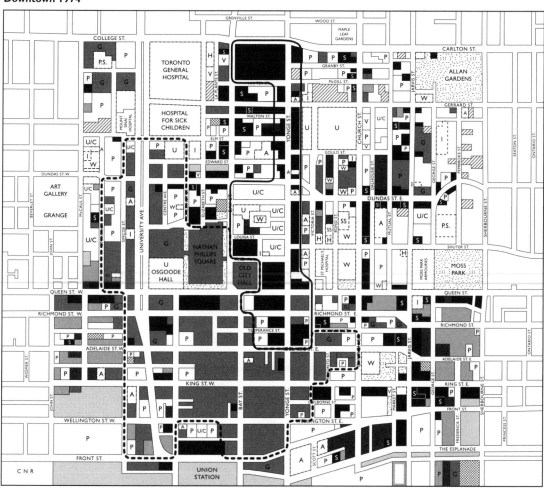

Residential
- ☐ Low Density Residential
- ▨ High Density Residential

Commercial
- ■ Retail and Services
- S Auto Services and Sales
- ■ Private Offices
- G Government Offices

Industry
- ▨ Industry
- W Indoor Warehousing
- ☐ Outdoor Storage

Institutions
- PS Public School
- HS High School (Public)
- SS Separate School
- PrS Private School
- U University and Colleges
- A Places of Amusement
- L Library
- W Places of Worship

Institutions
- H Hospitals
- I Other Institutions
- D Defence Establishments

Utilities
- ▨ Public Utilities

Open Space
- ▨ Public Parks
- ▨ Private and Other

Parking
- P Parking

Transportation
- ▨ Transportation
- TTC TTC Subway

Vacant Lands
- V Vacant
- U/C Under Construction and Demolition

- ▬ ▬ ▬ Downtown Office and Financial District
- ▬▬▬ Downtown Shopping District

Source: Toronto (1974: 196–7).

Table 11.1   **Selected Indicators of Change in Downtown Toronto, 1951–1971**

	1951	1956	1961	1966	1971
Core area retail sales as % of Metropolitan Toronto total	43		30	23	
Core area employment		272,000	272,000	264,000	293,000
% of Metropolitan Toronto total		44	40	37	32
Inner core area* employment		160,000	166,000	167,000	192,000
Commercial and government offices					
Land (million sq. ft)			5.8		6.7
Floor space (million sq. ft)			22.1		30.2
Density			3.8		4.5
Commercial retail					
Land (million sq. ft)			5.0		4.4
Floor space (million sq. ft)			8.7		7.5
Density			1.7		1.7
Industry and warehousing					
Land (million sq. ft)			3.7		2.3
Floor space (million sq. ft)			9.7		7.4
Density			2.6		3.0
Core area office floor space** (million sq. ft.)	7.8		14.2	17.7	24.5
Central district† office floor space†† (million sq. ft.)	8.1		16.2	20.7	28.6
% of Metropolitan office floor space††	97		93	89	80
Selected office-based 'industries' in central district as percent of CMA total					
Advertising agencies	94		87		73
Law firms	88		78		70
Accountants	79		69		34
Engineering consultants	77		60		41
City of Toronto Employment in separately located head and sales offices of manufacturing companies as % of CMA total			81		64

*Inner core area: a narrow south-north strip along the Yonge St axis within the core area.

**Core area: waterfront to just north of Bloor St, and Bathurst St in west to the Don River in east; gross floor space.

†Central district: core area and its extension north of Bloor to Eglinton Ave.

††Net floor space.

Sources: Toronto (1974); Royal Le Page; Statistics Canada, *Industries of Canada*, Catalogue No. 31–209; various directories.

Vancouver, attempted to decentralize offices. Research on offices stressing the diversity of activities and potential for sub-agglomerations legitimized decentralization policies.

Another strand of writing emerged in the 1960s in response to the urban renewal projects and urban expressway developments of the 1950s. This literature was highly critical of efforts to modernize the city centre. Jane Jacobs articulated this view in a 1958 article, 'Downtown is for People', and in *Death and Life of Great American Cities* (Jacobs, 1961). Other writers, largely investigative journalists, zeroed in on developers and city councils that 'sold out' (Aubin, 1977; Gutstein, 1975; Stein, 1972). Common to these voices was an attack on large-scale projects and buildings produced by big developers for big businesses with the aid of governments. Small-scale buildings of mixed age, mixed land uses, and small businesses were celebrated. These writings, together with the research on the potential diversity of linkages, provided conceptual underpinnings for the political movements attempting to reshape city centres in the 1970s through office decentralization measures and residential construction programs.

Uneven Development: From the Mid-1970s to the Mid-1990s

The central areas of Canadian cities went through another round of change between the mid-1970s and the mid-1990s. The intensity of these changes, however, varied according to the city and the time. In some cities the central areas were dramatically affected by growth (as in Toronto, Vancouver, Calgary), whereas other downtowns showed more stability (Quebec City, Halifax, Ottawa) or struggled while losing social and economic pride of place in the metropolitan area (Edmonton, Winnipeg, Kitchener, Hamilton). Some downtowns, like those of Toronto and Montreal, saw relatively little change in the second half of the 1970s, while those of Calgary, Vancouver, and Edmonton were covered with construction cranes. After 1981, the cranes came down in the western cities and moved back east, where downtown Toronto experienced great amounts of development. Although less than in Toronto, downtown Montreal also witnessed growth. Then in the 1990s, construction in downtown Toronto almost came to a halt, while Vancouver's downtown became the place of major change through construction.

From Office Development to Diversity

Throughout the 1970s and 1980s office development was the most visible element of change. In the booming downtowns, new office towers were accompanied by substantial increases in office employment, most likely constituting more than half of all employment in the central area of the large cities by the end of the 1980s.[4] While data on changes in the downtown areas are not easy to obtain, we know that in Ottawa, for example, central area office floor space increased from 1 to 1.5 million square metres (10.7 to 15.6 million square feet) in the 1980s, and in Toronto's core area (the area between the Don River and Bathurst and the waterfront and just north of Bloor Street) office floor space increased by a staggering 4.1 million square metres (44.8 million square feet) between 1971 and 1996, most of it added in the 1980s. In Toronto's core area, overall employment increased from 293,000 in 1970 to a peak of nearly 400,000 in 1989, and then fell to 383,000 in 1991 and probably to as low as 350,000 in 1996 according to Metropolitan Toronto Planning Department surveys.

Not all changes in the central areas were office-related, as David Ley (1996: 153-6) has pointed out. Many central areas witnessed the expansion of hospitals, universities and colleges, museums, art galleries, public libraries, spectator sports complexes (and fitness centres), and theatres and restaurants. Almost all cities with a waterfront saw enormous amounts of public, and some private, investment in recreation facilities and new infrastructure (Desfor et al., 1988; Hamilton and Simard, 1993). Also, many central areas, especially those of Toronto and

Vancouver, witnessed a considerable amount of residential construction and population increase, including the rather large government-orchestrated socially mixed housing areas known as False Creek (Vancouver) and St Lawrence Neighbourhood (Toronto). While many of the changes did not introduce new elements to downtowns, the revaluation of waterfronts and the reintroduction of residential populations marked significant turnarounds. Also, conversion of vacated or underused manufacturing space to office, entertainment, and residential functions constituted a new phenomenon. In some cities a great deal of downtown development was not driven by office growth but by the reuse of the older fabric for tourism and recreation (or ceremonial purposes). Elsewhere, downtowns experienced decline. Several studies (Bunting and Millward, 1999; Curtis, 1996; Filion and Bunting, 1993; Millward and Bunting, 1999) have documented the frustrating efforts to revitalize downtown Kitchener. It is not that Kitchener–Waterloo is an economic disaster area; on the contrary, it consistently registers one of the lowest unemployment rates in Canada. There is, however, clear evidence that Kitchener–Waterloo businesses and residents prefer newer, 'suburban-type' settings (Bunting and Filion, 1999).

The Roots of Downtown Diversity

What conceptualizations of central areas have theoreticians suggested for understanding these diverse changes? One theoretical framework has been advanced by Marxist scholars. Here the phenomenal increase in office floorspace is seen as being related to crises in the capital accumulation process (Harvey, 1978). When the industrial sector has difficulties finding markets for its products and thus offers mediocre or negative return on investment, capital switches into another 'circuit of accumulation', namely finance and real estate capital.[5] A related concept is that of the spatial movement of capital (Harvey, 1982: 190–203, 373–438). In this view, industrial capital is leaving North American cities in the lurch because it can earn more in low-wage countries. The same goes for capital switches from the 'Rustbelt' to the 'Sunbelt' in the US, or from the inner city to the suburbs. Older cities then have a hard time competing and must resort to tourism, fairs, convention centres, entertainment, and similar kinds of economic activities with low-wage and often part-time employment.

A second major framework focusing on the diversity of change is the 'global city' thesis advanced by Saskia Sassen (1991, 1994). In this perspective, multinational or transnational corporations are engines of urban development with global reach.[6] These companies congregate in a few locations across the globe—London, New York, Tokyo, for example. Together with service firms, collectively called 'business services' or, more glamorously, 'producer services' (such as law firms, accounting firms, management and computer consultants, advertising agencies), they form a spatially small cluster of businesses held together by intensive face-to-face linkages. These businesses employ highly paid executives, managers, and professionals. While routine office activities with low-paid female clerical workers get dispatched to the suburbs, well-paid 'downtown' professionals and executives need an army of low-paid service workers to run shops, restaurants, theatres, and other personal services. Cities not closely linked to the global business network have been bypassed by the new wave of core area development induced by global business expansion.

Another perspective, articulated by David Ley (1996), largely in the context of the gentrification debate, emphasizes the rise of urban professionals who have played an increasing role as advisers in both business and government. This 'new middle class' does not broker authority but influences economy and society through knowledge-based activity (Gouldner, 1979).[7] It is this class, or at least a powerful fraction of it, that in the mid-1970s redirected the course of central area development in Toronto and Vancouver and, to a lesser extent, in other cities. Conservation-minded and preoccupied with culture, the new middle class clearly expressed itself in strategic planning documents such as the 1975 Vancouver *Livable Region* plan (GVRD, 1975) and the

Toronto *Central Area Plan*, which attempted to control office development through down-zoning and to encourage residential development throughout the downtown area (Toronto, 1975, 1979).

Downtowns in the 1990s

In Vancouver, as in Toronto, the central area has been broken down into a myriad of planning districts and use designations (see Figure 11.1), which is a far cry from the broad-brush high-density commercial, residential, and institutional designations of 1950s and 1960s master or official plans. The new generation of plans recognizes downtown areas' diversity, with their specialized shopping, hospitals and medical treatment centres, theatres and cinemas, hotels, and museums and art galleries. Equally diverse is the social make-up of downtown residents. Most Canadian central areas host the majority of a metropolitan area's homeless and street prostitutes, although with the increasing claims by those with money and/or power on the downtown core, many marginal people are shuffled away to inner-city areas outside the central area and into run-down, older suburban motel strips. This displacement is the outcome of rising land values that cause the replacement of the facilities marginal people use downtown.

Contemporary downtowns do not account for as large a share of a metropolitan region's activities as they did in the past. In the case of Toronto, the core area with its nearly 400,000 jobs amounts to less than 25 per cent of all jobs in the census metropolitan area, and this proportion is shrinking every year. The region outside the central area has a huge variety of jobs, including as many office jobs as the central area. Location patterns have become complex. If many kinds of offices show a central area tendency, such as the administrative offices of banks, media companies, and large law firms, other offices show a strong preference for the suburb. This is the case with engineering and computer consultants and the head and sales offices of manufacturing companies.[8] Non-central areas also host an astonishing number of public-sector jobs (in hospitals, schools, court-houses, and government administrative offices) and personal service jobs. Above all, the suburbs are where airports are located, and airports have become magnets for the suburbanization of a host of economic activities.

Suburban Downtowns

The enormous increase in the population of Canadian metropolitan areas from the 1940s onward was facilitated by the large-scale peripheral expansion of built-up areas, as is discussed in detail in Chapter 13. This lateral expansion consisted mainly of residential areas serviced by schools and commercial strips along arterial roads, and somewhat later by a carefully planned hierarchy of shopping centres. Another feature of peripheral expansion was 'industrial areas' to accommodate factories, distribution warehouses, and, in some favoured locations, offices. By the late 1960s some of these offices within or at the edges of industrial areas formed clusters near expressway access points; these clusters of low-rise, widely spaced office buildings were then labelled 'office parks'.

From the perspective of planners, suburbs in the 1970s, despite their large industrial areas, had insufficient numbers of jobs to provide employment to their residents. Suburban activity concentrations, mostly in the form of commercial strips and shopping malls, lacked higher-order services, such as specialized educational institutions and hospitals, and specialized entertainment facilities, such as live theatres. High-order office activities were also absent. Further, suburbs, especially when they grew to house populations of several hundred thousand, were seen to lack identity and focus. More to the point for suburban municipal governments was the growing need to increase the non-residential real estate tax base to pay for costly infrastructure and services. Planners also saw deficiencies in the suburban living and working environments: the large distances between the suburbs and specialized downtown services and cultural institutions; the quality and availability of public transit; and inadequate facilities for senior citizens. For all these reasons, planners started to advocate the creation of suburban downtowns.

In general, suburban downtowns were intended to be mixed-activity nodes, that is, they were to have office jobs, a range of high-order services including such cultural activities as theatre; they were to have prominent public buildings, including city or town halls; and they were to be compact in physical form and pedestrian-oriented. They were also to have a residential population and serve as foci of local surface transit. The larger of these suburban downtowns were proposed to accommodate between 30,000 and 40,000 jobs, while the smaller ones were targeted to contain 10,000 to 20,000 jobs. These suburban downtowns were 'to replicate the traditional activities and qualities of downtown and to generate a sense of suburban community identity' (Relph, 1991: 421; see Garreau, 1991, for an alternative US definition).

In the 1970s a number of circumstances came together to set in motion the creation of hierarchies of intra-suburban centres and subcentres. The larger suburbs often had dynamic personalities as mayors who saw suburban office towers not only as means to fill the tax coffers but also, together with new city halls, as symbols of public acknowledgement of prestige. At the same time, some central cities, especially Toronto and Vancouver, attempted to control central downtown office development by directing offices to the suburbs. The planning profession in particular was keen to impose a structure on the 'sprawling', 'amorphous' metropolis. Suburban downtowns started to emerge in a number of metropolitan areas, for instance, in Laval and in the Fairview area of Pointe Claire, both in the Montreal metropolitan region, and in Ottawa's Kanata. But the idea of municipalities actively creating 'suburban downtowns' became established more firmly in Toronto and Vancouver than anywhere else in Canada and, since these two urban centres now provide 20 years of experience in these attempts, they will be discussed in detail.

Toronto

In the mid-1970s the municipality of Metropolitan Toronto 'encouraged the creation of a small num-

ber [of suburban centres with densities] ... sufficiently high to attract and maintain a wide range of central area types of activities and to support related improvements to the transportation system' (Metro Toronto, 1976: 93), thus to increase the number and range of jobs in, and provide a focus for, the suburban communities around them (Figure 11.4). Metro's 1980 *Official Plan* (Metro Toronto, 1980) designated two 'major centres' (in North York and Scarborough) that were meant to contain a wide range of functions and up to 40,000 jobs. Since the 'major centres' were intended to reduce the need to travel downtown to high-order services and jobs, the success of Metro's policy would depend on whether the suburban 'downtowns' could attract high-order functions, services, and jobs that traditionally had located in the central downtown area.

The suburban municipalities of North York and Scarborough actively supported the creation of their major centres. North York, with a population of 550,000, improved its hard services within an old shopping strip, served by two subway stations on a northward extension of the Yonge subway immediately north of Highway 401. In 1979 North York revised its official plan (North York, 1979) to offer incentives for new buildings housing a range of shops, personal services, office functions, and apartments within a three-kilometre Yonge Street corridor. It built a new civic complex in the southern half of the corridor, with a theatre complex, the Ford Centre, next to it. North York's centre has grown consistently so that in 1995 it contained 638,000 square metres (about 6.9 million square feet) of office space (Filion and Burke, 1997) with a total employment of 27,900, of which 82 per cent were office jobs (Metro Toronto, 1997). The centre was quite diverse, containing over a thousand jobs in each of retailing, services, and institutional activities (Table 11.2). It also hosted 6,800 apartments with a total of over 10,000 residents (Filion and Burke, 1997). The City Centre contains the offices of major municipal functions (City Hall and Board of Education) and public facilities such as a major library and an aquatic sport centre. A third subway station was built in the mid-1980s and most of the

Figure 11.4 **Location of Toronto Suburban Downtowns**

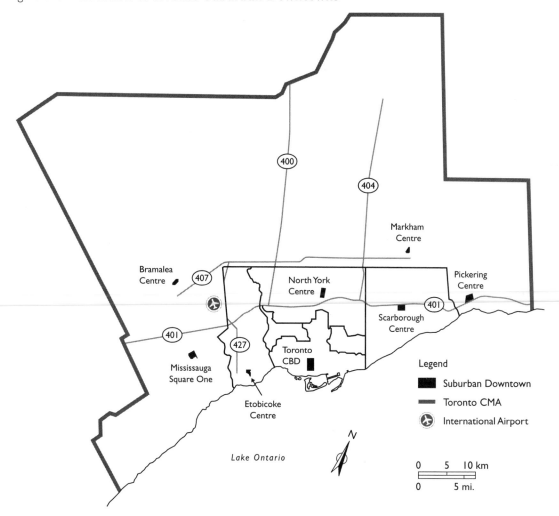

development is in the southern half of the corridor, within easy walking distance of two subway stations, though only 22 per cent of all rush-hour trips to and from the centre are by transit (Filion, 1997). Nonetheless, it is convenient to visit this centre by public transit and its bustle, with some on-street shopping, restaurants, and pubs, gives the pedestrian a feeling of being in a downtown-like area.

Scarborough, with a population of almost 400,000, started creating its own 'Town Centre' by constructing a municipal and school board office

building next to a new regional mall. The emerging centre is bounded on one side by Highway 401. New roads were built to serve the centre's greenfield site. In comparison to North York, Scarborough has been conservative in the building densities and range of activities that its plan and zoning by-laws permitted, so that development, after promising beginnings, has been spasmodic since the mid-1980s. The overall density of this complex is so low that owners of one office building operate a shuttle bus to and from the mall, 400 metres away, as walking, especially in

Table 11.2   **Toronto's Designated Major Centres**

	Office Space (sq. metres)		1995 Employment		
Location	1976	1990	Office	Retail	Total
CBD	4,110,000	6,430,000	233,800	22,700	367,800
North York	90,000	390,000[b]	22,800	1,400	27,900
Scarborough	60,000	220,000[c]	10,200	3,200	19,500
Eglinton	250,000	430,000	13,300	1,500	19,400
St Clair	270,000	370,000	9,800	600	12,100
Other 2 centres	30,000	110,000	8,200	1,500	15,500
Total: Centres	700,000	1,530,000	64,400	8,300	94,400
6 office parks	762,000	1,202,000	52,500	5,900	80,400
Other Metro	1,100,000	2,008,000	242,900	96,800	629,200
Total Metro	6,672,000	11,170,000	593,600	133,700	1,171,800
Square One	34,000	237,000[d]	N/A	N/A	12,000[a]
Other 3 centres	25,000	120,000[a]	N/A	N/A	N/A
Other GTA	377,000	1,579,000[a]	N/A	N/A	N/A
Total GTA	7,108,000	13,106,000	N/A	N/A	2,200,000[a]

[a] Approximation.
[b] 638,000 in 1995.
[c] 247,000 in 1995.
[d] 286,000 in 1995.
Sources: Filion and Burke (1997); Metro Toronto (1992, 1995, 1996).

winter, is too uncomfortable. A light rail transit line built to the centre from the eastern terminus of the Bloor-Danforth subway has not met expectations. It has been occasionally unreliable and a trip downtown or to all but one of Metro's other office centres entails two line changes. Transit accounts for 18 per cent of all rush-hour trips to and from the centre. In 1995 the centre contained 247,000 square metres (or about 2.7 million square feet) of office space and 1,200 apartments, and total employment of 19,500 (Table 11.2), but over 3,000 of the jobs

were in retailing and 4,700 in manufacturing and warehousing. Offices accounted for only 52 per cent of the centre's jobs (Metro Toronto, 1997).

Outside the City of Toronto (the former Metro Toronto) other new suburban downtowns are at various stages of development: in Mississauga to the west; in Brampton to the northwest; in Markham to the north; and in Pickering to the east. Three of these began as privately developed shopping centres to which developers added office space. But in the 1980s municipal governments became more aggressive in controlling and promoting the development of these emerging subcentres and, in some cases, added new and sometimes remarkable city halls. These new suburban downtowns or city centres vary in complexity. Mississauga's City Centre is by far the largest and has the widest variety of functions: a very large shopping mall (about 93,000 square metres or one million square feet in the mid-1990s), an attention-catching city hall with a public square, a large public library, a live-theatre complex, restaurants, cinemas, and other entertainment facilities. A new transit terminal serves as a hub for an emerging public transit system. About 12,000 jobs are found in the shopping mall and the 286,000 square metres (3.1 million square feet) of office floor space. Mississauga City Centre also includes a hotel and over 1,000 apartments in high-rise buildings.

Vancouver

Vancouver's employment and commercial functions were highly centralized in the early 1970s, with the City of Vancouver having 39 per cent of the Greater Vancouver Regional District (GVRD) population but 59 per cent of its jobs, while the CBD alone contained 60 per cent of the Greater Vancouver Regional District's commercial floor space. In 1976 the GVRD adopted *The Livable Region: 1976–1986*, a plan with the objective of minimizing the need for commuter and other travel across the region. The policy included the following four measures: (1) encouraging increased housing densities near the CBD; (2) decentralizing jobs and services to four regional town centres (RTCs) in the suburbs; (3) improving public transportation, including a new light-rail line from the CBD to Surrey's RTC; and (4) seeking to balance jobs and population in each part of the GVRD (Artibise et al., 1990). Initially, there would be four regional town centres: New Westminster, Metrotown in Burnaby, and two initially undetermined sites, which ended up as Surrey (the Whalley–Guildford centre as it was then known) and Port Coquitlam (Hutton and Davis, 1984) (see Figure 11.5). Each regional town centre was to become sufficiently large and varied to con-

tain 7,000 to 10,000 jobs and each was to serve a residential population of 100,000 to 150,000. Shopping would require about 65,000 square metres (700,000 square feet) of space and create 1,500 to 2,000 jobs, community and cultural services would create 1,000 to 2,000 more jobs, there would be over 93,000 square metres (one million square feet) of office space for about 5,000 jobs, and, finally, there would be 2,000 to 3,000 housing units within walking distance of each regional town centre to house a walk-in clientele for the centre and up to one-fifth of its workers (Spaeth, 1975).

Having to compete with development in the central downtown and elsewhere, development started slowly in the regional town centres. From 1976 to 1981, commercial space increased faster in both the CBD and elsewhere in the suburbs than in the RTCs. Trying to create four such centres at the same time may have been too ambitious (Hutton and Davis, 1984). Nonetheless, two additional town centres, Richmond and Lonsdale, were designated (see Figure 11.5). In 1986 the elevated skytrain rapid transit system opened, stimulating office growth in Burnaby's Metrotown but bringing little development to New Westminster (also served by the skytrain).

By 1991, the RTCs had attracted 962,000 square metres (10.3 million square feet) of retail space and in 1992 had 662,000 square metres (7.1 million square feet) of office space, ranging from 11,000 square metres (118,000 square feet) in Port Coquitlam's Regional Town Centre to 223,000 square metres (2.4 million square feet) in Burnaby's Metrotown (Table 11.3). Although the CBD continued to dominate the region in office space, its share of the Greater Vancouver Regional District's office space had decreased to 43 per cent, while the total RTC share had risen to 13 per cent (from 8 per cent in 1983). The Greater Vancouver Regional District's new *Strategic Plan* (GVRD, 1995) continued to advocate the concentration of shopping facilities and offices in pedestrian-oriented regional town centres to reduce the need for car travel across the region. Also, in 1994 the skytrain line reached the Surrey City Centre.

Figure 11.5   **Location of Vancouver Suburban Downtowns**

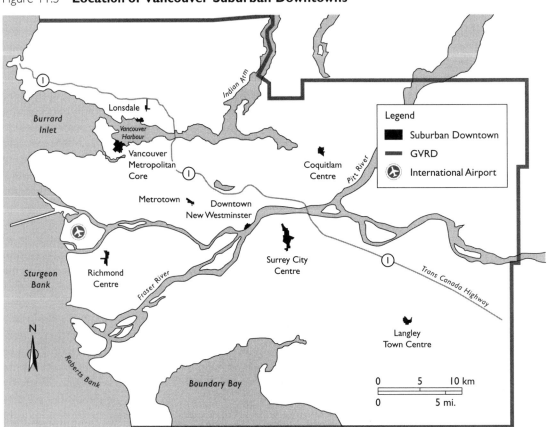

Burnaby's Metrotown, 12 km southeast of Vancouver's central business district and near the mid-point of the skytrain line, fulfils many functions associated with the regional centre concept. It contains a large retail complex, a range of commercial services, and the largest cluster of offices in the GVRD outside the City of Vancouver. It can be accessed by rapid transit, has shops and restaurants along its sidewalks, and operates more like a downtown than any of the other regional town centres. Richmond Town Centre, 16 km south of the CBD and a five-minute drive from the airport, contains a mix of retail and office facilities, as well as the Workmen's Compensation Board Hospital and Richmond General Hospital, which have attracted a huge concentration of health services to the centre's office buildings. Vancouver International Airport has enabled Richmond to become a hospitality and aerospace centre, and it could become a convention centre. Richmond also has substantial waterfront industrial land served directly by shipping, which, with the airport, has made it an important distribution centre for western Canada and enabled it to attract the head or regional offices of some large companies. Richmond Town Centre is approaching a balance of retail and office space, but its future regional role may be inhibited by BC Transit's announcement in 1995 that a rapid transit link

Table 11.3   **Vancouver's Regional Town Centres**

	Office Space (sq. m.)		Retail Space (sq. m.) 1991	Employment 1991–2
	1983	1991–2		
CBD	1,596,000	2,183,000	1,305,000	173,000
Broadway	318,000	418,000		
Metrotown	77,000	223,000	227,000	17,000
Richmond	52,000	139,000	281,000	20,400
Lonsdale	30,000	111,000	92,000	15,300
Other 3 RTCs	129,000	182,000	362,000	27,400
Total RTCs	288,000	655,000	962,000	80,100
Other	1,285,000	1,770,000	3,700,000	561,000
Total GVRD	3,487,000	5,026,000	5,967,000	814,100

Sources: GVRD (1991, 1993a, 1993b).

between it and the CBD, promised earlier, will not be built.

Lonsdale's regional town centre is very close to the CBD and has a striking waterfront setting, but its links to the CBD are a circuitous trip via the First Narrows Bridge (Lion's Gate Bridge) or by 'seabus' across Burrard Inlet. In addition, there is a limited amount of land for development. New Westminster's downtown existed long before it was designated a regional town centre and the municipality has encouraged apartment development within walking distance. However, there has been so little office development in recent years that it seems likely to function mainly as a local service centre in the future. Surrey council initially sought to create a dumbbell-shaped regional town centre but, in 1991, decided to cluster future downtown-type development in one-half of the centre. With more concentrated growth this RTC may be able to capitalize on

its skytrain link to Metrotown and the CBD. Coquitlam's RTC has yet to attract significant office development.

A critical element in the development of suburban downtowns in other cities, which is missing from the Greater Vancouver Regional District, is a highway network with intersecting ring and radial highways or intersections between highways and rapid transit lines, where exceptional access triggers the development of mixed-use centres at key interchanges. The skytrain provides a fast and reliable radial link between the CBD and the Metrotown, New Westminster, and Surrey regional town centres, but the link from the CBD to Richmond's regional town centre is along congested city streets. In 1995 BC Transit announced expansions that will include a partial north-south cross-town link between Port Coquitlam and New Westminster (BC Transit, 1995). If this light-rail transit link were extended from New Westminster to Richmond centre and the airport, it would create two or three sites with outstanding four-way access.

Head Offices and Other Trends in Suburban Downtowns

Municipalities and regional governments attempting to create suburban downtowns must recognize that a downtown is not merely a cluster of office buildings in an office park, nor is it a mall containing shopping, a few movie theatres, and some restaurants. A downtown has serendipitous variety and offices that serve more than the immediate community. The CBD of a large metropolis attracts the head offices of large corporations, such as the 220 companies that are most influential in Canada in terms of revenue, profits, exports, and jobs (Matthew, 1999). Clearly, such head offices are a phenomenon of large urban centres as Canada's three largest metropolitan areas have 148 (67 per cent) of the 220, and these are generally found in their CBDs. Although there is a sprinkling of head offices in suburbs across Canada, only Toronto, Vancouver, and Montreal have more than two of the top 220 companies in their suburbs. But have those high-order offices been attracted to suburban downtowns?

The head offices of the four large corporations in Montreal's suburbs are scattered, with two in Longueuil, one in Laval, and one in St Laurent. Only one of Vancouver's six suburban head offices of large corporations is in a regional town centre (Lonsdale); the rest are scattered. Toronto has 22 of these head offices in its suburbs, 10 in the suburbs that are within the City of Toronto (the former Metro Toronto suburbs) and 12 in the outer suburbs. Only two of the 12 head offices in the outer suburbs are in planned suburban downtowns: one in Markham's City Centre and one in Brampton's Bramalea Centre. In the former Metro itself, one of the head offices is in the Scarborough Centre, one is in Etobicoke's Centre, and three are in North York's City Centre, which suggests that Metropolitan Toronto's attempts have been more successful than those of the outer suburbs. More significant is

the fact that 15 of the 22 metropolitan Toronto head offices are within 1.5 kilometres of interchanges on Highways 401, 404, 407, or 427, which indicates how critical highway access is for suburban offices that serve more than local markets. Overall, only eight of the 32 large corporation head offices in the suburbs of Canada's three largest CMAs are in planned suburban downtowns, and only six of the 15 planned suburban downtowns have even one of the head offices.

As population continues to rise in Canada's metropolitan centres and their central business districts continue to evolve, we must know why attempts to create suburban downtowns have been more successful in some cases than in others. The Toronto and Vancouver CMAs both have populations over 1.5 million, sufficient to provide clienteles for suburban downtowns, and both cover large enough areas that travel time to their CBDs can be inconvenient for many suburban residents. Although Montreal is Canada's second largest CMA, suburban downtowns have not been a feature of its expansion, possibly because both its population and office complex are growing far more slowly than Toronto's and Vancouver's and its planners have not been as active in promoting suburban downtowns.

The absence of suburban downtowns in other Canadian CMAs indicates that minimum sizes of population and spatial area are preconditions to the formation of suburban downtowns. Alternatives to the CBD may not be needed in an urban centre whose population is under 1.5 million and where travel time from any part of the urban area to the CBD is less than 30 minutes. Furthermore, suburban downtowns may not be able to attract a critical mass of businesses and clients unless downtown congestion, particularly traffic congestion, makes it noticeably more time-consuming to visit the CBD than a suburban downtown with similar services. Another relevant aspect of size may be competition for space in the CBD. Strong competition drives up space costs and very high rents can prevent many offices from locating or remaining in the CBD. This is most likely to occur in an expanding metropolis that has not only a strong downtown cluster of retail, entertainment, and cultural facilities, but also a rapidly growing office complex that includes a network of interdependent head offices, services, and institutions, all competing for space. In addition, if an urban area's central office complex is to grow steadily it must have a role that extends beyond the needs of the individual metropolis, such as Toronto's dominance of national finance or Vancouver's gateway role.

For a centre truly to be a suburban downtown it must contain a wide range of retail, personal, hospitality, and business services occupying at least 100,000 square metres (1.1 million square feet) of shopping space and 500,000 square metres (5.4 million square feet) of office space, and, as most recent trends suggest, it must offer a variety of entertainment and cultural options. Given reliance on cars and the need to park them, it is unlikely that a transit and pedestrian orientation can be fully achieved in suburban downtowns. Still, a suburban centre can 'feel' like a downtown, provided it has shops, restaurants, and pubs leading directly off the sidewalk to foster relaxed social interactions for a clientele that includes the centre's workers, residents, and visitors. Achieving this will be no mean feat on sites designed to maximize consumer flow and, above all, to accommodate automobiles.

From the Past to the Future

In the larger Canadian cities small central nuclei had grown into rather extensive central downtowns by World War II. As these central areas expanded, their contents changed from a relatively unsorted set of multiple functions to strongly differentiated districts. At the same time most manufacturing activities left or were displaced. By the 1960s, office buildings and white-collar jobs had clearly become the dominant central downtown functions. However, other important activities and symbols remained, and in the 1970s the expansion of offices at the expense of other functions was challenged in the political arena, leading to the adoption of development control measures.

The formation of commercial/high-order service nuclei outside of the core area eventually included the shopping mall and, in the 1980s, the suburban downtown. These suburban downtowns were strongly supported by some regional governments and by the municipal governments of the concerned suburbs. The success of the suburban downtowns is not easy to judge. How we see them depends very much on our perspective. Suburban residents are often ambivalent. They are proud of their suburban downtown's prestigious buildings and readily patronize its shopping facilities and recreational and cultural activities, but they resent the traffic this generates, which they perceive as a threat to the suburban way of life they have chosen. Urbanites, on the other hand, complain about the lack of density and pedestrian activity, the car dependency, and the inadequate range of high-order functions in the suburban downtowns. All told, suburban downtowns are probably best viewed today as centres in evolution. Central downtowns have evolved over many decades if not a century; suburban downtowns have had little more than 20 years to develop. However, whether downtowns, both suburban and central ones, will continue to grow is not clear.

Office-based jobs, which have driven growth in most of the Canadian central and now also suburban downtowns, may not provide the impulses they have in the past. In the future, there may be fewer of these jobs because of rationalization and productivity improvements. Many traditional offices might disappear as employees telecommute. Increasing residential development, including the conversion of unwanted older office buildings to residential space, while seen as desirable because of a better work/home balance and the promise of a richer street life, may be a Trojan horse in the central downtown areas. Sooner or later residents will complain about traffic and other overspill of business operations. Business may then flee to the isolation of suburban office parks or 'employment areas', where ample parking and inadequate public transit encourage the use of the automobile. It is quite likely that central downtowns may not see any substantial growth in office floor space and employment in the twenty-first century. Still, this does not spell the end of downtown. Culture, education, entertainment, tourism, and a variety of specialized high-order activities will remain and expand in the central downtown area. This will include the many different facets of the media and 'creative' businesses and institutions (see Chapter 15). Downtowns, whether central or suburban ones, are very important nodes in the economy of the metropolis—but they are also part of a city's identity. Just like high-rise office towers are imbued with many meanings, downtowns are of symbolic or affective importance, adding further complications to the struggle over their futures. Either way, whether we speak of central or suburban downtowns, it is important to recognize that both a lot of doubt and a lot of interest surround their prospects.

Notes

1. Especially at major street intersections and subway stations, where Toronto's zoning by-law provisions were aimed to encourage office development. A formal planning district called 'central area' was created with the 1969 adoption of a new City of Toronto *Official Plan*. The new office nodes at Yonge/St Clair, Yonge/Eglinton, and Davisville were not part of the 'central area'. To placate resistance from nearby élite residential areas, they were designated as 'district commercial centres'. However, one can argue that these office nodes were an integral part of the 'central area' or 'central district' office agglomeration.

2. Table 11.1 also shows continuous, but differential, office decentralization. Already in 1961 the percentage of engineering consultants', accountants', and architects' offices in the 'central district' had fallen to levels below 70 per cent.

3. These lines of inquiries became very important in the United Kingdom, Sweden, the Netherlands, and Canada. In these and other countries, including Germany and France, governments became concerned about congestion in the centres of some of the larger cities. In several cases (especially London and Paris) office development bans were issued; national governments wanted offices to disperse from the capitals to the periphery (UK, Sweden, Netherlands) and in other cases municipal and/or national governments stimulated the development of suburban office parks or subcentres (e.g., Croydon in London, La Défense in Paris, Bürocity Nord in Hamburg).

4. Office employment began to change again in these 20 years: while earlier in the century female clerical employees formed an ever greater proportion of the office workforce, the 1970s and 1980s saw a rise in female non-clerical office employees. Managerial-professional occupations increased dramatically, with women taking up many of these jobs, while clerical employment stopped growing by the early 1990s. By 1981, female office employees were the majority (when all office occupations are summed) even in Toronto's conservative financial district (Huang, 1989).

5. At least one prominent Canadian example illustrates this kind of capital switching: in the early 1960s Seagram distilling company money financed part of the Toronto-Dominion Centre in Toronto. The resulting real estate development company, Fairview (later Cadillac-Fairview), went on to develop many more office buildings and shopping centres in North America (Collier, 1975). Generally, however, it is difficult to show a direct connection between excess capital in the industrial sector and office development (for studies in the US, see Beauregard, 1994; Feagin, 1987). It seems that most of the capital used for development comes through financial intermediaries such as banks and insurance companies; and these, most likely, form pools of capital from a variety of sources.

6. A hierarchy of cities results from location decisions of transnational firms. At the top of this hierarchy are truly 'world cities', such as London, New York, and Tokyo. At the subsequent level are other internationally influential centres, such as Paris, Los Angeles, and Hong Kong. Toronto and to a lesser extent Montreal and Vancouver are one level below this (see, for instance, Knox and Agnew, 1989: 61).

7. They have become so pervasive, and since they share many traits, they can be considered to constitute a class. The American sociologist Alvin Gouldner (1979) refers to them as the 'New Class', inserted between the 'old class' of capitalists and the 'working class'. Gouldner and many who have adopted his conception make a distinction between a cultural new class, the new class proper, and a technocratic new class, with the members of the cultural new class largely employed in the public sector. This distinction is not very important; there is a lot of empirical evidence that 'experts' switch between sectors. Also, they usually share the same kind of 'talk' or discourse at universities. These professionals or experts study and plan a wide variety of sub-spheres of economy and society: from the rationalization of car production to the expert firing of employees, and from the planning of health care to the planning (and researching) of cities, cultural policies, or foreign aid. Many discourses hide the real power of this class by talking about 'knowledge workers' or, even worse, 'information workers'.

8. 'Producer services' show widely divergent location patterns within metropolitan areas. Law firms and advertising agencies are still strongly represented in the downtown areas. (Law firms in Edmonton's CBD and inner city: 80 per cent in 1988, in Vancouver's CBD: 75 per cent in 1991, and in Toronto's central district: 57 per cent in 1981; advertising agencies in Toronto's central district: 74 per cent in 1981, in Vancouver's CBD: 65 per cent in 1991, and in Edmonton's CBD and inner city: 59 per cent in 1988.) On the other hand, computer/data-processing consultants and service firms, as well as engineering consultants, are highly decentralized, with downtown areas accounting for less than 50 per cent and even only 30 per cent of all those kinds of firms in the metropolitan areas of Toronto, Vancouver, and Edmonton. The inner-city share of employment in 'separately located head sales and auxiliary offices' of manufacturing firms has declined steeply in the case of Toronto, from 81 per cent in 1961 to 48.5 per cent in 1981 and about 25 per cent in 1991. Comparisons are difficult between metropolitan areas because of the use of different data sources and different definitions of 'downtown'. Data used here originate partially from Ley (1996) and Michalak and Fairbairn (1993).

References

Artibise, A., et al. 1990. *Choosing Our Future: Town Centres and the Livable Region*. Vancouver: Greater Vancouver Regional District.

Aubin, H. 1977. *City for Sale: International Financiers Take a North American City by Storm*. Montreal: Éditions L'Étincelle.

BC Transit. 1995. *In Transit, Moving People: A Ten-Year Development Plan for BC Transit*. Surrey, BC: BC Transit.

Beauregard, L. 1972. 'Le centre-ville/the City Centre', in Beauregard, ed., *Montreal: Guided 'Excursions'/Field Guide*. Montreal: Les Presses de l'Université de Montréal.

———. 1981. *La Rue Saint-Jacques à Montréal: une géo-graphie des bureaux*. Montreal: Université de Montréal.

Beauregard, R.A. 1994. 'Capital Switching and the Built Environment: United States, 1970–1989', *Environment and Planning A* 26: 715–32.

Bourne, L.S. 1967. *Private Redevelopment of the Central City: Spatial Processes of Structural Change in the City of Toronto*. Chicago: University of Chicago, Department of Geography, Research Paper No. 112.

Bunting, T., and P. Filion. 1999. 'Dispersed City Form in Canada: A Kitchener CMA Case Study', *Canadian Geographer* 43: 268–87.

——— and H. Millward. 1999. 'A Tale of Two Cities 1: Comparative Analysis of Retailing in Downtown

Halifax and Kitchener', *Canadian Journal of Urban Research* 7: 139–66.

Collier, R.W. 1974. *Contemporary Cathedrals: Large-Scale Developments in Canadian Cities.* Montreal: Harvest House.

Curtis, K.R. 1996. 'Revitalizing Kitchener's CBD: Public Planning Initiatives and Effects', in P. Filion, T. Bunting, and K. Curtis, eds, *The Dynamics of the Dispersed City: Geographic and Planning Perspectives on Waterloo Region.* Waterloo: Department of Geography Publication Series.

Desfor, G., et al. 1988. 'Redevelopment of the North American Waterfront: The Case of Toronto', in B.S. Hoyle et al., eds, *Revitalising the Waterfront: International Dimensions of Dockland Redevelopment.* London: Bellhaven Press.

Dicken, P., and P.E. Lloyd. 1990. *Location in Space: Theoretical Perspectives in Economic Geography*, 3rd edn. New York: HarperCollins.

Feagin, J.R. 1987. 'The Secondary Circuit of Capital: Office Construction in Houston, Texas', *International Journal of Urban and Regional Research* 11: 172–92.

Filion, P. 1997. 'Planning Suburban Employment Centres in the Dispersing City: The Greater Toronto Area's Mixed Record'. Waterloo: University of Waterloo, mimeo.

——— and T. Bunting. 1993. 'Local Power and Its Limits: Three Decades of Attempts to Revitalize Kitchener's CBD', *Urban History Review* 22: 4–16.

——— and S. Burke. 1997. 'Greater Toronto Multi-Use Nodes: Instruments of Intensification or Agents of Sprawl', presented at the annual meeting of the Urban Affairs Association, Apr. 1997, Toronto.

Freeman, B. 1976. 'Hamilton's Civic Square: The First 11 Years', *City Magazine* 1, 8: 26–41.

Gad, G. 1979. 'Face-to-face Linkages and Office Decentralization Potentials: A Study of Toronto', in P.W. Daniels, ed., *Spatial Patterns of Office Growth and Location.* New York: John Wiley and Sons.

———. 1991. 'Toronto's Financial District', *Canadian Geographer* 35: 203–7.

——— and D. Holdsworth. 1984. 'Building for City, Region and Nation: Office Development in Toronto, 1834–1984', in V.L. Russell, ed., *Forging a Consensus: Historical Essays on Toronto.* Toronto: University of Toronto Press.

——— and ———. 1987. 'Corporate Capitalism and the Emergence of the High-Rise Office Building', *Urban Geography* 8: 212–31.

Garreau, J. 1991. *Edge City: Life on the New Frontier.* New York: Doubleday.

Goddard, J.B. 1973. *Office Linkages and Location: A Study of Communication and Spatial Patterns in Central London.* Oxford: Pergamon.

Gouldner, A.W. 1979. *The Future of Intellectuals and the Rise of the New Class.* New York: Seabury Press.

Gutstein, D. 1975. *Vancouver Ltd.* Toronto: James Lorimer.

GVRD (Greater Vancouver Regional District). 1975. *The Livable Region 1976/1986: Proposals to Manage the Growth of Greater Vancouver.* Vancouver: Greater Vancouver Regional District.

———. 1991. *Greater Vancouver Key Facts.* Burnaby: GVRD Development Services.

———. 1993a. *Major Centres in Greater Vancouver.* Burnaby: GVRD Strategic Planning Department.

———. 1993b. *Greater Vancouver Office Users Survey and Development Prospects.* Burnaby: GVRD Strategic Planning Department.

———. 1995. *Livable Region Strategic Plan.* Burnaby: GVRD Strategic Planning Department.

Haig, R.M. 1926. 'Toward an Understanding of the Metropolis', *Quarterly Journal of Economics* 40: 179–208, 402–34.

Hamilton, W.G., and B. Simard. 1993. 'Victoria's Inner Harbour 1967–1992: The Transformation of a Deindustrialized Waterfront', *Canadian Geographer* 37: 365–71.

Hartshorn, T.A., and P.O. Muller. 1989. 'Suburban Downtowns and the Transformation of Metropolitan Atlanta's Business Landscape', *Urban Geography* 10: 375–95.

Harvey, D. 1978. 'Urbanization Under Capitalism: A Framework for Analysis', *International Journal of Urban and Regional Research* 2: 101–31.

———. 1982. *Limits to Capital.* Oxford: Basil Blackwell.

Hoover, E.M., and R. Vernon. 1959. *Anatomy of a Metropolis: The Changing Distribution of People and Jobs within the New York Metropolitan Area.* Cambridge, Mass.: Harvard University Press.

Horwood, E.A., and R.R. Boyce. 1959. *Studies of the Central Business District and Urban Freeway Development*. Seattle: University of Washington Press.

Huang, S. 1989. 'Office Suburbanization in Toronto: Fragmentation, Work Force Composition and Laboursheds', Ph.D. thesis, University of Toronto.

Hutton, T., and H.C. Davis. 1984. *The Role of Location in Regional Town Centre Planning and Metropolitan Multinucleation: The Case of Vancouver*. Vancouver: University of British Columbia, Planning Papers, CP#7.

Jacobs, J. 1958. 'Downtown is for People', in Fortune Magazine, *The Exploding Metropolis*. Garden City, NY: Doubleday.

———. 1961. *The Death and Life of Great American Cities*. New York: Random House.

Knox, P.L., and J. Agnew. 1989. *The Geography of the World Economy*. London: Edward Arnold.

Lemon, J.T. 1996. *Liberal Dreams and Nature's Limits: Great Cities of North America Since 1600*. Toronto: Oxford University Press.

Ley, D. 1996. *The New Middle Class and the Remaking of the Central City*. Oxford: Oxford University Press.

Matthew, M.R. 1999. 'The Role of Regional Town Centres as Vancouver's Gateway and Control Roles Expand'. Windsor: University of Windsor, Department of Geography, mimeo.

Metro Toronto. 1976. *Concept and Objectives*. Toronto: Metropolitan Toronto Planning Department.

———. 1980. *Official Plan for the Urban Structure: Metropolitan Toronto*. Toronto: Metropolitan Toronto.

———. 1992 *Office Space and Employment Characteristics: Greater Toronto Area*. Toronto: Metro Toronto Planning Department.

———. 1995. *Key Facts: 1995*. Toronto: Metro Toronto Planning Department.

———. 1996. *Employment in Metropolitan Toronto: 1995*. Toronto: Metro Toronto Planning Department.

———. 1997. *Planning Data Base*. Toronto: Metro Toronto Planning Department.

Michalak, W.Z., and K.J. Fairbairn. 1993. 'The Location of Producer Services in Edmonton', *Canadian Geographer* 37: 2–16.

Millward, H., and T. Bunting. 1999. 'A Tale of Two Cities 2: Comparative Analysis of Retailing in Downtown Halifax and Kitchener', *Canadian Journal of Urban Research* 8: 1–21.

Murphy, R.E., and J.E. Vance. 1954. 'Delimiting the CBD', *Economic Geography* 30: 189–222.

——— et al. 1955. 'Internal Structure of the CBD', *Economic Geography* 31: 21–46.

Nader, G.A. 1976. *Cities of Canada, Volume Two: Profiles of Fifteen Metropolitan Centres*. Toronto: Macmillan of Canada.

North York (City of). 1979. *D–11–48: Yonge Street Centre Area*. North York: City of North York.

Pacey, E. 1979. *The Battle of Citadel Hill*. Hantsport, NS: Lancelot Press.

Relph, E. 1991. 'Suburban Downtowns of the Greater Toronto Area', *Canadian Geographer* 35: 421–5.

Robbins, S.M., and N.E. Terleckyj. 1960. *Money Metropolis: A Locational Study of Financial Activities in the New York Region*. Cambridge, Mass.: Harvard University Press.

Sassen, S. 1991. *The Global City: New York, London, Tokyo*. Princeton, NJ: Princeton University Press.

———. 1994. *Cities in a World Economy*. Thousand Oaks, Calif.: Pine Forge Press.

Scott, A.J. 1982. 'Industrial Patterns and Dynamics of Industrial Activity in the Modern Metropolis', *Urban Studies* 19: 111–42.

Spaeth, J.D. 1975. *Regional Town Centres: A Policy Report*. Burnaby, BC: Greater Vancouver Regional District.

Stein, D.L. 1972. *Toronto for Sale: The Destruction of a City*. Toronto: New Press.

Strange, C. 1995. *Toronto's Girl Problem: The Perils and Pleasures of the City, 1880–1930*. Toronto: University of Toronto Press.

Toronto (Core Area Task Force). 1974. *Core Area Task Force: Technical Appendix*. Toronto: City of Toronto Planning Board.

Toronto (City Planning Board). 1975. *Proposals. Central Area Plan Review Part 1: General Plan*. Toronto: City of Toronto Planning Board.

Toronto (City of). 1979. *Official Plan, Part 1: Office Consolidation*. Toronto: City of Toronto Planning and Development Department.

Vancouver (City of). 1993. *Central Area Plan: Goals and Land Use Policy*. Vancouver: City of Vancouver Planning Department, adopted by Vancouver City Council, 3 Dec. 1991.

Weber, A. 1909. *Theory of the Location of Industries*. Chicago: University of Chicago Press.

Chapter 12

The Inner City

David Ley

Finding and Defining the Inner City

It has been said that all classifications are useful rather than true, and this statement applies with particular force to the classification of geographical regions. So a regional study, like this one, must begin both by defining its region and also by acknowledging at once that any such definition is arbitrary. While there are, undoubtedly, important themes shared by the ring of old neighbourhoods around the central business district (CBD) that we call the inner city, no single criterion, nor even a combination of criteria, permits boundaries to be drawn around urban areas with any claim to total adequacy.

In Canada the federal government has most often undertaken the nearly impossible task of defining the inner city, in part to target and monitor its own programs and policies. This was, indeed, the purpose of the first comprehensive definition, which used the common-sense criteria of age and spatial proximity to downtown to define the inner cities of Canada (McLemore, Aass, and Keilhofer, 1975). An urban census tract was included within the inner city if the percentage of its housing stock built before 1946 was double the metropolitan average, and/or if the tract was surrounded by others that were so defined. In this manner, isolated tracts with older housing were excluded while central tracts with newer housing (where redevelopment had occurred) were included. Based on the 1971 census, these criteria identified inner-city districts in 10 large cities with populations ranging from 18,000 (St John's) to 644,000 (Montreal), and accounting for between 10 per cent and 24 per cent

of the metropolitan total. A second government document adopted a more flexible means of regionalization (Brown and Burke, 1979). The identification of inner-city districts in the 23 census metropolitan areas (CMAs) then in existence was delegated to local field officers who were asked to employ the criterion of residential age but to qualify it according to local considerations and perceptions. Overall, the inner city so defined comprised some 30 per cent of the metropolitan population in 1971 and 25 per cent in 1976. But with a less standardized classification there were considerable departures around the mean, so that in 1976 the inner city, according to this definition, ranged from only 7 per cent of the metropolitan population in Victoria to 40 per cent in Montreal, a somewhat disturbing range.

A third attempt at inner-city definition by a federal department employed a narrower classification, including the CBD 'and the surrounding areas of mixed land uses, with high density residential development' (Ram, Norris, and Skof ,1989). Trends in 12 CMAs were examined over the 1951–86 period, and the inner-city definition was fixed throughout to aid comparison. While understandable, this decision had the effect of freezing inner-city boundaries, even though inner-city processes (e.g., property aging) were spreading beyond the area demarcated in 1951 and CBD expansion was removing housing from the core. The predictable outcome of these restrictive conditions was that the inner city's share of the metropolitan population in the 12 cities fell from 16 per cent in 1951 to 4 per cent in 1986, and by 37 per cent in absolute terms.

The Changing Profile of the Inner City

What form of descriptive profile of the inner city emerges from these earlier attempts at region-building? Table 12.1 displays a set of variables comparing the inner city of Winnipeg with the metro-

politan area as a whole in 1971. With 17 per cent of the metropolitan population, Winnipeg's inner neighbourhoods in general contained smaller households with fewer children and a higher proportion of the elderly. Household incomes were more than 20 per cent below the metropolitan average and unemployment rates, at 10 per cent, exceeded the mean by two-fifths. Educational attainment was lower in the inner city, with proportionately more blue-collar workers and fewer white-collar and professional workers—though these labour force differences were not that marked. There was, however, a significantly higher proportion of foreign-born residents than in the CMA as a whole. To accommodate this mainly tenant population, housing was more likely to consist of apartments and dwelling units with fewer rooms than in the CMA as a whole, with annual rents some 20 per cent lower.

With few exceptions the statistical profile of Winnipeg's inner city was shared in general terms by other CMAs in 1971 (McLemore, Aass, and Keilhofer, 1975). While the inner city–CMA contrast is apparent, it is nonetheless more muted than we might have expected across a number of variables, for although the demographic, ethnic, and housing variables do show a clearly defined gradient, the socio-economic differentials are slighter. There are two further points we need to make here. First, it bears repeating that the stark image of polarization between inner cities and suburbs in the United States is not repeated at this scale in Canada, though we shall see later that pockets of poverty are certainly a significant feature of the Canadian inner city. In many ways the Canadian city in 1971 continued to reflect the social area models of Burgess and Hoyt; demographic, housing, and life-cycle variables were distributed concentrically, following Burgess, and thus highlight a distinctive inner-city profile, while socio-economic variables displayed a sectoral pattern, following Hoyt, thereby obscuring a distinctive status for the inner city (see Chapter 9 for a description of these models).

A second important issue is the consideration of historic trends. What trends were discernible

Table 12.1   **Characteristics of the Inner City and Census Metropolitan Area of Winnipeg, 1971**

	Inner City	CMA
Population (% of CMA)	89,160 (17%)	540,240
Age groups:		
Less than 19	28%	34%
65 and over	15%	10%
Average household size	2.7	3.2
Average household income	$7,335	$9,380
Education:		
less than grade 9	42%	31%
university graduates	5%	6%
Occupational groups:		
blue-collar	28%	25%
white-collar	39%	44%
professional	17%	19%
Unemployment	10%	7%
Born outside Canada	29%	20%
Type of dwelling:		
single-detached	40%	63%
apartments	53%	32%
Dwellings owner-occupied	37%	59%
Rooms per dwelling	4.8	5.2
Average annual gross rent	$921	$1,142
Overcrowding (over 1 person per room)	6%	6%

Source: McLemore, Aass, and Keilhofer (1975)

prior to 1971 and what have been discernible since? There is some evidence that in the 20 years up to 1971, differentials were becoming more marked in the case of income and family size. One demographic consequence was population decline, but stability in the numbers of households. Across 23 CMAs, inner-city population fell by 11 per cent between 1971 and 1976, but households increased by 2 per cent (Ley, 1981), a trend that continued through the 1970s (Filion, 1987). In the 1980s, a significant shift occurred: between 1981 and 1986, and for the first time in 35 years, the inner-city population of 12 CMAs grew, by an average of 5 per cent (Ram, Norris, and Skof, 1989). A more detailed examination of Toronto's core area revealed net growth of over 12,000 residents in the decade after 1976 (Bourne, 1992), and this population shift has been sustained in most central cities through the 1990s. It is attributable in large measure to redevelopment, particularly of formerly industrial land such as the St Lawrence and Harbourfront sites in Toronto and False Creek in Vancouver. This trend can be expected to continue with ongoing projects in such districts as the Expo Site and Coal Harbour in Vancouver, the railway lands in Toronto, Little Burgundy in Montreal, and the Halifax waterfront, where in each instance industrial land is being recycled to mixed uses that include a substantial component of medium- or high-density housing units.

Meanwhile, the age profile of the inner city continues to highlight young adults, aged 20–35; this cohort already accounted for 37 per cent of residents by 1986, while people living alone amounted to 56 per cent of inner-city households (Ram, Norris, and Skof, 1989). The tendency of inner-city residents to display higher attainment in advanced education has accelerated; in 1971 inner-city neighbourhoods were 25 per cent overrepresented by residents of 15 years or over with a university education, but during the 1970s the rate of expansion of degree holders in the inner city was double that of the CMA (Filion, 1987). Other socio-economic measures are correlated with this, notably occupations, for by the 1990s inner-city residents show an overrepresentation of some 20 per cent in the proportions of professional and manage-

rial jobs in the five largest cities; indeed, inner-city residents employed in these sectors grew by over 150,000 between 1971 and 1991, while inner-city residents employed in other fields fell by over 200,000 (Ley, 1996a). These changes indicate the much discussed process of gentrification, known earlier in central Canada as 'white-painting', the movement of middle-class professionals into lower-cost inner-city districts, accompanied by the renovation or redevelopment of the housing stock. We shall have more to say about this process later, but for now it is necessary to add two important qualifiers.

First, despite gentrification, there has not been a marked elevation of inner-city incomes relative to the CMA mean, except where there are double-income professional households (Bourne, 1993; Rose and Villeneuve, 1998). This is a product of the rapid growth of two-wage-earner families in the suburbs, a function of the precise income definition used—the inner city performs more strongly on per capita income measures—and is also related to the presence of pre-professional and, increasingly, post-professional retired (or empty-nest) households drawn to inner-city living (Ley, 1996a). Whatever the cause, across Canada's nine largest cities, increases in median household income in the inner city during the 1970s attained 93 per cent of the increase achieved in the CMAs; in Toronto the rise in inner-city earnings exceeded that of the CMA (Filion, 1987). This pattern was sustained through the 1980s, for, aside from Toronto, average household incomes for central cities fell further behind levels for their CMAs, although the rate of decline has itself fallen (Bourne 1997). Second, in CMAs that have experienced slow growth and the erosion of a traditional industrial base without significant downtown office development, the inner city has felt limited reinvestment pressure and persists as the home of a much broader grouping of poor households. In Winnipeg, Regina, and Saint John, for example (but not in Vancouver, Toronto, or Halifax), disproportionate and intensifying concentrations of the unemployed, the elderly, and female lone-parent households all coexist in the same inner-city districts (Broadway, 1992).

A final trend to be mentioned here is the growing ethnic pluralism of metropolitan areas (Figure 12.1). In 1971, ethnic diversity was heavily localized in the central city, particularly its inner neighbourhoods, but by the mid-1990s a far more complex pattern had emerged, with immigrants spilling over into suburban municipalities and discrete suburban nodes forming, such as the South Asian community in north Surrey, in the eastern sector of metropolitan Vancouver (Figure 12.2). The growing immigrant content of large CMAs is part of a broader process of internationalization, to which we shall return later.

The Inner City as Perceived: The Biography of a Concept

As well as a seemingly objective profile, the inner city also has a subjective identity. Middle-class society in Western nations has commonly stigmatized the inner city, and this perception of a spoiled identity has directed middle-class attitudes and actions.

As presently understood, the inner city dates back to nineteenth-century industrialization and the construction of high-density and frequently shabbily built housing for blue-collar workers around the new factories, warehouses, and construction sites that offered semi-skilled and unskilled jobs for migrants to the city. The pace of growth, the limitations on mass transportation until the 1890s, and the paucity of municipal by-laws contributed to high residential densities, few public services, and little regulation of environmental quality. The blue-collar labour force lived close to their place of work in often unhealthy conditions. The alienating environment of English inner cities was condemned in the mid-nineteenth century by observers with political commitments as varied as those held by Charles Dickens, Frederick Engels, and Benjamin Disraeli. Conditions no less horrendous were present in the United States. In New York City infant mortality rates rose steadily through the nineteenth century from 135 per thousand births in 1810 to 240 in 1870. There was, of course, a geography to such conditions, and in the first decade of the twentieth century the Pittsburgh Survey recorded a fourfold differential in mortality rates between wards of that city, with the gravest rates occurring in the crowded immigrant districts located cheek by jowl with the iron and steel plants.

The deprivation and pathologies of the inner city led to middle-class avoidance, and rumour and stereotyping took the place of real knowledge (Ward, 1976). The substance and often the rhetoric of nineteenth-century images of the inner city have continued to recent decades, most notably in the United States in the polarized separations between racial minorities in the inner city and the middle class in the suburbs (Ley, 1974). And behind the images survive realities of continuing inequality. Infant mortality rates in Detroit have shown a fourfold variation between the inner city and the suburbs; inner-city rates are those of the Third World, while suburban rates reach the healthy standards of Northern Europe (Bunge and Bordessa, 1975).

To what extent do we find reflections of this tenacious image of the inner city as a spoiled identity in Canada? Tabloids in Canadian cities sensationalized conditions in the inner city and provided a regular reinforcement of an image bound around poverty and pathology. Rapid urban growth, particularly in the 1901–11 decade, and the arrival of immigrants from a plethora of sources seemed to be imitating earlier American experience. As superintendent of All Peoples' Mission in Winnipeg, J.S. Woodsworth observed and reflected on the impact of this rapid and largely unregulated growth, and found much he could recognize from Upton Sinclair's chronicle of the evils of the poor in Chicago recounted in *The Jungle* (Woodsworth, 1972 [1911]: 45). His own Mission visitors were reporting similar conditions in Winnipeg (ibid., 70):

> Shack—one room and a lean-to. Furniture—two beds, a bunk, stove, bench, two chairs, table, barrel of sauerkraut. Everything very dirty. Two families lived here. Women were dirty, unkempt, bare-footed, half-clothed. Children wore only print-slips.... The supper was on the table—a bowl of warmed-over potatoes for each person, part of a loaf of brown bread, a bottle of beer.

Figure 12.1   **Distribution of Immigrants in Vancouver CMA, 1971**

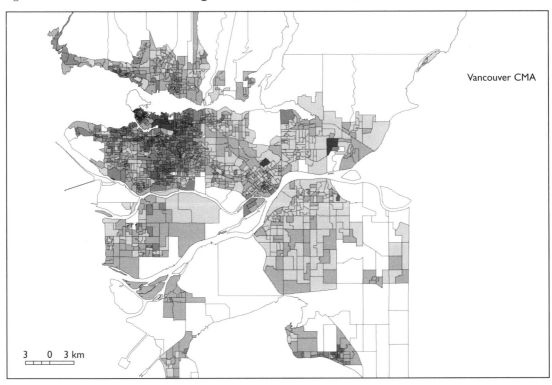

Vancouver CMA

3   0   3 km

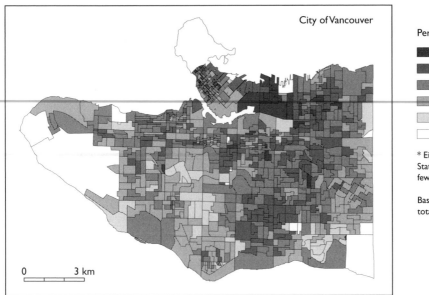

City of Vancouver

Per cent Immigrants

- 50.0 – 100.0%
- 40.0 – 49.9
- 30.0 – 39.9
- 20.0 – 29.9
- 0.0 – 19.9
- No data*

* Either data suppressed by
Statistics Canada or EA with
fewer than 150 persons/sq. km.

Base population:
total 1971 population.

0   3 km

Figure 12.2   **Distribution of Immigrants in Vancouver CMA, 1996**

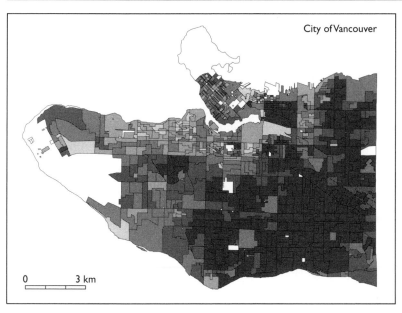

Vancouver CMA

3   0   3 km

City of Vancouver

Per cent Immigrants

■ 50.0 – 100.0%
■ 40.0 – 49.9
■ 30.0 – 39.9
■ 20.0 – 29.9
□ 0.0 – 19.9
□ No data*

* Either data suppressed by
Statistics Canada or EA with
fewer than 150 persons/sq. km.

Base population:
total 1996 population.

0   3 km

Source: Hiebert (1999). Reprinted by permission of the publisher. All rights reserved.

Montreal was the largest city, with close to half a million inhabitants by 1911, and labour conflict, municipal corruption, and poverty conditions led a businessman, Herbert Ames, to embark on a social survey and, like Woodsworth, to launch a reform campaign (Ames, 1972 [1897]). As elsewhere, rapid industrialization was associated with rapid urbanization and the city's population very nearly doubled in the 1850s and increased almost fivefold from 1852 to 1901 (Hanna, 1986). Factory hands flooded the city from the Francophone hinterland, from Britain, and from Ireland. Housing demand and marginal wages increased densities and decreased housing quality; the high level of working-class home-ownership existing in the 1840s was speedily reduced. Spatial sorting of residential districts occurred, of which the most striking was the social precipice in the city's west end, strongly correlated with elevation above and below an escarpment. The decisive statistic, which integrated all others, was the death rate, and here the figure for Montreal exceeded that even of New York and London; indeed, infant mortality at 293 per thousand births in 1859 was considerably in excess of the level in New York (Olson, Thornton, and Thach, 1987). Ames estimated that the overall death rate below the hill was 70 per cent greater than in the middle-class district above it.

As elsewhere, working-class districts were juxtaposed with local factories, and residential patterns overall were strongly influenced by the location of the place of work. Different districts had not only a distinctive class character, but also an ethnic and occupational emphasis. For example, one of the largest employers in the city was the repair and manufacturing shops of the Grand Trunk Railway in Pointe Saint-Charles, with a workforce of 2,000–3,000 during the first two decades of the twentieth century (Hoskins, 1987). Some 90 per cent of this large workforce lived within a walking distance of less than two miles from the shops in 1902. The distribution of machinists, one of the better-paid trades, dominated by Anglophones, showed a tight clustering around their workplace (Figure 12.3), creating a significant bonding between home and

work and contributing to a community resonating with the culture and landscape of what Ames called 'the real industrial class'.

One should not oversimplify the spatial differentiation that existed within the working class. Not all of the inner city consisted of poorer households, nor were all poorer households inner-city residents—significant working-class suburbanization existed in Montreal (Lewis, 1985), Toronto (Harris, 1991), Hamilton (Harris and Sendbuehler, 1994), and Vancouver (Holdsworth, 1979). But a combination of working-class households, environmental degradation, and poverty converged upon the inner city to create the popular stereotype of the slum behind the industrial waterfront and around the rail yards of Canada's cities. A fourth variable, ethnic and racial status, compounded the difference between, and ignorance of, the inner city by the middle class, an ignorance assailed by Woodsworth and Ames, like the British and American reformers before them. Whether the 'outgroup' was the Irish Catholics of Griffintown in Montreal, the Jewish garment workers in Toronto's Spadina district (Hiebert, 1993), or the Chinese and Japanese in Vancouver, the presence of exotic populations added to the strange and menacing image of the inner-city slum. Race and place were bound together in a value-laden perception. In the early-twentieth century, the idea of Vancouver's Chinatown as a place of stigma perniciously led to a widely publicized harassment of the district by public officials, a practice that simply confirmed its unsavoury status, its otherness, for the population at large (Anderson, 1991).

This unsavoury image, reinforced by social scientists obsessed with social disorganization in the inner city, has proven extraordinarily tenacious and provided a substantial motivation to urban renewal and slum clearance programs in Canada as in other Western nations in the post-1945 period. In city after city, old housing and high densities were sufficient to warrant the arrival of the federal bulldozer and the onset of the renewal process (Moore and Smith, 1993). But slowly, a new perception of the inner city began to form. In the early 1960s two important American social planners, Jane Jacobs

Figure 12.3   **Residential Location of Grand Trunk Railway Shop Machinists, Montreal, 1901**

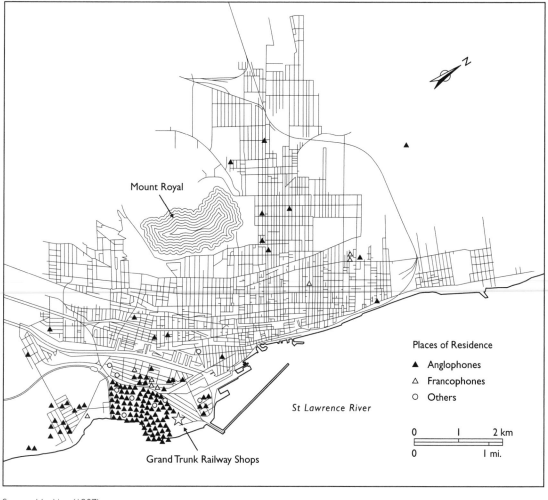

Source: Hoskins (1987).

(1961) and Herbert Gans (1962a), published ethnographic accounts of the inner city that severely challenged the dominant wisdom. Age and density, they showed, could be an asset rather than a disadvantage, sheltering a community where tight social networks and local institutions sustained a supportive social milieu unequalled in the frequently brutal landscapes of urban renewal. By the early 1970s Jacobs had moved to Toronto and presented her optimism for the Canadian inner city in different media, including a documentary commissioned by the National Film Board (Jacobs, 1971). Old buildings, social and land-use diversity, ethnic neighbourhoods, farmers' markets, pedestrian travel and public transportation, human-scale living environments, urban parks and waterfronts—Jacobs's broad vision celebrated exuberance, the cosmopolitan character of the inner city. To it was opposed the blandness of the freeway and high-rise city of the renewal planner or, indeed, the conformity of the distant suburban tract home.

The sometimes romantic vision of cosmopolitan vitality in the inner city has proven attractive to a significant minority of the professional middle class in metropolitan Canada since 1970. City living has gained a cachet it has not enjoyed since the eighteenth century in the perceptions of gentrifiers who have transformed the face of many older neighbourhoods. Consider the responses of new middle-class townhouse dwellers in the Vancouver inner-city district of Fairview Slopes (Mills, 1989): 'We both considered ourselves city people. I think that we like the amenities that cities have to offer, I think we like that sense of taking advantage of what we consider to be urban things ... in being close to theatres and that kind of city life.' For these boosters of inner-city living, the suburb now generates a sense of desperation: 'I hope and pray that if I ever have to move on the basis of some really altered circumstances, I'll still be able to live in the city. I do not want to live in the suburbs, I don't think it would ever suit me.'

Inner-City Diversity

Both the progressive reformers of the early-twentieth century and the social scientists who followed them erred in their perception of the inner city. Their portrayal of social disorganization was too one-sided, and it remained for a later generation to identify the social order that existed even in slum neighbourhoods (Suttles, 1968). Moreover, a second error had been perpetrated in generalizing the conditions of the slum to the entire inner city. The truth is that central-city neighbourhoods display considerable diversity. One American account suggested five types of dwellers and districts in the inner city (Gans, 1962b): areas of upper-class cosmopolitans, young singles, coherent ethnic communities, the deprived, and the trapped and downwardly mobile.

A thoughtful classification of inner-city districts in Canada recognizes this diversity (Table 12.2). Areas are categorized not on the basis of their social characteristics, but rather according to the dominant processes of identifiable change. As a result, neighbourhoods with different social characteristics may find themselves in the same category. Four processes are identified: decline, stability, revitalization, and massive redevelopment.

Districts in Decline

In these districts, physical deterioration of the housing stock is associated with population loss and with poverty and social problems among the remaining population. Property values increase slowly and may even decline; residents are primarily tenants and turnover may be rapid. This set of traits characterizes areas that in the United States reach the ultimate stage of deterioration—widespread housing abandonment. Where scattered examples occur, such as in parts of the North Ends of Winnipeg (Hiebert, 1992) and Halifax, or Saint-Henri and Pointe Saint-Charles in Montreal, or the Lower Ward of Toronto in the 1960s (Mann, 1970), they are found in former working-class neighbourhoods where poor housing and the collapse of the local industrial economy have contributed to low levels of demand and property disinvestment. The deindustrialization of Montreal's 'city below the hill' has been particularly devastating (DeVerteuil, 1993). By 1986, the collapse of the economic base in the industrial southwest resulted in unemployment of over 20 per cent and demographic flight, as the population fell by one-half from its 1961 level of 107,000. The same economic catastrophe hit the Francophone waterfront neighbourhoods east of downtown (Sénécal, 1995), and in each instance recreational and tourist initiatives have featured prominently in redevelopment plans. The Lachine Canal, a former industrial thoroughfare that runs through the heart of the southwest, has been declared a National Historic Park, while in the east, new tourist and leisure amenities have been constructed around the anchor of the Olympic Stadium.

Nonetheless, these initiatives have scarcely dented the most extensive concentration of deep poverty in any Canadian inner city (Figure 12.4).

Table 12.2   **Typology of Inner City Neighbourhoods**

	Decline	Stability	Revitalization	Massive redevelopment
Population	Continuing loss of population	No significant losses or gains	Little change	Gain in population
Socio-economic status	Decreasing	Stable	Increasing	Increasing
Family status	Increasing proportion of non-family units & elderly	Maintenance of population mix	Maintenance of population mix	Loss of families, gain of singles
Ethnicity	Varies: can be influx of deprived ethnic group or breaking down of traditional community	Sometimes strong ethnic community	Sometimes loss of ethnic groups	Seldom important
Community organizations	Poorly organized, unstable	Varies	Increasingly well organized	Usually unorganized
Physical conditions	Worsening	Stable	Improving	Improved housing, possible environment problems
Housing/land costs	Increasing much less than metro average	Increasing at same rate as metro average	Increasing more rapidly than metro average	Increasing more rapidly than metro average
Tenure	Increasing tenancy	Varies, but often high ownership	Little change	Tenancy
Non-residential functions	Loss of commercial-industrial functions with no replacement	Maintaining a mix of functions	Maintaining a mix of functions	Losing some commercial functions, but gaining others
Pressure for redevelopment	Low	Low	Strong, but controlled	High

Source: McLemore, Aass, and Keilhofer (1975)

East of downtown Montreal is a solid block of over 20 census tracts in acute distress where more than 40 per cent of families fall below Statistics Canada's low-income cut-off (Ley and Smith, 1997; Séguin, 1997). (The large concentration of poverty to the north-west of the City of Montreal boundary visible on Figure 12.4, is an anomaly. It results from the assignment of the low-income level of a small apartment district to an extensive, predominantly non-residential census tract.) No comparable regions of such

Figure 12.4   **Incidence of Families in Poverty, Montreal, 1991**

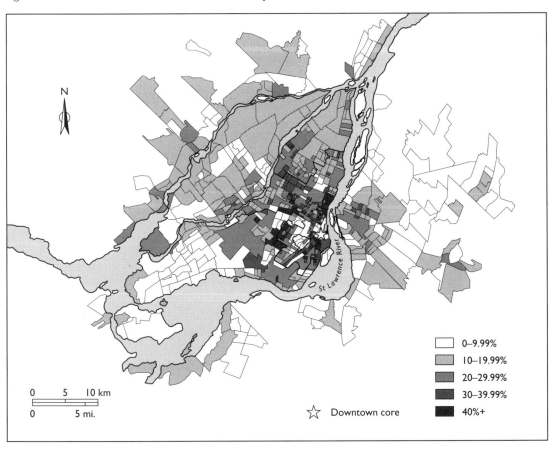

☐	0–9.99%
▨	10–19.99%
▨	20–29.99%
▨	30–39.99%
■	40%+

☆ Downtown core

Source: Ley and Smith (1997).

deep poverty exist in other major cities, though smaller concentrations exist, such as a compact set of five tracts in Vancouver's inner eastside, spreading out from the traditional skid row, an old district dominated by lodging houses and residential hotels and with an entourage of bars, soup kitchens, missions, and pawn shops serving a single-male population, including more or less resident elderly and handicapped men and younger, more transient males (Ley, 1994). In Vancouver, two railway stations and the bus station bound the Downtown Eastside on the south and west; in 1965 it included the city's major concentration of residential hotels, over 40 cheap cafés,

26 beer parlours, two liquor stores, and 11 Christian missions. In the late 1980s the district still contained 80 per cent of the city's premises with a full liquor licence. The western provinces have substantial numbers of Aboriginals living around skid row, at least on a seasonal basis; in Winnipeg surveys suggested a figure of up to 60 per cent (Rowley, 1978). Unemployment may be high, around 85 per cent, in the Winnipeg case, and may be associated with heavy drinking; over 70 per cent of men interviewed had received treatment at a detoxification centre.

Districts in decline are heavily supported by the state and voluntary groups; some 40 social service agencies operate in Vancouver's skid row, and proximity to these services (including social housing) offers a strong locational tie for residents. In Vancouver (unlike Winnipeg) the largest portion of the population consists of stable, elderly men without drinking problems, who have lived in rooms or social housing units for some years, although over the past two decades residents have become more diverse and include the mentally ill, some immigrants, teenage runaways, and even some families. In addition, the district's coherence has been strengthened by strong neighbourhood associations that have challenged the permissiveness typical of skid row and improved social services, enforced building codes, controlled excesses at liquor outlets, and sponsored the construction of a number of non-profit housing projects.

Other pockets of poverty and decline in the inner city are associated with a more dispersed rooming- and lodging-house population in the zone of housing conversions. They include group homes for deinstitutionalized psychiatric patients and other community-based facilities. This is a group at considerable risk, which comprises perhaps a third of the nation's homeless population, estimated in 1986 to fall between 130,000 and 250,000 (Dear and Wolch, 1993). This is a rough approximation. As discussed in Chapter 23, in the absence of reliable surveys we lack more precise or up-to-date data on the extent of homelessness in Canada. Due to the availability of suitable housing, proximity to necessary services, and the presence or absence of exclusionary zoning, group homes are frequently concentrated in specific inner-city districts. The Toronto district of South Parkdale contained no fewer than 49 group homes, or more than a quarter of the city's total, overwhelmingly serving psychiatric patients (Joseph and Hall, 1985). Such a concentration of poor and handicapped residents in aging lodging-houses provides a local context for neighbourhood decline, as private reinvestment is unlikely to occur in a locale with a perceived stigma.

Poverty districts are associated with other marginalized populations, including such historically persistent communities as the racial and ethnic minorities of Vancouver's Chinatown or the North Ends of Winnipeg and Halifax. As we shall note later, poverty is also concentrated around the massive public housing projects of the 1950s and 1960s, and where these were built in suburban sites, notably in Metro Toronto, they contribute to the existence of significant suburban poverty nodes, often associated with the location of the most destitute immigrants and refugees (Murdie, 1994). Poverty is linked as well to regional economies, for the structural unemployment of Atlantic Canada and parts of Quebec is manifested in a higher than average incidence of urban poverty. Montreal, Trois-Rivières, Quebec City, and, above all, Saint John are all CMAs with twice as many census tracts showing extreme scores on an impoverishment factor as the national average (Davies and Murdie, 1993).

One of the reasons why poverty is less visible in urban Canada is that the various indicators of poverty do not necessarily overlap in the same district (Broadway, 1989). For example, the impoverishment factor mentioned above was dominated by the presence of female-headed families but overlapped only slightly with two other poverty indicators, male unemployment and the presence of the elderly. This generalization, however, conceals considerable local variation. Indeed, in Winnipeg's North End, which has among the most extreme scores on impoverishment in urban Canada (Davies and Murdie, 1993), the geographical coincidence of poverty, female lone-parent families, and low educational attainment in neighbourhoods with a high Aboriginal population together define a state of multiple deprivation that approximates the conditions identified by the underclass theorists in the United States (Ricketts and Sawhill, 1988; Wilson, 1987). But this conjunction of events is unusual. In Toronto and even Montreal, analysis of the 1991 census revealed only a single case where all four deprivation indicators used in American underclass studies—high levels of male unemployment, female-headed families, non-completion of high school, and government transfer payments—overlapped in a particular census tract (Ley and Smith, 1997).

Districts of Stability

In contrast are inner-city districts where the stability of the urban landscape suggests that the pressures for change are slight. Such areas have a stable population and socio-economic status, with limited land inflation and pressures for redevelopment; home-ownership rates may well be high, and property is well maintained; the presence of a cohesive social order is indicated by the objective and symbolic indicators of community, such as strong voluntary organizations and a well-defined sense of place.

Districts such as these have been labelled 'urban villages', implying the existence of strong neighbourhood social networks, a complete range of local social institutions, and a tradition of mutual aid. The concept of the urban village emerged from an ethnographic study of Italians in the West End of Boston (Gans, 1962a). Despite the slum appearance associated with the age of the district and its high densities, the West End had a strong sense of local community. Its social basis was a result of the chain migration that had brought immigrants of comparable socio-economic status through kin networks to the same district. Similarly, there is a significant voluntary component to the map of ethnic segregation in Canadian cities, though such community has unfolded within the context of usually below-average economic status. It has not always been so, and earlier in the twentieth century, racial discrimination played an important role in the residential distribution of Jewish and Asian immigrants (Anderson, 1991; also see Chapter 9).

The high levels of immigrant home-ownership (Ray and Moore, 1991) contribute to a well-maintained housing stock, with substantial home improvement, or incumbent upgrading, completed most often with family and friends. In Vancouver's Grandview-Woodlands neighbourhood, a working-class area with a well-defined Italian presence, interviews revealed a marked sense of pride for one's home and considerable satisfaction with the upkeep practised by neighbours; indeed, without government grants over 90 per cent of interviewees had made major repairs in the previous five years

(Mercer and Phillips, 1981). The national policy of multiculturalism has encouraged such stable ethnic communities to celebrate further their identity and pride in the built environment. To the earlier ethnic icons of the parish church, the corner store and the pool hall have been added for some groups an ethnic cultural centre and annual street festivals, consolidating and celebrating a multiple identity. Along the main business thoroughfare of Grandview-Woodlands, an earlier ethnic modesty has given way to the amplification of ethnic symbols in brightly coloured shop awnings, frequently with the green, white, and red motif of the Italian flag, distinctive signage, and Mediterranean design elements. In such districts, indicators of community solidarity appear in the distribution of ethnic churches, temples, mosques, or gurdwaras (Beattie, 1998) and the incidence of voluntary organizations (Owusu, 1998), demonstrating the existence of dense social networks and strong ties.

The mutuality of identity and landscape, strengthened by the legitimating power of multiculturalism, has in some instances heightened the sense of ethnic proprietorship of neighbourhoods. This collective view of ethnic turf, aided by the icons of present and past cultural difference, may well be recognized by municipal councils and written into zoning and other protective by-laws (Anderson, 1991). Where older and less inclusive administrative styles have persisted, however, ethnic communities continued to have a precarious status before more powerful interests; not untypical was the demolition of much of Montreal's Chinatown in the 1970s to make way for a large complex of government offices.

In recent decades examples of stable working-class communities of British origin have been rare (but see Lorimer and Phillips, 1971), though stable Francophone districts remain on the east island of Montreal. Until the 1980s, the bastions of stability of British-origin groups in the inner city were the upper middle-class and élite districts, close to downtown, which are such a persistent feature of the Canadian city (Ley, 1993). In the 1970s, close to 70 per cent of Shaughnessy residents claimed British origin. This inner-city district is the wealthiest in Vancouver; it has over 70 per cent home-ownership and, until the mid-1980s, enjoyed little population turnover. Households were stable, indeed, many adults were living in the district where they had grown up. The landscape of the area advertises its identity; manicured, curving streets, architect-designed homes on large lots, and a supportive institutional cast of prominent Anglican, United, and Lutheran churches, private schools, and exclusive social clubs, with a distinctive concentration of up-market shops, including galleries and specialty home-furnishing stores on the edge of the district.

The old élite neighbourhood is repeated as a type across the country from the Uplands in Victoria to the South End in Halifax; with few exceptions, these districts have shown remarkable longevity in the twentieth century. By 1899, the southern half of Rosedale in Toronto was already a substantial élite community, and it has retained its status since. In Calgary the inner district of Mount Royal, developed before 1920 by the Canadian Pacific Railway as an exclusive neighbourhood, has upheld its social cachet. Since 1920 élite districts have expanded but they have rarely been displaced, and their locational stability is remarkable, considering urban growth and redevelopment pressures. The Toronto CMA, for example, grew sixfold from 1921 to 1981, with attendant pressures for residential redevelopment and downtown expansion, yet the innermost Rosedale tracts have experienced little decline in social stability.

Such stability has been accomplished through restrictive planning controls. In Westmount (close to downtown Montreal), municipal autonomy added political muscle to land-use protection, while Shaughnessy, thwarted in its efforts at political secession early this century, was nonetheless successful in acquiring protective zoning through a special act of the British Columbia legislature. Not unusual was a restrictive covenant, mandatory for home-owners in Calgary's Mount Royal, the terms of which included a prohibition on commercial land uses, minimum lot sizes and house prices, and the requirement that single-family dwellings be the

exclusive use. In each district vigilant home-owners' associations oversaw the conformity of the built environment with an élite protocol.

In the acute land pressures of the 1980s some social and land-use changes have influenced even élite districts. Modest infill has increased densities, though it has not diminished prices or status. More significant is an emerging transition in the complexion of the élite themselves. In Westmount, Francophones are replacing the departing Anglophone business élite, while in Shaughnessy new Asian wealth, particularly from Hong Kong, is evident (Ley, 1995; Mitchell, 1993). Other in-town élite districts similarly reflect the growing reality of multiculturalism and the growing diversity of Canada's international relations.

Districts of Revitalization

The inner-city typology identified revitalizing districts as a recent phenomenon and involving small areas only (McLemore, Aass, and Keilhofer, 1975). However, from small beginnings in the 1960s, revitalization expanded substantially in the 1970s and 1980s. The process involves up-filtering, the movement of middle-class households into formerly working-class or lower-middle-class districts, in contrast to the down-filtering, or declining status of residents, found in deteriorating districts (Knox, 1995: 305–9). The British term 'gentrification' is commonly applied to this transition. In its original and narrow definition, gentrification described the renovation of older housing stock, such as has occurred in areas like Don Vale (Cabbagetown) in Toronto, Plateau Mont-Royal in Montreal, and New Edinburgh in Ottawa. However, even in these districts, renovation is associated with infill and localized redevelopment. In cities like Vancouver and Victoria, where the building material of older homes is wood rather than brick, condominium redevelopment is the normal form that revitalization takes. Whether the dominant process is renovation or redevelopment, revitalizing districts are characterized by often spectacular short-term increases in land and housing costs, modest gains in home-ownership rates, and a well-educated and dominantly childless population of young professional households.

While revitalization is discernible in smaller cities like Kitchener (Bunting, 1987), Saskatoon (Phipps, 1983), and Halifax (Millward and Davis, 1986), it is particularly evident in Canada's major cities (Caulfield, 1994; Ley, 1996a). The rate of change quickened appreciably in the 1970s, and during that decade the level of social status gain in the inner city was four times greater than it had been during the 1960s (Ley, 1988). In the five largest CMAs, a net increment of some 60,000 residents with jobs in high-status, white-collar occupations occurred in inner-city neighbourhoods during the 1971–81 period. Almost 100,000 more joined them during the 1980s. While far larger numbers were added in the rest of the CMA, in relative terms inner-city gains were more substantial, so that by 1981 the inner cities actually contained a greater proportion of these high-status workers, a trend that has continued into the 1990s.

Revitalization does not seek out districts indiscriminately, and in major cities discernible patterns occur across the map (Figure 12.5). Trends in social status change are recorded by quintile, and the highest rate of change in Toronto shows clear tendencies towards concentration around such high-ranking cores as Don Vale (tracts 67, 68 on Figure 12.5) and Riverdale (tracts 69, 70, and 71), and Centretown (tracts 48, 49) and Sandy Hill (tracts 50, 51) in Ottawa. A correlation of increases in social status scores from 1971 to 1981 with a range of neighbourhood attributes identified the typical profile of a gentrifying district during that period (Ley, 1988). The best predictor of revitalization was the proximity of a census tract to an existing élite area; in the case of Toronto, for example, six of the seven locations of early gentrification wrapped around the edge of Rosedale and the Annex, established higher-status districts. Typically, the process unfolds on their downtown and somewhat downmarket fringes, where, although incomes would be about average for the city, dwelling values and rents would be above average. At the same time a revitalizing neigh-

bourhood would likely have distinctive residential architecture, be near a university and/or major hospital, and be close to parkland and/or accessible waterfront. In 1970 its population would have included a high proportion of small households, including students and the elderly, but with relatively few blue-collar workers or non-English speakers. A number of neighbourhoods undergoing revitalization during the 1970s shared many of these attributes: Kitsilano and Fairview Slopes in Vancouver; the Annex and Don Vale in Toronto; Centretown and Sandy Hill in Ottawa; lower Outremont, Milton-Parc, and the St-Denis Corridor in Montreal; and the South End in Halifax.

Particularly where the renovation (rather than redevelopment) of older houses is the dominant process, gentrification commonly (but not inevitably) takes place in stages (Gale, 1980). In the initial stage existing residents are joined by pre-professionals (students), artists, media groups, and certain other professionals, who are generally liberal or radical in their lifestyle and politics. This picture describes the character of Kitsilano and Cabbagetown in 1968-72 and Toronto's Queen Street West and Montreal's Rue St-Denis a decade later. These households are attracted in part by the social and cultural diversity of the inner city and its affordable housing. Careful research in Montreal has pointed out that this cohort is not gender-neutral, but that professional women play an important role, particularly in the early but also the later stages of gentrification (Dansereau and Beaudry, 1986; Rose, 1987, 1996). While the incomes of early gentrifiers are modest, they help redefine the character of a district and prepare the way for its commercialization and more substantial transition. As the neighbourhood is discovered, subsequent purchasers are buying into an inflating market as the neighbourhood's image changes. Later buyers include wealthier professionals such as doctors and lawyers, who tend to be more sensitive and protective concerning their investment, and the social mix favoured at an earlier stage is now regarded more ambivalently or resisted altogether. At this stage also, pioneering professionals shift their focus to other districts, usually

Figure 12.5 **Change in Social Status in Inner Toronto and Ottawa, 1971–1991**

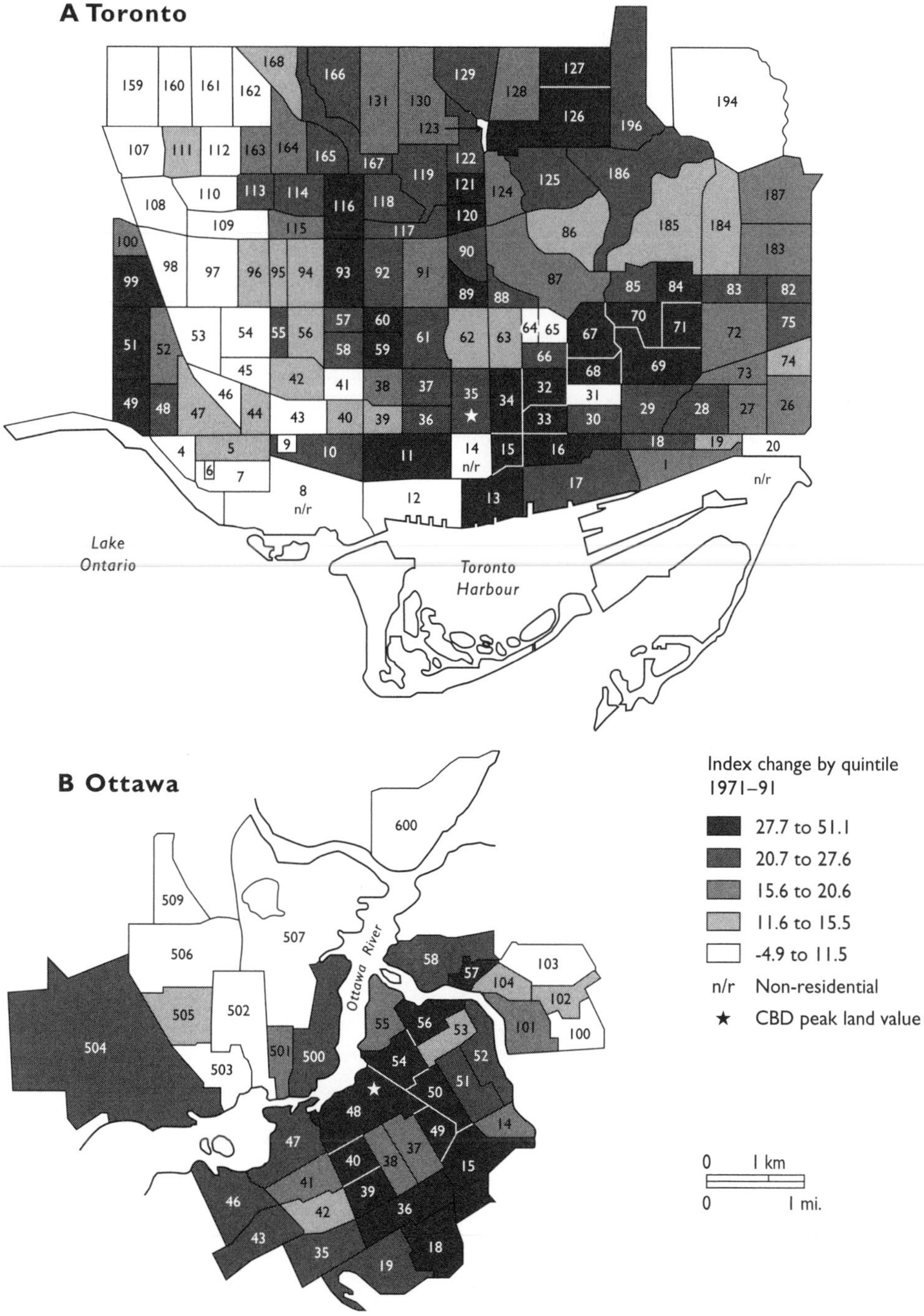
A Toronto
Lake Ontario
Toronto Harbour
B Ottawa
Ottawa River
Index change by quintile 1971–91
27.7 to 51.1
20.7 to 27.6
15.6 to 20.6
11.6 to 15.5
-4.9 to 11.5
n/r Non-residential
★ CBD peak land value
0 1 km
0 1 mi.

Source: Ley (1996b).

nearby, and a spatial diffusion of gentrification may be observed. In Toronto, for example, escalating prices in Don Vale (tracts 67, 68 in Figure 12.5) have caused middle-class demand to spill over to River-dale to the east (tracts 69–71) (Dantas, 1988).

The local impacts of gentrification are multi-faceted, and include the transformation of retailing (Tunbridge, 1986) and institutions such as schools and churches (Ley and Martin, 1993). But the most dramatic impact is on the housing market, where in extreme cases prices have doubled in only two years (Don Vale, 1979–81; Fairview Slopes, 1980–1). There has been a predictable displacement of ten-ants and replacement of home-owners from afford-able housing as a result (Ley, 1996a). Relocation occurs, if possible, nearby, though tenants typically pay higher rents for smaller units following their forced move. The loss of affordable housing in the inner city has been precipitous. In Vancouver, some 7,500 rental units were demolished between 1973 and 1981, primarily in districts undergoing condo-minium redevelopment. The Toronto situation is even more serious; 18,000 tenancies were lost in the deconversion of joint owner-tenant properties back to single-family use in the 1976–85 period, while from 1981 to 1986 over 9,000 rental apartments were lost through various forms of upgrading (Howell, 1986). Housing at the bottom end of the market, including rooming-houses and residential hotels, has been most vulnerable, and though gen-trification is not the only factor implicated, it does play a major role. Thus in Ottawa, municipal data record the loss of 40 per cent of the city's rooming-house units in only three years, from 1976 to 1979. Predictably, 70 per cent of these losses took place in Sandy Hill and Centretown, the wards where gen-trification was the most marked.

Areas of Massive Redevelopment

The more subtle landscape changes of gentrification in the 1970s and 1980s followed, and were in many ways a reaction against, the massive urban redevel-opment that took place in a number of inner-city districts in the 1950s and 1960s. In that earlier period housing stock was aging, while downtown employment growth sustained a lively demand, and permissive zoning maps allowed extensive apart-ment construction. Simultaneously, the public sec-tor, acting on the basis of its perception of urban slums (discussed earlier), was activating a significant slum clearance and urban renewal program across the country.

Massive redevelopment entailed population growth but, in private-sector building, a changing household composition as well. In districts like Vancouver's West End or St James Town in Toronto (Sewell, 1993), high-rise rental construction led to a loss of families and their replacement by small one- and two-person households of a somewhat higher social status than those who were displaced. While the housing units were generally of good quality, high densities from a concentration of proj-ects did not enhance cohesive social organization, particularly with rapid tenant turnover. In St James Town, following the creation of the highest-density precinct in Canada in the 1960s, the 1971 census showed a population increase of 32 per cent, with 71 per cent of residents (almost all tenants) having lived in their units less than two years. The imper-sonality of such transience and massive change per-mitted social problems to emerge in an unregulated environment, including prostitution in Vancouver's West End and in Oliver in Edmonton.

The location of apartment development, par-ticularly high-rise development, was strongly site-specific. In Toronto apartments were built in nodes with good access to the CBD, close to environmen-tal amenities and biased towards higher-income sec-tors (Bourne, 1967). This trend was maintained in other cities, also. The West End, adjacent to Stanley Park and the English Bay beaches, had been Vancouver's first élite district, as had Parliament Hill and Oliver in Edmonton, the sites of that city's major concentration of rental high-rise apartments (McCann, 1975). Even in smaller cities like Victoria, high-rises have been drawn to in-town locations with generous amenity; despite above average rents, waterfront settings show the lowest vacancy rates in the city, while developers have neglected lower-cost

Figure 12.6   **New Apartment Units in Victoria, 1968–1971**

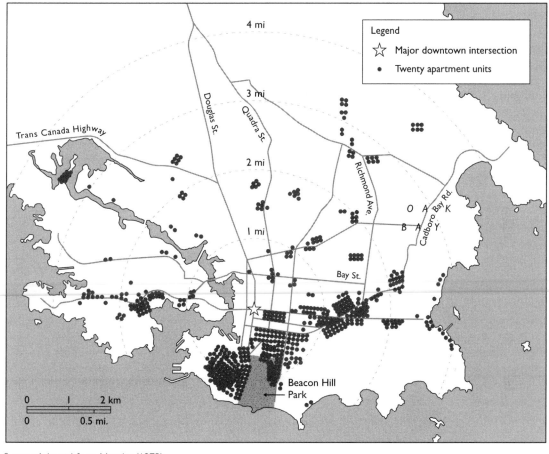

Source: Adapted from Murphy (1973).

(but lower-status) sites (Murphy, 1973). The distribution of apartments constructed during the 1968–71 building boom in Victoria demonstrates each of the spatial regularities found in larger cities (Figure 12.6). A third of new units were built within a mile of the main downtown traffic intersection, while outlying concentrations tended to be built on major arteries. A strong locational bias south of downtown abutted ocean frontage and Beacon Hill Park, while the disproportionate concentration on the sector leading east to Cadboro Bay Road runs through the old, élite, Rockland district and towards the present high-status areas of Oak Bay.

Public-sector redevelopment showed a predictably different pattern. While population densities generally rose, there was not necessarily a decline in the proportion of family households. Nor was there an increase in socio-economic status. High levels of unemployment and poverty in concentrated locations rarely led to a positive social environment. Slum clearance by the state was empowered in the National Housing Act of 1944, and its first project was the clearance and redevelopment of Regent Park North east of downtown Toronto (Moore and Smith, 1993; Sewell, 1993). The 1,300 mainly medium-density units were joined by more than

700 additional units in row houses, low-rise apartments, and five high-rise projects in Regent Park South 10 years later. The result is a massive and demoralizing concentration of poverty, an outcome repeated in the vast Jeanne-Mance project in Montreal, the North End of Halifax, the Raymur project in Vancouver, and elsewhere.

The scale of urban renewal involved massive dislocation of existing land uses and residents (Barcelo, 1988). In Montreal some 15,000 inner-city dwellings were demolished by the city in the decade from the mid-1950s to the mid-1960s; from 1960 to 1976 seven urban expressways were constructed. Relocation problems were often severe, and there was considerable reluctance to move. Some of these difficulties were well illustrated by the much smaller Rose-Blanshard renewal project in Victoria, which displaced 157 poor households (Robertson, 1973). The city's relocation officer identified these difficulties in correspondence with City Hall in the autumn of 1967. Among the tenants, he found 'many problem family units ... the matter of relocating these persons will present a most formidable difficulty'. But there were also obstacles in purchasing from some owners (Robertson, 1973: 55):

> With regard to the holdout realty owners still on the site, the majority of these are occupants who will not sell until they are offered sufficient money to be able to purchase comparable accommodation elsewhere. They cannot do this with the sums of money I am authorized now to pay them. This group of owners are unlikely to be intimidated by any means the Urban Renewal Authority can employ.

The high-handed hint of intimidation was not unusual in relations between renewal officials and the poor. A renewal document published by the City of Vancouver in 1956 observed that 'the Chinese (residential) quarter to the east of Main Street is at present of significance only to the people who live there' (Anderson, 1991). This was an insufficient reason for its survival, and large areas were bulldozed in an urban renewal program that displaced 3,300 residents. The insensitivity of slum clearance and the community mobilization it engendered, together with the social and design failure of massive renewal housing projects, led eventually to the suspension of these schemes. In 1969 a federal task force reported sternly on the public housing projects that were a common outcome of urban renewal, calling them 'ghettos of the poor' and places of 'stigma' and 'alienation'. During the 1970s federal policy shifted decisively away from large-scale clearance and rebuilding to more incremental policies of housing rehabilitation and neighbourhood enhancement; whereas in 1970 all federal moneys were committed to renewal, by 1979 the ratio of rehabilitation and improvement funds to renewal was of the order of 50 to one.

This is not to say that publicly inspired residential redevelopment did not occur in the inner city in the 1970s and 1980s. Large schemes housing hundreds or even thousands of residents were undertaken in a number of cities, including Toronto (St Lawrence, Harbourfront) and Vancouver (False Creek South). But there were significant departures from the 1950s and 1960s; densities are considerably lower, there is a social mixing of income groups, design standards are much higher, and, most important, construction on former industrial land has obviated the need for resident displacement (Hulchanski, 1984; Ley, 1987).

The Inner City: Explaining a Chaotic Concept

We have seen that the inner city becomes more diffuse as an object of study as we approach it empirically. There are no unequivocal grounds for delimiting it as a geographical region, and while we may set out objective or subjective indicators to establish a profile, both a statistical and a perceptual overview obscure important internal diversity between districts and also overlook the dynamic elements of sometimes rapid urban change. Moreover, a variety of transitional processes occur within the same city. Over a few square kilometres in inner Halifax, decline, stability, incumbent upgrading, and

Figure 12.7   **Process of Change in Single-Family Homes in Inner Halifax, 1977–1984**

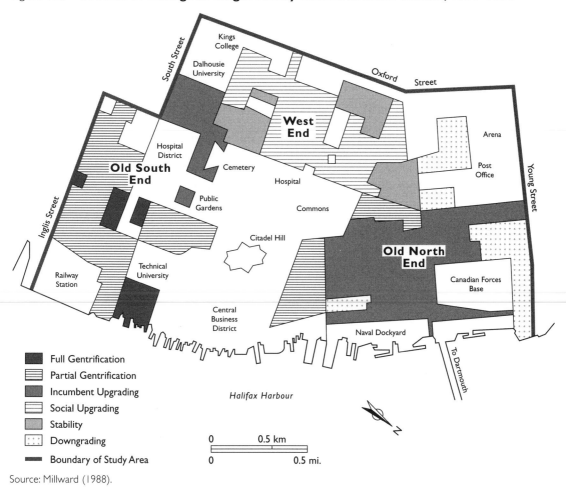

Source: Millward (1988).

gentrification have been identified as present simultaneously in the housing stock (Figure 12.7). Nor is there any necessary relationship between household change and change in the housing stock; renovation, for example, occurs both in gentrifying and non-gentrifying districts.

There are, nonetheless, brave souls who have sought to contain this diversity within a single explanatory account. The Chicago School referred to such ecological processes as invasion and succession to account for the concentration of social groups within 'natural areas' of the city. The principal sorting process was the competitive bidding of different residents for urban land; this perspective of consumer sovereignty characterized the neoclassical models of urban land economics that explained the inner-city landscape in terms of a set of preference curves. But both the Chicago School and the neoclassical theorists had a simple view of the inner city as consisting of undifferentiated poorer residents living at high densities, while the middle class opted for more space in the suburbs. In contrast, a more recent Marxist interpretation emphasizes supply rather than demand functions. Accounts of the inner city are bound to relations between the basic categories of capital and labour and the unequal power each holds; consumer sovereignty is devalued before the agency of capital to mould landscapes according to its own purposes.

Other explanations resist dominantly, or even exclusively, the economic emphasis of these perspectives. It is argued that the marketplace does not comprise the only dimension along which urban land is valued. How can one account for the location of Stanley Park in Vancouver on potentially the most desired residential setting in the city without referring to more plural values, which include amenity, recreation, and a broader public interest? Or how to explain the survival of Shaughnessy as an in-town élite area, with aberrantly low densities,

without an understanding of the symbolic power of this old élite district? The symbolic value of Shaughnessy has been translated into a vigorous politics of neighbourhood defence, and the same politics of turf has been exercised in poorer districts, with varying results. Urban politics implicates legal as well as political processes, and introduces a set of public and private institutions (the state, the courts, financial institutions, land development corporations) that, with residents, together engage in a set of negotiations, the outcome of which is an often unpredictable urban landscape.

Explanatory accounts of inner-city neighbourhoods, then, profitably recognize both the diversity of places and the range of processes acting upon them. An assessment of reasons for inner-city decline identified nine more or less competing explanations (Table 12.3). A convincing case could be made for

Table 12.3   **A Typology of Explanations of Inner-City Decline**

Explanation	Dominant Process(es)
Natural evolution	Urban growth, ecological succession, down-filtering
Preference structure	Middle-class flight to the suburbs
Obsolescence	Aging of built environment and social infrastructure
Unintended effects of public policy	Suburban subsidies, including construction of freeways and aids to new single-family home-ownership
Exploitation (1)	City manipulated by more powerful suburbs
Exploitation (2)	Institutional exploitation: red-lining by financial institutions; tax concessions; suburbanization of factories
Structural change	Deindustrialization and economic decline
Fiscal crisis	Inequitable tax burden; high welfare, social, and infrastructure costs
Conflict	Racial and class polarization

Source: Adapted from Bourne (1982).

the salience of any of these explanations, while at different periods they have risen or fallen in importance. Moreover, there is a geographic specificity to the incidence of these processes; between regions, for example, we cannot expect cities to share a common age or economic structure; between nations, the explanations require certain institutional and intergroup relationships that are not constant, not even between Canada and the United States (see Chapter 3). We should expect inner-city decline at a certain period in a particular place to be contingent on the intersection of a range of processes, some local, some national, some international.

Theoretical explanations are not necessarily geographically portable; an attempt to assess recent inner-city trends in Canada using a primarily American literature that discusses centrifugal (suburbanization) versus centripetal (inner-city revitalization) processes concluded that these competing 'models purporting to illuminate the evolution of the social fabric of the North American city lose much of their explanatory power when faced with a Canadian object of study' (Filion, 1987). A related study came to the same conclusion: 'immense regional and intraurban diversity remains. No single model of urban structure is sufficient to capture this diversity' (Bourne, 1987). A statistical comparison of four different explanations of inner-city revitalization concluded that each was of some relevance and that a more satisfactory strategy was to integrate them in a higher-order concept (Ley, 1986).

The Inner City and Societal Change

The relative failure of any single-variable account to provide an adequate explanation of inner-city landscapes and cultures suggests the wisdom of an integrated perspective, while the fact that the profile of the inner city is geographically and historically contingent indicates the necessity for fully contextual interpretation of the variable and evolving pattern of land uses and land users. Integration and contextualization together prescribe a distinctive regional geography of the Canadian inner city in transition.

What would that regional geography look like? (Bunting and Filion, 1988; Ley, 1996a). It would recognize at first the nineteenth-century origins of the inner city in a rapidly industrializing and urbanizing society. In a largely unregulated urban milieu where industry promised rapid investment returns, industrial land use was dominant and was able to invade almost any territory, even the neighbourhoods of the élite (Goheen, 1970). Until the adoption of the electric streetcar in the 1890s, mass transit was very limited, and this technological obstacle ensured that the industrial workforce lived within a short distance of their place of work on the waterfront or around the rail yards. Down-filtering of the inner-city housing stock provided rich returns to landlords and former owner-occupants, so that resistance to neighbourhood change was limited. The pace of immigration, often fuelled by crises in Europe, kept down industrial wages while inflating housing demand. With sustained demand, incentives for improvement of the housing stock for the poor were limited, and municipal by-laws and enforcement standards were permissive. Inadequate standards were also evident in environmental regulation, as Ames noted in the case of sanitation in the city below the hill in Montreal, and as is apparent in the polluting smoke pall that conceals so many details of the urban landscape in early photographs of Canadian cities.

But if the middle class withdrew they did not necessarily withdraw far. In the case of the élite, it was only a kilometre or two before roots were put down in a Shaughnessy or a Rosedale or, taking advantage of elevation, in the city above the hill in Montreal. These high-status neighbourhoods were quickly leap-frogged by the middle class and even the respectable working class in the new territory opened up by the electric streetcar. Mass production of the motor car had, by the 1920s, reduced still further the tyranny of distance for a significant segment of the workforce. Following municipal reform during the so-called Progressive era between 1890 and 1930 a more active local state, with the tool of zoning, began the regulation of urban land use and, for privileged districts, provided the means for ensuring protection against undesirable change. But urban boosterism remained the dominant ethos, and pro-development decisions came naturally to politicians who were also businessmen and who shared a common ideology of growth and progress.

In the postwar era the societal contexts impacting the inner city in Canada became more complex. Both suburbanization and the closure of old industries in the zone in transition around downtown were part of a restructuring of the central-city economy. Another element was the explosive growth of the service sector and (in the terminology of central place theory) the development of the CBD as the highest-order centre in the regional and national space-economy, the preferred location of the corporate complex of head offices and producer services, including finance and business services. Equally important was the burgeoning public sector and related non-profit professions, notably in teaching and health care. These employment trends have been faithfully translated into the downtown office boom that first became discernible in the late 1960s; since then a tripling of downtown office space in major cities is testimony to the employment growth.

The occupational profile of the (highly diverse) service sector raises further issues. First, about 40 per cent of jobs typically offer good-paying employment in managerial, professional, and related fields, the so-called quaternary sector. Second, in its vast clerical, secretarial, and retailing branches, the service economy offers expanded openings to female employment; rapidly, too, women are entering the quaternary occupations. These labour market changes are intimately bound up with the recent transition in the inner-city housing market. Blue-collar workers were already a disappearing minority in many inner-city neighbourhoods by 1970; it was often groups outside the labour market, including students and the elderly, that were displaced by gentrification, together with poorer segments of the service class. The in-migrants to the inner city had the financial freedom to move to the suburbs, as did many of their contemporaries, but they chose not to. Non-traditional family relations have been an important element in a positive valuing of the gen-

trified inner city (Mills, 1988). It is close to work and downtown adult attractions accessible to a childless household with discretionary income and with time freed from home maintenance and child-rearing.

This new middle class of professional and administrative workers has provided a key social group in inner-city restructuring of parts of the largest Canadian CMAs in the past 25 years (Ley, 1996a). Through infill housing it has consolidated the status of the old élite districts, and from these bastions its more adventurous and non-conformist members have contributed to ever advancing waves of residential renovation and redevelopment. As well as the housing stock, neighbourhood social infrastructure has been transformed; churches, schools, and thrift stores are neglected, to be replaced by leisure and fitness centres, pubs and restaurants, and shops oriented to purchasers with an eye for specialized and designer products.

The transformed retail landscapes of Spring Garden Road in Halifax, Rue St-Denis or Ste-Catherine in Montreal, Yorkville or Harbourfront in Toronto, and Granville Island or Fourth Avenue in Vancouver are all part of a broader transition towards the construction of landscapes of consumption in the inner city. In Toronto, a concentrated leisure and recreational landscape runs continuously from Ontario Place and Exhibition Park through the public facilities of Harbourfront and the Toronto Islands' Park, to the Skydome stadium, the CN Tower, and Roy Thomson Hall. New parks, new museums, refurbished theatres, concert halls, and historic districts, casinos, the cycle of annual festivals, and the periodic infusion of an Expo, the Olympics, or Commonwealth Games—all have transformed parts of the inner city into a consumption cornucopia. And in these landscapes that proclaim so eloquently the power of the pleasure principle, the state is fully implicated. In the early 1980s, Vancouver's planning director declared with considerable awe that major inner-city projects presented to senior governments for funding—a trade and convention centre, a domed stadium, an international exposition, a rapid-transit line, and several smaller projects—bore a combined price tag of almost $2 billion. A decade later all have been built. Arguably, the state is the most powerful single actor in the construction of the contemporary inner city.

At the municipal scale, civic politics underwent considerable change in the early 1970s in a number of major cities. The political power of the new middle class was expressed in their defence of neighbourhoods before the encroachment of freeways and high-density redevelopment, a curious mix of radicalism and NIMBYism. Local councils downzoned inner-city districts to lower densities, and senior government responded by abandoning urban renewal for policies of neighbourhood conservation and rehabilitation. Inner-city districts faced the brunt of land-use change, and in the inner cities locational conflict was most acute. Pro-development councils were challenged, and urban politics and land-use decision-making entered a more plural and combative phase (see Chapter 24).

Reform politics in the cities contained a significant environmental and social justice edge, but in the 1980s these gains have often been eroded as the federal and most provincial governments have retreated from their earlier involvement. The result is a growing income polarization in the inner city. Bourne's analysis for the Toronto CMA (Table 12.4) reveals an above-average incidence of low-income families in the City of Toronto (former boundaries) and the highest level of income polarization (Bourne, 1993, 1997). A rough measure of economic disparity may be derived by comparing mean and median incomes. The disparity index in Table 12.4 shows that in the new suburbs income variation was modest, while it was higher in the older municipalities and reached by far its highest level in the old City of Toronto itself. Polarization, moreover, was intensifying during the latter half of the 1980s. There is considerable evidence that conditions have continued to worsen in recent years; in every province and CMA the incidence of the low-income population rose between 1990 and 1995. In Vancouver, one of the nation's wealthier CMAs, the average family income was eroded by 10 percent in constant dollars between 1990 and 1995 (GVRD, 1998). Within the City of Vancouver, the share of families who fell below the low-income cut-off had risen from a fifth in 1986 to one-quarter in 1996, appreciably above the metropolitan level of 19 per cent. But most striking of all was the fact that despite the overall downturn in economic fortunes, the income category with the most pronounced growth through the first half of the 1990s was the top category, families earning in excess of $70,000 (Figure 12.8).

So the contemporary Canadian inner city includes a confusing mix of wealth and poverty, extremes of half-million-dollar condominiums and renovated houses against the homelessness of tens of thousands of urban Canadians, perhaps a third of them mental patients released from institutions by cost-cutting governments (Smith, 1998) (see Chapter 23 on this). Another growing and vulnerable homeless subculture consists of teenage runaways; a Winnipeg study revealed that half of them had suffered sexual abuse at home, while a third had contracted a sexually transmitted disease (IUS, 1990). For the poor, including single parents, the unemployed, the elderly, and some recent immigrants and refugees, the ongoing embourgeoisement of the inner city is translated into acute problems of affordability, with the severe contraction of housing at the bottom end of the market. And among, but not limited to, this group in the 1990s is emerging an alarming incidence of social pathology, including child abuse, drug addiction, prostitution, juvenile delinquency, and the ravages of high levels of HIV-AIDS in districts like Vancouver's Downtown Eastside and Winnipeg's North End. Polarization is not only a feature within cities but also between them, as local advantage and disadvantage are accentuated by the probing and testing pressures of globalization. Compare, for example, the growing divergence of housing and property markets in Vancouver and Toronto, the most internationalized of Canadian cities, with trends elsewhere in the urban system (Olds, 1996; Tutchener, 1998). The rapid growth of immigration after 1986 and its concentration in Toronto and Vancouver have encouraged distinctive house price trajectories in these cities that reflect an interna-

Table 12.4   **Variations in Household Income, Toronto CMA, 1985, 1990**

| Municipality | Household Income ($) | | | | Index of Income Disparity[a] | | % Low-Income Families[b] | |
| | Average | | Median | | | | | |
	1985	1990	1985	1990	1985	1990	1985	1990
Toronto CMA	100 (43,025)	100 (59,450)	100 (36,890)	100 (50,049)	16.6	18.8	10.6	14.6
Older central municipalities								
City of Toronto	91 ⎫		79 ⎫		34.1 ⎫		16.5 ⎫	
North York	81 ⎬	83	81 ⎬	77	16.2 ⎬	31.7	11.8 ⎬	21.7
York	75 ⎭		75 ⎭		16.6 ⎭		15.6 ⎭	
Older suburbs								
Etobicoke	102 ⎫		102 ⎫		17.2 ⎫		9.6 ⎫	
North York	101 ⎬	95	94 ⎬	94	24.3 ⎬	22.7	12.9 ⎬	17.5
Scarborough	95 ⎭		103 ⎭		8.4 ⎭		11.7 ⎭	
Newer suburbs								
Oakville	124 ⎫		129 ⎫		12.0 ⎫		4.7 ⎫	
Mississauga	109		114		10.8		7.5	
Brampton	105		117		4.8		6.5	
Vaughan	128 ⎬	122	131 ⎬	126	13.9 ⎬	13.4	6.1 ⎬	8.5
Richmond Hill	116		120		12.9		5.2	
Markham	140		143		14.8		4.3	
Pickering	118 ⎭		131 ⎭		5.2 ⎭		5.9 ⎭	

[a] An index of income skewness (I), where $I = \dfrac{(\text{average} - \text{median income})}{\text{median income}} \times 100\%$.

[b] Using Statistics Canada's definition of the minimum income needed to sustain a family.

Source: Adapted from Bourne (1993, 1997).

tional property market, unlike the regional and national processes that dominate other urban housing markets.

The contemporary regime impacting the inner city includes several key words: state privatization, municipal entrepreneurialism, and economic internationalization. Together they define the parameters of globalization and the world city, which John Friedmann set out with such chilling precision in 1986 (Friedmann, 1986; Knox and Taylor, 1995). While far from a complete prognosis, Friedmann's emphasis on post-industrial service economies, internationalized property markets, polarized income profiles, high levels of immigration, consumer amenities for national and international tourists, and government services unable to meet growing social needs provides an essential contextual template for interpreting the contemporary inner city.

Figure 12.8 **Average Family Income Groupings, Vancouver CMA, 1990 and 1995**

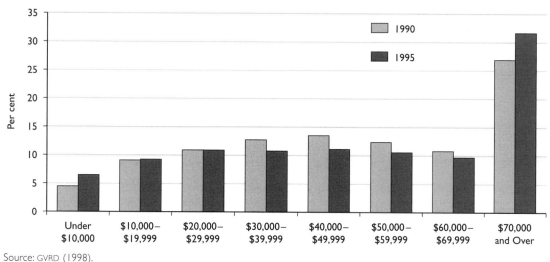

Source: GVRD (1998).

References

Ames, H. 1972 [1897]. *The City Below the Hill*. Toronto: University of Toronto Press.

Anderson, K. 1991. *Vancouver's Chinatown: Racial Discourse in Canada, 1875–1980*. Montreal and Kingston: McGill-Queen's University Press.

Barcelo, M. 1988. 'Urban Development Policies in Montreal, 1960–1978', *Quebec Studies* 6, 2: 26–40.

Beattie, L. 1998. 'Neighbourhood Change and the Ethnic Church: Cultural Maintenance and Service Provision', paper presented to the conference of the Canadian Association of Geographers, Ottawa.

Bourne, L. 1967. *Private Redevelopment of the Central City*. Chicago: University of Chicago, Department of Geography, Research Paper No. 112.

———. 1982. 'The Inner City', in C. Christian and R. Harper, eds, *Modern Metropolitan Systems*. Columbus, Ohio: Charles Merrill.

———. 1987. 'Evaluating the Aggregate Spatial Structure of Canadian Metropolitan Areas', *Canadian Geographer* 31: 194–208.

———. 1992. 'Population Turnaround in the Canadian Inner City', *Canadian Journal of Urban Research* 1: 66–89.

———. 1993. 'Close Together and Worlds Apart: an Analysis of Changes in the Ecology of Income in Canadian Cities', *Urban Studies* 30: 1293–317.

———. 1997. 'Social Inequalities, Polarization and the Redistribution of Income within Cities: a Canadian Example', in B. Badcock and M. Browett, eds, *Developing Small Area Indicators for Policy Research in Canada*. Adelaide, Australia: University of Adelaide Key Centre for Social Applications of GIS, Monograph Series 2.

Broadway, M. 1989. 'A Comparison of Patterns of Urban Deprivation Between Canadian and U.S. Cities', *Social Indicators Research* 21: 531–51.

———. 1992. 'Differences in Inner-city Deprivation: An Analysis of Seven Canadian Cities', *Canadian Geographer* 36: 189–96.

Brown, P., and D. Burke. 1979. *The Canadian Inner City: A Statistical Handbook*. Ottawa: CMHC.

Bunge, W., and R. Bordessa. 1975. *The Canadian Alternative: Survival, Expeditions and Urban Change.* Downsview, Ont.: York University, Geographical Monographs No. 2.

Bunting, T. 1987. 'Invisible Upgrading in Inner Cities: Homeowners' Reinvestment Behaviour in Central Kitchener', *Canadian Geographer* 31: 209–22.

———— and P. Filion, eds. 1988. *The Changing Canadian Inner City.* Waterloo: University of Waterloo, Department of Geography Publication Series No. 31.

Caulfield, J. 1994. *City Form and Everyday Life: Toronto's Gentrification and Critical Social Practice.* Toronto: University of Toronto Press.

Dansereau, F., and M. Beaudry. 1985. 'Les mutations de l'espace habité Montréalais: 1971–1981', *Les Cahiers de l'ACFAS* 41: 283–308.

Dantas, A. 1988. 'Overspill as an Alternative Style of Gentrification: The Case of Riverdale, Toronto', in T. Bunting and P. Filion, eds, *The Changing Canadian Inner City.* Waterloo: University of Waterloo, Department of Geography Publication Series No. 31.

Davies, W., and Murdie, R. 1993. 'Measuring the Social Ecology of Cities', in L. Bourne and D. Ley, eds, *The Changing Social Geography of Canadian Cities.* Montreal and Kingston: McGill-Queen's University Press.

Dear, M., and J. Wolch. 1993. 'Homelessness', in L. Bourne and D. Ley, eds, *The Changing Social Geography of Canadian Cities.* Montreal and Kingston: McGill-Queen's University Press.

Deverteuil, G. 1993. 'Evolution and Impacts of Public Policy on the Canadian Inner City: Case Study of Southwest Montreal, 1960–1990', MA thesis, University of British Columbia.

Filion, P. 1987. 'Concepts of the Inner City and Recent Trends in Canada', *Canadian Geographer* 31: 223–32.

Friedmann, J. 1986. 'The World City Hypothesis', *Development and Change* 17: 69–84.

Gale, D. 1980. 'Neighborhood Resettlement: Washington D.C.', in S. Laska and D. Spain, eds, *Back to the City.* New York: Pergamon.

Gans, H. 1962a. *The Urban Villagers.* New York: Free Press.

————. 1962b. 'Urbanism and Suburbanism as Ways of Life', in A. Rose, ed., *Human Behavior and Social Processes.* London: Routledge & Kegan Paul.

Goheen, P. 1970. *Victorian Toronto, 1850 to 1900.* Chicago: University of Chicago, Department of Geography, Research Paper No 127.

GVRD (Greater Vancouver Regional District). 1998. *Money, Money, Money: Analyzing the Region's Family Income, Composition of Income and Incidence of Low Income.* Burnaby, BC: GVRD Policy and Planning Department, Item 5.1.

Hanna, D. 1986. *The Layered City: A Revolution in Housing in Mid-Nineteenth Century Montreal.* Montreal: McGill University, Department of Geography, Shared Spaces No. 6.

Harris, R. 1991. 'A Working-Class Suburb for Immigrants, Toronto, 1909–1931', *Geographical Review* 81: 318–32.

———— and M. Sendbuehler. 1994. 'The Making of a Working-Class Suburb in Hamilton's East End, 1900–1945', *Journal of Urban History* 20: 486–511.

Hiebert, D. 1992. 'Winnipeg's North End', *Canadian Geographer* 36: 92–7

————. 1993. 'Integrating Production and Consumption: Industry Class, Ethnicity and the Jews of Toronto', in L. Bourne and D. Ley, eds, *The Changing Social Geography of Canadian Cities.* Montreal and Kingston: McGill-Queen's University Press.

————. 1999. 'The Changing Social Geography of Immigrant Settlement in Vancouver', *BC Studies* 121 (Spring).

Holdsworth, D. 1979. 'House and Home in Vancouver: Images of West Coast Urbanism, 1886–1929', in G. Stelter and A. Artibise, eds, *The Canadian City: Essays in Urban History.* Toronto: Macmillan.

Hoskins, R. 1987. *An Analysis of the Pointe St. Charles Shops of the Grand Trunk Railway.* Montreal: McGill University, Department of Geography, Shared Spaces No. 8.

Howell, L. 1986. 'The Affordable Housing Crisis in Toronto', *City Magazine* 9, 1: 25–9.

Hulchanski, D. 1984. *St. Lawrence and False Creek: A Review of the Planning and Development of Two New Inner City Neighbourhoods.* Vancouver: University of

British Columbia, School of Community and Regional Planning.

IUS (Institute of Urban Studies). 1990. 'Needs Assessment on Homeless Children and Youth', *IUS Newsletter* 30: 6.

Jacobs, J. 1961. *The Death and Life of Great American Cities*. New York: Random House.

———. 1971. *City Limits*. Ottawa: National Film Board.

Joseph, A., and B. Hall. 1985. 'The Locational Concentration of Group Homes in Toronto', *Professional Geographer* 37: 143–54.

Knox, P. 1995. *Urban Social Geography: An Introduction*, 3rd edn. New York: Longman.

——— and P. Taylor, eds. 1995. *World Cities in a World System*. Cambridge: Cambridge University Press.

Lewis, R. 1985. *The Segregated City: Class and Occupation in Montreal, 1861–1901*. Montreal: McGill University, Department of Geography, Shared Spaces No. 3.

Ley, D. 1974. *The Black Inner City as Frontier Outpost: Images and Behavior of a Philadelphia Neighborhood*. Washington: Association of American Geographers, Monograph Series No. 7.

———. 1981. 'Inner City Revitalization in Canada: A Vancouver Case Study', *Canadian Geographer* 25: 124–48.

———. 1986. 'Alternative Explanations for Inner City Gentrification: A Canadian Assessment', *Annals, Association of American Geographers* 76: 521–35.

———. 1987. 'Styles of the Times: Liberal and Neoconservative Landscapes in Inner Vancouver, 1968–1986', *Journal of Historical Geography* 13: 40–56.

———. 1988. 'Social Upgrading in Six Canadian Inner Cities', *Canadian Geographer* 32: 31–45.

———. 1993. 'Past Elites and Present Gentry: Neighbourhoods of Privilege in Canadian Cities', in L. Bourne and Ley, eds, *The Changing Social Geography of Canadian Cities*. Montreal and Kingston: McGill-Queen's University Press.

———. 1994. 'The Downtown Eastside: "One Hundred Years of Struggle"', in S. Hasson and Ley, eds, *Neighbourhood Organizations and the Welfare State*. Toronto: University of Toronto Press.

———. 1995. 'Between Europe and Asia: The Case of the Missing Sequoias', *Ecumene* 2: 185–210.

———. 1996a. *The New Middle Class and the Remaking of the Central City*. Oxford: Oxford University Press.

———. 1996b. 'The New Middle Class in Canadian Central Cities', in J. Caulfield and L. Peake, eds, *City Lives and City Forms*. Toronto: University of Toronto Press.

——— and B. Martin. 1993. 'Gentrification as Secularisation', *Social Compass: International Review of Sociology of Religion* 40: 217–32.

——— and H. Smith. 1997. *Is There an Immigrant Underclass in Canadian Cities?* Vancouver: University of British Columbia, Centre of Excellence for Immigration Research, Working Paper 97–106.

Lorimer, J., and M. Phillips. 1971. *Working People: Life in a Downtown City Neighbourhood*. Toronto: James Lewis and Samuel.

McCann, L. 1975. *Neighbourhoods in Transition*. Edmonton: University of Alberta, Department of Geography, Occasional Papers No. 2.

McLemore, R., C. Aass, and P. Keilhofer. 1975. *The Changing Canadian Inner City*. Ottawa: Ministry of State for Urban Affairs.

Mann, W. 1970. 'The Lower Ward', in Mann, ed., *The Underside of Toronto*. Toronto: McClelland & Stewart.

Mercer, J., and D. Phillips. 1981. 'Attitudes of Homeowners and the Decision to Rehabilitate Property', *Urban Geography* 2: 216–36.

Mills, C. 1988. 'Life on the Upslope: the Postmodern Landscape of Gentrification', *Society and Space* 6: 169–90.

———. 1989. 'Interpreting Gentrification: Postindustrial, Postpatriarchal, Postmodern?', Ph.D. dissertation, University of British Columbia.

Millward, H. 1988. 'Classification of Residential Upgrading Processes: A Halifax Case Study', in T. Bunting and P. Filion, eds, *The Changing Canadian Inner City*. Waterloo: University of Waterloo, Department of Geography, Publication Series No. 31.

——— and D. Davis. 1986. 'Housing Renovation in Halifax: Gentrification or Incumbent Upgrading?', *Plan Canada* 26: 148–55.

Mitchell, K. 1993. 'Multiculturalism, or the United Colors of Capitalism', *Antipode* 25: 263–94.

Moore, P., and P. Smith. 1993. 'Cities as a Social Responsibility: Planning and Urban Form', in L. Bourne and D. Ley, eds, *The Changing Social Geography of Canadian Cities*. Montreal and Kingston: McGill-Queen's University Press.

Murdie, R. 1994. 'Blacks in Near-Ghettoes?', *Housing Studies* 9: 435–57.

Murphy, P. 1973. 'Apartment Location: The Balance Between Developer and Community', in C. Forward, ed., *Residential and Neighbourhood Studies in Victoria*. Victoria: University of Victoria, Western Geographical Series No. 5.

Olds, K. 1996. *Developing the Trans-Pacific Property Market: Tales from Vancouver via Hong Kong*. Vancouver: University of British Columbia, Centre of Excellence for Immigration Research, Working Paper 96–102.

Olson, S., P. Thornton, and Q. Thach. 1987. *A Geography of Little Children in Nineteenth-Century Montreal*. Montreal: McGill University, Department of Geography, Shared Spaces No. 10.

Owusu, T. 1998. 'Immigrant Associations and Adaptation: The Case of Ghanaians in Toronto', paper presented to the conference of the Association of American Geographers, Boston.

Phipps, A. 1983. 'Housing Renovation by Recent Movers into the Core Neighbourhoods of Saskatoon', *Canadian Geographer* 27: 240–62.

Ram, B., M. Norris, and K. Skof. 1989. *The Inner City in Transition*. Ottawa: Ministry of Supply and Services, for Statistics Canada.

Ray, B., and E. Moore. 1991. 'Access to Homeownership Among Immigrants in Canada', *Canadian Review of Sociology and Anthropology* 28: 1–27.

Ricketts, E., and I. Sawhill. 1988. 'Defining and Measuring the "Underclass"', *Journal of Policy Analysis and Management* 7: 316–25.

Robertson, R. 1973. 'Anatomy of a Renewal Scheme', in C. Forward, ed., *Residential and Neighbourhood Studies in Victoria*. Victoria: University of Victoria, Western Geographical Series No. 5.

Rose, D. 1987. 'Un aperçu feministe sur la restructuration de l'emploi et sur la gentrification: le cas de Montréal', *Cahiers de géographie du Québec* 31, 83: 205–24.

———. 1996. 'Economic Restructuring and the Diversification of Gentrification in the 1980s: A View from a Marginal Metropolis', in J. Caulfield and L. Peake, eds, *City Lives and City Forms*. Toronto: University of Toronto Press.

——— and P. Villeneuve. 1998. 'Engendering Class in the Metropolitan City: Occupational Pairings and Income Disparities Among Two-Earner Couples', *Urban Geography* 19: 123–59.

Rowley, G. 1978. 'Plus ça change ... A Canadian Skid Row', *Canadian Geographer* 22: 211–24.

Séguin, A.-M. 1997. 'Poverty and Social Exclusion in the Montreal Metropolitan Area', paper presented to the conference of the Canadian Association of Geographers, St John's.

Sénécal, G. 1995. 'Le quartier Hochelaga-Maisonneuve à Montréal', *Canadian Geographer* 39: 353–62.

Sewell, J. 1993. *The Shape of the City: Toronto Struggles with Modern Planning*. Toronto: University of Toronto Press.

Smith, H. 1998. 'Social Polarisation at the Community Level: Evidence from Vancouver's Gastown and Downtown East Side', paper presented to the conference of the Canadian Association of Geographers, Ottawa.

Suttles, G. 1968. *The Social Order of the Slum*. Chicago: University of Chicago Press.

Tunbridge, J. 1986. *Of Heritage and Many Other Things: Merchants' Location Decisions in Ottawa's Lower Town West*. Ottawa: Carleton University, Department of Geography, Discussion Papers No. 5.

Tutchener, J. 1998. 'Globalisation and Residential Real Estate in Canadian Cities', MA thesis, University of British Columbia.

Ward, D. 1976. 'The Victorian Slum: An Enduring Myth?', *Annals, Association of American Geographers* 66: 323–36.

Wilson, W.J. 1987. *The Truly Disadvantaged: The Inner City, The 'Underclass' and Public Policy*. Chicago: University of Chicago Press.

Woodsworth, J. 1972 [1911]. *My Neighbour*. Toronto: University of Toronto Press.

Chapter 13

Suburbs

Peter J. Smith

Of all the ways in which Canadian cities have been transformed in the half-century since World War II, none has had such far-reaching effects, or wrought such immense changes to the Canadian way of life, as suburbanization. There were certainly suburbs before 1946, reaching back into the eighteenth and nineteenth centuries, but the era of large-scale suburban development and wholesale suburban living was very much a product of the new postwar economy (Bourne, 1993).[1] Since then, urban growth has largely been *sub*urban growth, and the urbanization of Canada's population, which is one of the truly fundamental changes of the twentieth century, has actually meant its *sub*urbanization. Between 1946 and 1996, Canada's urban population increased by about 15 million, a threefold increase that accounted for over 90 per cent of the country's total population growth. Most of this growth occurred on the margins of existing cities, in their *suburbs*.

These few facts are enough on their own to make suburbanization a highly significant phenomenon, but suburbs are more than just a mechanism by which cities grow. They are profoundly important social phenomena as well, 'the fullest, most unadulterated embodiment of contemporary culture', as Jackson (1985: 4) puts it, and the prime arena in which cultural changes of all kinds play themselves out. And when cultural change is combined with rapid population growth, as has so often been the case in Canada, the consequences are enormous, for cities at large no less than for their suburbs. As suburbs grow and change, so, too, do the cities that house them, a pattern of mutual adjustment that goes far to explain why Canadian cities are indeed 'in

transition'. In fact, the whole concept of transition has particular relevance for the suburbs. There are, for example, the critical transitions that occur with the very act of suburban development, when rural land is first converted into urban use and environmental systems are irrevocably modified. In a rather different sense, suburbs themselves can be thought of as a transitional kind of development, which Rowe (1991), in a neat double entendre, calls the 'middle landscape'—a landscape that falls between the extremes of densely built-up urban core and open countryside in form and appearance as much as in location. Then there are the temporal transitions to which suburban development inevitably gives rise, the transitions in metropolitan form and social organization as small, compact, essentially pedestrian cities evolved into vast sprawling agglomerations in thrall to the automobile. Established suburbs, too, go through complex transitions over time, a mix of demographic, social, economic, and physical changes constantly reshaping the suburban pattern. All have large geographical and planning implications that this chapter aims to explore.

Suburbs in Metropolitan Context

Suburbs are an integral part of the modern city. Every city in Canada has its suburbs, and any model of city structure must express that reality. It also follows, thinking of cities as economic and social systems, that suburbs are inextricably linked with all the other elements that together make up the city. Although they serve their own definite purposes (else why bother to distinguish them), those purposes are determined in relation to the larger whole. Suburbs cannot exist apart from the cities to which they belong.

These are extremely broad principles, of course, and for all their theoretical importance do not begin to capture the complexity and variety of suburban experience. Worse than that, they appear to be at odds with the way that suburbs are so often represented. A large literature treats cities and suburbs as though they are separate entities—separate and quite different. Sometimes, suburbs are even described as parasites, implying that their relationship with cities is neither necessary nor healthy. And although this confusion can often be put down to a loose use of the words 'city' and 'suburb', there is a truly fundamental problem here as well, the conceptual problem of determining exactly what a suburb is and how it differs from all the city's other parts. Suburbs today come in surprisingly rich diversity, embracing such 'a wide variety of communities and landscape forms' (Pratt, 1994: 605) that their common properties are quite obscured. It is even hard to tell where reality ends and myth takes over, so hedged about are suburbs in popular perception with outworn clichés and inadequate stereotypes (Bourne, 1996).

In contrast to the ambiguity that clouds the concept of the suburb today, its original usage was simplicity personified. 'Sub' in this context means near, and the English word 'suburb' was derived from the Latin, *suburbanum*, meaning a villa or country estate near Rome. In similar vein, the first modern suburbs appeared in the eighteenth century, when wealthy merchants began to take up second residences within carriage drive of London and other large commercial cities.[2] Before long, many of these merchants were living permanently outside the cities where their businesses were located. They were creating the first true dormitory suburbs, small communities of large, spaciously laid-out houses in a near-rural setting. Fishman (1987) has labelled them 'bourgeois utopias', living prototypes of the suburban ideal whose influence throughout the Anglo-American world has been both lasting and profound.

From this limited beginning, under the impact of industrialization and urbanization and the economic and social changes that followed in their wake, suburbs gradually came to be associated with a highly varied array of development forms and conditions. Ironically, however, the more diverse suburbs became, the more difficult it was to generalize about them on any basis except their location. Hence Donaldson (1969: ix) could write that 'A *suburb* is defined simply as a community lying within commuting distance of a central city.' Leaving aside for the moment the question of what Donaldson means by 'central city', his definition depends on a single (misleading) criterion,[3] for although commuting distance has the advantage of being more technical than such vague descriptions as 'near' or 'close', it is still a loose way of characterizing suburbs. With modern transport facilities, commuting distances can well exceed 80 kilometres and the potential commuting zone around any large city is likely to include at least some functionally separate communities (see Chapter 14). Hamilton and Guelph, for instance, lie within commuting distance of Toronto, and people do indeed commute from both places, but neither would tolerate being counted among Toronto's suburbs. Nor need they be. A location within commuting distance may be a *necessary* condition for suburban development but it is by no means a *sufficient* one.

What additional criteria might then be called on? One frequently mentioned is political independence, which brings us back to Donaldson's remark about the central city. This is actually a technical term and refers to the city as an administrative unit with its own municipal government and precise territorial limits. As a general rule, as cities grow they try to expand their territories by annexing land from the counties or townships that surround them. When these moves are resisted, however, as they commonly are, development spills beyond the city's boundaries. Rural municipalities then become urbanized and new urban municipalities established, until the original city, now the *central* city, is more or less encircled by its outlying communities. But while these communities are quite properly described as suburbs, it does not follow that a suburb must necessarily be independent from its central city, certainly not in Canada where a great deal of suburban development actually falls under central city jurisdiction.

As a matter of more general concern, if suburbs are to be characterized in relation to some well-defined areal unit, the central city is not the most appropriate choice; it is simply too arbitrary and inconsistent. A better, if still imperfect alternative is to be found in the concept of the *inner city*, which this book adopts. If the inner city is thought of as the city's core area, into which the original, pre-suburb city has been engrossed, it is equally logical to think of suburbs as constituting an outer zone of development, regardless of the pattern of municipal government. This elementary observation is the basis for the model put forward in Figure 13.1, and although it does not sweep away all the conceptual fog it does at least seize on a characteristic that all suburbs share. It is also axiomatic that development in the outer zone will have occurred as a direct result of the need to accommodate the city's growth. For a century or more, Canada's cities have expanded chiefly by adding new suburbs, advancing ever further into their surrounding countryside and engulfing such towns and villages as lie in their path. Since local planning controls came into force in the 1950s, much of this expansion has been directed to the margins of existing built-up areas—the zone of contiguous suburbs in the model—but beyond that, in the rural-urban fringe, pockets of suburban development are typically spattered across an otherwise rural landscape. The boundary between suburbs and countryside is not a line so much as a broad indeterminate zone, over which the pressures of suburbanization are widely dispersed. This is especially true of the largest and most rapidly growing metropolitan regions, such as Toronto or Vancouver, though all Canadian cities, whatever their size or growth history, conform more or less to the pattern shown in Figure 13.1.

The demand for new suburbs, then, is primarily a function of population growth, a truism that conceals a most complex reality. In the first place,

suburban population growth itself is a complex phenomenon, driven partly by its own natural increase and the eventual creation of new suburban households and partly by net migration from a variety of sources: from the inner city, from rural areas and small towns, and from other cities and their suburbs in Canada and elsewhere. In addition, established residents move frequently within the suburban zone, for many different reasons (Barrett, 1973; Michelson, 1977; Phipps and Cimer, 1994; Simmons, 1974). Their relocation patterns are extremely diverse as well, but the general tendency, when combined with the population growth factors, is towards outward movement—to the subdivision offering start-up homes for first-time home-buyers, perhaps, or the élite new community for older, upwardly mobile families.

On the inner margin of the suburban zone, meanwhile, there are growth pressures of a different kind. Sooner or later, the oldest surviving suburbs must expect to merge with the inner city, except perhaps when they are politically independent. The Montreal suburb of Mont-Royal, which originated as a planned community in 1910 (McCann, 1996), exists as a separate municipality to this day and by that criterion is as suburban as it ever was. But how about Montreal's Maisonneuve district? It, too, originated as a suburban municipality but joined with Montreal as long ago as 1918 (Linteau, 1985). Rosedale is another example, annexed by Toronto in 1905 after having been 'plotted out as a high-class suburb' in the 1860s (Careless, 1984: 96). Then there is Shaughnessy Heights in Vancouver, which set out in 1907 to be 'the most prestigious residential suburb in the city' (Duncan, 1994: 60)—*in* the city, not outside it. Should any of these be considered suburbs today, or are they now part of the inner city? In terms of the indicators discussed by David Ley in Chapter 12, the latter would seem to be the case, though Ley also makes it clear that there are no agreed criteria for delimiting inner cities. Nor, whatever criteria are used, are their limits irrevocable. Boundaries, once again, are zones rather than lines, transitional zones of indefinite character, no longer as suburban as they once were but not yet

Figure 13.1   **Suburbs in the Generalized Structure of a Typical Canadian City (not drawn to scale)**

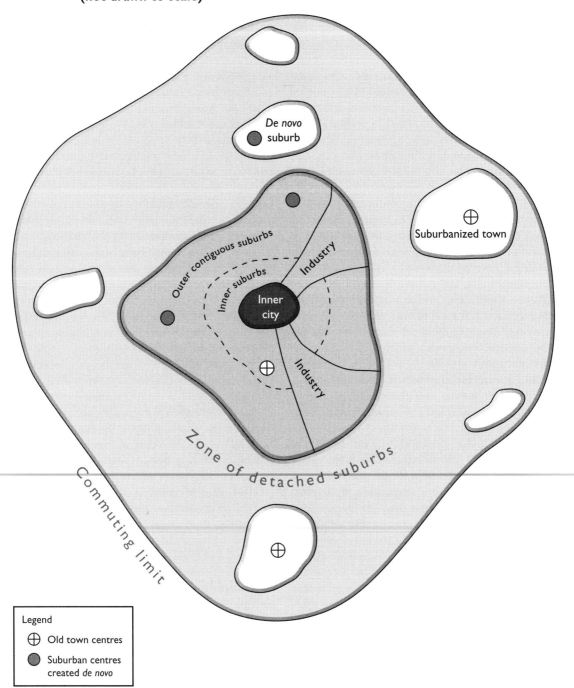

unmistakably of the inner city. These zones are for-ever shifting as well, gradually advancing outward as the innermost suburbs are absorbed and the inner city expands.

Of course, simply substituting 'inner city' for 'central city' in definitions like Donaldson's does not throw much light on the nature of suburbs or their place in the constantly changing city. For this it is necessary to consider other characteristics, beginning with the commonly held view that sub-urbs are economically and culturally dependent on the cities that spawned them. Jobs are a crucial aspect of this relationship, so to that extent depend-ency is already implied in the concept of commut-ing. More generally, though, it relates to services of all kinds, and particularly those highly specialized services (medical, educational, retail, entertainment, and so on) that require large populations to support them and have traditionally been provided from a single central location.

These are obviously important ideas that still have much validity to them (Bourne, 1989; Rose and Villeneuve, 1993), but they, too, need to be qual-ified. Modern suburbs are not always as dependent on their parent cities as conventional theory sup-posed, not even for employment. Already, more than a century ago, the greatest industrial expansion was occurring on the outskirts of cities, usually in sepa-rate municipalities. Thus was born the industrial suburb, a new kind of urban community that simul-taneously broadened and obscured the whole notion of a suburb. Although these new communities were physically close to their parent cities and were usu-ally connected to them by some form of rail transit that fostered commuting, they possessed a degree of economic independence that was not typically sub-urban; they were places to work as well as places to live.[4] Since then, as Chapters 15 and 17 explain, the suburbanization of jobs has accelerated enormously and commuting patterns have become more com-plex as a consequence. For all that we think of sub-urbs as places where most of the residents work somewhere else—and the examples presented in Table 13.1 indicate this is still a reasonable view to take—that 'somewhere else' is not necessarily the

inner city or even the central city; it could be any-where within the greater metropolitan area.

By the same token, and this, too, is made clear by Table 13.1, the suburbanization of jobs has not affected all suburbs equally. In some cases, especially among smaller suburbs with little or no local indus-try, 80 per cent or more of the labour force will work elsewhere, mainly in the central city (and probably the inner city). Distance from the urban core is sometimes a factor as well, as we can see by comparing the Victoria suburbs of Oak Bay and Sidney or the Toronto suburbs of East York and Oakville. Perhaps the most important factor of all, though, is the degree of 'urbanization', especially among larger suburbs that tend to become increas-ingly independent and self-sufficient as they mature (Muller 1976). The largest—and several in Canada have populations in the 100,000–600,000 range—function much like cities in their own right, even to the extent of being structured around their own multipurpose cores. In the contemporary dispersed city, these suburban downtowns act as major devel-opment nuclei, competing in many respects with the central business district (see Chapter 11), just as suburban locations are frequently preferred these days for specialized service facilities of all kinds, from airports to universities. These trends have given rise to a new generation of suburbs, repre-sented in Table 13.1 by Richmond, Mississauga, and Laval, among others—functionally diverse suburbs that are significantly less dependent on their central cities, for either services or jobs, than was once the case, while yet being thoroughly integrated into their respective metropolitan economic systems.

A further weakness of the conventional depend-ency thesis is its implicit assumption that suburbs are mere appendages of cities and contribute little to them in return. In fact, though, by supplying good-quality living space for a large and continually increasing population, suburbs perform a most vital function. They are also generally thought of—and here they become ideological constructs as much as practical ones—as facilitating a much desired lifestyle, a belief that has long set suburbs apart in popular imagining. The 'good life' may be no more

Table 13.1   **Place of Employment of Active Labour Force of Selected Suburbs in 1991, and Population of the Same Suburbs in 1996**

Census Metropolitan Area and Suburbs	Place of Employment, 1991					Population 1996
	Suburb of Residence (including at home)		Central City	Elsewhere in CMA	Outside CMA	
Victoria CMA:						
Oak Bay	18%	(11%)	52%	23%	7%	17,865
Sidney	48%	(7%)	24%	24%	4%	10,701
Vancouver CMA:						
White Rock	28%	(9%)	14%	54%	3%	17,210
West Vancouver	32%	(15%)	37%	27%	4%	40,882
Burnaby	35%	(5%)	39%	23%	3%	179,209
Richmond	53%	(7%)	31%	13%	3%	148,867
Edmonton CMA:						
Beaumont	16%	(4%)	64%	17%	3%	5,810
St. Albert	30%	(5%)	62%	4%	4%	46,888
Fort Saskatchewan	59%	(5%)	29%	8%	4%	12,408
Ottawa-Hull CMA:						
Rockcliffe Park	13%	(11%)	70%	10%	7%	1,995
Kanata	25%	(5%)	45%	27%	3%	47,909
Nepean	29%	(5%)	56%	12%	3%	115,100
Toronto CMA:						
East York	11%	(4%)	57%	30%	2%	107,822
North York	37%	(5%)	30%	30%	2%	589,653
Oakville	43%	(6%)	18%	31%	7%	128,403
Mississauga	53%	(4%)	19%	25%	3%	544,382
Montreal CMA:						
Mont-Royal	19%	(10%)	55%	23%	3%	18,282
Châteauguay	32%	(4%)	27%	36%	5%	41,423
Dorval	32%	(6%)	25%	41%	2%	17,572
Laval	38%	(5%)	33%	26%	3%	330,393
St John's CMA:						
Mount Pearl	23%	(4%)	69%	4%	3%	25,519

Note: This illustrative table provides only a partial list of the suburbs that comprise each individual CMA. All suburbs featured in the table were independent municipalities in 1991 and 1996. East York and North York were subsequently amalgamated with Toronto and the other inner suburbs to form a greatly enlarged central city.

Sources: Statistics Canada, Census Catalogues 93–323, *Place of Work: The Nation* (1993) and 93–357–XPB, *A National Overview: Population and Dwelling Counts* (1997).

certain in suburbia than anywhere else, but it is a compelling dream nonetheless (Wright, 1983).

At the historic core of the suburban mystique is the idea that suburbs are more akin to the country than to the city, and so permit a healthier, more satisfying, better adjusted way of life. There are clear overtones here of the Arcadian myth, a vision of a pastoral paradise that was one of the many offshoots of the great Romantic movement that swept the Western world after 1750.[5] In accordance with Romantic ideals, suburbs came to be associated with an environment that was both closer to nature, in the literal sense, and more 'natural', meaning more in harmony with people's physical, social, and spiritual needs. Where the city was the place of work and commerce, a scene of great energy and busyness, crowds and noise, and in its residential quarters, poverty, squalor, and disease, the suburb was the blessed antidote, a place of respite and regeneration and of wholesome domesticity (Mumford, 1938). These were obviously powerful images and they had a profound influence on early planning theory, most notably in Frederick Law Olmsted's concept of the Romantic suburb, which he pioneered at Riverside, Illinois (Fisher, 1986), and in its English counterpart, the garden suburb, as first devised by Raymond Unwin (Creese, 1966; Miller, 1992). Central to both, and of continuing importance ever since, was a vision of the suburb as a place where family life and social life would both flourish, a vision of healthy families living in healthy, village-like communities. This was the ideal that Olmsted, Unwin, and their many followers sought.[6]

For a time, while suburbs were still small and exclusive and clearly separated from their parent cities, a quasi-rural atmosphere was readily maintained. This all changed, however, as the transition to the age of the 'mass suburb' took effect and suburbs began to appear in forms that made them accessible to ordinary people, in sociological terms, to the 'masses'. The change did not happen overnight, and in Canada it did not become fully established until after World War II, but long before then the modern suburb had been set on a new and irreversible course that was itself the product of two overpowering forces. The first was the explosive growth of urban population and the concomitant emergence of a huge new middle class. Combined with an increasingly affluent working class, this soon created a demand for new houses and new communities that only mass production could satisfy. On top of that, the second force was the constant stream of technological innovations that helped bring suburban living within reach of the mass of the population: the many advances in construction methods, going back to the 1830s in Chicago, when the balloon-frame house was invented (Wright, 1983); the adoption of new and cheaper house styles, such as the bungalow, introduced into Britain from India in the 1860s (King, 1997); the increasingly sophisticated techniques of land development and capital financing even before Levittown became a synonym for the large-scale, 'corporate' suburb (Doucet and Weaver, 1991; Gans, 1967);[7] and perhaps most important, from a geographical and planning standpoint, the successive changes in modes of public and private transportation, beginning with the horse-drawn omnibus in the 1820s and progressing from there to electrified streetcars and subway trains, to high-speed suburban railways and, most overwhelmingly of all, to the automobile and its paraphernalia of highways and expressways, bridges and interchanges.[8] All helped facilitate the spread of suburban development on an ever-expanding scale and gave rise, in the process, to an ever-more complex social geography. As Olsen (1976: 236) explains, writing about Victorian London: 'The new suburb was a highly efficient means both of functional and social segregation: functional in that it enabled home-life and work to be carried out in two distinct and often distant places, social in that it enabled each class to be tidily sorted into its own homogeneous neighbourhood.'

For all its segregating tendencies, however, suburban development, then and since, has been shaped by tastes and values typically thought of as middle-class. During the Victorian period, in particular, the suburb was the very embodiment of bourgeois ideology and a highly visible metaphor for the cult of respectability that permeated Victorian life. What could be more respectable, after all, than owning one's own home on its own plot of ground? And providing there a secure place for one's family, a safe, quiet, and, above all, private place? What Boyer (1994) refers to as the privatization of urban space was one of the fundamental transformations wrought by the suburban revolution, and none better fitted the Victorian sense of rectitude and propriety. The quest for private space might be inherently paradoxical; 'a collective attempt to live a private life' is how Mumford (1938: 215) described it, but it was of elemental importance to the geography of suburbia. Low-density development became the norm and the prime attribute of suburbia as a distinct kind of environment. The spaciousness of the suburbs, especially in contrast to the congested city core, was also a major factor in their rapid expansion and huge extent, since so much more land was needed to house a given number of people. In our own day that same spaciousness is sometimes attacked as wasteful sprawl, yet its appeal is as powerful as ever. The ideals of space and privacy and the freedom they convey, the sense of independence and personal control, are not easily forgone, certainly not by Canadians. They are core values that the suburban way of life seeks to satisfy.

At the same time, as the architect Moshe Safdie (1970: 224) has observed, there is a 'contradictory desire in our utopia', a desire for openness and for small communities on the one hand, and for the amenities and opportunities of the large city on the other. Herein lies what Safdie calls the 'paradox of suburbia', meaning that the larger a city becomes and the further it spreads in a low-density form, the more difficult it is to gratify both desires—or either of them, for that matter. The transportation problems simply become too great.

In other respects, also, patterns of suburban life have changed dramatically in recent years, forced to adapt to a host of new circumstances far removed from the original suburban ideals. Falling birth rates, working wives, an aging population, single-parent families, corporate downsizing, Third World immigration, these are just some of the factors that have come into play. Suburbs now have to accommodate a much greater variety of people and lifestyles, household arrangements and housing forms, often at densities that make a mockery of the traditional notions of space and privacy. And although many suburban communities are as privileged and sheltered as ever (as evidenced, for example, by the growing popularity of 'gated communities'), the picture is quite different for suburbs as a whole. The distinction between suburbs and inner city, from which they have so long been set apart, has become increasingly blurred as well. Even in a relatively new city like Edmonton, where suburban residents are definitely younger and more affluent on average than those in the inner city, and more likely to belong to conventional families living in their own detached houses, many people in the suburbs do not fit this description, while many in the inner city do (Table 13.2). Old people and poor people, single parents and recent immigrants, renters and non-family households—all are still found in higher proportions in the inner city, but in absolute terms there are many more of them in the suburbs. And all, in their several ways, contribute to the great changes that have occurred in suburban character.[9]

The Variety of Canadian Suburbs: Order Out of Diversity

'American suburbs', writes Jackson (1985: 5), 'come in every type, shape and size: rich and poor, industrial and residential, new and old.' So, too, do Canadian suburbs, except that their variety is greater even than Jackson suggests. This is brought out by Figure 13.2, which uses the device of the morphological matrix to identify basic variations on 15 key attributes of contemporary suburbs, grouped into five more general clusters. Each attribute is explained in turn, though it should be kept in mind throughout the discussion that every suburb is a composite of all fifteen attributes.

I. Physical Development Characteristics

The first attribute, physical development pattern, harks back to Figure 13.1 and the distinction made

Table 13.2   **Comparison of Suburbs and Inner City, Edmonton, 1991**

	Suburbs	Inner City
% of population 0–14 years of age	24.9%	12.1%
% of population 65 years or older	6.4%	13.0%
Family households as % of all private households	79.5%	39.8%
Single-parent families as % of all family households	14.8%	19.2%
Mean household income per census tract		
(a) median	$47,272	$31,396
(b) range	$29,252–$108,130	$17,938–$48,679
% of population in low-income family units	15.8%	36.8%
% of private dwellings owner-occupied	68.3%	24.6%
Single-detached houses as % of all private dwellings	64.8%	25.9%
% of population whose mother tongue is a non-official language (single responses only)	15.9%	25.1%
Recent immigrants as % of total population	10.3%	16.3%
Population increase 1986–91	7.6%	3.9%
% of total CMA population	73.8%	13.2%

Note: In Tables 13.2, 13.3, and 13.4 suburbs are defined as (a) census tracts within the City of Edmonton largely or entirely developed since 1950, when neighbourhood unit planning was officially adopted; (b) census tracts that originally formed part of suburban municipalities subsequently annexed by Edmonton; and (c) outlying communities in which over 50 per cent of the labour force is employed elsewhere within the Edmonton CMA.

Source: Statistics Canada, Census Catalogues 95–377 and 95–378, *Profile of Census Tracts in Edmonton: Parts A and B* (1993).

there between 'contiguous' and 'detached' suburbs. The former lie within the continuous built-up zone that extends out from the inner city, while the latter are physically separated from other suburbs in a pattern of discontinuous or fragmented development popularly referred to as 'urban sprawl'. The matrix also recognizes a third, transitional category called 'merging suburbs' to cover those situations where suburbs that were once clearly detached are being encroached upon as the city grows. Their eventual fate, of course, is to be absorbed into the greater mass of contiguous suburbs, though this process may take decades to complete. The mix of suburbs in individual cities also varies, which has important implications for metropolitan form. The greater the proportion of detached suburbs, as in Toronto or Vancouver, the more dispersed the city will be, whereas metropolitan regions where most of the suburban population lives in contiguous suburbs will have a much more concentrated form. Calgary is a prime example.

In addition to their differences in development pattern, suburbs also vary by size and age, though these are relative concepts. Thus, Mississauga and North York, both of which had well over a half-million people in 1996 (Table 13.1), are large suburbs

Figure 13.2   **Morphological Matrix of Suburban Characteristics**

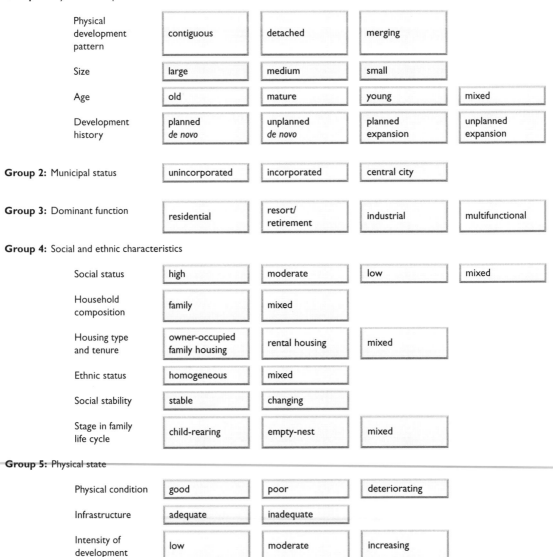

Group 1: Physical development characteristics

Physical development pattern	contiguous	detached	merging	
Size	large	medium	small	
Age	old	mature	young	mixed
Development history	planned *de novo*	unplanned *de novo*	planned expansion	unplanned expansion

Group 2: Municipal status — unincorporated | incorporated | central city

Group 3: Dominant function — residential | resort/retirement | industrial | multifunctional

Group 4: Social and ethnic characteristics

Social status	high	moderate	low	mixed
Household composition	family	mixed		
Housing type and tenure	owner-occupied family housing	rental housing	mixed	
Ethnic status	homogeneous	mixed		
Social stability	stable	changing		
Stage in family life cycle	child-rearing	empty-nest	mixed	

Group 5: Physical state

Physical condition	good	poor	deteriorating
Infrastructure	adequate	inadequate	
Intensity of development	low	moderate	increasing

by anyone's standards, but there are others, such as Burnaby (180,000) in Vancouver and Mill Woods (85,000) in Edmonton, that can equally be considered large in their local contexts, especially when compared with the many suburban communities whose populations are a few thousand at most. In principle, then, the distinction between large and small suburbs is easily made, though it can be a source of confusion in another respect. This is illustrated by Mill Woods, a comprehensively planned district comprising 24 separate neighbourhoods. So, is Mill Woods one suburb or 24, since each neighbourhood can be considered a suburban community in its own right? In fact, both answers are correct, because the larger the suburb the more likely it is to develop its own hierarchical structure: to form suburbs within suburbs within suburbs.[10] In systems terms, and also in planning terms, this makes eminent sense, but it does underline the importance of scale to the characterization of suburbs. Early editions of *The Dictionary of Human Geography*, for instance, defined suburb as 'a socially homogeneous residential district within an urban area', a definition that would have disqualified both Mill Woods and Burnaby, let alone Mississauga and North York. Although each contains many relatively homogeneous units—its 'small' suburbs—at the overall or 'large' scale, homogeneity is out of the question.

The significance of this point can be seen immediately with respect to the attribute of age. Every city has some suburbs that developed relatively early ('old' suburbs), others that developed quite recently ('young' suburbs), and some at an intermediate stage that the matrix describes as 'mature'. If a suburb is of a neighbourhood scale or less, and especially if it was developed after about 1950, it is highly likely that it will all be of the same age. For large suburbs, however, that is all but impossible. Even Mill Woods, where construction has been going on continuously since 1970, has neighbourhoods that are mature by Edmonton standards alongside others that are still quite new, while Burnaby, which one local planning official describes as a mature suburb when viewed as a whole (Ito, 1995: 122), has residential districts ranging from the 1920s to the present. The matrix would classify them both as 'mixed' suburbs, a mixture of young, mature, and, in Burnaby's case, relatively old communities.

Development history, the final attribute in this set, combines two characteristics. The first is summed up in the distinction between 'planned' and 'unplanned' suburbs, while the second distinguishes development that occurred 'de novo' (meaning an entirely new community was created on what planners call a 'greenfields' site) from the 'expansion' and suburbanization of once-independ-

ent towns. Together these yield four types of suburbs, all of which are fairly common across Canada. It can also be observed that *de novo* development is normal for contiguous suburbs, though detached suburbs sometimes fall into this category as well. Kanata outside Ottawa is an excellent example. More commonly, detached suburbs grow around the nucleus provided by an existing town, usually a rural service centre that is utterly transformed in consequence (Evenden, 1991a; Sinclair and Westhues, 1974). Such growth is also likely to be spontaneous rather than planned, though there are certainly instances in Canada, Ottawa being the best case in point, where metropolitan planning policy has supported the construction of detached suburbs (Coleman, 1969; Wright, 1978). Generally, however, suburban development is a market-driven process that local planning systems attempt to control as best they can. In this pragmatic sense, a suburb can be considered planned if it adheres to established principles of community design and meets local standards of environmental quality, particularly as prescribed by zoning and subdivision regulations. This requires the suburb to have been built in accordance with an approved plan governing the arrangement of land uses, the layout of streets and other transport facilities, the type, density, and appearance of the intended development, and the provision of physical and community services such as schools, playgrounds, shops, and sewers. By this definition, virtually all suburban development in Canada today is planned, though evidence of earlier unplanned development still abounds.

2. Municipal Status

Quite apart from their physical development characteristics, all suburbs come under some form of municipal government, even those that are not politically independent. In fact, municipal government varies widely across Canada, though the three categories adopted for the matrix are sufficiently broad to cover all situations.

The first category, 'unincorporated suburbs', refers to communities, mostly quite small, that have established themselves outside a central city in a rural municipality under whose jurisdiction they remain. In the past, this pattern was often associated with the worst characteristics of unregulated fringe development (Russwurm, 1975), rural municipalities then being poorly equipped to cope with the suburban invasion. This generally changed in the 1950s and 1960s, when even unincorporated developments came to be closely regulated by local planning authorities. The best of them, like Sherwood Park, a detached Edmonton suburb that originated *de novo* in 1954, were carefully designed as well. Sherwood Park now has about 40,000 people and many of the trappings of an independent city, yet it is still legally part of Strathcona County.

In the most extreme cases, fringe municipalities become so thoroughly suburbanized that a rural form of government is no longer appropriate. Burnaby, Nepean, Mississauga, and Laval are examples from Table 13.1 of erstwhile rural municipalities that have been reconstituted as cities. In the matrix they are classed as 'incorporated suburbs', though this category more usually applies to smaller places that have either expanded from a pre-existing town or obtained incorporation after the suburb became established. In an important variation on the Arcadian myth, these communities are often looking to protect a way of life that they value for its imagined small-town similarities. Political independence gives them the control they feel they need.

The third and final category applies to suburbs under central city jurisdiction, a circumstance that comes about in one of two ways: either the suburbs originate within the central city or they are absorbed into it *ex post facto*. Calgary is the most striking illustration of the former situation, reflecting a two-pronged strategy that the city and the metropolitan planning authority have pursued since the 1950s. On the one hand, an aggressive annexation program provided ample land for the city's expansion; on the other, development in the surrounding municipalities was deliberately restricted (Brown, 1991; Brown, Miller, and Simpkins, 1989). Saskatoon, Regina, and Edmonton adopted similar courses, though with less success in Edmonton

(Smith, 1991a). Even there, however, most of the largest suburbs, including Mill Woods, developed inside the central city.

In the second situation, suburbs form initially outside the central city and are then annexed by it, sometimes on the suburb's initiative but more usually because the city itself wishes to expand. All Canadian cities have grown in this way at some time, though none more spectacularly than Montreal, which annexed 20 suburban municipalities between 1883 and 1918 (Linteau, 1985). A few Canadian cities have also undergone comprehensive consolidations, though in these cases the initiative has come from above, from provincial governments. The earliest example was the so-called Unicity of Winnipeg that the government of Manitoba created in 1971 by amalgamating Winnipeg with all 11 of its suburban municipalities (Brownstone and Plunkett, 1983). Halifax had a similar reorganization imposed on it in 1996 (Nicolai, 1997). Then came the Toronto amalgamation of 1998, which introduced yet another variation. This time, only the innermost ring of municipalities was consolidated, while the more distant suburbs, which account for almost half of the metropolitan population, were left intact (Tomalty, 1996). In all these cases, however, the fact that once-independent communities were now incorporated into a central city did not necessarily mean that they ceased to be suburbs; their established character was not so easily erased.

3. Dominant Function

Throughout their long history, suburbs have been thought of as serving primarily a dormitory or 'residential' function, and it is certainly true that any suburb must provide living space for its residents. In determining a suburb's functional type, however, other attributes have to be considered as well, particularly size and municipal status. A suburb that developed within a central city, for instance, is almost certain to be purely residential, because modern zoning practices will have ensured that living areas and work areas are clearly separated. Outside the central city the pattern is more diverse, especially among suburbs that are politically independent. All four of the matrix's functional types are represented in this group, though the distinctions are sometimes fuzzy. Thus, communities in the 'resort/retirement' category will function much like regular residential suburbs, except that they have special qualities that make them equally attractive to recreationists and retirees. Usually, in fact, as typified by the Vancouver suburb of White Rock, such communities are known as resorts long before they become popular with commuters. 'Industrial suburbs', too, although distinguished by their independent industrial bases, depend on relatively high levels of commuting, both in and out. Table 13.1 gives partial evidence for this, in such cases as Kanata, Oakville, and Mount Pearl, though there are also instances (Fort Saskatchewan, for example) where the level of local employment is so high that it is doubtful if they should be classed as suburbs at all.

Similar uncertainty can occur with respect to 'multifunctional suburbs', those relatively large, urbanized suburbs that have broadly based economies of their own. Generally, as illustrated by such places as Burnaby, Nepean, and Laval, 30-40 per cent of the suburb's labour force will be employed locally, but the proportion is sometimes much higher than that—in Richmond, for example, or Mississauga (Table 13.1). Function used to be a simple way of distinguishing suburbs, but not any more.

4. Social and Ethnic Characteristics

Based on standard indicators of social status, such as income, occupation, and education, suburbs run a broad gamut, which the matrix simply divides into 'high', 'moderate', and 'low'. In practice, particularly at the neighbourhood scale, the great majority of Canadian suburbs fall into the moderate category, though in every city there are some that rank relatively high—Uplands, for example, an élite community in the incorporated suburb of Oak Bay, Victoria (Forward, 1973)—and some that rank relatively low. It is also to be expected, once again, that larger suburbs will themselves house communities of widely different status. These points are illustrated

for Edmonton in Figure 13.3 and Table 13.3, and although the data refer to census tracts, which are not always a good fit with neighbourhoods or other recognized social units, they do substantiate the wide range of social characteristics that apply in Canada's suburbs today, as well as give evidence of the tendency to social segregation that has long prevailed in suburbs everywhere. Only one variable, average household income, is presented in Figure 13.3, but it correlates well with other indicators and so is a reasonable surrogate for social status in Edmonton's case. It certainly picks out the great wedge of neighbourhoods in the southwest sector, following the North Saskatchewan River, that are well-known as Edmonton's most prestigious, along with the exclusive detached suburbs of St Albert and Sherwood Park, outside the central city. Also clearly identified is the ring of older, low-status communities that almost encircles the inner city. Needless to say, these are also the communities with the highest levels of suburban poverty (as indicated by percentage of population in low-income families). Newer census tracts within the central city fall generally into the moderate category, though larger units, like Mill Woods in the far southeast, are best described as mixed.

The next pair of attributes, household composition and housing type and tenure, are closely related to social status, and like it are more variable than traditional stereotypes allow. While it is certainly true that suburbs generally are still pre-eminently the domain of family households, not only is family more broadly defined these days (to include both married and common-law couples, with or without children living at home, and single parents living with at least one child), but non-family households are also a large component of many suburban neighbourhoods. In Edmonton, for example, they account for between a quarter and a half of all households in about a third of all suburban census tracts. Housing type and tenure are even more variable, ranging from tracts that fit the conventional image of suburbs as places where families live in their own, mostly detached houses to those where most people live in rental accommodation of one

Table 13.3   **Indicators of Social, Household, and Ethnic Character for Suburban Census Tracts in Edmonton, 1991**

Indicator	Quartile			
	Lowest	Second	Third	Highest
A. *Social characteristics*				
1. Average household income	$29,252–$41,999	$42,000–$47,271	$47,272–$53,999	$54,000–$108,130
2. % of population in low-income family units	2.1–10.8%	10.9–16.9%	17.0–24.2%	24.3–41.5%
3. % of labour force in managerial, professional, and related occupations	8.6–22.4%	22.5–27.7%	27.7–35.4%	35.5–67.8%
4. % of population 15 years and older with university degree	1.7–6.5%	6.6–10.5%	10.6–16.5%	16.6–52.9%
B. *Household and housing characteristics*				
1. % of private households in census families	45.4–70.9%	71.0–82.2%	82.3–86.9%	87.0–95.1%
2. % of private dwellings owned by occupiers	5.5–55.9%	56.0–66.9%	67.0–78.4%	78.5–98.4%
3. % of private dwellings in single-detached houses	0.2–49.9%	50.0–63.5%	63.6–77.9%	78.0–98.7%
C. *Ethnic characteristics*				
1. % of population whose mother tongue is a non-official language (single responses only)	3.7–13.1%	13.2–16.9%	17.0–22.7%	22.8–35.5%
2. % of population who are recent immigrants (1971–91)	0–5.7%	5.8–10.1%	10.2–15.9%	16.0–26.4%

Note: Ranges indicate lowest and highest values for census tracts within each quartile.
Source: Statistics Canada, Census Catalogues 95–377 and 95–378, *Profile of Census Tracts in Edmonton: Parts A and B* (1993).

form or another (Table 13.3). The latter are also most mixed in household composition, as well as tending to have the lowest average household incomes. This suggests that the mixing of housing types that has become so typical of suburban neighbourhoods is largely market-driven, a sign of the market's adaptation to today's more varied household arrangements and housing needs. Yet it is a trend that urban planners have long supported as well. The particular

housing mixes found in Canadian suburbs may not achieve the broad social balance that theorists like Lewis Mumford (1968) and Humphrey Carver (1979) aspired to, but the practice is nonetheless regarded as socially desirable.

Another characteristic of Canadian society with significant suburban ramifications is the ethnic diversity that has resulted from the changed immigration patterns of the past 25 years or so. The effects

Figure 13.3   **Household Income per Suburban Census Tract, Edmonton, 1991**

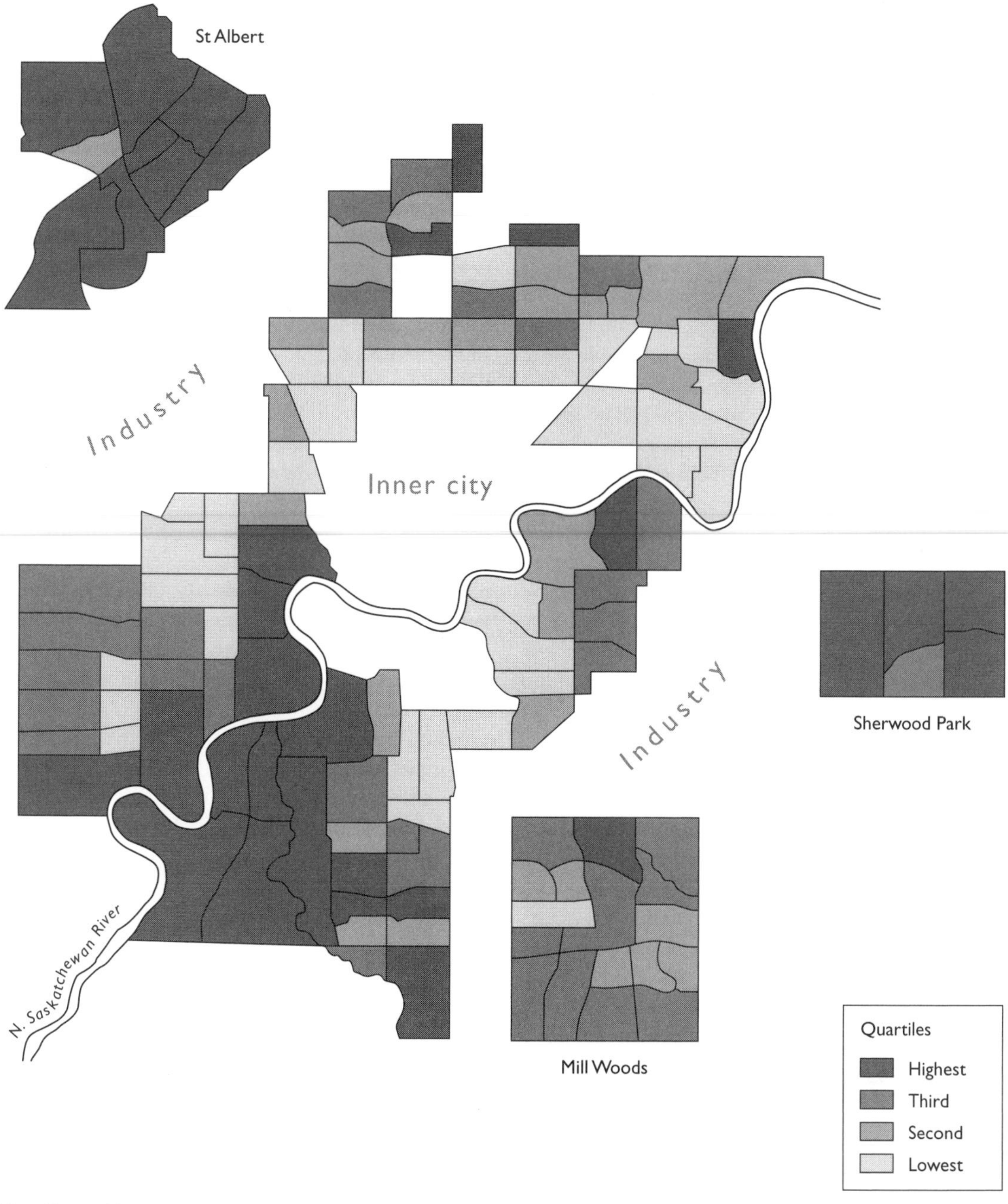

St Albert

Industry

Inner city

Industry

Sherwood Park

N. Saskatchewan River

Mill Woods

Quartiles

Highest
Third
Second
Lowest

Note: Ten outlying census tracts defined as suburban (see Table 13.2) have been omitted.

Source: Statistics Canada, Census Catalogues 95–377 and 95–378, *Profile of Census Tracts in Edmonton: Parts A and B* (1993).

are by no means uniform, however, and although many suburbs are now home to people of widely differing cultural, racial, and linguistic backgrounds, others have remained essentially untouched. The latter, which the matrix labels 'homogeneous', are typified by Beauport, an almost totally Francophone suburb of Quebec City, and by Mount Pearl, an equally strongly Anglophone suburb of St John's; in both cases, immigrants accounted for a mere 1 per cent of the population in 1991. In 'mixed' suburbs, by contrast, substantial (though widely varying) proportions of the population will have been born outside Canada—44 per cent in the Toronto suburb of Scarborough in 1991; 42 per cent in Saint-Laurent, a Montreal suburb; 35 per cent in Richmond. And while some of these people were brought up speaking either English or French as their native language, most were not. In Scarborough, 25 per cent of the population reported some foreign language as their mother tongue; in Richmond it was 28 per cent; and in Saint-Laurent a high 34 per cent. Saint-Laurent also has an unusually large Anglophone population (26 per cent), making it perhaps the most polyglot suburb in Canada.

All of these examples have been taken from relatively large, politically independent suburbs, but ethnic mixing occurs at a much smaller scale as well, in neighbourhoods and census tracts. Edmonton provides an example again, and although it is dangerous to reduce something as complex as ethnicity to simple indicators, those used in Table 13.3 and Figure 13.4 are highly suggestive. For one thing, they make it clear that suburban census tracts vary greatly in the degree to which they have been affected by immigration; for another, they establish a definite geographical pattern to these differences. In other words, they suggest that recent immigration trends have resulted in an increased tendency to ethnic segregation within Edmonton's suburbs. Two particularly striking pieces of evidence are the relatively high concentration of people from foreign-language backgrounds in the northern and southeastern sectors of the city, including Mill Woods, and their virtual avoidance of the detached

suburbs, not just St Albert and Sherwood Park but those that lie still further away, beyond the limits of Figure 13.4. In ethnic terms, most of Edmonton's most nearly homogeneous communities are outside the central city.

The final pair of attributes in this fourth group introduces the complex issue of social and demographic change. First, and most broadly, the matrix distinguishes between suburbs whose social character is essentially stable, which most suburbs will be most of the time, and those that are changing in some vital respect. Inner suburbs, for instance, may increasingly become home to lower-income groups and to recent immigrants. We can see some indication of both tendencies in Figures 13.3 and 13.4. In addition, and regardless of any propensity to social change, all suburban communities undergo critical demographic changes as they age and the family life cycle runs its course. As children grow up and leave home, so the overall character of the suburb will shift from being strongly child-oriented (the child-rearing stage) to being primarily adult (the empty-nest stage) (Michelson, 1977). This effect may be offset to some degree by the natural turnover of population, if parents also leave and are replaced by families with children, but the demographic consequences are still substantial, in part because contemporary families are smaller on average than those of the baby-boom generation. This is illustrated for Edmonton in Table 13.4, which shows how the family life cycle (as indicated by the relatively high proportions of empty-nest families in census tracts developed before 1971) manifests itself in a decreasing, aging, and relatively immobile population. Eventually, of course, when none of the original residents remain, the whole cycle will begin again, unless other development factors have intervened in the meantime to render the suburbs less attractive to families with children.

5. Physical State

The final set of attributes treats suburbs as built environment, especially in respect of those qualities that

Figure 13.4   **Proportion of Suburban Census Tract Population Whose Mother Tongue Is Neither English nor French, Suburban Census Tracts, Edmonton, 1991**

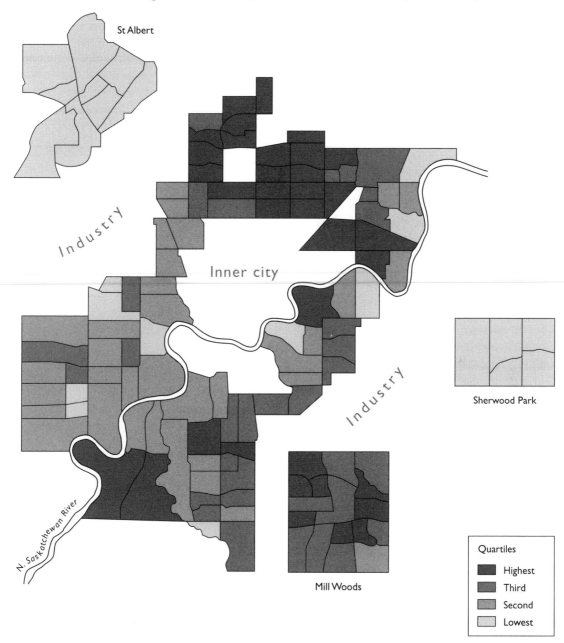

Note: Ten outlying census tracts defined as suburban (see Table 13.2) have been omitted.

Source: Statistics Canada, Census Catalogues 95–377 and 95–378, *Profile of Census Tracts in Edmonton: Parts A and B* (1993).

Table 13.4   **Indicators of the Family Life-Cycle Effect for Suburban Census Tracts in Edmonton, 1991, Stratified by Period of Development**

| Indicator | Period of development | | | | |
	1946–60	1961–70	1971–80	1981–91	Total
1. *Rate of population change 1986–91*					
Decrease (more than 2%)	13	11	9	—	33
Little change (± 2%)	11	6	14	—	31
Moderate increase (2%–10%)	3	9	23	4	39
Large increase (more than 10%)	2	—	10	20	32
Total	29	26	56	24	135
2. *% of non-movers (people living in same residence for at least 5 years, by quartile)*					
Highest: 55.1–72.4%	14	11	9	—	34
46.6–55.0%	6	9	18	1	34
39.7–46.5%	8	3	17	6	34
Lowest: 5.7–39.6%	1	3	12	17	33
Total	29	26	56	24	135
3. *% of population 65 years and older (by quartile)*					
Highest: 10.9–24.3%	25	7	2	—	34
5.0–10.8%	4	16	9	5	34
3.0–4.9%	—	2	28	5	35
Lowest: 1.2–2.9%	—	1	17	14	32
Total	29	26	56	24	135
4. *% of census families without children living at home (by quartile)*					
Highest: 40.5–50.8%	21	9	3	1	34
29.8–40.4%	8	13	9	4	34
23.5–29.7%	—	2	20	12	34
Lowest: 17.2–23.4%	—	2	24	7	33
Total	29	26	56	24	135

Source: Statistics Canada, Census Catalogues 95–377 and 95–378, *Profile of Census Tracts in Edmonton: Parts A and B* (1993).

bear directly on family and community life. In the matrix, these have been narrowed down to three, though the first two, 'physical condition' and 'infrastructure', commonly go hand in hand. Moreover, although the matrix divides both attributes into 'good' and 'poor' categories, this distinction was more important in the past than it is today. From the late-nineteenth century on, many low-income families, a high proportion of them immigrants, sought cheap land outside the boundaries of towns and cities all across Canada. Here, beyond the reach of municipal regulations, they could build their own houses out of whatever materials they could obtain, on plots of land large enough to practise a semi-subsistence way of life. They had created their own Arcadia, though it came with a cost: houses were generally crude, often no more than shacks; there were no services of any kind; and access to the city and to jobs was a matter of walking or cycling to the nearest streetcar terminus or factory complex (Harris, 1992, 1996; Harris and Sendbuehler, 1992). Then, in the 1940s and 1950s, these working-class suburbs, as they are sometimes called, were overrun in the great surge of postwar expansion. Some, like Forest Lawn in Calgary and Jasper Place in Edmonton, even became incorporated in a vain, Canute-like attempt to hold back the tide (Smith, 1991a). They were tax-poor, though, and amalgamation with a central city was the only way they could meet the environmental and servicing standards that residents and regulators were coming to demand (Smith and Diemer, 1978). Although they have left some mark on the suburban landscape—they explain about half of the low-income census tracts in Figure 13.3, for example—the more rigorous enforcement of building codes and planning regulations normally ensures that contemporary suburbs at least reach acceptable standards of health, safety, and service infrastructure. Further physical changes may still occur, however, particularly under conditions of social downgrading or inadequate maintenance, and this the matrix allows for as well. The oldest and poorest suburbs are particularly at risk, not just of deteriorating but of losing their suburban status altogether.

This same issue, the transition of inner suburbs into inner city, also affects the last attribute, identified in the matrix as 'intensity of development' to avoid confusion with population density, which is a separate concept. Although changes in intensity (as indicated, for example, by an increased number of dwelling units per hectare) may lead to changes in population density, so, too, will demographic changes of the kind discussed earlier, where there is no change at all to the built environment.

Historically, suburbs have been associated with development of relatively low intensity, typified by spacious house lots, extensive community open space, and generously laid-out streets. That pattern has by no means been universal, however. Since at least the 1950s, particularly in planned neighbourhoods, it has been standard practice to incorporate more intensive types of housing into the suburban environment: apartment buildings, both walk-up and high-rise (Hancock, 1968, 1994); row housing in almost endless variety; and even more specialized forms of accommodation such as retirement villages and extended-care facilities (Holdsworth and Laws, 1994). Sometimes these occur in sufficient concentrations for the overall intensity of development to be characterized as 'moderate' rather than 'low', though these are vague descriptions. It is also possible, and here the idea of transition comes into play, for a suburban neighbourhood to become more intensively developed over time (Halseth, 1996). This can come about in several ways: owners may enlarge and upgrade their houses as family circumstances change (Evenden, 1991b, 1997); houses of modest size may be replaced by larger ones, again as a mark of social upgrading (Majury 1994); and additional housing units may be fitted into existing spaces, by breaking down large residential properties, perhaps, or adding 'granny flats' for elderly parents, or building over surviving fragments of open ground. When this last process, which is known as 'infilling', occurs in older, inner suburbs, it may also signal that the transition into inner city has begun, especially if it is accompanied by redevelopment; that is, if houses are being demolished and apartments or some other kind of multiple-housing structure erected in their place. In such situations, the increased intensity of development is a telling indicator of fundamental changes in neighbourhood character.

Planning Challenges of Suburban Growth and Change:Development Issues and Conflicts

Just as suburbs have been the prime arena for urban growth since the end of World War II, so, too, have they been the principal focus of urban planning activity (Smith and Moore, 1993). The sheer scale of suburban development, and its importance to Canadian society and the national economy, made that all but inevitable. It also gave planners of the postwar generation an unprecedented opportunity to refine the art of community design, which they had been schooled to think of as central to their discipline. In no other aspect of urban development have the interests of business and government, public and planners, coincided to such powerful effect. Indeed, considering that the suburban development system began from next to nothing in the 1940s, it is remarkable how quickly it was able to rise to the challenge of accommodating the mass of the new urban population in well-built houses and well-equipped communities. This was a huge achievement.

For all its material contribution, however, large-scale suburban development was no panacea, nor could the mass suburb deliver all that the Arcadian myth had seemed to promise. To the contrary, almost from the outset there were those who were highly critical of the new suburbs, seeing them as dreary and monotonous wastelands, petticoat ghettos that marginalized women, limited and limiting in all those aspects of life that make for a vital society (Clark, 1966). And although these particular concerns have faded somewhat over time, as suburbs and the development system both matured, there have always been others to take their place. It is one of the great ironies of the suburban experience that where earlier generations had condemned the city and looked to suburbs as the ideal escape,

now the city was being idealized and suburbs condemned (Fowler, 1992; Sewell, 1984). In the eyes of contemporary critics, suburban development is unsound in every respect, environmentally, financially, and socially. In its stead, they wish to return to a form of city they regard as more truly urban, a nostalgic and romanticized vision of a diverse, compact, endlessly interesting city that is as mythic in its way as the Romantic suburb ever was. It is also a vision that has powerful forces arrayed against it, not just the development industry in all its ramifications but the ordinary people of Canada, the vast majority of whom still see suburbs as providing their best choice of living place. The dilemma for our local planning systems—and it is but one manifestation of the universal dilemma of planning in democratic societies—is how best to ameliorate established suburban forms and patterns of expansion while maintaining the freedom of choice that is one of our most precious liberties.

Among the many problems that the processes of suburban growth and change have given rise to, the following are particularly noteworthy from a geographical and planning standpoint.

(1) Suburban growth is everywhere treated as though it can be sustained indefinitely, which is a logical impossibility. Indefinite expansion implies unlimited resources, above all, an inexhaustible supply of land on which to build. But no resource is more finite than land. In the vastness of prairie space perhaps the practical limits to development may seem remote enough to verge on the infinite, but elsewhere they are real and pressing. Where would future suburbs be built in a Vancouver of 5 million people or a Toronto of 10 million? The whole idea of limits to growth has received scant attention in Canada, and certainly no city has faced up to its long-term implications.

(2) Unchecked suburban expansion is invariably accompanied by environmental damage and the loss of irreplaceable natural resources (Detwyler and Marcus, 1972). Natural hazards are often ignored as well, despite the risks to life and property and the high cost of remedial measures, such as Winnipeg's Red River Floodway. But even when

prospective development areas are safe to build on, as they mostly are around Canada's cities, they may have other qualities that make development undesirable. They may provide critical wildlife habitat, for example, or be ecologically significant in some other respect; they may pose a threat to nearby lakes, streams, and wetlands through contaminated run-off or accelerated erosion; they may be the site of a valuable natural resource—an aquifer recharge area, or a sand and gravel deposit, or land uniquely suited to some agricultural specialty. Or they may just have great scenic value, offering those semi-wild landscapes that Canadians so prize in their urban environments. Why, then, are such areas not protected as a matter of course? There is no shortage of appropriate techniques: analytical techniques for identifying areas of special character and assessing their importance, and regulatory and design techniques for mitigating the impact of development on environmental systems. The general principle of sustainable development has gained wide acceptance, too, even if its practical implications are not well understood.[11]

The fundamental question always remains, however. Do the benefits of environmental protection outweigh the costs? The issue here is not just that protective measures are often expensive in themselves, but that they may cause the cost of development to rise as well. There may even be long-term costs to the entire community, if a city is forced into a less efficient growth pattern, say, or if significant development opportunities have to be forgone. Protecting prime agricultural land is particularly problematic, because it is the easiest land to build on and the most economical to develop. This has huge implications for house prices and local housing markets, and while senior governments are sometimes willing to impose extraordinary protective measures, such as the Ottawa green belt or the special agricultural zoning that applies in Quebec and British Columbia, municipal governments are typically loath to take any action that might discourage development or add to its cost.

(3) Environmental considerations aside, the unit cost of low-density suburban development is already high when all the related costs for land and infrastructure are factored in. The situation is at its worst under conditions of unstructured sprawl such as prevail around most of the largest cities, but even moderately intensive, contiguous suburbs like those of Edmonton consume more in public expenditures than they generate in property tax revenues. This means that the suburban way of life, a privileged way of life in many eyes, is actually being subsidized by other taxpayers (Lewinberg, 1996). The planning problem, which is coming to receive a great deal of attention in Canada, is how to make suburban development self-supporting, or more nearly so, without pricing it out of the market for all but the most affluent.[12] One suggestion, which developers have favoured for many years, is that municipalities should lower their servicing standards: permit narrower streets, for example, or locate schools so as to draw on larger catchment areas. The general solution that has won most support, however, is intensification, meaning that suburban land could be used more efficiently and economically if it were more intensively developed (Tomalty, 1997). Sustainable development principles are often invoked as well, in the sense that higher housing densities are presented as a necessary trade-off if environmentally sensitive sites are to be spared. Whether these views will ever become popular is an open question, though. Intensification calls for trade-offs of its own, particularly in terms of space and privacy, those most valued properties of suburban environment (Leung, 1996; Simpson, 1996).

(4) A similar conflict of values bedevils the argument that intensification would help ease the transportation problems that are an inevitable and increasingly burdensome consequence of continuous suburban expansion. There is the sheer physical difficulty of moving ever-larger numbers of people and vehicles over ever-greater distances on ever-more congested facilities, to say nothing of the costs that then accrue—not just the construction and maintenance costs generated by a seemingly insatiable demand for new and improved facilities, especially for automobile traffic, but all the associated costs in energy consumption and atmospheric pol-

lution, in travel time and operating expenses, in injury, death, and property damage, and even in emotional well-being as stress and 'road rage' take their toll. But while a more intensive pattern of suburban development could certainly achieve some improvement, by reducing travel distances, for instance, and by making mass transit more feasible, it is not likely to bring about the revolution in public attitudes and travel behaviour that the problems require. Suburban residents will not readily give up the freedom and convenience that the private automobile is still able to provide.

(5) A transportation problem of a rather different kind results from the suburbanization of jobs, and especially from their segregation in dedicated business parks and industrial zones. This pattern has definite advantages from a planning standpoint, but for the poor, living in the inner city or inner suburbs, the isolation of suburban workplaces is a serious obstacle—a geographical obstacle—in the way of employment. Women are particularly affected because they are most likely to be at the mercy of inadequate and inconvenient public transit services (Mensah, 1994). One obvious solution would be to build low-income housing close to suburban industrial districts, but that is impractical now that the government of Canada has abandoned its social housing programs (see Chapter 16). Other possible approaches depend on jobs being provided at more accessible locations, such as suburban town centres, or even within certain residential districts, a practice that planners call 'mixed development' (England, 1996). Even with such measures, however, the spatial mismatch between employment opportunities and the homes of the poor seems destined to remain an intractable problem.

(6) Political fragmentation, such as prevails in most large Canadian cities, typically gives rise to uncoordinated patterns of development that are both inefficient and inequitable. Not only are suburban municipalities free to compete, even fight, with each other and with their central cities—for territory, for development, for status—but they also vary widely in their resources and in their ability and willingness to share the burden of area-wide needs.[13]

Welfare costs, for instance, are heavily loaded onto central cities where social problems are concentrated, while affluent residential suburbs deny any responsibility. Servicing standards and costs are also likely to vary among suburban municipalities, and there may be costly gaps and overlaps in service provision. As well, land-use practices prohibited in one community may be tolerated by a neighbour, adding yet another dimension to the basic pattern of spatial inequality. And although there are well-recognized mechanisms for coping with all of these problems, notably the various arrangements for metropolitan government (see Chapter 18), their effect has been undermined in recent years by increasingly vigorous demands for municipal autonomy and the subsequent 'retreat from regional planning' (Frisken, 1982). As far as most suburban municipalities are concerned, if there are costs and inefficiencies to political fragmentation, which they will almost certainly dispute, they are outweighed by the benefits that come from local control and self-determination. The right of local communities to govern their own affairs is cardinal in democratic politics, and fiercely defended whenever attacked. That lesson received one of its most dramatic demonstrations in 1997, in the fight that Toronto's inner suburbs waged against their enforced amalgamation with the central city.

(7) Suburbs are not static creations. Sooner or later, they all become subject to pressures for change: economic, social, and demographic pressures to which they adjust as best they can. Suburban life, suburban social relations, even suburban built environments all will be affected in numerous ways. We might think, for example, of the recent proliferation of home-based businesses, which is not only changing suburban work patterns (see Table 13.1) but the very meaning of suburban residence (Gurstein, 1996); or the rapid increase in new-immigrant populations in suburbs such as Scarborough and Richmond, and the social tensions to which that has given rise (Ray, Halseth, and Johnson, 1997); or the aging populations of the earlier postwar suburbs and the consequent imbalance between service needs and service facilities. Neighbourhoods designed for active families find them-

selves with half-empty schools and deserted play-grounds, while outlying neighbourhoods, where the school-age population is concentrated, wait for years for the same facilities. This is just one example, but it illustrates how difficult it is for suburban communities to keep up with changing needs and circumstances, and how difficult it is to adapt their built environments to new activity patterns. Planned suburbs, in particular, were neither meant nor expected to change. When forced to do so, as the Edmonton suburb of West Jasper Place was to accommodate West Edmonton Mall, the disruption is severe (Smith, 1991b).

On technical grounds alone, coping with change is always a challenge, but when a political dimension is added, as it generally is these days, the problems become formidable indeed. Change is usually resisted, and often feared, in established communities, and political opposition and organized protest have become accepted means of giving vent to community concerns. This has been made manifest through a host of issues: the passion with which residents defend neighbourhood schools threatened with closure or resist the construction of 'monster houses' that would overwhelm a neighbourhood's established character (Majury, 1994);[14] the prolonged fights that erupt when arterial roads become congested and gridlocked and the residents of outer expanding suburbs seek relief at the expense of inner, long-established ones (Leo, 1977); and the regularity with which development proposals are attacked as LULUs (locally unwanted land uses), no matter how socially desirable they may be. Meeting today's diverse housing needs in forms that are both appropriate and affordable is particularly problematical. To some extent, as evidenced by the growing popularity of such things as retirement villages and adults-only condominiums, often in the form of gated communities, these needs are being accommodated in newly developing suburbs, but a peripheral location is not suitable for everyone. If applied to disadvantaged groups, it becomes just another way in which they are marginalized in contemporary society (Laws, 1994). Yet trying to provide for these people within developed communities is

rarely welcomed either. The current trend to 'de-institutionalization', for example, has provoked numerous battles in the neighbourhoods where group homes and other special facilities are proposed (Dear 1992). And while this response can be condemned as self-interested NIMBYism, it is also every community's democratic right to try to prevent unwanted changes. The resultant conflict is something that local planning systems, through their elected bodies, must grapple with daily. Where suburban planning was once seen as a relatively straightforward technical activity, focused on the design of good-quality environment, now it is a thoroughly political activity as well.

Suburban space has thus become contested space, far removed from those utopian images of bliss and harmony that were once its touchstone. In itself, however, this neither invalidates the suburb as a form of urban development nor robs it of its intrinsic appeal to the people it serves. On the contrary, it is a mark of the importance that most suburban residents attach to their homes and environs and the way of life they permit. For all their flaws—and they are large—there is no practical alternative to the suburbs for the mass of the urban population, nor will there be for as far as anyone can see into the future. The real challenge is not to do away with suburbs, as some critics seem to imply, but to adapt them more effectively to changing needs and circumstances and to changing public attitudes and expectations about suburban development, suburban environment, and the suburban way of life. In this respect, Canadian suburbs, and hence Canadian cities, must remain constantly *in transition*.

Notes

1. Historical, geographical, and planning perspectives on Canadian suburban development are provided by Baerwaldt and Reid (1986), Carver (1978), Evenden and Walker (1993), Linteau (1987), Sewell (1977), and Smith and Moore (1993). There are also numerous books and articles that treat various aspects of suburban planning and development in individual cities. These

include works on Victoria (Forward, 1973), Vancouver (Evenden, 1978, 1995; Hardwick, 1974; Perkins, 1993; Wynn and Oke, 1992), Calgary (Harasym and Smith, 1975), Edmonton (McCann and Smith, 1978; Smith, 1995; Wang and Smith, 1997), London (Sancton and Montgomery, 1994), Hamilton (Harris and Sendbuehler, 1992; Weaver, 1978), Toronto (Clark, 1966; Harris, 1992, 1996; Lemon, 1985, 1996; Paterson, 1985, 1991; Sewell, 1993), Ottawa (Elliott, 1991; Timusk, 1976; Wright, 1978), Montreal (Charbonneau, Hamel, and Barcelo, 1994; Hanna, 1980; Lewis, 1991; Linteau, 1985; McCann, 1996; Van Nus, 1984), Halifax (Morton, 1995), and St John's (Cooper, 1975).

2. As used here, the term 'modern suburbs' refers to suburbs as they developed in the Anglo-American world over the past 200 to 250 years. There is also a much older, largely European tradition best expressed in the French term 'faubourg'. This is medieval in origin and describes a pattern of exclusion and social marginalization in which unwelcome people and businesses were refused entry to the city but were allowed to congregate outside its walls and gates (Saalman, 1968). By the nineteenth century, French faubourgs were largely working class and industrial, often little better than slums and viewed with distaste and even fear by bourgeois society (Merriman, 1991). Their reputation, in fact, was much like that of North American inner cities today.

3. To give Donaldson his due, he did add two important qualifications, both of which are considered later in this section. The second part of his definition reads as follows: 'Usually, but not always, suburbs are dependent on central cities economically and culturally; usually, but not always, they are independent of these cities politically' (Donaldson, 1969: ix).

4. Paul-André Linteau's study of Maisonneuve is the classic account of an early Canadian industrial suburb (Linteau, 1985).

5. American authors usually refer to this as the Jeffersonian myth and relate it to a strong anti-

urban tradition particularly associated with Thomas Jefferson; for examples, see Donaldson (1969) and Jackson (1985).

6. Even in Canada, where industrialization was less advanced and cities were newer and smaller, these attitudes had an important influence, extending into the postwar period; see, for example, Carver (1962), Delaney (1991), Holdsworth (1984), Morton (1995), Purdy (1997), and Weaver (1978).

7. Terms like 'corporate suburb', 'corporate city', and 'corporate society', often have a pejorative connotation, implying that power is excessively concentrated in a few élite 'corporations', governmental as well as commercial, which are then able to impose their narrow self-serving values on an unwitting public. See, for example, Lorimer (1978) and Reid (1991). In more neutral terms, a corporate suburb is one developed as a unified project, in which all phases of planning and construction are controlled by a single corporation.

8. The relationship between suburban expansion and transport facilities has been a popular line of inquiry since Warner's path-breaking study of Boston (Warner, 1962). Canadian examples include Armstrong and Nelles (1986), Doucet (1982), Evenden (1978), Frisken (1994), and Linteau (1985).

9. The following authors examine various aspects of the changing character and growing diversity of Canadian suburbs, though sometimes in the context of a broader study: Balakrishnan and Hou (1996), Carlyle (1991), Dansereau (1993), Dowling (1996), Fairbairn and Khatun (1989), Le Bourdais and Beaudry (1988), McGahan (1994), Ray, Halseth, and Johnson (1997), Rose and Villeneuve (1993), Skaburskis and Geros (1997), Taylor (1987), and Vischer (1987).

10. The concept of hierarchically structured suburbs has been established in planning theory since at least the 1950s. Mill Woods, for example, is organized as a three-level hierarchy of neighbourhoods, communities, and district, corresponding to small, medium, and large sub-

urbs in the matrix (Wang and Smith, 1997). Calgary and Scarborough also afford excellent examples (Harasym and Smith, 1975; Smith and Moore, 1993).

11. Although environmental protection and resource conservation in the face of suburban expansion are generally subsumed under the rubric of sustainable development these days, they have been major themes of the planning literature for many decades. Important examples are Hough (1995), Kaiser, Godschalk, and Chapin (1995), and McHarg (1969). For case studies of Canadian planning approaches and experience, see Coleman (1969), Crawford (1993), Grant (1994), Hossé (1978), Livey (1995), Pierce (1981), Reid (1990), Robinson (1995), Smith (1989), Tamminga (1996), Tomalty (1994), White (1996), Wolfe and Glenn (1992), and Yip (1994). Rees and Roseland (1991) provide a useful review of the sustainable development concept.

12. This issue is best illustrated in a set of reports commissioned by Canada Mortgage and Housing Corporation: *The Integrated Community: A Study of Alternative Development Standards*, 1996; *Changing Values, Changing Communities: A Guide to the Development of Healthy Sustainable Communities*, 1997; and *Conventional and Alternative Development Patterns —Phase 1: Infrastructure Costs*, 1997, and *Phase 2: Municipal Revenues*, 1997.

13. For case studies of the problems and conflicts resulting from political fragmentation in a variety of Canadian cities, see Batey and Smith (1981), Des Rosiers (1992), Frisken (1990), Millward (1996), and Smith and Bayne (1994).

14. 'Monster' or 'mega' houses are larger than normal for a particular neighbourhood. Usually they replace an existing smaller house by taking advantage of the circumstance that most houses are not built to the maximum size permitted under zoning regulations.

References

Armstrong, C., and H.V. Nelles. 1986. 'Suburban Street Railway Strategies in Montréal, Toronto and Vancouver, 1896–1930', in G.A. Stelter and A.F.J. Artibise, eds, *Power and Place: Canadian Urban Development in North American Context*. Vancouver: University of British Columbia Press.

Baerwaldt, W., and B. Reid. 1986. 'Re-reading Suburbia', *City Magazine* 8, 1: 17–29.

Balakrishnan, T.R., and F. Hou. 1996. 'Neighbourhood Status Persistence and Change in the Canadian Metropolitan Areas', *Canadian Journal of Urban Research* 5: 183–98.

Barrett, F.A. 1973. *Residential Search Behavior: A Study of Intra-urban Relocation in Toronto*. Toronto: York University-Atkinson College, Geographical Monographs No. 1.

Batey, W.L., and P.J. Smith. 1981. 'The Role of Territory in Political Conflict in Metropolitan Fringe Areas', in K.B. Beesley and L.H. Russwurm, eds, *The Rural-Urban Fringe: Canadian Perspectives*. Downsview: York University-Atkinson College, Geographical Monographs No. 10.

Bourne, L.S. 1989. 'Are New Urban Forms Emerging? Empirical Tests for Canadian Urban Areas', *Canadian Geographer* 33: 312–28.

———. 1993. 'The Changing Settlement Environment of Housing', in J.R. Miron, ed., *House, Home, and Community: Progress in Housing Canadians 1945–1986*. Montreal and Kingston: McGill-Queen's University Press.

———. 1996. 'Reinventing the Suburbs: Old Myths and New Realities', *Progress in Planning: Contemporary Perspectives on Urbanization* 46, 3: 163–84.

Boyer, M.C. 1994. *The City of Collective Memory: Its Historical Imagery and Architectural Entertainments*. Cambridge, Mass.: MIT Press.

Brown, E.C. 1991. 'A History of Calgary's Uni-city Form of Government', *Alberta and Northwest Territories Journal of Planning Practice* 11: 45–52.

———, R.M. Miller, and B.D. Simpkins. 1989. 'The City of Calgary's Comprehensive Annexation', *Alberta and Northwest Territories Journal of Planning Practice* 8: 39–78.

Brownstone, M., and T.J. Plunkett. 1983. *Metropolitan Winnipeg: Politics and Reform of Local Government*. Berkeley: University of California Press.

Careless, J.M.S. 1984. *Toronto to 1918: An Illustrated History*. Toronto: James Lorimer.

Carlyle, I.P. 1991. 'Ethnicity and Social Areas within Winnipeg', in G.M. Robinson, ed., *A Social Geography of Canada*. Toronto: Dundurn Press.

Carver, H. 1962. *Cities in the Suburbs*. Toronto: University of Toronto Press.

———. 1978. 'Building the Suburbs: A Planner's Reflections', *City Magazine* 3, 7: 40–5.

———. 1979. 'The Private and the Social Habitat', *Contact: Journal of Urban and Environmental Affairs* 11, 3: 33–42.

Charbonneau, F., P. Hamel, and M. Barcelo. 1994. 'Urban Sprawl in the Montréal Area—Policies and Trends', in F. Frisken, ed., *The Changing Canadian Metropolis: A Public Policy Perspective*. Toronto and Berkeley: Canadian Urban Institute and the Institute of Governmental Studies Press.

Clark, S.D. 1966. *The Suburban Society*. Toronto: University of Toronto Press.

Coleman, A. 1969. *The Planning Challenge of the Ottawa Area*. Ottawa: Department of Energy, Mines and Resources, Geographical Paper No. 42.

Cooper, R.G. 1975. 'Mount Pearl New Town', *Living Places* 11, 4: 2–9.

Crawford, P. 1993. 'Preserving Rural Character in an Urban Region: Rural Planning in the Township of Langley', *Plan Canada* 33, 2: 16–23.

Creese, W.L. 1966. *The Search for Environment: The Garden City Before and After*. New Haven: Yale University Press.

Dansereau, F. 1993. 'Neighbourhood Differentiation and Social Change', in J.R. Miron, ed., *House, Home, and Community: Progress in Housing Canadians 1945–1986*. Montreal and Kingston: McGill-Queen's University Press.

Dear, M. 1992. 'Understanding and Overcoming the NIMBY Syndrome', *Journal of the American Planning Association* 58: 288–300.

Delaney, J. 1991. 'The First Garden Suburb of Lindenlea, Ottawa: A Model Project for the First Federal Housing Policy, 1918–24', *Urban History Review* 19: 151–65.

Des Rosiers, F. 1992. 'Urban Sprawl and the Central City', *Plan Canada* 32, 6: 14–18.

Detwyler, T.R., and M.G. Marcus. 1972. *Urbanization and Environment: The Physical Geography of the City*. Belmont, Calif.: Duxbury Press.

Donaldson, S. 1969. *The Suburban Myth*. New York: Columbia University Press.

Doucet, M.J. 1982. 'Politics, Space and Trolleys: Mass Transit in Early Twentieth-Century Toronto', in G.A. Stelter and A.F.J. Artibise, eds, *Shaping the Urban Landscape: Aspects of the Canadian City-Building Process*. Ottawa: Carleton University Press.

Doucet, M., and J. Weaver. 1991. *Housing the North American City*. Montreal and Kingston: McGill-Queen's University Press.

Dowling, R. 1996. 'Symbolic Constructions of Place in Suburban Surrey, British Columbia', *Canadian Geographer* 40: 75–80.

Duncan, J. 1994. 'Shaughnessy Heights: The Protection of Privilege', in S. Hasson and D. Ley, *Neighbourhood Organizations and the Welfare State*. Toronto: University of Toronto Press.

Elliott, B.S. 1991. *The City Beyond: A History of Nepean, Birthplace of Canada's Capital 1792–1900*. Nepean, Ont.: City of Nepean.

England, K. 1996. 'On Intensification and Women-Friendly Cities', in J. Emeneau, ed., *A Practitioner's Guide to Urban Intensification*. Toronto: Canadian Urban Institute.

Evenden, L.J. 1978. 'Shaping the Vancouver Suburbs', in Evenden, ed., *Vancouver: Western Metropolis*. Victoria: University of Victoria, Western Geographical Series Vol. 16.

———. 1991a. 'Fleetwood in Surrey: The Making of a Place', in P.M. Koroscil, ed., *British Columbia: Geographical Essays in Honour of A. MacPherson*. Burnaby, BC: Department of Geography, Simon Fraser University.

———. 1991b. 'The Expansion of Domestic Space on Vancouver's North Shore', in G.M. Robinson, ed., *A Social Geography of Canada*. Toronto: Dundurn Press.

————, ed. 1995. *The Suburb of Happy Homes: Burnaby, Centennial Themes*. Burnaby, BC: Simon Fraser University.

————. 1997. 'Wartime Housing as Cultural Landscape: National Creation and Personal Creativity', *Urban History Review* 25, 2: 41–52.

———— and G.E. Walker. 1993. 'From Periphery to Centre: The Changing Geography of the Suburbs', in L.S. Bourne and D.F. Ley, eds, *The Changing Social Geography of Canadian Cities*. Montreal and Kingston: McGill-Queen's University Press.

Fairbairn, K.J., and H. Khatun. 1989. 'Residential Segregation and the Intra-Urban Migration of South Asians in Edmonton', *Canadian Ethnic Studies* 21: 45–64.

Fisher, I.D. 1986. *Frederick Law Olmsted and the City Planning Movement in the United States*. Ann Arbor: UMI Research Press.

Fishman, R. 1987. *Bourgeois Utopias: The Rise and Fall of Suburbia*. New York: Basic Books.

Forward, C.N. 1973. 'The Immortality of a Fashionable Residential District: The Uplands', in Forward, ed., *Residential and Neighbourhood Studies in Victoria*. Victoria: University of Victoria, Western Geographical Series Vol. 5.

Fowler, E.P. 1992. *Building Cities That Work*. Montreal and Kingston: McGill-Queen's University Press.

Frisken, F. 1982. 'Old Problems, New Priorities: Changing Perspectives on Governmental Needs in an Expanding Region', in Frisken, ed., *Conflict or Cooperation? The Toronto-Centred Region in the 1980s*. Downsview, Ont.: Urban Studies Programme, York University.

————. 1990. *Planning and Servicing the Greater Toronto Area: The Interplay of Provincial and Municipal Interests*. North York, Ont.: York University, Urban Studies Working Paper No. 12.

————. 1994. 'Provincial Transit Policymaking for the Toronto, Montréal and Vancouver Regions', in Frisken, ed., *The Changing Canadian Metropolis: A Public Policy Perspective*. Toronto and Berkeley: Canadian Urban Institute and the Institute of Governmental Studies Press.

Gans, H.J. 1967. *The Levittowners: How People Live and Politic in Suburbia*. New York: Pantheon Books.

Grant, J. 1994. 'Rhetoric and Response: Sustainable Development in Residential Environments', *Environments: A Journal of Interdisciplinary Studies* 22, 3: 3–12.

Gurstein, P. 1996. 'Telework and Its Impact on Urban Form', in J. Emeneau, ed., *A Practitioner's Guide to Urban Intensification*. Toronto: Canadian Urban Institute.

Halseth, G. 1996. 'Mapping Residential Redevelopment in a Canadian Suburb', *Canadian Journal of Urban Research* 5: 137–46.

Hancock, M.L. 1968. 'Flemingdon Park, a New Urban Community', in L.O. Gertler, ed., *Planning the Canadian Environment*. Montreal: Harvest House.

————. 1994. 'Don Mills, a Paradigm of Community Design', *Plan Canada* 34, 4: 87–90.

Hanna, D.B. 1980. 'Creation of an Early Victorian Suburb in Montréal', *Urban History Review* 9, 2: 38–64.

Harasym, D.G., and P.J. Smith. 1975. 'Planning for Retail Services in New Residential Areas Since 1944', in B.M. Barr, ed., *Calgary: Metropolitan Structure and Influence*. Victoria: University of Victoria, Western Geographical Series Vol. 11.

Hardwick, W.G. 1974. *Vancouver*. Toronto: Collier-Macmillan Canada.

Harris, R. 1992. ' "Canada's All Right": The Lives and Loyalties of Immigrant Families in a Toronto Suburb, 1900–1945', *Canadian Geographer* 36: 13–30.

————. 1996. *Unplanned Suburbs: Toronto's American Tragedy, 1900 to 1950*. Baltimore: Johns Hopkins University Press.

———— and M.P. Sendbuehler. 1992. 'Hamilton's East End: The Early Working-class Suburb', *Canadian Geographer* 36: 381–6.

Holdsworth, D.W. 1984. 'House and Home in Vancouver: Images of West Coast Urbanism', in G.A. Stelter and A.F.J. Artibise, eds, *The Canadian City: Essays in Urban and Social History*. Ottawa: Carleton University Press.

———— and G. Laws. 1994. 'Landscapes of Old Age in Coastal British Columbia', *Canadian Geographer* 38: 174–81.

Hossé, H.A. 1978. 'The Greenbelt and Ottawa's "Urban Containment" ', in R. Wesche and M.

Kugler-Gagnon, eds, *Ottawa-Hull: Spatial Perspectives and Planning*. Ottawa: University of Ottawa Press, Department of Geography and Regional Planning Occasional Papers 4.

Hough, M. 1995. *Cities and Natural Process*. London: Routledge.

Ito, K. 1995. 'Metrotown: A Time and a Place', in L.J. Evenden, ed., *'The Suburb of Happy Homes': Burnaby, Centennial Themes*. Burnaby, BC: Simon Fraser University.

Jackson, K.T. 1985. *Crabgrass Frontier: The Suburbanization of the United States*. New York: Oxford University Press.

Kaiser, E.J., D.R. Godschalk, and F.S. Chapin. 1995. *Urban Land Use Planning*. Urbana: University of Illinois Press.

King, A.D. 1997. 'Excavating the Multicultural Suburb: Hidden Histories of the Bungalow', in R. Silverstone, ed., *Visions of Suburbia*. London: Routledge.

Laws, G. 1994. 'Community Activism around the Built Form of Toronto's Welfare State', *Canadian Journal of Urban Research* 3: 1–28.

Le Bourdais, C., and M. Beaudry. 1988. 'The Changing Residential Structure of Montréal 1971–1981', *Canadian Geographer* 32: 98–113.

Lemon, J.T. 1985. *Toronto Since 1918: An Illustrated History*. Toronto: James Lorimer.

———. 1996. *Liberal Dreams and Nature's Limits: Great Cities of North America Since 1600*. Toronto: Oxford University Press.

Leo, C. 1977. *The Politics of Urban Development: Canadian Urban Expressway Disputes*. Toronto: Institute of Public Administration of Canada, Monographs on Canadian Urban Government No. 3.

Leung, H.-L. 1996. 'Designer Suburbs', in J. Emeneau, ed., *A Practitioner's Guide to Urban Intensification*. Toronto: Canadian Urban Institute.

Lewinberg, F. 1996. 'Some Thoughts about Intensification', in J. Emeneau, ed., *A Practitioner's Guide to Urban Intensification*. Toronto: Canadian Urban Institute.

Lewis, R.D. 1991. 'The Development of an Early Suburban Industrial District: The Montréal Ward of Saint-Anne, 1851–71', *Urban History Review* 19: 166–80.

Linteau, P.A. 1985. *The Promoter's City: Building the Industrial Town of Maisonneuve 1883–1918*. Toronto: James Lorimer.

———. 1987. 'Canadian Suburbanization in a North American Context—Does the Border Make a Difference?', *Journal of Urban History* 13: 252–74.

Livey, J. 1995. 'Urbanizing York Region', *Plan Canada* 35, 2: 25–8.

Lorimer, J. 1978. *The Developers*. Toronto: James Lorimer.

Majury, N. 1994. 'Signs of the Times: Kerrisdale, a Neighbourhood in Transition', *Canadian Geographer* 38: 265–70.

McCann, L.D. 1996. 'Planning and Building the Corporate Suburb of Mount Royal, 1910–1925', *Planning Perspectives* 11: 259–301.

——— and P.J. Smith. 1978. 'The Residential Development Cycle in Space and Time', in Smith, ed., *Edmonton: The Emerging Metropolitan Pattern*. Victoria: University of Victoria, Western Geographical Series Vol. 15.

McGahan, P. 1986. *Urban Sociology in Canada*, 2nd ed. Toronto: Butterworths.

McHarg, I.L. 1969. *Design with Nature*. Garden City, NY: Doubleday/Natural History Press.

Mensah, J. 1994. 'Gender, Spatial Constraints, and the Employment Activities of Low-income People in a Local Labour Market', *Canadian Journal of Urban Research* 3: 113–33.

Merriman, J.M. 1991. *The Margins of City Life: Explorations on the French Urban Frontier, 1815–1851*. New York: Oxford University Press.

Michelson, W. 1977. *Environmental Choice, Human Behavior, and Residential Satisfaction*. New York: Oxford University Press.

Miller, M. 1992. *Raymond Unwin: Garden Cities and Town Planning*. Leicester: Leicester University Press.

Millward, H. 1996. 'Greater Halifax: Public Policy Issues in the Post-1960 Period', *Canadian Journal of Urban Research* 5: 1–17.

Morton, S. 1995. *Ideal Surroundings: Domestic Life in a Working Class Suburb in the 1920s*. Toronto: University of Toronto Press.

Muller, P.O. 1976. *The Outer City: Geographical Consequences of the Urbanization of the Suburbs*.

Washington: Association of American Geographers, Resource Paper No. 75–2.

Mumford, L. 1938. *The Culture of Cities*. New York: Harcourt, Brace and Company.

———. 1968. *The Urban Prospect*. New York: Harcourt, Brace and World.

Nicolai, A. 1996. 'From Halifax, Amalgamated', *New City Magazine* 17, 3: 14–15.

Olsen, D.J. 1976. *The Growth of Victorian London*. London: Batsford.

Paterson, R. 1985. 'The Development of an Interwar Suburb: Kingsway Park, Etobicoke', *Urban History Review* 13: 225–35.

———. 1991. 'Housing Finance in Early 20th Century Suburban Toronto', *Urban History Review* 20: 63–71.

Perkins, R. 1993. 'What's Happening in the Suburbs of Greater Vancouver?', *City Magazine* 14, 3: 19–24.

Phipps, A.G., and J.J. Cimer. 1994. 'Late-1980s Voluntary Residential Mobility in Windsor and Niagara Falls, Ontario', *Canadian Journal of Urban Research* 3: 148–65.

Pierce, J.T. 1981. 'The B.C. Agricultural Land Commission: A Review and Evaluation', *Plan Canada* 21: 48–56.

Pratt, G. 1994. 'Suburb', in R.J. Johnston, D. Gregory, and D.M. Smith, eds, *Dictionary of Human Geography*, 3rd ed. Oxford: Basil Blackwell.

Purdy, S. 1997. 'Industrial Efficiency, Social Order and Moral Purity: Housing Reform Thought in English Canada, 1900–1950', *Urban History Review* 25, 2: 30–40.

Ray, B.K., G. Halseth, and B. Johnson. 1997. 'The Changing Face of the Suburbs: Issues of Ethnicity and Residential Change in Suburban Vancouver', *International Journal of Urban and Regional Research* 21: 75–99.

Rees, W.E., and M. Roseland. 1991. 'Sustainable Communities: Planning for the 21st Century', *Plan Canada* 31, 3: 15–26.

Reid, B. 1990. 'Suburbs in Transition: The Urbanization and Greening of Surrey', *City Magazine* 11, 4: 38–41.

———. 1991. 'Primer on the Corporate City', in K. Gerecke, ed., *The Canadian City*. Montreal: Black Rose Books.

Robinson, P.A. 1995. 'Protecting the Environment in a Rapidly Urbanizing Community', *Plan Canada* 35, 6: 22–5.

Rose, D., and P. Villeneuve. 1993. 'Work, Labour Markets and Households in Transition', in L.S. Bourne and D.F. Ley, eds, *The Changing Social Geography of Canadian Cities*. Montreal and Kingston: McGill-Queen's University Press.

Rowe, P.G. 1991. *Making a Middle Landscape*. Cambridge, Mass.: MIT Press.

Russwurm, L.H. 1975. 'Urban Fringe and Urban Shadow', in R.C. Bryfogle and R.R. Kreuger, eds, *Urban Problems*. Toronto: Holt, Rinehart and Winston of Canada.

Saalman, H. 1968. *Medieval Cities*. London: Studio Vista.

Safdie, M. 1970. *Beyond Habitat*. Cambridge, Mass.: MIT Press.

Sancton, A., and B. Montgomery. 1994. 'Municipal Government and Residential Land Development: A Comparative Study of London, Ontario, in the 1920s and 1980s', in F. Frisken, ed., *The Changing Canadian Metropolis: A Public Policy Perspective*. Toronto and Berkeley: Canadian Urban Institute and the Institute of Governmental Studies Press.

Sewell, J. 1977. 'The Suburbs', *City Magazine* 2, 6: 19–55.

———. 1984. 'Old and New City', *City Magazine* 6, 4: 11–14.

———. 1993. *The Shape of the City: Toronto Struggles with Modern Planning*. Toronto: University of Toronto Press.

Simmons, J.W. 1974. *Patterns of Residential Movement in Metropolitan Toronto*. Toronto: University of Toronto Press.

Simpson, R. 1996. 'Residential Intensification: The Wrong Planning Debate', in J. Emeneau, ed., *A Practitioner's Guide to Urban Intensification*. Toronto: Canadian Urban Institute.

Sinclair, P.R., and K. Westhues. 1974. *Village in Crisis*. Toronto: Holt, Rinehart and Winston of Canada.

Skaburskis, A., and D. Geros. 1997. 'The Changing Suburb: Burnaby, B.C. Revisited', *Plan Canada* 37, 2: 37–45.

Smith, D. 1989. 'Local Area Conservation: How One Suburban Municipality Utilizes Environmental

Planning to Conserve Its Natural Heritage', *Plan Canada* 29, 5: 39–42.

Smith, P.J. 1991a. 'Community Aspirations, Territorial Justice, and the Metropolitan Form of Edmonton and Calgary', in G.M. Robinson, ed., *A Social Geography of Canada*. Toronto: Dundurn Press.

———. 1991b. 'Coping with Mega-Mall Development: An Urban Planning Perspective on West Edmonton Mall', *Canadian Geographer* 35: 295–305.

———. 1995. 'Planning for Residential Growth Since the 1940s', in B. Hesketh and F. Swyripa, eds, *Edmonton: The Life of a City*. Edmonton: NeWest Publishers.

——— and P.E. Bayne. 1994. 'The Issue of Local Autonomy in Edmonton's Regional Plan Process: Metropolitan Planning in a Changing Political Climate', in F. Frisken, ed., *The Changing Canadian Metropolis: A Public Policy Perspective*. Toronto and Berkeley: Canadian Urban Institute and Institute of Governmental Studies Press.

——— and H.L. Diemer, 1978. 'Equity and the Annexation Process: Edmonton's Bid for the Strathcona Industrial Corridor', in Smith, ed., *Edmonton: The Emerging Metropolitan Pattern*. Victoria: University of Victoria, Western Geographical Series Vol. 15.

——— and P.W. Moore. 1993. 'Cities as a Social Responsibility: Planning and Urban Form', in L.S. Bourne and D.F. Ley, eds, *The Changing Social Geography of Canadian Cities*. Montreal and Kingston: McGill-Queen's University Press.

Tamminga, K. 1996. 'Restoring Biodiversity in the Urbanizing Region: Towards Pre-emptive Ecosystems Planning', *Plan Canada* 36, 4: 10–15.

Taylor, S.M. 1987. 'Social Change in Hamilton 1961–1981', in M.J. Dear, J.J. Drake, and L.G. Reeds, eds, *Steel City: Hamilton and Region*. Toronto: University of Toronto Press.

Timusk, C. 1976. 'Kanata: A New Community Approaches its Tenth Year', *Contact: Journal of Urban and Environmental Affairs* 8, 3: 222–32.

Tomalty, R. 1994. 'An Ecosystem Approach to Growth Management', *Environments: A Journal of Interdisciplinary Studies* 22, 3: 13–25.

———. 1996. 'Megacity Madness', *New City Magazine* 17, 3: 9–13.

———. 1997. *The Compact Metropolis: Intensification in Vancouver, Toronto and Montréal*. Toronto: ICURR Publications.

Van Nus, W. 1984. 'The Role of Suburban Government in the City-Building Process: The Case of Notre Dame de Grâces, Quebec, 1876–1910', *Urban History Review* 13: 91–103.

Vischer, J.C. 1987. 'The Changing Canadian Suburb', *Plan Canada* 27: 130–40.

Wang, S., and P.J. Smith. 1997. 'In Quest of "Forgiving" Environment: Residential Planning and Pedestrian Safety in Edmonton, Canada', *Planning Perspectives* 12: 225–50.

Warner, S.B. 1962. *Streetcar Suburbs: The Process of Growth in Boston 1870–1900*. Cambridge, Mass.: Harvard University Press.

Weaver, J.C. 1978. 'From Land Assembly to Social Maturity: The Suburban Life of Westdale (Hamilton), Ontario, 1911–1951', *Social History* 11: 411–40.

White, R. 1996. 'Designing More Sustainable Suburban Communities: Calgary's Approach', *Plan Canada* 36, 4: 16–19.

Wolfe, J.M., and J.M. Glenn. 1992. 'The Effects of Regional County Municipal Plans and Agricultural Zoning in the Region of Montréal', *Plan Canada* 32, 6: 9–13.

Wright, G. 1983. *Building the Dream: A Social History of Housing in America*. Cambridge, Mass.: MIT Press.

Wright, J.M. 1978. 'The Regional Municipality of Ottawa–Carleton: Planning Objectives, Concepts and Principal Policies', in R. Wesche and M. Kugler-Gagnon, eds, *Ottawa–Hull: Spatial Perspectives and Planning*. Ottawa: University of Ottawa Press, Department of Geography and Regional Planning Occasional Paper 4.

Wynn, G., and T. Oke, eds. 1992. *Vancouver and Its Region*. Vancouver: University of British Columbia Press.

Yip, S. 1994. 'Applying Sustainable Development Principles to Residential Community Planning', *Plan Canada* 34, 2: 31–4.

Chapter 14

The City's Countryside

Christopher R. Bryant, Philip M. Coppack, and Clare J.A. Mitchell

The countryside that has evolved around our cities over the course of the twentieth century can rightly be called the city's countryside, for it provides the stage on which several acts of city life are played out. The collection of environments comprising the city's countryside (Bryant, Russwurm, and McLellan, 1982) provides the support base for a variety of activities and functions tied into the city, including recreational activities, the production of commodities, and residential development. The city's countryside is therefore a complex environment with multiple dimensions.

The changing relationships between city and countryside reflect a complex set of processes operating at the regional scale and within the broader fabric of society. In the second half of the twentieth century, they reflect the shift from an industrial to a post-industrial society. The nature of the relationship between Canadian cities and their countrysides shares much with that of the United States, but the specific geographic forms that have resulted differ because of differences in context, particularly in terms of the political and cultural environments. The differences in form between the Canadian and Western European situations are even larger because of greater differences in context—economic, political, and cultural. An example is the greater role played by public transportation in the major metropolitan regions of Western Europe. Furthermore, the settlement structure of European countries is considerably older and more densely populated than that of North America.

The changing relationship between the city and countryside in Canada, and the resulting changing form of the settlement pattern, is manifest in changing lifestyles, land use, and demographics. Any system that undergoes change experiences a certain degree of stress, and this is as true of the city's countryside as of any other environment. These stresses are manifest in conflicts between different uses of the land and between the various groups (e.g., recreationists, new and long-time residents, farmers, and industrialists) using the surroundings of the city. When those stresses involve significant divergences between individual and collective values associated with, say, the land resource, then public intervention in the form of management and planning may be necessary.

In this chapter we explore the evolution, form, and processes underlying the structure of the city's countryside. First, we consider two generic frameworks that deal with the formation and settlement of the city's countryside in Canada in the context of post-industrial society. Second, we introduce a framework that allows us to address the issue of regional and subregional specificity in the city's countryside by focusing on the multiplicity of environments in this complex geographic zone. The heterogeneity of this geographic space has been increasingly emphasized as a new focus has emerged, that of the role of local actors and processes. Finally, we consider the implications of the changing relationships and settlement form for planning and management and how the public sector has responded to the challenges that these present.

City-Countryside Relationships

Forces and Processes of Change in Post-Industrial Society

Settlement structure in its broadest sense incorporates the built environment; the various land uses resulting from human activity (e.g., residential, industrial, commercial, agricultural, recreational); the various functions supported by both the bio-physical and the built environment (e.g., work, play, living); and the interactions that tie the different elements together into some sort of functioning system. Settlement structures evolve as the result of a multitude of decisions taken by individuals, households, firms, agencies, and governments at all levels. These decisions reflect sets of values, and changes in these values, that are influenced by forces operating and interacting at a number of levels. While factors influencing decisions at, say, the individual household or firm level are significant, the total set of decisions being made cannot be understood without first understanding the broader context in which they occur (Bryant, 1995).

The most significant change in the broader context is the transition from an industrial to a post-industrial society that was recognized during the mid-twentieth century (Bell, 1973). Much has been written about this transition; generally it has been characterized by the growth and development of a variety of service sectors, the growing importance of knowledge as capital, the increasing openness in the economic system, huge advances in communications technology, and the growth of a whole host of new consumer 'needs' (Bryant, 1988; Bryant and Johnston, 1992).

How have these broad changes been reflected in the evolving settlement system in the city's countryside? Human activities function within 'systems of exchange' involving, for example, the transfer of ideas, commodities, and information. These systems operate at, and across, a variety of different geographic scale levels. The changes have worked their way through the various systems of exchange and have modified their boundaries. One of the key

results has been the development of an extended urban life-space around cities and the development of the city's countryside.

A whole range of geographic scales exist, from the macro (international and national) through the meso (e.g., urban field, regional city) to the micro (e.g., firm, individual). Socio-economic systems function through various forms of interaction or various systems of exchange. Interaction occurs between units that reside at the same geographic scale (e.g., between households or between firms within the same broad region) and between 'units' at different scales of geographic analysis. Thus, an individual firm can be tied into both a national system and an international system of production and consumption. Some systems of exchange can be very localized, such as the production of farm produce for sale in pick-your-own outlets around Toronto and Montreal, where the market is predominantly made of local urban and exurban residents (Bryant and Marois, 1998). Other systems of exchange are more regional, such as the commuting flows that tie residence in the city's countryside to the work environment in the urban core. Still others are tied into national and international systems of exchange (e.g., wheat production around Regina and Saskatoon in Saskatchewan).

The exchanges or interactions that link decision-making units within or between different geographic scales of analysis include flows of people (e.g., commuting patterns), goods (e.g., farm produce), information, money, capital, and ideas. These exchanges can be influenced by changing values, technologies, and institutions. Although the broad changes can be seen as 'megatrends' (Naisbitt, 1982), the broad trends characterizing the transformation of society, it is important to realize that their influence is transmitted both upward and downward through the various systems of exchange to produce the changing settlement structure we observe in the city's countryside.

The broad trends associated with the evolution of post-industrial society have been summarized elsewhere in terms of: (1) the development of 'new needs' in society; (2) the changing nature of communication technology; and (3) the changing nature of production technology (Bryant, 1988; Bryant and Johnston, 1992). All of these trends can be linked to various changes that have occurred, and continue to occur, in the settlement structure of the city's countryside.

New needs are related to increasing levels of disposable household income, changing personal health-care values, greater values placed on education, and changing values regarding lifestyles and quality of life. Not all people have adopted or developed these values to the same extent, of course, and we have to recognize the variety of combinations of values and needs held by different individuals and groups in society (Walker, 1987).

Of all the changing values to emerge during the post-industrial period, those influencing lifestyle and quality of life have had the greatest impact on the city's countryside. According to Harvey (1990), contemporary societies value the past, a sense of place, consumption of landscape, and roots. These values are tied to the emergence of 'postmodernism', a general philosophy and lifestyle inseparably related to globalization of the post-industrial economy. As Harvey (1990, 427) writes:

The more global interrelations become ... and the more spatial barriers disintegrate, so more rather than less of the world's population clings to place and neighbourhood or to nation, region, ethnic groupings, or religious belief as specific marks of identity. Such a quest for visible and tangible marks of identity is readily understandable in the midst of fierce time-space compression. There is still an insistent urge to look for roots in a world where image streams accelerate and become more and more placeless.

In the city's countryside, we can easily observe the effects of these values. For example, people seeking country living can be observed in exurban residential development, both in its scattered form and in the smaller settlement nodes. The development of outdoor recreational opportunities has grown remarkably over the past few years. Parks, go-

kart tracks, horse-riding establishments, ski trails, ski slopes, and other recreational opportunities, such as theme parks (e.g., Canada's Wonderland, north of Toronto), are now commonplace in the city's countryside. Furthermore, frequent trips to the countryside for the 'rural' experience of shopping in a small town are embedded in the commuting field of a major city (Bunce, 1981; Coppack, 1988a; Mitchell, 1998). The development of pick-your-own farm produce outlets, which are common around Metropolitan Toronto (Johnston and Bryant, 1987) and increasingly around Montreal (Bryant and Marois, 1998), also reflects the search for new experiences by city-based consumers.

Changes in communications technology have been fundamental to the development of the settlement system in the city's countryside (Bryant and Lemire, 1998). The development of truck transportation and the supporting public investment in highway infrastructure in Canada have been critical to the dispersal of industrial and commercial activities to suburban locations and smaller towns and cities found in the city's countryside of the larger metropolitan centres (on employment dispersion, see Chapter 15, and on retail dispersion, Chapter 17). But the development and rapid diffusion of the private automobile really characterized the scattered residential development that took hold in the city's countryside in the 1950s and 1960s. This settlement form differs considerably from that found around many Western European cities, where public transportation played a much more significant role in the early stages of the spread of urban influences into the countryside. The private automobile continues to play a role in the development of the city's countryside in Canada, but public transportation has also become a factor in some metropolitan regions (e.g., the GO Transit system centred on Toronto and the metropolitan subway system in Montreal that has facilitated the growth of such suburban centres as Longueuil, where the South Shore terminal is located, and St-Bruno and Mont-St-Hilaire, because of their highway links to Longueuil).

Improvements in goods transportation systems have significantly altered the boundaries of the systems of exchange in which many of the economic activities in the city's countryside function. For example, agricultural activities in the city's countryside can be influenced as much by competition from producing regions on the other side of the world as by pressures from a nearby expanding urban centre.

These transportation technologies have their roots in technologies that developed in industrial society. Other communications technologies, namely telecommunications, fax, e-mail, and the Internet—in fact, all the artefacts of our 'information society'—have been more closely associated with the development of post-industrial society. These new and rapidly evolving forms of communication have radically altered the lifestyles and relationships between residence and workplace for some people. It is not uncommon for some executives whose workplace is in downtown Toronto to spend two days each week working at home, some 100 kilometres from the office, another one or two days in the office, and the rest of the week travelling. However, this type of work pattern has not yet been adopted in sufficient proportions to make a noticeable dent in rush-hour traffic congestion for people working in Vancouver, Toronto, or Montreal—people who hold twentieth-century attitudes regarding employee-employer-workplace relationships. (Chapter 8 discusses further the impact of new communications technologies on urban residents.)

Finally, although many of the *changes in production technology* also have their roots in the technological changes of industrial society, there has been an increasing emphasis placed on knowledge as capital in these developments. In particular, research and development plays an increasingly important role. At one end of the spectrum, some technological changes simply continue patterns of substitution of capital for labour (e.g., farm mechanization). These patterns go back to the nineteenth century and can still be seen operating in many agricultural areas in the city's countryside in Canada. Other industrial technologies, such as assembly-line production, helped fuel the development of industrial production in the peripheries of urban centres because they

needed large areas of land at relatively cheap rates. At the other end of the spectrum, the advanced technology of the microchip and microprocessor have placed more and more emphasis on the need for a professional and specialized workforce with all the associated values that a highly educated workforce demands. Now, the industrial park is giving way to the 'prestige business park'. Small towns in the city's countryside can extol the virtues of a high 'quality of life' for the professional personnel of the newer industries, while offering all the advantages of proximity to the facilities and amenities of a major urban centre. (Some of these factors are discussed in Chapter 12 and noted as contributing to residential revitalization in the inner city.)

Settlement Organization in the City's Countryside

Since at least the 1920s, the concept of extended fields of urban influence over rural areas has been a central focus in urban and rural-urban fringe research. Several concepts have been developed to describe and explain these extended fields of interaction. Each concept reflects the central idea of a *nodal city region* and a rural periphery woven into a 'city-region' tapestry (Dickinson, 1947) or what has been called a *meso-scale* urban form (Preston, 1977) (Figure 14.1).

Meso-scale urban forms centred on one dominant urban node are appropriately referred to as regional cities; however, urban meso-forms can take on different spatial configurations, all of which involve the idea of the nodal region. These meso-scale urban structures, with their central cities and surrounding countrysides, together form one layer in a series of nested nodal regions that operate at different geographic scales (Figure 14.1). The hierarchy of nodal regions starts inside the city with activity nodes connected by flows (e.g., the central business district and its ties with suburban areas through commuting flows) and ranges up through the regional city scale comprised of one city core and its countryside to the urban field as a collec-

Figure 14.1   **Hierarchy of Nodal Regions**

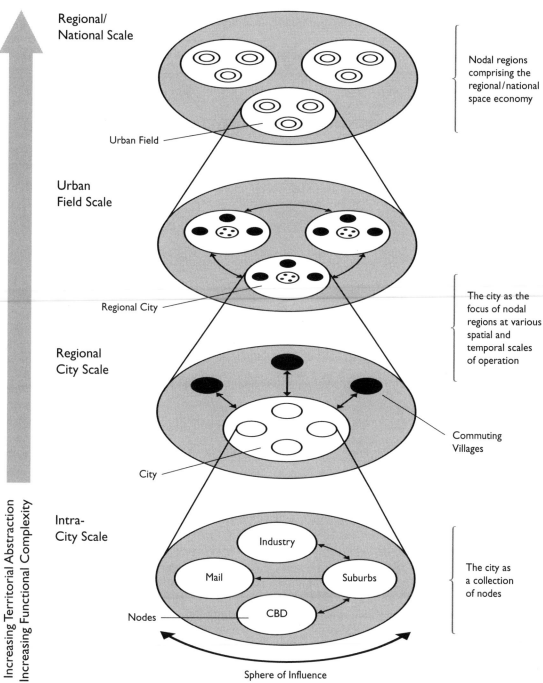

Regional/
National Scale

Urban Field

Urban
Field Scale

Regional City

Regional
City Scale

City

Intra-
City Scale

Nodes

Industry

Mail

Suburbs

CBD

Sphere of Influence

Nodal regions
comprising the
regional/national
space economy

The city as the
focus of nodal
regions at various
spatial and
temporal scales
of operation

Commuting
Villages

The city as
a collection
of nodes

Increasing Territorial Abstraction
Increasing Functional Complexity

tion of regional cities. Finally, the whole national space economy can be seen as a collection of urban fields that may or may not (as in Canada's case) blanket the space economy.

In general, most concepts of the city's country-side are built on the idea of the functional region, the area over which a given core influences its immediate environs. For example, the labour—or commuter—shed (the area from which a city draws it labour pool) spreads far beyond the political boundary of the City of Toronto or even the GTA (Greater Toronto area) (Coppack and Robins, 1987; Ricour-Singh, 1979). In areas such as Ontario's 'Golden Horseshoe' at the western end of Lake Ontario, the density of cities is such that a series of overlapping functional regions exists, leading to what has been termed 'megalopolitan' development (Gottman, 1961).[1]

In the decades following World War II, two phenomena have contributed to the development of the city's countryside. First, up to the mid-1960s, the process of metropolitanism accelerated, with suburban development spreading rapidly in the US and at a somewhat slower pace in Canada. Second, from the mid-1960s to the present, rural areas have seen an influx of city dwellers, either as permanent residents and cottagers, or as visitors to small communities within approximately two hours of the respective urban centres. This 'extra-metropolitan' development has generated several conceptual models, among them that of the dispersed city (Burton, 1959; Dahms, 1984; Hart, 1975), the regional city (Gertler, 1972; Russwurm, 1976, 1977), and the urban field (Coppack, Russwurm, and Bryant, 1988; Friedmann, 1973; Friedmann and Miller, 1965; Hodge, 1967, 1972). The idea of the city-centred functional region based on shopping and work interaction was also the basis of the government of Ontario's planning and development frameworks of the late 1960s and early 1970s, such as the *Design for Development* strategy and the *Toronto-Centred Region* concept (Ontario, 1966, 1970, 1974). It has also been central in the ongoing debates concerning the organization of the Greater Montreal Region (Trépanier, 1998).

The evolution of the city's countryside is the result of powerful technological, social, economic, and demographic forces, especially those related to population redistribution into rural areas. The outcomes of these forces can be conceptualized into a four-stage historical model that, while concentrating on population redistribution, has at its heart all of the factors mentioned above (Bryant, Russwurm, and McLellan, 1982; Bryant and Lemire, 1998; Coppack and Preston, 1988). This historical and descriptive model (Figure 14.2) shows how population and economic activities were first polarized and then decentralized as technological, economic, cultural, and demographic forces changed in step with the evolution of post-industrial society.

In the first stage (1), a process of polarization proceeded apace with both population and economic activity focusing on larger urban nodes. This was the result of a complex set of forces revolving around the mechanization of agriculture and the associated displacement of agricultural labour from rural areas, and of the willing search for the 'bright lights' of the city by rural people looking to better their lives by leaving low-paying farm jobs for higher-paying industrial and urban jobs. This movement was accentuated by the development of industrial agglomeration economies in the cities. The development of a transportation and, eventually, communications network capable of moving people and goods easily and cheaply within city and country alike reinforced this polarization pattern and allowed wider use of the city by adjacent rural populations.

The influx of people to the city, somewhat paradoxically, set the stage for the eventual development of the city's countryside. As people moved into the city, suburban development occurred, leading to residential enclaves and commercial and industrial nodes around the city periphery. These, in turn, acted as stepping-stones to development further afield (for example, workers who live an hour's drive into the countryside and are employed in industrial or office developments in the City of Toronto fringe or in adjacent municipalities such as Markham, Vaughan,

Figure 14.2 **Stages of Growth of the Regional City**

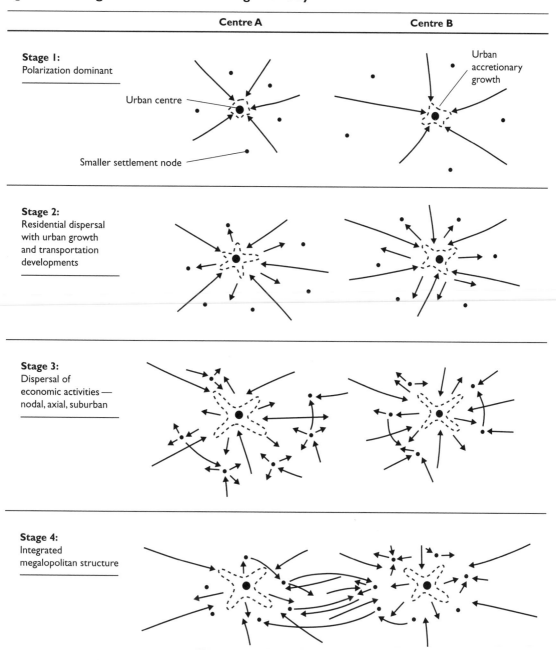

Source: Bryant, Russwurm, and McLellan (1982).

and Mississauga). While the physical or formal edge of the city may have been well defined, usually by the built-up area and political boundary, the actual influence of the city spread much further afield. The commercial activities of the suburbs provided employment and retailing opportunities to an increasingly mobile rural population close to the city. The resulting patterns of commuting and shopping tied the rural surroundings ever closer to the city cores. This situation is typified by the second stage (2) of the model and represents the early stages of regional city development.

Eventually, as the settlement form matured in the third stage (3), industrial and residential nodes developed further out into the countryside proper and, where urban areas of influence overlap, the development of an integrated megalopolitan structure occurred (the fourth stage on Figure 14.2). Ontario's 'Golden Horseshoe' area since the 1980s was clearly in the transitional phase between stages three and four. Here, clear structural distinctions between one urban area and another, or between urban and rural areas, are increasingly difficult to discern. While political boundaries might proclaim spatial divisions, patterns of economic, social, and population interaction tell a much different story. However, there are still powerful centralizing forces at work, illustrated by the continued dominance of the built-up area centred on Toronto in relation to employment pull and the heavy volumes of road traffic on such key arteries as Highways 401, 400, 403, and 407. Such continued centralizing pressures are fuelled by the development industry and local planning policies and by the continued substantial public investment in highways and the public transportation system. Together, these factors slow down the achievement of a truly decentralized multinodal urban system.[2]

It is not surprising that stages three and four have not developed to their fullest extent around isolated or relatively small urban centres such as Regina, Saskatoon, or St John's. The most complex and highly developed cities' countrysides are found in those regions that have experienced continuing trends of meso-scale polarization in the space economy and demographic concentration within the broad functional regions centred on Toronto, Montreal, and Vancouver.

The forces underlying this model and its concomitant settlement form are complex; furthermore, they may also be historically specific to a large extent. For example, the decentralizing patterns depended on the technological innovations of the automobile and its supporting infrastructure. Concentration of industry, likewise, had to wait for an improved accessibility to sources of energy, as well as changes in transportation and production technologies.

In recent years, the relationship between the concentrated built-up urban areas and their rural peripheries has become more intimate. Changing demographic and economic circumstances have given us an older, more affluent population. Rapid advances in communications and transportation technology (see Chapter 8) have led to increased levels of accessibility, while new needs and demands have prompted the pursuit of new and different lifestyles oriented towards the consumption and use of rural resources (Cloke, 1983; Moss, 1978). Residential enclaves have sprung up on the peripheries of Canada's cities—commuter refuge from the stress of earning a living in the city. Old mills turn into 'Olde Mills' as grist mills are transformed into gift shops catering to well-heeled city dwellers seeking to purchase nostalgia and experience rural ambience for a day.

The process of economic reorientation in small towns and rural areas in the city's countryside has both positive and negative ramifications. Traditional values are eroded, but often replaced with new and equally worthwhile ones (Bryant, 1995; Gilg, 1985; Mathieson and Wall, 1983; Westhues and Sinclair, 1974). Economic activities change as country stores give way to specialized tourist retailing, and, while we may mourn their passing, their transformation has given a new lease on life to many small towns (Dahms, 1984, 1985, 1988). Ironically, the search for historical character and rural atmosphere by newcomers has guaranteed the continued existence and preservation of many towns in the city's countryside.

Form of the City's Countryside

Two of the most useful constructs for visualizing the form of the city's countryside are the regional city and the urban field. The urban field can be seen as a wider-reaching and more complex behavioural space comprised of three basic dimensions (Figure 14.3). First, the settlement form itself is comprised of a multi-centric arrangement of high-density urban clusters of all sizes, centred on a core city and surrounded by open space. Second, a twofold set of relationships exists between the nodes based on: (1) physical flows of goods, services, and people—such as shopping, recreation, work trips; and (2) non-physical flows, such as electronic money transfers, information, and ideas (which may also be seen as commodities, but transfer mores, values, and attitudes between urban and rural environments). In addition, there are the periodicities over which the interactions occur. These revolve around the daily

system (such as goods delivery and commuting), the weekend/weekly system (such as recreational day trips, overnight travel, and cottaging), and the seasonal system of flows that permeate the other two periodicities and define the outer limits of the field (Coppack, 1988b).

The regional city includes the concentrated built-up core and commuting zone of the urban field. There is some utility in considering the rural-urban fringe portion of the regional city as a series of land-use zones with specific characteristics (the inner fringe, outer fringe, urban shadow, and rural hinterland). However, not all regional cities exhibit all these zones and not all zones are characterized by all attributes, nor are all zones easy to discern.

The first two zones, the inner and outer fringes, comprise the rural-urban or simply urban fringe, and represent those areas close to the city (in terms of travel time and accessibility) in the most direct state of transition. These areas are exemplified by land uses such as idled farmland that will become residential or industrial subdivisions, cemeteries, scrapyards, and some 'nuisance' activities such

Figure 14.3   **The Form of the Urban Field and Regional City**

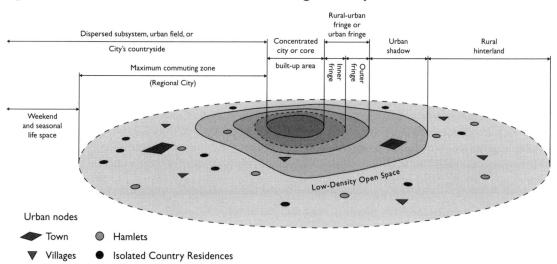

Source: Bryant, Russwurm, and McLellan (1982).

as abattoirs and stockyards that are incompatible with most urban land uses (Russwurm, 1977). All these land uses are also attracted by the relatively cheaper land costs and availability of space. Yet, while there are clearly discernible land uses—uses, for example, that would be easily seen on an aerial photograph—there are also more subtle and less discernible characteristics to the urban fringe. Ownership of land is frequently in the hands of farmers. Some are waiting for their land to fetch urban prices before selling; others continue to farm, resisting, coping with, or adapting to the pressures in the urban fringe.

Further out, in the urban shadow, urban influence is much more subtle and less visible, but nonetheless real. Typical of this shadow area are scattered country residential enclaves—single homes or country estates adjacent to small towns. These residents may commute an hour or more to the central urban node for employment, recreation, medical services, and the like. Beyond this shadow zone is the rural hinterland, where, again, urban influence is present but subtle, and the regional city proper merges into the urban field. Here, small rural communities play host to thousands of urban visitors seeking rural ambience on summer weekends. These communities may even find themselves host to large manufacturing establishments that traditionally were bound to large urban centres. The decisions by Honda, Suzuki, and Stelco to locate in small Ontario communities (Alliston, Ingersoll, and Nanticoke respectively) are examples. These plants are removed from, but easily accessible to, the inputs and markets of the larger urban centres.

Beyond and overlapping the rural hinterland of the regional city lies a zone of seasonal use. Here the metropolitan influence is seen in cottage communities, ski resorts, and other recreational environments. Many of these cottage areas are fast turning into retirement enclaves as people choose to move from city to periphery.

The zonal characterization is, of course, a generalization that reflects the meso-scale forces of urban development pressures and broad accessibility patterns. However, within these broad zones there is considerable heterogeneity, reflecting the presence of significant local processes of community differentiation (Bryant, 1995).

The Environments of the City's Countryside

The model of the city's countryside presented below deals with how it functions and its observable features. The conceptual model of the environments in the city's countryside is comprised of nine environments (Figure 14.4). These environments can be organized into three distinct dimensions 'wired' together by systems of exchange. The first major dimension, the physical dimension, contains two environments—the non-built environment (which includes 'natural' open space and managed open space) and the built environment. This dimension represents the *form* of the city's countryside. Many of the demands of the evolving regional city and urban field are directed at the land base in this physical environment. This is where most of the concerns about the impacts and stress created by the evolving settlement system have been expressed.

The second major dimension, the structural system, is comprised of three human environments—the living, working, and play environments. These are superimposed on the physical dimension. Together, the environments of the structural dimension give rise to the *functions* in the city's countryside. The living environment involves a range of actors, including temporary, overnight inn-guests, cottagers, and permanent long-term or new residents. They live in spatially diverse places ranging from scattered country homes, cottages, and guesthouses to homes in the urban core itself. The play environment describes the leisure needs and demands of the residents, tourists, and recreationists, who seek rural places as one element in their recreational and leisure behaviour-space. The work environment is structured by the traditional agriculture/extraction, manufacturing, and services/retail sectors, each influenced by a heterogeneous set of considerations that give rise to a complex, integrated pattern of economic activity and exchanges.

Figure 14.4   **A Multidimensional Framework for the City's Countryside**

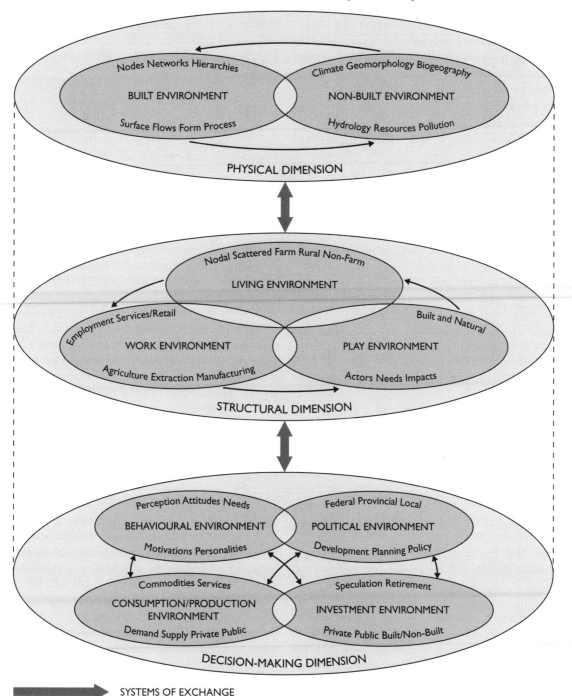

The third major dimension is the decision-making dimension, comprised of four environments —consumption/production, investment, political, and behavioural. The investment environment is one of the cornerstones of the work environment because it involves allocation of the factors of production—land, labour, and capital. In the city's countryside, particular attention is paid to the land base—the demand for land and the various functions it supports are the principal manifestations of the changing values that underlie the evolving form of the regional city. The political and behavioural environments comprise the control subsystem that guides and constrains function and hence form. The political environment is most easily thought of as the formal control system and includes federal, provincial, and municipal authorities. All actions and behaviour in the city's countryside can be thought of as passing through the filter of planning and development policy in the formal control environment, although only a subset of all possible actions is effectively open to scrutiny. Real development is the result of a multitude of actors—private and public, individual, corporate—and is influenced by informal processes as much as by formal processes (Bryant, 1995).

The behavioural environment thus represents what might be called informal control. How people live reflects their perceptions of their environments, demands, needs, and means, as well as their motivations, personalities, and demographic, social, and cultural attributes and those of the social system in which they function. The behavioural environment is truly a creation of its resident groups and individuals. Thus, in short, the decision-making environments, made up of countless decisions taken at various scales and levels, provide the *process* that drives the city's countryside.

At one level, all of these environments are superimposed on each other and overlap, and so give rise to a complex mosaic of land uses, functions, and values. But at another level, they are bound together by flows of ideas, commodities, and people at different scales in time and space to form a dynamic, integrated, functioning whole. Using some of the concepts outlined above, we shall now explore some selected attributes of the city's countryside in Canada. We shall concentrate on three of the more important attributes: population structure and change, the characteristics of urbanites in the city's countryside, and small settlements.

Empirical Attributes of the City's Countryside

Population Structure and Change

The most evident manifestation of the evolution of the city's countryside is seen in population structure and change. The population of the city's countryside can be categorized into several components to represent the main elements of the regional city (Tables 14.1 and 14.2). The *concentrated population* refers to the main concentration of the built-up area; the *dispersed population* (or permanent countryside population) refers to the city's countryside. This dispersed or countryside population can be further divided into farm and non-farm; the non-farm group can again be divided into *dispersed or rural non-farm scattered* and *dispersed non-farm nodal* settlements (dispersed nodal settlements are settlements with populations from 50 to 10,000). With this in mind, population data are discussed below for Canada's regional cities by province, for rural non-farm population change for the period 1941 to 1981, a period of rapid urban expansion and growth.

The absolute numbers, relative shares, and proportional change components for 52 regional cities across Canada are summarized in Tables 14.1 and 14.2 (Russwurm, Coppack, and Bryant, 1988).[3] The 52 regional cities in Canada have accounted for an increasing proportion of the nation's population since 1941 (Table 14.1); the ratio of their 1981 to 1941 population was 2.46 compared to the national population ratio for 1981 to 1941 of 2.11. Other interesting trends occurred within the regional cities where: (1) the concentrated urban populations levelled off at about 80 per cent of total regional city population by the end of the period represented (Table 14.1); (2) the rural non-farm scattered

Table 14.1   **Regional City Populations and Percentage of Total Population, 1941, 1961, and 1981**

		Atlantic[a]	Quebec	Ontario	Prairies	BC	Canada[a]
Regional City Population (000s)	1941	514	2,436	3,112	803	604	7,469
(% of total population)		(45.5)	(73.1)	(82.2)	(33.2)	(73.8)	(65.5)
	1961	751	4,134	5,344	1,529	1,234	12,992
		(50.7)	(78.6)	(85.7)	(48.1)	(75.8)	(73.0)
	1981	986	5,128	7,668	2,473	2,069	18,324
		(44.1)	(79.6)	(88.9)	(58.4)	(75.4)	(75.5)
Regional city population by component (%)							
1. Concentrated	1941	61.3	75.5	71.4	76.5	79.8	73.2
	1961	66.2	81.9	77.2	87.1	81.1	79.6
	1981	61.0	80.2	78.6	85.9	80.9	79.5
2. Dispersed population							
2.1 Dispersed non-farm nodal	1941	17.1	9.0	9.3	4.4	5.1	8.8
	1961	20.9	8.3	9.3	4.5	5.1	8.6
	1981	31.3	9.5	10.5	7.4	6.6	10.4
2.2 Rural non-farm scattered	1941	2.5	1.9	4.7	1.9	6.6	3.5
	1961	5.2	3.3	6.8	1.9	12.2	5.5
	1981	6.0	8.2	8.3	4.9	13.2	7.8
2.3 Farm	1941	19.0	13.5	14.7	17.2	8.4	14.3
	1961	7.7	6.5	6.7	6.5	3.9	6.4
	1981	1.6	2.1	2.6	2.5	1.7	2.3

[a]Newfoundland population excluded in 1941 and 1961. Newfoundland joined Canada in 1949; its 1961 population was 415,074.
Source: Adapted from Russwurm, Coppack, and Bryant (1988: Table 7.3, 112).

population component of the dispersed part of the regional cities increased absolutely by over five times (a population increase of 163.7 per cent between 1941 and 1961, and of 107.1 per cent between 1961 and 1981 [Table 14.2]), while farm population declined to two-fifths of its 1941 value (Table 14.2); and (3) the dispersed non-farm nodal population growth rate, while slowing after 1961 (Table 14.2), nonetheless maintained a steady increase in its share of total regional-city population (Table 14.1). By 1981, the city's countryside had about four exurbanite (or rural non-farm scat-

tered) people for every farm person. In the aggregate, for the 52 regional cities in 1981, out of every 100 people, 80 lived in the concentrated category, 10 in dispersed towns and villages, eight in scattered non-farm locations, and two on farms (Table 14.1). But there were also pronounced provincial differences, reflecting both the degree to which post-industrial and urbanization forces have affected regional economies and the different densities of settlement.

Another perspective is offered by considering the countryside surrounding two CMAs, Toronto

Table 14.2   **Population Change Rates (per cent), Canada and Provinces, 1941–1981**

		Atlantic[a]	Quebec	Ontario	Prairies	BC	Canada[a]
Region							
	1941–61	31.2	57.9	64.6	31.3	99.1	54.8
	1961–81	17.8	22.4	38.3	33.1	68.4	33.7
Regional Cities (Total)							
	1941–61	46.1	69.7	71.7	90.4	104.3	76.0
	1961–81	8.8	24.0	43.5	61.7	67.7	39.8
1. Concentrated							
	1941–61	57.8	84.1	85.6	116.9	107.7	90.1
	1961–81	6.9	21.6	46.1	59.5	67.4	40.4
2. Dispersed population							
	1941–61	27.6	25.4	37.0	4.2	91.0	32.8
	1961–81	51.2	35.1	34.6	77.2	69.1	42.1
2.1 Dispersed non-farm nodal							
	1941–61	78.4	55.7	72.0	97.1	103.2	77.4
	1961–81	50.7	41.9	62.0	165.2	117.5	63.0
2.2 Rural non-farm scattered							
	1941–61	300.0	189.4	151.7	81.3	205.0	163.7
	1961–81	51.3	207.4	74.8	262.0	81.1	107.1
2.3 Farm							
	1941–61	−40.8	−18.2	−21.4	−28.3	−5.9	−45.2
	1961–81	−72.4	−60.4	−44.3	−38.4	−25.0	−49.6

[a]Newfoundland and St. John's were excluded for 1941 to 1961 calculations; Newfoundland joined Canada in 1949.
Source: Russwurm, Coppack, and Bryant (1988: Table 7.2, 111).

and Saskatoon. These two CMAs represent extremes in the Canadian urban system. Toronto is located in the industrial heartland in Ontario and is the largest city in Canada. Saskatoon, located in the agricultural hinterland of the country, is much smaller but is also one of the most rapidly growing cities in Canada. Despite differences in urban rank, the patterns of population structure are very similar, though at different scales and intensity. Within 100 kilometres of the City of Toronto, by 1981 virtually no truly rural areas—where the economy is domi-

nated by farming—could be found (Russwurm, Coppack, and Bryant, 1988). While the trend towards declining farm populations and increasing rural non-farm population is also observable around Saskatoon, the rural non-farm population has been much more restricted spatially, reflecting the area's overall rural nature, the small size of the concentrated city, and land banking policies that have been in effect since the 1930s.

As a final example, we consider a local municipality from the Kitchener-Waterloo area. In the regional city of Kitchener–Waterloo the percentage of the population classified as 'rural non-farm' in one of its constituent townships (Wilmot) more than doubled between 1951 and 1981 (from 28.1 to 52.7 per cent) (Thomson and Mitchell, 1996). A recent survey of the township's residents further revealed that 60 per cent had moved from the urban core of the regional city to the rural countryside. While many factors prompted this relocation, the aspiration to live in a 'rural environment' was the most important response offered by more than 80 per cent of the sample. This finding, along with conclusions drawn in other studies (Beesley and Walker, 1990; Bourne, 1995; Coppack, 1988a; Dahms, 1984; Russwurm and Bryant, 1984), reaffirms that the appeal of the countryside is a driving force promoting the migration of urban residents into the city's countryside. Certainly from a population perspective, this demonstrates once again that the countryside is most definitely the city's countryside.

Characteristics of Urbanites and Small Settlements in the City's Countryside

Since population change tells much about the dynamics that drive regional city development, it is instructive to investigate the attributes of the people involved in this settlement evolution. Several studies have investigated the characteristics of exurbanites. In a study of the Guelph, Stratford, and Kitchener–Waterloo regional cities in Ontario, Beesley (1988), for example, analysed attributes of exurbanites using four major criteria: the specific regional city to which they belonged; their distance from the regional city's urbanized core; the settlement type in which they resided; and whether the respondents were of urban or rural origin. A summary of key results is given in the form of attribute profiles in Table 14.3.

Others also have used the origin of residents to classify people living in the city's countryside. Expanding on the work of Menzies (1994), Thomson and Mitchell (1998) suggest that the countryside is home to three groups of people, differentiated

according to their residential history: 'ruralites', with deep roots in the area; 'newcomers', transplanted city dwellers who maintain their primary contacts with the urban core; and 'homecomers', former city dwellers who may be new to a particular fringe area but whose roots are rural.

The presence of these three groups has been documented in Alberta (Momsen 1984; Red Deer Planning Commission, 1975) and, more recently, in southern Ontario. A survey of 100 households within the regional city of Kitchener–Waterloo revealed that the majority of rural residents (60 per cent) had relocated from an urban centre. Of these, nearly three-quarters had some former rural living experience and thus were classified as 'homecomers', with a much smaller percentage (30 per cent) designated as 'newcomers'. Research also revealed significant variations in the demographic characteristics of these groups and their activity patterns. As Thomson and Mitchell (1998: 197) concluded:

With a strictly urban background, newcomers are more strongly linked to the core of the regional city for their social and economic needs than they are to the fringe area in which they live. In contrast, those with a purely rural background are more connected to their immediate neighbours and more likely to patronize local businesses than newcomers without any previous rural experience. Acting as a bridge between the two is a group of residents who have taken on some of the activity patterns of rural residents within the field. While some retain employment ties to the core, others have turned their attention to communities within the countryside for their shopping, employment or social needs.

For visitors to the city's countryside, the tendency is to seek characteristics associated with what Bunce (1994: 34) has called the 'countryside ideal', 'a complex mix of myth and reality, encompassing at one end of the spectrum profound philosophical questions about modern civilisation and at the

Table 14.3   **Characteristics of Urbanites in the City's Countryside: Selected Attributes**

Spatial Criteria and Subgroups	Characteristics
Regional City	
Guelph Regional City	– higher education – newer, higher-value homes – urban background – perceive community as changing, unsafe, and with noisy roads – satisfied with local medical services and facilities – rate Guelph moderately high as place to live – journey to cities to shop and visit
Kitchener CMA Regional City	– perceive local community as attractive, safe, with quiet roads and privacy – satisfied with local fire protection – optimistic about the future of their local community – journey to cities to shop and visit
Stratford Regional City	– married – employed – older homes – perceive local community as unattractive, unchanging, and not private – rate Stratford and Metropolitan Toronto relatively high as place to live – satisfied with local taxes
Distance	
Near (<20 km)	– upper household income group – single-detached, custom-built, larger homes, large lot and home and property in upper-value category – urban background – strong community attachment – perceive local community as happy, well-kept, attractive, natural, a very good place to live with a lot of privacy, rich and very satisfactory – satisfied with local community as a place to live, the local goods and services, and police protection services – evaluate the local community now, past, and future, and the Kitchener CMA urban area good as a place to live – journey to cities to work, shop, and visit
Intermediate (20–40km)	– newer homes – satisfied with local taxes and the services received for local taxes – evaluate local community now and past moderately high
Far (>40 km)	– older homes – perceive local community relatively negatively – satisfied with local welfare, garbage disposal, and recreation services – rate Guelph and Kitchener moderately high

Table 14.3   **(continued)**

Settlement Type	
Scattered (compared to nodal)	– young and employed, upper personal and/or household income group
	– newer, custom-built, single-detached homes, on larger lot, in upper-value category
	– recent urban background
	– perceive local community as rural, young, well-kept, attractive, natural, private, agricultural, wealthy, and very satisfactory but far from conveniences and with heavy traffic on main roads
	– generally less satisfied with local government and services
	– rate local community of the past and Metropolitan Toronto relatively high
	– journey to cities to work, shop, and visit
Rural-Urban Dichotomy	
Urban (compared to rural)	– higher education
	– upper personal and/or household income group
	– newer homes, larger lots, upper-value category
	– recent urban background
	– improved quality of life
	– perceive local community as happy, attractive, a very good place to live, wealthy, and very satisfactory
	– not particularly satisfied with local fire protection, garbage disposal, or road maintenance
	– rate local community and Guelph high
	– journey to cities to work, shop, and visit

Source: (Beesley, 1988: 138–9).

other, simple escapism'. In North America, Bunce suggests, the farm, and its associated agrarian ideology, and the town, with its associated economic and social heritage, rank high as a desirable way of life for the urban resident. While this desire may prompt some to relocate to the rural fringe, others satisfy their quest to experience the 'romantic sensibility' (Park and Coppack, 1994: 163) of the past by taking periodic jaunts into the countryside.

Several recent surveys of visitors to small communities within the Toronto area have demonstrated that an important motivation for patronizing these small towns was to experience the 'atmosphere' of the 'rural' environment offered there. For example, in separate surveys of Elora and Stratford, Ontario, visitors tended to rank scenery, country atmosphere, historical character, and shops and restaurants as strong attractions for their visit (Coppack, 1988a; Mitchell, 1988).

The growing number of visitors to picturesque and historic towns has provided a large part of the necessary market threshold for both the re-emergence of ubiquitous economic functions (Coppack, 1985) and the emergence of specialized, high-order amenity functions. These are goods and services that frequently reflect local tradition and heritage (e.g., pottery, home-grown produce, woodcarvings) and whose ability to attract visitors is attributed to their location within an appealing 'amenity environment'. Park and Coppack (1994: 164) define this as 'the attraction invested in landscape, place and locality, premised on characteristics perceived as pleasant, particularly those characteristics of an intangible nature which serve psychological rather than physical needs.' What the consumer purchases, therefore, is not simply a quilt, for example, but the knowledge that the quilt, which itself reflects local heritage, was purchased in a pleasing environment reminiscent of a bygone era.

Entrepreneurs in many parts of Canada have capitalized on society's desire to experience the past. In southern Ontario, for example, Dahms (1991a, 1991b) and Mitchell (1993, 1998) have documented the evolution of several communities whose development has occurred around the sale and marketing of heritage and tradition. In the community of St Jacobs, a local entrepreneur and his development company have transformed the village into a thriving tourist destination. The community is located approximately two hours west of Toronto, and within the regional city of Kitchener–Waterloo. It is home to more than 100 businesses providing a variety of specialized goods and services, many of which are produced on site (e.g., ornamental ironwork, quilts, and stained glass). More than one million people visit the community annually and contribute between $18 million and $20 million to the local economy (Mitchell, 1998).

Investment in the 'commodification' of heritage can reap significant financial benefits for local entrepreneurs. The presence of tourists within a community, however, may have a significant impact on the quality of life for local residents (Dahms, 1991b; Doxey, 1975; Mitchell, 1998). Mitchell describes this impact in a five-stage model of 'creative destruction'. The model predicts that the creation of the new landscape of commodified tradition ultimately will result in destruction of the old, idyllic rural landscape upon which development initially was based. The process of creative destruction is at work in the village of St Jacobs. Here resident attitudes towards tourism have deteriorated over the past three decades as visitor num-

bers have escalated. While the extent of capital investment in St Jacobs is atypical, the study does point to some of the disbenefits associated with development of the regional city.

The search for the countryside ideal and the associated resurgence of retail functions in places like St Jacobs is related to many of the ideas contained within the conceptual models presented earlier in the chapter (Figure 14.4)—for example, the existence of complex interactions involving people, money, goods, and ideas within the regional city and urban field; the multiple roles that small communities play in the city's countryside; and the existence of residential, play, and production environments operating on a physical resource base that incorporates both the natural and built environments.

Future of the City's Countryside

It is appropriate in closing to consider planning and development in the city's countryside. This is an area where change is the only constant. Too often, it is an area that is seen in simplistic terms because of the relative lack of the built infrastructure we associate with the city core. It should be clear that comprehensive planning and development in the city's countryside can only take place within a policy framework that recognizes the multidimensional nature of that particular part of the urban system. And, although we have not considered the structure and stresses created within the rural resource base, especially in the agricultural sector, any planning and development for the settlement structure has to deal with these concerns (see, for example, Bryant and Johnston, 1992; Johnston and Bryant, 1987). The familiar refrain of 'environment as a resource', rather than the more simplistic idea of land as a commodity, must be echoed once again. At the same time, dealing with resource issues from a largely sectoral perspective, as has been the case generally (for example, the development of agricultural land-conservation policies, or aggregate mineral policies), ignores the interrelatedness at a regional level between the concentrated urban areas and the city's countryside.

Four key points must be noted if responsible planning and development policy of the city's countryside is to become a reality (Coppack and Russwurm, 1988). First, while the city's countryside may be in large part a product of the city, it does not follow that city planning and policy can prevail in the countryside. The differences in roles, uses, and nature are too pronounced for such an approach. The city's countryside has much less built infrastructure spread over a far greater areal extent and impinging on a much larger number of 'natural' environments. Thus, physical planning for land uses takes on a much different complexion, requiring consideration of the multiple roles played by places and resources in rural areas. In the concentrated urban area, given the complexity of its built environment, the roles of particular areas are relatively clear-cut—for example, industrial, retail, and residential areas, despite transitional zones and the increased mixing of uses in the last quarter of the twentieth century. In rural areas, small communities support residential, recreation, commercial, tourism, and heritage functions, as well as providing a home for rare species and other uses, often at the same time and in the same place. Until the recent influx of exurbanites, the social structure of the countryside was more homogeneous within communities and areas, although sometimes quite different between communities and areas. Furthermore, rural communities have usually been established for long periods of time and often have extended family and social networks (Walker, 1987). This stands in contrast to the city, where much of the growth has occurred since the mid-twentieth century and migration activity has usually been very pronounced.

Second, economic development of the city's countryside requires a more innovative and enlightened approach than that practised to date. Frequently, the conventional approach has viewed rural areas as either chronically backward and terminally ill, or as 'urban-areas-in-waiting'. Inadequate attention has been paid to the other, more positive, roles that the city's countryside plays in the urban lifespace. This is particularly the case for city-core governments, whose tendency to see the countryside

and its resources (especially its space) as bride-to-be and dowry (e.g., through successive annexations) has caused endless friction with politicians and polity alike in the countryside. Seemingly endless debates are carried on regarding how to reorganize the major metropolitan regions into more effective administrative units. The Greater Toronto Area initiatives and debates are well known (Office for the Greater Toronto Area, 1992a, 1992b). The debates in the Montreal region have been just as extensive (Trépanier, 1998). In both regions, attempts to create larger regional structures have always met with resistance, and the single largest challenge is how to deal with real regional issues of management and planning without crushing the local community processes that have given such a rich variety to the city's countryside. Furthermore, it is perhaps time that we recognized that different non-traditional development options, such as tourism, exurban residential enclaves, and retirement communities, exist. These can only occur when complementary, conflicting, and compatible activities are identified within the multidimensional and multi-use nature of the city's countryside. Also, it must be recognized that city core and country are one entity, with no dominant partner, even though in political and economic terms the city core wields considerable influence. However, as society changes and new attitudes towards rural areas prevail, the strength and bargaining position of the countryside will increase concomitantly.

Notes

1. The mismatch of 'formal' and 'functional' urban regions gives rise to fundamental management and political problems. Further discussion of these problems is found in Chapter 18.

2. Notable here are the differences in the form of post-World War II cities in the US as opposed to the form of Canadian cities. See Chapter 3, which is devoted to this theme.

3. These were defined for all cities that in 1976 had a concentrated population of 40,000 or more (as well as Charlottetown, Granby, and Chilliwack

in order to represent important areas otherwise not included) by including all census subdivisions (i.e., municipalities and Indian reservations) within a 50 km radius (60 km for Toronto, Vancouver, and Montreal); areas of overlap were assigned on the basis of 1971 commuting flows.

References

Beesley, K.B. 1988. 'Living in the urban field', in Coppack, Russwurm, and Bryant (1988).

———— and G. Walker. 1990. 'Resident paths and community perceptions: a case study of the Toronto urban field', *Canadian Geographer* 34, 4: 318–30.

Bell, D. 1973. *The Coming of Post-Industrial Society: A Venture in Social Planning*. New York: Basic Books.

Bourne, L. 1995. *Urban Growth and Population Redistribution in North America: A Diverse and Unequal Landscape*. Toronto: Centre for Urban and Community Studies, University of Toronto, Major Report 32.

Bryant, C.R. 1988. 'Economic activities in the urban field', in Coppack, Russwurm, and Bryant (1988).

————. 1995. 'The role of local actors in transforming the urban fringe', *Journal of Rural Studies* 11, 3: 255–67.

———— and T.R.R. Johnston. 1992. *Agriculture in the City's Countryside*. London: Pinter Publishers; Toronto: University of Toronto Press.

———— and D. Lemire. 1998. 'Le développement local et la dynamique métropolitaine au Canada: le rôle des localités dans la restructuration de l'espace des régions métropolitaines', in J.-M. Lacroix, ed., *Urban Policies in North America. Proceedings of the 5th International Colloquium of the Centre d'études canadiennes*. Paris: Centre d'études canadiennes, Université de Paris III/Sorbonne Nouvelle.

———— and C. Marois. 1998. 'Franges et agricultures périurbaines dans la région de Montréal', in C. Manzagol and C.R. Bryant, eds, *Montréal 2001: Visages et défis d'une métropole*. Montreal: Les Presses de l'Université de Montréal.

————, L.H. Russwurm, and A.G. McLellan. 1982. *The City's Countryside*. Toronto: Longman.

Bunce, M. 1981. 'Rural sentiment and the ambiguity of the urban fringe', in K.B. Beesley and L.H. Russwurm, eds, *The Rural-Urban Fringe: Canadian*

Perspectives. Toronto: York University, Atkinson College, Geographical Monograph No. 10.

————. 1994. *The Countryside Ideal: Anglo-American Images of Landscape*. London and New York: Routledge.

Burton, I. 1959. 'Retail trade in a dispersed city', *Transactions of the Illinois State Academy of Science* 52: 145–50.

Cloke, P.J. 1983. *An Introduction to Rural Settlement Planning*. London: Methuen.

Coppack, P.M. 1985. 'A stage model of central place dynamics in Toronto's urban field', *East Lakes Geographer* 20: 1–13.

————. 1988a. 'Reflections on the role of amenity in the evolution of the urban field', *Geografiska Annaler* 70B: 353–61.

————. 1988b. 'The evolution and modelling of the urban field', in Coppack, Russwurm, and Bryant (1988).

———— and R.E. Preston. 1988. 'Central place structure of the urban field', in Coppack, Russwurm, and Bryant (1988).

———— and D. Robbins. 1987. 'Commuting patterns in the Toronto area, 1971', *Ontario Geography* 29: 63–78.

———— and L.H. Russwurm. 1988. 'The future of the urban field', in Coppack, Russwurm, and Bryant (1988).

————, ————, and C.R. Bryant. eds. 1988. *Essays in Canadian Urban Process and Form III: The Urban Field*. Waterloo: University of Waterloo, Department of Geography Publication Series No. 30.

Dahms, F. 1984. 'Demetropolitanization or urbanization of the countryside? The changing functions of small rural settlements in Ontario', *Ontario Geography* 24: 35–62.

————. 1985. 'Ontario's rural communities—changing, not dying', in A.M. Fuller, ed., *Farming and the*

Rural Community in Ontario: An Introduction. Toronto: Foundation for Rural Living.

———. 1988. *The Heart of the Country: From the Great Lakes to the Atlantic Coast—Rediscovering the Towns and Countryside of Canada.* Toronto: Deneau.

———. 1991a. 'Economic revitalisation in St. Jacobs, Ontario: Ingredients for transforming a dying village into a thriving tourist destination', *Small Town* (May–June): 12–18.

———. 1991b. 'St Jacobs, Ontario: from declining village to thriving tourist community', *Ontario Geography* 36: 1–13.

Dicken, P. 1986. *Global Shift: Industrial Change in a Turbulent World.* London: Harper and Row.

Dickinson, R.E. 1947. *City, Region and Regionalism: A Geographical Contribution to Human Ecology.* London: Kegan Paul Trench Truber.

Doxey, G. 1975. 'A causation theory of visitor-resident irritants: methodology and research inferences', in *The Impact of Tourism: Sixth Annual Conference Proceedings of the Travel Research Association.* San Diego, Calif.: Travel Research Association.

Friedmann, J. 1973. 'The urban field as a human habitat', in S.P. Snow, ed., *The Place of Planning.* Auburn, Ala.: Auburn University Press. Reprinted in L.S. Bourne and J.W. Simmons, eds, 1978 *Systems of Cities.* Toronto: Oxford University Press, 1978.

——— and J. Miller. 1965. 'The urban field', *Journal of the American Institute of Planners* 31: 312–20.

Gertler, L. 1972. *Regional Planning in Canada: A Planner's Testament.* Montreal: Harvest House.

Gilg, A. 1985. *An Introduction to Rural Geography.* London: Edward Arnold.

Gottman, J. 1961. *Megalopolis.* New York: The 20th Century Fund.

Hart, J.F. 1975. *The Look of the Land.* Englewood Cliffs, NJ: Prentice-Hall.

Harvey, D. 1990. 'Between space and time; reflections on the geographical imagination', *Annals of the Association of American Geographers* 80: 418–34.

Hodge, G. 1967 'Emerging bounds of urbanism', *Community Planning Review* 18: 4–9.

———. 1972. 'The emergence of the urban field', in L.S. Bourne and R.D. MacKinnon, eds, *Urban Systems Development in Central Canada.* Toronto: University of Toronto Press.

Johnston, T.R.R., and C.R. Bryant. 1987. 'Agricultural adaptation; the prospects for sustaining agriculture near cities', in W. Lockeretz, ed., *Sustaining Agriculture Near Cities.* Ankeny, Iowa: Soil and Water Conservation Society.

Mathieson, A., and G. Wall. 1983. *Tourism: Economic, Physical and Social Impacts.* London: Longman.

Menzies, S. 1994. 'The church on the fringe', *Mandate* 25, 2: 5–8.

Mitchell, C.J.A. 1988. 'Recreation and culture in the urban field', in Coppack, Russwurm, and Bryant (1988).

———. 1993. 'Cultural tourism and community economic development: A case study of St. Jacobs, Ontario', in G. Nelson and E. Alder, eds, *Proceedings of the Heritage Planning in an Urban Context Seminar.* Waterloo: Heritage Resource Centre, University of Waterloo.

———. 1998. 'Entrepreneurialism, commodification and creative destruction: a model of post-modern community development', *Journal of Rural Studies* 14, 3: 273–86.

Momsen, J. 1984. 'Urbanization of the countryside in Alberta', in M.F. Bunce and M.J. Troughton, eds, *The Pressures of Change in Rural Canada.* Toronto: York University, Atkinson College, Geographical Monograph No. 14.

Moss, G. 1978. 'Rural settlements', *Architects Journal* 18 (Jan.): 100–39.

Naisbitt, J. 1982. *Megatrends.* New York: Warner Books.

Ontario, Government of. 1966. *Design for Development: Statement by the Prime Minister of the Province of Ontario on Regional Development.* Toronto: Government of Ontario.

———. 1970. *Design for Development: The Toronto-Centred Region.* Toronto: Government of Ontario, Ministry of Treasury, Economics and Intergovernmental Affairs.

———. 1974. *Central Ontario Lakeshore Urban Complex.* Toronto: Queen's Printer.

Office of the Greater Toronto Area. 1992a. *Shaping Growth in the GTA: A Commentary Report.* Toronto: Office of the Greater Toronto Area.

———. 1992b. *A Vision for the Countryside: Report of the Provincial-Municipal Countryside Working Group*. Toronto: Office of the Greater Toronto Area.

Park, C., and P. Coppack. 1994. 'The role of rural sentiment and vernacular landscapes in contriving sense of place in the city's countryside', *Geografiska Annaler* 76B, 3: 162–72.

Preston, R.E. 1977. 'A perspective on alternate settlement forms', in L.H. Russwurm, R.E. Preston, and L.R.G. Martin, eds, *Essays on Canadian Urban Process and Form*. Waterloo: University of Waterloo, Department of Geography Publication Series No. 10.

Red Deer Regional Planning Commission. 1975. *Household Survey of Country Residents*. Red Deer, Alta.: The Commission.

Ricour-Singh, F. 1979. *Poles and Zones of Attraction*. Ottawa: Ministry of Supply and Services, Statistics Canada Census Analytical Study, No. 99–754.

Russwurm, L.H. 1976. 'Country residential development and the regional city form in Canada', *Ontario Geographer* 10: 79–96.

———. 1977. *The Surroundings of Our Cities*. Toronto: Holt, Rinehart and Winston.

——— and C. Bryant. 1984. 'Changing population distributions and rural-urban relationships in the Canadian urban field, 1941–1979', in M.F. Bunce and M.J. Troughton, eds, *The Pressures of Change in Rural Canada*. Toronto: York University, Atkinson College, Geographical Monograph No. 14.

———, P.M. Coppack, and C.R. Bryant. 1988. 'Population in the urban field', in Coppack, Russwurm, and Bryant (1988).

Thomson, L., and C.J.A. Mitchell. 1996. 'Counter-urbanization in Waterloo Region: the lure of the countryside', in P. Filion, T. Bunting, and K. Curtis, eds, *The Dynamics of the Dispersed City: Geographic and Planning Perspectives on Waterloo Region*. Waterloo: University of Waterloo, Department of Geography Publication Series No. 47.

——— and ———. 1998. 'Residents of the urban field: a case study of Wilmot Township, Ontario, Canada', *Journal of Rural Studies* 14, 2: 185–201.

Trépanier, M.-O. 1998. 'Les défis de l'aménagement et de la gestion d'une grande région métropolitaine', in C. Manzagol and C.R. Bryant, eds, *Montréal 2001: Visages et défis d'une métropole*. Montreal: Les Presses de l'Université de Montréal.

Walker, G.E. 1987. *The Invaded Countryside: Structures of Life in the Invaded Fringe*. Toronto: York University, Atkinson College, Geographical Monograph No. 14.

Westhues, K., and P.R. Sinclair. 1974. *Village in Crisis*. Toronto: Holt, Rinehart and Winston.

Part 4

Land Use and Activities

In the preceding chapters we have gained insight into city structure by opening windows on different segments of the city. When considered together, these windows increase our understanding of the total urban panoramic. In Part Four we turn our attention to specific functions or activities, along with their respective land-use patterns, that take place in cities. The chapters here focus on three major functional sectors: work, housing, and retail. In Chapter 15, Pierre Filion and Tod Rutherford discuss the changing nature of the city's employment base. In Chapter 16, Richard Harris examines trends in housing, while Chapter 17, by Ken Jones, is devoted to the urban retail scene. Consistent with our theme, each of these chapters is concerned with the kinds of change or transition that characterize the subsector in question.

The sequence in which the following three chapters appear is important. It begins with the assumption that cities are first and foremost places of specialized economic production, that is, places where jobs are available and work takes place. In the simplified scheme of things, suggested in Figure IV.1, work then becomes the first functional sector in the city. Working may entail the actual production of a tangible good or semi-finished product, or it may involve the delivery of a less tangible service or consultation. The workplace may serve a mar-

Figure IV.1   **Land Use and Activities**

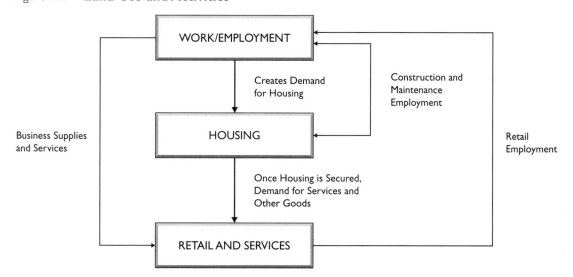

ket within its local area or it may be aimed at a broader national or international market. Either way, the presence of work calls for a resident labour force. Employees and their families need places of residence for shelter and sustenance, and for the reproduction of a future labour force. Put simply, employment creates a demand for housing. Housing then becomes the second functional sector in a city system. Types of housing in demand will be directly related to the nature of employment, and hence workers' characteristics, in a given area—income level, education and values, job security. The well-educated professionals with above-average income who make up the advanced service sector will be attracted to housing varieties and neighbourhood types at the upper end of the real estate market.

Members of the growing low-order service sector, in contrast, will have few housing options, primarily because of income and commuting constraints.

Once we have work and housing in place, there are still unsatisfied demands. A third realm of urban activity is represented by the retail sector, which accommodates household needs. This sector has grown dramatically since the war in response to the average household's rise in disposable income. More recently, as increased numbers of women work outside the home, there is a concomitant increase in demand for goods and services once produced within the home. The frequency of exchanges between stores and households means that success for retail and related activity is largely dictated by location.

Chapter 15

Employment Transitions in the City

Pierre Filion and Tod Rutherford

Patterns of employment have changed profoundly over the last quarter-century. Transformations since the early 1970s have been such that a writer has recently forecast the 'end of work' (Rifkin, 1995), while others speak of a deepening polarization between a small number of high-skill, well-paid jobs and a large proportion of unskilled, low-wage 'McJobs' (Economic Council of Canada, 1990). Certainly, the last 25 years have witnessed significant changes in the type and pattern of employment. Foremost in many Canadians' experience has been increasing unemployment as both average unemployment rates and duration have risen markedly since the 1960s (Betcherman, 1996). There has also been a rapid increase in the proportion of service jobs and a related fall in primary- and secondary-sector employment. With this shift towards services has come escalating 'non-standard' employment, that is, part-time self-employment and temporary employment, raising concern over the quality of this type of work. Concurrently, there have been marked intra-metropolitan employment shifts. With the deep fall in central-city and older-suburban manufacturing employment, the bulk of job growth has taken place in new suburban areas. This chapter highlights the connection between these employment shifts and transformations affecting the urban structure of Canadian cities. It also acknowledges the variety of workplace location preferences and explains certain sectors' predilection for central sites.

The rapidity and salience of these and other changes to Canadian employment have led to an intense debate about processes underlying this restructuring. This is the object of the first section of the chapter, which not only explores general patterns in Canadian employment during the 1990s, but also examines competing explanations for these trends. These explanations focus on the apparent decline of manufacturing and of advanced economies previously structured along Fordist principles, and postulate the rise of a new post-industrial, post-Fordist era (Allen, 1989; Sayer and Walker, 1992). The following sections highlight employment shifts within census metropolitan areas (CMAs), with a particular focus on the Toronto CMA because of the diversity of its employment structure reflecting its prominent position within the Canadian economic system. Attention is on both employment suburbanization and the ongoing attraction of central areas for certain enterprises. The chapter closes with an examination of urban employment issues stemming from late-twentieth-century economic transitions.

Employment Changes Since 1971

There is growing consensus that patterns of Canadian employment have undergone a significant qualitative shift since the early 1970s (see Donner, 1991; Norcliffe, 1994; Rutherford, 1996; Betcherman, 1996; Sharpe and Haddow, 1997). While the Canadian economy has enjoyed one of the strongest rates of job creation among advanced economies, with the total number of those in full-time employment increasing by nearly one-third (from 9.30 to 13.75 million) between 1975 and 1997, this rate has slowed in each decade since the 1960s, with unemployment and non-standard employment increasing substantially. Thus, while the average unemployment rate in the 1960s was approximately 4 per cent, by the 1990s this level had risen to over 9 per cent. Over the same period, average annual employment gains fell from 3.1 per cent between 1961 and 1973 to a low 0.6 per cent between 1989 and 1997 (Sharpe and Haddow, 1997). As a result, the percentage of the unemployed who were out of work over one year, which was well under 5 per cent in the 1970s, had more than doubled to over 12 per cent by 1994 (Betcherman, 1996). Youth unemployment has been especially severe in the 1990s. Rates for those between 15 and 19 years old jumped from 14 per cent in 1989 to 24 per cent in 1997. Reality is even worse than these data suggest. Official unemployment rates measure only those actively seeking work and thus do not account for those who have withdrawn from the labour market. A more reliable measure is provided by employment rates (the percentage of the total population in employment), which fell from just over 62.5 per cent in 1989 (a historical high) to under 59 per cent in 1997 (Smith, 1997).

The period since 1975 has also been notable for a marked employment shift from large to small firms and to self-employment. For example, between 1973 and 1992, the share of manufacturing employment in plants with 100 or less employees increased from 28.8 per cent to 37.9 per cent, while that of those with more than 500 workers fell from 32 per cent to 24.8 per cent (Baldwin, 1996). The rise in self-employment has been especially marked in the 1990s with private- and public-sector downsizing. From 1989 to 1997, the share of those in self-employment rose from 13.8 per cent to 18.1 per cent, while those working for private employers fell from 70 to 67.1 per cent and public-sector employment declined from 16.1 to 14.7 per cent (Gardner, 1997; Smith, 1997).

Concern has centred not only on the number of jobs but also on their quality (see Myles, 1991). Thus, the proportion of those in non-standard employment consisting of independent contracting, part-time and short-tenure jobs has risen from less than 24 per cent in 1975 to nearly 30 per cent by 1994, while those working 'normal' hours (30–49 hours/week) fell from 73.4 per cent in 1981 to 69.1 per cent in 1991 (see Krahn, 1995).

All these employment changes are linked to real wage stagnation and income polarization. Real wage growth over a 10-year period has dropped from 42.5 and 36.8 per cent, respectively, in the 1950s and 1960s to just over 2 per cent in the 1980s. The 1990s are in fact experiencing a fall in real wages. Income polarization is evidenced by the 1967-91 decline from 42 to 32 per cent in the proportion of the labour force earning between 75 and 150 per cent of median income (Betcherman, 1996). This distribution indicates that an increasing number of individuals make either little or a lot of money and that fewer people are earning middle-range incomes.

Since the 1960s, manufacturing's share of Canadian employment has fallen precipitously, from 27 per cent in 1961 to only 15 per cent in 1992, while services now account for over 72 per cent of total employment (Britton, 1996). Indeed, between 1971 and 1991, service employment grew by a massive 77 per cent (Coffey, 1996). The fall in goods production employment has been especially notable since the late 1980s, which reflects the combined impact of free trade and domestic recession (see Gertler, 1996). Between 1989 and 1997, while goods production lost more than 104,000 jobs, gains in the service sector exceeded 900,000 (Smith, 1997). Manufacturing employment has shrunk from 1.79 million in 1978 to 1.67 million in 1994, a drop of 6.7 per cent. When compared to 1989, when total manufacturing employment peaked at 1.97 million, this decline reaches 15 per cent (Statistics Canada, 1998).

Some have argued that Canada is simply 'deindustrializing'—that is, experiencing an inexorable employment and output shift away from goods production (see, for example, Niosi, 1978). Reality is less clear-cut, however. Over the medium to long term, employment shifts are partly explained by manufacturing productivity increases.[1] The introduction of labour-saving technology, such as robots and computer-controlled machinery, has boosted workers' output, making it possible to produce more with a given, or even reduced, workforce. In the steel industry, for example, output per person tripled between 1960 and 1994: in 1960 it took 36,500 people to produce 6 million tons of steel; by 1994, 33,300 employees could produce nearly 16 million tons. The impact of labour-saving devices is reflected in much less of a fall in manufacturing's share of gross domestic product (GDP), from 20 per cent in 1971 to 18.5 per cent in 1994, than in its employment share.

The leading perspective on employment shifts from goods to services has been Bell's 'post-industrial' thesis, developed in the 1970s. Bell proposed a three-stage model, each dominated by different types of economic outputs. Over the pre-industrial stage, the economy was dominated by personal domestic production; during the industrial stage, by manufacturing, transport, distribution, and banking; and in the post-industrial stage, by human and professional services such as health care and education (Bell, 1973; see also Allen, 1989).

Bell's thesis has been substantially amended since the 1970s. Gershuny and Miles (1983), for example, have demonstrated the difficulty in distinguishing service from manufacturing employment. They tie much of the increase in service-sector employment to heightened demand for intermediate or producer services, such as accountancy, marketing, computer programming, and engineering and design consulting. These categories were previously classified as manufacturing employment but since the 1960s have developed as separate service-sector entities. This observation suggests that much of the apparent service-sector growth results simply from a reclassification of what used to be goods-sector activities. What is more, many 'services' are directly dependent on goods production (primary resources, manufacturing, and construction) and many traditionally defined services are in fact goods (material objects). For example, hotels, which fall within the service sector, offer shelter, a type of good. Employment in banking and finance often depends on the circulation of goods and com-

modities. Now, as in the past, a high proportion of employment gravitates to industrial goods, but the last decades have witnessed an employment shift from the production to the financing, marketing, and selling of these goods (Sayer and Walker, 1992).

In this light, the argument that advanced societies can unambiguously be classified as post-industrial becomes more problematic. An alternative thesis posits a transition from Fordist to post-Fordist systems of production and labour market structuring (see Norcliffe, 1994; Swift, 1995; Rutherford, 1996). In this view, Fordism was based on mass production as a form of work organization relying on assembly-line techniques—especially in the automobile, steel, and consumer durables sectors. The resulting standardization of production assured vast economies of scale. The success of Fordism lies in its capacity to match massive productivity increases with a corresponding rise in consumption. The balance was achieved thanks to the presence of mechanisms that assured consistently high consumer demand. Foremost among these was the success of trade unions in raising their members' standard of living. The combined effect of climbing productivity and high unionization rates within the manufacturing sector made it possible for blue-collar workers to acquire homes, cars, and appliances—to attain middle-class consumption standards. Trade unions were not the only instrument that stimulated consumption over the Fordist era. The development of the welfare state provided the old and the poor with the means to engage in a measure of consumption. In addition, to preclude recessions triggered by falling consumption, governments, inspired by Keynesian principles, pumped money into the economy at the first signs of a faltering demand by launching infrastructure, housing, and other job-creation programs. Together, these mechanisms adjusted, or regulated, the production and consumption spheres and thus reduced the occurrence and impact of recessions. This regulation system fuelled a 'virtuous circle' of productivity and consumption gains until the late 1960s, when productivity advancement slowed as the limits of Fordist assembly techniques were reached and worker resistance increased. Henceforth, profits declined and consumption growth became sluggish. Commitment to Keynesianism waned in the late 1970s as government deficits ballooned and double-digit inflation set in. Rising prices were due to an ongoing increase in demand that was no longer accompanied by proportional productivity increases.

To many observers, the restructuring of advanced economies since the 1970s has marked a transition towards post-Fordism (see Harvey, 1989; Scott, 1988). Post-Fordism is grounded in flexible production technologies and employment, a shift from mass markets towards more segmented markets, and new forms of 'network-based' industrial organizations that emphasize reciprocal relations between firms. In addition, advanced producer services foster continual innovation and supply market intelligence (Coffey, 1992). This restructuring is also associated with greater international competition. In Canada, free trade agreements have accelerated the exposure of manufacturing to continental and, increasingly, global markets (Norcliffe, 1994; Britton, 1996). Many sectors also indicate a trend towards greater flexibility, consisting in a widened range of tasks employees are expected to undertake and more reliance on non-standard employment as employers seek to 'fine-tune' their labour requirements to demand. Increased outsourcing to an array of temporary/part-time and 'self-employed' workers results in 'two-tier' labour markets (Swift, 1995). This practice is particularly common in the service sector, where trade union representation is weaker than in manufacturing (Galarneau, 1996). In the early 1990s, 6 per cent of the manufacturing labour force was either part-time or temporary in status, compared to over 20 per cent in services. Overall, pay is lower (by 22 per cent) and both income and work conditions are more bifurcated in services than in manufacturing (see Economic Council of Canada, 1990; Grenon, 1996).

The post-Fordist emphasis on flexibility has caused firms to subcontract production processes that used to be carried out in-house. This has resulted in an intensification of inter-firm linkages and the emergence of industrial districts grouping firms that interact with each other (Marshall, 1920; Porter, 1990; Scott, 1988). As we shall see, with transportation improvements such districts can cover considerable areas.

The combination of post-Fordism and globalization accounts for the present employment and social structure. With the loss of much of their standardized production, Canadian cities have seen their blue-collar middle class shrink. Many of the unskilled or semi-skilled workers who in the recent past would have held stable and well-paying manufacturing employment must now settle for the insecurity and low wages of menial service jobs. As Canadian cities deindustrialized over the last decades, the service sector experienced rapid expansion driven by changing consumer habits and the rapid rise of the tourism and convention industry in large Canadian cities. In a sense, we witness the expansion of a low-income service class whose role is to cater to the demands of the wealthy and of what remains of the middle class (Reich, 1992). At the other end of the income spectrum, individuals with skills that are adapted to the needs of those economic sectors that perform strongly under post-Fordism and globalization do extremely well financially. This is the case of highly skilled workers employed within sectors making heavy use of information. In Canada, industries that rely heavily on research and development—the aircraft, pharmaceutical, and software industries, for example—and those that invest considerably in market intelligence—such as the financial sector—employ large numbers of well-qualified and highly remunerated workers.

The Employment-Urban Interface

Employment and workplace characteristics—such as employment growth and decline, income level, location and patterning of major centres of employment, physical structure and layout of workplaces—reflect on cities in a variety of ways. For a start, there is a close association between employment and demographic expansion. This connection is evidenced by the strong correlation between metropolitan region employment and demographic growth (as demonstrated in Chapter 5). Another dimension of the employment-urban interface is the employment sphere's influence on consumption patterns. A labour force's income, education, and values all reverberate on a city's housing, cultural, entertainment, and recreation activities, retail activity, and demand for public-sector services. Urban social structure (the respective importance and location within an agglomeration of different income groups) is, of course, in large part a function of income distribution (see Chapter 9). Terms of employment, too, have an impact on consumption, as illustrated by difficulties for a highly unstable labour force to achieve home-ownership.

Because they occupy a large share of a city's space, workplaces have a determining effect on urban land-use patterns. The higher the share of its employment found in low-density industrial or business parks, rather than, say, in a compact high-rise central business district (CBD), the larger is the overall space needed by the urban region. In this same vein, by placing the heaviest (that is, the rush-hour) load on urban transportation networks, workplaces dictate the mode, capacity, and locational requirements of urban transportation facilities (see Chapter 8). A further facet of the employment-urban interface is the dependence of municipalities on workplaces for their tax base and, hence, for their fiscal health.

The city is not only at the receiving end of employment trends; it can also contribute to these trends. As city's built environment (buildings and infrastructures, including transportation systems) has an impact on the nature of employment. Compact and transit-oriented urban areas generate fewer construction jobs and less demand for durable goods, especially automobiles, than cities that are dispersed and fully dependent on cars. Seventy years ago, Le Corbusier argued that were Americans to choose to live in high-density, apartment-dominated cities rather than in single-family suburbs, collectively they could sharply reduce the amount of time they must devote to their employment because dense urban environments require far less human energy to create and maintain (Le Corbusier, 1973 [1933]).

In dispersed cities, abundant indoor and outdoor space consumption mitigates the shift to services by promoting an intense use of the car and the accumulation of goods. Herein lies a paradox of the contemporary city. While the importance of services grows at the expense of that of goods production—as evidenced by the highly visible replacement of inner-city industrial areas by residential and recreational uses—urban development assumes a form that perpetuates a heavy dependence on durable goods, particularly the car. This form of urbanization is thus one of the factors sustaining Fordist production—the assembly of durable goods—in the post-Fordist era. Without this type of urbanization, the shift towards service consumption would have been more pronounced.

The next section documents the interface between employment and the city in more detail. Specifically, we highlight intra-urban employment location trends and examine the consequences on the city of decelerated job creation as well as of a polarization in income and work conditions. The focus is on Toronto, although employment decentralization trends in Montreal and Vancouver are also reported. As Canada's largest CMA, Toronto's employment base is highly diversified. It is at once the country's premier administrative and manufacturing centre. On a North American scale, it hosts the third largest concentration of corporate head offices, after New York and Chicago, and ranks second, after Detroit, in the auto assembly and parts industry (GTA Task Force, 1996: 52–4). By virtue of its economic diversity and size, the Toronto CMA offers a broad range of employment and workplace sites and is thus ideally suited to a study of intra-urban employment trends. Yet, we must caution about generalizing the Toronto experience to urban Canada as a whole. Size and diversity set Toronto CMA apart. Trends such as employment decentralization and service-sector growth unfold there on a larger scale than elsewhere in Canada. In addition, Toronto's sustained prosperity since the war, with the notable exception of a disproportional decline over the 1989–92 recession, is uncharacteristic of most other Canadian CMAs.

Intra-Urban Employment Location Trends

Factors of Decentralization

In the pre-war city, most office and a high proportion of retail employment opted for the CBD, the most accessible place within the city (because at a convergence of public transit routes when this was the predominant form of urban transportation). Manufacturing, which accounted for a far larger proportion of employment than it now does, located along waterways and railways to secure access to supplies from outside the metropolitan region and to export products along the same routes. Industry clustered within industrial districts to ease linkages with other establishments. Old sectors within contemporary cities host the remnants of such districts. This is the case of the Montreal and Toronto garment districts, which bring together within a few blocks textile wholesalers and numerous garment establishments.

Since World War II, retail, manufacturing, and, later, offices have increasingly favoured peripheral locations. Several factors feed this trend. One is the attempt to secure proximity to the suburbanizing labour force and client base. Transportation also promotes decentralization. Exponential rise in car and truck use accompanied by massive urban expressway and arterial road investment revolutionized urban transportation. Henceforth, inter-firm linkages and market access have mostly involved truck journeys, and everywhere, with the exception of the CBDs of large metropolitan regions, the car has become the chief commuting mode. This transportation system reduces proximity requirements both among interdependent firms and between workplaces and their labour shed. Within large agglomerations, any location with ready accessibility to an expressway is suitable for workplaces (Birch, 1975; Cameron, 1973; Steines, 1977; White, Binkley, and Osterman, 1993: 193). A further transportation-related inducement to locate in the suburbs is the attraction of airports for firms that depend on air transportation. In the postwar city, the influence of canals, railways, and harbours on industrial location has been in large part superseded by that of arterial roads, expressways, and airports. Figure 15.1 shows both the proximity of Greater Toronto Area industrial districts to expressways and a concentration of such sites around Pearson Airport.

The need to accommodate large volumes of vehicles on site increases the amount of space all workplaces require and hence raises the appeal of low-cost peripheral sites relative to more expensive central locations. In this same vein, single-storey buildings, which are prodigal land consumers, are best suited to Fordist assembly-line techniques. Interestingly, recent establishments that rely on more flexible forms of production opt for the same type of buildings to avoid the use of lifts. An accelerated pace of production promotes the grouping of all operations on a single floor where supplies are easily delivered by trucks and finished products loaded on this same form of transportation.

Another factor of decentralization is the abundance of land zoned for employment purposes. Municipalities, anxious to maximize economic development and property tax entries, are excessive in their workplace land designation. This explains a considerable oversupply of land zoned for employment purposes within the Greater Toronto Area, particularly in peripheral municipalities (see Figure 15.2). With time, suburban employment sites have become increasingly differentiated, which allows them to accommodate different types of workplaces. Along with run-of-the-mill industrial and office parks, suburbs now offer prestige locations with expressway visibility, elaborate landscaping, and select corporate neighbours, as well as so-called 'suburban downtowns' with upscale office buildings (see Chapter 11).

The rising proportion of people working from their home—currently 9 per cent work some or all of their regularly scheduled work hours at home—constitutes a further factor of employment decentralization (Lowe, 1997; MacDonald, 1997). People working at home fall into numerous categories, from managers and professionals employed by large corporations to individuals setting up home busi-

Figure 15.1   **Greater Toronto Area Major Industrial Concentrations**

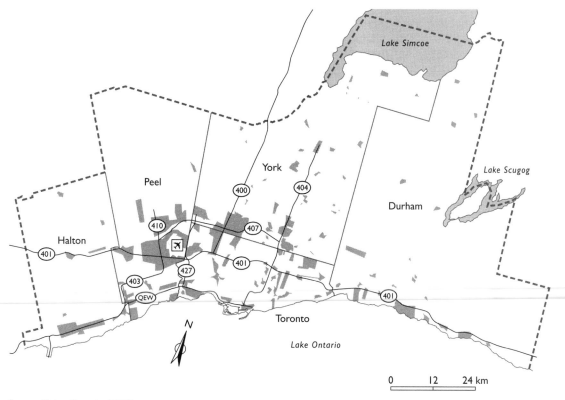

Source: Metro Toronto (1996).

nesses as a low-return alternative to unemployment (Nadwodny, 1996). Thanks to advances in electronic communications it becomes possible to reduce the number of journeys to the office and thus live further from employment concentrations. Increasingly, new condominium buildings and suburban subdivisions are wired so as to facilitate telecommuting (*Toronto Star*, 1998).

Table 15.1 portrays employment decentralization trends over the 1981–91 period in Canada's three largest CMAs for three urban sectors: central city, inner suburbs, and outer suburbs.[2] As expected, all three CMAs experienced a considerable increase both in the number and proportion of jobs in the outer suburbs. Yet, compared to impressive 1981–91 rates of outer-suburban growth (from 52.3 per cent

in Vancouver to 92 per cent in Toronto), ratios of jobs to employed outer-suburb residents have remained relatively stable. Over these 10 years, this ratio underwent a modest change from 0.86 to 0.83 in Toronto, 0.51 to 0.57 in Montreal, and 0.72 to 0.73 in Vancouver. This suggests that outer-suburban population and employment growth have occurred at rates that are roughly similar.

Table 15.1 also points to the stability of inner-suburban job and employed resident numbers in Toronto and Montreal. Note, however, that as outer-suburban expansion unfolds, the inner suburbs' share of CMA employment falls (more so in Toronto, where outer-suburban development far outpaces that of Montreal). Vancouver is an exception, with inner-suburban employment experiencing a remark-

Figure 15.2   **Industrially Designated Land in the City of Toronto and GTA Regional Municipalities**

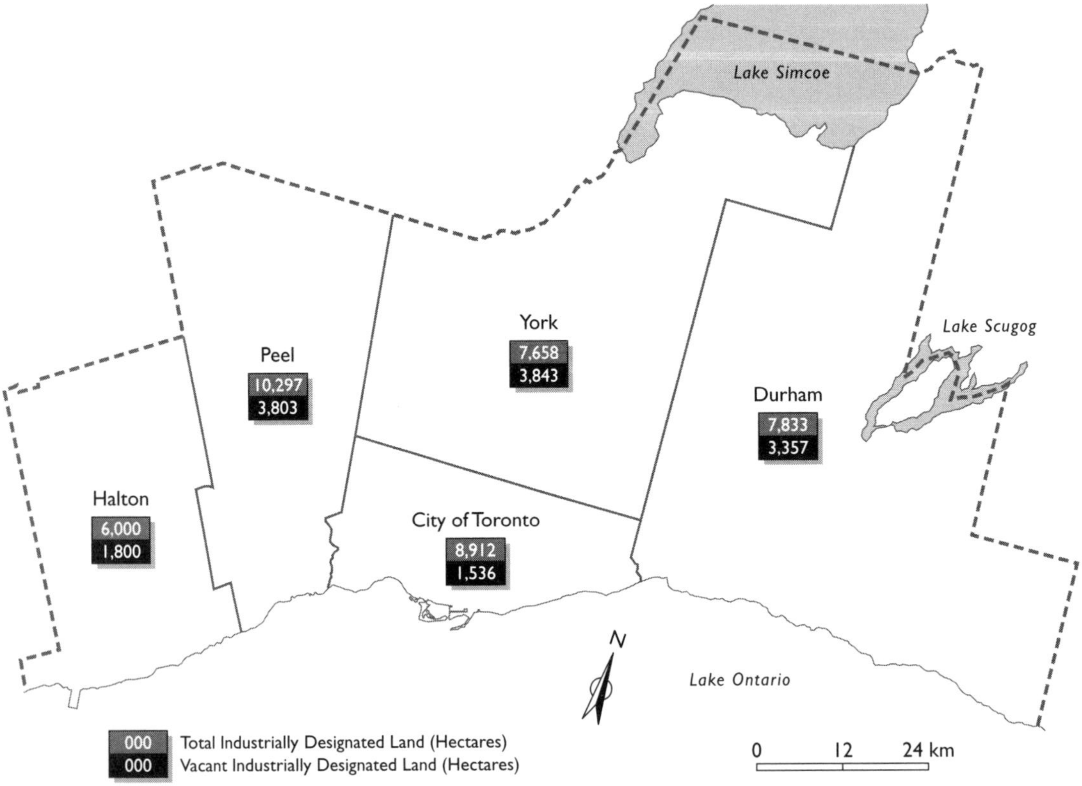

Lake Simcoe

Lake Scugog

Peel
10,297
3,803

York
7,658
3,843

Durham
7,833
3,357

Halton
6,000
1,800

City of Toronto
8,912
1,536

Lake Ontario

N

000 Total Industrially Designated Land (Hectares)
000 Vacant Industrially Designated Land (Hectares)

0   12   24 km

Source: Metro Toronto (1996: 18).

able increase. Doubtless, this is due to the presence in 1981 of plentiful undeveloped land within the area defined here as Vancouver's inner suburbs, in contrast to Toronto's and Montreal's inner suburbs having been mostly built up. The three central cities have seen the number of jobs rise over the 1981–91 period—by 16.2 per cent in Toronto, 10.9 per cent in Vancouver, and 5.1 per cent in Montreal. This is mostly a reflection of CBD office expansion during the 1980s. But this increase was not sufficient to prevent a fall in the central cities' proportions of CMA jobs. This observation also pertains to office space. For example, despite an important wave of downtown Toronto office construction, this district's share

of metropolitan region office space fell from 55 per cent in 1976 to 40.2 per cent in 1994 (Metro Toronto, 1995). In brief, the picture to emerge is one of employment decentralization, mitigated by central-city job increases and the ability of inner suburbs to hold on to their employment.

It is noteworthy that over the last 50 years the main tendency in urban employment location has been ongoing decentralization. This signifies that, for the most part, both Fordist and post-Fordist economic trends have been associated with suburbanization. Therefore, it appears that the profound work-related transformation induced by the passage to post-Fordism has generally not involved a de-

Table 15.1   **Employment Distribution Trends, 1981–1991, Toronto, Montreal, Vancouver**

Toronto	Outer Suburb		Inner Suburb		Central City		Total	
	Jobs (% of CMA)	Employed Resident (% of CMA)	Jobs (% of CMA)	Employed Resident (% of CMA)	Jobs (% of CMA	Employed Resident (% of CMA)	Jobs	Employed Residents
1981	376, 320 (23.6%)	435,560 (27.7%)	648,750 (40.7%)	814,585 (51.8%)	567,975 (35.7%)	321,285 (20.4%)	1,593,045	1,571,430
Ratio jobs/employed residents	0.86		0.80		1.77			
1991	722,710 (35.7%)	875,485 (42.9%)	643,785 (31.8%)	822,775 (40.3%)	659,855 (32.6%)	341,460 (16.7%)	2,026,350	2,039,720
Ratio jobs/employed residents	0.83		0.78		1.93			
Per cent change 1981–91	92.0%	101.0%	−0.8%	1.0%	16.2%	6.3%	27.2%	29.8%
Montreal								
1981	244,895 (19.4%)	481,470 (37.0%)	370,570 (29.3%)	351,855 (27.0%)	647,135* (51.3%)	468,500* (36.0%)	1,262,600	1,301,825
Ratio jobs/employed residents	0.51		1.1		1.38			
1991	381,370 (26.7%)	666,670 (45.2%)	367,085 (25.7%)	352,770 (23.9%)	679,925 (47.6%)	455,105 (30.9%)	1,428,380	1,474,545
Ratio jobs/ employed residents	0.57		1.04		1.49			
Per cent change 1981–91	55.7%	38.5%	−0.9%	0.3%	5.1%	−2.9%	13.1%	13.3%
Vancouver								
1981	155,220 (24.9%)	216,980 (34.9%)	180,530 (28.9%)	194,150 (31.2%)	288,375 (46.2%)	210,700 (33.9%)	624,125	621,830
Ratio jobs/employed residents	0.72		0.93		1.37			
1991	236,375 (29.4%)	324,940 (41.4%)	248,40 5 (30.9%)	225,670 (28.8%)	319,935 (39.8%)	233,955 (29.8%)	804,715	784,565
Ratio jobs/employed residents	0.73		1.1		1.37			
Per cent change 1981–91	52.3%	49.8%	37.6%	16.2%	10.9%	11.0%	28.9%	26.2%

*1991 City of Montreal boundaries.
Sources: Statistics Canada (1983, 1993).

parture from Fordist workplace location patterns. We will see, however, that there are exceptions to this rule.

Dispersion and Clustering

Decentralization does not eradicate clustering (the tendency for workplaces belonging to a same category to opt for nearby locations). But save within CBDs and surviving pre-war industrial districts, clustering assumes a more diffused pattern than over the preceding phase of urbanization. This distribution derives from a relaxation of the need for proximity within the car- and truck-oriented metropolis. Clustering now assumes the form of overrepresentation of certain categories of workplaces within portions of an agglomeration, rather than that of the contiguous presence of related enterprises as in the past. Clustering is tied to the intensification of linkages that follow from the post-Fordist trend towards the formation of extensive networks of firms. There are obvious advantages for establishments that engage in frequently repeated exchanges to minimize distance between each other. This is particularly the case since, for all the urban accessibility improvements of the last 50 years, in large metropolitan regions the capacity of firms to extend their linkages is compromised by endemic congestion. This is one factor accounting for observed clusters in portions of the City of Toronto within the following industrial sectors: metal goods, clothing, furniture and fixtures, mechanical equipment and machinery, and electrical and electronic products (Gertler, 1996: 10–11).

This alone does not fully explain clustering, however. Clustering results also from differences in location need according to workplace category. The search for similar site characteristics by one type of workplace can translate into their location in the same part of a metropolitan region. We now consider the location needs of different types of workplaces within the suburban environment, excluding older inner-suburban employment districts to which we turn later when discussing the appeal of more central locations for certain establishments.

(1) Warehousing and assembly-line production, consumers of ample space, favour suburban industrial parks. These establishments enjoy a great deal of location latitude within the suburban realm by virtue of their primary reliance on a semi-skilled blue-collar labour force, available throughout the suburbs, and on expressways for linkages and market accessibility.

(2) Suburban back and satellite offices perform operations formerly carried out in large CBD offices, but they can easily operate outside that area's concentrated environment and thus avoid its high rents. Back and satellite offices can opt for a variety of suburban locations (Metro Toronto, 1988: 7). Like warehousing and standardized production, they tap a labour force that is ubiquitous within the suburban environment, in this case, semi-skilled office workers (Nelson, 1986).

(3) Establishments that rely heavily on air delivery and travel for supply, distribution, and face-to-face information linkages naturally favour sites that enjoy good airport accessibility.

(4) Workplaces that employ a highly specialized labour force occasionally seek proximity to their skilled employees. This phenomenon is most manifest in Silicon Valley in the San Francisco area, where numerous computer establishments converged in the same district, close to their highly specialized labour force. This spatial pattern eases the possibility for workers to change workplaces and is partly the outcome of employees leaving their firm to launch new computer enterprises. In Canada, we find high-tech industry concentrations in Markham, in the northeastern part of Toronto CMA, and in Kanata, in the western segment of the Ottawa metropolitan region, as well as a cluster of pharmaceutical establishments in the Montreal CMA's Ville Saint-Laurent and West Island district. This symbiosis between employee residence and workplace location rests on workers' predilection for short commutes and on firms' sensitivity to the preferences of these highly sought-after workers. Despite the role of cars and expressways in easing metropolitan-wide accessibility, labour markets are not fully integrated at the scale of large CMAs. Data from

Toronto indicate that within a metropolitan region with a continuously built area extending roughly 85 by 30 kilometres, 89.5 per cent of commutes take place within municipalities that are 10 kilometres or less from the home municipality (calculated from Statistics Canada, 1993).

(5) The need to be easily accessible to their customer base guides the location choice of client-oriented establishments (retail as well as public- and private-sector services). The tendency for retail to follow population as it moves outward is expressed by the contrast between a considerable increase in retail floor space in the suburbs and modest variations in per capita amounts of retail floor space between different portions of the Toronto metropolitan region (Metro Toronto, 1995: 4-8) (see Chapter 17).

(6) Some suburban workplaces seek visible and/or prestigious sites. These include exclusive business parks, locations abutting expressways where corporate identification can be seen daily by tens of thousands of passersby, and new suburban downtowns. In large metropolitan regions, such as Toronto, these downtowns have been successful in their efforts to attract upscale office buildings. Among establishments willing to pay a premium for visible and prestigious suburban sites, we find head offices, warehouses, and production facilities of large national and international corporations (Hemson Consulting, 1987: 7–8).

Other categories of workplaces prefer central city and older suburban sites over more peripheral locations. The premier central-city workplace concentration is the CBD, reputed for its agglomeration economies (see Chapter 11). CBD workplaces indeed enjoy unparalleled face-to-face contact possibilities with nearby establishments and strong synergy whereby other activities in the immediate area generate positive effects. For example, retail and hospitality services (hotels, restaurants, bars, recreation and exercise centres) benefit from the presence of nearby offices, while a well-developed retail and service sector heightens a CBD's appeal for offices. Part of the attraction of CBDs stems from their position at the focal point of public transit systems, which enables workplaces to tap a large pool of potential workers.

In addition, high public transit use makes it possible for large cities' CBDs to devote less land to the car and concentrate more activities than suburban locales do, and thus offer unequalled pedestrian-based synergy and face-to-face contact possibilities. Moreover, many employers are lured to the CBD and other central-city and older-suburb sites by the proximity of a sought-after labour force. Whereas the technologically oriented middle class tends to prefer suburban residential areas (hence the suburban predilection of high-tech industries), the segment of the middle class involved in social science and artistic activities has spearheaded the gentrification of inner-city neighbourhoods (Castells and Hall, 1994; Ley, 1996). At the bottom of the income range, low-wage service and manufacturing establishments take advantage of the disproportional percentage of recent immigrants residing in central cities and older suburbs. Lastly, the prestige of a downtown address is another attraction for workplaces.

In large metropolitan regions, CBDs have benefited from the rapid growth of the service sector. These districts indeed group a broad range of services that have enjoyed rapid expansion over the post-Fordist era: management; business services; cultural activities; specialized retail; and tourism and convention-related establishments.

CBD prosperity is not spread evenly across Canada's urban hierarchy. As a rule, CBDs of smaller CMAs do not fare as well as those of large metropolitan regions. In small metropolitan regions, downtowns are often in a state of advanced economic deterioration, with numerous empty premises and lots signalling the severe employment and retail activity loss they have endured (Bunting and Millward, 1999; Millward and Bunting, 1999). This decline is explained by the difficulty these CBDs experience in competing with suburban locales. In smaller agglomerations, too, CBDs were never of a sufficient size to generate the rich linkages and strong synergy effects that would have given them an edge over new suburban developments. In addition, transit underdevelopment in these CMAs deprives their CBDs of the accessibility advantages it confers to large CMAs' downtown areas.

Industrial establishments that retain their central location are another source of employment within the central city and older suburbs. Some firms remain in the central city and older suburbs because of their integration to an industrial district's intense linkage network, as in the case of Montreal's and Toronto's inner-city garment districts. These firms are tied to their present location by intense inter-firm linkages with close-by establishments. Attachment to older parts of the agglomeration also stems from important sunk capital and dependence on site-specific infrastructures, such as harbour facilities. Reliance on boat delivery has caused Redpath to expand its waterfront refinery close to downtown Toronto. Workplaces also opt for these portions of the CMA to maintain market proximity. As in more peripheral settings, retail and services locate in the central city and older inner suburbs to be close to their clients. For example, the areas immediately surrounding large metropolitan regions' CBDs host concentrations of printing establishments supplying downtown offices.

The central city and older inner suburbs also appeal to certain new industrial enterprises. These are firms that can operate within subdivided, often multi-storey, industrial premises and benefit from the proximity to certain suppliers and markets as well as to the central city and older-suburb labour force. In Toronto, cultural and media industries are perceived as suited to central locations by virtue of their proximity to the inner-city pool of creative workers, easy access to downtown theatres and galleries, and flexibility in terms of physical plant needs (Toronto, 1991: 6–8). The segmentation of markets, including cultural markets, that characterizes post-Fordism propels the growth of these industries, as evidenced by the multiplication of cable channels over the last years.

The multimedia industry illustrates the enduring appeal of cities' central areas for enterprises engaged in the development of customized products and reliant on a labour force combining creativity and technical skills. This industry includes firms using a multimedia approach to graphic design, software development, and publishing, as well as establishments engaged in the development of multimedia products for platforms such as CD-ROMs and the Internet. By virtue of its access to the most advanced communications technology, this industry would appear to face minimal locational constraints and could thus be expected to assume a dispersed location pattern. But recent research paints an entirely different picture (Brail, 1997, 1998): much of the industry concentrates in Toronto's core area. Forty-one per cent of Ontario's 418 multimedia firms are located within the former City of Toronto boundaries—the central part of the Toronto CMA. Different factors account for this clustering. First, many of these firms are involved in the development of highly customized products for corporate clients. Securing such clients and tailoring products to their specifications involve repeated face-to-face contacts—hence the advantage of a location, such as central Toronto, within easy reach of corporate headquarters. Second, there is a great deal of subcontracting within this industry. Multimedia firms often contract out musical composition, voice-overs, and cinematography. This constitutes another source of frequent meetings, to assure conformity between subcontracted work and multimedia firms' requirements. Third, these firms rely on contract workers for much of their creative work, and individuals engaged in creative pursuits show a predilection for inner-city locations. It is thus logical for multimedia firms to locate close to a group of workers essential to their product development. Finally, former industrial buildings on the east and west side of downtown Toronto offer abundant affordable floor space for such firms.

The persistence of central-city appeal for workplaces is expressed in variations in gross square foot rent for industrial and office space, suggesting the existence of a differential rent in central areas. As Figure 15.3 indicates, many central districts have industrial rents above the Toronto metropolitan region average. This tendency is even more pronounced for office space, with all CBD districts scoring well above the agglomeration average. Along with the ongoing appeal of the CBD, Figure 15.4 points to an extension of high office space rents to

Figure 15.3   **Industrial Rents in the Greater Toronto Area (average annual rent per square foot in available premises, by industrial districts for which data are available)**

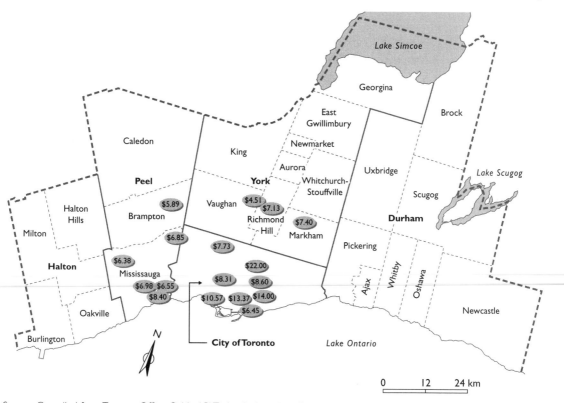

Source: Compiled from Toronto Office Guide, ICI Technologies <http://www.officeguide.com>, retrieved January 1998.

the north, with North York Centre values equalling those of downtown Toronto (in large measure a function of the absence of older office structures in recently developed North York Centre).

Overall, the emerging metropolitan-wide picture is one of advancing but incomplete decentralization. Workplaces have clearly been involved in the decentralization trend that has marked postwar urban Canada. But this pattern has not translated in a random distribution of different types of workplaces throughout the ever-expanding territory of metropolitan regions. Rather there is an enduring tendency for workplaces belonging to a same category to opt for similar locations. Nor does decen-

tralization necessarily mark the decline of central locations. Particularly in large metropolitan regions, the CBD and surrounding districts have maintained their attraction for certain workplaces.

Urban Employment Issues

This section focuses on issues illustrating how present employment trends affect critical aspects of urban life: the environment; the use of space within cities; municipalities' fiscal capacity; and cities' social structure. It closes with a brief critique of strategies municipal administrations adopt to stimulate economic development.

Figure 15.4   **Office Rents in the Greater Toronto Area (average annual rent per square foot in available premises, by office districts for which data are available)**

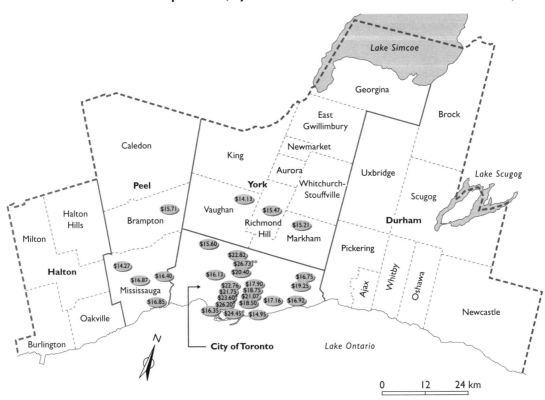

*Downtown Toronto office districts

**North York Centre office district

Source: Compiled from Toronto Office Guide, ICI Technologies <http://www.officeguide.com>, retrieved January 1998.

Employment and Urban Dispersion

The influence of workplaces on urban structure—density, land use, and transportation patterns—derives from the large proportion of space taken by such sites, the type of location they favour, and the transportation modes they promote. By opting for areas that are poorly accessible by public transportation because of their low density (with as few as 6.5 employees per hectare in a fully developed southeastern Scarborough manufacturing and warehousing district) and fragmentation into large mono-functional zones, workplaces have contributed to an ongoing rise in car use (Metro Toronto, 1988: 72). Figure 15.5 depicts the near-total reliance on the automobile of suburban industrial and office parks.

There is an environmental paradox to suburban employment sites, most particularly industrial and office parks. At first appearance, with their abundant green space, they seem to be environmentally benign (Castells and Hall, 1994: 1). But closer examination refutes this impression. With their heavy car and truck reliance, they are major

Figure 15.5   **A.M. Peak Modal Splits, Selected Business Parks, 1996**

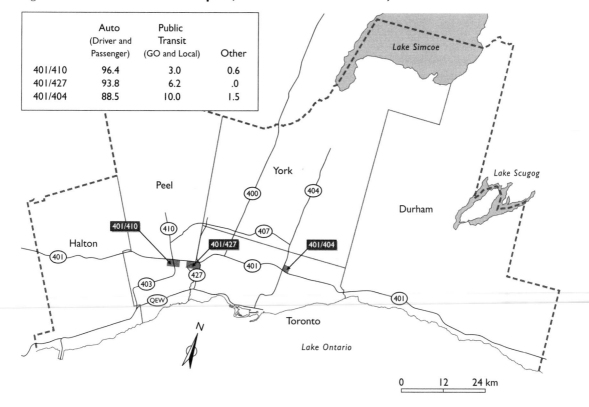

	Auto (Driver and Passenger)	Public Transit (GO and Local)	Other
401/410	96.4	3.0	0.6
401/427	93.8	6.2	.0
401/404	88.5	10.0	1.5

Source: Transportation Tomorrow Survey, special tabulations.

contributors to air pollution, and the vast amount of land they consume makes them important contributors to urban sprawl and to the resulting loss to urbanization of rural and natural land.

To moderate the growing office predilection for suburban office parks and self-standing locations, as well as the high level of car dependence associated with these locations, Metro Toronto (now the City of Toronto) and the Office for the Greater Toronto Area have promoted the creation of sub-

urban downtowns. These were intended to reproduce, at a reduced scale, environments conducive to pedestrian and transit use, as in the CBDs. But the Greater Toronto Area's three largest suburban downtowns (those of Mississauga, North York, and Scarborough) reveal environments still dominated by parking lots and wide arterial roads, which are thus inimical to pedestrian movement and achieve public transit modal splits closer to those of car-oriented suburban regional municipalities than to those of transit-dependent downtown Toronto (see Table 15.2) (see Chapter 11).

Vacant Industrial Sites

Deindustrialization has resulted in an abundant inventory of vacant industrial land and buildings, particularly in central cities and inner suburbs. Older industrial areas are particularly vulnerable because their establishments are often at the tail end of their life cycle and their installations are often obsolete. For example, in the former City of Toronto approximately 75 per cent of the industrial inventory is considered to be unsuitable to contemporary needs; this proportion is below 10 per cent in most outer suburbs (Metro Toronto, 1996: 15). Efforts to prevent the deindustrialization of inner-city industrial belts generally fail. The former City of Toronto has actively engaged in attempts to preserve its industrial zones in the face of advanc-

ing suburbanization and deindustrialization. In 1977, it created an Industrial (I) zoning category to prevent commercial activities from locating within these zones (Toronto, 1991: 1). As traditional industries vanished, the City of Toronto targeted emerging sectors such as film and fashion. But it soon became apparent that it was impossible to maintain industrial activities in all areas zoned for this purpose. Numerous sites and buildings zoned 'I' remained vacant despite reindustrialization efforts.

The outlook on the reuse of former industrial sites is a function of their location within a metropolitan region, of a particular region's economic performance, and of its urban structure. Simply put, redevelopment prospects are most favourable for sites located close to the CBD, in agglomerations that both are prosperous and boast a healthy downtown. Conversely, reuse is seriously compromised in poorly accessible sites and in the central areas of dispersed agglomerations. Redevelopment obstacles

Table 15.2   **1996 A.M. Peak Modal Split: Downtown Toronto, Suburban Downtowns and GTA Suburban Regional Municipalities (in Percent)**

	Automobile, Driver	Automobile, Passenger	Local Transit	Go Rail	Walk and Cycle
Downtown Toronto	27.8	7.0	42.8	16.1	6.1
Suburban Downtowns					
North York Centre	56.9	12.9	24.3	0.6	5.1
Scarborough Centre	72.3	12.4	13.7	0.4	1.0
Mississauga Centre	82.6	10.4	6.2	0.2	1.4
GTA Suburban Regional Municipalities					
Durham	65	12	4	4	10
York	65	13	7	1	7
Peel	64	14	6	3	8
Halton	68	12	2	5	8

Source: Transportation Tomorrow Survey, <http://www.jpint.utoronto.ca>. Date of retrieval, 6 Aug. 1998, and special tabulations.

are further compounded by a metropolitan region's lagging economic performance.

Decontamination expenses represent another barrier to the reuse of industrial land. At a given level of contamination, these expenses vary according to the nature of replacement uses, each requiring specific soil cleanliness standards (CMHC, 1993; Royal Commission on the Future of the Toronto Waterfront, 1990). These are much higher for residential than industrial reuse. In the absence of public-sector subsidies, considerable decontamination expenses rule out the redevelopment of sites that cannot attract land uses capable of generating sufficient market value to cover such costs. Developers are also wary of the unpredictability of soil decontamination expenses. Despite its location within two kilometres of downtown Toronto, the Ataratiri project, which was intended to house 14,000 people on former industrial land, was abandoned in large part because of excessive decontamination costs (Earnst and Young, 1992; Millward, 1990).

In highly accessible sites, especially when unburdened by contamination, office, mixed-use, and housing-focused redevelopments are attractive possibilities. These options are consistent with the present intensification objectives of municipal planners, who seek to temper sprawl by augmenting density within the built perimeter. Successful examples of residential reuse include St Lawrence Market in Toronto, the Angus site in Montreal, and False Creek in Vancouver (Cybriwsky, Ley, and Western, 1986; Dansereau, Germain, and Éveillard, 1996). The former City of Toronto took an innovative approach to the reuse of deindustrialized districts close to the CBD. Newly adopted zoning for these areas makes fullest use of the mixed-use concept. Provided that the external integrity of heritage industrial buildings is preserved, controls on possible uses therein are minimal. These structures can contain residential units as well as industrial and commercial activities (Toronto, 1996a, 1996b, 1997).

Another option is to seek new industrial firms to replace departing establishments. This transition can take place within existing buildings—typically in units created within large installations—or in new facilities. In the latter case, the tendency is for a closely packed industrial landscape, often composed of multi-storey buildings, to make way for a suburban-like industrial park with single-storey structures and plentiful green and vehicular space.

A further possibility is to encourage retail development. This alternative is particularly suited to land abutting arterial roads. Presently, the Toronto Economic Development Corporation revitalization strategy for industrial land close to Toronto's port includes 'big-box' stores (*Toronto Planning Digest*, 1996).

In extreme circumstances, when a non-appealing location or high anticipated decontamination expenses deter investors, all the above options are ruled out. Reuse may then entail a dramatic decrease in intensity of use, such as turning these sites into parks, naturalized areas, sport fields, or golf courses.

Employment and Municipal Decline

Employment loss can spark a spiral of municipal decline. Workplace closures translate into an immediate drop in municipal tax revenues. There are further ramifications. As employment falls, so do retail, housing market activity, and property assessment. In Ontario, this situation is exacerbated by local or regional governments' responsibility for a portion of welfare payments. Ballooning welfare rolls then aggravate municipalities' fiscal imbalance. All of this translates into higher tax rates, which make it difficult to attract workplaces. Such a situation is common in resource and old industrial centres. The central municipalities of large metropolitan regions are also vulnerable. For example, the City of Toronto (1998 boundaries) was disproportionately affected by employment losses during the 1989–92 recession. As a result, central cities and inner suburbs often experience a decline or hesitant growth of their commercial/industrial assessment. Economic difficulties and other reasons, such as infrastructure obsolescence, account for these municipalities' tendency to post higher tax rates than new suburbs do (see Figure 15.6).

Still, welfare programs, less racism, and a frequent involvement of regional governments in the

Figure 15.6   **Effective Property Tax Rates* on GTA Commercial and Industrial Properties, 1994 (% of market value)**

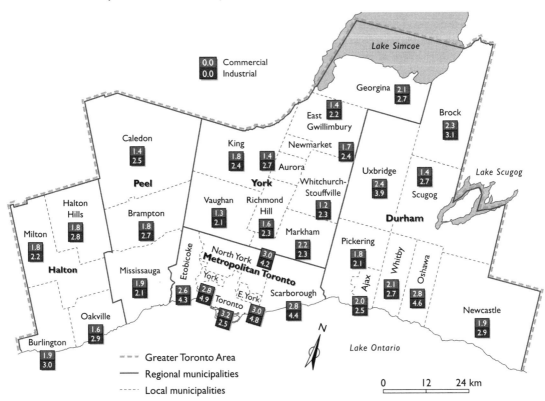

*Includes taxes for lower-tier purposes, upper-tier purposes, and education.
Source: GTA Task Force (1996: 78).

The Changing Nature of Work

delivery of services account for lesser gaps in municipalities' financial capacity in Canadian than in US metropolitan regions. For example, no Canadian metropolitan region experiences the stark fiscal discrepancy between Detroit and its suburbs.

As seen in the first section, overall job creation rates have decelerated since the advent of post-Fordism and young people are disproportionately afflicted by resulting unemployment (Bernier, 1996). At the same time, post-Fordist work arrangements polarize incomes. While incomes at the peak of the pay scale have increased appreciably, most spectacularly among executives of large corporations, middle-range incomes have stagnated and those at the bottom have fallen precipitously (Yalnizyan, 1998).

These changes within the employment sphere impact on different aspects of urban life. Unable to afford a dwelling of their own, increasing numbers of low-income people (including families) are compelled to share accommodation. This is the case for unemployed or underemployed young adults who are forced to remain in their parents' home (Miron, 1988). Meanwhile, housing for the poor, rooming-houses in particular, is disappearing rapidly in some cities, partly as a consequence of the ease with which moderately wealthy households attracted to inner-city housing can outbid poor individuals in the residential market. In consequence, low-income households are relegated to a shrinking portion of urban residential space, while growing numbers of street people heighten the visibility of poverty. Marginalization and polarization equally reverberate on other forms of consumption. At one end of the spectrum, food banks cannot cope with ever-rising needs, while at the other, demand for luxury cars and other expensive goods and services is robust.

With lay-offs, early retirement, and difficulties for young adults to enter the job market, formal work is becoming absent from the lives of an increasing proportion of individuals. Decades ago, sociologists and some planners heralded the advent of a leisure society where rising productivity would yield a progressive shortening of the time individuals devote to formal work, without adverse consequences for consumption levels (Dumazedier, 1976; Krauss, 1971; Pearson, 1969). As we are now well aware, things have unfolded very differently. For some, work demands have amplified, but others have found themselves altogether shut out from the workplace. This raises a critical planning issue: How can the city be adapted to the increasing presence of individuals with plentiful available time, some of whom, such as retirees with a substantial pension, are financially comfortable, while others live well below the poverty line? Cities have been planned in a functional fashion, with virtually all land being allocated to residential, production, or consumption uses and their respective infrastructure requirements. What little city-owned leisure space there is generally caters to the needs of children. What is more, movement in most districts urbanized since the war is difficult without the use of a car. The unavailability of areas where teenagers can congregate informally has long been identified as a shortcoming of a near-exclusive planning focus on fiscally lucrative activities. This predicament now extends to the growing ranks of those who are without employment. There is a need to rethink urban planning so that cities can be better adapted to the presence of

various categories of unemployed individuals. This would entail catering to the accessibility needs of low-income individuals in postwar environments where the car has become indispensable and providing locales for both organized and spontaneous activities of interest to the unemployed.

Employment Creation Strategies

There is a tradition of local governments engaging in employment creation efforts by marketing their municipality to employers and providing incentives to incoming and expanding firms. These efforts originally concentrated on manufacturing, largely because of its high service-sector spin-off effects. But, as stressed in this chapter, employment has diminished within this sector, reducing the effectiveness of these municipal initiatives. Many local governments then turned to public- and private-sector service employment strategies. But outcomes were compromised by government cut-backs and the effect of automation and rationalization within the service industry as a whole. This raises questions about future targets of local strategies for employment creation. While traditional sources of employment seem to be losing their capacity to create jobs, there is no shortage of community needs awaiting responses. Many of these needs stem from the economic marginalization caused by high unemployment. This leads some to propose a community economic development strategy that would generate jobs targeted at social and environmental demands left unmet by the market (Daly and Cobb, 1994; Henderson, 1991; Rifkin, 1995). But the present public-sector financial stringency casts doubts on possible sources of income for those involved in community development initiatives (Filion, 1998).

Conclusion

This chapter has examined urban and employment trends, more specifically how post-Fordism plays itself out in a dispersing urban structure. It has shown that the contemporary urban structure, characterized by the persistence of a concentrated realm within a predominantly dispersed environment, accommodates the needs of different categories of workplaces. It has also demonstrated that this urban form is itself in large part an outcome of workplace location patterns. High-rise office buildings are an essential constituent of large cities' CBDs. Meanwhile, industrial and business parks, as well as retail and service concentrations, have emancipated suburbs from their former employment and service dependence on the central city. The form urban development takes and how people organize their lives within cities owe much to employment trends. Where city dwellers live is largely dictated by where they find work, and for most the commuting trip is the main daily journey. And the time and money available for urban consumption are a consequence of the nature of a metropolitan region's employment.

We can anticipate two major urban consequences from likely future employment evolution. The first will be ongoing dispersion fuelled by electronic communications and the changing nature of work reflected in increasing home-based work. Yet for all its apparent entrenchment, one should remain aware of the fragility of present and coming employment and, therefore, of urban dispersion. Dispersion hinges on the availability of low-cost fuel and the continuing household and public-sector ability to foot the bill for the expensive infrastructures associated with this form of urbanization, two preconditions with a highly uncertain future. The second consequence of employment trends for the city will be a yawning income and social gap due to a segmentation of the labour force into relatively permanent and well-paid workers and disposable low-paid employees. In the absence of government remedies, metropolitan regions will increasingly mirror this polarization, with worsening discrepancy between high- and low-income districts, a conversion of many middle-income neighbourhoods into either low- or high-income areas, and rising homelessness.

Notes

1. While Canada's manufacturing productivity rose more slowly than that of other advanced industrial nations since the 1960s, it has nonetheless considerably exceeded service-sector productivity improvements (Britton, 1996).

2. As defined here central cities refers to the City of Toronto (pre-1998 boundaries, before Metro's amalgamation), the City of Montreal (1991 boundaries), and the City of Vancouver. The inner-suburb category includes, in the Toronto CMA, the remainder of the City of Toronto (all pre-1998 Metro Toronto municipalities with the exception of the then City of Toronto), in the Montreal CMA, Island of Montreal municipalities apart from the City of Montreal, and in the Vancouver CMA, all municipalities abutting the City of Vancouver, including those that face this city on the north side of the Narrows. In all three cases, the outer suburb encompasses the remainder of the CMA.

References

Allen, J. 1989. 'Is There a Service Economy', in J. Allen and D. Massey, *The Economy in Question*. Milton Keynes: Open University Press.

Bell, D. 1973. *The Coming of the Post-Industrial Society*. New York: Basic Books.

Betcherman, G. 1996. 'Globalization, Labour Market and Public Policy', in R. Boyer and D. Drache, eds, *States Against Markets: The Limits of Globalization*. London: Routledge.

Birch, D.L. 1975. 'From Suburb to Urban Place', *Annals of the American Academy of Political and Social Science* 422: 25–35.

Brail, S. 1997. 'The Emerging Multimedia Industry: Impacts on Toronto's Urban Industrial Landscape', paper given at the Urban Affairs Association annual meeting, Toronto, Apr.

———. 1998. 'The Paradox of Technological Change: "New" Media in "Old" Urban Areas', paper presented at the annual meeting of the American Association of Geographers, Boston, Mar. Available at <http://www.geog.utoronto.ca/deptinfo/BRAIL 2.html>, date of retrieval, 19–8–98.

Bunting, T., and H. Millward. 1999. 'A Tale of Two CBDs 1: The Decline and Revival of Downtown Retailing in Halifax and Kitchener', *Canadian Journal of Urban Research* 7: 139–66.

Cameron, G.C. 1973. 'Intraurban Location and the New Plant', *Papers of the Regional Science Association* 31: 125–43.

Castells, M., and P. Hall. 1994. *Technopoles of the World: The Making of Twenty-First-Century Industrial Complexes*. New York: Routledge.

CMHC (Canada Mortgage and Housing Corporation). 1990. *Relationship Between Urban Soil Contamination and Housing in Canada*. Ottawa: CMHC.

Coffey, W. 1992. 'The Role of Producer Services in Systems of Flexible Production', in H. Ernste and V. Meier, eds, *Regional Development and Contemporary Industrial Response: Extending Flexible Specialisation*. London: Belhaven.

———. 1996. 'The Role and Location of Service Activities in the Canadian Space Economy', in J. Britton, ed., *Canada and the Global Economy: A Geography of Structural and Technological Change*. Montreal and Kingston: McGill-Queen's University Press.

Cybriwsky, R.A., D. Ley, and J. Western. 1986. 'The Political and Social Construction of Revitalized Neighborhoods: Society Hill, Philadelphia, and False Creek, Vancouver', in N. Smith and P. Williams, eds, *Gentrification of the City*. Boston: Allen and Unwin.

Daly, E.D., and J.B. Cobb. 1994. *For the Common Good: Redirecting the Economy toward Community, the Environment and a Sustainable Future*, 2nd ed. Boston: Beacon Press.

Dansereau, F., A. Germain, and C. Éveillard. 1996. 'Le quartier Angus, un exemple de mixité sociale programmé', *Plan Canada* 36, 1: 33–8.

Donner, A. 1991. 'Recession, Recovery and Redistribution: The Three R's of Canadian State Macro-Policy in the 1980s', in D. Drache and M. Gertler, eds, *The New Era of Global Competition*.

Montreal and Kingston: McGill-Queen's University Press.

Dumazedier, J. 1967. *Toward a Society of Leisure*. New York: Free Press.

Economic Council of Canada. 1990. *Good Jobs, Bad Jobs: Employment in the Service Economy*. Ottawa: Economic Council of Canada.

Earnst and Young. 1992. *Ataratiri Project: Audit of the Project Management System and Controls Other Than the Property Acquisition Process*. Toronto: Earnst and Young.

Filion, P. 1998. 'Potential and Limitations of Community Economic Development: Individual Initiative and Collective Action in a Post-Fordist Context', *Environment and Planning A* 30: 1101–23.

Galarneau, D. 1996. 'Unionized Workers', *Perspectives on Labour and Income* 8, 1: 43–52. Statistics Canada, Catalogue 75–001–XPE.

Gardner, A. 1997. *The Self-Employed*. Ottawa and Toronto: Statistics Canada and Prentice-Hall, Focus on Canada Series, Catalogue 71–005.

Gershuny, J. and I. Miles. 1983. *The New Service Economy*. London: Frances Pinter.

Gertler, M.S. 1996. *Industrial Activity in Metropolitan Toronto: The Incidence of Clusters and Network Relations*. Toronto: Metro Toronto, Metro Planning, Research and Information Services.

Grenon, L. 1996. 'Are Service Jobs Low-Paying', *Perspectives on Labour and Income* 8, 1: 29–34, Statistics Canada, Catalogue 75–001–XPE.

GTA (Greater Toronto Area) Task Force. 1996. *Report*. Toronto: Queen's Printer for Ontario.

Harvey, D. 1989. *The Condition of Postmodernity*. Oxford: Basil Blackwell.

Hemson Consulting. 1987. *Outlook for Office Employment and Space in the Central Core*. Toronto: City of Toronto.

Henderson, H. 1991. *Paradigms in Progress: Life Beyond Economics*. Indianapolis: Knowledge Systems Inc.

Krahn, H. 1995. 'Non-Standard Work on the Rise', *Perspectives on Labour and Income* 7, 4: 35–42. Statistics Canada, Catalogue 75–001–XPE.

Kraus, R.G. 1971. *Recreation and Leisure in Modern Society*. New York: Appleton-Century-Crofts.

Le Corbusier. 1973 [1933]. *The Athens Charter*. New York: Grossman.

Ley, D. 1996. *The New Middle Class and the Remaking of the Central City*. Oxford: Oxford University Press.

Lowe, G. 1997. 'Computers in the Workplace', *Perspectives on Labour and Income* 9, 2: 29–36. Statistics Canada, Catalogue 75–001–XPE.

MacDonald, G. 1997. 'Home Is Not Where the Work Is', *Globe and Mail*, 4 Apr.

Marshall, A. 1920. *Principles of Economics*, 8th edn. London: Macmillan.

Metro Toronto (Metropolitan Toronto Planning Department, Policy Development Division). 1988. *Metropolitan Plan Review: Industrial Areas (Report No. 5)*. Toronto: Metro Toronto.

———— (Metro Planning). 1995. *Metro Facts: 1994 Metro Toronto Employment Survey—Summary Results*, vol. 26. Toronto: Metro Toronto, Mar.

———— (Metro Planning). 1996. *Towards an Industrial Land Strategy (Industrial Land Strategy Study, Phase 1, Overview Report)*. Toronto: Metro Toronto.

Millward, H., and T. Bunting. 1999. 'A Tale of Two CBDs 2: The Internal Retail Dynamic of Downtown Halifax and Downtown Kitchener', *Canadian Journal of Urban Research* 8: 1–27.

Millward, R.E. 1990. *Ataratiri: Principles, Directions and Strategies*. Toronto: City of Toronto, Housing Department.

Miron, J.R. 1988. *Housing in Postwar Canada: Demographic Change, Household Formation, and Housing Demand*. Montreal and Kingston: McGill-Queen's University Press.

Myles, J. 1991. 'Post-Industrialism and the Service Economy', in D. Drache and M. Gertler, eds, *The New Era of Global Competition*. Montreal and Kingston: McGill-Queen's University Press.

Nadwodny, R. 1996. 'Canadians Working at Home', *Canadian Social Trends* 40: 16–22. Statistics Canada, Catalogue 11–008E.

Nelson, K. 1986. 'Labor Demand, Labor Supply and the Suburbanization of Low-Wage Office Work', in A.J. Scott and M. Storper, eds, *Production, Work, Territory*. Boston: Allen and Unwin.

Niosi, J. 1978. *Is the Canadian Economy Closing Down?* Montreal: Black Rose.

Norcliffe, G. 1994. 'Regional Labour Market Adjustments in a Period of Structural Transformation', *Canadian Geographer* 38: 2–17.

Pearson, N. 1969. *Planning for a Leisure Society*. Guelph, Ont.: University of Guelph, Centre for Resources Development Publication No. 18.

Porter, M.E. 1990. *The Competitive Advantage of Nations*. New York: Free Press.

Reich, R.B. 1992. *The Work of Nations: Preparing Ourselves for 21st Century Capitalism*. New York: Vintage.

Rifkin, J. 1995. *The End of Work: The Decline of the Global Labour Force and the Dawn of the Post-Market Era*. New York: Putman.

Royal Commission on the Future of the Toronto Waterfront. 1990. *Soil Contamination and Port Redevelopment in Toronto*. Papers of the Canadian Waterfront Resource Centre, No. 3. Toronto: The Commission.

Rutherford, T. 1996. 'The Socio-Spatial Restructuring of Canadian Labour Markets', in J. Britton, ed., *Canada and the Global Economy*. Montreal and Kingston: McGill-Queen's University Press.

Sayer, A., and R. Walker. 1992. *The New Social Economy: Reworking the Division of Labour*. Oxford: Basil Blackwell.

Scott, A. 1988. *New Industrial Spaces*. London: Pion.

Sharpe, A., and R. Haddow, eds. 1997. *Social Partnerships for Training: Canada's Experiment with Labour Force Development Boards*. Ottawa and Kingston: Centre for the Study of Living Standards, Caledon Institute of Social Policy, and School of Policy Studies, Queen's University.

Smith, J. 1997. 'The Labour Market: Mid-Year Review', *Perspectives on Labour and Income* 9, 3: 7–20. Statistics Canada, Catalogue 75–001–XPE.

Statistics Canada. 1983. *Place of Work—Census Metropolitan Areas*. Ottawa: Minister of Supply and Services, Catalogue 92–908.

————. 1993. *Place of Work—The Nation*. Ottawa: Minister of Industry, Science and Technology, Catalogue 93–323.

————. 1998. *Historical Labour Force Statistics 1997*. Ottawa: Minister of Industry, Catalogue 71–201–XPB.

Steines, D.N. 1977. 'Causality and Intraurban Location', *Journal of Urban Economics* 4: 69–97.

Swift, J. 1995. *Wheel of Fortune: Work and Life in an Age of Falling Expectations*. Toronto: Between the Lines.

Toronto, City of. 1991. *Future of City Industry Study (Cityplan 91, Report 22)*. Toronto: City of Toronto.

———, Planning and Development Department. 1996a. *King-Parliament Official Plan II*. Toronto: City of Toronto.

———, Planning and Development Department. 1996b. *King-Spadina Official Plan Part II*. Toronto: City of Toronto.

———, Urban Development Services. 1997. *King-Parliament Community Improvement Plan: A Plan to Assist Reinvestment and Revitalization*. Toronto: City of Toronto.

Toronto Star. 1998. 'Home Office Boom Has Condos, Houses Wired', 6 Feb., B1, B4.

Toronto Planning Digest. 1996. Untitled news item, 10, 10: 5.

White, S.B., L.S. Binkley, and J.D. Osterman. 1993. 'The Sources of Suburban Employment', *Journal of the American Planning Association* 59, 2: 193–204.

Yalnizyan, A. 1998. *The Growing Gap*. Toronto: Centre for Social Justice.

Chapter 16

Housing

Richard S. Harris

Housing makes up about 30 per cent of the land area of Canadian towns and cities. As a result, houses help to define the character of different places: the urbane row 'plexes' of Montreal, the graceful limestone homes of old Kingston, the comfortable bungalows of Vancouver, the ambitious condominiums of Toronto. For their occupants, dwellings such as these have all kinds of significance (Harris and Pratt, 1993). Housing is the largest item in most people's budgets. Including furnishing and household expenses (such as heat and property taxes) it absorbs on average almost 25 per cent of household income. For home-owners, the dwelling is by far the household's largest capital asset. Most Canadians value highly the comfort, privacy, and personal autonomy that housing provides. But sometimes four walls hide the private misery of loneliness and, for too many women and children, the daily degradation of battery and abuse. For better or worse, we spend most of our lives at home and we care a lot about how we are housed.

This chapter reviews how Canadians are housed. It considers the changing ways in which housing has been produced and sold, how it is occupied by different types of people and then used. It highlights geographical variations at both the regional and local scales, variations that are important in themselves and for the development of public policy. Before looking at these substantive issues, however, we need to consider the various ways in which housing may be viewed.

Perspectives on Housing

Housing touches many aspects of our lives. It has been studied by academics with varied points of view. In this chapter it is not possible to consider all of this variety. For our purposes it is useful to identify four major traditions of thought.

Neoclassical Economics and Demography

Housing is like any commodity: being useful, it has a price. As such, it is a matter of concern to economists, many of whom take a neoclassical viewpoint (Fallis, 1985; Goldberg, 1983). Economists analyse housing in terms of supply and demand, with consumer demand leading the market. If more people want housing, they bid up prices. Contractors, seeing a profitable opportunity, build more. Because economists emphasize housing demand, they are very sensitive to the importance of demographics. In *Boom, Bust, and Echo*, the economist David Foot (Foot and Stoffman, 1996) has claimed that changing demographics can explain 'two thirds of everything', including shifts in housing demand. Most writers would give somewhat greater weight to the influence of immigration and incomes. Miron (1988), for example, has argued that rising incomes enabled many young singles and couples to form households instead of staying at home with their parents. This trend helped increase the number of households in Canada in the postwar years. Associated with a demand for small rental units, it underlay the apartment boom of the 1960s. In this manner, changing patterns and levels of demand called forth an appropriate response from the suppliers of housing. On the other hand, neoclassical economists point out that if demand flags, so do prices, profits, and the rate of construction. Thus, it is possible to explain the construction downturns of the early 1980s and 1990s in terms of economic recessions that, especially in the earlier downturn, were also coupled with high interest rates. Demand was stifled, and supply almost dried up.

Changes in the types of units built are also thought to be led by demand. Condominiums illustrate the point. Condominiums are a fairly new form of multi-unit home-ownership in which the household owns a dwelling unit but not the land on which it sits (Hulchanski, 1993). Typically, their owners share the cost of paying someone else to maintain the building. A neoclassical explanation of condominium growth would emphasize the emergence of growing numbers of 'empty-nesters' and of DINKs (Double Income, No Kids), who can afford to own property but who do not want the responsibilities of maintenance. As consumers express new preferences and make new choices, suppliers respond.

From this point of view, the 'hidden hand' of a self-regulating market is the best means of co-ordinating the actions of thousands of businesses and households. Since the price mechanism is vital to this process, attempts to interfere with prices are criticized. Rent controls, for example, are attacked on the grounds that, by depressing prices, they inhibit new construction and create a shortage that benefits no one (Fallis, 1985: 202–6; Goldberg, 1983: 67–8). Proponents of this view argue that the housing industry has provided good housing to most Canadians and that significant problems are faced by only a small minority—those on very low incomes (Goldberg, 1983: 88–91). It follows that, at most, governments should concern themselves with the housing of this minority, otherwise leaving housing to the private sector.

This approach has yielded many insights. It offers plausible answers to policy questions such as: 'What effect have rent controls had on the housing market in a specific city?' It gives us tools to analyse how households trade off the convenience of access to work against the advantages of a larger home on a larger lot (Bassett and Short, 1980, ch. 3). However, the assumption that consumers of housing make

free choices gives insufficient weight to the ways that the housing industry can shape demand. More generally, it makes no serious attempt to explain how housing markets are shaped by the wider society. On these issues we must turn to other points of view.

Sociopolitical Views

A number of writers have developed a sociopolitical view that emphasizes the existence within the housing market of a variety of interest groups (Bassett and Short, 1980, chs 5–7). These groups, sometimes referred to as 'actors' or 'institutions', include builders, developers, real estate agents, mortgage lenders, landlords, and local governments.

All groups are seen to wield some degree of economic and political power. Lenders can grant or deny mortgage credit. This is important because the great majority of home-buyers need a mortgage. In 1991 half (49 per cent) of home-owners owned their homes outright, but most would have had a mortgage when they first bought.[1] Local governments zone land and may exclude types of housing (and hence types of households) that may be perceived to be undesirable. The common targets are low-income households, who pay little in property taxes but who make relatively heavy demands on municipal services. Landlords can refuse to rent to people they perceive to be undesirable on economic or social grounds. Common targets have included single parents and visible minorities. (Racial discrimination is illegal but difficult to prove.) Real estate developers, who create whole subdivisions, define what types of residential environments are available (Filion and Alexander, 1994; Lorimer, 1978). In the process, arguably, each group can shape people's preferences. Again, condominiums are an example.

The demand for condominiums has been fostered, and in part created, by large developers who have seen the chance to make large profits. Perhaps the most successful promoter in Canada has been Martin Atkins. In 1985 alone he marketed 1,006 of the 1,865 condo units sold in Toronto. Journalist Ian

Brown (1986: 50) observed that 'Atkins is the man responsible not only for Toronto's current bout of condo fever, but for making real an entirely new conception of what urban life ought to be.' From this point of view consumer demand is constrained and shaped by actors on the supply side of the housing market. This point of view introduces social and political dimensions to the subject. It is incomplete, however, because it does not set the housing market within the context of the changing structure of the economy as a whole. A third perspective is especially concerned with this issue.

Political Economy

Political economists, mostly Marxists and neo-Marxists, see the social groups active within the housing market as part of a wider structure of class interests (Bassett and Short, 1980, ch. 9; Feagin and Parker, 1990). They agree that the housing industry has power over consumers, but they stress that such power is limited by the larger, impersonal logic of capital accumulation. Each group must act in economically rational terms or go to the wall. In one sense this argument parallels the neoclassical economist's emphasis on the market's 'hidden hand'. But instead of viewing this process as beneficent, political economists see it as immoral. Housing, they argue, is provided to those who can afford it, and not necessarily to those in need. Capitalism creates poorly paid workers who cannot afford decent accommodation. Problems and crises are inherent in, and not incidental to, the housing market and will always exist. It follows that the state cannot solve the housing problem until it has dealt with the structured inequalities of the wider society.

Political economists argue that capital accumulation creates a dynamic of historical change within society, and hence within the housing market. According to one interpretation, a crisis of profits in the 1930s brought on a new 'regime of accumulation' (Belec, Holmes, and Rutherford, 1987). This regime depended on allowing wages to rise so as to create demand for the products of industry. It is sometimes labelled 'Fordist' because it was heralded by the policies of the Ford Motor Company, which in the 1910s introduced higher pay in order to reduce labour turnover on the assembly line. Housing was important to this new regime. Until the middle of the twentieth century, many Canadians acquired homes by subjecting themselves to a rigorous regimen of thrift. In Canada, as elsewhere, the state helped to change this pattern. The Dominion Housing Act of 1935 was a first step, consolidated by later National Housing Acts. These encouraged people to acquire homes on long-term credit. In the postwar years, mortgaged home-ownership reflected and sustained economic growth not only through housing construction but also by creating demand for a wide range of consumer goods.

Some political economists believe that we are now in a period of transition to a new, 'post-Fordist' regime of accumulation, one of greater social polarization and inequality. From this point of view, the condo boom not only reflects new consumer preferences and the activities of clever promoters, but also a larger process of economic restructuring, one that entails, as its counterpoint, a growth in poverty and homelessness.

The recent growth of poverty has affected women more than men. It is associated with the ghettoization of working women into low-paying occupations, high divorce rates, and increasing numbers of female single-parents. These trends have highlighted the fact that the housing experience of men and women is different (Rose and Wexler, 1993). None of the perspectives considered up to now have much to say about the nature and causes of this difference, but feminism does.

Feminism

Feminists believe that housing reflects, and helps to shape, gender relations in society as a whole. Although these relations are changing, they are still marked by elements of patriarchy (male dominance). Feminists note that although the home has long been viewed as the place of women, it has been built and designed by men with men's interests in mind (Watson, 1986). From this point of view the suburban single-detached home, often described as the Canadian dream, is viewed with some scepticism (Hayden, 1984). It may be comfortable to return to after a day in the factory or office but it can be boring because it constitutes an isolated work environment for the (typically female) homemaker. Moreover, such a home makes it difficult for women to get into the workforce. Its size makes for a lot of housework, while the fact that it is so often situated in a low-density suburb is a further problem. Such suburbs are poorly serviced by transit and women do not have as ready access to automobiles as men (Wekerle, 1985). This view would suggest that higher-density apartments or condominiums may be a preferable alternative. This is especially true of inner-city units, which are likely to be better serviced by transit and to have better access to a variety of social services (Rose and LeBourdais, 1986). Some feminists, however, have suggested that co-operatives are better still, especially if they contain facilities such as day care and involve co-operative housekeeping (Johnson, 1994).

The feminist point of view is the youngest and still developing. Recent research has emphasized the problems of generalizing about, and imposing uniform standards on, all women (Strong-Boag et al., 1999). Historically, for example, Strong-Boag's (1991) research indicates that the isolation experienced by women in the early postwar period was greater than today. It also shows that, having experienced the Great Depression and war years, women of the time judged this isolation very differently from their daughters today. One implication of the feminist point of view is that the distinctiveness of men's experience must also be examined. Margaret Marsh (1991), for example, has suggested that the origins of the modern suburb lie partly in the rise of male domesticity. Around the turn of the century, middle-class men began to show much more interest in home hobbies and do-it-yourself activities, and this began a trend. As yet, however, little attention has been paid to the distinctive experiences of men.

These four ways of looking at housing have often been presented as alternatives. Certainly they lead to different political conclusions. In some respects, however, as the condominium example indicates, they can also be viewed as complements. A thorough explanation of the condo boom would have to pay attention to the changing demographic structure of the population and to changes in patterns of child-rearing as these in turn affect housing preferences. It could not afford to ignore the actions of sharp promoters such as Martin Atkins, who did rather more than respond to a latent consumer demand. It would be incomplete without being interpreted as part of a larger process of social change, including changes in the situation of women and men. Arguably, the political economy perspective is the most comprehensive, but all have something to offer.

The Production, Financing, and Sale of Housing

Housing is produced in a different way from any other commodity. Canadians have grown accustomed to the assembly line, in which the product is moved past stationary workers. In the housing industry, the product (that is, the dwelling) is stationary and the tradesmen—bricklayers, carpenters, electricians—move from site to site (McKellar, 1993). In this regard, as in others, the industry can appear anachronistic. The rate of technological change has been slow and increases in labour productivity quite modest. Many attempts at innovation have fallen by the wayside. In the early-twentieth century some companies (including Sears) experimented with pre-cut home 'kits'; in the 1970s, others tried European-style 'systems building' using precast concrete slabs and modules. Each met with limited success, and then with failure. These failures were due in part to the fact that house-building is unusually cyclical. The fixed capital tied up in machinery and factories lies expensively idle during downturns.

Another feature of the home-building industry is the small average firm size. In 1984 there were 8,994 companies making single-family homes in Canada; the following year these companies built, on the average, fewer than 10 dwellings each (Clayton Research Associates, 1988: 15; McKellar, 1993). The contrast with most other industries is striking. Most builders are too small to afford new technology, but they are flexible. Little capital is needed to become a builder, especially if specialized work using expensive equipment (such as backhoes for digging foundations) is contracted out. This industry has, for many decades, provided good opportunities for immigrant entrepreneurs. The Sharps are an extreme example. In the 1920s Max Sharp, a German Jew, immigrated to Canada and settled in Toronto (DeMont, 1989). With little in the way of capital or skills he built a family home, which he then sold for a profit. Over the next two decades he built, occupied, and sold many more homes, at the rate of about one a year. In the 1950s Isadore, his son, took over the now-profitable contracting business. Today, 'Izzy' Sharp owns the Four Seasons chain of hotels and is one of the richest people in Canada. For every success of this kind, there are, of course, innumerable failures. But this family's history highlights the unusual potential for self-made mobility and profit within the housing and real estate industry.

Although change in house-building has been slow, over the length of the past century it has been considerable. Three developments are especially noteworthy. First, speculative builders (those who build first and then try to find buyers) have grown in importance. A century ago, affluent households usually commissioned homes from custom builders. Low-income households built their own homes, often with help from family or neighbours. In the building boom of 1900–13 about a third of all new homes in Toronto were self-built, and in western cities the proportion was probably higher (Harris, 1996). Today, custom work makes up an unknown, but certainly smaller, fraction of new construction. Owner-building is important chiefly in the Atlantic region (Rowe, 1989).

A second change has been the growing importance of housing finance. Until at least the 1940s, many households bought their first home from savings. Those who used credit obtained it from other individuals, whether family, friends, or strangers with whom they were put in contact by a local lawyer (Harris and Ragonetti, 1998). They 'put down' at least half of the purchase price from their savings. Typically, the mortgage had to be repaid within five years. In the 1930s, to encourage new construction and help pull the economy out of depression, the federal government passed the first in a series of Housing Acts that revolutionized the home finance system. In 1946 the Central (now Canada) Mortgage and Housing Corporation (CMHC) was set up, mainly to grant and insure mortgage loans. First-time home-buyers were encouraged to buy property on credit as soon as they could. In stages, mortgage terms have been relaxed so that 25-year mortgages on 80-90 per cent of the purchase price are now common. Institutional lenders (at first insurance companies, credit unions, and *caisses populaires*, and more recently banks) have come to dominate the mortgage market except among immigrants, for whom personal loans are still common (Murdie, 1986).

A third change has been the rise of the developer. A century ago, different agents were involved at different stages in the process of land development. Land was subdivided, sold to individual speculators, sold again on a piecemeal basis to many small builders, built upon, and then sold again to the eventual owners. The result was a varied, sometimes chaotic, residential landscape in which small and large dwellings might be juxtaposed. Some housing and some areas are still built in this way. But, especially in the larger metropolitan areas, much is now built by developers who control the entire process from land subdivision through to final sale (Figure 16.1). Developers began to emerge by the 1920s (Weiss, 1987). They shaped areas like Kingsway Park in Etobicoke (Toronto) (Paterson, 1984) and Westdale in Hamilton (Weaver, 1978). After World War II, they were favoured by a tax system that allowed rapid depreciation of investments in built infrastructure. They have become dominant in building offices, shopping centres, apartments and condominiums, and, to a lesser extent, single-family homes. From coast to coast, the result is the planned subdivision.

Figure 16.1   **The Structures of Residential Building Provision**

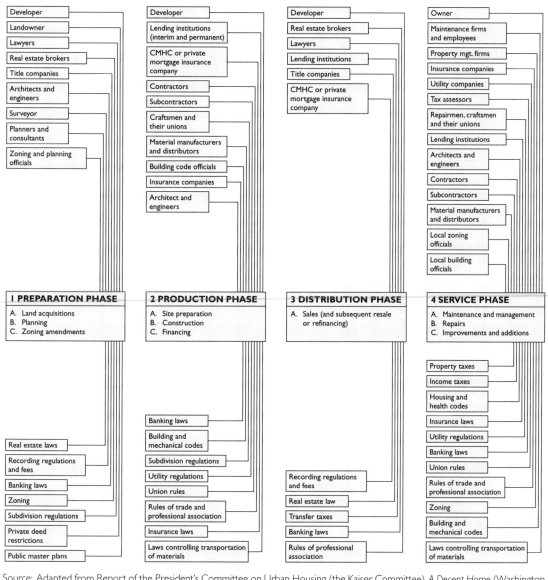

Source: Adapted from Report of the President's Committee on Urban Housing (the Kaiser Committee), *A Decent Home* (Washington, 1968), 115.

For many years these subdivisions were uniform in appearance. Beginning in the 1980s, the revival of historical styles has created some local diversity. Some styles (e.g., Georgian) and materials (e.g., brick veneer) seem popular everywhere. Others, such as Toronto's Gothic gables and polychromatic brickwork and Vancouver's cedar siding, are restoring some local qualities to the suburban scene.

Working against the trend towards large-scale development is the growing importance of home renovation. In 1966, renovations to the existing stock of housing accounted for 18 per cent of housing investment in Canada. (The remainder was for new construction.) By 1976 this proportion had increased to 23 per cent and by 1986 to 33 per cent (Fallis, 1993: Table 2). If the land component of new construction is excluded, renovation expenditures began to exceed new construction in 1981 (Clayton Research Associates, 1988: 6). Renovation activity is more significant than published data suggest. An unknown but high proportion of such work takes the form of do-it-yourself. It is catered to by a type of building supply dealer that has emerged since the 1940s. Oriented to consumers, not contractors, it stocks a variety of materials. Home Depot, an American chain that has made incursions into Canada, is the extreme example. Other renovation work is done informally by contractors who are paid by an exchange of services or 'under the table'. In such cases, the investment of labour is not recorded. In many ways, renovation work is carried out in the manner of new construction in, say, 1900. As renovations become more important, the growth of large developers/contractors and of institutional lending will be slowed.

Changes in production have been accompanied by an evolution in marketing and sales. Only the speculative builder has to market homes: a custom builder already has a client while owner-builders are not building to sell. The rise of speculative building has created a growing need to sell homes. In the earlier years of this century most builders and home-owners sold on their own. They relied on the classified section of the local newspaper, supplemented with a sign outside the dwelling. Starting in the 1920s, large builders began to build model homes, and this is now routine. Many offer variations on a few basic models and build only when a client has signed a contract. (This blurs the line between speculative and custom building.) Some new homes and most existing homes are sold, and some apartments are rented, through agents. In major cities, multiple listing services (MLS) provide a computerized listing of properties for sale that includes information on the price and characteristics of each dwelling. Real estate agents use MLS listings to identify properties that might be of interest to their clients. Placing a property on the MLS guarantees that it will be brought to the attention of many agents and potential buyers. This advantage comes at a price to the seller: a commission of about 6 per cent of the sale price. This commission usually represents the major cost of moving for a home-owner, and is one reason why home-owners move less often than tenants.

The Occupation of Housing

To occupy housing people form themselves into households. This process is by no means as simple as it may appear (Miron, 1988, 1993b). The household may correspond to a social entity such as an individual, or a nuclear family, but often it does not. Historically, many families took in single boarders or boarding families (Modell and Hareven, 1973). As late as 1931, 19 per cent of all urban households in Canada contained lodgers and a further 6 per cent contained lodging families (Harris, 1994: 35). The combined total of 25 per cent had halved by 1951 and has dropped steadily since. Lodging was common when incomes were low or when population growth created a shortage of dwellings. 'The family' itself might include the grandparents or siblings of the parents. Such arrangements have always been most common among immigrants. The household is malleable, responding to changes in economic circumstances, social mores, and market conditions.

Household formation also depends on incomes and the age composition of the population. Very high rates of household formation in the 1960s and early 1970s were due to rising incomes. Miron (1988) has estimated that as much as one-third of the 1951–81 increase in households was due to the changed living arrangements that affluence made possible. But this increase was also due to the emergence into adulthood of the postwar baby-boom generation. As this age cohort first entered the housing market they sought rental accommodation and helped to fuel the apartment boom of the 1960s. As they got jobs, saved money, and had children (though fewer than their parents) they sought to acquire homes. They pushed house prices up rapidly during the 1970s and, especially, the second half of the 1980s, but also ensured that ownership rates remained high even in the face of the price boom (Foot and Stoffman, 1996: 27–40). In the 1990s, as the echo generation tried to enter the housing market, there should have been at first a demand for apartments. But high youth unemployment, an increase in the proportion of those who enrol in some type of post-secondary education, and rising tuition have forced many to stay or return home (Mitchell and Gee, 1996). As ever, incomes as well as demographics determine how dwellings are occupied.

Filtering and Neighbourhood Change

New households do not usually occupy new housing. Most are formed by young people with modest incomes and savings. Little housing is built for those on low, or even moderate, incomes. Today, especially in the larger urban centres, apartments are built towards the top end of the market. Except in the least accessible and cheapest locations, new homes for owner occupancy cost as much as the average home in any given city. In 1996, for example, the average cost of a new single-detached home was $125,760, while existing homes sold in that year, at an average of $99,534, were notably cheaper.[2] The cheapest homes and apartments are generally older, lack some modern conveniences, and may be deteriorated. Such older accommodation is typically occupied by new households and by lower-income households in general.

For many years it was assumed that the housing market worked in an orderly way to provide housing for new and low-income households. Expensive new homes would be occupied by the affluent, who would vacate older but adequate homes that would then be occupied by those on moderate incomes, leaving the most modest homes for the poor (Figure 16.2). A new home in an expensive suburb would generate a 'chain' of moves. Each household in this chain would move upmar-

ket, while the housing units themselves would 'filter' down (Bourne, 1981: 149–60). The concept of filtering (although not the term itself) was used by E.W. Burgess and the Chicago sociologists in the 1920s. They assumed that low-income immigrants would occupy housing that had filtered down from the more affluent native-born. This older housing was concentrated in the inner city, where most immigrants therefore settled.

The filtering model assumes that boundaries between housing submarkets are permeable. *Submarket* refers to the fact that in terms of price and quantity, the housing market is not a continuum but is organized into more or less discrete segments. Units within each submarket are approximately equivalent, but those in different submarkets are not. Since housing is immobile, each urban area defines its own submarket (see below). Locally, tenure, house type, and, in large metropolitan areas, location define further subcategories. For a low-income family with young children looking to rent an at-grade dwelling in a city's east end, the availability of new housing for purchase, of small high-rise apartments, or of vacancies in the far west side of the city is unhelpful. Filtering can link submarkets: a family may move from an older east-end townhouse into a new west-end home. But when filtering is blocked, slowed, or reversed then serious housing problems can ensue, especially at the lower end.

The filtering model is a more accurate description of market processes in the US than in Canada. It is true that until the 1970s, filtering was common in Canadian cities. In the first half of this century, for example, it characterized the City of Toronto, though not always the suburbs (Harris, 1996: 255). Inner cities came to house a disproportionate number of low-income people and immigrants. In Vancouver the Chinatown and east-side districts, in Toronto the Kensington-Spadina neighbourhoods, and in Montreal the St Urbain corridor all exemplify this process. In cities like Hamilton and Winnipeg this pattern continues. Elsewhere the partial gentrification of inner-city areas, including those just mentioned, has slowed or even reversed the process. Affluent households are buying old

Figure 16.2   **Patterns of Urban Filtering in Canada, 1945–2000**

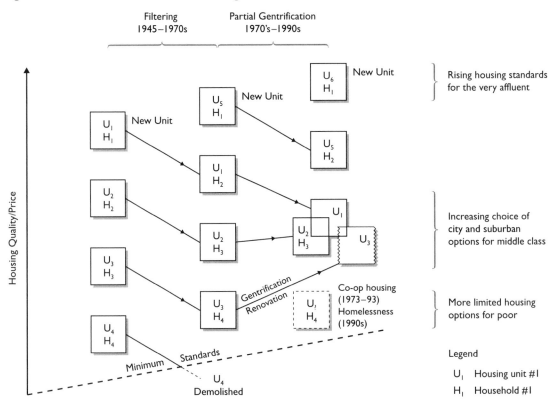

homes and, through renovation, making them new (Ley, 1997) (see Chapter 12). One consequence has been the loss of cheap rental housing and the displacement of immigrant workers' families and others on low incomes (City of Toronto, 1986). To some extent the demand for cheap housing is still met by older bungalows and apartments built in the 1920s and by apartments built in the 1950s and 1960s. These accommodate lower-income households. Toronto's St Jamestown is a case in point. But as the growing ranks of the homeless can testify, this is insufficient. Reverse filtering (such as that fuelled by gentrification) has disrupted what was always a fragile mechanism for providing housing to the poor (Figure 16.2).

Residential Mobility and Neighbourhood Change

Broadly speaking, it is clear why some affluent households settle in the inner city and, generally, why households move. People move when they perceive their existing dwelling to be less desirable than an alternative. Many factors can contribute to a feeling of dissatisfaction or stress (Brown and Moore, 1970). These include job relocation or changes in family size, household income, or neighbourhood quality. Growing households need more space and soon relocate; shrinking, empty-nest households may 'overconsume' housing for many years before moving. As households earn more they will usually wish to improve their home or neighbourhood; when their income falls they may soon be compelled to move on, especially if they rent. Households move to get out of deteriorating neighbourhoods, since this affects both the quality of their daily life and also the value of their property; those on moderate incomes may also be displaced in gentrifying areas if rents and/or property taxes go up. Above all, however, people move to follow their jobs. Thus, in moving to the suburbs after World II, Canadians were moving closer to suburbanizing jobs and also acquiring the larger homes on larger lots that growing families needed and that rising incomes could support (Clark, 1966). The slow deterioration and congestion of inner-city neighbourhoods also added a push.

Gentrification may be explained, too, by changes in job location and household structure (Ley 1997). The more visible aspects of gentrification—singles and gay bars, upscale specialty stores, cosmopolitan restaurants—speak of a new lifestyle of discriminating consumerism. Determining these patterns has been the growth of office employment in central cities, coupled with the desire of employees to live fairly close by. Changes in household structure have caused a new generation to evaluate inner-city living more favourably than did their parents. More households now contain two earners and/or no children, and to these a central location may make sense even if neither person works downtown. It may be a compromise location for those working at opposite ends of the city and offers the safest bet should one or the other lose a job. A central location also makes sense for the growing number of single persons and single parents, since inner areas are better served by transit and the kinds of community services (notably day care) that such households need (Rose, 1989; Rose and LeBourdais, 1986; Wekerle, 1985).

The growth of two-earner families has complicated the process of residential mobility and created a difference in commuting behaviour between men and women (Hanson and Pratt, 1995). With two earners, and usually two workplaces outside the home, the adults in the household must compromise about where to live. Women compromise more than men. A high proportion of women are employed part-time and/or in jobs—such as clerical work—that are available in many locations (Armstrong and Armstrong, 1994). Many households still decide where to live mainly on the basis of where the man works. The woman then seeks employment close by, partly so as not to interfere too much with her greater responsibility for housework and child-rearing at home (Michelson, 1984). Of course, more women now have full-time work or careers, often in the growing CBD. Single or married, they have a strong incentive to live close to work. Lacking a 'wife' at home, they must minimize commuting time to leave time for household chores. Easily maintained downtown condominiums or apartments have a particular attraction (Rose, 1989). For a variety of reasons, then, whether they are part-time workers seeking work close to home or have careers that encourage them to find a home close to work, women do not commute as far as men.

Social Differences in Housing Occupancy

Social groups differ in the type of housing they occupy. The major social groups in Canada are those defined on the basis of class (or socio-economic status), ethnicity, and gender, and these characteristics are likely to go a long way in determining the individual's housing situation, chiefly through the effect of income. Middle-class professionals, for example, earn more than clerical workers, and a male professional more than his female counterpart (Armstrong and Armstrong, 1994). Some 'social' housing is provided to the needy (see below), but the private market allocates housing on the basis of price. Differences in household income (and wealth) are critical in determining what type of housing—and in what location—a person can afford.

Business owners, managers, and, to a lesser extent, middle-class professionals tend to live in relatively large and well-equipped homes. They are also especially likely to own their own homes. In Canada, as in many countries, there are strong tax incentives for home-ownership. For example, unlike other assets, homes are exempt from capital gains tax. Dowler (1983) has calculated that tax subsidies of this kind are several times as large as the amounts that have been channelled to social housing. Except for those who move often and those who dislike the responsibility of maintaining a home, most households prefer to buy rather than rent their dwelling. Since their incomes are generally more than sufficient, most business owners and managers own their own homes (Harris and Hamnett, 1987). Housing conditions are generally poorer among blue- and white-collar workers. Levels of working-class home-ownership are also lower, although higher than might be expected on the basis of income. It seems that blue-collar workers have especially strong aspirations to own their own homes. It may be that for people who are vulnerable to lay-offs and who have little control over their work environment, owner-occupation offers financial security and a place of personal autonomy (Harris and Pratt, 1993). Those with the lowest incomes, including unskilled workers and the welfare-dependent poor, occupy the worst, typically rental, accommodation. Some districts of poor-quality rental housing are badly deteriorated. Slums that result in housing abandonment, however, are much less common in Canadian than in US cities. This is because social disparities are not as great in Canada, in part because the social safety net is stronger. But disparities are currently rising as a result of recent government cut-backs.

Differences in the housing situation of men and women have probably grown in recent years, and have only begun to receive serious attention (McClain and Doyle, 1983). In the 1950s, when most adults lived in husband-wife households, men and women occupied the same dwellings. The home meant different things to the woman than to the man: she was more likely to view it as a workplace and perhaps a showplace for homemaking talents, while he viewed it more as a haven from work (Harris and Pratt, 1993). But both lived in the same structure. With rising divorce rates and more single-parent households, most of which are headed by women, this is no longer true. An increasing proportion of households living below the poverty line, typically in poor-quality rental housing, are headed by women (Rose and Wexler, 1993; Watson, 1986).

Ethnic groups also differ in their housing situation. Little has been written about ethnic differences in housing occupancy in Canada. This is a curious paradox in a society that thinks of itself as multicultural. In the past—although not so clearly in the present—immigrants of all nationalities had low incomes and lived in modest housing. Perhaps because they brought a strong desire to establish themselves in their adopted country, however, they tried hard to improve their situation and acquire property. They were willing to live in crowded conditions, taking in boarders to save capital (Kirk and Kirk, 1981). In some respects, however, it may be misleading to generalize about immigrants. Some immigrants—including many recent newcomers from Hong Kong—have been quite affluent, and have not had to sacrifice much in order to acquire homes. Then again, not all cultures seem to have attached equal value to home-ownership. Folk wisdom suggests that Italians and Portuguese value ownership very highly, but the same may not be true of the Chinese and Vietnamese. It has been suggested, as well, that there is a cultural difference in this regard between Canada's two 'charter' groups: one reason why Montreal has long had a lower rate of home-ownership than Toronto may be that French Canadians attach less value to owning a home. Recent research has challenged this view (Choko, 1998; Choko and Harris, 1990). In general, however, it is clear that cultural as well as economic factors influence the types of housing people aspire to and occupy.

The Uses of the Home

Once built and occupied, homes are used by their occupants daily, and for many purposes. Over the past century the home has become more important for recreation. Gas barbecues and in-ground swimming pools testify to the recreational uses of the back yard. The phonograph, radio, television, audio, video and computer, and lately the Internet have increased the attraction of the home itself. Homes have grown and developed new rooms, in part to house these new technologies, with many consequences for the character and quality of daily life (Simon and Holdsworth, 1993).

Unpaid Work

Apart from being a place for recreation, the home has always been an important workplace (Bradbury, 1993; MacKenzie and Rose, 1983). The running of all households, even those blessed with the latest in home technology, requires a great deal of labour. People, clothes, floors, and dishes have to be kept (fairly) clean. Food has to be bought and cooked. Children create other tasks: changing diapers, teaching, transporting, listening, and consoling. Some technologies have reduced the amount of housework done in the home. Doing the wash by hand and fetching water from a well were time-consuming tasks. But the differences between past and present may be overstated (Cowan, 1983). Appliances have been used as much to raise standards—of cleanliness and culinary expertise—as to save work. While they have reduced the time spent on old work they have created new work. Washers, blenders, microwaves, and so forth must be bought and maintained. As automobiles have made it possible to build homes at lower densities, suburbs have forced people to buy, use, and maintain cars to get to work, shop, and attend school. Today we spend less time cleaning, but more time shopping, than our grandparents. The net effect on the amount of work done is not as clear as it might seem.

Unpaid work is also performed upon the home. Owner-building is the extreme case, where the owner invests 'sweat equity' instead of hiring labour or buying the finished dwelling (Harris, 1998). Today, do-it-yourself home maintenance and renovation are more common. This includes everything from replacing a light-bulb to building an addition. Some maintenance is carried out by almost every household, including tenants. Occasionally landlords may offer rent discounts to tenants who work on their apartments (Krohn, Fleming, and Manzer, 1977). In general, however, owner-occupants have the greatest opportunities and incentives to do such work. Some people buy a home anticipating that their own work will save money and, incidentally, allow for self-expression. Sometimes the direction of causality is opposite. Ownership changes people's lifestyle in ways that they may not anticipate, encouraging house maintenance and improvement as part of a more home-centred life (Michelson, 1977: 268–9). Although pure owner-building has become quite rare in urban areas, more modest forms of do-it-yourself work are common. It is impossible to be precise about the relative importance of this work because so much of it goes unrecorded. The upward trend, however, is clear.

Work done within, and upon, the home is still very much part of a gender division of labour. Since at least the late-nineteenth century, men have commuted and worked on the home, while women have laboured within it, whether for love or money. This pattern is slowly breaking down. It is true that many women spend a good deal of time working outside the home. Surveys show, however, they still do more than their share of housework, even in households where both the man and the woman work full-time (Armstrong and Armstrong, 1994; Michelson, 1984). More than men, they juggle their work to accommodate their domestic responsibilities (Hanson and Pratt, 1995). Some women have been attracted to teleworking since this type of work is least disruptive to domestic responsibilities: women make up about 45 per cent of the total labour force but 55 per cent of those who work for pay at home (Gurstein, 1995: 12). This is part of a legacy of patriarchy that influences most aspects of social life, but it is especially apparent in the use of the home.

Paid Work

The home has always been used as place of paid employment. Historically, many households derived income from the home itself by taking in lodgers. In 1901, almost 10 per cent of the income of urban households in the United States was obtained from boarders. Although lodging has declined since World War II, other types of home employment seem to be on the increase. The proportion of mothers with young children who are in the labour force has grown rapidly. Since the number of day-care spaces has not kept pace, many young children are cared for informally in home day care. The women who provide this service use their homes to obtain a modest but (partially) tax-free income (MacKenzie and Truelove, 1993). There has also been a resurgence of industrial 'homework': people employed in piece-work labour at home. This is especially apparent in the garment industry in Toronto and Montreal (Johnson and Johnson, 1982). Computers and telecommunications have made possible a new type of home employment. The 1980s and 1990s saw an increase in small businesses, many run out of people's homes, and also of teleworkers, employees who 'telecommute' from their homes. In the mid-1990s small businesses and teleworkers each accounted for about one-third of all home-based workers (Gurstein, 1995: 11). In 1994 a survey showed that these home-based workers relied on communications technology, notably computers (92 per cent), voice mail (77 per cent), and e-mail (40 per cent) (Gurstein, 1995: 31). Although accurate data are lacking, full and part-time homeworkers might have accounted for 10 per cent of the labour force (see Chapter 15 on the evolution of work).

Homeworkers place new demands on their homes and neighbourhoods. The 1994 survey showed that many had altered their homes to accommodate work needs, typically by improved lighting and wiring. Almost a third of respondents had renovated existing space, while 12 per cent had added a new room (Gurstein, 1995: 34). Their use of neighbourhood facilities had also changed. Compared with when they were not working or when they had not been employed, home-based workers made more use of local banks, post offices, and copy centres and less use of cafés, parks, and recreation centres. In working at home, many con-

travened local zoning regulations. In terms of health and safety, the regulation of paid work in the home is a growing issue.

A Geographical Perspective

In Canada, more than in most countries, it can be misleading to generalize about housing. In general it is true that Canadians live in some of the best, and best-equipped, housing in the world. Almost all urban dwellings are structurally sound and have the basic conveniences (for a northern climate) of piped water, electricity, and central heating. The form these houses take, however, and how much they cost varies a great deal from place to place.

The Uniqueness of Each Place

The size of Canada, coupled with the immobility of housing, guarantees that housing market conditions will vary enormously from place to place (Bourne and Bunting, 1993). A shortage in one place cannot be met by a surplus elsewhere, unless the places in question happen to be within easy commuting distance. The major urban areas in Canada, however, are strung out like islands in an archipelago over a distance of five thousand kilometres. Urban housing markets are largely independent of one another. Prices in Calgary rose rapidly during the OPEC-induced oil boom of the 1970s and then slumped in the early 1980s (Figure 16.3). In Vancouver they spiked during a speculative boom in 1980–1, fell, and then rose steadily for over a decade as Asian immigration fuelled population and economic growth. In Toronto and southern Ontario they boomed during the prosperous 1980s, fell by a quarter during the recession of the early 1990s, and are now slowly recovering. In Montreal and Winnipeg, for different reasons, they have been depressed for a generation. Single-industry towns have the most volatile housing markets of all, but even the larger cities are profoundly affected by shifts in capital investment.

The history of European settlement, moving from east to west, has helped distinguish local hous-

Figure 16.3 **Trends in House Prices, Selected Canadian Cities, 1974–1997**

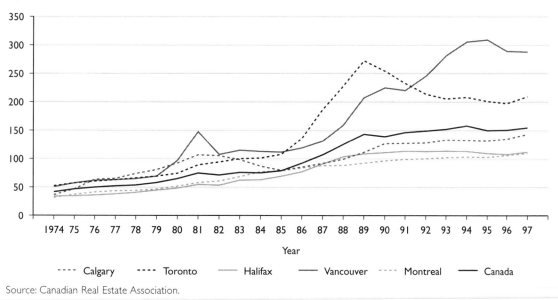

Source: Canadian Real Estate Association.

ing submarkets. Eastern cities have the highest proportion of older housing. Changes in transportation technology and in standards of living have allowed for residential development at lower densities over the course of the past century. As a result, eastern cities have a higher proportion of dense, multi-occupancy housing stock associated with high levels of tenancy. In contrast, in Winnipeg, Edmonton, Calgary, and Vancouver, which grew up around the streetcar and the automobile, neighbourhoods of single-detached homes may be found close to the CBD. Moreover, as each city was developed by different immigrants, different architectural styles came to predominate. Nineteenth-century Montrealers favoured 'plexes', superimposed dwellings with separate entrances; Torontonians occupied gabled row houses in a late Gothic style; Vancouverites drew heavily on California bungalow and British 'Tudorbethan' models (Choko, 1998; Holdsworth, 1977). The historical geography of the country has helped to create a unique housing stock, and different housing markets, in each urban centre.

Generic Differences Between Places

If each place is unique, some geographical variations in housing are generic in character. They are specific to certain *types* of places. The most basic difference, implied in the scope of this book, is that between rural and urban. Land and housing in urban centres are more expensive and more regulated than in rural areas. As a result, urban housing takes up a high proportion of residents' incomes, is less likely to be owner-built or occupied, and contains a high proportion of attached, multi-family dwellings. In 1991, for example, the home-ownership rate was much lower in urban (57 per cent) than in rural areas (84 per cent).

The difference between urban and rural housing is more one of degree than of kind. City and country are the ends of a spectrum that includes a range of types of settlement. Small towns have higher levels of home-ownership than cities but lower levels than villages or farms (where, of course, home and work are often one and the same). Similarly, the suburbs of any city typically contain a relatively high pro-portion of detached, owner-occupied homes (Choko and Harris, 1990). This is due in part to lower land prices and also to the fact that the more recent sub-urbs have been developed at a time when household incomes were higher and ownership more affordable. These city-suburban differences in home-ownership are associated with geographical variations in the uses to which the home is put. On average, owners do more unpaid work in the home than tenants. Moreover, because a higher proportion of owner-occupants have children, they are likely to spend more time on child-rearing. As a result, more unpaid work is carried out in suburban than in inner-city homes, with apparent consequences for public space. For example, in suburbs, parks and sidewalks are fre-quented by children; in cities, they are mostly an adult domain. In this manner, generic differences between city and suburb encompass not only the housing mar-ket but also the way of life of local residents.

Given these generic differences, urbanization has had a significant impact on the types of hous-ing that Canadians occupy. It has increased the pro-portion of people living in multi-unit structures, notably after the apartment construction booms of the 1920s and 1960s. It has also helped to depress the level of owner-occupation. Over the past half-century this effect has been roughly counterbal-anced by a growth in real incomes (Harris, 1986). Thus, in Canada as a whole, the proportion of households that owned their own homes fell from 66 per cent to 62 per cent between 1951 and 1981, partly due to a rapid rate of urbanization that did not taper off until the 1970s (Bourne, 1993). It changed little during the 1980s, so that in 1991 it stood at 63 per cent. The rate within urban areas fluctuated, but over the period as a whole it held steady at about 56 per cent. Trends in housing, then, must be understood in the context of the changing character of population settlement.

Housing and the State

In Canada, housing is produced by the private sec-tor and mostly owned by private corporations or individuals. Its production, occupation, and use, however, are profoundly influenced by the state. The 'private' tenure categories of 'owner-occupation' and 'tenancy', for example, are defined by property law. Their meaning changes with new legislation, such as rent controls (Hulchanski, 1993).

The Growth, and Faltering, of Government Activity

All three levels of government have played a grow-ing role in the housing market over the past cen-tury. Municipalities were the first to become involved because housing conditions were worst in the cities. The rise of industry in the nineteenth century concentrated people in growing urban cen-tres such as Montreal, Toronto, and Hamilton. Workers' wages were low and living conditions were poor. Overcrowding and poor sanitation helped spread infectious diseases, threatening the health of all city dwellers. The prevalence of wood-frame construction led to serious fires. Municipal-ities realized that urban conditions demanded regulation of the built environment, especially housing, and consequently began to exert control over how houses were built, maintained, and occu-pied (Hodge, 1986). Suburbs, especially those occu-pied by immigrants and workers, were slower to adopt controls, but most had done so by the 1950s (Harris, 1996: 141–67).

In the twentieth century, local governments have also taken control over land use. A century ago it was typical for land parcels to be developed piece-meal. Stores or small factories were built on other-wise residential streets. Investment in property was uncertain. A merchant might build a fine brick home at the suburban fringe only to have his invest-ment threatened by a labourer building a shack next door. Land subdividers began to realize that there might be a demand for regulated subdivisions from which undesirable land uses were prohibited. At first they used legal covenants that prevented or man-dated certain types of land use, which prohibited the use of certain building materials (usually wood) or specified minimum construction costs. Other covenants more directly affected who could rent or buy property. In Westdale, an interwar suburb of Hamilton, a typical covenant specified that 'none of the lands described . . . shall be used, occupied by, or let or sold to Negroes, Asiatics, Bulgarians, Austrians, Russians, Serbs, Rumanians, Turks, Armenians, whether British subjects or not, or foreign-born Italians, Greeks or Jews' (Weaver, 1978: 421). Target groups have varied with time and place, and it is not clear how common such covenants were before they were declared unconstitutional in the late 1940s (Walker, 1997: 182–245). After World War II municipalities took over the functions of land-use planning, although there has been a recent resurgence in the use of private covenants (Filion and Alexander, 1994). Today planning departments control land use through zoning plans that specify the use to which each piece of land may be put (Figure 16.1) (Hodge, 1986). These plans are not always followed to the letter. In older districts, 'nonconforming' uses may persist. Anywhere in the city, zoning can be changed in response to pressure from developers or local residents. In many provinces such changes have to be brought before a public hearing, and such hearings are a staple of local politics.

Federal involvement in housing dates from the 1930s (Bacher, 1993; Belec, Holmes, and Rutherford, 1987). At that time little housing was built, while many home-owners lost their homes because they could not pay their mortgages. Here was a national housing crisis. To help create jobs, the federal government loaned money for home renovations (Hobbs and Pierson, 1988). More importantly, in 1935 it passed a Dominion Housing Act through which it insured and helped to provide mortgage loans (Figure 16.4). The main purpose was to rejuvenate the building industry; most buyers were quite affluent (Belec, 1997). In 1946 the government set up the CMHC, whose loan activity has been important for the postwar development of suburban owner-occupied homes (Poapst, 1993).

Mortgage assistance was justified by the supposed filtering-down of benefits to lower-income groups, but it did not solve the housing problem.

By comparison with the US, Canada was slow to develop a housing program for those in greatest need (Harris, 1999). Only after 1964, when the federal government made the financial terms attractive, did several provinces establish housing agencies. In the next five years these provincial agencies created a short boom in public housing construction (Patterson, 1993). Some public housing was built in the inner city, as part of slum clearance and urban renewal projects. Typically, in such cases, more units were destroyed than created. Those units occupied by seniors were uncontroversial. 'Family' projects, however, soon ran into opposition from local residents, even though they were concentrated in areas where housing conditions were poor. Part of the problem was the size of the projects, which encouraged stigmatization. This is a problem that has worsened over time as public housing has come to contain an increasing concentration of visible minorities. In Toronto, for example, Blacks occupied only 4 per cent of all of the housing units managed by the Metro Toronto Housing Authority in 1971, soon after construction (Murdie, 1994). By 1986 the proportion had soared to 27 per cent, more than five times the proportion of Blacks in the Toronto population as a whole. Resident opposition to public housing and high unit subsidy costs prompted the government to abandon construction for families and to cut back on building for seniors (Patterson, 1993).

From the early 1970s the federal government has directed more modest amounts of money towards what is now referred to as 'social housing' (Figure 16.4). This takes the form of municipal nonprofit or co-operative housing. Co-ops differ from public housing because they are socially mixed and ownership is shared among residents. Since most co-ops have been built in socially diverse neighbourhoods, they have been able to avoid social stigma (Harris, 1993; Skelton, 1994). As CMHC program reviews showed in the 1980s, however, social and class diversity in these projects inevitably reduced the number of low-income households that were housed (CMHC, 1984). Since then the federal government has steadily divested itself of

Figure 16.4   **Evolution of Federal Housing Programs, 1945–1993**

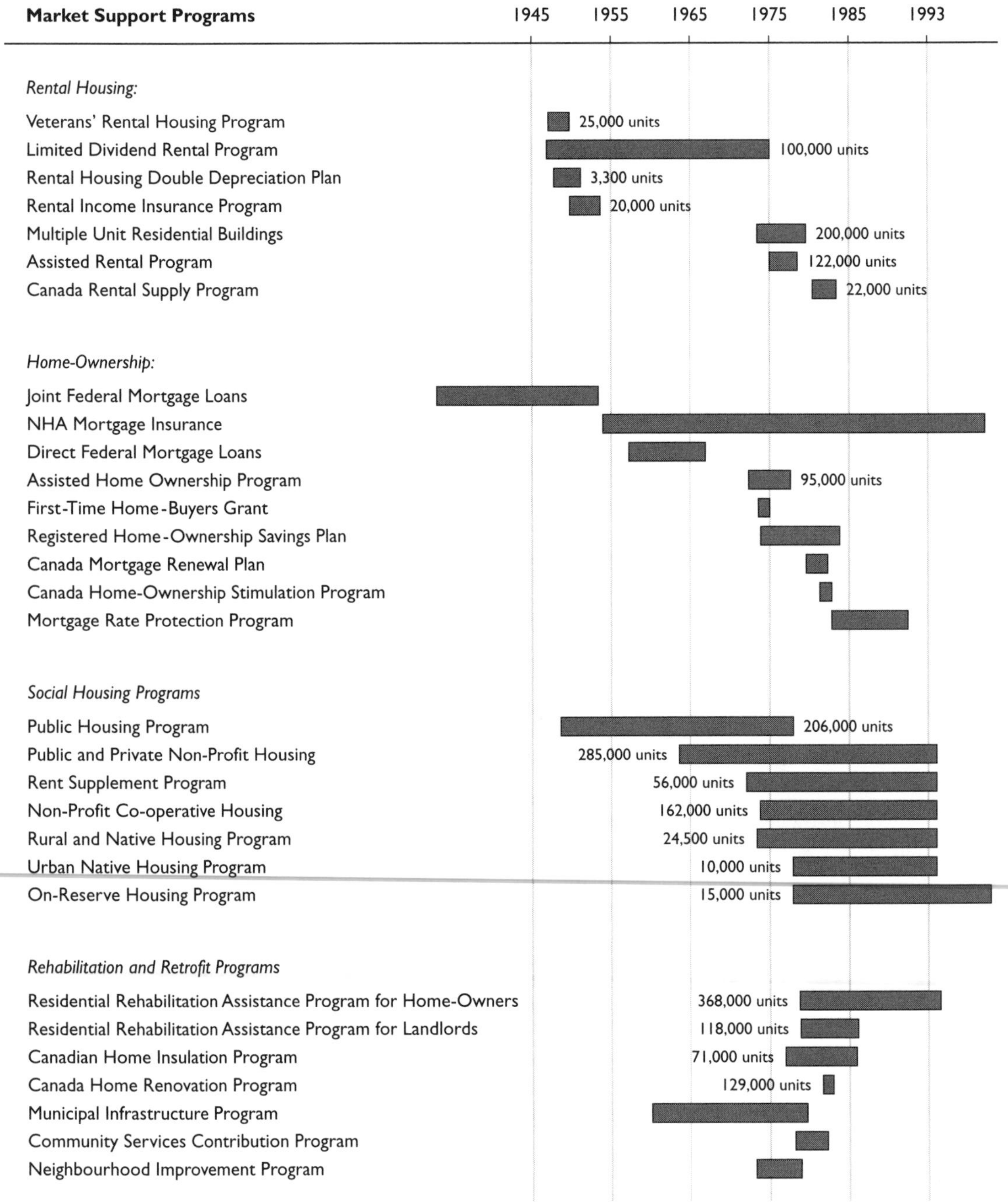

Market Support Programs	1945	1955	1965	1975	1985	1993

Rental Housing:

Veterans' Rental Housing Program — 25,000 units

Limited Dividend Rental Program — 100,000 units

Rental Housing Double Depreciation Plan — 3,300 units

Rental Income Insurance Program — 20,000 units

Multiple Unit Residential Buildings — 200,000 units

Assisted Rental Program — 122,000 units

Canada Rental Supply Program — 22,000 units

Home-Ownership:

Joint Federal Mortgage Loans

NHA Mortgage Insurance

Direct Federal Mortgage Loans

Assisted Home Ownership Program — 95,000 units

First-Time Home-Buyers Grant

Registered Home-Ownership Savings Plan

Canada Mortgage Renewal Plan

Canada Home-Ownership Stimulation Program

Mortgage Rate Protection Program

Social Housing Programs

Public Housing Program — 206,000 units

Public and Private Non-Profit Housing — 285,000 units

Rent Supplement Program — 56,000 units

Non-Profit Co-operative Housing — 162,000 units

Rural and Native Housing Program — 24,500 units

Urban Native Housing Program — 10,000 units

On-Reserve Housing Program — 15,000 units

Rehabilitation and Retrofit Programs

Residential Rehabilitation Assistance Program for Home-Owners — 368,000 units

Residential Rehabilitation Assistance Program for Landlords — 118,000 units

Canadian Home Insulation Program — 71,000 units

Canada Home Renovation Program — 129,000 units

Municipal Infrastructure Program

Community Services Contribution Program

Neighbourhood Improvement Program

Source: CMHC, Canadian Housing Statistics, various years, from Tom Carter, 'Current Practices for Procuring Affordable Housing: The Canadian Context', *Housing Policy Debate* 8, 3(1997): 593–631.

responsibility for social housing. As part of larger budget-cutting initiatives, in 1993 it announced a phase-out of capital funding for new projects and in 1996 declared its intention to abandon any role in the management of existing units, other than on Native reserves. The Canadian government is now less active in the housing field than that of any of the leading industrialized nations, including the United States (Harris, 1999; Wolfe, 1998).

Recent federal initiatives have shifted the housing debate to the provinces. Provincial governments have generally played a minor role in housing. They participated to varying degrees in the public housing and co-operative housing programs (McAfee, 1984). Quebec has been the most active, especially since the establishment of the Quebec Housing Corporation in 1966. In the 1970s other provinces took initiatives. Ontario, for example, developed a program to help moderate-income households buy homes, and Quebec has also been active in this area. For some time the most significant provincial activity was the regulation of rents. Following the introduction of federal wage and price controls in 1974, every province by 1976 had some form of rent regulation. Most still do. Typically, rent increases are limited to a fixed amount each year, although the rate of increase has sometimes been allowed to vary with inflation and appeal procedures permit exceptions. There has been a great deal of debate about the effects of controls (Miron and Cullingworth, 1983). They have helped sitting tenants and lowered landlord profits, and have probably reduced the level of apartment construction. Partly as a result, vacancy rates in most cities fell below 2 per cent from the mid-1970s to the mid-1980s, but have lately risen to around 4 per cent (Silver and van Diepen, 1995).

Federal cutbacks have put the spotlight on the provinces. The response has varied (Wolfe, 1998). At one extreme, Quebec and British Columbia still support social housing, but their commitment is compromised by fiscal difficulties. In Ontario, the Harris government has announced its intention to sell the better public housing units and to decentralize the construction and management of social housing to local municipalities. Quebec, too, has embarked on a program of decentralization. Alberta, the province best able to take initiatives, has never been inclined to do so. For the next several years, fewer publicly subsidized housing units will be built than at any time since 1964. For those who are lucky, the ultimate housing safety net will be their parents' home (Mitchell and Gee, 1996). The less fortunate may end up on the street.

The Changing Activities of the State

If the role of the state in the housing market has grown (and shrunk), it has also changed. In the past century, four shifts have occurred. First, there has been a steadily growing concern for the price, as opposed to the quality, of housing. In the 1900s, housing reformers were preoccupied by the health and fire hazards of overcrowded, poor-quality, inner-city housing (Purdy, 1997). Their efforts brought regulations that raised standards of construction and maintenance. Today, Aboriginal Canadians are the only group among whom many people live in seriously inadequate conditions. In 1991, 23 per cent of Aboriginal households occupied dwellings that were inadequate by contemporary standards, and 8 per cent lacked basic bathroom facilities (Ark Research Associates, 1996: 47). Among other Canadian households, the equivalent proportions were only 9 per cent and 0.8 per cent. Since World War II, a decline in average household size has almost eliminated overcrowding. As late as 1951, almost one-fifth of dwelling units contained more than one person per room. By 1971 this proportion had fallen to 9 per cent and by 1991 to 1 per cent. Today, the key housing issue is that of affordability, a rising problem throughout the postwar period. In 1946 only 15 per cent of all consumer expenditures went for shelter; by 1986 the proportion had risen to 23 per cent. Especially during the 1980s, high interest rates and rapid price increases made it difficult for many young households to afford their own homes. Only the increasing labour force participation of women, coupled with a growing willingness to purchase smaller condominium dwellings, prevented ownership rates from falling.

The most serious problems of affordability are experienced by renters. The usual indicator of affordability is the proportion of households that spend more than a specified proportion of their income on housing. Over the years the generally accepted proportion has risen from 20 per cent to 30 per cent—an indicator of the growing problem of affordability and also a sign that any figure is arbitrary (Hulchanski, 1995). On the 30 per cent criterion, in 1991 most (60 per cent) of the households with affordability problems were tenants, even though tenants made up a minority (37 per cent) of urban households (Lo and Gauthier, 1995). Among major metropolitan areas, affordability problems were most common in Victoria (44 per cent) and Vancouver (41 per cent) and least common in Ottawa-Hull (31 per cent). Across the country, lone parents (51 per cent) were more likely to have an affordability problem than were people living alone (44 per cent), couples with children (22 per cent), or couples without children (21 per cent). (For detailed information on affordability trends in all major Canadian metropolitan areas, see CMHC, 1998.)

The extreme sign of affordability problems is homelessness (Fallis and Murray 1990). A recent increase in homelessness is due to the increasing polarization of incomes, the loss of cheaper housing stock with the gentrification of the inner city, and new policies that have left more mentally ill people to fend for themselves. But, ironically, among these causes must be included the activities of government itself. Around the time of World War I many of the poorest households found shelter by building their own (modest) homes in the suburbs (Harris, 1996). In raising housing standards, municipalities have helped to eliminate this possibility and raised the cost of housing (Figure 16.2) (Somerville, 1995). For several reasons, then, affordability and homelessness have become the housing policy issues of our time.

Second, more and more experts have come to recognize that the usefulness of any house depends on its geographical setting. Local governments soon recognized the importance of externalities for the control of land use. Federal and provincial governments were slower to acknowledge the importance of geographical patterns. The first national program of public housing was to house war workers in the early 1940s. Many projects included a range of social supports, including day care (Bacher, 1993: 134–5). By comparison, later public housing projects were poorly designed. Large and isolated, they were easily stigmatized while making daily activities—including shopping—a major chore. Following public criticism, some lessons were learned (Dennis and Fish, 1972; Patterson, 1993). The social housing and neighbourhood improvement programs of the 1970s and 1980s have shown greater care in the placement of new housing in relation to existing housing, and also in relation to community services.

Beginning in the 1970s, urbanization and household formation slowed. Levels of new construction began to fall, gentrification gathered momentum, and more resources were devoted to the rehabilitation of existing stock. Accordingly, a third, recent change is that planners and policymakers are becoming more interested in monitoring, managing, and adapting existing dwellings (Moore and Skaburskis, 1993). The challenge is greatest in the rental sector. Apartments built during the construction booms of the 1920s, 1950s, and even the 1960s are deteriorating. Rehabilitation is expensive and might further erode the endangered stock of cheap rental housing. In the context of serious affordability problems for renters, the management of this aging rental stock has become a key policy issue (Fallis, 1993).

A fourth policy shift has concerned the types of households that are housed. Home improvement grants in the 1930s helped make the home more attractive and functional for women raising children (Hobbs and Pierson, 1988). In the postwar years, CMHC activity attempted to house husband-wife families, each with 2.4 children. Recently, however, family and household structures have become more diverse. Husband-wife households make up a declining proportion of the total, and among these a declining proportion include children—70 per cent in 1971 but only 60 per cent by 1991. There has been a rapid growth in single-parent families and individuals aged over 65 who maintain their own households, including those who live alone (Rose and Wexler, 1993). The private sector has met some of this need. Many seniors can afford housing suited to their needs, and contractors have responded by building golf-and-country estates, adult-only condominiums, and congregate-care retirement complexes (Holdsworth and Laws, 1994). Other seniors, however, along with single parents and others with limited incomes or special needs, have been poorly served (McClain, 1993). All rely on community services and public transit, which provides good service only to inner-city districts (Rose and LeBourdais, 1986). Some are attracted by non-traditional types of housing developed with more amenities and at higher densities (Johnson, 1994). There is scope here for the intensification of development in older suburbs. Some housing co-ops have taken this type of initiative, but the private sector has not. Since cutbacks mean that few co-ops will be built in the near future, local planners must try to make it easier for builder-developers to meet the need.

Policies and Transitions

It has been said that Canada has housing programs but no housing policy (Dennis and Fish, 1972). At the federal level, programs have not been conceived and implemented as a whole to achieve a specific purpose. Provinces have sometimes followed the federal lead, but often not, and never with any consistency. Municipalities have responded differently to local circumstances. Interventions have routinely failed to achieve what was intended. The overall picture is one of an incoherent hodgepodge of activity.

Stepping back from the shifting details, we can see that a pattern does emerge. This is most apparent when we examine the effects, rather than the proclaimed goals, of state activity. The main effect has been to facilitate the emergence of a corporate capitalist economy. One of the main reasons why the federal government became involved in the housing market was to better manage the economy (Dennis and Fish, 1972: 3–4). Home-building is labour-intensive; encouraging construction is a good way of reducing unemployment. It also has a large economic 'multiplier': buyers of new units need new appliances, cars, and so forth. Moreover, since most new homes are mortgaged, and since mortgages account for the majority of consumer debt, housing finance is a convenient tool of monetary policy. Altogether, then, Canadian governments have used housing to help to manage the economy as a whole.

Within the housing sector, since the 1930s there has been a consistent bias towards capitalist forms of housing provision and ownership (Bacher, 1993). 'The building industry' has been favoured over owner-builders, even in the 1940s and 1950s when the latter accounted for about a quarter of housing starts (Harris, 1998); large developers have been encouraged in preference to small builders (Lorimer, 1978); financial institutions have been favoured over the individual lender, even though the latter held more than half of all mortgage debt as late as the 1950s (Harris and Ragonetti, 1998). For many decades individual lenders provided almost all the mortgage money available to buyers of older and cheaper homes, and they are still important in immigrant districts (Murdie, 1986). Market bias has been at best a mixed blessing. It has led to the production of safe, energy-efficient, and roomy housing for the majority of Canadians, but it has helped create monotonous neighbourhoods and a mountain of consumer debt, while doing little directly to help lower-income households.

A similar bias may be found in terms of housing occupancy. Governments have encouraged owner-occupation. The most significant subsidy has been the non-taxation of capital gains or imputed rent, implicit expenditures that far outweigh spending on 'social housing' (Dowler, 1983; Steele, 1993). The effects are regressive. Owners are more affluent than tenants; affluent home-owners receive the greatest subsidies of all. The effect of this implicit policy is that the poor subsidize the rich. The larger effect of promoting home-ownership has been to bolster the consumer economy. With CMHC mortgage support, and following agency design guidelines, suburban land has been developed in the form of low-density single-detached homes. In such environments, households must buy cars and other durables in large quantities, incurring larger debts. Housing 'policy' has boosted the demand for goods and credit, further promoting the consumer economy (Belec, Holmes, and Rutherford, 1987).

The biases of government policy are likely to continue. The business interests that have shaped policy still hold sway. There is a lobby for publicly subsidized housing, including low-income tenants, single parents, and ex-psychiatric patients, but these groups have little political influence. In the winter of 1998, when a fiscal surplus had raised the possibility of new federal spending initiatives, no politician was talking about social housing. Past policies, indeed, the whole history of Canadian housing, has created a powerful inertia. The majority of Canadian households own their own homes. They constitute a large and powerful electorate that would resist any attack on the tax subsidies they currently enjoy.

Individually and collectively, Canadians are experiencing a period of great transition, at work and at home. Their needs for and expectations of housing are changing. In an era of less government it is clear that the great majority are going to have to manage and fend for themselves.

Notes

1. Statistics Canada, *Canada Year Book* (Ottawa: Minister of Supply and Services, 1990), 7.7.
2. These figures relate only to homes sold and financed under the provisions of the National Housing Act. In general, NHA homes are a little cheaper than the average. These, and comparable data for specific cities, are reported in Canada Mortgage and Housing Corporation, *Canadian Housing Statistics 1996* (Ottawa: CMHC, 1997).

References

Ark Research Associates. 1996. *The Housing Conditions of Aboriginal People in Canada 1991.* Ottawa: CMHC.

Armstrong, P., and H. Armstrong. 1994. *The Double Ghetto*, 3rd edn. Toronto: McClelland & Stewart.

Bacher, J. 1993. *Keeping to the Marketplace: The Evolution of Canadian Housing Policy.* Montreal and Kingston: McGill-Queen's University Press.

Bassett, K., and J. Short. 1980. *Housing and Residential Structure: Alternative Approaches.* London: Routledge & Kegan Paul.

Belec, J. 1997. 'The Dominion Housing Act', *Urban History Review* 25, 2: 53–62.

———, J. Holmes, and T. Rutherford. 1987. 'The Rise of Fordism and the Transformation of Consumption Norms: Mass Consumption and Housing in Canada, 1930–1945', in R. Harris and G. Pratt, eds, *Social Class and Housing Tenure.* Gavle, Sweden: National Swedish Institute for Building Research.

Bourne, L.S. 1981. *The Geography of Housing.* London: Edward Arnold.

———. 1993. 'The Changing Settlement Environment of Housing', in Miron (1993a).

——— and T. Bunting. 1993. 'Housing Provision, Residential Development and Neighbourhood Dynamics', in L.S. Bourne and D. Ley, eds, *The Social Geography of Canadian Cities.* Montreal and Kingston: McGill-Queen's University Press.

Bradbury, B. 1993. *Working Families: Age, Gender, and Daily Survival in Industrializing Montreal.* Toronto: McClelland & Stewart.

Brown, I. 1986. 'The Apprenticeship of Marty Atkins', *Toronto* 1, 4: 50–7, 70.

Brown, L.A., and E.G. Moore. 1970. 'The Intra-Urban Migration Process: A Perspective', *Geografiska Annaler* 28: 1–13.

Choko, M. 1998. 'Ethnicity and Home Ownership in Montreal, 1921–1951', *Urban History Review* 26, 2: 32–41.

——— and R. Harris. 1990. 'The Local Culture of Property: A Comparative History of Housing

Tenure in Montreal and Toronto', *Annals of the Association of American Geographers* 80: 73–95.

City of Toronto, Planning and Development Department. 1986. *Trends in Housing Occupancy*. Toronto: City of Toronto, Research Bulletin No. 26.

Clark, S.D. 1966. *The Suburban Society*. Toronto: University of Toronto Press.

Clayton Research Associates. 1988. *The Changing Housing Industry in Canada, 1946–2001*. Ottawa: CMHC.

CMHC (Canada Mortgage and Housing Corporation). 1984. *Social Housing Review*. Ottawa: CMHC.

———. 1998. *Renter to Buyer: CMHC's 27-Year Historical Affordability Report 1970–1997*. Ottawa: CMHC.

Cowan, R. 1983. *More Work for Mother: The Ironies of Household Technology from the Open Hearth to the Microwave*. New York: Basic Books.

DeMont, J. 1989. 'Sharp's Luxury Empire', *Macleans* 102, 23: 30–3.

Dennis, M., and S. Fish. 1972. *Programs in Search of a Policy*. Toronto: Hakkert.

Dowler, R. 1983. *Housing-Related Tax Expenditures: An Overview and Evaluation*. Toronto: Centre for Urban and Community Studies, University of Toronto, Major Report No. 22.

Fallis, G. 1985. *Housing Economics*. Toronto: Butterworths.

———. 1993. 'Postwar Changes in the Supply-Side of Housing', in Miron (1993a).

——— and A. Murray. 1990. *Housing the Homeless and Poor*. Toronto: University of Toronto Press.

Feagin, J.R., and R. Parker. 1990. *Building American Cities: The Urban Real Estate Game*. Englewood Cliffs, NJ: Prentice-Hall.

Filion, P., and M. Alexander. 1994. 'Restrictive Covenants: Hidden Obstacles', *Plan Canada* 35, 1: 33–7.

Foot, D., and D. Stoffman. 1996. *Boom, Bust, and Echo: How to Profit from the Coming Demographic Shift*. Toronto: Macfarlane Walter and Ross.

Goldberg, M. 1983. *The Housing Problem: A Real Crisis?* Vancouver: University of British Columbia Press.

Gurstein, P. 1995. *Planning for Telework and Home-based Employment: A Canadian Survey on Integrating Work into Residential Environments*. Ottawa and Vancouver: CMHC and Centre for Human Settlements, University of British Columbia.

Hanson, S., and G. Pratt. 1995. *Gender, Work, and Space*. New York: Routledge.

Harris, R. 1986. 'Home Ownership and Class in Modern Canada', *International Journal of Urban and Regional Research* 10, 1: 67–86.

———. 1993. 'Social Mix, Housing Tenure and Community Development', in Miron (1993a).

———. 1994. 'The Flexible House: The Housing Backlog and the Persistence of Lodging, 1891–1951', *Social Science History* 18, 1: 31–53.

———. 1996. *Unplanned Suburbs: Toronto's American Tragedy, 1900–1950*. Baltimore: Johns Hopkins University Press.

———. 1998. 'Owner-Building', in W. van Vliet, ed., *Encyclopedia of Housing*. Beverly Hills, Calif.: Sage.

———. 1999. 'Housing and Social Policy: A Historical Perspective on Canadian-American Differences', *Urban Studies* (forthcoming).

——— and C. Hamnett. 1987. 'The Myth of the Promised Land: The Social Diffusion of Home Ownership in Britain and North America', *Annals of the Association of American Geographers* 77, 2: 173–90.

——— and G. Pratt. 1993. 'The Home, Home Ownership and Public Policy', in L.S. Bourne and D. Ley, eds, *The Social Geography of the Canadian City*. Montreal and Kingston: McGill-Queen's University Press.

——— and D. Ragonetti. 1998. 'Where Credit is Due: Residential Mortgage Finance in Canada, 1901–1954', *Journal of Real Estate Finance and Economics* 16: 223–38.

Hayden, D. 1984. *Redesigning the American Dream: The Future of Housing, Work and Family Life*. New York: W.W. Norton.

Hobbs, M., and R.R. Pierson. 1988. ' "A Kitchen That Wastes No Steps": Gender, Class and the Home Improvement Plan, 1936–1940', *Histoire sociale/ Social History* 21, 41: 9–37.

Hodge, G. 1986. *Planning Canadian Communities*. Toronto: Methuen.

Holdsworth, D. 1977. 'House and Home in Vancouver: Images of West Coast Urbanism, 1881–1929', in

A.F.J. Artibise and G. Stelter, eds, *The Canadian City: Essays in Urban History*. Toronto: McClelland & Stewart.

———— and G. Laws. 1994. 'Landscapes of Old Age in Coastal British Columbia', *Canadian Geographer* 38, 2: 174–81.

Hulchanski, J.D. 1993. 'New Forms of Owning and Renting', in Miron (1993a).

————. 1995. 'The Concept of Housing Affordability: Six Contemporary Uses of the Housing Expenditure-to-Income Ratio', *Housing Studies* 10, 4: 471–92.

Johnson, L.C. 1994. *Housing the New Family: Reinventing Housing for Families*. Ottawa: CMHC, Centre for Future Studies in Housing and Living Environments.

Johnson, L., and R.E. Johnson. 1982. *The Seam Allowance: Industrial Home Sewing in Canada*. Toronto: Women's Press.

Kirk, C.T., and W.K. Kirk. 1981. 'The Impact of the City on Home Ownership: A Comparison of Immigrants and Native Whites at the Turn of the Century', *Journal of Urban History* 7: 471–87.

Krohn, R.G., B. Fleming, and M. Manzer. 1977. *The Other Economy: The Internal Logic of Local Rental Housing*. Toronto: Peter Martin.

Ley, D. 1997. *The New Middle Class and the Remaking of the Central City*. New York: Oxford University Press.

Lo, O., and P. Gauthier. 1995. 'Housing Affordability Problems Among Renters', *Canadian Social Trends* (Spring): 14–17.

Lorimer, J. 1978. *The Developers*. Toronto: James Lorimer.

McAfee, A. 1984. 'Four Decades of Geographical Impact by Canadian Social Housing Policies', in B. Barr, ed., *Studies in Canadian Regional Geography: Essays in Honour of J. Lewis Robinson*. Vancouver: Tantalus.

McClain, J. 1993. 'Housing as a Human Service: Accommodating Special Needs', in Miron (1993a).

———— and C. Doyle. 1983. *Women and Housing*. Ottawa: Canadian Council on Social Development.

McKellar, J. 1993. 'Building Technology and the Production Process', in Miron (1993a).

MacKenzie, S., and D. Rose. 1983. 'Industrial Change, the Domestic Economy and Home Life', in J. Anderson et al., eds, *Redundant Spaces in Cities and Regions*. London: Academic Press.

———— and M. Truelove. 1993. 'Access to Public Services: The Case of Day Care', in L.S. Bourne and D. Ley, eds, *The Social Geography of the Canadian City*. Montreal and Kingston: McGill-Queen's University Press.

Marsh, M. 1991. *Suburban Lives*. New Brunswick, NJ: Rutgers University Press.

Michelson, W. 1977. *Environmental Choice, Human Behaviour and Residential Satisfaction*. New York: Oxford University Press.

————. 1984. *From Sun to Sun: Daily Obligations and Community Structure in the Lives of Employed Mothers and Their Families*. Totowa, NJ: Rowman and Allanheld.

Miron, J. 1988. *Demographic Change, Household Formation and Housing Demand: Canada's Postwar Experience*. Montreal and Kingston: McGill-Queen's University Press.

————, ed. 1993a. *Housing Progress in Canada since 1945*. Montreal and Kingston: McGill-Queen's University Press.

————. 1993b. 'Demographic Change, Household Formation and Housing Demand: Canada's Postwar Experience', in Miron (1993a).

————. and B. Cullingworth. 1983. *Rent Control: Impacts on Income Distribution, Affordability and Security of Tenure*. Toronto: Centre for Urban and Community Studies, University of Toronto.

Mitchell, B., and E.M. Gee. 1996. 'Young Adults Returning Home: Implications for Social Policy', in B. Galaway and J. Hudson, eds, *Youth in Transition: Perspectives on Research and Policy*. Toronto: Thompson.

Modell, J., and T. Hareven. 1973. 'Urbanization and the Malleable Household: An Examination of Boarding and Lodging in American Families', *Journal of Marriage and the Family* 35: 467–79.

Moore, E.G., and A. Skaburskis. 1993. 'Measuring Transitions in the Housing Stock', in Miron (1993a).

Murdie, R.A. 1986. 'Local Strategies in Resale Home Financing in the Toronto Housing Market', *Urban Studies* 28, 3: 465–83.

———. 1994. 'Blacks in Near-Ghettoes? Black Visible Minority Population in Metropolitan Toronto Housing Authority Public Housing Units', *Housing Studies* 9, 4: 435–58.

Paterson, R. 1984. 'The Development of an Interwar Suburb: Kingsway Park, Etobicoke', *Urban History Review* 13, 3: 225–35.

Paterson, J. 1993. 'Housing and Community Development Policies', in Miron (1993a).

Poapst, J.V. 1993. 'Financing of Postwar Housing', in Miron (1993a).

Purdy, S. 1997. 'Industrial Efficiency, Social Order and Moral Purity: Housing Reform Thought in English Canada, 1900–1950', *Urban History Review* 25, 2: 30–40.

Rose, D. 1989. 'A Feminist Perspective on Employment Restructuring and Gentrification: The Case of Montreal' in J. Wolch and M. Dear, eds, *The Power of Geography: How Territory Shapes Social Life*. Boston: Unwin Hyman.

——— and C. Lebourdais. 1986. 'Changing Conditions of Female Single Parenthood in Montreal's Inner City and Suburban Neighborhoods', *Urban Resources* 3, 2: 45–52.

——— and M. Wexler. 1993. 'Post-War Social and Economic Changes and Housing Adequacy', in Miron (1993a).

Rowe, A. 1989. 'Self-help Housing Provision: Production, Consumption, Accumulation and Policy in Atlantic Canada', *Housing Studies* 4, 2.

Silver, C., and R. van Diepen. 1995. 'Housing Tenure Trends 1951–1991', *Canadian Social Trends* (Spring): 8–12.

Simon, J., and D. Holdsworth. 1993. 'Housing Form and Use of Domestic Space', in Miron (1993a).

Skelton, I. 1994. 'The Geographic Distribution of Social Housing in Ontario, Canada: Comparing Public Housing and Locally Sponsored, Third Sector Housing', *Housing Studies* 11, 2: 189–206.

Somerville, T.S. 1995. *Measuring the Effects of Municipal Regulations on House Price and Rents*. Ottawa: CMHC.

Steele, M. 1993. 'Incomes, Prices and Tenure Choice', in Miron (1993a).

Strong-Boag, V. 1991. 'Home Dreams: Women and the Suburban Experiment in Canada, 1945–60', *Canadian Historical Review* 72, 4: 471–504.

———, I. Dyck, K. England, and L. Johnson. 1999. 'What Women's Spaces? Women in Australian, British, Canadian and US Suburbs', in R. Harris and P. Larkham, eds, *Changing Suburbs: Foundation, Form, and Function*. London: Chapman and Hall.

Walker, J.W. St G. 1997. *Race, Rights, and the Law in the Supreme Court of Canada*. Toronto: Osgoode Hall.

Walson, S. 1986. *Housing and Homelessness: A Feminist Perspective*. London: Routledge & Kegan Paul.

Weaver, J. 1978. 'From Land Assembly to Social Maturity: The Suburban Life of Westdale (Hamilton), Ontario, 1911–1951', *Histoire sociale / Social History* 11: 411–40.

Weiss, M. 1987. *The Rise of the Community Builders*. New York: Columbia University Press.

Wekerle, G. 1985. 'From Refuge to Service Center: Neighbourhoods that Support Women', *Sociological Focus* 18, 2: 79–95.

Wolfe, J. 1998. 'Canadian Housing Policy in the 1990s', *Housing Studies* 13: 121–34.

Chapter 17

Dynamics of the Canadian Retail Environment

Ken Jones

The retail landscapes of urban Canada reflect the immense diversity of social classes, incomes, ethnicity, lifestyles, and business formats that comprise our cities. Arterial strips, neighbourhood shopping streets, suburban plazas, downtown shopping areas, and revitalized boutique districts are some of the most visible elements of the metropolitan landscape. Names like The Bay, Wal-Mart, Canadian Tire, Club Monaco, Harry Rosen, and Sam the Record Man are instantly recognized by most Canadians. Other retail organizations have regional prominence (e.g., Provigo, Jean Coutu, London Drugs, Sobey's, and Loblaws). Canada's retail environment is a product of two distinct and competing retailing systems—the planned shopping centre hierarchy and the remaining unplanned retail areas. The chains dominate the planned shopping centres, while the independents normally are restricted to unplanned central city or retail strip locations.

Retailing is a major component of the Canadian economy. In 1997, total retail sales measured $233 billion or 28.1 per cent of the gross national product (Statistics Canada, 1998). Thirteen per cent of the Canadian workforce, 1,381,000 persons, are employed in the retail sector, and 804,000 Canadians work in shopping centres (Statistics Canada, 1995). In our society, retailing is pervasive. For many, shopping is a major leisure activity. Retail sales absorb approximately one-third of our disposable income and the image of our cities is shaped in large part by the nature and vibrancy of their retail environments.

This chapter will describe and interpret the various elements that comprise and shape our urban retail system, stressing geographical, locational

dimensions. First, a brief review of the literature associated with intra-urban retailing will be presented. This section will serve to familiarize the reader with the basic structure of urban retailing and will comment on the factors that relate to urban retail development and change. Second, an examination of the evolution of the Canadian intra-urban retail system will be provided. Here the focus is on the development of the shopping centre, the rebirth of the central city, the growth of the big-box retailers, and the role and positioning of the specialty retail area. Next, a general morphology of the contemporary urban retail structure will be introduced. This discussion examines both the functional and market characteristics that make up the various components of the evolving urban retail fabric. The chapter concludes with an integrated framework for evaluating the intra-urban retail system and outlines a series of trends related to the future disposition of non-store retailing in Canada and the movement towards globalized retailing.

Intra-Urban Retailing: A Review

The geographic literature related to urban retailing can be grouped into four research perspectives. The first focuses on both the identification and classification of various structural elements of the retail landscape. The second explores the spatial dynamics of retail change. The third emphasizes an understanding of the development and operation of various retail structures—shopping centres, central area retail districts, retail strips, and specialty retail areas. The final research perspective is directed towards applied investigations. Here, geographers are active in assessing new retail locations for major retail firms and are using various spatial models to analyse shopping centre impacts.

The development of a systematic classification of retail structures is based to a large extent on the pioneering works of Proudfoot (1937) and Berry (1963). These studies differentiated shopping environments on the basis of their locational and functional characteristics and provided a framework for interpreting the retail structure. Proudfoot's work described the existing retail pattern for the pre-1945 city and identified five types of retail structure—the central business district (CBD), outlying business centres, principal shopping thoroughfares, neighbourhood shopping streets, and isolated store clusters. Berry's well-known classification of the retail hierarchy summarized the early postwar city. Here, the dominant business elements of centres, ribbons, and specialized areas are interpreted in terms of central place postulates. More recently, Davies (1976) developed an integrated model of urban retail form based on the simultaneous overlapping of nucleations, ribbons, and specialty retail area characteristics. According to Davies, the retail pattern of the city centre can be viewed in broad terms as a nucleation structured in a series of zonal belts of retail activity. Finally, Jones (1984) provided a reworking of the Berry model. In this interpretation, the urban retail system is subdivided into two structural forms—strips and centres. Each of these systems is then further differentiated according to its location in either an inner-city or suburban environment.

The literature related to urban retail change can be traced back to the empirical work of Simmons (1966). Simmons's conceptual model of retail change examined how socio-economic conditions and elements of urban growth influence the development of the intra-urban retail system. In this model, temporal and spatial variations in income, technological development, and urban demographic growth and change affect consumer mobility and preferences, and eventually cause an adjustment in the nature and distribution of retail structures. In Britain, the works of Bromley and Thomas (1993),

Shaw (1978), and Sibley (1976) examined the long-term patterns and evolutionary processes associated with retail change. They concluded that changes in retail pattern were viewed as the outcome of the aggregate adaptive behaviour of independents and multiple-unit chains. More recently, changes in the retail system have been examined from the perspective of the supply side (Laulajainen, 1987). In these analyses, the final disposition of the retail system is viewed as the outcome of the spatial strategies of, and interplay between, developers, retailers, and planners—the actors who ultimately shape the future form of the urban retail landscape.

Retail structural analysis has had a long tradition in urban geography. In the 1950s and 1960s, North American studies of retail structure dominated the literature. These studies explored suburban retail strip development, retail mix and usage patterns, inner-city retail decline, the emergence of the shopping centre, and the specialty retail phenomenon. In the 1970s and 1980s, the interest in retail studies shifted to the United Kingdom. British geographers, in an attempt to formulate responsive retail planning policies, studied a wide variety of urban retail issues. These included inner-city blight, retail decentralization, the quality of inner-city retail areas, the impact of hypermarkets, and the future role of planned regional shopping centres.

Finally, applied studies have tended to focus on particular elements or projects associated with the retail system. Because of their nature, most of these studies adopt a micro-based, case-study approach. Typically, these analyses are undertaken to provide advice to retail corporations concerning the investment potential of particular locations or to aid government agencies in assessing the social, economic, or environmental impact of a specific development. In the literature, the works of Applebaum (1968), Davies and Rogers (1984), and Lea (1989) illustrate these forms of study. In the private sector, because of disclosure problems, most of this literature remains hidden, but in the public domain numerous consulting and planning reports document the role of the applied retail geographer in assessing and planning the course of urban retail development.

Evolution of the Canadian Urban Retail System

The contemporary retail landscape of urban Canada is the product of a series of complex structural changes. In addition, the retail structure is perhaps the most responsive element in the urban landscape. The entry and exit rate of retailers into the market-ing system is highly volatile. A recent study of non-metropolitan urban areas (Yeates, 1998) found that the average retail turnover rate between 1995 and 1997 (measured as either going out of business, relo-cation, or change of ownership) for five Ontario communities was an incredible 40 per cent. This high degree of volatility was confirmed by an analy-sis that calculated the aggregate failure rate of retail enterprises along 175 major retail streets in Metro-politan Toronto for the 1994–6 period. In this case the degree of retail turnover was a staggering 33 per cent (CSCA 1998). In some categories, such as fash-ion, the failure rates over the three-year period were in the 40 to 44 per cent range, while the lowest turnover rates were experienced by pharmacies (24.5 per cent) and laundries (19.7 per cent). Very minor shifts in the income, demographic, lifestyle, and/or competitive characteristics of an area will lead to quite rapid changes in both form and struc-ture of the retail environment. Conceptually, the retail fabric of our cities has been created in response to the dynamic interplay of demographic, techno-logical, behavioural, and entrepreneurial change (Figure 17.1). At the most basic level, retailers locate in response to market conditions. If the popula-tion/income mix or market potential is appropriate, retail development will occur.

The spatial pattern of these retail groupings relates to the technology of the time. When mobil-ity is low, retail activities concentrate; when mobil-ity increases, retail activities disperse. At a finer level, consumer and entrepreneurial decisions can deter-mine which retail areas grow and which decline. Consumer preferences for both retail goods and destinations can reflect a whole set of considerations that can be broadly defined as lifestyle-related. Certain urban shopping areas move in and out of fashion for particular consumer groups. At the sup-ply side, investment decisions are based on the entrepreneur's assessment of the future disposition of the retail system. Will a certain downtown rede-velopment project be successful? How will the competition react? What will be the demographic composition and demands of a community in 10 years? What demographic cohorts will experience growth? What demographic cohorts will experi-ence decline?

The Pre-World War II System

The intra-urban retail system has experienced sev-eral transformations in the last 60 years. These trans-formations were tied to successions in types of urban structure and transportation: the compact pre-automobile city; the dispersed automobile city; and the emerging information city.

In the pre-war city, both aggregate consumer mobility and car ownership were low. In response, many consumers shopped daily for food and 'going

Figure 17.1   **The Determinants of Retail Structure**

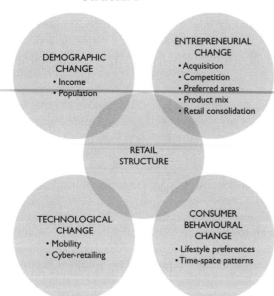

downtown to shop' was viewed as a normal activity. An examination of the pattern of retail activities in urban Canada prior to 1950 reflected this reality. Nearby corner stores were a necessity and downtown retailing flourished. It was the 'Age of the Department Store'. To illustrate, in 1930 all divisions of the T. Eaton and Robert Simpson companies controlled an impressive 10.5 per cent of total retail sales in Canada (Royal Commission on Price Spreads, 1935). Because of the reliance on public transit along major arterials, inner-city retail strips were a significant element in the retail landscape. These strips extended into the residential portions of the city and consisted of almost continuous rows of shops that served essentially local convenience-oriented needs.

Relatively low mobility in the pre-war city explains retail location patterns. Day-to-day shopping was carried out close to the home in corner stores and neighbourhood commercial strips. Meanwhile, high-order goods were typically purchased downtown, the uncontested public transit accessibility hub at a time when this was the dominant form of urban transportation (Jones and Simmons, 1993).

The Emergence of the Shopping Centre

In 1950, the next era of retail development in urban Canada began with the opening of Park Royal Shopping Centre in Vancouver. For the next 40 years, the planned shopping centre, the automobile, and suburbanization were the major forces shaping the retail structure of urban Canada. By 1997, shopping centre sales accounted for approximately 45 per cent of total non-automotive retail sales in the country (International Council of Shopping Centers, 1997) and were responsible for almost all the growth in shopping goods activity during the post-war period. Shopping centre development in Canada has undergone four periods of evolution since its inception. In the 1950s, shopping centre developers adopted a *consequent* development strategy. In this environment, the shopping centre was constructed after the housing stock in a given area was in place and the details of the market were known.

Most plazas were small, unenclosed, and automobile-oriented, and were developed independently to serve the convenience needs of the community. During this early period, retail planning controls were in most cases non-existent and often a form of uncontrolled retail sprawl development resulted. A major factor in these patterns was the reluctance of the major Canadian department store chains to move to the suburbs. Both Eaton's and Simpsons adopted a wait-and-see attitude and were content to remain securely located in the downtown cores of Canadian cities.

The 1960s saw a shift in this attitude with the emergence of *simultaneous* shopping centre development. In this stage, both the centre and the housing stock were built at the same time and the shopping centre was viewed as the centre of the 'planned' community. In Canada, the first development to adopt this approach was Don Mills Plaza in Toronto (1959). This linkage between residential and commercial land uses helped to foster the emergence of several large development companies. These included Cadillac Fairview, Bramalea, and Trizec. The philosophy of simultaneous development became accepted at all levels, from the large regional complexes (e.g., Fairview Mall, Bramalea City Centre, and Scarborough Town Centre in Toronto) to the neighbourhood plazas that form the centre of small residential communities. It is also interesting to note that during this period the shopping centre became an institution. The shopping centre industry in Canada established both policies and procedures, such as the percentage lease whereby the rent is a percentage of sales revenues. A host of specialties emerged to deal with a variety of shopping centre concerns—design, law, leasing, marketing, landscaping, parking, tenant mix, energy conservation, and lighting. In effect, an entire industry was created.

By the end of the 1960s, the shopping centre industry in Canada was well established and a level of corporate control over the prime shopping centre locations in Canada had been assured. Table 17.1 depicts the current list of major shopping centre developers in Canada, most of which are a legacy of

Table 17.1   **Major Canadian Shopping Centre Owners/Management Companies, 1997**

Owner/Management Co.	Headquarters	Total No. of Centres	Total Gross Leasable Area (sq. ft.)
Cambridge S.C.	Toronto	54	27,691,925
Cadillac Fairview	Toronto	36	21,107,533
20 Vic	Toronto	14	11,490,504
OMERS	Toronto	19	11,382,822
First Professional	Toronto	48	11,284,500
Ivanhoe	Montreal	33	9,567,698
Centrecorp	Toronto	76	8,939,574
Olympia and York	Toronto	69	8,654,884
Pioneer	Edmonton	41	7,382,606
Atlantic S.C.	Stellarton, NS	40	7,055,059
ONTREA Inc.	Toronto	10	6,993,717
Westcliff	Montreal	20	6,550,244
Enterprise	Toronto	36	6,361,457
RioCan	Toronto	41	5,717,489

Source: Maclean-Hunter (1997).

this period. These developers are arguably the most important players in determining the spatial structure of the retail distribution system in Canada. It is important to note that the shopping centre system that emerged from the 1960s was essentially homogeneous in nature. One shopping centre at any one level of the hierarchy looked much the same as the next. It had the same layout and design, it felt the same, it offered the same range of goods, services, and tenants in the same standardized environment.

In large part, this sameness was the product of the corporatization of the shopping centre. Beginning in the early 1960s, a synergy developed between corporate chain retailers and shopping centre developers that continues to the present. Throughout North America, the planned shopping centre provided the principal vehicle for the entry and ultimate dominance of the retail chain in the urban marketplace (Doucet, Jacobs, and Jones, 1988). By 1986, slightly more than half of all retail chains and department stores in Canada were located in shopping centres—51.7 per cent or 17,795 outlets. Certain types of retail chains were disproportionately oriented to shopping centres. In terms of total sales, women's clothing (91 per cent), luggage and leather goods (89 per cent), children's clothing (87 per cent), jewellery stores (85 per cent), and shoe stores (83 per cent) were the retail activities that showed the greatest propensity for shopping centre locations.

The relationship between the retail chain and the shopping centre is reflected in the redistribution of retail space in many metropolitan environments. For example, in Metropolitan Toronto (since

1998, the City of Toronto), which has kept an inventory of retail space since 1953, the share of the total retail space found in planned shopping facilities rose from 2.4 per cent in 1953 to 40.8 per cent in 1971, 54.5 per cent in 1986, and 55.3 per cent in 1994 (Simmons et al., 1996).

The early 1970s saw a gradual shift to a third stage in some larger metropolitan markets—the *catalytic* shopping centre. In this case, the shopping centre was viewed as a growth pole to stimulate future residential development. In a typical case, a super-regional shopping centre was built in a 'greenfield' at the intersection of two major expressways and would precede residential development by three to five years. Scarborough Town Centre and Mississauga Square One are prime examples of this trend in the Toronto region. In part, these developments were in keeping with the 'bigger is better' philosophy that permeated North American business decision-making in this period. The success of these centres was also contingent on both large development companies with extensive land banks and the willingness and ability of national chains to enter a location and wait for the market to develop.

The 1960s and 1970s were also characterized by the commercial revitalization of central cores, as these areas became a prime focus for shopping centre development. In Canada, the first attempt at a downtown shopping centre was in London, Ontario (Wellington Square, 1960), and by the end of the 1970s most major cities in Canada had an enclosed shopping facility in the downtown core. In most cases, these developments were joint ventures that involved the developer, a major department store (often Eaton's), and an important financial institution. To date, over 30 city centres in Canada have experienced this form of development, which has reshaped the retail form of Canada's downtowns (see Table 17.2).

The end of the 1970s saw the market saturation of the suburban shopping centre in Canada. Developers pursued a series of alternative growth strategies. First, a number of selected shopping centres were rejuvenated. This process generally involved the enclosing and 'remixing' of first-generation

regional shopping centres that had been constructed in the 1960–5 period. Second, through a strategy termed 'infilling', a number of smaller towns became targets for enclosed regional or community malls on their periphery. As a consequence, a number of downtown cores in these smaller communities experienced severe decline. A third option, adopted by major developers such as Cadillac Fairview, Olympia and York, Bramalea, Oxford, Cambridge, Trizec, and Daon, was to become active in the high-growth markets of the United States. It became commonplace for Canadian retail-commercial developers to become major players in Los Angeles, New York City, Dallas, Minneapolis, and Denver.

The 1980s saw the emergence of a fourth form of shopping centre development—the shopping centre as an *entertainment or tourist attraction*. The overt mixing of retailing and recreation in a major shopping centre is an innovation particular to Canada. The 350,000 square metre (3,800,000 square foot) West Edmonton Mall is by far the most ambitious example of this type of mega-project with its dozens of tourists attractions. These include an ice-skating rink, wave pool, submarine rides, marineland, aviary, Fantasyland Hotel, children's amusement park, and a mock 'Parisian' shopping boulevard. The Eaton Centre, recognized as one of Toronto's most popular tourist attractions, illustrates this phenomenon. These environments assume a recreational as well as a shopping purpose. Also in the 1980s, many inner-city shopping centres and redeveloped waterfront properties have been targeted partly at tourists and recreational shoppers. Over the last decade, entertainment has become a more important component of many shopping destinations as multi-screen theatres or virtual-reality complexes become shopping centre anchors.

By far the most active form of shopping centre development in Canada during the 1980s was the revitalization of existing properties. Developers have found that shopping centres have a distinct life cycle. After approximately 10 to 15 years, most centres are in need of renovation. Since their initial construction, the demography and income level of their trade area has changed, their competitive environment has

Table 17.2   **Major Downtown Redevelopment Projects in Canada**

Project	Major Tenant*	Location	Size (000 sq. ft)	Date (Renovation)	Developer/ Manager
1. Galleria London (Wellington Square)	Eaton's/The Bay	London	770	1960 ('83) ('89)	RHK Capital
2. Place Ville-Marie		Montreal	184	1962 ('85) ('87)	Trizec-Hahn
3. Place Bonaventure		Montreal	169	1967	Canada Lands Co.
4. Place Alexis Nihon		Montreal	395	1967	Enterprise
5. Highfield Square	Eaton's	Moncton	269	1968	Atlantic S.C.
6. Scotia Square		Halifax	286	1969	Atlantic S.C.
7. Toronto Dom. C.		Toronto	121	1969 ('74) ('84)	Cadillac Fairview
8. Midtown Plaza	Eaton's/Sears	Saskatoon	695	1970 ('72)	Cadillac Fairview
9. City Centre	Eaton's/Zellers	Sudbury	600	1971 ('75) ('80) ('86)	Pioneer
10. City Centre	Wal-Mart	Thompson	156	1971	Thompson Mall Inc.
11. Pacific Centre	Eaton's/Renfrew	Vancouver	954	1971 ('75) ('85)	Cadillac Fairview
12. Commerce Court		Toronto	145	1972, 1990	CIBC Dev. Corp.
13. Lloyd Jackson Sq.	Eaton's	Hamilton	620	1972 ('83) ('88)	Yale Properties
14. Royal Centre	Zellers	Vancouver	263	1973 ('92)	Cambridge S.C.
15. Manulife Centre		Toronto	284	1973 ('88)	Manuf'ers' Life
16. Station Mall	Sears/Zellers	Sault Ste Marie	458	1973 ('81) ('86)	Algocen
17. Market Square		Kitchener	318	1974	MSK Develop.
18. Cumberland Terr.		Toronto	106	1974	Hammerson
19. Kesfus Mall		Thunder Bay	217	1974 ('80) ('84)	Pioneer
20. Place Québec		Quebec City	100	1974	For Sale
21. Edmonton C.	The Bay/Renfrew	Edmonton	496	1974 ('84)	Oxford
22. Peterborough Sq.		Peterborough	341	1975 ('84)	Fairfield
23. Lethbridge C.	The Bay	Lethbridge	332	1975 ('88)	Cambridge S.C.
24. Hudson Bay C.	The Bay	Toronto	425	1975 ('82)	Bloor at Yonge Dev.
25. Eaton Centre	Eaton's/The Bay	Toronto	3,200	1977 ('79) ('89)	Cadillac Fairview
26. Toronto Dom. Sq.	Eaton's/The Bay	Calgary	1,220	1976	Eaton's/Oxford
27. Scotia Fashion C.		Calgary	86	1976	Trizec/Hahn
28. Brunswick Sq.		Saint John	152	1977 ('87)	Brunswick Sq.

Project	Major Tenant*	Location	Size (000 sq. ft)	Date (Renovation)	Developer/ Manager
29. First Can. Place		Toronto	202	1978 ('83)	Olympia-York/First Place Tower
30. Place du Centre		Hull	90	1978	Westcliff
31. Cornwall Sq.	Sears	Cornwall	253	1979	Cadillac Fairview
32. College Park		Toronto	165	1979 ('83)	Tor. College Park Ltd.
33. Eaton Place	Eaton's	Winnipeg	960	1979	Oxford
34. Holt Renfrew C.	Holt Renfrew	Toronto	221	1979	Morguard
35. Brandon Gallery	Eaton's	Brandon	235	1980	Cambridge S.C.
36. King Value Centre	Sears	Kitchener	251	1980	ESC Capital
37. Algo Centre		Elliot Lake	179	1980	Algocen
38. Gateway Mall	Sears/Zellers	Prince Albert	337	1981	Oxford
39. Cornwall C.	Eaton's/Sears	Regina	614	1981 ('83)	Cadillac Fairview
40. Atrium on Bay		Toronto	135	1982	Brookfield
41. Chatham C.	Sears	Chatham	235	1982 ('83)	Cambridge S.C.
42. Sarnia Eaton C.		Sarnia	256	1982	Cadillac Fairview
43. Rideau Centre	Eaton's/The Bay	Ottawa	1,100	1983	Viking/Rideau
44. Market Square		Saint John	227	1983	Hardman Group
45. Guelph Eaton C.		Guelph	276	1984	Pioneer
46. Manulife C.	Holt Renfrew	Edmonton	182	1983	Manuf'ers' Life
47. Eaton Market Sq.		Brantford	211	1986	Laing
48. Le Faubourg Ste Catherine		Montreal	239	1986 ('87)	Les Cours Montreal
49. Portage Place	Holt Renfrew	Winnipeg	286	1987	Cadillac Fairview
50. Edmonton Eaton C.	Eaton's	Edmonton	520	1987	Enterprise
51. Les Cours Mont-Royal		Montreal	185	1988	Mutual Life
52. Le Centre Eaton	Eaton's	Montreal	290	1988	Receivership
53. Promenades de la Cathedrale	Eaton's/The Bay	Montreal	175	1988	Omers
54. Park Place	Sears	Lethbridge	465	1988	Oxford
55. Victoria Eaton C.	Eaton's	Victoria	402	1989	Cadillac Fairview
56. Place Montreal Trust	Marks & Spenc.	Montreal	211	1988	Caisse de Dépot/ Cadillac Fairview

*As of 23 August 1999 the 64-store Eaton's department store chain was placed under bankruptcy protection. It is expected that the 16 Eaton's locations listed here will be either converted to other retail uses or re-leased to other Canadian or US department store chains.

Source: Maclean-Hunter (1997).

been altered, and their 'book value' has been depreciated to zero. Revitalization offers a number of advantages to the developer. Existing shopping centres are well situated in a known market, they experience fewer zoning or environmental regulatory problems, and renovation typically involves lower construction and financial costs than the construction of new structures does. Most of these renewal projects involve the re-tenanting of the centre and result in an increase in the total number of retail units. Even if no additional retail space is added, because of the reduction in store size (the outcome of small boutiques replacing larger stores) the actual number of stores in a centre can increase dramatically. Revitalization has taken a number of forms. These include expansions, enclosures, re-tenanting, renovations, or various combinations of the above.

Figure 17.2 illustrates the process whereby shopping centre maturation contributed to major shifts in the growth of new retail forms. In essence, the intra-urban shopping centre hierarchy developed between 1950 and 1970 led to a dichotomous retail system. The new suburban system was planned, functionally homogeneous, and the domain of the retail chains. In contrast, the older inner-city areas remained unplanned and were dominated by independent merchants. By the mid-1970s, shopping centre developers recognized that they had created a series of standardized, often overly sanitized, shopping environments. Their response was threefold. First, through shopping centre renovation, they instituted new, upscale design features in many of their major centres. Second, they began to experiment with new marketing approaches, such as the shopping centre as an entertainment vehicle. Third, they returned to the inner city, often with the assistance of local government authorities, to develop planned central-city shopping centres (e.g., Pacific Centre, Vancouver), festival retail developments in waterfront locations (e.g., Market Square, Saint John), or historic properties (e.g., Le Vieux Port, Montreal; Warehouse District, Winnipeg).

Concurrently, in many cities across Canada, provincial authorities reinvested in old inner-city shopping districts through a variety of business

Figure 17.2 **Shopping Centre Maturation and Urban Retail Change**

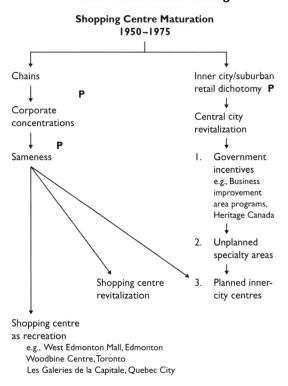

P = Problem areas

improvement programs. Grant programs, often subsidized by a tax levy, were used to upgrade the physical appearance of retail strips, improve public parking, and provide assistance for a wide range of business activities, such as advertising, marketing, and financial management (Holdsworth, 1985). In part, these programs were used to offset some of the consequences of shopping centre competition on traditional retail areas. In other cases, inner-city areas rejuvenated 'naturally'. In this scenario, selected inner-city strips in major metropolitan areas developed a specialty focus. These areas provided an alternative shopping environment to the shopping centre. They stressed assortment and quality of merchandise and merchant expertise, and offered the vitality of an uncontrolled shopping environment. In some districts, such as Toronto's Yorkville and Vancouver's Gastown, this process was initiated in the 1960s (see Chapter 12 on the inner city).

The Arrival of the Big-Box Retailers and Power Centres

The 1990s have seen virtually no shopping centre growth in Canada (Doucet and Jones, 1997; International Council of Shopping Centers, 1997). Shopping centres experienced a decline in sales associated with a variety of factors—the economic recession of the early 1990s; high cross-border shopping over the 1990–2 period due to a strong Canadian dollar; decline in the real incomes of consumers; the aging of the Canadian population and corresponding shifts in retail expenditure patterns (Foot and Stoffman, 1995). All of these factors led to a downturn in consumer spending (Kidd, 1996). The introduction of major competition in the form of big-box retailers and power centres and the arrival of Wal-Mart precipitated a consumer shift from the traditional department stores and regional malls to the free-standing discount department store/superstore (see Table 17.3).

The changes in the competitive environment have modified the tenant mix of the regional shopping centre. Hardware, food, sporting goods, toys, electronics, furniture, office supplies, arts and crafts, pet stores, and optical wear have been the categories under the most pressure from the invasion of the mostly US-based big-box retailers. These large destination retailers, such as Home Depot, Sports Authority, Toys R Us, Office Depot, Chapters, Business Depot, Michaels, Lenscrafters, and Petsmart, which stress competitive pricing, assortment, and brand merchandise, increasingly dominate our retail markets (Jones, Evans, and Smith, 1994). In the Greater Toronto Area (GTA), between 1990 and 1997, 175 big-box retailers entered the market and added over 600,000 square metres (6.5 million square feet) of retail space to the system. During the same period, the shopping centre system in the GTA grew by only approximately 90,000 square metres (one million square feet) (CSCA, 1998). Exacerbating

Table 17.3   **Big-Box Retailers in Canada, 1994–1998**

Category	No. Units (1994)	No. Units (1998)
Warehouse Clubs		
Price Club/Costco	46	56
Automotive		
Canadian Tire	34	100
Home Improvement		
Home Depot	19	31
Reno Depot	7	7
Revy	2	8
Office Products		
Business Depot/Staples	25	192
Office Depot/Office Place	8	37
Computers/Electronics		
Adventure	28	26
Computer City	3	7
Future Shop	45	100
Books		
Chapters	0	29
Indigo	0	3
Sporting Goods		
Sport Chek	40	39
Sports Authority	5	5
Sportmart	11	0
Home Furnishings		
Brick	45	50
Idomo	5	3
Ikea	8	7
Toys and Games		
Toys R Us	58	61
Arts and Crafts		
Michaels	16	17
Bedding Supplies		
Pacific Linen	20	20

the problem for the shopping centre is the higher sales productivity of the big-box retailer. For the GTA, it is estimated that big-box retailers control approximately 8 per cent of total retail selling floor space but account for 15 per cent of all non-automotive sales (CSCA, 1998). In large part, the regional shopping centre has become marginalized and increasingly dominated by fashion merchandisers and personal services. In response, in many shopping centres, rents have fallen, vacancies have increased, many shopping centre properties have become overvalued, and the ownership of many shopping centre development companies has changed hands.

The Role and Positioning of Specialized Retail Areas

There have always been specialized retail clusters within metropolitan areas. The growth in the importance of these types of districts, however, is new. Several reasons account for the recent increase in specialty retailing. These include: a general consumer reaction to the sterility of suburban plazas; an expansion of consumer demand; and changes in demographics and lifestyles. Specialty retailing tends to be an inner-city phenomenon and is often spatially associated with gentrified residential areas or waterfronts. These retail districts attract weekend shoppers from all over the region.

The pattern of specialty retailing can be either dispersed or concentrated. The former includes merchants who offer a highly specialized product (e.g., model trains, comic books, historical documents) and who rely on consumer motivations that can be best described as esoteric. These retailers have no need to form specialty clusters since they offer one-of-a-kind merchandise and their customers will travel long distances to purchase the product. Other specialty retailers cluster in order to reach a certain set of consumers. These comprise clusters of antique and art dealers, furniture stores, high-fashion retailers, suppliers of electronic equipment, restaurants, and automobile showrooms.

Jones and Simmons (1993) have identified five distinct types of specialty clusters: specialty product

areas, fashion centres, factory outlets/off-price centres, historic or theme developments, and ethnic strips. These areas can be either planned or unplanned and serve four distinct sets of consumer demands. First, they may cater to individuals who have a preference for high-quality, status-oriented brand labels and tend to demand high-cost, *exclusive* goods. In other cases, they may serve consumers who are bargain conscious and have a propensity to shop for *discount* merchandise. Third, they may be associated with *lifestyle* purchases that can be linked to cultural heritage, peer pressure, or age. Finally, they may satisfy certain shopping needs that are purely *esoteric* and predicated on the need to acquire or collect a particular item.

Specialty product areas provide an environment for comparison shopping, where choice offered by a group of stores selling similar goods attract consumers. Some areas, such as Granville Island Market in Vancouver and Harbourfront Antiques in Toronto, serve the entire metropolitan market (and enjoy high tourist appeal); others serve a portion of this market. Those areas serving an entire metropolitan market tend to locate near the city centre, though automobiles and furniture districts, because of their space requirements, locate at the periphery in low-rent areas. The neighbourhood specialty strip is typically found in older residential area that have experienced gentrification (e.g., The Beaches, Toronto; Rue St-Denis, Montreal; Old Strathcona, Edmonton). It provides higher-quality food and fashion goods and new forms of personal services.

Fashion and factory outlet centres are on the opposite sides of the spectrum. The former deliver designer products in an upscale environment (e.g., Bay-Bloor/Yorkville, Toronto; Sherbrooke West/Crescent, Montreal); the latter, perhaps last year's styles or imitations, are most usually located in low-overhead stores. Both forms of retail development attract the recreational shopper. Fashion streets are often the most expensive and visible shopping locations within the metropolis (e.g., Fifth Avenue, New York City; Michigan Avenue, Chicago) with close links to the high-income sectors and/or executive employment locations. These high-fashion streets have been particularly attractive to European chains, and in a number of instances these retail environments have been incorporated into mixed-use projects that integrate offices, hotels, and entertainment.

The factory outlet or off-price centre is the most recent variant in the evolution of the suburban shopping centre. In these locations costs are reduced by strategies such as less glamorous mall design, reduced customer service, minimal mall/store fixturing, and a reliance on merchandise that is end-of-the-line, overruns, or seconds. In Canada, these centres are not as prominent as in the United States.

Historic redeveloped properties or theme malls have become a feature of revitalization in older parts of the city, especially waterfront and warehouse districts. The Historic Properties in Halifax, Quebec City's Lower Town, Toronto's Queen's Quay Terminal Warehouse, and Winnipeg's Warehouse District suggest that a variety of developments are possible. Historic or architecturally important buildings provide the focus. In some developments existing building stock is used, and in others new structures are created. In either case, these environments take on the appearance and function of planned shopping centres.

In the United States, these forms of inner-city shopping areas have become commonplace and have added a new, upscale dimension to the retail fabric of central cities. One developer, James Rouse, has been prominent in this form of retail renewal. Examples of the 'Rouse Model' include Faneuil Hall, Boston; The South Street Seaport, New York City; HarborPlace, Baltimore; and The Gallery on Market Street East, Philadelphia. In other cases, a property of some importance is renovated as a specialty theme mall. Examples of these forms of development include Trolley Square, Salt Lake City; Union Station and Georgetown Park, Washington; Jax's Brewery, New Orleans; Old Colony Mill, Keene, New Hampshire; and Ghiradelli Square, San Francisco.

Specialized retailers capitalize on another amenity: small towns and villages in attractive rural settings. Unplanned versions of these recreational retailing clusters have also emerged in smaller communities that provide close-by markets to large metropolitan regions: Niagara-on-the-Lake, Elora, and St Jacobs in Ontario; Knowlton in Quebec. These retail environments are seasonal and are comprised of independent merchants, although in certain instances land costs/rental rates have put extreme pressure on the traditional character of these areas (see Chapter 14).

Ethnic strips are normally associated with the point of entry of an immigrant group in the city. At first, the retail component expands to serve the needs of the immediate neighbourhood. In this phase certain types of services dominate, in particular food and fashion retailers, restaurants, and personal services linked to the cultural heritage of the community. Eventually, the strip evolves to cater to members of the ethnic group throughout the metropolitan area. In time, these areas may also become tourist attractions, as is the case with Kensington Market and Chinatown in Toronto.

The rapid growth of specialty retailing areas has added a new aspect of competition within the urban retail system. The addition of specialty retailing to the retail strip presents the consumer with an alternative to the conventional shopping centre. It also has generated a series of negative externalities based on the growing retail traffic in certain inner-city neighbourhoods. Independent merchants have normally satisfied specialty retail demands, but more specialized chains are now taking aim at the market niches that such unplanned street environments and theme malls provide. In response, the conventional malls are attempting to develop more distinct images, and in some of our major urban areas (e.g., Toronto and Vancouver) ethnic shopping centres are emerging (Wang, 1996). A new level of complexity has been added to both the geography of urban retailing and the retail location decision.

Downtown

The downtown constitutes a distinct retail environment. This district, previously the unchallenged centre of high-order retail activity, has had to adapt to successive retail transitions over a century. This area's high-density built environment also distinguishes it from the rest of the metropolitan region, which places a premium on downtown space and forces all establishments, including retail, to be parsimonious with their use of land. Finally, downtown's accessibility potential sets it apart from suburban locales. It enjoys unparalleled transit accessibility, while being less accommodating to cars than suburbs, where parking is free and plentiful.

The central business district of a city combines almost all the retail clusters described above: it is the highest-order unplanned centre and it serves the entire metropolitan region. Usually, it incorporates a series of diverse retail areas. These can include skid row retailing that features bars, cheap restaurants, and adult entertainment; high-fashion streets; major inner-city shopping centres; entertainment districts; traditional shopping streets; underground retail concourses; ancillary malls associated with mixed-use developments; and historic redeveloped specialty retail areas.

In many major US cities and in many smaller centres in Canada, the downtown retail environment has been threatened by the continued development of planned suburban shopping destinations within an essentially no-growth market. In other centres, including most major Canadian metropolitan areas, the downtown was viewed as a retail investment opportunity by shopping centre developers and department store chains. In a retail context, Eaton's was the major player in the retail redevelopment of over 20 Canadian cores (Table 17.2). Yet, despite these investments, the relative share of CBD retail sales in our urban areas is declining. In Toronto, the central core now accounts for 9.7 per cent of the retail floor space and 6.9 per cent of retail employment in the Greater Toronto Area (Simmons et al., 1996).

In both Canada and the US, the key to downtown survival is the vibrancy of the economic base of the community or region as a whole. The downtowns of blue-collar industrial cities (that is, Hamilton, Sudbury, Windsor) are most vulnerable. Downtowns are more successful in cities, like London or Saskatoon, that act as regional service centres. Obviously, a number of factors contribute to the success of downtown retailing. These include a strong public transit system that focuses on the core, a concentration of office/government employment in the downtown area, inner-city high-rise apartment or condominium development, a safe, unthreatening inner-city environment, and the willingness of major retailers (normally department stores), developers, and financial institutions to invest in the central area.

Towards A Classification of the Urban Retail System

An attempt to generalize and classify urban retailing should be balanced by the realization that the retail landscape within metropolitan areas is difficult to categorize. Neighbourhoods change, access patterns evolve, consumer preferences are modified, and new retail forms are developed. In effect, new retail typologies emerge daily. Many retail stores and districts are continuously undergoing change. If a store does not work with one type of product, the retailer can shift the product mix or alter the image or advertising. It is not uncommon for the same location to go through dozens of variations in function and/or form over a 20-year period.

Four different approaches have been taken to produce a taxonomy of the urban retail structure. These relate to the *morphology* or spatial form of the cluster, the *functional composition* of the business types in the cluster, the composition of the *market* served, and the *ownership* patterns that differentiate planned and unplanned centres. Most taxonomies include each of these characteristics to some degree.

In this chapter, a revised version of the taxonomy developed by Jones and Simmons (1993) is presented (Figure 17.3). The system considers four criteria for classifying urban retailing. Retail areas are differentiated according to their morphology, location, and market size and type. Each urban retail area initially has been defined as either a centre or a strip. Then, in sequential stages, all areas are placed into inner-city and suburban categories, and centres are further subdivided into planned and unplanned classes. Within

Figure 17.3   **A Typology of the Contemporary Urban Retail System**

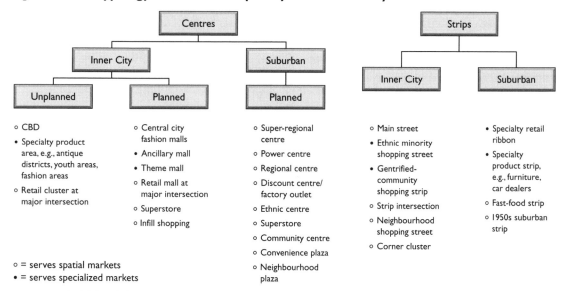

○ = serves spatial markets
• = serves specialized markets

Note: In this classification the term 'planned' refers to a retail environment that is developed, designed, and managed as a unit and where the tenancy and common areas are under corporate control.

the system, each retail area then is assigned a position in the intra-urban retail hierarchy that reflects the size of market it serves and is defined further as satisfying either spatial or specialized markets.

Inner-city retailing has been dominated historically by the unplanned shopping area. In this classification three unplanned forms are possible—the CBD, specialty product areas, and major retail clusters at major intersections served by public transit. The first two serve metropolitan markets, the latter more local demands. Planned inner-city shopping areas are a recent phenomenon and have become a common feature in urban Canada since the mid-1970s. In the downtown two types of planned centres have emerged—the central city fashion mall, which often has been the focus of major urban revitalization projects, and the ancillary retail complex, which has become the normal underground use in major office, hotel, and condominium developments in Montreal and Toronto.

Since the 1970s, four other planned centre types have emerged in the inner city. These include: theme malls, infill shopping centres, retail mall developments at major intersections, and superstores or hypermarkets. Theme malls are a recent phenomenon and normally are tourist-oriented, occupy waterfront locations, and promote a distinct specialty product theme and atmosphere. The infill centre is a typical suburban shopping centre transplanted into the inner city. These centres were developed when the major development firms were faced with a saturated suburban market and new growth opportunities were restricted to neglected inner-city areas. The development of planned centres at major inner-city intersections represented a modernization of traditional retailing at these shopping nodes. These centres took advantage of the established public transit linkages and the traditional regional shopping focus these areas provided. The superstore represents the return of the major supermarket chains to previously abandoned inner-city locations. Typically, these single retail units occupy a minimum of 4,500 square metres (50,000 square feet), offer discount prices and wide product assortment, and rely on extensive trading areas.

The classification of planned suburban shopping centres is essentially hierarchical, ranging from the neighbourhood plaza to the super-regional shopping centre. This hierarchy can be measured by several criteria, such as number of stores, number of establishments, floor surface, total selling area, number of parking spaces, customer volumes, trade area size, rental rates, and sales per square foot values. Since the 1960s there have been three additions to the planned suburban retail system. First, during the late 1960s the super-regional shopping centre emerged. These centres, anchored by a minimum of two major department stores, comprise over 90,000 square metres (a million square feet) of gross leaseable area and serve a market of approximately 500,000 customers. Second came the advent of the discount or off-price centre. These malls afford 'no-frill' shopping and cater to a market segment attracted to bargain-oriented shopping. This discount trend is reflected in the growth of three other retail forms—the factory outlet, the flea market, and the warehouse/superstore. More recently, other variants of the suburban shopping centre have evolved. The mega-mall/recreational complex has been launched in Edmonton (Johnson, 1987) and new suburban shopping complexes are becoming increasingly directed towards distinct market segments—the family market, the young urban professional market.

The retail strip can be effectively differentiated according to its location in the inner city or the suburbs. In the inner city six retail forms can be identified (see Figure 17.3). Main streets (the downtown strip), strip intersections, neighbourhood shopping streets, and corner store clusters have served essentially the same functions since the early 1900s. The main street still remains the foremost focus of retail activity for most large Canadian cities although its proportion of total urban retail sales has declined. In the downtowns of smaller metropolitan regions, high vacancy rates attest to both relative and absolute retail activity decline. Neighbourhood retail areas continue to serve the daily needs of local populations and reflect the cultural and lifestyle characteristics of the resident population of the areas they serve. These neighbourhood strips are some of the most volatile elements in the urban retail landscape. The ethnic and gentrified-community shopping strips have developed specialized retail functions. They have evolved to serve metropolitan-wide markets particularly with respect to restaurants, fashion goods, and specialized products (e.g., art and antiques).

In the suburbs, four distinct forms of strip retailing have evolved (see Figure 17.3). All reflect the dominance of the automobile. The first comprises the 1950s suburban strip shopping mall phenomenon. These 'unplanned' developments represented the first stage in the retail expansion to the suburbs and were restricted to major suburban arterial locations. Normally, they are characterized by a series of small centres with limited parking that abuts the front of these properties. Some suburban arterials have taken on a specialty focus. Typically, these specialized clusters include fast-food restaurants, automobile dealers, furniture warehouses, home improvement retailers, and discount merchandisers.

In the late 1980s and continuing into the 1990s, big-box retailers (also known as category killers) and power centres have been added to the urban retail system. This part of the hierarchy can include a variety of retail forms, but all are based on low margins and high sales per square foot that are supported by low land costs and labour inputs—hence high volumes and low unit prices. Typically, these retailers occupy industrial lands and prefer highly accessible, expressway/highway locations. In the typical power centre, one would find a free-standing Price Club/Costco and Home Depot, and a variety of other category killers (Chapters, Sports Authority, Business Depot, Adventure Electronics, and Michaels) (see Figure 17.4).

This classification provides a conceptual framework for understanding the complexity of the urban retail environment. In evaluating this typology, it should be remembered that the downtown makes up between 10 and 15 per cent of stores and the outlying shopping centres perhaps another 20 per cent. In total, these major nodes, with their larger stores and chain focus, account for close to half the sales

Figure 17.4 **Typical Power Centre**

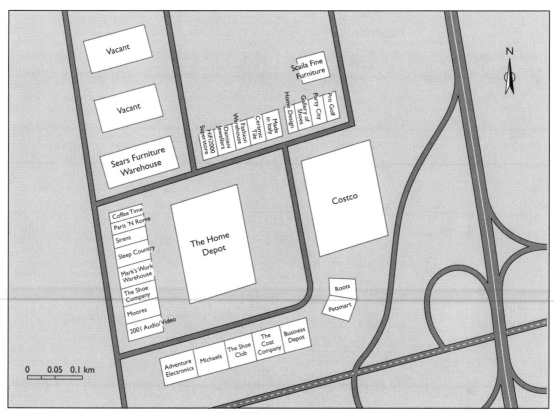

in the metropolitan region. However, approximately two-thirds of urban retailers operate in a variety of other shopping environments where they serve both specialized and convenience-oriented needs.

Conclusion

The urban retail system is structurally complex. In attempting to understand this environment, three distinct approaches should be integrated (Figure 17.5). First, it is necessary to describe and develop an inventory of the basic functional characteristics and spatial distribution patterns of the retail structure. The focus should be on such basic dimensions as retail type, number of stores, employment, ownership, and store turnover rates. The second and third approaches

examine the retail system from the traditional perspectives of demand and supply. The geographer has been more comfortable examining the spatial aspects of demand. Here, consumer behaviour and attitudes are measured empirically in terms of retail expenditure patterns, distance decay relationships (the rate at which the use of a shopping facility declines with distance), and images of various retail environments. The market typically is assessed in terms of location, areal extent, income level (market size), demographic composition, and lifestyle characteristics. The third component, retail supply, normally has been overlooked in most geographic appraisals of the urban retail landscape. But by concentrating on entrepreneurial decisions, the form, spatial distribution, and dynamics of urban retailing could be better under-

Figure 17.5   **An Integrated Framework for the Study of the Intra-Urban Retail System**

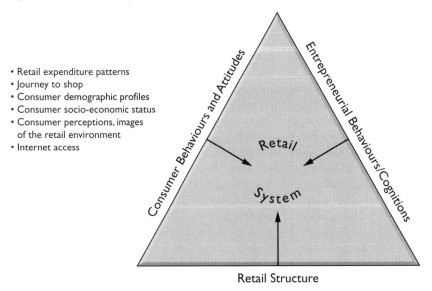

• Retail expenditure patterns
• Journey to shop
• Consumer demographic profiles
• Consumer socio-economic status
• Consumer perceptions, images
  of the retail environment
• Internet access

• Perception of market
  segments, market shares,
  average expenditures
• Locational considerations,
  site/situation criteria
• Buying practices
• Retail inventory
• Retail turnover
• Cyberstores

• Retail inventory
• Number of stores,
  number of establishments
• Retail square footage
• Total retail sales
• Retail employment

• Parking spaces
• Retail change
• Ownership patterns
• Degree of government
  involvement

stood. Important questions to be addressed include: How do particular retailers react to specific market segments? How does the retail firm decide what retail merchandise to stock in a particular area? How are locational strategies formulated? What is the relationship between the retail chain and the shopping centre developer? What determines the retailer's ability to pay for a particular location? By conceptualizing the retail system in these terms, our ability to understand and contribute to the development and planning of this complex and volatile environment will be significantly increased.

Several changes will likely impact the Canadian urban retailing system over the next decade. First, as our population ages, new retail types and forms will emerge. The growth of this market segment will place new demands on the system requiring increased convenience, new merchandising mixes,

and the growth of new specialty chains that specifically cater to the 'greying' population (e.g., nutrition and health food stores). Second, corporate concentration throughout the Canadian retail system will continue to increase. This retail consolidation will occur both through acquisition and by the arrival in Canada of major American and European retailers. This trend reflects the growth of an international retail system (Yeates, 1999) and the realities of the North American Free Trade Agreement. The sectors most affected will be department stores and fashion retailers. Third, on a number of dimensions, the retail structure of our metropolitan areas has become increasingly polarized. It can be anticipated that the dichotomy between inner-city and suburban retailing will increase. Certain areas will cater exclusively to particular market segments, and shopping environments will be developed to serve distinct lifestyle groupings—normally the affluent. Structurally, there will be a continued growth in both large power centres and free-standing destination retailers, as well as in small convenience centres. Fashion retailers and most shopping mall tenants will demand small floor surfaces, while 'stand-alone' superstores will become the preferred format for food, drug, furniture, electronics, recreation and leisure, toy, and home improvement retailers. Finally, new issues will influence the operation of our retail system. These may include the issue of property rights and shopping centre access; the consequences of 'overstoring' on new retail development; the role of planning legislation on the final disposition of our urban retail future; the impact of Internet retailing; and privacy issues related to the proliferation of large databases that capture the purchasing patterns of the individual consumer.

Cyber-shopping will have the greatest impact on the urban retail system. Currently, the technology is still in its infancy, but it will reshape the retail landscape, whether through CD-ROM catalogues, cyber-shopping malls, retailer-specific home pages, or advanced forms of virtual shopping. The number of Internet sites established primarily to sell goods and services now exceeds 12,000 and is growing at a rate of 500 per month, and 1,200 cyber-malls exist on the Internet (Jones and Biasiotto, 1997). For 1998, Internet-sourced retail sales worldwide are estimated at $12 billion, 1 per cent of retail sales for that year and seven times more than for 1997. Online purchases are expected to reach 9 per cent of all retail sales by 2001 (Cramer Communications, 1999). According to a study conducted by the Financial Executives Institute and Duke University, 56 per cent of US companies will sell products online by the year 2000, up from 24 per cent in 1998

(Duke-Fuqua School of Business, 1999). Currently, consumers are concerned about various security issues that relate to potential fraud associated with the transmission of credit card information, computer viruses, and the inability to authenticate cyber-merchants. Consumers complain about slow transmission times, inadequate delivery systems, and the uncertainty of product return policies. But the Internet does offer a number of compelling advantages. It permits 24-hour access, 365 days a year. It is not restricted by location and introduces an element of privacy into the purchase of goods and services. From a retailer's perspective the Internet eliminates store rents and reduces the need for sales staff—two of the largest cost items.

Most of the leading retail Web sites are associated with suppliers/manufacturers (Dell Computers) and/or non-store retailers (Amazon Books). Certain product lines are highly compatible with Internet shopping. These include books, computer software and hardware, flowers, and music/CDs. Other retail categories that will have a significant Web presence and will indeed become commonplace, electronic, non-store purchases over the next decade include: new and used automobiles; specialty foods; health products; airline tickets; and travel/hotel packages. Within a generation, Internet shopping will attain mainstream status.

The retail environment is continually washed by waves of innovation. New products, new store types, new technologies, and new locations emerge, and new market segments are identified. There is constant interplay among categories of actors—retailers, consumers, developers, all levels of government, and, increasingly, technology providers. In this system winners and losers are quickly identified as the retail landscape constantly evolves.

References

Applebaum, W. 1968. *A Guide to Store Location Research*. Reading, Mass.: Addison-Wesley.

Berry, B.J.L. 1963. Commercial Structure and Commercial Blight. Chicago: University of Chicago, Department of Geography, Research Paper No. 85.

Bromley, R.D.F., and C.J. Thomas, eds, 1993. *Retail Change: Contemporary Issues*. London: UCL Press.

Cramer Communications. 1999. 'Internet Statistics' <http://www.cramercomm.com/stats.html>, retrieved May 1999.

CSCA (Centre for the Study of Commercial Activity). 1998. *Toronto Area: Strip Retail Survey Summary Tables—1997*. Toronto: Ryerson Polytechnic University, Centre for the Study of Commercial Activity.

Davies, R.L. 1976. *Marketing Geography: With Special Reference to Retailing*. London: Methuen.

——— and D.S. Rogers, eds. 1984. *Store Location and Store Assessment Research*. Chichester: John Wiley & Son.

Doucet, M.J., A.H. Jacobs, and K.G. Jones. 1988. 'Megachains in the Canadian Retail Environment', *International Journal of Retailing* 3: 5–23.

Doucet, M.J., and K.G. Jones. 1997. *Shopping Centre Dynamics in the Greater Toronto Area*. Toronto: Ryerson Polytechnic University, Centre for the Study of Commercial Activity, RP1997–4.

Duke-Fuqua School of Business. 1999. '56 Percent of US Firms to Sell Online by 2000' <http://www.nua.ie/surveys/?f=VS&art_id=905354818&rel=true>, retrieved May 1999.

Foot, D.K., and D. Stoffman. 1996. *Boom, Bust, and Echo: How to Profit from the Coming Demographic Shift*. Toronto: Macfarlane Walter and Ross.

Holdsworth, D. 1985. *Reviving Main Street*. Toronto: University of Toronto Press.

International Council of Shopping Centers. 1997. *The Scope of the Shopping Centre Industry in Canada: 1997*. New York: ICSC.

Johnson, D.B. 1987. 'The West Edmonton Mall—From Super-Regional to Mega-Regional Shopping Centre', *International Journal of Retailing* 2: 53–69.

Jones, K.G. 1984. *Specialty Retailing in the Inner City*. Toronto: York University Department of Geography, Monograph 15.

——— and J. Simmons. 1993. *Location, Location, Location: Analyzing the Retail Environment, 2nd edn*. Toronto: Nelson Canada.

———, W. Evans, and C. Smith. 1994. 'New Formats in the Canadian Retail Economy', *Journal of Shopping Centre Research* 1, 1: 161–208.

——— and M. Biasiotto. 1997. *Internet Retailing: Current Hype or Future Reality?* Toronto: Ryerson Polytechnic University, Centre for the Study of Commercial Activity, RP1997–9.

Kidd, K. 1996. 'Where Have All the Shoppers Gone?', *Globe and Mail Report on Business Magazine* (Dec.): 38–50.

Laulajainen, R. 1987. *Spatial Strategies in Retailing*. Dordrecht, Holland: D. Reidel.

Lea, A.C. 1989. 'An Overview of Formal Methods for Retail Site Evaluation and Sales Forecasting', *Operational Geographer* 7, 2: 8–17.

Maclean-Hunter. 1997. *Canadian Directory of Shopping Centres 1998*. Toronto: Maclean-Hunter.

Proudfoot, M.J. 1937. 'City Retail Structure', *Economic Geography* 13: 425–8.

Royal Commission on Price Spread. 1935. *Report*. Ottawa: King's Printer.

Shaw, G. 1978. *Process and Pattern in the Geography of Retail Change with Special Reference to Kingston-upon-Hull*. Hull: University of Hull, Occasional Papers in Geography, No. 24.

Sibley, D. 1976. *The Small Shop in the City*. Hull: University of Hull, Occasional Papers in Geography, No. 22.

Simmons, J.W. 1966. *Toronto's Changing Retail Complex*. Chicago: University of Chicago, Department of Geography, Research Paper No. 104.

———, M. Biasiotto, D. Montgomery, M. Robinson, and S. Simmons. 1996. *Commercial Structure of the Greater Toronto Area: 1996*. Toronto: Ryerson Polytechnic University, Centre for the Study of Commercial Activity, RP1996–4.

Statistics Canada. 1995. *Historical Labour Force Statistics*. Ottawa: Minister of Industry, Catalogue 71–201.

———. 1998. *Retail Trade: December 1997*. Ottawa: Minister of Industry. Catalogue 63–005–XPB, vol. 69 (12).

Wang, S. 1996. *New Development Patterns of Chinese Commercial Activity in the Toronto CMA*. Toronto: Ryerson Polytechnic University, Centre for the Study of Commercial Activity, RP1996–8.

Yeates, M. 1998. *Commercial Structure and Change in Non-Metropolitan Urban Areas*. Toronto: Ryerson Polytechnic University, Centre for the Study of Commercial Activity, RP1998–2.

———, ed. 1999. 'Metropolitan Commercial Structure and the Globalization of Consumer Services', *Progress in Planning* (forthcoming).

Part Five

Governance and Planning

Urban management is centrally important and necessary to the life of the city. The three chapters included here are closely connected and focus on the specialized agencies and processes involved in administering the city. In Chapter 18, Andrew Sancton describes the local level of government. He examines the areas of intervention under the jurisdiction of municipal administrations. These include urban infrastructure planning, development, and maintenance, as well as land-use control. These administrations are also responsible for so-called local services: public transit, waste collection and disposal, fire protection, policing, parks and recreation, libraries, public health, and schools. Many of these responsibilities are subject to strict provincial government directives. Chapters 19 and 20 are about urban planning, which is largely practised within the municipal government sphere, hence within the context portrayed in the previous chapter. The strong focus on planning reflects the importance of its influence on the form cities take. In Chapter 19, Jill Grant retraces the history of planning in Canada and describes planning processes and outcomes. This chapter is about where Canadian planning has come from and how it operates. Chapter 20, by Walter Jamieson, Adela Cosijn, and Susan Friesen, concentrates on some of the major issues that confront contemporary Canadian planning practice and explores innovations meant to promote its adaptation to present circumstances.

Together, these three chapters relate the evolution of municipal government and planning. As indicated in Table V.1, there is a close parallel between the historical accounts of Chapters 18 and

19. From World War II to the late 1960s and early 1970s, municipalities took a strong pro-development stand and adopted program-based and expert-driven approaches to the delivery of services. It is within this context that planning departments were set up. Over this period, planners, as well as other experts, were bestowed influence and prestige. The role of planning was to accommodate and co-ordinate the rapid urban expansion then taking place. After this, there was a rather abrupt transition in urban administration in general and in the practice of urban planning. Across Canada, municipal and planning agendas were transformed by municipal reformers advocating respect for the extant built environment and public participation. Turning to the contemporary scene, Chapters 18 and 20 both paint a troubled picture of the present situation. Chapter 18 emphasizes the difficulties confronting local and regional governments in a climate of downloading, reduced financial capacity, and economic uncertainty. It relates these circumstances to the growing efforts to encourage economic development, which take place at the expense of other areas of municipal intervention. Meanwhile, Chapter 20 discusses contemporary planning issues, such as enduring environmental problems, loss of place identity, and difficulties in achieving genuine public participation. Some of these issues are expanded upon in Part Six, 'Pressing Issues'.

The municipal government and planning difficulties mentioned here and discussed at length in the following pages reflect limits to the public sector's capacity to guide the evolution of cities. Municipalities and planning systems are confronted

Table V.1	**The Evolution of Municipal Decision-Making and Urban Planning**	
	Municipal Administration	Urban Planning Agenda
1950s to late 1960s and early 1970s	Pro-development, reliance on programs and expertise	Creation of planning systems, influence of professional planners, pro-development
From the late 1960s and early 1970s to the present time	Urban reformism, public participation and conservation	Public participation and protection of inner-city conservation neighbourhoods, suburban car-orientation
Present context	Downloading, financial stringency	Continued car-orientation, loss of sense of place and heritage, urban design planning, participation problems, but also innovations

with the demands of developers (often active on the municipal political scene) and with residents' self-interests and enduring predilection for suburban styles of development. These difficulties also pertain to society-wide trends, such as enhanced international competition that makes it difficult to enforce regulations, environmental or otherwise, for fear that this might cause the relocation of firms. Still, Chapter 20 ends on an optimistic note by looking at the positive implications of planning innovations, for example, the development of environmentally friendly neighbourhoods.

Chapter 18

The Municipal Role in the Governance of Canadian Cities

Andrew Sancton

Everywhere in Canada over recent years municipal governments have been under great stress (Hobson and St Hilaire, 1997). They appear to have been the victims of constant downloading from federal and provincial governments. Their structures and practices have been the subject of intense scrutiny as provincial authorities and local residents have assumed that considerable money can be saved if only the right reforms are put in place. Nowhere has the stress been greater than in Ontario, where the Progressive Conservative government led by Premier Mike Harris has simultaneously forced the creation of Canada's most populous municipality and drastically reorganized the functional and financial framework for all the province's municipalities and school boards.

Recent changes in Ontario and other provinces have forced Canadians to re-examine the most fundamental assumptions about the governance of our cities. The main objective of this chapter is to explore these assumptions and to analyse how they are being affected by the constant barrage of change that now faces everyone—from mayors to bus passengers—in any way connected to Canadian municipal government. The chapter is divided into four sections: the historical background and constitutional status of Canadian local government; functions and funding; politics and parties; and issues relating to reorganization, of which Toronto's recent amalgamation is the most dramatic example.

History and Constitutional Status

Canada's municipal system—even in Quebec—is grounded almost entirely in British law and prac-

tice, with some later additions from the United States. Prior to the nineteenth century in Britain the first municipal corporations were established by royal charter or act of Parliament in order partially to remove certain defined urban territories from the control of traditional feudal authorities. By this device urban property-holders were able to set up their own taxing system, to build their own streets and public markets, and to enforce their own regulations concerning local trade and commerce. In these early days, attaining municipal status was often a major victory, if not for the whole community, at least for established merchants and property-owners. During the nineteenth century, Parliament extended the municipal system throughout Britain. The central government had become increasingly strangled by hundreds of its own local boards and commissions, which had been created to cope with the multitude of problems resulting from rapid industrialization. A comprehensive system of municipal government was seen as a valuable mechanism for helping finance, implement, and co-ordinate central policies at the local level.

Reasons for establishing municipal government in Canada were similar to those that emerged over the centuries in Britain (Isin, 1992). Municipalities met the needs of both local élites and central governments. As in Britain, early Canadian municipal governments were not particularly democratic. The franchise was generally restricted to male property-owners or leaseholders. Much of the impetus to democratize Canadian local government—including the idea of holding direct elections for the office of mayor—came from the United States.

The constitution of Canada[1] establishes two orders of government: federal and provincial. By Section 92(8) of the Constitution Act, 1867, 'Municipal Institutions in the Province' are included as one of the 'Classes of Subject' for which 'In each Province the Legislature may exclusively make Laws'. Municipal institutions are mentioned in the 1867 Act because they were already established in the three British colonies—Canada (Ontario and Quebec), New Brunswick, and Nova Scotia—that initially comprised the Canadian federation.

The oldest incorporated municipality in Canada is Saint John, New Brunswick, which received a royal charter in 1785. The legislature of Lower Canada incorporated Montreal and Quebec City in 1832; Hamilton and Toronto were incorporated by the legislature of Upper Canada in 1833 and 1834 respectively. Following the unification of Upper and Lower Canada in 1840, the new legislature established comprehensive systems of municipal government for both parts of the colony. The Municipal Corporations Act of 1849 (the Baldwin Act) was the most important legislation for what is now Ontario; the equivalent legislation for Quebec was approved in 1855 (Higgins, 1986: 40–7).

In both Ontario and Quebec each distinct urban area was to be governed by a single municipality, usually called a city but sometimes a town. Rural areas were to be governed by both counties and smaller units contained therein: townships or parishes, towns, and villages. This system survived intact for more than a century in both provinces. It still exists in many parts of Ontario. Other Canadian provinces have generally adopted similar systems of municipal government, except that they have generally done without counties as upper-tier units of rural government.

When an area is incorporated as a municipality under provincial legislation, it acquires a legal identity, just as a business does when it is incorporated as a limited company. Incorporation necessarily involves the specification of three features essential to a municipality's existence: a precisely defined territory; a mechanism, usually an elected council, by which the municipality can make legally enforceable decisions; and a list of governmental functions legally within its jurisdiction. Because municipalities owe their existence to provinces whereas the federal and provincial governments owe theirs to the constitution, the municipal level of government in Canada is in a legally inferior position (Hoehn, 1996). Such a position is reflected by the fact that, legally speaking, the federal and provincial governments are directly linked to the Crown and carry out their activities in the name of the reigning monarch, while municipal corporations act legally only on their own behalf; they are not acting for Her Majesty the Queen.

In 1997, the constitutional status of Canadian municipalities was tested in the courts. Five of the six municipalities being merged by the Ontario legislature to create the enlarged City of Toronto challenged the constitutionality of the Act in question. In his judgement rejecting the municipalities' case, Mr Justice Borins clearly stated 'four principles which apply to the constitutional status of municipal governments':

i) municipal institutions lack constitutional status;
ii) municipal institutions are creatures of the legislature and exist only if provincial legislation so provides;
iii) municipal institutions have no independent autonomy and their powers are subject to abolition or repeal by provincial legislation;
iv) municipal institutions may exercise only those powers that are conferred upon them by statute. (Borins, 1997)

Unlike the provinces, the federal government has no legislative authority with respect to municipalities. Nevertheless, the federal government is an extremely important institution for determining the quality of our urban life (Andrew, 1994). Through its monetary, fiscal, and trade policies, it plays a central role in defining the nature of urban economic activity. Its policies concerning taxation and intergovernmental transfers have much to do with determining the capacity of provincial governments to respond to municipal demands for additional funds for urban services. Federal jurisdiction over railways, ports, and airports is of crucial importance to many aspects of urban development; so is the fact that the federal government is the biggest single landowner in urban Canada. For some of our urban neighbourhoods, the most significant determinant of their future character will be federal immigration policy.

The importance of provincial governments for cities goes far beyond their constitutional responsibility for municipal government. Provinces control health care, education, and social services. Hospitals, schools and universities, and centres providing special services to the young, the old, or the handicapped are all important features of urban life. Although provinces usually do not operate such institutions directly, they have become responsible for assuring their financial survival. Provincial highways are crucial arteries for urban transportation; their extension and expansion often determine the future direction of urban development. Provincial policies relating to the subsidization of housing (Fallis et al., 1995), sewage treatment, water-supply systems, public transit (Perl and Pucher, 1995), and other urban services can have a huge influence on large-scale strategic land-use decisions usually made at the local level.

Functions and Funding

The exact functional responsibilities of municipalities vary widely across the country. Even within the same province, municipalities of similar size and character often do not have the same list of functions. In Quebec, municipalities have virtually no involvement with hospitals or social services. In Ontario, municipalities operate homes for the aged, provide child day care for low-income families, and are responsible for the delivery of welfare payments. They have no formal responsibility for local hospitals but are often expected to make significant contributions to their capital fund-raising campaigns. Most urban municipalities in Canada have direct control over parks and recreation, but in Vancouver this task is performed by a directly elected local

commission. In Quebec, local police forces are generally under the direct control of the municipality. In Ontario and other provinces, the municipalities generally pay the bill while the forces themselves are controlled and directed by commissions not directly accountable to the municipal government (Martin, 1995).

Almost without exception, Canadian provinces have assigned the following functions to municipalities: fire protection; local roads and streets; the collection and disposal of residential solid waste; sewage systems; the taxation of land and buildings; and the regulation of local land use. The common thread in this list of functions is property. This has led many in Canada—practising municipal politicians, journalists, and academics—to conclude that municipalities are the units of government concerned with regulating, servicing, and taxing our built environment. For many politicians, other functions are at best frills and at worst the unjustifiable result of provincial policies aimed at unloading costly social functions on unwilling municipalities and their overburdened taxpayers.

Land-use planning is often considered the government function that best exemplifies the close connection between municipalities and the built environment. It is almost impossible to generalize about land-use planning procedures in the various provinces. All provinces provide for municipal adoption, in one form or another, of an overarching plan that is supposed to provide a framework for future development and detailed land-use regulation (Smith, 1995). Similarly, they all provide for some form of municipal control on the subdivision of land for new development and on the uses to which land can be put. However, the degree of provincial control over these processes varies widely. Regardless of legal arrangements in the various provinces, the political agendas of municipalities throughout the country are dominated by land-use issues. In the real world of inter-municipal competition for investment and provincial regulations aimed at ensuring affordable housing or co-ordinating the development of large-scale infrastructures, little room exists for radical differences in land-use policies among municipalities sharing similar characteristics within the same province. Nevertheless, there are important decisions to be made in each locality about such matters as the number, size, and location of suburban shopping malls; the preservation of heritage buildings and streetscapes; the extent to which downtown business and commercial functions will be allowed to spread into adjoining residential neighbourhoods; the timing and density of new suburban development. All these matters relate to land-use planning. They are at the heart of Canadian municipal politics. (For fuller discussions of planning in Canada, see Chapters 19 and 20.)

One of the major difficulties in attempting to describe municipal functions in Canada is that, in most cities, the municipal government does not have direct responsibility for many important functions of government subject in some degree or other to local control. Instead, such functions are under the control of what are generally known as special-purpose bodies. Exact definitions of such bodies are notoriously difficult. In their purest form they are very much like municipalities. They are established by provincial legislation; they have a defined territory; they have the right to raise their own revenues; members of their governing body are directly elected by the public. The main difference is that, while municipalities are responsible for a number of governmental functions, special-purpose bodies only deal with a particular function or set of closely related ones. School boards are the best Canadian example.

Most other special-purpose bodies lack one or more of the characteristics listed above. They have no taxing authority or legal right to claim municipal funds; their members are appointed rather than elected; or certain of their decisions are subject to approval by municipal councils. In assessing the real political power of various special-purpose bodies, it is important not to rely exclusively on an examination of their legal status. For a wide range of reasons, municipal councils might be extremely reluctant to attempt to change police, transit, or library policies, even though in some circumstances they might be legally entitled to overrule the relevant special-purpose body.

Funds for services delivered by municipalities and special-purpose bodies come from three main sources: an annual tax on the assessed value of real estate; grants—either conditional or unconditional—from provincial government; and user fees. The relationship between the property-tax burden and the level of provincial grants has in recent years become a significant political issue in most Canadian provinces. In principle, there seems to be less disagreement about the desirability of user fees, especially for environmentally sensitive services such as water supply and sewage (Bird and Slack, 1993). Nevertheless, there are serious practical problems to extending them further. For example, charging user fees for garbage collection seems to work out satisfactorily in smaller communities where people tend to know each other. No large Canadian city has attempted such charges, presumably because of the fear that some city residents will attempt to avoid the charge by dumping their garbage in unauthorized locations.

Issues relating to property taxes, provincial grants, and special-purpose bodies all come together in attempts to 'disentangle' the provincial-municipal relationship. Quebec experienced a massive disentanglement in 1980: the province cancelled most grant programs to its municipalities and drastically restricted the authority of school boards to levy property taxes, thereby allowing municipalities to make up for the lost grants by taking over the property-tax revenues previously collected by the school boards. Municipalities were quite happy with this arrangement until 1990, at which time the province decided that school boards would henceforth be expected to cover much of the cost of maintaining school buildings by increasing their property-tax levies (Kitchen and Auld, 1995: 14).

More recently, other Canadian provinces, including British Columbia, Alberta, and Newfoundland, have all taken significant steps to reduce the authority of school boards to levy taxes. New Brunswick has abolished school boards altogether. Nowhere, however, has the disentanglement process been more wide-ranging and controversial than in Ontario. The process was begun by Premier David

Peterson's Liberals and was intensified under Premier Bob Rae's NDP government in the early 1990s. The main objective under the NDP was to make municipalities more clearly responsible for the so-called 'hard' services (the regulation of land development and the provision of sewers, roads, and water-supply systems) while ensuring that the province took over most of the remaining municipal responsibilities for the 'soft' services, especially all aspects of income security (welfare). A negotiated agreement was worked out between Ontario's municipalities and the provincial government in 1993, but the Association of Municipalities of Ontario (AMO) refused to ratify it because of the government's imposition of financial cutbacks under what it called the 'Social Contract'. Significant as this agreement was, had it been implemented it would have had no impact whatever on the funding of education.

When Harris's Conservative government came to office in 1995, it approached the issue from a quite different perspective. Its objective was to gain control of the educational system by drastically reducing the authority of school boards (Ibbitson, 1997). Eliminating their right to levy taxes was a crucial element in this plan. In early 1997, the Conservative government announced that education costs would no longer be funded by the residential property tax and that the province would take over the non-residential property tax. The effect of this decision would have been to force municipalities to use the residential property-tax funds no longer needed by the school boards to pay for many services previously funded in large measure by the province. In particular, municipalities were to pay *half* the costs of providing *all* welfare payments within their borders, up from 20 per cent of the costs of short-term welfare for people generally considered to be employable. Protests against this decision were so strong, even among the government's supporters, that it was forced to retreat. Starting in 1998, municipalities are to pay 20 per cent (not half) of all welfare costs, that is, municipalities are now contributing to the cost of welfare for single parents and disabled people as well as those who are theoretically employable. Despite the gov-

ernment's retreat from its initial position, nowhere else in Canada do municipalities face such a heavy financial commitment for welfare-related programs.

This new state of affairs is demonstrated in Table 18.1, which shows 1998 budgeted revenues and expenditures for London, Ontario, a single-tier unit of municipal government not forming part of the political and administrative structure of any of Ontario's counties or regional municipalities. The table has a number of significant features. Its main object is to show, in descending order, the extent to which each of the various functions of local government in London draws on the general revenues of the municipal corporation, that is, proceeds from the property tax and from other municipal revenues not tied to a particular municipal function.

Two kinds of local special-purpose bodies (conservation authorities and the local public health unit) serve areas extending beyond London's city limits. For these it is impossible to determine the extent of their total expenditures and revenues relating only to London. What is known, and what is reported in the third column of the table, is the extent to which they are funded from London's general revenues. For purely municipal functions and for functions performed by special-purpose bodies operating only within the city boundaries, the table reports in the first column the total expenditures for each function. The second column shows the revenues—mainly user charges and conditional grants—generated by each function. For these functions, the figure in the third column is the result of subtracting the figure in the second from that in the first. As a direct result of the recent changes, welfare is now the largest expenditure item in London local government, but the municipal council has virtually no discretion as to how the money is spent. The rules and regulations related to the receipt of welfare are still made by the province.

Had the provincial government not retreated from its initial position, the welfare burden on municipalities would have been much greater. If the government had reduced the proposed municipal share from 50 to 20 per cent without making other changes to its financial plans, it would have found

Table 18.1   **Budgeted Local Government Expenditures by Function, London, Ontario, 1998 ($000s)**

Function	Total Expenditure	Revenue from Conditional Grants and User Charges	Expenditures from Property Tax and General Revenues
Welfare and employment services	147,458	95,602	51,856[1]
*Police	42,001	660	41,343
General municipal government	42,515	6,630	35,884[2]
Fire Protection	27,432	189	27,244
Debt charges, capital levy, and contribution to reserves	24,565	0	24,565
Housing	17,300	0	17,300[3]
Road maintenance, traffic control, and parking	15,366	3,666	11,690
*Public transit	27,612	17,711	9,901
*Library	11,224	1,414	9,811
Solid waste management	9,993	479	9,514
*Public health	n/a	n/a	8,146
Land ambulance	7,000	0	7,000[4]
Parks	5,051	58	4,494
Property assessment	3,700	0	3,700[5]
Child day care	6,891	3,957	2,934
Land-use planning	2,393	187	2,206
Recreation	10,704	8,762	1,943
*Economic development and promotion	1,744	102	1,642
Services for the handicapped	1,762	259	1,573[6]
*Art gallery & museums	1,448	329	1,118
*Watershed conservation	n/a	n/a	1,020
Animal control	1,224	553	671
*Convention centre	3,593	2,597	656
Community grants	648	0	648
Services for the elderly	16,318	15,791	526[7]
Building controls	3,393	3,111	282
Centennial Hall	617	518	94[8]

Table 18.1   **(continued)**

*Electricity	249,700	249,700	0
Water	38,855	38,855	0
Sewage collection and treatment	25,366	25,366	0

*Indicates this function is not under the direct control of city council but rather under the control of a local special-purpose body of one type or another.

n/a Indicates that expenditures and revenues relating only to the City of London are not available because the relevant special-purpose body operates beyond the city's boundaries.

1. In future years, municipalities are to pay only 20 per cent of total approved costs. These numbers do not reflect such a policy because, for 1998, the government of Ontario is simply billing municipalities for its 20 per cent share of long-term welfare programs that the province is still administering. The 'net' figure in the right-hand column does, however, represent the municipality's real costs for this service.
2. Includes the following items: the City Administrator's Department, excluding fire and ambulance services; the Finance Department, excluding Centennial Hall; legal services, including all the functions of the city clerk; all costs associated with elected officials; various management costs of the Community Services Department, totalling about $3 million; management and general facility costs of the Environmental Services Department, totalling about $10.5 million; and various financial management charges, including tax revenue write-offs and insurance charges, totalling about $9 million.
3. This amount represents what the province will bill the city in 1998 for social housing costs. In future years the city will take over the administration of this function.
4. This amount represents what the province will bill the city in 1998 for land ambulance costs. In future years the city will take over the administration of this function.
5. This is the city's 1998 share of province-wide assessment costs.
6. Transportation services for the physically handicapped and the blind.
7. Includes Dearness Community Services and the cost of reduced transit fares for senior citizens.
8. A multi-purpose hall owned and operated by the city.

Sources: City of London, *1998 Budget Summary*, approved by Council, 22 June 1998, together with more detailed information provided by city staff; City of London, *1998 Water Budget*; City of London, *1998 Sewer Budget*; and City of London, Hydro-Electric Commission, *1998 Budget*, 13.

itself seriously overextended, especially in light of the personal income tax cuts it was implementing. The province thus sought alternatives to income tax to fund public services. The government therefore further adjusted its original plan by setting a *provincial* residential property-tax rate for education purposes, instructing the municipalities to continue collecting it on behalf of the school boards. The tax is designed to raise approximately half the amount that school boards previously raised through their own levies on residential property. Although new to Ontario, such a tax is quite common in other Canadian provinces, notably British Columbia, Alberta, Manitoba, New Brunswick, and Prince Edward Island. Whatever the virtues of the new arrangements might be, they hardly make the overall system more accountable or easier for taxpayers to understand. For most who pay property tax in Ontario, more than half the amount they will be paying will still be going to education and welfare, programs over which municipal councils have virtually no direct control.

It is an article of faith among Canadian municipal politicians that they have been the victims of fiscal 'downloading', that is, federal and provincial governments have reduced grants and/or have expected municipal governments to take over functions for which they were previously responsible. If such downloading has taken place and if municipal governments have not otherwise reduced spending, we should expect local government spending to increase as a proportion of total government spending. The truth of this claim depends almost entirely on what year is chosen as a reference point. For example, in 1913 local governments accounted for 36 per cent of government spending in Canada; provinces for only 17 per cent. By 1948 the percentages were 14 and 18, respectively (Crawford, 1954: 59). It would appear that a rather dramatic form of 'uploading' occurred between 1913 and 1948.

Table 18.2 presents annual data from Statistics Canada showing the percentage of total government expenditures accounted for by each level of government for the period 1965-94. To eliminate double or triple counting, transfers from other levels of government to a particular level are deducted from total expenditures for that level. Readers are reminded that expenditures of school boards are included as local government expenditures. The main story told by this table is that, since 1965, the federal government's share of total expenditures has remained roughly constant at around 50 per cent; the provincial share has increased from 30 to 40 per cent; and the local share has decreased from 18 to 11 per cent. Once again, this looks more like uploading from local to provincial rather than any form of downloading. A closer look at the table shows that, starting in 1984, the local share of total government expenditures (exclusive of transfers) began increasing again—albeit fairly slowly—from its low point in 1983. Indeed, between 1984 and 1994 local expenditures (exclusive of transfers) grew by 96.4 per cent while the equivalent figures for the federal and provincial levels were 51.4 per cent and 86.8 per cent, respectively.

The table shows that hard evidence for downloading does exist—as long as we recognize that its scale is modest; that provinces seem to have absorbed more of the federal downloading than they have passed on; and that, in 1994, the local share of overall government spending was still lower than it was at any time in Canadian history before 1975. It is always possible, of course, that the statistics do not tell the real story. Perhaps the federal government and the provinces have indeed withdrawn from a significant number of essential functions and/or reduced their grants to local governments for such functions. Perhaps local governments have absorbed the additional burdens with minimal increases in costs by eliminating frills and becoming more efficient. If this is what has happened—and many local politicians make precisely such a claim—then the reality of downloading would not be reflected in the percentages shown in Table 18.2. Determining the validity of the claim is virtually impossible. For every alleged example of downloading, a counter-example of increased provincial financial responsibility can usually be found; for every example of increased local efficiency, there are similar examples at other levels.

Now that federal and provincial budgets are generally balanced, it is doubtful that local spending will continue to increase faster than spending at other levels. The level of property taxes in Canada is already the highest among OECD countries.[2] Provincial governments seem as unwilling as ever to widen the variety of taxes available to local governments. Grants to local governments might begin to grow again in relative terms, but it is unlikely that total local expenditures (exclusive of transfers) will. This is especially true in light of projections that the greatest demands for increased government expenditures in the foreseeable future will result from the aging of the population. Health, pension, and long-term care costs are generally not local responsibilities.

While local governments in general might not become more powerful, there is little doubt that municipal governments *are* increasing their strength in relation to local special-purpose bodies. The decline in the authority of school boards has already been noted. In Ontario, local police services boards have recently been placed under tighter municipal control. The provincial government now appoints

Table 18.2   **Total Expenditures (excluding transfers) by Federal, Provincial, and Local Canadian Governments, 1965–1994 (%)**

Year	Federal	Provincial	Local
1965	50.8%	30.6%	18.6%
1966	50.0	31.6	16.5
1967	51.2	32.2	16.5
1968	50.6	33.0	16.4
1969	49.9	34.3	15.7
1970	49.5	35.7	14.8
1971	49.9	36.1	14.0
1972	50.7	35.7	13.6
1973	51.5	35.8	12.7
1974	51.8	35.6	12.7
1975	51.7	36.9	11.4
1976	51.6	36.2	12.1
1977	50.8	37.0	12.2
1978	50.4	37.4	12.2
1979	50.6	38.3	10.9
1980	51.4	37.2	11.4
1981	51.3	37.5	11.2
1982	51.3	38.3	10.4
1983	52.4	37.4	10.1
1984	53.8	36.4	9.8
1985	51.6	38.5	10.0
1986	50.9	38.8	10.3
1987	51.6	37.9	10.5
1988	50.5	38.8	10.8
1989	50.3	38.7	11.0
1990	49.7	39.1	11.2
1991	48.6	40.3	11.1
1992	48.7	40.3	11.1
1993	48.2	40.5	11.4
1994	48.4	40.3	11.4

Source: Calculated from Statistics Canada CANSIM data located at: <http://datacentre.epas.utoronto.ca> (labels D464264, D464244, D464287, D464285, D464803, D464801).

only a minority of the members and the local council must now approve all police budgets, although the board does have the right of appeal to a provincial regulatory body. In 1997, the government announced that statutory protection for local library boards would be removed. In an unexpected decision at the end of that year it decided to withdraw the proposed legislation. In any event, there can be no disputing the fact that the changes sponsored by Ontario's Conservative government affecting provincial-municipal relations have significantly strengthened municipal governments in relation to their associated special-purpose bodies. In so doing, the provincial government has alienated professional organizations representing teachers and police officers. Most such organizations—including ones for public librarians—have traditionally argued that municipal politicians should not be given untrammelled authority to control local non-property-related functions that require the expertise of skilled professionals.

Significantly, school boards in Canada have generally lost authority to their provincial governments, not to local municipalities. Hospitals, long-term care institutions, and personal social services are still almost completely insulated from municipal control. Notwithstanding the recent changes, police in Ontario still have considerable protection against municipal involvement in how their operations are to be carried out. In short, municipalities are a long way from having complete control over local public services within our urban areas. They are still, above all, the agencies of government that look after property.

Politics and Parties

During the 1970s in many Canadian cities it seemed that municipal politics was going through a period of fundamental change. Citizen groups were mobilizing against developers and were often winning their battles to protect neighbourhoods and green space. Their political representatives were being elected to council and were occasionally in control. Although adherents of the so-called 'new reform movement' might have had a relatively clear conception of the ideal urban environment, they had no common view concerning the role of municipal government in bringing it about. Some were genuinely committed to various forms of neighbourhood self-government. Others wanted to use local issues primarily as a way of mobilizing the working class for larger and more important battles to be fought out in the national arena. Most were concerned only with the particular issues at hand and became involved in municipal politics simply because it was the municipal government, in the first instance at least, that would be making the relevant decisions (Caulfield, 1988). Nobody in the new urban reform movement argued in favour of the principle that decisions by municipal governments should be considered final and should not be appealed to provincial supervisory bodies. Nobody articulated a vision of a genuinely multifunctional municipal government, the control of which would be contested at election time by competing political parties. Such views were more often expressed by academics (Plunkett and Betts, 1978: 147–52) and authors of provincially sponsored reports (Manitoba, 1976: 61–7). In fact, many new urban reformers seemed profoundly suspicious of any political institutions, including municipal governments and local political parties, with the potential to overrule the expressed preferences of local neighbourhoods and their leaders (or delegates).

The new urban reformers were successful in changing the way many Canadians viewed their cities. They were responsible for the implementation of elaborate new mechanisms to ensure that individuals and citizen groups had ample opportunity to express their views about proposed changes to the physical environment in their areas. They helped change the style of the municipal political process so that sensitivity to neighbourhood concerns became an avowed objective of just about everybody, including municipal managers and engineers. But the functions and capabilities of municipal government changed very little. If anything, new provincial regulations relating to such matters as environmental assessments had the effect of reducing the capacity of municipal governments to manage their own affairs (on this theme, see Chapter 24).

Sharp divisions between new reformers and old-guard pro-development municipal politicians are now hard to find. This means that we seem further away now from municipal party politics in Canada than we were in the 1970s. Outside Quebec, Vancouver is the only major Canadian city whose council is in any way controlled by a political party. Because of Vancouver's at-large election system, the 'right' organizes itself as the Non-Partisan Association (NPA) to finance expensive city-wide contests and present a complete slate of candidates. In the 1996 municipal elections the NPA won all 11 council seats—not an encouraging development for the future health of Vancouver's municipal party system.

In Montreal, a municipal party system has been in place since the mid-1950s (Quesnel, 1994). The most successful municipal political party in Canadian history is Jean Drapeau's Civic Party, which completely controlled Montreal city council from 1960 to 1986. By embodying Montrealers' intense civic pride, Drapeau remained firmly in control through the turbulent late 1960s and early 1970s. By the time the Montreal Citizens Movement (MCM) took over in 1986, the provincial legislature had amended municipal election law to provide for public funding of recognized municipal political parties and to allow the printing of their names on the ballot.

The MCM victory in 1986 was by no means a victory for the urban radicals who had been prominent in the party since its initial electoral breakthrough in 1974. In preparing to succeed Drapeau, most members of the party had increasingly moderated their political positions. Those who did not either drifted away altogether or found themselves on the margins of party decision-making (Thomas, 1988). One of the many ironies of the MCM victory was that it was as massive (54 of 57 council seats) as most of Drapeau's. Jean Doré was re-elected mayor in 1990, his party winning 42 of 50 council seats. In 1994, Doré was defeated by Pierre Bourque, a relatively unknown former director of the city's botanical gardens who had hastily put together a municipal party known as Vision Montreal. Although the party won a clear majority of council seats, it had problems maintaining its cohesion over its first term. Still, facing three opposing parties, one of which was a seriously weakened MCM, it won a second term in 1998.

During the 1960s and 1970s there was a widely held belief that the emergence of political parties at the municipal level in Canada was both desirable and inevitable (Masson and Anderson, 1972). At the end of the 1990s it is clear that increasing urbanization and the complexity of urban problems do not themselves create and nurture local political parties. We are no closer to having established party systems in our major cities now than we were 25 years ago. Why were the earlier expectations never realized?

The answer seems to lie in the fact that, notwithstanding the growing importance of cities and their problems, municipal government remains limited in its functions and autonomy (Peterson, 1981). The great societal issues that create and sustain political parties in our national politics—building the Canadian nation on the basis of the National Policy for the Conservatives, establishing our independence from Britain and bilingual identity for the Liberals, and building the welfare state as a response to the Great Depression for the CCF/NDP—are not present in local politics. Provincial politics, too, provide a forum for debates over societal issues: priorities in the distribution of public-sector resources, the role of governments, and the constitutional role of provincial governments.

This is not to say that there are no divisive issues in local politics. In the 1980s and 1990s we have become increasingly familiar with the NIMBY (Not In My Back Yard) syndrome. Residents of particular areas fight bitterly with municipal governments and other public and private institutions trying to build potentially dangerous, noisy, disruptive, or ugly installations in their immediate areas. Citizens rarely become more aroused politically than when someone wants to turn their quiet neighbourhood street into a multi-lane thoroughfare or the nearby vacant field into a landfill site.

Important as such issues are at the time, they are rarely capable of building an ongoing city-wide coalition of like-minded people sharing similar interests and political priorities. Without such coalitions there can be no indigenous local political parties. Whether Progressive Conservatives, Liberals, and New Democrats decide to become more openly involved in local politics will probably have more to do with the exigencies of national and provincial politics than with their assessments of the need for change in our municipalities.[3]

There is every reason to believe that municipal politics in Canada will continue to focus on issues relating to the use and development of land. Depending on the economic circumstances of the particular community in question, there will be more or less pressure to accommodate the wishes of particular developers who invariably will promise that their proposed projects will improve the community, attract further investment, and provide jobs. In prosperous economic times, citizen groups opposing particular developments are in a relatively strong position (as they were in Toronto in the early 1970s and the late 1980s); in times of economic downturn, pressures for growth and development are irresistible and the political leverage of citizen groups all but disappears.

Municipal Reorganization

Major Canadian municipalities such as Montreal, Toronto, and Vancouver were originally incorporated as a result of specific legislation relating only to them. Montreal and Vancouver remain legally isolated from the general municipal systems subsequently established in their provinces. The more common arrangement was for cities to be incorporated according to procedures outlined in such general legislation. The important point, however, is that cities in Canada, until the 1950s at least, were not linked in any legal or political way to the towns, villages, and countryside that surrounded them. Conventional wisdom held that city problems and rural problems were different. Arrangements for municipal government were structured accordingly.

In the early twentieth century Montreal was unquestionably Canada's pre-eminent city. Municipal incorporation in parishes surrounding the City of Montreal was relatively easy. As the residential and industrial property market boomed, new municipalities sprang up by the dozens. As many sunk into bankruptcy (in some cases by design) because of excessively optimistic investment in expensive infrastructure, they were annexed by the City of Montreal. The territory of the central municipality grew dramatically; so, too, did its debt, because the standard condition of annexation was that the city absorb all outstanding financial obligations of its new component parts. In 1920, when four more suburban municipalities were in desperate financial straits, the city refused to solve the crisis through annexation. As a result, the provincial legislature established Canada's first metropolitan government, the Island of Montreal Metropolitan Commission, whose main initial function was to control the borrowing of the member suburban municipalities. Optional functions were added later, including the building of a 'metropolitan boulevard', but most municipalities resisted and progress was virtually non-existent (Sancton, 1985: 26–30).

As in Montreal, the City of Toronto's boundaries also grew dramatically as a result of annexation in the early twentieth century. But in Ontario the provincial government itself moved in to control the problem of excessive borrowing by the remaining Toronto suburbs as well as for all Ontario municipalities. Toronto did not get metropolitan government until 1953 with the creation of the Municipality of Metropolitan Toronto. The Metro level of government in Toronto soon became much more important than its equivalent in Montreal. Metro Toronto was charged with providing the roads, sewers, water supply, and overall planning for the gigantic suburban expansion of the 1950s and 1960s. It did its job well and became known worldwide as a Canadian success story (Rose, 1972). In 1960 the Manitoba legislature implemented its version of metropolitan government by creating the Corporation of Greater Winnipeg (Brownstone and Plunkett, 1983: 21–5). In 1969 the Quebec legisla-

ture greatly strengthened and enlarged Montreal's system of metropolitan government by creating the Montreal Urban Community (Sancton, 1985: 116).

The essentials of the metropolitan government systems in Montreal, Toronto, and Winnipeg were the same. The central city and surrounding municipalities kept their existing boundaries. They each gave up some of their functions to the new level of government, which was controlled by its own council. In Montreal and Toronto (until 1988), members of the metropolitan council came from the local councils, while in Winnipeg they were directly elected. Costs of the new metropolitan functions were apportioned to each member municipality in proportion to its share of the total taxable property assessment in the area covered by the metropolitan authority.

Constituent municipalities in the metropolitan authorities surrendered the relevant functions with varying degrees of reluctance. Some of them correctly calculated that a modest loss of authority was a small price to pay to maintain their existence and their ability to continue to control such matters as local zoning, streets, and parks and recreation. Rapidly growing areas, especially in suburban Toronto, experienced real gains from metropolitan government. Infrastructure to support new development was built on a scale far surpassing the financial capabilities of the municipality itself. Using the established tax base of the central city, Metro Toronto effectively created vast portions of what became the cities of North York, Scarborough, and Etobicoke.

From the mid-1960s until the late 1970s, provincial governments in many provinces made dramatic changes to the organization of municipal government. Ontario, British Columbia, and Quebec introduced new upper-tier structures. At the same time as it created regional governments, Ontario merged numerous municipalities at the lower tier. In 1972, the Manitoba legislature merged the Corporation of Greater Winnipeg and its 12 constituent municipalities into one 'Unicity' (Brownstone and Plunkett, 1983).

Policy-makers justified this dramatic assault on traditional structures for municipal government on three main grounds. First, they argued that, especially in fast-growing areas, a local political authority was needed to plan future development around existing population centres. The main implication of this belief was that, contrary to previous practice, city and countryside would now have to be joined, for planning functions at least.

Second, they believed economies of scale could be captured both by moving services from lower-tier municipalities to the regional or metropolitan level and by merging lower-tier municipalities into larger units so that even the most local of services could be delivered by larger units. Associated with this belief was the argument that more highly trained administrators were needed at the municipal level and that their inevitably hefty salaries could only be paid for by relatively large units.

Third, many policy-makers in this field were convinced that larger municipal units would increase equity as measured by both relative tax burdens and levels of service. Municipalities benefiting from abnormally high concentrations of revenue-producing industrial and commercial property would now have to share their good fortune. Those that might have been unable to afford such items as sophisticated sewage treatment facilities or good public libraries would find their service levels upgraded, probably to the standards in place in the best-served community with which they had been merged.

Unfortunately, each of these arguments contained inherent flaws, which caused serious problems for those politicians making them (Sharpe, 1981). Merging city and countryside caused significant problems for both sides. If the central city were relatively strong within the new region, as it is in the Regional Municipality of Hamilton-Wentworth, outlying areas felt that effective regional government would inevitably serve the city's interests and not theirs. If suburban areas seemed to be politically stronger, as was the perception in Winnipeg's Unicity, then the central city felt its concerns always took second place behind those of suburban shopping centres or new residential subdivisions. If the boundaries for the region extend far out into the countryside, as they do for the Regional Municipality of Ottawa–Carleton, the different concerns of both sides are all too obvious. If they are tightly drawn around largely built-up areas, which became the case for Metropolitan Toronto, then genuine regional planning is impossible.

No structural arrangement is likely to mitigate the inherently different interests of city, suburb, and countryside; hence, democratic regional planning is likely to be exceptionally difficult regardless of the structural arrangements. There are obvious problems with the traditional municipal system in Canada in which city and countryside are kept separate. But this system at least has some inherent flexibility in that both sides recognize the inevitability from time to time of annexations of rural land to the city for purposes of new urban development.

In Ontario annexations no longer take place in areas covered by two-tier regional government. Because the top tier provides the major infrastructure, all municipalities are seen as having the potential to support at least some significant urban development. But what about the boundaries of the regions themselves? Since the first regional government in Ontario was introduced, not a single one has experienced any external boundary change.

The biggest problem with two-tiered regional governments is political. Two-tier regional government fragments municipal government functionally by splitting it into two distinct levels. Most Canadian two-tier systems were originally structured so that all members of the upper-tier council have also been members the lower-tier councils. The advantage of this system has been that the upper tier has had to be extremely responsive to the expressed desires of the politicians who run the constituent units. The main disadvantage has been that politicians and voters have focused most of their attention at the lower tier, leaving the regional bureaucrats and, in some cases, the indirectly elected chairperson very much in control and not clearly accountable.

Conventional wisdom offers a standard solution to the accountability problem: provide for the direct election of upper-tier councillors who will sit only at that level. Such was the electoral system for the two-tier Corporation of Greater Winnipeg (1960–71) prior to Unicity and for the Municipality of Metropolitan Toronto between 1989 and 1997 (Mellon, 1993). It has also been the system in the Regional Municipality of Niagara since its creation in 1968 and in Ottawa–Carleton since 1994. For reasons outlined by Paul Peterson (1981: 109–30), most citizens have enough difficulty becoming involved in the affairs of a single municipal tier. Adding another makes it doubly difficult. Direct elections to both levels increase the potential for jurisdictional squabbles between the two tiers at the political level, if not the bureaucratic.

The 1990s have brought a dramatic resurgence of interest in municipal reorganization, especially in eastern Canada. But nowhere has anyone seriously proposed the creation of new full-fledged two-tier systems of municipal government. In Cape Breton and Halifax in Nova Scotia, in Miramichi in New Brunswick, and in London, Kingston, and Chatham–Kent in Ontario, municipal governments have been created that include vast expanses of undeveloped rural land. But each is a single-tier system built on the urban government of a particular city or cities. Presumably the perceived extravagances of Ontario's two-tier regional governments prevented them from being used as a model for organizational restructuring in the 1990s, a period in which the need to save public funds is apparently the guiding imperative (Sancton, 1996).

During the 1990s, the established two-tier systems of municipal government were under attack in both Montreal and Toronto, and for similar reasons. Both were seen—especially by elected politicians in the constituent municipalities—as unduly complex and rigid. More importantly, the upper-tier authorities covering the central cities, the Montreal Urban Community and the Municipality of Metropolitan Toronto, only included 56.8 per cent and 53.7 per cent of their respective 1991 census metropolitan areas (Sancton, 1994: 76). With such limited territorial scope they could hardly be expected to perform some of their main original objectives, notably strategic land-use planning and economic development for the entire metropolitan area.

The Quebec government acted first. In 1992, the Liberal Minister of Municipal Affairs appointed Claude Pichette to chair a 12-person Task Force on the Montreal Region. When it reported in December 1993, the task force recommended the creation of a new 21-member council for the Montreal Metropolitan Region, the territory of which would cover the entire census metropolitan area (Quebec, 1993). Most of the council members would be mayors of constituent municipalities chosen by regional groups of mayors but, because they are so populous, the cities of Montreal, Laval, and Longueuil would be directly represented by both their mayors and by some members of their councils. Existing upper-tier authorities within the region, including the Montreal Urban Community, would be transformed into 'inter-municipal service agencies' and would be expected to be of less importance than both the municipalities and the Montreal Metropolitan Region.

The Liberals took no action on the report prior to their electoral defeat in 1994. The succeeding Parti Québécois government appointed a Ministre pour la métropole who conducted his own set of public consultations on the issue. The end result was the passage of legislation in mid-1997 establishing a 40-member Commission de développement pour la métropole (CDM). It is to be presided over by the minister. Of the remaining 39 members, two-thirds are to be elected municipal politicians (half from within the territory of the Montreal Urban Community and half from other municipalities within the census metropolitan area) and the other one-third are to be appointed by the minister from among representative socio-economic groups. The CDM is to have advisory functions only, especially in relation to issues concerning economic development, planning, transportation, and the environment. All existing municipal organizations—including the Montreal Urban Community—remain in place, although the CDM itself is supposed to make recommendations for streamlining this remarkably cumbersome set of municipal structures (Trépanier, 1998: 107–12). By late 1998, however, no members of the CDM had been appointed and the provincial government was having second thoughts about its desirability.

In April 1995, the NDP government in Ontario appointed a three-person task force chaired by Anne Golden to make recommendations about municipal government in the Greater Toronto Area. Its mandate was similar to that of the Pichette task force for Montreal and, in terms of municipal structures, its recommendations—made public in January 1996—were almost identical (Ontario, 1996). As with Pichette, a provincial election intervened between the time of the task force's appointment and the time the recommendations were acted on. The Harris Conservative government, which had reduced by half the time available to the Golden task force, was reluctant to establish a Greater Toronto Council that would clearly link the outer suburbs of the GTA, the source of much of its political support, to the problems of the central city. It was also concerned about the apparent complexity caused by Golden's recommendation that 'flexible service districts' provide some of the services currently the responsibility of the metropolitan and regional governments.

Since Harris had promised during the election campaign that 'one way or another the metropolitan level of government in Toronto had to go' (Ibbitson, 1997: 244), he could not follow the example of the Quebec government and simply add a weak GTA authority on top of what was already there. The decision in late 1996 to merge the constituent units of the Municipality of Metropolitan Toronto into one new City of Toronto was highly controversial. Because the government announced its decision only a few weeks before proclaiming its new regime for allocating provincial and municipal responsibilities (the 'megaweek' announcements in January 1997), many have concluded that amalgamation was a financial necessity flowing from downloading. In fact, the notion that the amalgamation would save money was more a justification after the fact for a decision that had already been made on other grounds.

The Golden task force had assumed that municipalities would no longer be delivering welfare payments. This was a crucially important explanation for its position that the existing metropolitan and regional governments were no longer necessary. But when the provincial government realized that it had

to *increase* municipal responsibility for welfare in order to take control of the educational system, such governments could hardly be abolished. The option of making welfare a direct responsibility of a Greater Toronto Council seemed completely unpalatable, although the government did eventually decide that GTA welfare costs would be pooled among all constituent municipalities. In any event, for the government it seemed administratively simpler *not* to abolish the metropolitan and regional governments. Since the Premier was committed to doing *something* within Metropolitan Toronto, the option of merging the constituent municipalities appeared increasingly attractive, especially since one of them, the City of Toronto, was proving uncooperative. In October 1996, Mayor Barbara Hall had even gone so far as to express public support for unionized city employees who participated in the Toronto 'Days of Action' protest against the Conservative cutbacks (Ibbitson, 1997: 243).

The government's amalgamation decision sparked a firestorm of protest during the first half of 1997. Much of it was led by the 'new reformers' of the 1960s and 1970s, who believed that the council of the amalgamated city would be less considerate of the interests of neighbourhoods than those of the existing lower-tier municipalities. Despite protests, referendums, and filibusters, the government went ahead. In November, the mayor of North York, Mel Lastman, soundly defeated Barbara Hall to become the first mayor of the new amalgamated City of Toronto. He took office on 1 January 1998, the day Metro Toronto's two-tier system of municipal government ceased to exist.

Later in 1998, the Conservative Minister of Municipal Affairs introduced legislation to establish a Greater Toronto Services Board (GTSB). Its responsibilities would be similar to that of the CDM in Montreal, except that it would also have operating responsibilities for commuter trains. Suburban mayors are profoundly suspicious, especially since they are still bitterly opposed to the government's previous decision to force them to share in the City of Toronto's welfare costs (Frisken, 1998: 198–200). For the suburbs, even the modest plans for the creation of the GTSB suggest that more such perceived outrages are on the horizon.

When the GTSB is established, its territory outside the new City of Toronto will be under the jurisdiction of *three* tiers of municipal government. This matches the legislation for Montreal, except that there the CDM is not to be as functionally important as the proposed GTSB and there is no municipal involvement in the provision of welfare payments. That a Parti Québécois government would add to the complexity of the Quebec state is perhaps not surprising; that a Conservative government would create a single municipality of more than two million people within Metro and then go on to superimpose a GTSB on top of the area's existing regional governments is something that no Conservative supporter could ever have predicted. Far from slavishly following an ideological agenda with respect to municipal organization in Toronto, the Harris Conservatives have patched together a set of policies inspired, it seems, only by a desire to take control of the educational system and to keep an off-the-cuff electoral promise that was not part of its official platform. None of this can be encouraging for those who might expect the Greater Toronto Area, Canada's largest urban region, to be the beneficiary of careful, deliberative provincial policy-making.

Conclusion

The dramatic decisions of the provincial government in 1996 and 1997 have demonstrated once again that Ontario's municipalities have little real autonomy, either legal or political. That a provincial legislature can make drastic changes in the municipal organization of Toronto in the face of the declared opposition of municipal councils and of local public opinion as expressed through referendums is as much evidence for such a statement as one could ever expect to attain. It is important to note, however, that in other provinces—Quebec and British Columbia are the most obvious examples—municipalities in urban areas seem at least to be treated as serious political entities. But we do not yet know how, if at all, the Ontario policies will affect the future actions of other provincial governments.

Defenders of the Ontario policies—including those who might wish to emulate them in other provinces—will say that larger municipalities subject to fewer provincial regulations will have the policy-making capacity to make significant independent decisions about such important matters as roads, public transit, garbage disposal, and social housing. They will argue that we are witnessing the emergence of an era in which municipalities are significantly more important in shaping the quality of our urban lives. But, even if this is true, pressures will be intense for municipalities to compete with each other economically, especially through the lowering of local taxes. People concerned about such issues as transit, housing, and the environment will likely respond by urging provincial governments to implement new regulations and/or new programs of conditional grants. As long as we remain an urban nation and as long as provinces have as much constitutional authority as they have, it is hard to imagine that they will remain aloof from the most important of our urban issues.

Whenever Canadian provincial governments have imposed municipal structural reform on their cities, they have claimed that they have interfered with municipal autonomy to make municipal governments stronger and to make it easier for them to govern more independently in the future. But the very act of intervention dramatically undermines the legitimacy of the new institutions that are created. Municipal governments imposed from above are unlikely to take root in the communities they are supposed to serve. As we observe developments in our newly amalgamated cities—Toronto and Halifax, for example—we shall have an unparalleled opportunity to determine whether or not the structure of municipal government makes a difference to the quality of Canadian urban life.

Notes

1. The constitution of Canada is defined (partially at least) in Section 52(2) of the Constitution Act, 1982.

2. As reported by the Canadian Tax Foundation in *Canadian Tax Highlights* 1, 11 (16 Nov. 1993):

83. The report uses 1992 data from the Organization for Economic Co-operation and Development (OECD), whose membership includes 24 countries with the world's most productive economies.

3. During the debate about amalgamation in Toronto in 1997, it was frequently asserted that the creation of a large city council with its 57 members would likely encourage the emergence of political parties. In the court challenge to the amalgamation legislation, Andrew Sancton and James Lightbody submitted opposing affidavits that, in part at least, addressed this issue.

References

Andrew, C. 1994. 'Federal Urban Activity: Intergovernmental Relations in an Age of Restraint', in F. Frisken, ed., *The Changing Canadian Metropolis: A Public Policy Perspective*. Berkeley, Calif.: Institute of Governmental Studies Press.

Borins, S. 1997. Decision of Ontario Court of Justice (Motions Court), July re. municipal amalgamation in Toronto.

Bird, R.M., and N.E. Slack. 1993. *Urban Public Finance in Canada*. Toronto: Wiley.

Brownstone, M., and T.J. Plunkett. 1983. *Metropolitan Winnipeg: Politics and Reform of Local Government*. Berkeley: University of California Press.

Caulfield, J. 1988. ' "Reform" as Chaotic Concept: The Case of Toronto', *Urban History Review* 17: 107–11.

Crawford, K.G. 1954. *Canadian Municipal Government*. Toronto: University of Toronto Press.

Fallis, G., et al. 1995. *Home Remedies: Rethinking Canadian Housing Policy*. Toronto: C.D. Howe Institute.

Frisken, F. 1998. 'The Greater Toronto Area in Transition: The Search for New Planning and Servicing Strategies', in D.N. Rothblatt and A. Sancton, eds, *Metropolitan Governance Revisited: American/Canadian Intergovernmental Perspectives*. Berkeley, Calif.: Institute of Governmental Studies Press.

Higgins, D.J.H. 1986. *Local and Urban Politics in Canada*. Toronto: Gage.

Hobson, P.A.R., and F. St Hilaire, eds. 1997. *Urban Governance and Finance: A Question of Who Does What*. Montreal: Institute for Research on Public Policy.

Hoehn, F. 1996. *Municipalities and Canadian Law: Defining the Authority of Local Governments*. Saskatoon: Purich.

Ibbitson, J. 1997. *Promised Land: Inside the Mike Harris Revolution*. Toronto: Prentice-Hall.

Isin, E.F. 1992. *Cities Without Citizens: The Modernity of the City as a Corporation*. Montreal: Black Rose.

Kitchen, H., and D. Auld. 1995. *Financing Education and Training in Canada*, Canadian Tax Paper No. 99. Toronto: Canadian Tax Foundation.

Manitoba, Government of. 1976. *Committee of Review, City of Winnipeg Act, Report and Recommendations*. Winnipeg: Government of Manitoba.

Martin, M.A. 1995. *Urban Policing in Canada: Anatomy of an Aging Craft*. Toronto: University of Toronto Press.

Masson, J., and J.D. Anderson, eds. 1972. *Emerging Party Politics in Urban Canada*. Toronto: McClelland & Stewart.

Mellon, H. 1993. 'Reforming the Electoral System of Metropolitan Toronto: Doing Away with Dual Representation', *Canadian Public Administration* 36: 38–56.

Ontario, Government of. 1996. *Greater Toronto: Report of the GTA Task Force*. Toronto: Publications Ontario.

Perl, A., and J. Pucher. 1995. 'Transit in Trouble? The Challenge Posed by Canada's Changing Urban Mobility', *Canadian Public Policy* 21: 261–83.

Peterson, P.E. 1981. *City Limits*. Chicago: University of Chicago Press.

Plunkett, T.J., and G.E. Betts. 1978. *The Management of Canadian Urban Government*. Kingston: Queen's University Institute of Local Government.

Quebec, Government of. 1993. *Montréal: A City-Region*. Report of the Task Force on Greater Montréal. Quebec: Government of Quebec.

Quesnel, L. 1994. 'Party Politics in the Metropolis: Montreal 1960–1990', in F. Frisken, ed., *The Changing Canadian Metropolis: A Public Policy Perspective*. Berkeley, Calif.: Institute of Governmental Studies Press.

Richmond, D., and D. Siegel, eds. 1994. *Agencies, Boards and Commissions in Canadian Local Government*. Toronto: Institute of Public Administration of Canada.

Rose, A. 1972. *Governing Metropolitan Toronto: A Social and Political Analysis, 1953–1971*. Berkeley, Calif.: University of California Press.

Sancton, A. 1985. *Governing the Island of Montreal: Language Differences and Metropolitan Politics*. Berkeley: University of California Press.

———. 1994. *Governing Canada's City-Regions: Adapting Form to Function*. Montreal: Institute for Research on Public Policy.

———. 1996. 'Reducing Costs by Consolidating Municipalities: New Brunswick, Nova Scotia and Ontario', *Canadian Public Administration* 39: 267–89.

Sharpe, L.J. 1981. 'The Failure of Local Government Modernization in Britain: A Critique of Functionalism', in L.D. Feldman, ed., *Politics and Government of Urban Canada*. Toronto: Methuen.

Smith, P.J. 1995. 'Urban-Planning Systems for Metropolitan Canada', in J. Lightbody, ed., *Canadian Metropolitics*. Toronto: Copp Clark.

Thomas, T.L. 1997. *A City with a Difference: The Rise and Fall of the Montreal Citizen's Movement*. Montreal: Véhicule Press.

Trépanier, M.-O. 1998. 'Metropolitan Governance in the Montreal Area', in D.N. Rothblatt and A. Sancton, eds, *Metropolitan Governance Revisited: American/Canadian Intergovernmental Perspectives*. Berkeley, Calif.: Institute of Governmental Studies Press.

Chapter 19

Planning Canadian Cities: Context, Continuity, and Change

Jill Grant

To understand the role of planning in Canadian cities, we must situate planning practice within the context of cultural values and processes. Planning has become embedded in Canadian society as one of the means by which we transpose cultural values onto our townscapes and landscapes: its strengths and weaknesses mirror those of the society that employs it. This chapter briefly explores the history of planning in Canada, beginning with a discussion of colonial settlement. It describes the context and process of planning and considers how the contemporary urban landscape reflects a century of planning policies, regulations, and practices.

Early History

While archaeologists continue to search for evidence of the earliest human occupation of North America, consensus indicates that people had arrived in Canada by at least 12,000 years ago. Early sites were small and temporary, usually near good sources of food and water. Millennia later, when Europeans traversed the Atlantic to claim Canada as their possession, the land was already well populated with a diverse array of settlements. In the agricultural heartland around the Great Lakes and along the fish-rich west coast, substantial communities housing hundreds of people greeted the newcomers.

Extending their political and military domain to the New World, Europeans soon began their own settlements in Canada. Some of the earliest communities initiated by those who came to reap the rich harvests of the sea and land developed in an essentially organic fashion, with no evident plan.

These settlements, like Quebec City (see Figure 19.1[1]), reflected the patterns of medieval towns and villages: paths and roads followed the lay of the land to serve necessary economic and social functions.

By the eighteenth century, England and France enhanced control of their North American colonies. Establishing towns became a keystone of colonial policy: control the land through new settlements. True to the popular baroque traditions of the time, the Europeans designed streets, squares, and markets

Figure 19.1

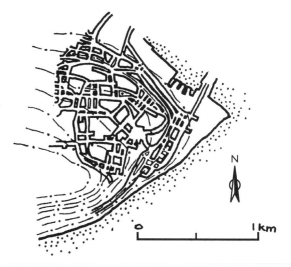

Quebec City, founded by the French in 1608, offers an example of an organic layout. Streets followed lines that connected sites of work, commerce, and housing and reflected the rough topography of the site.

in an elegant geometry: eastern cities like Halifax, Charlottetown (see Figure 19.2), and the French fortress at Louisbourg reveal such influences. This approach to planning reflected the triumph of authority over landscape; despite the grade of the hill or the presence of waterways, the formal pattern laid out by military engineers dominated. Legal systems provided for private property ownership, imposing an economic order that would continue to influence the shape and development of communities for centuries to come.

As settlers moved westward, the surveyor's grid overlaid the landscape, whether on the flat meadows of the prairies or the rocky knolls of the Canadian Shield; cities like Winnipeg, Edmonton, and Vancouver (see Figure 19.3) reveal the pragmatic rigour of the grid. By the end of the nineteenth century, the grid extended to cover most of the West, with surveyors dividing the land for ready sale to new immigrants. Early in Canadian urban history, the rationality of the market and of the engineer had a dramatic effect on the shape of settlements in Canada; later, comprehensive community planning and land-use regulation would provide additional mechanisms to reinforce the impacts of economic imperatives and technological specifications (Gunton, 1991; Hodge, 1991; Kemble, 1989; Wolfe, 1994).

Figure 19.3

Vancouver, first settled in 1862, illustrates the rigidity of the survey grid (which changes orientation and grain from time to time). From the Ontario-Manitoba border westward, the surveyor set the template for the Canadian city.

Figure 19.2

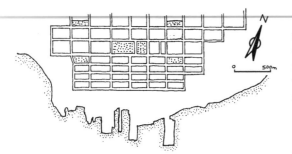

Charlottetown was laid out in a baroque design (similar to that of Philadelphia) by British soldiers in 1768. Like Halifax and Saint John, it shows the simple elegance of narrow blocks, central square, and survey baseline along the harbour.

When people generate their communities through the course of their everyday lives, form generally follows function. In other words, the layout of the organic settlement reflects the traffic patterns people create in going to work, market, or worship. Such patterns are found in early Canadian indigenous settlements and fishing villages and in the areas outside the planned cores of eastern colonial cities. The obverse is also clear in Canadian planning history: authorities plan settlements according to abstract principles where form controls function. The military and civic authorities of the early colonial period imposed rigorous and rational grids on the land in a pattern that reflected centralized control. Community activities had to accommodate the design. Both patterns are found in early Canadian settlements.

Town Planning Arrives

The modern town planning movement in Canada gained its impetus from the urban problems of the late-nineteenth and early-twentieth centuries. National immigration policies brought a million newcomers to Canada, increasing pressure on local governments to respond to the stresses created in cities ill-equipped to accommodate the inflow. The urban population of Canada increased from 1.1 million (25 per cent of the total) to 4.3 million (50 per cent of the total) between 1881 and 1921 (Rutherford, 1984). Housing conditions were abysmal, with intense crowding, poor sanitation, and considerable risk of fire. Aging housing stock in older parts of the cities was in decline. Poor immigrants flocked to the cities, creating an urban working class of meagre means and rough character. Slums had begun to appear. Racism and intolerance were growing. Labour unrest presented a serious threat in some communities during and after the depression of the 1880s.

Street railroads encouraged suburban and strip development radiating out from the core. Railways often cut off port cities from their waterfronts, redirected development patterns, and sometimes created neighbourhoods 'on the bad side of the tracks'. Cities in eastern Canada began to decline as rails carried capital and immigrants to the West.

A survey of working-class conditions in Montreal in 1897 illustrated the prospects faced by many urban dwellers: high mortality rates, long work hours, no access to education, subsistence wages (Copp, 1974). Epidemic diseases presented a risk, not only to the poor but to all urban residents. Investigative journalists exposed poor urban conditions, convincing many Canadians that some remedial action was necessary.

Other than building roads, local governments provided relatively little in the way of services until late in the nineteenth century. However, interest in the new filth theory of disease increased recognition that inadequate sewer services, poor water supply, and uncollected garbage contributed to epidemics. Consequently, after the 1870s many municipalities began programs to ensure clean water and to remove waste from streets and yards. Cities invested in massive infrastructure projects for sewers, piped water systems, and garbage collection, often providing excess capacity in anticipation of future population and economic growth (Rutherford, 1984). Municipalities were broadening their mandates to encompass a wider range of responsibilities, and thus setting the context in which planning would become an integral part of their activities.

As wealth concentrated in large corporations, cities became centres of power and prosperity, as well as dens of poverty. Centralization of industry and wealth in the largest cities led to growth in some settlements at the expense of others. The Maritime economy, once the backbone of the Canadian colonies, was in collapse by the late-nineteenth century as industries moved westward. Montreal and Toronto became the economic hubs of the nation, centres of manufacturing and commerce. Cities across Canada sought strategies either to enhance their economic prospects or to maintain their influence. The urban reform movement reacted against the corruption and inefficiency of city governments; in response, many municipalities changed their administrative systems, bringing in a new city manager structure and implementing a career public service model (Rutherford, 1984). With new structures in place and experts on hand to advise council members on appropriate interventions, cities had the tools to build on their strengths and solve some of their most pressing problems.

Popular interest in urban reform, scientific management (as used by Henry Ford in developing the production line in the US), and garden cities (as constructed by Ebenezer Howard and his colleagues in the UK) generated support for the idea of town planning: a rational way of dealing with urban problems. Facing the end of the open frontier, national leaders became anxious to conserve resources for future prosperity. Confronting competition from other cities (and countries) to attract investment and residents, local government leaders sought to promote their cities as the best places to live and work. Thus, at both the national and local levels, by the 1910s government leaders came to see town planning as a tool they could use to achieve their economic, political, and social aims.

Planning schemes for Canadian cities began to appear in the first decade of the twentieth century. For instance, the Ontario Association of Architects and the Toronto Guild of Civic Art commissioned a plan for Toronto in 1906, and John Lyle prepared another in 1911 for the central city (Sewell, 1993). Plans were drawn for a number of other cities, including Calgary and Regina, but none were implemented (Gunton, 1981). Beautification leagues appeared across the country, even in small communities. (Readers of the L.M. Montgomery novels about Anne of Green Gables may recall that even Avonlea, Prince Edward Island, had a village beautification society.) In larger cities, civic art groups prepared schemes for elaborate urban beautification projects inspired by the American City Beautiful movement (Van Nus, 1984).

As early as 1912, several provinces adopted legislation to allow towns and cities to prepare planning schemes. Responding to the growing interest in town planning, the Commission of Conservation (established in 1909 to promote conservation of resources) invited Thomas Adams, a veteran of British garden city planning, to visit Canada in 1913. The same year, following a decade of boosterism and wild speculation, western land markets collapsed, saddling cities with acres of serviced but valueless land. The national government became convinced that Canada needed some form of town planning: in 1914 the government hired Adams to lead a town planning division in the Commission of Conservation. For the next several years Adams toured the country writing planning legislation, promoting town planning, and developing model suburbs (Armstrong, 1959; Simpson, 1985; Stein, 1994a, 1994b).

Adams came to town planning through his activities with the Garden City Association in Britain. Inspired by Ebenezer Howard's (1985 [1898]) vision

of a self-sufficient community that offered the best of town and country, the garden city movement grew rapidly in England at the turn of the twentieth century. A former farmer, councillor, and journalist trained in surveying, Adams saw in the garden city an answer to the congestion of the inner city and the sprawl of the large city (Adams, 1974 [1934]). As manager of the first British garden city project at Letchworth, Adams helped translate the vision into reality. His pragmatic approach contributed to the success of the project, but also allowed some of Howard's idealistic tenets (like public ownership of land) to be sacrificed in order to secure project financing (Simpson, 1985).

While war raged in Europe, Adams set about visiting almost every Canadian province (most several times). He developed a model town planning act and assisted several provinces in their attempts to adopt it into law. He designed plans for new and renewed communities, including Temiscaming in northern Quebec (1917), Lindenlea (a suburb in Ottawa that was not built according to plan), and the Richmond district in Halifax (1918). Adams's plans reveal his interest in diagonal streets (efficient routes to connect destinations) and boulevards (amenity open space). While critics have dismissed his designs as uninspired (Perks and Jamieson, 1991), we see in his clean lines a commitment to efficiency, economy, and functionality.

Adams's plan for the Richmond district in Halifax created a unique urban experiment. In 1917, an ammunition ship exploded in the narrows of Halifax harbour, killing over 1,600 and razing 325 acres. The Halifax Relief Commission brought in Adams and other planning experts in March 1918. Adams and his team, including Horace Seymour, prepared a planning scheme that featured residential boulevards and diagonal streets to direct traffic through the area (see Figure 19.4). Architects designed row housing with hydrostone cladding (a mix of gravel, stone, sand, and cement moulded under pressure), in an old English effect (similar to styles favoured in the early British garden cities). Although the Relief Commission had hoped to provide low-cost housing for displaced families, construction

Figure 19.4

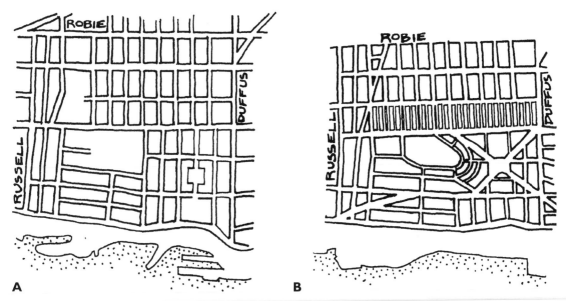

Thomas Adams's 1918 plan for the Richmond district of Halifax brought together elements of the British garden city and the American City Beautiful movement, while exemplifying Adams's unique commitment to pragmatic functionality. (Plate A shows the district before the explosion; Plate B is Adams's design.)

delays and material costs put the rents for new housing above the means of most (Weaver, 1976).

As town planning activity proliferated under Adams's ministrations, a growing number of surveyors, architects, and engineers were drawn to the practice. In an effort to professionalize their activities, in 1919 a small group gathered in Ottawa to establish the Town Planning Institute of Canada (Sherwood, 1994). Thomas Adams served as the first president. The Institute grew rapidly, publishing a journal and organizing conferences to promote the vision, share knowledge, and develop professional standards.

Changes in government and shifting national priorities undermined the commitment to town planning in the 1920s, although not before zoning had gained a foothold as a tool for protecting property values. In the wake of the Russian Revolution and in view of the faith of socialists in long-term planning, the Canadian government reassessed its agenda; even Adams's assurance that planning sup-

ported the market failed to persuade a government increasingly fearful of socialism. The Commission of Conservation was disbanded in 1921; Adams headed to New York in 1923 (Armstrong, 1959; Simpson, 1985).

The most significant planning tool initiated by planners in the 1920s did catch on, only to further undermine town planning efforts for the next three decades. The first zoning by-law in Canada was prepared for Kitchener in 1924 by Horace Seymour (Bloomfield, 1985). By the 1920s, zoning had become popular in American cities as a way of controlling land use (and land values) and increasing the predictability of development. During the mid-1920s through to the early 1950s, zoning effectively replaced local planning in Canada. Instead of developing overall town planning schemes for cities, local politicians adopted zoning by-laws that confirmed the status quo while providing mechanisms to enable land-use changes under specific conditions.

As Moore (1979) argues, zoning worked well with patronage and populist politics and thus proved attractive to business interests, ratepayers, and councillors. By contrast, attempts to adopt plans in cities like Toronto were ignored or defeated during the 1920s. Planning vision yielded to property interests.

Economic growth in the late 1920s led to a brief resurgence in interest in planning. Vancouver hired the American planner, Harland Bartholemew, to craft a plan (heavily influenced by City Beautiful principles). However, with the economy in collapse after 1929, town planning fell into abeyance; through the Depression the government reaffirmed its faith that the market could create wealth (and thereby good cities).

The Great Depression of the 1930s led to government interest in planning in the US, but not in Canada. The federal government consistently refused to put funds into planning schemes for new towns or to take initiatives that might challenge the market. In 1935, the League for Social Reconstruction, a group of prominent Canadians, published *Social Planning for Canada*, the framework for a welfare state (League for Social Reconstruction, 1935). While that document did not immediately influence government, the ideas incorporated in it began to percolate into public discussion as Keynesian economics grew in popularity. As Gunton (1991) argues, the federal government began to adopt planning measures only after the worst of the crisis had passed. Beginning in 1935 this government took small steps towards addressing housing need by adopting the Dominion Housing Act, followed by the National Housing Act in 1938; finally, as war loomed in Europe, the federal government began to accept a limited role in remedying urban problems.

Postwar Reconstruction and the Revival of Planning

With World War II under way, the federal government reasserted its leadership role in managing resources. In this context, it began planning at both national and local scales. It established the Wartime Housing Corporation to address the pressing need for housing for military and munitions workers. Various committees and agencies planned for postwar reconstruction and reintegration of returning soldiers into the economy and society. The federal government laid the groundwork, first in housing and then in other spheres of activity, for urban planning to be established following the war (Hulchanski, 1986; Sewell, 1994; Wolfe, 1994).

The postwar period saw a rapid expansion in community planning activities. The national mood of postwar optimism for a better future, faith in science, and trust in government service created an atmosphere in which city planning seemed logical, appropriate, and necessary. The 1950s and 1960s witnessed the rise of rational comprehensive planning in Canada and the revival of the planners' professional organization, renamed the Canadian Institute of Planners. Many communities prepared master plans—long-range documents to govern future growth. Governments at all levels hired experts to study problems and offer rational solutions in a climate of popular support for public-sector interventionism. While some of the work in this period set the stage for the modernization of Canadian cities, some of the decisions, in hindsight, appear deeply flawed.

Mortgage insurance policies established through the Central Mortgage and Housing Corporation (CMHC, since renamed Canada Mortgage and Housing Corporation) indirectly encouraged cities to prepare plans and to adopt approved site planning standards and zoning practices: homes built according to CMHC guidelines received speedy mortgage approvals. CMHC guidelines set the parameters for minimum site planning standards nationwide. During the 1960s, many cities across the country established planning departments and hired staff planners (often trained in the new university planning programs funded with federal and provincial assistance). City planning became institutionalized within the local civil service (Carver, 1962, 1975; Hodge, 1991).

Meanwhile, developers actively explored the housing markets created through the greater purchasing power of a growing middle class. Outside

Figure 19.5

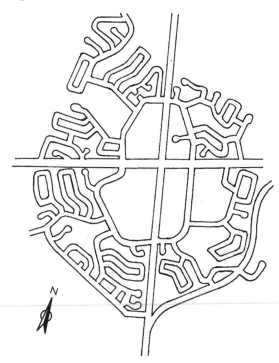

Don Mills in Toronto became the paradigmatic Canadian suburb. From the late 1950s onward, its winding streets were copied across the nation.

Toronto, Macklin Hancock built Don Mills, a suburb of ranch-style houses, looping streets, neighbourhood units, and open spaces with pathways. Drawing on the popular garden city design precepts of the 1950s, Don Mills presaged a new era in suburban design in Canada (Figure 19.5). Developers from coast to coast copied elements of the award-winning and economically lucrative project. Within a generation, the features of Don Mills became the hallmark of Canadian suburbia, a landscape dominated by the values of privacy, family, amenity, growth, and progress (Hancock, 1994; Hodge, 1991; Sewell, 1977, 1993).

Don Mills represented the epitome of modernist garden city principles: separation of uses; low-density development; a hierarchy of streets; shopping concentrated in retail malls and strips; loops, crescents, and cul-de-sacs; buffers of green space or high-density housing to protect single-detached housing; extensive open space systems. The neighbourhood unit, developed by Clarence Perry (1929), formed the basis of spatial and community organization. Although no other community experienced quite the same level of success and fame as Don Mills, elements of the model were copied holus-bolus across the country. Developers endlessly cloned the suburban form, boiled down to its essentials (wide lots, winding streets, and shopping strips), and communities entrenched the principles that supported it into their plans and land-use regulations. Several new resource-based towns, such as Kitimat, British Columbia, and Thompson, Manitoba, employed garden city principles to create a new urban form.

The success and replication of the suburban model through the 1960s and 1970s reflects a confluence of factors. The federal government promoted suburban design elements and regulations through its site planning guidelines and mortgage insurance programs; with programs to support the development industry, the federal government encouraged the mass production of housing by companies committed to economies of scale in servicing land and building homes. Local governments eager to facilitate development adopted CMHC standards in their local land-use and subdivision regulations. Planners trained in the new planning schools and reading the latest planning journals and books believed in the principles of the garden city and neighbourhood unit, and tried to promote them in their work. Builders recognized the profit potential and popularity of the new suburban model, and thus sought to meet demand. Householders, influenced by the visual imagery and rhetoric of the new medium of television, saw in suburbia a reflection of their own middle-class aspirations. (For further information on Canadian suburbs, see Chapter 13.)

The modernist project as shown in the development of postwar suburbia had a 'flip side' in the approach taken to dealing with the central city.

Journalists and activists had been complaining about abysmal conditions in the slums of the larger cities since the late-nineteenth century, but governments were slow to respond. With the optimism of reformers and the resources of the growing welfare state in the postwar period, governments finally addressed urban blight. In the 1950s and 1960s, the federal government provided loans and grants to encourage cities to clear slums. Studies were commissioned to identify the worst areas and plans were developed to renew cities. Faith in progress and science and growing nationalism spawned confidence that Canadians could improve their cities and the lot of their inhabitants. Planning was seen as an essential tool in the arsenal for the war on the slums.

The first slum clearance project began in Toronto in 1948, at Regent Park North. During the 1947 Toronto election, residents approved the project by a three to two margin in a plebiscite; taxpayers generally supported such improvements, as did major newspapers' editorials. The project resulted in a larger number of housing units than had been on the site, but a lesser diversity of use. In this and dozens of other neighbourhoods across the country, land was expropriated, dilapidated buildings demolished, and new multi-family housing constructed. Plans for the renewed sites reflected popular planning principles of the time: large amounts of open space (predominantly grass or pavement), high-rise apartment towers and townhouse clusters, separation of pedestrian and vehicular traffic, no through streets. The 'towers in the park' of Le Corbusier, the great French architect and modernist planner, featured strongly in the site plans. Public subsidies kept the cost of new housing affordable, creating the first substantial amounts of public housing in the nation (Sewell, 1993).

The federal government provided funds for redevelopment studies through the 1950s, seeing slum clearance as part of a strategy of national development of urban infrastructure. Many of the redevelopment studies were very elaborate and scientific, in the fashion of the day. Gordon Stephenson, a professor of planning at the University of Toronto, did several. His Halifax report (1957), for example, examined and mapped substandard housing, fire calls, instances of tuberculosis, number of children in foster care, cases of juvenile delinquency, and other 'indicators' of urban blight. He overlaid maps of these indicators and through a rational analysis identified areas of the city that, he argued, warranted redevelopment. Halifax designated a 'central redevelopment area', secured funds from the federal government to expropriate land and demolish structures, and laid waste to large tracts of the city core. Unfortunately for Halifax (and several other cities that destroyed old neighbourhoods based on such analyses), the land sat vacant for the better part of a decade awaiting a developer ready to redevelop it (Collier, 1974).

Through to the early 1960s, support for these urban renewal projects remained strong in Canadian communities. Newspaper reports from the time show little evidence of protest even by those forced to relocate. However, as municipalities expanded the renewal net to ever more neighbourhoods, and people realized that these projects rapidly generated new communities of poverty, resistance began to develop. By the mid- to late 1960s, home-owners and tenants began to fight to try to save older neighbourhoods. Governments had already invested millions in redevelopment projects that seemed slow to produce much of a return. Public housing providers had planned or constructed nearly 20,000 units between 1960 and 1966, but the backlash from private-sector builders was significant. 'Slum clearance' and 'urban renewal', which first seemed such hopeful concepts, were dirty words by 1970. Planners often found themselves carrying the blame for the projects they had facilitated in their new roles as municipal civil servants.

As suburban growth blanketed the nation, many cities planned new urban expressways during the 1960s. Increasing automobile ownership and traffic jams convinced highway engineers of the need for better routes across town and from suburb to downtown. Federal and provincial governments invested massively in highways. Planners worked with the engineers in identifying optimal routes and in trying to persuade city residents of the viability of the plans. By the late 1960s many neighbour-hoods resisted the relocation and segmentation associated with expressway construction. Planning projects became the focus of civic action and pro-test; in such communities as Toronto and Winnipeg, reform-minded councillors were elected on plat-forms opposing planning projects (Higgins, 1986). With the defeat in 1971 of the Spadina Expressway project in Toronto, Canadian communities had a model that proved that citizen action could stop unwanted developments (Sewell, 1993).

The Participation Era

While originally the preserve of civil servants and developers' experts, the planning process opened in the late 1960s and early 1970s to provide room for public involvement. Governments responded to the new social context in which citizens were taking to the streets to insist on the right to participate in decision-making. Planning issues became public battles as residents fought to protect neighbour-hoods threatened by urban renewal, development projects, and highway alignments. Inspired by media images of the American civil rights movement and protests over the Vietnam War, citizens marched for a variety of causes in the late 1960s. Planning proj-ects soon faced considerable opposition. Author Jane Jacobs (1961) gave focus to the criticisms of modern planning, decrying the open spaces, high-rise towers, and formless street patterns that plan-ners were promoting. Rising commitment to civic action and interest in planning issues were felt strongly in planning practice in most of the devel-oped nations at this time (Grant, 1990, 1994).

The extent of public action overwhelmed politicians and led to revisions to planning acts and local planning practices to provide for public par-ticipation in the planning process (Grant, 1988). Citizens were granted new rights to participate in plan development and administration and to appeal council decisions. Many cities established neigh-bourhood planning offices to bring planning to the people. CMHC funded the Neighbourhood

Improvement Program (NIP) to allow municipalities to assist run-down neighbourhoods to plan their own infrastructure improvements. People across the country began to learn about planning and worked in partnership with politicians and plan-ners to formulate plans for their communities (see Figure 19.6).

The late 1960s also saw a resurgent interest in cities and a commitment to regional development. The federal government established the Ministry of State for Urban Affairs (MSUA) with a mandate to conduct research and promote vibrant cities. Other federal agencies encouraged regional planning for economic development through programs to help disadvantaged regions establish industrial infra-structure and economies of scale in various sectors (such as agriculture and fisheries). A number of provinces initiated regional planning for urban regions. While some of the strategies of planning were changing, the basic national goals of growth and rational development remained paramount in efforts at all scales, from national to local (Gertler and Crowley, 1977; Lang, 1972).

Figure 19.6

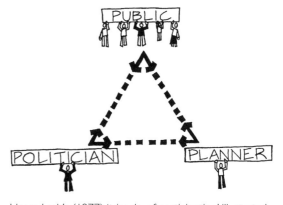

Harry Lash's (1977) 'triangle of participation' illustrated the new partnership among planners, politicians, and the public in planning. Lash's study was among many commissioned by the federal Ministry of State for Urban Affairs to encourage new approaches to promoting urban vitality.

The Newfoundland Resettlement Program: An Experiment in Urbanization and Regional Planning

Although Newfoundland is one of the smaller provinces, it hosted one of the boldest experiments in regional planning and urbanization during the late 1960s and early 1970s. Eager to turn around a legacy of poverty and unequal opportunity, the provincial and federal governments planned a major project to resettle the residents of remote fishing outports into 'growth centres'. Communities designated for growth would provide education, health care, and other government services not available in smaller settlements.

The resettlement project provided government with an opportunity to test theories of regional planning and economic development being promoted internationally at the time. Third World countries eager to share the wealth enjoyed by developed nations were encouraged to stimulate urban industrial centres. Foreign aid supported investment in infrastructure, such as dams, ports, roads, and power projects, that would integrate Third World economies into the global system. In planning the resettlement program, Canadian governments applied principles advocated by international experts, bankers, and diplomats.

While many of the objectives of the resettlement scheme were positive, the impacts on outport communities and their residents were tragic. Growth centre communities often failed to receive the promised upgrades on services and facilities. People mourned the identity and heritage left behind in the outports. Moreover, the project did not improve the circumstances of many of those who were relocated. Trends that undermined local self-reliance and the resources upon which it depended continued unabated. Within a few years the project was seen as a dismal failure. (Matthews, 1976)

Retrenchment and Recession

By the late 1970s, many of the initiatives of the participation era had come under attack. Citizen involvement had fallen off dramatically, yet developers felt that vocal members of the public had too many opportunities to delay viable projects. Costly regional development initiatives were not yielding expected returns and regional disparity grew apace. Extensive government investments in urban and regional development during the 1960s and early 1970s contributed to heavy debt burdens and growing tax levels. The federal government dissolved the MSUA in 1979, ended NIP, and reduced its regional development expenditure. In the shifting political climate of the late 1970s and early 1980s, Keynesian economics was under attack and conservative opinions were growing in influence, thus undermining support for participatory and interventionist planning.

The 1980s and 1990s brought economic reassessment: recession, debt crisis, and 'downloading'. Planning came under attack by those who believe that government regulation dampens a rational and free market. Provincial and regional planning functions were reduced in some jurisdictions (e.g., Prince Edward Island and Alberta); 'strategic planning', modelled on business approaches, replaced comprehensive planning; municipalities were amalgamated to create new megacities in several provinces (including Nova Scotia, New Brunswick, and Ontario). The context of planning changed dramatically as the values of rationality, individualism, and entrepreneurship became increasingly powerful and as governments yielded authority to market forces.

Although planning found itself under attack from many sides in the 1990s, its early principles proved so well entrenched within Canadian culture (and congruent with mainstream values) that they continued to dominate built form. Development interests suggested that planning regulations and processes slowed needed growth (despite the evidence that growth has long been a planning goal). Governments looking to reduce operating expenses cut planning positions, restructured operations, and streamlined procedures. Critics accused planning of destroying cities, of promoting exclusionary values, and of constructing urban spaces with no sense of place or character (Duany and Plater-Zyberk, 1992; Kunstler, 1993). 'Modernist' planning was blamed for many of the problems of the city, from traffic jams to abandoned inner cores. Experimental communities, such as Bamberton (near Victoria, British Columbia) and Seaton, Ontario, were proposed, following 'new urbanist' and 'sustainable' planning principles (with higher density, modified grid layouts, and pedestrian orientations). Yet, despite the criticisms of post-modernists, ordinary Canadians are still building and buying suburban forms that replicate the planning principles of the garden city. Fiscal realities and cultural values continue to exert powerful centrifugal forces on urban development. suburbia spreads while downtowns continue to face serious problems. Planning has become a well-established function of government, although its profile diminishes in response to the volume of criticisms levelled against it. It seems clear, though, that few would argue that government should not play some role in setting the rules and regulations for urban development.

The history of planning in Canada reveals the nexus between planning and growth in public consciousness. In times of growth, Canadians turn to planning as a means to control and channel change in ways that are beneficial to the community. In times of economic decline, Canadians blame planning for creating urban problems and preventing development. Our society has a love/hate relationship with planning and zoning. On the one hand, we want the security and predictability they offer for neighbourhoods; on the other hand, we resent how they can produce outcomes and landscapes we find offensive. We have come to rely on planning to regulate a complex set of economic and physical processes with partial knowledge and limited tools.

Planning has become institutionalized as a cultural apparatus for shaping change in the built environment, for imposing cultural values and preferences on the landscape. In times of changing values, planning stands condemned for its adherence to mores that are becoming outdated. Some in society are poised to 'throw the baby out with the bath water' and give up on planning: they would let the market govern land use on its own. Others argue for new planning approaches and values to respond to contemporary problems: they prefer to transform planning and those it serves. Few proclaim that planning is working quite effectively (although some hold that view). The debates between these differing positions occur not only within the profession but increasingly within the public arena. Regardless of the position one takes in this argument, one must acknowledge that the planning process generates particular types of outcomes in the built environment. In the next section we discuss the planning process and the type of cities that planning contributes to produce.

The Planning Process

Through the century of planning in Canada, the planning process has become more bureaucratic, legalistic, expensive, and esoteric. Planning is now deeply embedded in the philosophy and the mechanics of government. Planning and its regulations provide the ground rules that enforce dominant values on the landscape and that have shaped the typical urban and suburban forms we find in Canadian cities in the late-twentieth century. Because of its utility as a tool in the management of the land market, planning has been widely accepted (although extensively criticized). As it became more deeply entrenched in Canadian society and economy, planning lost much of its original vision and settled on a more constrained range of values than were originally promoted (see Table 19.1).

Planning operates within many contexts: legal, political, economic, social, organizational, and technical. Each of these domains exerts pressure and influence on those participating in the planning process. The legal context involves laws and regulations at national, provincial, and local levels. National legislation on issues such as environmental protection, environmental impact assessment, and fisheries and oceans can limit local planning

Table 19.1   **Professional Values in the History of Planning in Canada**

Key Values Associated with Planning	Early Town Planning Movement (1890s to 1920s)	Depression Era (mid-1920s to late 1930s)	Wartime and Recovery (1940–65)	Reflection and Citizen Action (1965–79)	Post-Modernism and Neo-Conservatism (1980 to present)
Efficiency	Planning legislation first promoted planning schemes to improve conditions; later, zoning became the favoured practice.	Zoning spread across the country as an efficient (and politically acceptable) strategy for controlling land.	Comprehensive planning gains popularity; plans and regulations adopted; economies of scale implemented.	Regional planning projects initiated to encourage growth; neighbourhood planning to accommodate protest.	Fiscal crisis led to fewer resources for planning; planning seen as 'inefficient' and impeding market flexibility.
Health	Sanitary reform led to the adoption of codes and practices to improve health.	Few improvements made; some declines due to poverty.	Established building codes and land standards; war against urban blight.	Expansion of welfare state benefits; concerns about pollution but limited action.	Healthy communities project promoted; interest in 'sustainable development'.
Amenity	Parks advocates promoted parkland development; the City Beautiful movement inspired art and architecture; the neighbourhood unit promised a good family environment.	Little interest from government; consultant planners were unable to sell their services.	Established standards for open spaces, parks, playgrounds; land standards ensured open environment, wide streets; highways and roads to accommodate traffic.	Established environmental assessment procedures; expanded parks; neighbourhood improvement program for infrastructure.	Interest in downtown revitalization and nostalgia for tradition led to strength of new urbanism movement; heavy focus on amenity and aesthetics.

Table 19.1   (continued)

Equity	Housing advocates unable to convince government to provide low-cost housing; planning separated from housing interests.	Few resources committed by government; fear of socialism.	Social housing projects implement small homes and 'towers in the park' in limited numbers; mass-produced housing for the middle class.	Created opportunities for greater citizen involvement; reaction to urban renewal; neighbourhood protection; social housing continues to be produced but is more mixed and on much smaller scale.	Promoting mixed use and mixed housing type developments to provide diverse housing; affordability remains a problem.
Dominant pattern	The garden city movement effectively brought these values together in a comprehensive theory (but partial practice).	Planning virtually disappeared as a government activity.	The 'modernist project' began in an effort to use planning to reshape the urban environment to meet goal of progress.	While modernist trends continued, there was greater reflection on the nature of planning and how citizens should participate in it.	Planning finds its major approaches and codes under attack as urban design and free market come to the fore.

options or require compliance with particular procedures. Federal standards, such as the building code or CMHC requirements for mortgage insurance, also influence local planning outcomes. Provincial laws set out the framework for local planning practices through enabling statutes and provincial land-use policies (on themes such as agricultural land or mine-land protection). Provincial legislation also regulates such matters as public participation rights, appeal processes, engineering standards, and environmental protection requirements. Municipal decisions result in plans, land-use by-laws, subdivision regulations, site planning standards, design guidelines, and minimum standards (upkeep requirements). As creatures of the provinces, however, municipalities may find their by-laws subject to review by provincial authorities.

The political context within which planning operates is highly contentious. Local politicians search for issues that will garner popular support (while coinciding with their personal values). To be elected they need both the support of voters and the financial assistance of those with resources. Planning issues often feature into campaigns: growth and development have proven a populist strategy through the years, although heritage conservation can also become a convincing option in some communities. The economics of campaign financing often forges alliances between politicians and development interests. Land development companies seek to create an environment sympathetic to their applications and hence may contribute to local political campaigns. In the absence in certain provinces of laws requiring candidates to disclose financial contributions in local elections, suspicion of undue influence from 'special' interests runs rife.

As the early advocates of planning realized, the economic context plays a key role. In a society where private property is a primary asset and where home-ownership is the major investment for most households, regulating the land market is essential. Planning and zoning have provided the tools to achieve this goal. The development industry as a prime component in the national economy has considerable influence over the process used in local planning and the

principles guiding planning practice. With the recent decline in the welfare state and a diminishing role for government intervention, planning finds itself even more affected by market factors.

The social context brings dominant cultural values and expectations to planning. Values related to privacy, family, domesticity, democracy, consumerism, and convenience shape the perceptions of all the players in the planning process, and thus influence the outcomes of planning decisions. Planning and zoning produce landscapes and townscapes that reflect those societal values (as well as professional values related to efficiency, health, amenity, and equity).

The organizational context of local government also affects planning processes and outcomes. Municipal bureaucracies develop their own cultures and logics that favour particular approaches to planning. Mechanisms for advancement within the organization may encourage some behaviours more than others. For instance, where councils are most responsive to citizen involvement, planners may be more eager to promote active participation; for instance, planners and politicians in Vancouver were recently accused of 'planning by polling' (Howard, 1995; Seelig, 1995). Some organizations seem disposed to innovation and experimentation while others discourage deviation from the status quo.

Finally, the technical context also influences planning process and outcomes. As new tools and approaches appear in the literature and in society at large, they offer planners alternative techniques for dealing with problems and issues. However, with science and rationalism continuing to dominate notions of professional competence, radical changes in approaches seem unlikely.

Thus we find that the land planning process occurs within these many contexts and that its various players are influenced by these contexts. The steps in the process are relatively straightforward. The provinces set the general rules for planning and zoning, and municipalities prepare and implement the plans and regulations. While the rules and procedures vary somewhat across the country, the basic processes are quite similar.

Provincial planning legislation enables municipalities or regions to prepare plans to regulate the development and use of land. Plan preparation typically involves a range of background studies documenting themes such as demographic trends, land-use patterns, traffic analysis, housing need, and commercial and industrial capacity. Public participation allows members of the community to share responsibility for developing the plan, for example, through planning advisory committees or in public meetings. Staff members synthesize the inputs from the process into a policy document variously called an 'official plan', 'community plan', or 'municipal planning strategy', and prepare the accompanying land-use regulations or zoning by-law and subdivision regulations. Plans and by-laws take effect upon motion of local councils and after review by provincial authorities.

Once plans are adopted, planning and development staff administer the regulations to ensure that developments comply with the plan and by-laws. (For example, are the proposed uses allowed within this zone? Is the proposed building a sufficient distance from the lot line? Are there enough parking spaces?) Projects that comply with the regulations are normally approved by staff relatively quickly. Projects that meet most but not all of the technical specifications may be considered for a 'minor variance'; staff are empowered to grant variances in many jurisdictions.

Larger or more complex projects may need additional reviews to ensure compliance with health, environmental, or traffic engineering regulations and to assess capacity of schools, fire, police, infrastructure, and commercial facilities. When developers assemble large parcels of land and apply for subdivision permits or comprehensive development districts, the development officer reviews the site plans and schematics for compliance with subdivision regulations and circulates them to appropriate departments and government agencies for evaluation and feedback.

Projects that require changes to permitted uses or that demand a comprehensive site plan receive much more detailed analysis and usually need council approval. Proponents of such projects normally retain consultants to provide background studies demonstrating the need for, and suitability of, the project. Community members have an opportunity to air their concerns and suggestions at public meetings or hearings. Planning staff review the project against plan policies and offer council advise on the suitability of the request; if they believe that the project fulfils the intent of the plan, they may recommend rezoning or acceptance of the development agreement. Council then decides whether to approve or reject the project. Because planning policies are often vague (and sometimes even contradictory)—e.g., 'ensure quality of life for all'; 'a vibrant commercial heart'; 'strong regional commercial centres' —the approval process offers many opportunities for contention and dispute (Grant, 1994).

Urban Outcomes

The planning process, operating within its complex context of legal, economic, political, social, technical, and organization influences, generates the outcomes that shape our urban and suburban realms. In the postwar period this created central cities with high skylines, concrete plazas, asphalt parking lots, and one-way street systems. It generated radiating strip commercial districts with corporate outlets and parking in front; and cookie-cutter suburbs named after parks, woods, and hills. While economic and social factors may have been the driving forces in shaping the postwar Canadian city, planning and land-use regulations provided the working ground rules by which spatial structures and patterns were forged.

The shape and fate of central cities in the second half of the twentieth century tended to reflect the growing influence of the automobile and the internationalization of the economy. Traffic patterns changed considerably. In the 1950s and 1960s, cities built highways to bring commuters downtown and facilitate transport activities around rail, air, and water. Traffic engineers often made streets into one-way systems in an effort to reduce traffic jams and improve flow; however, the indirect effect was to make the network opaque and to discourage visits to the downtown.

Seeing an opportunity to purchase inexpensive land on the urban periphery, and thus to provide abundant parking within an easy journey for consumers with growing disposable incomes, developers built shopping malls at key traffic junctions. The malls caught on quickly with consumers, providing a new recreational shopping experience. One by one major retailers in the city centre moved to the malls, leaving central commercial areas weakened (see Chapter 17 on retail location trends). While office functions continued in central business district skyscrapers, retail facilities declined markedly in most central cores. Abandoned buildings and growing parking lots changed the feel of downtown. The bustle of the central city in the early 1950s had, by the late 1970s, given way to clear signs of malaise. By the 1980s and 1990s, even office uses began to move to the periphery, again lured by inexpensive land and less traffic congestion (see Chapter 11 on central and suburban downtowns).

In the 1950s and 1960s, planning facilitated many of these changes by providing the land-use regulations and policies that reflected modernist ideals. Attempting to respond to the symptoms of urban blight, cities regulated height, massing, open space, parking, use, and, in some cases, design. By adopting policies and regulations on these matters, cities streamlined and 'depoliticized' the process of considering applications. At the same time, the planning process tended to standardize outcomes, with developers seeking the 'highest use' for their properties in the maxima that the rules would allow. Thus, high-rise towers in the park or plaza proliferated, and urban design accommodated the automobile.

As political and social concern about the effects of planning on the central city grew in the late 1960s and early 1970s, municipalities adjusted processes (and thus outcomes). They provided processes with more opportunities for public input and revised their regulations to modify the size and density of structures and uses allowed in the central city. Incentive programs tried to save or revitalize the 'main streets' of Canadian downtowns. Planners worked with neighbourhoods to renew infrastruc-

Figure 19.7

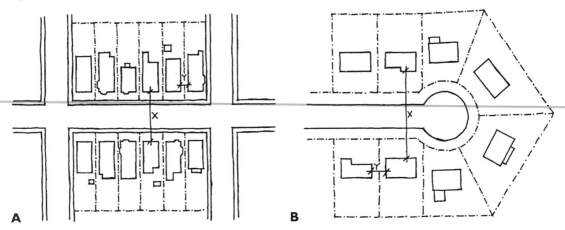

Planning standards adopted after World War II reduced the density and changed the characteristics of residential areas. Plate A shows pre-war development patterns in the old city: they resulted in narrow lots, narrow streets, grid layouts, and a mix of uses. Plate B indicates that with the adoption of new engineering and planning standards in the postwar period, development patterns tended to feature wide lots, wide and winding streets, and a separation of uses. The distance between facing (x) and abutting (y) homes almost doubled with the new standards, creating spacious but sprawling suburbs.

ture and reverse the process of decay. While some areas experienced gentrification and revival, others continued to endure the loss of economic strength and function. The numbers of schools, stores, and hospitals in inner-city areas continued to diminish as cities found it difficult to reverse the economic and cultural factors disposing people to move to the suburbs. Plan policies designed to protect and rebuild urban cores were seldom enough to repel the centrifugal forces that transferred industry, commerce, and housing to the urban periphery.

As products of an era in which planning regimes facilitated built form, the suburbs and the commercial strip developments of the postwar period aptly illustrate how planning and land-use regulation have contributed to the creation of standardized landscapes. Suburbia represented the postwar rejection of the industrial city: spacious lawns and winding streets replaced the narrow lots and grid layout of the central core (see Figure 19.7). The myths of the middle-class nuclear family, homemaker mom, two cars in the driveway, and neighbourhood school were embodied in building practices and land-use regulations that resulted in look-alike suburban areas from coast to coast.

Governments even built Arctic and Aboriginal settlements with similar houses and layouts, despite extreme differences in culture and climate. Zoning standards demanded wide lots, significant setbacks, and separation of housing types and uses. The market called for ranch-style bungalows and grassy lawns. Commercial uses were segregated to arterial roads to prevent through traffic from penetrating residential environments: in the process, though, the regulations generated the visual wasteland of strip development. An economic market shaped by corporate concentration and heavy brand-name advertising and a regulatory environment seeking to protect neighbourhoods from commerce led to rapid expansion of this urban form. Thus, suburban and new town maps from cities across Canada show similar patterns for areas built between the 1950s and 1980s, which contrast markedly with earlier building trends (see Figure 19.8).

Conclusion

While planning shares responsibility for exacerbating the problems of the city, it is not the driving force behind the changes witnessed during the twentieth

Figure 19.8

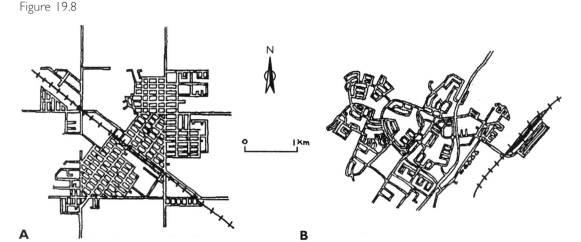

Dauphin, Manitoba (Plate A), and Thompson, Manitoba (Plate B), contrast new town planning styles. Built in 1896, Dauphin follows a grid that reflects its *raison d'être*: the railway line. Thompson, constructed in 1957 to house workers at an INCO nickel mine, follows the garden city principles so popular at the time.

century. Planning provides the tools to shape cities, but political leaders and community members decide whether and how to use planning. Canadian governments have chosen to rely on planning tools in a typically Canadian way: less intrusively than is the case in Britain, but with more insistence than is found in the United States. Institutionalized planning and land-use regulation support the economic market and political realities. Professional planners gave communities the expertise needed to impose cultural (and economic) values on landscapes. Despite decades of change, many of the dominant assumptions underlying planning remain strong; planning promotes efficiency, health, and amenity (with bones thrown to equity). Ideals related to family, domesticity, privacy, and growth continue to influence planning outcomes and thus affect the shape of the city.

Canadian cities are far from perfect: they consume too much land, energy, and resources and condone too much inequity. However, Canadian cities have improved in the twentieth century. Planning contributed to the processes whereby cities became better managed and for the most part healthier. Change has become somewhat more predictable, with its effects subject to some control.

Residents have confidence that they will not (or should not) face noxious uses in their neighbourhoods: cities that presently face environmental contamination, such as Hamilton, Ontario, and Sydney, Nova Scotia, see it as a serious issue for community action and government investment. Canadian cities cannot claim to enjoy the best features of European or Asian cities with their wealth of heritage and character; indeed, planning shares responsibility for perpetuating the ugliness of strip development and the repetitiveness of suburbia for which our cities are known. Still, Canadian cities have avoided the worst problems of American cities: viz., racism, gang-related violence, and wholesale abandonment of neighbourhoods. We cannot credit planning alone with either the successes or the failures of our urban landscapes. Instead, we must conclude that our artefacts (such as our cities) reflect our cultural values and commitments, as do the instruments (such as planning) that we use to create them.

Note

1. Illustrations in this chapter were prepared by Neil Emms.

References

Adams, T. 1974 [1934]. *The Design of Residential Areas: Basic Considerations, Principles, and Methods*. New York: Arno Press.

Armstrong, A. 1959. 'Thomas Adams and the Commission of Conservation', *Plan Canada* 1, 1: 14–32.

Bloomfield, E. 1985. 'Ubiquitous Town Planning Missionary: The Careers of Horace Seymour, 1892–1940', *Environments* 17, 2: 29–42.

Carver, H. 1962. *Cities in the Suburbs*. Toronto: University of Toronto Press.

———. 1975. *Compassionate Landscape*. Toronto: University of Toronto Press.

Collier, R. 1974. *Contemporary Cathedrals*. Montreal: Harvest House.

Copp, J.T. 1974. 'The Condition of the Working Class in Montreal, 1897–1920', in M. Horn and R.

Sabourin, eds, *Studies in Canadian Social History*. Toronto: McClelland & Stewart.

Duany, A., and E. Plater-Zyberk. 1992. 'The Second Coming of the American Small Town', *Plan Canada* (May): 6–13.

Gertler, L., and R. Crowley. 1977. *Changing Canadian Cities: The Next 25 Years*. Toronto: McClelland & Stewart.

Grant, J. 1988. 'They Say "You Can't Legislate Public Participation": The Nova Scotia Experience', *Plan Canada* 27, 10: 260–7.

———. 1990. 'Understanding the Social Context of Planning', *Environments* 20, 3: 10—19.

———. 1994. *The Drama of Democracy: Contention and Dispute in Community Planning*. Toronto: University of Toronto Press.

Gunton, T. 1981. 'The Evolution and Practice of Urban and Regional Planning in Canada', Ph.D. dissertation, University of British Columbia.

———. 1991. 'Origins of Canadian Urban Planning', in K. Gerecke, ed., *The Canadian City*. Montreal: Black Rose Books.

Hancock, M. 1994. 'Don Mills: A Paradigm of Community Design', *Plan Canada* 34, 4: 87–90.

Higgins, D. 1986. *Local and Urban Politics in Canada*. Toronto: Gage Educational Publishing.

Hodge, G. 1991. *Planning Canadian Communities, 2nd edn*. Toronto: Nelson.

Howard, E. 1985 [1898]. *Garden Cities of To-Morrow*. Powys, Wales: Attic Books.

Howard, R. 1995. 'Master Plan Provides Destination, but No Route', *Globe and Mail*, 22 Apr., A6.

Hulchanski, J.D. 1986. 'General Introduction to the Issue', Special issue on the history of Canadian housing policy, *Urban History Review* 15, 1: 1—2.

Jacobs, J. 1961. *The Death and Life of Great American Cities*. New York: Vintage Books.

Kemble, R. 1989. *The Canadian City, St. John's to Victoria: A Critical Commentary*. Montreal: Harvest House.

Kunstler, J. 1993. *The Geography of Nowhere: The Rise and Decline of America's Man-made Landscape*. New York: Simon and Schuster.

Lang, R. 1972. *Nova Scotia Municipal and Regional Planning in the 1970s*. Halifax: Nova Scotia Department of Municipal Affairs.

Lash, H. 1977. *Planning in a Human Way: Personal Reflections on the Regional Planning Experience in Greater Vancouver*. Ottawa: Ministry of State for Urban Affairs.

League for Social Reconstruction. 1935. *Social Planning for Canada*. Toronto: Thomas Nelson and Sons.

Matthews, R. 1976. *'There's No Better Place Than Here': Social Change in Three Newfoundland Communities*. Toronto: Peter Martin Associates.

Moore, P. 1979. 'Zoning and Planning: The Toronto Experience', in A. Artibise and G. Stelter, eds, *The Usable Urban Past*. Toronto: Macmillan of Canada.

Perks, W.T., and W. Jamieson. 1991. 'Planning and Development in Canadian Cities', in T. Bunting and P. Filion, eds, *Canadian Cities in Transition*. Toronto: Oxford University Press.

Perry, C. 1929. 'The Neighborhood Unit', in *Neighborhood and Community Planning*. New York: Regional Survey of New York and Environs, vol. 7.

Rutherford, P. 1984. 'Tomorrow's Metropolis Revisited: A Critical Assessment of Urban Reform in Canada, 1890–1920', in G.A. Stelter and A.F.J. Artibise, eds, *The Canadian City: Essays in Urban and Social History*. Ottawa: Carleton University Press.

Seelig, M.Y. 1995. 'Vancouver's CityPlan: Citizen Participation as a Political Cop-out', *Globe and Mail*, 27 Feb., A15.

Sewell, J. 1977. 'The Suburbs', *City Magazine* 2, 6: 19–55.

———. 1993. *The Shape of the City: Toronto Struggles with Modern Planning*. Toronto: University of Toronto Press.

———. 1994. *Houses and Homes: Housing for Canadians*. Toronto: James Lorimer.

Sherwood, D.H. 1994. 'Canadian Institute of Planners', *Plan Canada* (special issue) 34 (July): 20–1.

Simpson, M. 1985. *Thomas Adams and the Modern Planning Movement: Britain, Canada and the United States, 1900–1940*. London: Alexandrine Press Book.

Stein, D.L. 1994a. 'Thomas Adams, 1871–1940', *Plan Canada* (special issue) 34 (July): 14–15.

———. 1994b. 'The Commission of Conservation', *Plan Canada* (special issue) 34 (July): 55.

Stephenson, G. 1957. *A Redevelopment Study of Halifax, Nova Scotia*. Halifax: City of Halifax.

Van Nus, W. 1984. 'The Fate of City Beautiful Thought in Canada, 1893–1930', in G.A. Stelter and A.F.J. Artibise, eds, *The Canadian City: Essays in Urban and Social History*. Ottawa: Carleton University Press.

Weaver, J. 1976. 'Reconstruction of the Richmond District in Halifax: A Canadian Episode in Public Housing and Town Planning', *Plan Canada* 16, 1: 36–47.

Wolfe, J. 1994. 'Our Common Past: an Interpretation of Canadian Planning History', *Plan Canada* (special issue) 34 (July): 12–34.

Chapter 20

Contemporary Planning: Issues and Innovations

Walter Jamieson, Adela Cosijn, and Susan Friesen

Introduction: City Form, City Function, and the Planner's Role

Planners can be seen to function principally as mediators between social purpose and city form. Their primary work is to ensure that the form a city takes accurately reflects the priorities of all its citizens. Planners work to shape city form by interpreting social purpose and regulating individual ambitions to fit a conception of the public interest. This mission is made difficult by the fact that planners must sort through the competing individual and collective priorities of thousands of citizens. Adding further complexity is the concrete nature of the city, which, together with an enormous underlying investment of resources, results in an urban form that does not respond quickly to shifts in communal values and goals.

In confronting these challenges, some planners have come to recognize that tinkering with the form without addressing the function—the underlying driving forces—is ineffective. At the same time, planners question whether their role legitimately includes shaping human purpose as a part of changing city form. Arguably, the answer to this dilemma lies in involving citizens as informed participants in modifying the built environment. For example, sustainable development is an emerging social value that requires significant change in urban form. Planners seeking to remedy urban sprawl as a means of achieving sustainable urban development will need to assist people in defining sustainability and making choices about practising it.

The multi-dimensional nature of the planner's task is underlined by the reciprocity of the link between form and function: not only is city form shaped by people's values and behaviours, but the form a city takes influences human activities and expectations. People tend to pattern their daily lives around the structure of the physical environment they inhabit. This can have the effect of reinforcing the existing form and making it even more resistant to change.

The first part of the chapter outlines some of the key issues that Canadian planners face at the turn of the millennium. These issues clearly demonstrate that many of the attitudes and techniques applied to urban planning in the twentieth century are no longer effective and, worse, have led to unsustainable and inequitable urban forms and practices. They also reveal the interaction of conflicting needs, demands, and priorities, which renders the planner's task anything but simple. The second part of the chapter then provides examples that illustrate creative, innovative approaches to addressing these issues in the current context.

Contemporary Planning Issues

The following planning issues have been selected for discussion in this chapter:

- urban dispersion and car dominance;
- loss of sense of place;
- loss of natural and cultural environments;
- functional and social segregation;

- tension between the development industry and planners;
- growing mistrust of government and planning;
- ineffective public participation.

These issues illustrate and define the most urgent tasks confronting urban planners today. They are problems that have taken shape gradually in the course of the twentieth century. It is easy to understand why, over the first two-thirds of the century, planners did not foresee the damaging impacts that the automobile—and the concomitant dispersion of the built environment over vast unwalkable areas—would have on our cities. Perhaps we can comprehend, too, the destruction of natural and historical features in favour of the inexorable march towards 'modernity'. These developments were viewed as positive elements of the unbroken thread of 'progress', a key modernist concept.

Since the 1970s, however, important events have sounded a wake-up call for planners. Not only have citizens demanded a growing voice in the decisions affecting their lives, but a complex web of adverse environmental effects has borne witness to the cumulative consequences of past forms of planning. Depletion of non-renewable energy resources, as well as water and air pollution, can now clearly be linked to over-reliance on motor vehicles. No longer can citizens and planners ignore the limits to growth that were overlooked in earlier eras.

Put bluntly, the slowness of Canadian planning institutions to adapt to changing social, technological, and ecological imperatives has damaged our cities. The 'symptoms' of this planning malaise, listed above, are various. The first four issues are clearly related to post-1945 urbanization trends; by contrast, the last three reflect aspects of the planning process itself. Of course, true to the nature of planning, all of these various issues must be understood as overlapping and influencing each other.

Urban Dispersion and Car Dominance

Urban sprawl has become a source of concern as it became clear that it is unsustainable: it consumes scarce agricultural land, wetlands, forests, and valuable open spaces. It is also responsible for an ever-increasing dependence on motor vehicles, leading to pollution and disruption of ecosystems, as well as rising public infrastructure and service costs (OECD, 1996). There is also an important inequity dimension; this city form marginalizes those who do not have the financial means to access widely dispersed locations of residence, employment, recreation, and other services (Garreau, 1991).

One of the defining features of sprawl is the scattering of a large proportion of residents to suburban areas where people live, work, shop, and play. In the postwar period, consumer demand for single-family homes on large lots has resulted in low-density residential developments with concentrations of commercial, and other services in suburban shopping malls. At the same time, many Canadian cities have maintained vibrant central business districts (CBDs), which incorporate business, commercial, and a measure of residential uses. This physical structure of cities—multi-purpose CBD surrounded by low-density, dispersed suburban development—has led to a high dependency on automobiles for commuting, shopping, and other services and activities. The evolution of the Canadian city can be conceptualized as a series of concentric rings, with the original CBD as a hub. Over time, suburban development has 'leap-frogged' outward; as a result, outer suburbs are ever more distant from the CBD and from other suburban activity nodes (see Chapters 1 and 13).

The dispersed urban form facilitates the movement of motor vehicles at the expense of the safety and comfort of pedestrians and cyclists. While the effects of this form are most pronounced in suburban areas, they have also proven detrimental to inner-city vitality. Downtown districts deteriorate as services and activities are diverted to suburban malls and higher-income households move to the suburbs.

To reach any suburban activity node, pedestrians are forced to cross wide streets flowing with vehicle traffic. The physical layout of residential suburbs, typically based on a curvilinear street pattern, deters effective public transit services. As a result, people build their lives and homes around their vehicles, as is evident in typical suburban housing designs that feature multi-car garages prominently situated at the front.

Pedestrians and cyclists are equally challenged by the dominance of the automobile in many inner-city neighbourhoods and CBDs. While older districts are typically laid out on a scale more appropriate to walking and cycling, these areas have been forced to adapt to high volumes of traffic and to the need to accommodate large numbers of parked vehicles. This has led, in many cases, to the widening of streets. In some cities, expressways linking the suburbs to the CBD have cut through and effectively destroyed the fabric of inner-city neighbourhoods (Jacobs, 1961). Elsewhere, enormous tracts of land are dedicated to vehicle storage and buildings of historic value have been razed to expand parking capacity. These aspects of inner-city design translate into environments that are, at times, as impractical and unpleasant for pedestrians as any new, low-density suburban development.

Loss of Sense of Place

Reliance on private motor vehicles has contributed to a loss of sense of place. The human scale necessary to invite people to use public spaces and thus maintain face-to-face contact with one another is not typically used as an urban design criterion by developers and planners. As people walk less within their neighbourhoods, they talk less with their neighbours; consequently, their sense of community is fragmented into associations made at their commuting destinations. Identification with the place-based community in which they live is thereby diminished.

Combined with this is the visual similarity between and within urban districts. A Toronto subdivision looks much like one in Calgary or Vancouver; downtown high-rises across the country reflect a similarity of design; and strip malls are the same everywhere. This lack of distinction has important aesthetic implications, but also erodes the community attachment and pride essential to quality of life (Hiss, 1991).

Frequently, the lack of local distinctiveness reflects the fact that a major force shaping urban design is not concern for the quality of life of people inhabiting the built environment, but rather the premium placed on economic growth and profits. Building in the suburbs is cheaper and easier than inner-city redevelopment because the process can be more easily standardized and land costs are lower (OECD, 1996: 25–8). Large development companies reduce risk and increase profits as they employ a 'cookie cutter' approach to suburban construction; likewise, the growth of chain stores and food outlets relies on cloned buildings for marketing and product recognition purposes. In addition, rigid planning regulations often reinforce sameness and inhibit creativity and uniqueness. In this way, most of the urban environment is constructed in the absence of a coherent vision rooted in local values and with little regard for compatibility with natural surroundings (Alexander, 1979).

Loss of Environments

The rapid spread of urbanization in the twentieth century has resulted not only in the loss of natural environments but, increasingly, of cultural environments that formerly provided sense of place and made cities and neighbourhoods distinct from one another. During much of the century, there was a widespread misperception among planners that older urban areas were unhealthy, valueless 'slums'. Only since the 1960s has it been understood that older districts and buildings possess considerable social and cultural value (see Chapter 12). Heritage buildings reflect the political and social values of a particular era, offering meaning and historical continuity to communities.

Nonetheless, numerous heritage buildings and entire districts have been lost in the process of redevelopment. This destruction was brought about in part by a zoning system that made no provision for their protection and by the fact that advocates have not always been effective in making a convincing case for their conservation. Consequently, the value of heritage sites has not been fully appreciated by the general public and opposition to their destruction has often been ineffective, with predictable results.

Functional and Social Segregation

One of the defining characteristics of suburbanization is the segregation of land uses as well as income groups. Canadian city form has its origins in the social values and demands of the industrial period, and was given shape in response to the joint priorities of planners and developers. Planners saw land-use planning, which sets aside parcels of land according to their intended use, as the best way to bring order to city growth. On the other hand, developers benefited from the reduced risk and preparation costs resulting from segregated land-use planning.

The chief problem with this kind of development is that it places homes far from places of work and shopping and other daily activities, forcing reliance on motorized transport. It also suits certain age and income groups better than others. Suburbs are generally tailored to middle-class families with children. Therefore, singles and low-income groups have tended to gravitate to the inner city where public transit is more readily available, rental accommodation more abundant, and accessibility to public services easier. As the demographic, social, and economic structure of our society evolves, the dispersed suburban form becomes increasingly anachronistic, unaffordable and inconvenient for a majority, a bastion of socio-economic homogeneity for a minority.

Having discussed concerns arising from the practice of postwar urban planning, we now introduce three issues that concern the planning process and the perception of planning.

Tension between the Development Industry and Planners

Developers are often portrayed as risk-takers, constantly challenging the boundaries of municipal regulation. In reality, developers are typically risk-averse, finding security in regulation: rules define what they can and cannot do, and ensure that their competitors are bound by exactly the same constraints. In this way, regulation 'levels the playing field', but it also inhibits innovation. Changes in regulation can make room for design improvements, but may also introduce uncertainty and increase costs, and are therefore most often viewed negatively by the development industry.

In today's increasingly competitive economy—especially during times of low building activity—predictability is at a premium. Thus a conundrum is created in which developers reproduce the products they are confident will sell, asserting that 'this is what the market demands'; meanwhile, people buy mainstream products because, by and large, they have no alternative. For obvious reasons, this cycle is self-perpetuating. Developers are reluctant to build and people are hesitant to buy alternative housing designs because both parties seek to make secure investments (Perks and Wilton-Clark, 1996).

Planners attempting to tackle urban sprawl can in principle modify regulations to produce more compact and integrated patterns of development. Not surprisingly, developers generally voice their resistance to such changes. As planners seek to make regulations more flexible and adaptable to specific circumstances, they can expect anger and criticism from developers who see such changes as threats to the level playing field they cherish. In addition, for many developers, public participation in planning is time-consuming and unpredictable, thereby adding costs and uncertainty to urban development. This perception is a source of antagonism between planners and the development industry.

Growing Mistrust of Government and Planning

Many factors account for growing mistrust of government and its service providers. Because of its size and affluence, the priorities of the baby-boom generation[1] have dominated the public policy agenda as well as the property market for many years. This generation has come to anticipate both ongoing economic prosperity and the security of the welfare state. This security has recently been eroded by new demographic and economic realities, which have contributed to widespread dissatisfaction with government (Preteceille, 1997).

Although primary and secondary industries remain important to the Canadian economy, employment and economic growth are increasingly driven by services and information. With this 'post-industrial revolution', job security has become a thing of the past as companies restructure and downsize. At the same time, the welfare state is dismantled in the face of ballooning public debt. Baby boomers, on the threshold of their retirement years, are now faced with the prospect that government pensions and other social programs may not be there for them.

For their part, some members of younger generations confronted with insecure job prospects and little government protection from unemployment and poverty turn to the right-wing policies of deregulation, privatization, and self-sufficiency (Preteceille, 1997). These attitudes constrain opportunities for planning and regulation.

To add to this, the media's tendency to focus attention on the public and private blunders of politicians has contributed to public scepticism of those in positions of power (Glassman, 1997: 122). Public figures react by resorting to imprecise language and vague generalities, which further erodes public confidence. Planners' close association with politicians and the political process 'tars them with the same brush'. In addition, planners are a part of a government bureaucracy perceived by many as being bloated, inefficient, and self-serving (Tellier, 1994: 45).

The past few decades have also seen a steady rise in urban crime, frightening many people into moving to the suburbs and the surrounding countryside, which are perceived as safer (Coppack, 1988: 16). In some cities, personal space and security in the urban core have progressively been whittled away, replaced by a sense of loss of control and intense competition rather than common purpose. Insecurity translates into a lack of trust in governments, which are perceived as unresponsive and unaccountable.

Ineffective Public Participation

Public confidence in government and specifically in planning has been further eroded by the perception that the public participation process, touted as a means to ensure fair and equitable outcomes, is largely ineffective.

In the 1960s, citizens were no longer content to view democracy simply as the right to elect representatives. They wanted those they elected to consult them about important decisions and allow broader discussion on political issues (see Chapter 24). This perspective marked the beginning of a new era in planning, as public participation became an integral part of the planning process and environmental impact assessments were institutionalized.

At the time, some planners took on new roles as social activists, advocating on behalf of minority groups. They actively sought out diverse views rather than securing support for the majority stance as in the early postwar decades. They became increasingly adept at negotiating trade-offs with developers that would result in improved social conditions among disadvantaged groups. This type of activity was not always welcomed by developers and was sometimes viewed with scepticism and suspicion by the public, who sensed planner-developer collusion.

While public participation is an entrenched aspect of the planning process in the 1990s, many planners complain that attendance at public meetings is generally poor and that the public lacks interest for planning issues. Reasons for poor public participation can partly be found in the multiple demands on people's time and high expectations on the part of planners. Planners must accept that the immense weight they attach to certain issues may not be shared by society at large. In some cases, planners themselves lack commitment for public participation because of its time-consuming nature and competing claims on their time. Also, familiarity with issues and possible solutions can make planners impatient with the public process. In addition, public participation is sometimes 'hijacked' or dominated by special interest groups that have become adept at co-opting the process and crowding out the views of those who are less organized. This situation is exacerbated by many planners' insufficient skills at facilitating effective public participation.

The NIMBY (Not In My Back Yard) attitude, a phenomenon planners must contend with regularly, is a source of cynicism within the profession. Planners struggle with the contradictory nature of public support for a goal such as sustainable development and individual opposition to specific plans to attain the goal because of perceived negative impacts on personal well-being. Although it is true that people are self-interested—often at the expense of the common good—we infer that the incidence of NIMBYism would drop dramatically were citizens more confident in politicians and planners. Individuals might be willing to make sacrifices if they were assured that costs would be spread fairly throughout society and if they could see a direct relationship between their sacrifice and the desired outcome. However, the NIMBY syndrome has deep roots in the institution of private property and is therefore not likely to be eradicated easily.

Summary

This discussion demonstrates that urban planning in Canada is at a critical historical juncture: the mindset and methods that have defined planning in the twentieth century no longer provide the necessary tools to resolve contemporary problems. Recognition of the ills inherent in urban sprawl, together with citizen participation in public decision-making, has redefined the urban planning agenda in the new millennium.

Innovations and Solutions

Innovative approaches exist to address the important planning issues discussed above. The following examples, while rooted in specific locales, have been selected because of their applicability to a diverse range of urban settings. Moreover, while they do not exhaust the range of possible approaches, they illustrate the spirit of creativity and collaboration beginning to infuse Canadian planning practice.

New City Form

In response to the flaws inherent in urban sprawl, a design school known as 'neotraditionalism' or 'new urbanism' has achieved prominence since the early 1980s. The new urbanist approach is discussed here in some detail for two reasons. (1) Arguably, it is the most promising approach currently employed to address the problems generated by urban dispersion, car dominance, loss of sense of place, and antagonism between developers and planners. (2) It is undoubtedly the most discussed and high profile new planning technique being implemented in North America. The new urbanist design philosophy seeks to remedy many of the most profound shortcomings of the typical postwar planning model by focusing on sense of place and community, by returning to traditional forms of urban design, and—in theory, at least—by enhancing access to housing and services.

Central to the new urbanist vision is the desire to reinvest residential neighbourhoods with a sense of place. The term 'neotraditional' sums up the approach of this design movement: in essence, what is old is made new again. The concept of the 'neighbourhood unit', relied upon heavily by the new urbanists, was first articulated in the early part of this century by pioneering planners such as Briton Ebenezer Howard and Americans Clarence Perry and Clarence Stein. Enshrined in the landmark New York regional plan in the 1920s, the neighbourhood unit was predicated on the principle of a 'catchment area' extending no more than three-quarters of a mile from the neighbourhood focal point, the elementary school. Each unit would contain about 1,000 families or 5,000 people, based on the average family size of the period (Hall, 1992: 59). The neighbourhood unit was conceived not only as a practical design but also as a 'deliberate piece of social engineering which would help people achieve a sense of identity with the community and with the place' (ibid., 58).

The movement's most visible proponents are American urban planners Andres Duany and Elizabeth Plater-Zyberk. In 1990, Duany and Plater-Zyberk were retained by Carma Developers Ltd to design a neotraditional neighbourhood for the area in southeast Calgary to become McKenzie Towne, Phase I (see Figures 20.1 and 20.2). The McKenzie Towne project comprises 13 neighbourhood units—referred to by the designers simply as 'neighbourhoods'—organized around a mixed-use town centre. The focal point of each neighbourhood is a central park-like square. The goal of enhancing walkability within the neighbourhood is consonant with Perry's: the plan for McKenzie Towne drafted by Duany and Plater-Zyberk stipulates that '[n]eighbourhood size is determined, not by population, but by the distance from a neighbourhood square' (Calgary, 1993: 5). They use the distance that most people can walk comfortably in five minutes (about 450 metres) as a yardstick for the maximum radius of the neighbourhood boundary from the square. Density is slightly higher than

Figure 20.1 **McKenzie Towne, Calgary**

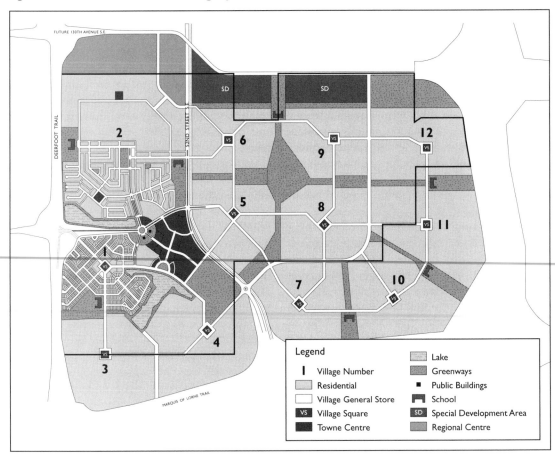

Source: City of Calgary, Outline Plan for East MacKenzie.

Figure 20.2   **McKenzie Towne, Village of Inverness & Towne Centre**

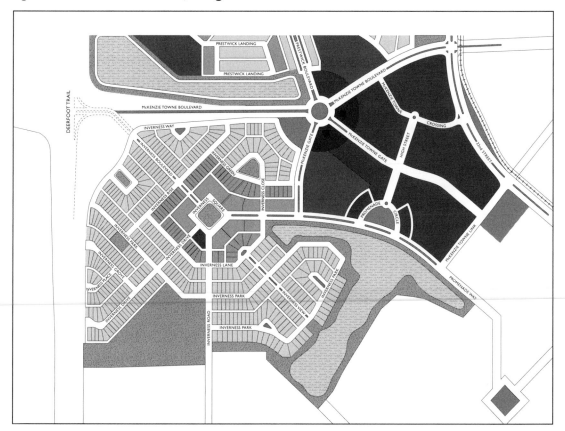

Source: City of Calgary, Outline Plan for East MacKenzie.

the average in typical Calgary residential communities—Duany and Plater-Zyberk prescribe a
neighbourhood population of between 1,500 and
2,000 people (ibid.)—and is variable throughout
the neighbourhood.

An explicit goal of neotraditional design is to
restore vitality to public spaces. Much of what we
consider to be 'sense of place' derives from the
activities taking place within the built environment.
The plan for McKenzie Towne therefore seeks to
create a physical environment that will invite residents to inhabit the many public areas—the streets,
the parks, the playgrounds and squares—in addition
to the private home. Careful attention is accorded

to the design of streets, with the intention to make
the streets 'feel like outdoor rooms' (ibid., 10). To
this end, garages are moved to the rear of houses,
where they are accessed via laneways. Houses are
sited closer to the street; many feature front porches
from which, it is hoped, residents will interact with
neighbours and passers-by. It is hoped that the
closer relationship between house and street will
play a safety role as well by increasing the number
of 'eyes on the street'. At the same time, the reduction in setbacks enhances the connection between
buildings and the public area of the street. This factor, in conjunction with careful architectural controls over building height, size, and materials, results

in a 'street wall' that encloses and defines the open-air 'room'.

Spatial definition, according to the new urbanists, is a precondition to the genesis of a sense of place. For this reason, streets and other public spaces in McKenzie Towne are enclosed and accentuated by buildings. On a larger scale, neighbourhoods are simultaneously connected and interspaced by linear areas called 'corridors'. Corridors may eventually contain larger traffic arteries, greenbelts, canals, light rail lines, or a combination of these. The importance of this principle lies in an effort to distinguish districts from each other—even from adjacent ones. New urbanism seeks to instil some idiosyncrasy and place-based character even in new suburban areas (Kunstler, 1996: 56).

An important aspect of both form and function in McKenzie Towne is its street pattern. An explicit intention of the modified grid design is to place a premium on the comfort, convenience, and safety of pedestrians. Block lengths are shortened to provide many choices of route for pedestrians and motorists alike. Carriageways on local streets are narrower than city-wide standards in order to slow traffic and reduce the distance pedestrians must travel when crossing. Sidewalks and planted boulevards are required on both sides of the street (Calgary, 1993: 23). In addition, on-street parking is deemed 'mandatory' in the McKenzie Towne plan, as '[t]his layer of parking provides a psychological shield of protection for the pedestrian on the sidewalk' (ibid., 13).

The grid street layout and circumscribed boundary of the neighbourhood are together intended to support public transit use. The McKenzie Towne plan situates a bus stop at the neighbourhood's centre; thus the stop is no more than a five-minute walk from the furthest home. It also recommends that the bus stop itself form part of the neighbourhood general store, so that riders can await the bus in 'comfort and dignity' (ibid., 9); this is an especially important consideration given Calgary's cold winter climate.[2]

The comprehensive plan for McKenzie Towne provides for a light-rail transit (LRT) station at the heart of the town centre when subsequent phases are built. This concept is congruent with a 'subset' of new urbanism, the so-called 'transit village', which takes its inspiration from the railway- and streetcar-focused settlement patterns of the early-twentieth century. However, development of the town centre and extension of Calgary's LRT network lie some distance in the future.

A key goal of neotraditional planning is to facilitate reintegration of uses (residential, commercial, employment, recreation) and socio-economic groups. To this end, McKenzie Towne incorporates a small general store and café adjacent to the neighbourhood square. Some houses are designed to accommodate a home office and a studio suite over the garage. Denser development of townhouses and walk-up apartments is concentrated around the square, with less dense single-family housing radiating out to the neighbourhood's borders. The hope is that people of all ages, social groups, and stages in life will find a place within the same community. Also, 'the assemblage of [13] neighbourhoods is to be as self-sufficient as possible with regard to daily needs.... McKenzie Towne will ideally contain a well-balanced combination of work, shopping, and living opportunities' (ibid., 5).

Implicit in these design principles is the possibility not only to increase neighbourhood diversity and vitality, but also to address certain equity issues not typically considered in residential suburb design. The most salient equity concerns are affordability and accessibility for all socio-economic groups. While the jury is still out on whether McKenzie Towne will succeed in creating a more equitable community, providing access to a range of basic needs for residents from all walks of life, this goal is central to the development concept.

Less expensive housing types, studio suites, and garden cottages are designed to blend aesthetically with surrounding, more expensive dwellings. The intent is to encourage informal contact between individuals of higher- and lower-income brackets while preserving the property values of expensive housing units. Ironically, Duany and Plater-Zyberk note that 'this housing should be sufficiently desirable that it will tend not to remain affordable upon resale. This is the mark of success and should not be avoided' (ibid., 12). Thus, the long-term status of affordable housing in McKenzie Towne seems in question.

Working against accessibility is the suburb's remote location from Calgary's central business district or any other substantial hub of employment and services. The eventual development of the town centre, complete with an LRT station, may remedy this shortcoming. But for the time being, no matter how transit-supportive, walkable, safe, pleasant, and community-oriented McKenzie Towne is intended to be, the private automobile remains most residents' chosen means of transportation to their distant places of employment, shopping, and recreation.

Neotraditionalism is a blossoming trend in neighbourhood design—an interesting and promising one, but a trend nonetheless. Predictably, given its growing notoriety (Walt Disney Co. opened Celebration, a Florida neotraditional community, in 1996), the virtues and shortcomings of new urbanism are hotly debated by designers and lay persons alike. One must be indulgent when assessing the potential of new urbanist design. Above all, it is important to separate the new urbanist concept of good design from its application in a rapidly growing number of Canadian communities; these developments often borrow only certain new urbanist principles and are executed with varying degrees of art and skill.

While many claims are made on behalf of new urbanism—that it reduces urban sprawl by producing a more compact settlement form, that it lowers the cost of providing and maintaining municipal infrastructure—the movement's primary goal is to infuse communities with a sense of place. Still, this has not prevented the adoption of new urbanist principles by groups advocating sustainability; indeed, the promotion of a pleasing, safe, walkable environment may also dampen the impulse to use the private car. In the transit village model, the LRT station as the centrepiece of a compact, mixed-use district is intended to promote sustainable practices. The *Sustainable Suburbs Study* (Calgary, 1995) incor-

porates virtually all the neotraditional design principles implemented in McKenzie Towne.

At the same time, however, neotraditional development at the urban edge does not slow urban sprawl. While this form of design contains nodes of high density and mixed uses, the overall density of a neotraditional neighbourhood is not much greater than that of a typical suburban subdivision. Moreover, the greenbelts and other open spaces interspersed among the houses contribute to spread development. Added to this is the 'hybrid' nature of some so-called neotraditional communities that blend certain aspects of new urbanism with standard suburban design in order to overcome consumer resistance towards the full neotraditional package (Shawcross, 1998).

At present, the implementation of neotraditional designs requires extensive co-operation and consultation among designers, developers, and municipal planning, engineering, and transportation departments. Duany and Plater-Zyberk's document for McKenzie Towne carefully lays out six interrelated plans and regulations to be adopted by Council and administered by the developer (Calgary, 1993: 14). This is in addition to the three-year period preceding Council's adoption of the Outline Plan during which design charettes (sessions including a number of individuals trying concurrently to formulate solutions for an architectural or planning problem) were held, consumer research was conducted, and all parties were made aware of the feasibility of the development (ibid., 19). The planning of neotraditional communities in Ontario has also involved lengthy and complex processes (Ontario, 1997). The incorporation of neotraditional design standards into such documents as Calgary's *Sustainable Suburbs Study* may eventually streamline and normalize the planning of neotraditional communities.

Many new urbanism communities are criticized for 'faking' the authenticity of past times and places. Critics contend that the 'place-making' undertaken by new urbanist designers creates 'synthetic revival' communities that have only ever existed as ideals in the popular imagination. Further, detractors argue that neotraditionalism promotes the 'privatization of public space', the ultimate outcome of which will be patrolled, gated communities (Crittenden, 1998: D3). These charges can easily be refuted. First, as noted, neotraditional design finds its roots in orthodox town planning principles of the early part of the twentieth century. Many of its chief tenets are from the work of pre-eminent urban designers such as Kevin Lynch and Christopher Alexander. Neither the ideas nor the patterns of development from which they arise are new; both are present in historical and existing urban forms. What is more, new urbanist principles explicitly encourage distinctive identity and idiosyncrasy within and between neighbourhoods. Housing design and scale are varied along the street wall and residents are given the choice of whether and how to develop outbuildings. No matter its shortcomings, the significance of the neotraditional movement lies in the fact that it proposes an alternative to the typical, soulless, suburban development of the post-World War II period, and in this it stands virtually alone.

A New Model of Public Participation

Politicians and planners pay lip service to sustainable development[3] and in particular to making cities sustainable. Although no single definition of sustainable development has emerged, virtually all models involve public participation (WCED, 1987: 65). All levels of government have formally integrated public consultation into planning and decision-making processes. At the same time, administrators have taken the view that social problems cannot be solved by throwing money at them: there is no longer sufficient money. For this reason they are turning to public involvement as a way of reducing crime, building a new preventive health-care system, and providing a host of other services.

In order to give substance to the commitment to public participation, an effective participatory process must be in place. Too often, rather than generating consensus, public participation results in insoluble disputes. Further, citizens frequently find that their wishes are flagrantly ignored despite a great deal of effort and involvement on their part (Grant, 1994). This can be due to special interest groups' and politicians' capacity to hijack participatory processes and use them to further their own ends. In some cases, solutions are predetermined and the public process becomes a formality or 'rubber-stamp' exercise (Forester, 1989). Also, in some communities, such as those with high numbers of immigrants, the concept of public participation is unfamiliar and the confidence and skills needed to become involved are lacking.

Despite these challenges, the need for a sound participatory process has never been greater. As cities become larger and more diverse and as public resources dwindle, it is imperative to draw on residents' creativity. Governments have the responsibility to ensure that public involvement is structured in a way that is inclusive and accessible, and that does not serve a manipulative function (Abbott, 1996). There is also a need for public participation processes that transcend individual neighbourhoods so as to address metropolitan-wide planning concerns. This would counter the present tendency for public participation to centre exclusively on neighbourhood concerns.

To assure the success of participation, planners require new skills and must be prepared to accept new roles. They must be adept in mediation, negotiation, and conflict resolution. In addition, they need to assume the role of educators. Through it all, they must keep an open and unbiased mind-set. In the process they will assist in building public confidence in government and providing a participatory structure that can tackle complex city-wide issues such as urban sprawl, crime, and environmental destruction, while not neglecting or minimizing more localized issues.

Many Canadian cities are grappling with the need to establish a higher level of public participation that addresses metropolitan-wide problems. The need for such a structure is at the centre of the discussion generated by the passage by the province of Ontario of Bill 103, The City of Toronto Act.[4] The bill has ignited debate about how to build a structure that allows local communities to retain control over local planning and service delivery, while providing a means for city-wide problem-solving, public participation, and accountability.

The City of Calgary 1995 GoPlan provides an excellent example of a city's attempt to achieve sustainability through broad-based public involvement. The impulse for the GoPlan process arose from increasing public concern about damage to river valleys, loss of arable land, air pollution, and traffic congestion. The GoPlan public participation process sought to involve all Calgarians in building a workable vision that would take account of the needs of all stakeholders and balance these needs with those of the natural environment and the realities of the greater political context. The plan also strove to integrate land use with transportation planning, thereby establishing a clear link between car use and urban sprawl. Calgarians had never seen a participation effort on the scale of GoPlan. It involved numerous public meetings, open houses, surveys, discussion papers, and widespread media publicity. Anyone who wanted to participate had ample opportunity to do so.

The GoPlan process came under some criticism for its expense, for creating expectations that cannot be met, and for being somewhat of a public relations 'circus'. These criticisms reflect a perception of the process as a one-time event rather than as a new approach to planning. Like many cities, Calgary has a well-established network of community associations suited to public participation at the community level. Although these organizations are not always fully inclusive and sometimes operate manipulatively, the fact remains that a solid structure is in place to allow broad-based participation in each Calgary neighbourhood. This neighbourhood-based structure was not adequate for the ambitious scope of the GoPlan process, however. Because this was not clearly understood, insufficient attention was paid to developing a permanent structure to accommodate ongoing city-wide participation, although a temporary structure was created for GoPlan.

GoPlan has spawned several important initiatives: the *Sustainable Suburbs Study*, Growth Area Management Plans, and work is under way to develop new road standards that will support higher density, reduce sprawl and encourage walking. The *Sustainable Suburbs Study* is intended to identify means of implementing the findings of the GoPlan, control the costs of growth, and encourage more sustainable development by modifying the design of suburban developments, the highest growth areas in the city. This study established a Round Table Working Group that included representation from key city departments, developers, school boards, the university, community associations, and the building industry. Outside advisers drawn from health and social service providers and the real estate industry were also consulted. The input of the round table was invaluable to the formulation of planning policies consistent with the objectives of the GoPlan. Still, rather than using the round table as the starting point for a permanent consultative process, City Council disbanded it after approving the study. As a result, the momentum of the GoPlan has not been sustained as there is no firm public perception of GoPlan as an ongoing process, despite the continued distribution of a newsletter meant to inform the public and solicit feedback. Yet, the Calgary GoPlan process marks the beginning of one Canadian city's journey towards more direct democracy to confront the complex issues that arise from rapid growth.

Use of New Computer Technologies

In searching for efficient, democratic structures to meet the needs of expanding cities, the potential role of technological advances in communication should not be overlooked. Effective public participation—and, arguably, the survival of democracy in a highly urbanized world—rests on a reliable and accessible means of information exchange in the public domain (Paton, 1994: 20). Many city administrations are using the Internet to inform the public about planning issues, zoning by-laws, regulations, and programs, and as a time-saving method of soliciting public input (O'Mara, 1997). The Internet also provides a forum for discussion, saving time and money for travel and meetings and making it possible for shut-in and otherwise silent people to participate (Mendels, 1998). This method of discussion also provides for the input of special interest groups without allowing them to control or dominate the process.[5]

Although accessibility limits the usefulness of the Internet as a public participation tool, its use is presently rising rapidly (Spicer, 1994). Internet services can now be delivered through television cables. This development may trigger an explosion of use. Increased access at little or no cost through public libraries and other public service systems also favours the use of the Internet for participation purposes.

New computer technologies are also used to collect and manage large amounts of information, which contribute to a more effective co-ordination of planning. For example, the City of Edmonton has recently embarked on a Crime Spots Project that uses a PC-based Geographic Information System (GIS) to identify city 'criminal hot spots' in real time. The Edmonton Police Service emergency dispatch system, which handles all calls for service and crime data, has been 'geocoded' within Emergency Service Zones defined at a city block resolution. The resulting maps allow police to allocate resources where they are most needed and pinpoint the type of services best suited for a particular area. For example, if a high level of family violence reports originate from a given locale, appropriate social services can be aimed at prevention and support within this area. It is also hoped that, over time, these GIS data will provide researchers with an understanding of the effects of certain key trends on crime incidence, for example: what spatial effects on crime trends have resulted from changes in resource allocation; what the effects on crime are of proximity to major thoroughfares, shopping centres, and other land uses; and what effects population characteristics have on crime rates. In order to establish these relationships, these data will be matched with other data sets such as those collected by Statistics Canada (Kennedy, 1998).

The Internet also offers a unique opportunity for planners and designers to use techniques like CAD (computer-aided design) to portray 'virtual' alternative cities, neighbourhoods, and buildings that can spark discussion and generate public demand for other ways of doing things.

Interactive media like the Internet represent an important break from mass media information systems such as television, radio, and newspapers, where media workers play the role of 'gatekeepers' controlling what, and how, information is presented. For example, on-line chat groups offer individuals the opportunity to say and ask what they want about almost any topic and to discuss information that would not normally be aired in traditional mass media. The viewer or reader is no longer a passive recipient of information but an active participant in discussions and in the definition of issues. Some have even suggested that telecommunications will make cable-TV town meetings possible and link citizens more directly to their elected representatives (Glassman, 1997).

New Use of Regulations and Funding Sources

Never before have planners been called upon to be as creative in employing regulation to shape and direct development. Federal and provincial funding cutbacks have shifted responsibility for the delivery of services to municipalities; however, the latter often lack the fiscal resources needed to meet these additional demands. At the same time, there is strong public opposition to increased taxation, making ingenuity and innovation a necessity. In general, cities are responding using a combination of four strategies: (1) looking for ways to redistribute taxes; (2) considering new forms of taxation; (3) making agreements with the private sector; and (4) allowing greater flexibility in regulation.

Historically, regulation has been used primarily to bring about conformity. There is now recognition that, despite commonalities, each city—even smaller communities within cities—has unique problems and characteristics that require adapted rules. The result is a new regulatory approach used to enhance heritage conservation, to promote reuse and redevelopment in downtown areas, and to curb urban sprawl by encouraging residential uses in inner-city neighbourhoods. Although the new approach is commonly referred to as deregulation, this is not in fact the case. Regulation is still relied upon and, indeed, there are often more rules than in the past. The primary difference is that regulation has departed from the 'one rule fits all' approach by becoming more customized and adaptable to specific circumstances. It is not yet clear how the new regulatory environment will shape city form. There is hope that it will support sustainable growth and revitalization and also provide the opportunity for cities to make themselves more distinct from each other by allowing for creative approaches and solutions. On the other hand, there are concerns that greater flexibility in regulation will lower standards and quality of life for some, procure windfalls for developers, and be the source of confusion in expectations and ultimately of court challenges.

The City of Victoria provides a good illustration of the selective implementation of these new regulatory strategies. In 1994, British Columbia made changes to the Municipal Act that gave local governments the ability to enter into Heritage Revitalization Agreements with heritage property owners. These agreements allow a municipality to vary almost any municipal regulation, including zoning, land use, density, siting, parking, and subdivision, in exchange for a commitment to heritage preservation. The legislation provides cities with the opportunity to make regulatory trade-offs. Victoria took advantage of these agreements. One year later it also approved a tax incentive policy to offer property tax relief for owners of heritage properties in the downtown. The policy is aimed at encouraging upper-floor redevelopment of heritage buildings to make them safer and to increase the popularity of downtown living (Goodacre, 1996).

Toronto is embarking on a similar course of action to revitalize two aging industrial areas, King-Parliament and King-Spadina. In the public participation process used to decide how to carry this out, the city was urged to abandon traditional land-use planning—with its emphasis on segregation of uses—and allow the market to decide land use. At the same time, however, concern was expressed that landowners and developers in other parts of the city might resent this apparent 'special treatment' for the targeted districts (Bedford, 1997). The mayor responded by assembling a 'think-tank'—including planners, developers, and economists—to decide on the approach to take. The group agreed that certain areas of the city demanded an approach to planning requiring more flexibility. This led to the creation of a new land-use designation: the Reinvestment Area (RA). This zoning category permits almost any mix of residential, live/work, commercial, and light industrial use. To minimize conflicts between uses, the city has adopted tighter noise transmission standards, placed some height and setback limits corresponding to the predominant building type, and introduced form controls to improve the scale relationship between new buildings and the street. Parking standards were lowered to encourage higher density. To protect important heritage buildings in these new RA zones, the city has replaced its earlier density bonus system with a scheme that allows new developments to exceed the prescribed building envelope up to certain specified limits. This permits them to obtain greater floor area and gives them the flexibility to design around existing heritage buildings (Bedford, 1997).

There is increased discussion about the need to change the property tax structure in order to curb urban sprawl and help cash-strapped municipalities pay for infrastructure and services no longer financed by senior governments. Presently, North American property taxes in urban areas are generally based on values derived from the development of the property rather than from the land itself. For this reason, open or sparsely developed land is taxed at a relatively lower rate than intensively built properties. This reduces the incentive to develop vacant lots and intensify development. It also means that property taxes in the inner city tend to be higher than in the suburbs even though service costs are higher in the suburbs due to larger size lots and greater distances.

According to the Canadian Property Tax Association, property taxes have overtaken income taxes as one of the single highest operating expenses of companies (CPTA, n.d.). Since property taxes are higher in the inner city many companies find it advantageous to build on the outer fringe of cities, thus adding to urban sprawl and contributing to the decay of downtown areas. There is a growing call to base property taxes in urban areas on the land rather than on improvements so as to encourage more intensive land use.

Some cities impose lot levies as a way of paying for expenses generated by new developments. Essentially, these levies pass on the cost of developing service infrastructure for new subdivisions to new homebuyers through lot costs, rather than having these costs spread throughout the tax base. Developers oppose these levies because they drive up their costs, increase house prices and thus reduce potential markets, and make new housing costs vary from one subdivision and from one city to another, skewing competition (Dempster, 1997).

Meanwhile, cities are increasingly confronted with problems and regulations imposed on them as a result of international agreements or with higher standards brought about by technological and industrial advancements. These changes can make existing planning regulation and guidelines almost irrelevant. Safety, building, and environmental standards and insurance costs all play a role in deciding what kind of infrastructure gets built. When these standards change suddenly they challenge planning regulation in ways that cannot always be anticipated.

There are numerous examples of this kind of problem. In British Columbia heritage conservation efforts and planning preservation goals have been seriously impaired by recent changes to the building code intended to ensure better preparation for earthquakes. The seismic upgrading needed to meet these new standards increases renovation costs by approximately 30 per cent. Owners seeking to improve their heritage properties must meet these new building standards, minimize costs, and conform to the city's heritage preservation guidelines. The end result is that while facades are preserved, the interiors of many heritage buildings are gutted (Barber, 1997).

Other cities face contradictory situations in which, for example, the fire department acquires larger trucks to improve service, while the city builds narrower roads in pursuit of sustainability. The new roads are then too narrow for the new trucks to negotiate safely. In the ensuing debate about public safety the outcome is generally in favour of wider roads rather than truck design changes, thus vitiating planning regulation. Finally, there is a great deal of speculation on how Canada's international commitment to reduce fossil fuel emissions will ultimately affect housing construction and transportation planning due to pressure to reduce motor vehicle emissions and energy use.

Conclusion

The discussion has highlighted the complex interconnectedness of urban planning concerns. Dispersion as a predominant city form evolved out of specific social impulses, given concrete shape by historically contingent planning principles. Far from being confined to the physical realm, however, the ramifications of this urban form are felt in the social, political, ecological, economic, and cultural domains as well. Municipal finances, transportation planning, immigration, and technology are all driving forces influencing city form, and all interact in reciprocal and unpredictable ways. Similarly, the public and private sectors overlap and depend on one another. Perhaps the many issues and activities that together make up the object of urban planning can best be conceived as a web wherein multiple strands and layers affect one another. Recognition of the interdependence of planning issues is not new. After all, urban planning practice arose out of a desire to direct and regulate individual activities in order to maximize the collective interest; the principle of zoning was originally conceived as a tool for 'social engineering', based on awareness of the connections between industrial activity, overcrowding, and ill health.

The twentieth century has seen unprecedented change in all spheres of human concern, from science and technology to the most basic values that constitute a framework for decision and action. We now face a situation wherein many of the foundational principles of urban planning are 'out of sync' and do not respond to the most pressing social concerns. As pointed out in this chapter, the dominant postwar planning paradigm that promotes urban dispersion and reliance on motorized vehicles has affected access equity, quality of life, heritage preservation, and ecological integrity. Ironically, even in the face of mounting evidence of its shortcomings, the postwar planning model still predominates. Awareness is growing, however, of the need to seek out innovative approaches that match current circumstances, some of the most promising of which we have described here.

Notes

1. The so-called 'baby-boom' generation is usually considered to consist of those born in the two decades immediately following the end of World War II (Forcese and Richer, 1988: 22).
2. Significantly, bus service was extended early to McKenzie Towne on the initiative of the developer. Carma was eager to ensure that the transit-supportive dimension of the neighbourhood be affirmed. The company therefore reached an agreement with the City of Calgary whereby bus service was extended to McKenzie Towne in advance of the critical number of residents being reached. Carma cost-shares the service with the city, paying the difference between the fares collected and the cost of service (David Harvey, personal communication, 19 June 1998).
3. The term 'sustainable development' achieved catch-phrase status in 1987 when the Brundtland Report, *Our Common Future*, was published under the auspices of the World Commission on Environment and Development (WCED). The report provides the following definition: 'Sustainable development is development that meets the needs of the present without compromising the ability of future generations to meet their own needs' (WCED, 1987: 43).
4. Bill 103 was commonly referred to as the 'Megacity Bill' because it amalgamated the municipalities of East York, Etobicoke, North York, Scarborough, Toronto, and York into one City of Toronto.
5. Interestingly, in 1997 the Internet quickly became a forum for debate around the creation of the Toronto 'megacity'. So far, while relatively disorganized, the Internet hosts numerous and varied voices.

References

Abbott, J. 1996. *Sharing the City: Community Participation in Urban Management*. London: Earthscan.

Alexander, C. 1979. *The Timeless Way of Building*. New York: Oxford University Press.

Barber, S. 1998. (Heritage Planner for the City of Victoria). Personal communication.

Bedford, P. 1997. 'When They Were Kings: Planning for Reinvestment', *Plan Canada* July, 18–23.

Calgary, City of. 1993. *Outline Plan for East McKenzie*. Calgary: City of Calgary.

———. 1995. *Sustainable Suburbs Study: Creating More Fiscally, Socially and Environmentally Sustainable Communities*. Calgary: City of Calgary.

Coppack, P.M. 1988. 'The Evolution and Modelling of the Urban Field', in P. Coppack, L.H. Russwurm, and C.R. Bryant, eds, *Essays on Canadian Urban Process and Form III: The Urban Field*. Waterloo: Department of Geography, University of Waterloo.

CPTA (Canadian Property Tax Association). n.d. <http://www.cpta.org/index.html>. Retrieved Oct. 1998.

Crittenden, G. 1998. 'Front Porch Challenge', *Globe and Mail*, 20 June, D1, D3.

Dempster, M. 1997. 'Land demand heats up', *Calgary Herald*, 13 Dec., A7.

Forcese, D., and S. Richer. 1988. *Social Issues: Sociological Views of Canada*, 2nd edn. Toronto: Prentice-Hall.

Forester, J. 1989. *Planning in the Face of Power*. Berkeley: University of California Press.

Garreau, J. 1991. *Edge City: Life on the New Frontier*. New York: Doubleday.

Glassman, R.M. 1997. *The New Middle Class and Democracy in Global Perspective*. New York: St Martin's Press.

Goodacre, R. 1996. 'Let's Make A Deal: Heritage Revitalization Agreements in Action', *CHC Bulletin Network* 3, 1: 1.

Grant, J. 1994. *The Drama of Democracy: Contention and Dispute in Community Planning*. Toronto: University of Toronto Press.

Hall, P. 1992. *Urban and Regional Planning*. New York: John Wiley and Sons.

Harvey, D. 1998. (Senior Vice-President, Marketing and Planning, Carma Developers Ltd, Calgary, Alberta). Personal communication.

Hiss, T. 1991. *The Experience of Place: A New Way of Looking at and Dealing with our Radically Changing Cities and Countryside*. New York: Vintage Books.

Jacobs, J. 1961. *The Death and Life of Great American Cities*. New York: Random House.

Kennedy, L. 1998. 'Edmonton Crime Spots Project Website'. <http://www.ualberta.ca/rimgrp/home.htm>. Retrieved Oct. 1998.

Kunstler, J.H. 1996. 'Home from Nowhere', *Atlantic Monthly* (Sept.): 43–66.

Mendels, P. 1998. 'Conventions Without Travel', *New York Times*, 4 Jan., 20, 22.

OECD (Organization for Economic Co-operation and Development). 1996. *Innovative Policies for Sustainable Urban Development: The Ecological City*. Paris: OECD.

O'Mara, W.P. 1997. 'Catching Up With the Net', *Planning* 63, 7: 20–2.

Ontario, Ministry of Municipal Affairs and Housing. 1997. *Breaking Ground: An Illustration of Alternative Development Standards in Ontario's New Communities*. Toronto: Queen's Printer for Ontario.

Paton, R. 1994. 'The Need to Reform Information Policies', *Canadian Speeches: Issues of the Day* (Apr.): 20–6.

Perks, W.T., and A. Wilton-Clark. 1996. *Consumer Receptivity to Sustainable Community Design: Designing an Alternative for the Residential Suburb in Calgary and Seeking the Consumer's Opinions and Choices*. Calgary: Faculty of Environmental Design, University of Calgary.

Preteceille, E. 1997. 'Urban Economic Restructuring and Public Policy', in F. Moulaert and A.J. Scott, eds, *Cities, Enterprises and Society on the Eve of the 21st Century*. London: Pinter.

Shawcross, S. 1998. (Director, IBI Group, Calgary, Alberta). Personal communication.

Spicer, K. 1994. 'Consumers Must Be the Drivers on Info Highway', *Canadian Speeches: Issues of the Day* (July): 45–9.

Tellier, P.M. 1994. 'The Urgency of Re-engineering the Public Service', *Canadian Speeches: Issues of the Day* (Apr.): 45–51.

WCED (World Commission on Environment and Development). 1987. *Our Common Future*. Oxford: Oxford University Press.

Part Six

Pressing Issues

The emphasis throughout this volume has been on urban change and transition. As expected, change can be a major source of crisis. This explains the focus of many of the preceding chapters on crises arising from the rapid changes that have characterized the postwar evolution of cities. However, the earlier chapters have not been primarily concerned with the identification of problems. Rather, their purpose has been to describe and explain one particular aspect of the contemporary Canadian city. Here, the following chapters are chiefly focused on urban problems. Chapter 21 examines cities' adverse environmental impacts, while Chapter 23 discusses homelessness in Canadian cities. Arguably, these chapters address the two foremost problems affecting the contemporary city. By contrast, Chapters 22 and 24 are about the role of residents in the adaptation of cities to emerging social trends.

Figure VI.1 illustrates how these problems are linked to the subject-matter of the preceding chapters, where issues of change and transition have been cast primarily in terms of growth, expansion, and restructuring. In this figure, the environment constitutes the macro level inasmuch as it is essential to the support of life and, therefore, of all human endeavours. This is the focus of Chapter 21. The next level, the meso scale, consists of the major influences affecting urban life: social, technological, and economic. The previous 20 chapters have considered change in one or more of these parameters of city structure. Finally, the micro level relates to life experienced in the 'everyday' geography of the city. Quality of everyday life results from citizens' efforts to improve living conditions in the city. While the

figure outlined here is a highly simplified representation that overlooks complex interactions between levels and between sources of influence, it does raise issues of change and adaptation alongside those of misadaptation, problems, and crises.

In Chapter 21, Mary Ellen Tyler exposes the environmental downside of the postwar urban development trends documented in earlier chapters: low urban density, large specialized zones, long journeys, dependence on the car and the truck. She isolates as major urban, indeed global, issues the lack of environmental sustainability resulting from colossal amounts of energy required for the operation of

Figure VI.1 **Pressing Issues**

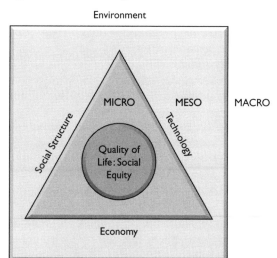

cities and the damages urban systems inflict on natural systems. As a second kind of contemporary urban crisis, homelessness can be perceived as the ultimate expression of social polarization and of a massive loss of unskilled employment. In Chapter 23, Tracy Peressini and Lynn McDonald demonstrate that homelessness is more the consequence of an absence of stable and sufficiently paid employment than of the inability of homeless people to function because of personal deficiencies such as addiction and mental illness. Thus, beyond the specificity of the homelessness phenomenon, this chapter constitutes an indictment of urban society's social and economic evolution over the last decades.

This final part of the book is also about solutions to urban problems. Tyler offers examples of measures promoting environmental protection within cities and Peressini and McDonald allude to social policy remedies to homelessness. The chapters here also address the adaptation of cities to an evolving social structure and to changing values. Brian Ray and Damaris Rose provide in Chapter 22 a succinct but powerful introduction to feminist conceptions of urban spatial organization, which leads to an overview of the alternative socialist-feminist theory of city structure. Once thought radical, feminist models of urban form are now widely accepted as a part of post-modern thinking about the city. Feminist logic has also made a very real difference in the way we think about, design, and develop urban areas. This ability to promote an alternative, feminist-based view of urban structure has led urban social theorists and activists to encourage and celebrate the visible presence within cities of 'other' less visible or less numerous marginalized groups—gays and lesbians and female immigrants, as highlighted by Ray and Rose, are but two examples. The chapter illustrates how these two groups have carved a place for themselves within the post-modern city.

The volume's last chapter, Chapter 24 by Paul Villeneuve and Anne-Marie Séguin, also pertains to the adjustment of cities to changing circumstances. In this case the focus is on political power. The chapter chronicles the mobilization of the so-called 'new middle class' and of different minority groups from the late 1960s and early 1970s, and examines their critical influence on the municipal political scene. But Villeneuve and Séguin equally demonstrate the complexity and limitations of attempts by social groups to adapt the city to their values. The influence of mobilized residents has been diluted by the enduring power of corporate interests and the reduced intervention capacity of governments (including municipal governments) as a result of their perilous fiscal circumstances.

Chapter 21

The Ecological Restructuring of Urban Form

Mary Ellen Tyler

Since earliest times, human ability to shape and control the physical and ecological environment has been continuously augmented. The natural world has been transformed and re-created at local and global scales by the human use of technology in the service of social, political, economic, and institutional goals. Nowhere is this truer than in cities. Historically, city-making has transformed biophysical systems into human-controlled and -constructed landscapes, which displace nutrient and biogeochemical cycles and are energy dependent, geomorphologically extreme, species poor, and climatically different. From ancient to modern times, the degree of this transformational change has varied only in the nature of its scale, toxicity, persistence, and variety. In the *Granite Garden,* author Anne Whiston Spirn (1984) cites air-quality problems in Rome in AD 61 and fourth-century BC water-quality problems in Greek cities. Similarly, Mayan settlements in the Peten region of Guatemala *circa* 1000 BC were characterized by ecosystem-level fluctuations in phosphorous, carbonates, and sediment flows resulting from human mobilization (Delcourt and Delcourt, 1991).

The Nature of the Urban Environment

Once viewed as simply the inevitable consequence of economic progress, urbanization has become a primary generator of environmental change. The rational conception of urbanism, which is usually associated with modern planning, starts with land as 'property' and proceeds to produce a physical pattern based on a juxtaposition of socio-economic functions. This model of urbanism—as real estate, zoning, and technological infrastructure—may function extremely well in response to sociopolitical and economic goals, but it has nothing to do with ecosystem science and ecological processes in the natural world.

In the language of everyday planning and development practice in North America, the term 'ecology' is generally reserved for the 'natural'—meaning not 'human made'. Flowing from this convention, the term 'environment' has been dichotomized into 'built' and 'preserved' and 'urban' space versus 'open' space. Urban systems and ecological systems are in effect quite dissimilar in their function, structure, behaviour, and system interrelationships. From a functional perspective, cities are much more like giant immobile organisms than energy self-sufficient ecological systems. Consistent with this concept of the city as an organism, Canadian urban environmental management activities have primarily focused on conservation strategies intended to create a more 'efficient' organism as defined by reduced consumption of resources, such as land. This is commendable, but it is not enough.[1]

Conservation aside, the biophysical environment in the Canadian urban context is more about engineering than ecology. Urban environmental processes are to be found in systems of public works infrastructure that artificially create system sinks, sources, and feedback loops for the control of water, organic decomposition, nutrient cycling, energy, heat, materials movement, edaphic (soil condition) gradients, and climate. Compared to natural ecosystems, which are energy self-sufficient, urban systems and their infrastructures are energy-dependent and consume massive amounts of both renewable and non-renewable energy resources. It has been estimated (Odum, 1993) that the amount of energy consumed per unit of area in an urbanized landscape is one thousand times greater than the amount required to support an equivalent area of forest. Only a profound structural change in the way urban systems are designed and built will redress this fundamental ecological imbalance.

Over the last 40 years, the Canadian environmental discourse (including sustainability) has been about natural resource economics. It has focused on the legal and public policy regulatory mechanisms for addressing regional level 'point source' air, water, and soil pollution problems resulting from industrial manufacturing and species-related habitat impacts associated with natural resource exploitation activities in the oil and gas, forestry, fishing, and mining sectors. Since the 1970s, the shift in the locus of the Canadian environmental discourse from geographic resource regions to cities, from industrial economic sectors to community amenity concerns, and from end-of-pipe industrial pollution to consumer behaviour has been profound. This urban, human-centred shift in the national environmental discourse marks the unprecedented accession of cities, rather than natural resources, as the primary locus for Canadian environmental policy and regulatory concern. For the first time, environmental management is as much the professional domain of planners, engineers, and architects as it is of miners, loggers, oil companies, and wildlife biologists.

It was not until the 1980s that the impact of urbanization on regional landscapes and ecological life-support systems in the populous agricultural areas of southern Ontario and the Lower Mainland of British Columbia was generally recognized as a particularly important Canadian environmental policy issue. It has really only been in the last 20 years that an urban and municipal focus for environmental concerns emerged around 'people-centred' issues such as environmental health, environmental amenity, and consumer household behaviour, including such

issues as water conservation, energy conservation (including car use), and residential curbside recycling. Popular urban environmentalism in effect became synonymous with individual socially responsible action as manifested through a personal ethos of environmental conservation.

Since the end of the 1960s, Canadian environmental concerns have paralleled the popular political and cultural ideologies of their times—from natural resource-based to human-centred, from rural and remote to urban, and from a federal government responsibility to an individual ethos. A fundamental question remains, however: has this evolution made any significant difference to the inherent ecological dysfunction of urban systems? Unfortunately, the answer seems to be 'no'.

An indication that little has changed in the ecological condition of Canadian urban systems can be found in the 'British Columbia Report' column in the *Globe and Mail* (1997), which addressed Vancouver's 'State of Environment' as follows:

> The GVRD's (Greater Vancouver Regional District) recent analysis found that the traffic on the bridges leading in and out of Vancouver during the worst moments of rush hour back in 1985 was a lighter load than the traffic encountered anytime from 5:30 a.m. to 6:30 p.m. in 1997. Rush hour now lasts all day. British Columbians have responded to this by car-pooling less, not more. In 1985 the vehicle occupancy rate was 1.25 people per vehicle; today it is 1.2 persons. We (the Lower Mainland of BC) now produce more greenhouse gases per capita than the Germans, British or Japanese.... What we don't like to mention in polite company is that British Columbia produces more garbage per person than any other province in Canada.... blue boxes notwithstanding, we actually produce more garbage than any other people on the planet: two kilos a day per person. British Columbians also consume more energy per person than anybody else does on Earth. Apparently we need twice as much as the Japanese and we consume one third more energy per capita than even those glut-

tonous Americans!...This is just not the way we like to think of ourselves, and that's the problem.

This view of Vancouver, the city that many Canadians think of as having the most desirable physical environment in the country, raises obvious concerns. If this is what is really happening to one of Canada's premier urban natural settings, then what is going wrong? Further, how can the next iteration of the Canadian environmental agenda address these compounding problems in the twentieth-first century, when fiscal restraint is high on provincial and municipal agendas? Growing recognition of rapid rates of all kinds of urban-induced environmental deterioration has led to a new subfield in the study of ecology referred to as 'urban ecology'. Urban ecology tells us what has gone wrong while suggesting strategies aimed at redressing the situation. The remainder of the chapter focuses on the current state of the art as regards the study and application of urban ecology in Canada. The first section sets the scope by sketching out major issues/problems. It is followed by a discussion of some of the advances in conceptual thinking that attempt to integrate the physical ecological environment with the better understood spatial economic built environment. This is followed by a discussion of the reporting and monitoring methods developed to assess the changing state of the urban environment, and of the advancing frameworks—thematic, activity-based regulation, and ecosystems—that now guide the planning and management of the urban environment. Two case examples stress the need for immediate 'demonstration' projects that prove the inherent feasibility and cost-effectiveness of ecologically based development strategies. The conclusion points to ecologically based design as a new framework for community design and urban development, which weds urban form with ecological processes.

An Overview of Urban Ecology Issues in a Canadian Context

The effects of urbanization on regional landscapes, topography, soils, hydrologic systems, and plant and animal communities were well documented by the mid-1980s (Hough, 1984; Spirn, 1984). To understand how urban activities affect ecological processes, the following discussion is intended to provide a brief overview of the effects of urbanization on water and the hydrologic cycle, land, energy, air quality, and climate.

Water

Between 1983 and 1994, the residential consumption of water in Canadian municipal systems increased by 23 per cent relative to an urban municipal population increase of 16 per cent. Most residential water use can be accounted for by lawn and garden watering (which can increase by 50 per cent the average daily seasonal use on hot summer days), drinking water, cooking and food preparation, household cleaning and laundry, bathroom hygiene (baths and showers), and toilet flushing. The term 'grey water' is used to distinguish water used in the household (other than directly consumed) from water used to carry human sewage ('black water'). Less than 5 per cent of all water treated at the municipal level is used for drinking.

The 1996 report on *The State of Canada's Environment* (Environment Canada, 1996) noted that 'urban water quality is generally good in Canada, but the quality differs considerably from place to place, as does the extent of monitoring.' The Office of the Ontario Provincial Auditor's *1994 Annual Report* identified that 120 of 490 municipal water treatment plants (serving approximately one million people) either had not met provincial guidelines on treated water quality or had not performed sufficient testing to determine if guidelines had been met (Office of the Provincial Auditor, 1994). Similarly, in 1993, the Greater Vancouver Regional District's *Drinking Water Quality Improvement Plan* suggested it could cost up to $500 million to bring water quality up to Health Canada's 1993 drinking water guidelines (GVRD 1993; Health and Welfare Canada, 1993).[2] Because of the potential for contamination, the level of municipal water and wastewater treatment has been steadily rising across Canada However, the level of treatment varies significantly depending on local circumstances (Environment Canada, 1998a). Figure 21.1 provides a 1994 overview of Canadian municipal wastewater treatment by region.

Hydrology

The deconcentrated form of Canadian urban growth over the last 30 years is characterized by construction of new residential subdivisions, town centres, regional shopping centres, and a massive hierarchy of road systems. All of this activity has removed class-one soils from agricultural productivity, filled in wetlands, changed the course and flows of rivers and streams, removed habitat for a variety of species, and modified local climates. The 'hard-surfacing' of the landscape effectively removes and compacts soil, which prevents the infiltration of water from snow

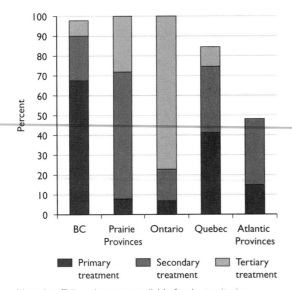

Figure 21.1 **Municipal Wastewater Treatment by Region, 1994**

Note: Insufficient data were available for the territories.
Source: Environment Canada (1998a); calculations based on data derived from Municipal Water Use database, Water Program, Environment Canada.

and rain. The physical footprint of the average residential suburban lot is estimated to be 80 per cent impervious after development (Dorney, 1989). As a result, urbanization effectively changes the hydrologic cycle at local and regional scales. In addition to the extraction of surface and groundwater, tons of dirt are removed through subdivision development. What is not initially released into the air as suspended particulate matter is washed directly into surface water bodies and wetlands or is indirectly deposited into surface waters when it is washed off hard urban surfaces by storm water and melt water and taken up as sediment in urban storm sewer systems.

An early Canadian study (Luckman, 1979) conducted on an urban storm-water catchment basin in London, Ontario, noted that microbiological concentrations (bacterial and viral) were approximately 100–1,000 times greater in urban storm-water run-off than in local stream-base flows. The United States Environmental Protection Agency (Toubier and Westmacott, 1989) calculated that a new medium-density 97.8-acre urban residential development in the northeastern United States was capable of generating storm-water run-off pollution loadings of three pounds of lead, 6.5 pounds of zinc, 47 pounds of phosphorus, 360 pounds of nitrogen, and 50,357 pounds of suspended solids.

Land

The urbanization of land consumes ecological capital in the form of biomass production, trophic (food web) energy systems, and flows of matter, nutrients, and water. It transforms land through a construction process that consumes massive amounts of energy and materials. Once an area is constructed, energy continues to be consumed in heating, cooling, and transportation. Between 1966 and 1986, Environment Canada's Canada Land Use Monitoring Program (CLUMP) monitored 25 Canadian cities with populations of 25,000 or more (Rump, 1989). During this 20-year period, approximately 301,440 hectares of rural land were converted to urban and urban-oriented uses. Approximately 58 per cent of this urbanized land was classified as having high capability for agricultural production. Land conversion for urban growth continues to be a part of Canadian urbanization. For example, the 1996 State of the Environment Report for Canada cites a study on the future of the Greater Toronto Area (GTA) by the IBI Group (1990). The study concluded that even under the most compact urban development pattern, urban growth rates in the GTA by the year 2021 will have consumed a further 350 square kilometres of land. This compact form estimate contrasts sharply with an estimated increase of 900 square kilometres for conventional development. Despite the effects of low-density suburbanization, the single-family house retains its popularity. For example, approximately 50 per cent of all housing starts in Canadian metropolitan areas in 1986, 1991, and 1994 were single-family detached dwellings (CMHC 1996).

The environmental effects of housing in urban regions are related to the amount of land consumed for residential purposes, which is largely determined by a development's density and spatial configuration. The amount of land and resources consumed is largely a function of the nature of the housing stock. For example, single-family detached dwellings have traditionally been built on large lots and at much lower numbers of units per square kilometre than is the case for high-rise or low-rise apartments, multiple-household dwellings, or semi-detached housing. But residential use is not the only factor in high levels of land consumption. The spatial and locational characteristics of residential land uses have an impact on urban transportation systems and storm sewer, sanitary sewer, water supply, and energy servicing infrastructure requirements. All these systems, in turn, have direct and indirect effects on air, water, soil, regional landscape habitats, and climatic processes. The pressure on air, water, energy, and land resources from residential and related land uses is magnified over time by ongoing urban residential growth. The cumulative effects of residential land development create environmental stress on regional resource and landscape systems such as watersheds.

There is nearly one car for every two Canadians, giving Canada one of the highest car-ownership ratios in the world (Environment Canada, 1993). The land and the cost of infrastructures required to support these approximately 12 million vehicles is significant. For example, in Canadian cities, approximately 42 per cent of the land area in downtown cores and 18 per cent of the land in metropolitan areas is occupied by motor vehicle-related infrastructure, such as roads, bridges, parking lots, and rights-of-way (Statistics Canada, 1991).

Air Quality

Given current housing trends, it is not really surprising that suburban-based car use is most often cited as the major contributor to declining air quality. An indicator of Canadian cities' dependency on road systems for the transportation of people as well as economic goods and services is the per capita urban gasoline consumption figures for Toronto (D'Amour, 1993). On a world scale, Toronto's per capita gasoline consumption is second only to the average of United States cities. One of the consequences of dispersed spatial form is its impact on public transit. Public transit accounts for less than 5 per cent of urban travel in Canadian cities (Environment Canada, 1996). Urban public transit use in Canadian cities remained essentially the same between 1990 and 1995, while use of the private automobile for urban travel in the same period increased by over 14 per cent (Environment Canada, 1998b). In 1990, the Healthy City Office of the City of Toronto reported that an estimated 16.5 kilotonnes of carbon dioxide, 63 tonnes of nitrogen oxides, and 103 tonnes of volatile organic compounds were released every day by motor vehicles in the Greater Toronto Area (Toronto, 1991: 3). In the process of preparing the first 'Regional Air Management Plan' for a Canadian city in 1994, the Greater Vancouver Regional District estimated that more than 600,000 tonnes of potentially harmful pollutants are emitted annually into Vancouver's airshed (GVRD, 1994b: 5).

Automobiles produced after 1988 emit an estimated 7.4 times less carbon monoxide, 4.9 times less general hydrocarbons, and 3.1 times fewer nitrogen oxides than cars assembled between 1975 and 1987 (Statistics Canada, 1992). But increased usage of the private car resulting from lifestyle choice and spatially deconcentrated urban regional form offsets the benefits of these technological improvements.[3]

Energy and Climate

Urban land use and urban automobile use are also connected to energy consumption and climatic change. For example, as illustrated in Figure 21.2, residential use and transportation accounted for almost half (49 per cent) of the total amount of energy consumed in Canada in 1994. The by-products of fossil fuel energy used in both urban residential heating and cooling and urban transportation include carbon dioxide (CO_2). Carbon dioxide emissions have been linked to global climate change as one of the 'greenhouse gases' that assist in regulating the surface temperature of the earth. Based on glacial ice-core sampling, current global atmospheric carbon dioxide concentrations are estimated to be the highest in the last 220,000 years (Environment Canada, 1998c). 'In 1995, Canada emitted 3.8 per cent more carbon dioxide from fossil fuel use than in 1994. This compares with an average increase of 1.5 per cent per year over the decade 1984–1995' (ibid.). Since 1955 the Canadian transportation sector alone has emitted a total of 1,166,153 tonnes of CO_2 into the atmosphere. Most of this, 999,208 tonnes, is attributable to the car. In 1993, CO_2 emissions from different forms of passenger transportation were estimated as 16 per cent of Canada's total emissions, while the residential sector accounted for an estimated 9 per cent (Environment Canada, 1995a). Together, these two representative sectors of car-oriented urban form make up one-quarter of Canada's total CO_2 emissions. A breakdown of CO_2 by sector is illustrated in Figure 21.3.

Figure 21.3   **Carbon Dioxide Emissions by Sector, 1993**

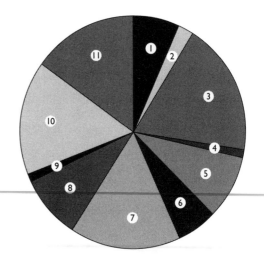

1. Non-combustion sources 7%
2. Pipelines 2%
3. Power generation 19%
4. Public administration <1%
5. Residential 9%
6. Commercial 6%
7. Industrial 16%
8. Other 9%
9. Agriculture 1%
10. Passenger transportation 16%
11. Other mobile sources 15%

Note: Percentages do not total to 100 owing to rounding.
Source: Environment Canada (1995).

Figure 21.2   **Energy Consumption by Sector, 1994**

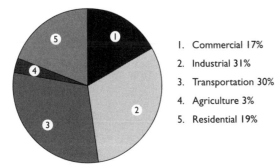

1. Commercial 17%
2. Industrial 31%
3. Transportation 30%
4. Agriculture 3%
5. Residential 19%

Source: Statistics Canada (1994).

Urban energy use is also a function of urban climate. The geographic location of urban regions and their macroclimatic contexts (such as seasonal temperatures, wind direction and speed, humidity, precipitation, and topography) influence and are in turn influenced by the spatial and structural form of the built environment and its associated land-use activities. The best-known urban climate phenomenon is the so-called 'urban heat island' effect (Marsh, 1991), as sketched out in Figure 21.4. This is the result of absorption and radiation of thermal energy from the hard surfaces of buildings and roads, combined with the energy-transforming and heat-generating activities associated with urban land-use activities. The net effect is the heating of the air surrounding urban areas. The city acts like a hot-water bottle releasing stored heat into the regional landscape. As a result, relative to the surrounding countryside (Marsh, 1991; Spirn, 1984):

- the average annual temperatures in cities can be 0.3–3C higher;
- the average annual humidity level can be 6 per cent lower;
- summer cloud cover can increase by 30 per cent and winter fog conditions by 100 per cent;
- 5–10 per cent less snowfall and 10-15 per cent more thunderstorms can occur on an annual basis.[4]

Figure 21.4 **The Urban Heat Island**

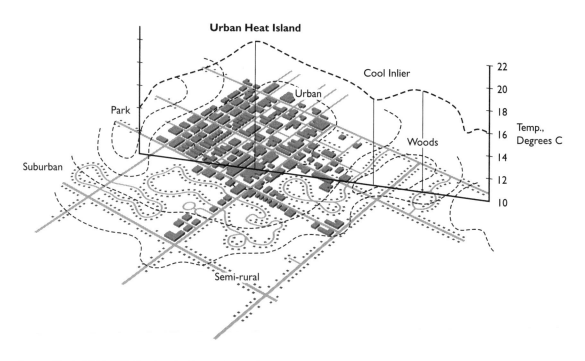

Source: Marsh (1991: 231). Reprinted with permission of John Wiley & Sons, Inc.

In sum, human health and ecological well-being are inextricably connected with environmental quality. Air, water, energy, and nutrients are essential life-support components for all living species, including human urban populations. The extent to which people continue to modify these fundamental ecological life-support systems in urban regions has a profound cumulative effect on climate, air, water and soil quality, biodiversity, and energy use.

Basic Concepts in Urban Ecology

The issues briefly sketched out above are not independent but rather highly interactive and cumulative. One of the most obvious examples is seen in the interaction between auto-induced air pollution and urban climate as manifest in summer heat inversions. Other interactions are more complex and continue to elude our understanding. All told, the cumulative effects of urban-industrial landscapes on human and ecological health are not well understood. Urban ecology is a very new field, which is not yet fully developed conceptually. The fundamental conceptual problem is one of integrating current knowledge and understanding of ecosystems with comparable bodies of knowledge about human-made urban systems. Much of the original development of the theory and practice of urban ecology in a Canadian municipal context was pioneered in southern Ontario by the late Dr Robert Dorney of the University of Waterloo in the 1970s. This original work was collected and published in 1989 (Dorney, 1989). This section will introduce three conceptual frameworks, from the simplest to the most complex, that have advanced the development of urban ecology theory.

Ecological Footprint

The city is a built environment created by human activities and intentions. These complex physical, socio-economic, and technological urban systems are interconnected and interactive in the way they function, but they are not self-sufficient with respect to the natural resources and life-support systems they require. As illustrated in Figure 21.5, cities depend absolutely on massive inputs from local hinterlands and distant regions. For example, the urban region of 1.8 million people that covers the Lower Mainland of British Columbia (from Vancouver to Hope) is 4,000 square kilometres in area. However, it actually has an 'ecological footprint' approximately 19 times this size, if the area required to provide the resources necessary to support this conurbation is calculated. This calculation for BC's Lower Mainland includes an estimated requirement of 23,000 square kilometres for food, 11,000 square kilometres for forest products (wood, paper), and 42,000 square kilometres for fossil fuel energy (Rees and Wackernagel, 1994; Wackernagel and Rees, 1996).

Urban Metabolism/Life-Support System

The city as a resource-consuming system is the synthetic equivalent of a large animal. It consumes oxygen, water, and organic matter in the form of imported food and fossil fuels. Similarly, it releases carbon dioxide, heat, and water vapour into the atmosphere and excretes waste by-products into its surroundings. The safe disposal of urban waste products, including household garbage, represents a huge

Figure 21.5 **The Urban Ecological Footprint**

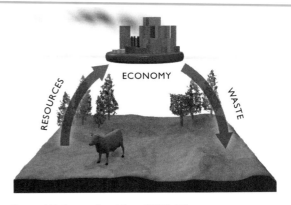

Source: Wackernagel and Rees (1996: 12).

and growing problem for cities everywhere (see Petts and Eduljee, 1994). Unlike animals, an urban 'metabolism' produces a multitude of waste by-products and synthetic compounds that are not, and in some cases cannot be, assimilated and recycled by ecological systems. This essentially linear (resources in-waste out) characteristic of urban systems is a function of their industrial design paradigm. Industrial cities function like machines, not like biological systems. Cities represent technological life-support systems created with the inherent assumption that a limitless supply of energy and resources from biological life-support systems is available to 'fuel' them. Over the last 30 years, most of the environmental concerns about urban-related industrial processing and manufacturing activities have focused on pollution problems created by waste by-products. However, the spatial scale and cumulative effect of disturbances to terrestrial and aquatic systems within regional landscapes as a result of urbanization has only recently been acknowledged as a primary concern for human populations and ecosystems at a global scale.

Air, water, soil, and energy are four fundamental biological life-support systems. Habitat, or biological 'life space', is created by the integration and interactions of these four systems. All ecological systems, regardless of type, have energy flows and nutrient cycling, vertical and horizontal spatial and functional organization, all exhibit change over time, and all have webs of critical interrelationships among life-support processes. Human sociocultural and technological systems, together with the physical and spatial structure of urban systems, also exhibit characteristic patterns of structure, function, change, and interrelationships. When the spatial and process interactions and functional relationships between urban and ecological systems are complementary and mutually reinforcing, a true 'urban ecology' can be achieved. However, when there is conflict or incompatibility, the results are detrimental to both human and ecological systems. Because of their mutual dependency on biological life-support systems, both human activities and ecological processes are ultimately indivisible—hence

the critical importance of designing, managing, and manifesting this indivisibility in the city.

Urban Sustainability/Sustainable City

The concept of urban sustainability has been around for some time. Its roots lie in the broader concept of environmental sustainability that goes back to the Bruntdland Commission (WCED, 1987), which identified a history of adverse social and environmental impacts resulting from economic decision-making. A 'sustainable' approach, in contrast, is intended to simultaneously incorporate social, environmental, and economic values into development decision-making. Urban sustainability is hard to categorize because it straddles the fence between conceptual framework and operational strategy. As a result, its definition is variable because, as MacLaren (1996: 186) puts it: '[there] is no single best definition since different communities are likely to develop slightly, or even significantly different conceptualizations of urban sustainability, depending on their current economic, environmental and social circumstances and on community value judgments.' According to Peter Newman, (1998: 299):

> Sustainability is both a vision and a set of practical steps. The vision has been framed by a global political process that saw the need to bring environmental considerations into the mainstream of economic policy and social policy, and the practical steps involve all aspects of professional practice at the local level.

Urban sustainability is concerned with the connections needed between environmental, social, and economic interests and with the implied balance of these three interests.

Mark Roseland (1992: 295) has noted in his work for the National Roundtable on the Environment and the Economy that 'the road to sustainable development is paved with failed efforts to incorporate the environment into everyday municipal decision-making.' A major obstacle in implementing urban sustainability initiatives can be attributed to the conflicting opinions of economists, environmentalists, and social advocates and to the fact that economic interests often gain more attention than environmental ones in the political process (Roger-Machart, 1997: 54). Likewise, it can be argued that if urban sustainability is examined only in environmental terms, it will be considered a luxury by the poor and unemployed. The implementation problem can be seen within the urban planning profession itself, where the planner must juggle three conflicting objectives: 'to grow the economy, distribute this growth fairly and in the process not degrade the ecosystem' (Campbell, 1995: 2). The difficulty in combining these goals has resulted in task specialization between three kinds of planners: the economic development planner, the environmental planner, and the equity planner. Unfortunately, this role division impedes the implementation of urban sustainability. Ideally, every planner should give equal importance to environmental protection, economic development, and social equity. All planners would then be driven by an ecological mandate and would promote initiatives favouring sustainability.

The quintessence of urban sustainability is its holistic embrace of environmental, social and economic needs. The concept implies that each of these should be given the same weight in the decision-making process. Many different initiatives can be adopted to promote sustainability. These can be grouped in three categories: lifestyle changes; the built environment; and industrial practices. The question to ask, however, is what kind of initiatives should individuals and communities adopt? To answer this question, governments, community organizations, and individuals must experiment with innovations having the potential to enhance sustainability. After all, publicized by demonstration projects, successful innovations may become mainstream, which is what is required if urban sustainability is to become a reality. More specifically, 'it is critical that at the local level we have a continuous flow of innovations in sustainability, both in symbolic gestures and in institutional responses that lead to mainstreaming. Otherwise the process cannot

start and it cannot become an accepted part of our cultures' (Newman, 1998: 311).[5]

Urban Environment Reporting

Over the last quarter-century, environmental reporting or accounting, as it is sometimes termed, has become a procedure used in virtually all developed countries to provide recognized statistical indicators about the changing state of the natural environment. This reporting process has been promoted because of a need to chart the evolution over time of key environmental trends, and is intended to identify those human activity-environmental change relationships requiring environmental management and institutional (policy, legislation) intervention. Effective environmental reporting contributes to improve the understanding of the interrelationships between human activities and natural environments. The previous section has also outlined some of the emerging conceptual frameworks that contribute to an understanding of the cumulative and complex ways in which the urban built environment interacts with the natural environment. Amplification and refinement of conceptual, analytical, and monitoring frameworks require that they be applied in real situations. This involves establishing a range of 'environmental performance criteria', the development of which begins with accurate and consistent reporting.

Canadian state of the environment (SOE) reporting emerged in the 1980s as a business-like approach to measuring environmental conditions and trends. SOE reporting is explicit in its recognition of the critical relationship between human activities in the environment and the state of the environment. In 1986, a national report was released by Statistics Canada entitled *Human Activity in the Environment*. This report used a 'Stress-Response Environmental Statistical System' (STRESS) methodology (Friend and Rapport, 1979; Statistics Canada, 1986). The STRESS system was an innovative approach at the time. It did not organize statistical information on human activity in the environment by the conventional reporting framework of specific 'medium' (air, water, land) or by economic sector (agriculture, forestry, fisheries). The object of the STRESS framework is to reflect dynamic environmental process by integrating environmental 'media' (air, water, and land) and specific 'activities' (such as agriculture, forestry, and fishing) with thematic types of 'stresses' imposed on the environment and the environment's responses to these stresses.

A national SOE reporting program was put in place with the passage of the Canadian Environmental Protection Act in 1988 and the STRESS approach became the basis for developing a national SOE reporting methodology. The 1991 report on *The State of Canada's Environment* contained a specific chapter on cities: 'Urbanization: Building Human Habitats' (Environment Canada, 1991). This initial urban environmental reporting exercise was limited because of a lack of municipal environmental data available at the national level. For the second national report in 1994, the State of the Environment Reporting Directorate of Environment Canada, in conjunction with the Federation of Canadian Municipalities, commissioned an overview survey of environmental reporting activities in Canadian municipalities (Maclaren et al., 1994). Forty out of 56 contacted cities responded to the survey. The most commonly collected data categories were land use, water quality, water consumption, water treatment, waste generation, waste disposal, and recycling. Perhaps the most telling finding was that 'There was considerable overlap in key environmental issues among municipalities; however, there was no consistent relationship between the types of environmental data collected and key issues identified by each municipality' (ibid., vol. 3, 33).

By the early 1990s, both international and local environmental agendas had shifted to sustainable development. Statistical reporting on human activities in the environment found new meaning as indicators of sustainability. A 'Measuring Urban Sustainability: Canadian Indicators Workshop' was held in 1995 under the auspices of Environment Canada, Canada Mortgage and Housing Corporation (CMHC), and the Intergovernmental Committee on Urban and Regional Research (ICURR) (Envi-

ronment Canada et al., 1995). Workshop participants from across Canada were asked: 'What are the key characteristics of urban sustainability? What are the most important issues involved in achieving sustainability in urban areas?' A master list of 15 indicator categories was identified:

- equity/income/distribution/poverty
- human health
- education
- public safety/crime
- community participation
- heritage/culture
- housing/shelter needs
- government/public services
- air quality
- water quality and use
- soil quality/contamination
- ecosystems/green space/biota
- land use/urbanization
- energy and resource
- consumption/conservation and solid waste.

The same fundamental problems of collection, availability, consistency, and interpretation associated with urban SOE reporting concern urban sustainability indicators. Indicators, by themselves, do not constitute an implementation strategy and their existence does not guarantee better decision-making. Indeed, a strong argument can be made that too many resources have been given over to statistical monitoring when the real issue lies with active intervention and demonstrable change.

Ecological Planning and Management at the Municipal Level

Canadian urban environmental planning and management have undergone three significant iterations over the past 20 years. These are marked by the adoption of the 'thematic spatial', 'activity-based regulatory', and 'ecosystem' frameworks. These represent progressively more complex and interconnected approaches to integrating the built and natural environments in the municipal planning process.

The Thematic Spatial Framework

The thematic spatial framework views human activities in the urban and regional environment as a matter of organizing the geographic distribution of compatible and incompatible types of land use. The legislative requirement for 'official' or 'master' plans based on land-use planning and zoning is representative of this framework. Within this framework, the urban environment is treated essentially as a public utility. This 'public works' focus is on the supply and spatial distribution of sewer and water, solid waste disposal, public parks, and open space. Historically, this framework has been the underpinning of most Canadian city and municipal planning.

Because of the widespread application of the thematic framework, the physical form of the Canadian urban environment reflects an engineered geometry and spatial land-use distribution geared exclusively to roads, sewer, water, utilities, and economic activity. This kind of urban environment represents the modernist 'city-as-a-machine-for-economic-productivity' model that has historically dominated North American urbanism. There are no ecosystem principles or ecological intentions at work in this model, apart from mowed green space and hazard land dedications of undevelopable lands (usually due to slope constraints and flood plains). Rather than assuring a true ecological function, landscape and waterfront settings for cities serve as passive aesthetic 'backdrops' for urban form.

Activity-based Regulation

This second framework moved urban environment from an exclusively geographic land-use context into the sphere of public policy with the introduction of tools intended to manage environmental behaviour. Activity-based regulation emerged in Canadian urban planning in the 1970s and became increasingly dominant through the 1980s. It represents the establishment and enforcement of environmental quality standards for water, sewage, solid waste disposal, and air, independent of geographic location. It also extends protection for environ-mentally significant and sensitive biotic and abiotic landscape features and processes on the basis that their environmental characteristics deserve to be protected. This recognition of ecological utility and the implied fiduciary responsibility for protecting it still remain controversial in Canada, especially so when applied on a grand scale in areas such as in southern Ontario and Greater Vancouver. In these highly urbanized regions, persistent growth has put intense pressure on the continued existence and function of wetlands, watersheds, terrestrial and aquatic habitats, and plant and animal populations, which have already been compromised once or more by agricultural and industrial activities.

When municipalities in Ontario decided to adopt urban environmental quality standards to protect local and regional ecological resources, they generally had to go to the Ontario Municipal Board (OMB) (a quasi-legal provincial agency whose mandate is to adjudicate on planning-related matters) to resolve their authority to do so. As a result, most current environmental practices in Ontario municipalities, such as environmental regulation by-laws, habitat protection in official plans, and ecological criteria for development approval, have evolved through external 'institutional sanction'. Examples include the Muskoka District's establishment of water quality criteria to regulate lakefront residential development approval in the 1980s and the Regional Municipality of Waterloo's designation and protection of environmentally sensitive policy areas (ESPAs) in its Official Regional Plan in the mid-1970s (Ouellet, 1996). The validity of both these measures was established through OMB adjudication.[6]

Non-legislated changes in the practice of land development have accompanied legislative change. Dorney's (1989) 'ecological planning' approach to urban development is a good example. Dorney portrayed the evolution of approaches to municipal environmental planning as involving the passage from 'flat earth planning' to 'contour planning' and to 'feature and constraint planning'. Flat earth planning refers to an engineering approach to land development that scrapes everything off the surface of the landscapes and replaces all landscape processes (drainage, energy) with infrastructure surrogates. Unlike the flat earth approach, contour planning acknowledges land-form and develops tracts of land using the opportunities and constraints presented by topography. Feature and constraint planning advances contour planning, first by acknowledging the presence of significant, characteristic, and sensitive ecological, historical, and cultural landscape features, then by attempting to retain and incorporate these landscape resources into the land development and development planning process. But Dorney's preferred ecological planning approach was one that went beyond the preservationist characteristics of feature and constraint planning to incorporate dynamic ecological processes and system components into landscape development. This emphasis on dynamic ecological process is at the core of the ecosystem framework.

The Ecosystem Framework

The ecosystem framework represents the third and most current phase in ongoing attempts at integrating ecological dynamics into urban planning and design. It illustrates the dramatic change in thinking that defines the environmental orientation of urban planning in the new century. This approach to urban planning is different from any other in that it begins with the pre-development natural ecosystem. In this way it is grounded in the boundaries and parameters of the natural environment rather than those of the fabricated domain. This makes it easier both to recognize and to plan for the complex and cumulative interactions that occur within and between the natural and built environments. Explained to the public as meaning simply that 'everything is connected to everything else', the 'ecosystem' approach was popularized in Canada by former Toronto mayor David Crombie in his Royal Commission on the Future of the Toronto Waterfront (1992). The ecosystem framework is concerned with ecological life-support systems. It has become synonymous with the concept of urban sustainability discussed earlier, and is a model in which social, economic, and

ecological needs are integrated in a systematic and complementary way. Tools and concepts, such as indicators and 'ecological footprints' (Wackernagel and Rees, 1996), have emerged as ways of assessing life-support system function in such critical areas as food production and energy. There is also a direct link to the reporting methods discussed above.[7]

The emergence of the ecosystem approach represents a significant alternative to the economic land-use framework that underlies most Canadian municipal planning. In a discussion paper prepared for the Royal Commission on the Future of the Toronto Waterfront, Doering et al. (1991:A5) identified some of the distinct characteristics of an ecosystem planning framework:

- 'interactions among components of the ecosystem are emphasized';
- 'the boundaries of analysis are expanded, when necessary, to recognize ecosystem processes that transcend geographic areas usually encompassed by plans';
- 'a long-term perspective (beyond the typical three-to-five-year political term) is stressed';
- 'key elements of environmental assessment processes are incorporated, including examination of alternatives and prediction of effects';
- 'ecosystem health, sustainability, and quality of life are more highly valued'.

Figure 21.6 exemplifies the ecosystem framework in application. It shows how the 1992 royal commission suggested that green space in the Caledon area (a part of the Toronto waterfront's watershed despite its location many kilometres to the northwest) should be set up. The ecosystem framework is significant because it views urban systems ecologically, as biological systems rather than as spatial economic engines of growth and/or capitalized real estate. Municipal boundaries, for example, were never conceived as ecosystem boundaries and critical ecosystem processes related to air, water, nutrient flow, energy, and plant and animal population dynamics cut across property lines and political boundaries. As pointed out by Doering et al. (1991:

Figure 21.6   **Town of Caledon: Proposed Green Space System**

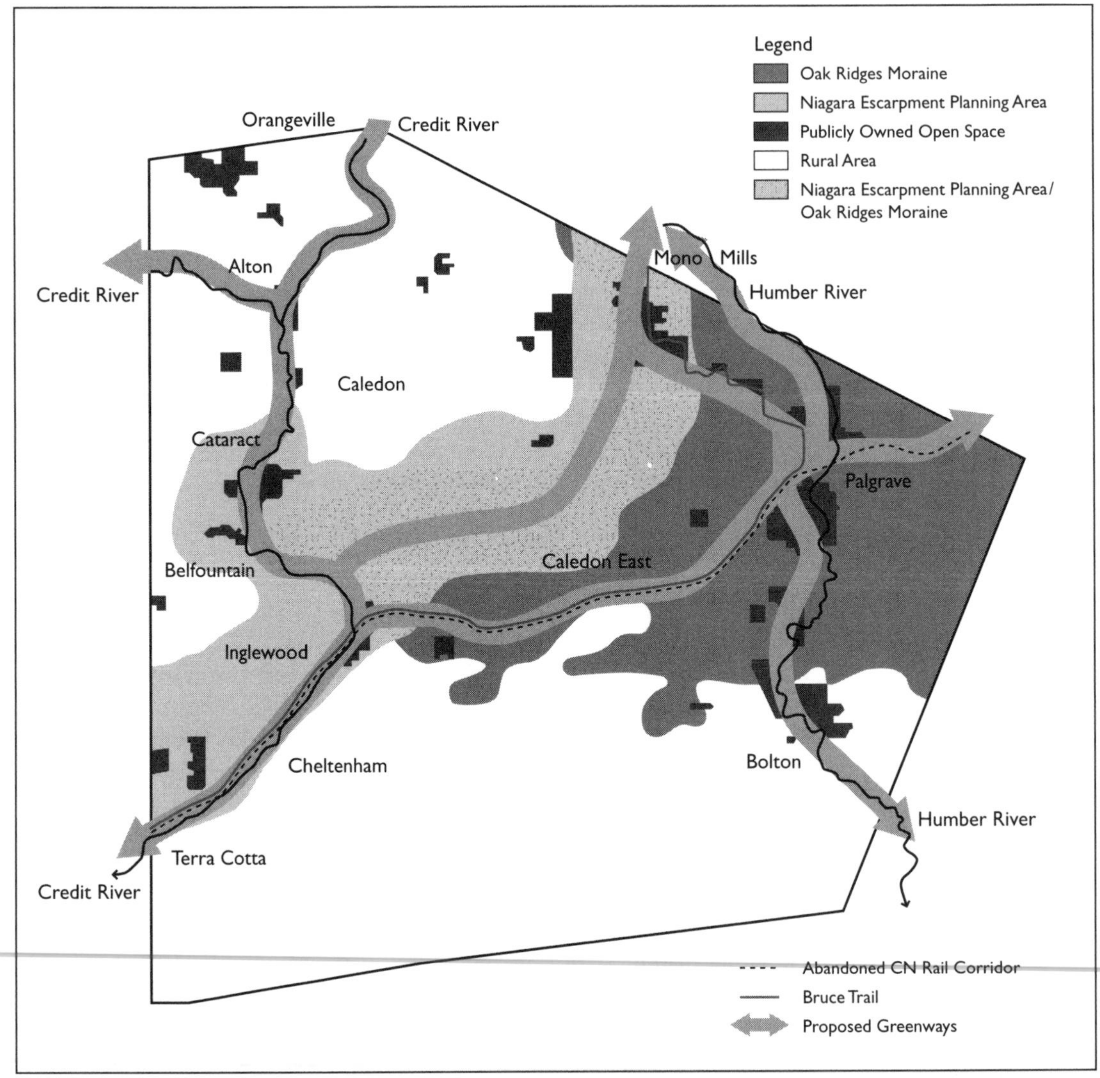

Source: Royal Commission on the Future of the Toronto Waterfront (1992: 200).

49): 'there is no legislative framework for land-use planning for areas defined on an ecosystem basis—watersheds, the Oak Ridges Moraine, or the Greater Toronto Bioregion'. Providing this will require a revolution in our thinking about cities. It may also require a re-examination of the fundamental question—what are we managing for?

The Ecological Restructuring of Urban Form: The Need for Demonstration

There is an urgent need to integrate the current Canadian institutional discourse on environmental reporting and indicators with institutional innovation in restructuring the planning and management of urban form. A number of problems with the current emphasis on indicators need to be addressed in this integration. Most important is the need for demonstration opportunities to bring into the mainstream the idea that ecological functions are valuable to urban systems for more than just aesthetic or ideological reasons.

There are no full-fledged examples of deliberate ecological infrastructure planning or design in a regional context. There are no examples of urban nutrient-cycle management. There are no examples of environmental zoning where urban microclimatic zones capable of extending the number of vegetation growing days are identified and protected, or of urban zoning by soil type productivity or by aquatic or terrestrial habitat productivity. Landscape ecology theory is not applied to create interconnected landscape systems or to identify critical spatial dimensioning for ecological processes at urban regional scales. For example, the 'new' urbanism movement (see Chapter 20) is definitely about changing development standards. However, changing development standards does not involve on its own any difference to the ecological performance of the built urban environment. Using less land for higher-density development does not de facto translate into improved ecological function; easing municipal roadway width standards or side-yard set backs to increase development densities or making new developments more transit-friendly by controlling development density and minimizing roads does not automatically enhance ecological function. There is nothing in these 'new' intensified approaches that deliberately integrates ecological function or ecosystem processes (such as energy transfer, water, soil, microclimate, habitat succession, and biological productivity) into their physical and functional design. Neither 'new' nor 'old' urban developments have been designed to meet pre-established site-specific ecological performance standards.

The advantages of ecological design must be demonstrated in Canadian cities if the ecosystem approach to urban ecology is to become a functioning social, economic, and biological reality. However, barriers to ecological innovation in the design and restructuring of the urban environment are immense. In a 1992 study, Perks surveyed key informants representing regulators, developers, financial agents, and municipal and provincial politicians involved in urban development in Alberta. Nine out of 10 informants, from all sectors represented, saw the most formidable obstacle to urban innovation as city utilities engineers and city transportation engineers, closely followed by city legal experts, community associations, and city fire services. Given that four of these agents are part of the municipal system responsible for development approval, the likelihood of local government-initiated ecological restructuring seems remote in the absence of a significant reason for change.

The value of urban ecology demonstration projects lies in their ability to restructure development at relatively small but operational urban scales that allow innovations to be 'tested' within specific social, economic, political, and ecological contexts. Demonstration projects also take on an important education function by serving as precedents for the wider application of the concepts they are demonstrating. Currently, a tremendous gap exists between our thinking about sustainability and the ecosystem approach and what is really on the ground. There is a critical need to give urban ecology ideas and urban ecological design physical manifestations in cities. Ultimately, if such demonstrations validate innovative practices, they will provide an impetus for their integration into the design and functioning of the city as a whole. Demonstrated implementations of policies and performance standards also serve as mechanisms for testing market-driven validation of sustainable innovations.

Despite growing awareness of the need for an ecosystem approach, there are few real-world demonstrations of new, ecologically based designs on a scale large enough to draw the attention of the public and development community. Still, alternative development styles at the scale of individual buildings or small parcels of open space are being pursued (see, e.g., Aberley, 1994; Roseland, 1997; Todd and Todd, 1994; Van der Ryn and Calthorpe, 1982; Van der Ryn and Cowan, 1996), and CMHC (1997) recently conducted a research study on the infrastructure costs and municipal revenues associated with alternative development patterns and standards. Two attempts to formulate ecosystem-based development standards, which have received significant attention, are the City of Waterloo's ecological buffer policy and Calgary's *Sustainable Suburbs Study*.

The City of Waterloo's Ecological Buffer Policy

The City of Waterloo's current policy approach to ecological 'function', as a land-use category, represents an early stage in the development of an urban ecological zoning system. An ecological buffer policy was initiated in response to suburban development pressure on agricultural lands in the upper Laurel Creek watershed on the west side of Waterloo. The concept of 'ecological buffer' as a land-use category is different from the conventional development standard set back, hazard land, and recreational open space and right-of-way dedications usually associated with greenfield development plan approval. Ecological buffers are not defined by human use but by ecological function. They are areas that have specific ecological functions necessary for maintaining local ecosystem processes. In the case of Waterloo, the specific ecological functions of concern were the critical hydrogeological processes connected with the maintenance of the upper Laurel Creek watershed ecosystem. For example, root-zone functions in the riparian zone adjacent to the stream channel regulate: the interface between surface run-off and stream channel flow; wetland functions including nutrient flow regulation; seasonal storage; soil moisture gradients and groundwater recharge; and root-zone and drip-line functions of forested areas, including nutrient storage and cycling, hydrogeological flow gradients, seasonal storage, filtration, and groundwater recharge. In the Waterloo policy, critical buffer zone areas were identified on the basis of extensive environmental study of the upper Laurel Creek watershed and incorporated into the Laurel Creek Development Plan as 'constraint lands' (Trushinski, 1995). This designation has three categories, each representing a relative degree (high, medium, low) of functional significance for specific buffer locations.

The significance of Waterloo's approach lies in its recognition of the existence of the landscape's ecological infrastructure and in attempts to maintain its function at the ecosystem level while still enabling urban development within the constraints of this framework. The Waterloo example demonstrates that the maintenance of ecological function and urban development can occur simultaneously and that, if used in innovative ways, conventional land-use planning tools such as zoning and development approval criteria can incorporate means to secure ecological processes. However, Waterloo had to engage in a comprehensive political, community, institutional, and interjurisdictional process to achieve this result. Institutional processes should not be underestimated in efforts to duplicate this urban ecological planning precedent (Cox et al., 1996).

The City of Calgary's *Sustainable Suburbs Study*

Issues of environmental concern, notably land, air, and water quality, grew massively in Calgary during its mid-1970s and mid-1990s economic and population booms. The urban form that accommodated Calgary's rapid population growth was low-density, suburban, sprawling, and automobile-dependent. Yet, between 1985 and 1994, provincial transportation grants to municipalities declined by $50 per capita while the city's 1995 transportation plan projected a 204 per cent increase in the number of vehicles on Calgary's roads over the next 30 years (Calgary, 1995: 10). At the same time the study identified motor vehicles as the source of 80 per cent of the city's air-quality problems. The city's demographics have also changed over time, with empty-nesters becoming the fastest-growing household type. However, the most significant impetus for rethinking conventional suburban development was the City of Calgary's estimate that over $1 billion in infrastructure (water, sewer, and roads) would be required to support projected population growth over the next 10 years. In response, the city's Planning and Building

Department produced the *Sustainable Suburbs Study*, which proposed a number of new policies and performance standards with the intention of demonstrating the viability of new standards in sustainable suburban forms of development.

The 'sustainable suburb' concept represents more fiscally affordable infrastructure standards, more socially diverse housing forms, and more environmentally conscious resource conservation in the built environment. Specifically, implementation of this concept has the potential to use 40 per cent less land to accommodate the same suburban population by changing average densities to 12.4 household units per gross hectare from 7.3 units per gross hectare (ibid., 12). This intensification of density creates a spatial form conducive to pedestrian movement and transit use.

In the Calgary study, the emphasis is primarily on resource conservation (using less land) rather than on incorporating ecological processes into urban form. For example: 'Construction of an average single family home generates 2.5 tons of construction waste' that can be recycled (ibid., 60). Still, ecological function is emphasized to some extent through the use of natural systems and constructed wetlands as alternatives to conventional storm water management infrastructure: 'Constructed wetlands are based on the concept of using plant material and microbes to naturally extract excess nutrients and pollutants from incoming water. When exposed to this natural process, contaminants are removed, settled out or transformed, resulting in cleaner discharge into natural watercourses' (ibid., 69).[8]

The prevailing belief that the ecological restructuring of urban form will necessarily be more expensive than current development practices is seriously challenged by Calgary's *Sustainable Suburbs Study*. In fact, it may well be that the high costs of conventional development infrastructure will become a major factor in promoting urban restructuring alternatives. In a rather ironic twist to conventional wisdom, it may be the high costs of public works that provide the catalyst to rethinking how the built environment can deal with energy, water, grey water, sewage, soil, habitat, environmental gra-

dients, biodiversity, food production, and trophic systems. This economic rethinking could lead to changes in zoning and land-use planning that would ensure that ecological performance becomes an integrated part of the urban development process. It could also lead to a new 'biogeoclimatically' appropriate form of urban design for Canadian cities.

Conclusion

Two of the most persistent myths in post–World War II Canadian urbanism are: (1) that environmental degradation is the price of economic progress, and (2) that urban growth is a 'free' economic good. The apparent corollary to both is that anything 'ecological' is de facto more expensive. However, as the previous discussion indicates, there is demonstrable evidence from Calgary, one of Canada's fastest-growing cities, that conventional forms of urban development may be more expensive than ecological alternatives. Urbanization is as much a technological phenomenon as it is a socio-economic process. Current urban form is a direct response to infrastructure engineering for roads and sewers and storm-water run-off. This massive infrastructure dependency and the form it creates must be restructured. In this context sustainability and urban ecology truly become environmental design problems.

The human built environment is by definition a sociocultural technological 'artifact', an artificial as opposed to 'natural' system. Thanks to this recognition, for the first time, the environment and sustainability clearly fall within the realm of the environmental design professions. It becomes possible to think about designing an 'artificial' or 'built' ecology. It becomes possible to think about the ecological performance of the built environment. It becomes possible to think about building systems as ecological systems, thereby changing the metaphor of the building and the city as machines to buildings as biological organisms and cities as ecological systems. The goal, according to the eminent Canadian architect, Arthur Eriksen (1993: 48), 'should be to have a living component in every building. Only then will the mechanistic city give way to the extended human organism that the city really is—a self-portrait of all its citizens.'

Ecological design offers the skills to address the question of what the 'new' urban forms of a sustainable society should be and to set out the possibilities for a new technology-society nexus that could enable new manifestations of adaptive form, function, and community to emerge in the wake of industrialism and modernism. Canadian cities are in transition. Among other things, it is a transition from an industrial model of urbanism to an ecosystem model of urbanism. It is a transition in which ecological, economic, and social performance become simultaneous and mutually reinforcing objectives for the built environment. It is a transition from administrative regulation to design as the dominant tool for urban development and restructuring. The emergence of ecological design as the focus of Canadian urbanism is a major shift in thinking that has only just begun, but it has the potential to change dramatically both the form and the function of Canadian cities.

Notes

1. Contrary to the popular wisdom of many grassroots urban environmental groups, saving a few small, species poor, disconnected remnants of agricultural landscapes from encroaching urban development will not change the scale of urban ecological dysfunction and urban system dependency on engineered infrastructure.

2. Despite the presence of water treatment plants and stringent municipal water-quality guidelines for Canadian cities, non-point urban surface run-off may contain contaminants from roadways, driveways, lawns, and gardens and a variety of other urban land-use surfaces. This storm drainage can carry animal feces, viral pathogens, hydrocarbons, micro-toxins, assorted chemicals, and heavy metals that may enter groundwater and surface water sources entirely untreated. For example, the Greater Vancouver Regional District's newsletter, *GVRD News* (July–Aug. 1994), describes urban storm-water

run-off as a 'toxic brew'. Although urban storm-water quality is not monitored at the municipal level across Canada, the dominant types of contaminants include nutrients (primarily phosphorus and nitrogen), organic compounds (diazinon, PCBs, benzene), sediments (sands, silts, clays), heavy metals (lead, zinc, mercury), petroleum residues (gasoline, grease, oil), and oxygen-demanding biological and chemical elements (Spirn, 1984; Tourbier and Westmacott, 1989). The Greater Vancouver Regional District covers an area of 3,200 square kilometres and had a population of 1.7 million people in 1993. It has 14,000 kilometres of private, municipal and regional sewers to collect wastewater. In 1993 this extensive network of infrastructure collected and moved 380 billion litres of wastewater (GVRD, 1994a). A four-year expansion of this system cost an estimated $650 million and included the upgrading of two treatment plants to secondary treatment level, which is twice as effective as the primary level of treatment and the equivalent of 95 per cent contaminant-free. 'Wastewater is 99 per cent water and less than 0.1 per cent waste. But that 0.1 per cent can be enough to endanger the health of humans, fish, birds and other shore and aquatic life' (ibid., 1994a: 2).

3. For example, Environment Canada compared the emissions of one urban transit diesel bus carrying 43 people with the emissions of 43 cars built after 1988 and thus equipped with pollution-abatement technology. Compared to the bus, these 43 cars would still produce '54 times more carbon monoxide, 8.4 times the hydrocarbons, and 2.4 times the nitrogen oxides produced by the bus carrying 43 people' (Statistics Canada, 1992).

4. While deforestation of the Brazilian rain forest has deservedly received much attention in the global greenhouse gas and climate change debate, little attention has been paid to global urbanization. A 1993 input-output pilot study of Canadian greenhouse gas emissions was done by Statistics Canada. The results showed

that households were important contributors to greenhouse gas emissions by virtue of their consumer patterns. Forty-four per cent of Canada's estimated industrial emissions are associated with the production of household commodities, including electrical power and other utilities. According to this accounting method, each $1,000 of electricity consumed by households produce almost five tonnes of CO_2 equivalents (Smith, 1993).

5. Editors' note: Sherri Hanley, School of Planning, University of Waterloo, contributed editorial assistance in the discussion of the sustainable city concept.

6. This was also the case of the more recent 1993 efforts of the City of Waterloo, Ontario, to regulate land use and development in the upper Laurel Creek watershed on the basis of municipal environmental policy guidelines and a multi-stakeholder round table process, which is discussed in the next section of the chapter.

7. The conceptual approach used in the preparation of the third national SOE report centred on sustainable development and the application of an ecosystem framework. The template for the 1996 report used life-support systems, the efficient use of non-renewable resources, productive capacity of species and ecosystems, and biological diversity as the benchmarks for evaluating environmental change and as indicators of sustainability at the national level.

8. Similarly, the United Nations Environment Program (Heywood and Watson, 1995: 447) suggests that ecological systems provide 'free services'. For example:

> wetlands provide substantial capabilities to assimilate wastes and to purify water that flows through them: microbial diversity can be important for the degradation of hazardous wastes; adequate functioning of soil microbiota is partially responsible for the maintenance of soil fertility, while the contribution of intact forests in controlling soil erosion is well known.... Thus, landscape-level conversions, particularly those involving hydrological changes associated with clearing forested watersheds, can increase flows and the variance of flows, making flood control more difficult and expensive. In aquatic ecosystems, even the addition of a single species can greatly affect water quality.

References

Aberley, D., ed. 1994. *Futures by Design: The Practice of Ecological Planning.* Gabriola Island, BC: New Society Publishers.

Calgary, City of. 1995. *Sustainable Suburbs Study: Creating More Fiscally, Socially and Environmentally Sustainable Communities.* Calgary: City of Calgary, Planning and Building Department.

Campbell, S. 1995. 'Green Cities, Growing Cities? Ecology, Economics and the Contradictions of Urban Planning', *Journal of the American Planning Association* 62: 296–312.

CMHC (Canada Mortgage and Housing Corporation). 1996. *Canadian Housing Statistics.* Ottawa: CMHC, Statistical Services Division.

————. 1997. *Conventional and Alternative Development Patterns—Phase 1: Infrastructure Costs; Phase 2: Municipal Revenues.* Ottawa: CMHC.

Cox, J., C. Hendrickson, I. Skelton, and R. Suffling. 1996. 'Watershed Planning for Urbanization to Avoid Undesirable Stream Outcomes', *Canadian Water Resources Journal* 21: 237–51.

D'Amour, D. 1993. *Towards an Investigation of Sustainable Housing.* Ottawa: Canadian Mortgage and Housing Corporation, Sustainable Development and Housing Research Paper No. 2.

Delcourt, H.R., and P.A. Delcourt. 1991. *Quaternary Ecology: A Paleoecological Perspective.* New York: Chapman and Hall.

Doering, R.L., D.M. Biback, P. Muldoon, N.H. Richardson, and G.H. Rust-D'Eye. 1991. *Planning For Sustainability—Towards Integrating Environmental Protection into Land-Use Planning.* Royal Commission on the Future of the Toronto Waterfront Working Paper No. 12. Toronto: Queen's Printer for Ontario; Ottawa: Supply and Services Canada.

Dorney, R.S. 1989. *The Professional Practice of Environmental Management,* ed. L.C. Dorney. New York: Springer-Verlag.

Environment Canada. 1991. *The State of Canada's Environment.* Ottawa: Minister of Public Works and Government Services.

———. 1993. *Environmental Implications of the Automobile,* SOE *Bulletin No. 93–1.* Ottawa: Environment Canada, State of Environment Reporting Program.

———. 1995. *Technical Supplement to the Environmental Indicator Bulletin on Canadian Passenger Transportation,* SOE *Technical Supplement 95–3.* Ottawa: Environment Canada, State of the Environment Reporting Program.

———. 1996. *The State of Canada's Environment.* Ottawa: Minister of Public Works and Government Services.

———. 1998a. *Urban Water: Municipal Water Use and Wastewater Treatment,* SOE *Bulletin No. 98–4.* Ottawa: Environment Canada, State of the Environment Reporting Program.

———. 1998b. *Canadian Passenger Transportation,* SOE *Bulletin No. 98–5.* Ottawa: Environment Canada, State of the Environment Reporting Program.

———. 1998c. *Climate Change,* SOE *Bulletin No. 98–3.* Ottawa: Environment Canada, State of the Environment Reporting Program.

———, Canada Mortgage and Housing Corporation, and Intergovernmental Committee on Urban and Regional Research. 1995. *Developing Indicators of Urban Sustainability: The Canadian Experience.* Ottawa: Environment Canada, Proceedings of the Measuring Urban Sustainability: Canadian Indicators Workshop, Toronto, 19–21 June.

Erickson, A. 1993. 'Revitalizing Our Cities', *Plan Canada* (Nov.): 47–8.

Friend, A., and D. Rapport. 1979. *Towards a Comprehensive Framework for Environmental Statistics: A Stress-Response Approach.* Ottawa: Statistics Canada, Catalogue 11–510.

Globe and Mail. 1997. 'British Columbia Report', 12 Sept., A23.

GVRD (Greater Vancouver Regional District). 1993. *Drinking Water Quality Improvement Plan: Discussion Paper.* Vancouver: GVRD.

———. 1994a. 'Wastewater Program a Massive and Costly Operation: Stormwater Could Be More Hazardous than Sanitary Sewer', *GVRD News* 2 (July–Aug.).

———. 1994b. 'Views Sought on First Regional Air Management Plan in Canada', *GVRD News* 5 (Mar.–Apr.).

Health and Welfare Canada. 1993. *Guidelines for Canadian Drinking Water Quality.* Ottawa: Minister of Supply and Services.

Heywood, V.H., and R.T. Watson. 1995. 'Biodiversity and Ecosystem Functioning: Ecosystem Analyses', in *Global Biodiversity Assessment.* New York: United Nations Environment Program.

Hough, M. 1984. *City Form and Natural Process: Towards a New Urban Vernacular.* New York: Routledge.

IBI Group. 1990. *Greater Toronto Area Urban Structure Concepts Plan: Summary Report.* Toronto: Greater Toronto Co-ordinating Committee.

Luckman, B.H. 1979. *Urban Runoff and Water Quality Monitoring in the Carling Street Catchment Basin, London, Ontario.* London, Ont.: University of Western Ontario, Department of Geography, Geographical Paper No. 39.

MacLaren, V. 1996. 'Urban Sustainability Reporting', *Journal of the American Planning Association* 62: 184–200.

———, M. Campbell, W. Dickenson, and E. Young. 1994. *Municipal State of Environment Reporting in Canada: Current Status and Future Needs,* 3 vols. Ottawa: Environment Canada, State of Environment Reporting Program.

Marsh, W.M. 1991. *Landscape Planning and Environmental Applications.* 2nd edn. New York: John Wiley and Sons.

Newman, P. 1998. 'From Symbolic Gesture to the Mainstream: Next Steps in Local Urban Sustainability', *Local Environment* 3: 299–308.

Office of the Provincial Auditor. 1994. *1994 Annual Report*. Toronto: Queen's Printer for Ontario.

Odum, E.P. 1993. *Ecology and Our Endangered Life-Support Systems*. Sunderland, Mass.: Sinauer Associates.

Ouellet, P. 1996. 'Environmentally Sensitive Policy Areas as a Tool for Environmental Protection', in P. Filion, T. Bunting, and K. Curtis, eds, *The Dynamics of the Dispersed City: Geographic and Planning Perspectives on Waterloo Region*. Waterloo: University of Waterloo, Department of Geography Publication Series.

Perks, W.T. 1992. *Innovative Site Development Standards and Practices: Review of Industry Perceptions, Phase 1 Progress Report*. Calgary: Alberta Municipal Affairs.

Petts, J., and G. Eduljee. 1994. *Environmental Impact Assessment for Waste Treatment and Disposal Facilities*. Chichester, UK: Wiley.

Rees, W., and M. Wackernagel. 1994. 'Ecological Footprints and Appropriated Carrying Capacity: Measuring the Natural Capital Requirements of the Human Economy', in A.-M. Jansson, M. Hammer, C. Folke, and R. Costanza, eds, *Investing in Natural Capital: The Ecological Economics Approach to Sustainability*. Washington: Island Press.

Roger-Machart, C. 1997. 'The Sustainable City: Myth or Reality', *Town and Country Planning* 66, 2: 53–5.

Roseland, M. 1992. *Towards Sustainable Communities*. Ottawa: National Round Table on the Environment and the Economy.

———, ed. 1997. *Eco-City Dimensions: Healthy Communities, Healthy Planets*. Gabriola Island, BC: New Society Publishers.

Royal Commission on the Future of the Toronto Waterfront. 1992. *Regeneration: Toronto's Waterfront and the Sustainable City, Final Report*. Toronto: Queen's Printer for Ontario; Ottawa: Supply and Services Canada.

Rump, P. 1989. Canada Land Use Monitoring Program (CLUMP) Files. Personal communication. Ottawa: Environment Canada, State of the Environment Reporting Branch.

Smith, R. 1993. 'Canadian Green House Gas Emissions: An Input-Output Study', in *Environmental Perspectives*. Ottawa: Statistics Canada, Catalogue 11–528E.

Spirn, A.W. 1984. *The Granite Garden: Urban Nature and Human Design*. New York: Basic Books.

Statistics Canada. 1986. *Human Activity and the Environment 1986*. Ottawa: Supply and Services Canada, Catalogue 11–509.

———. 1991. *Human Activity and the Environment 1991*. Ottawa: Ministry of Industry, Science and Technology, Catalogue 11–509E.

———. 1992. 'Motor Vehicles and Air Pollution', *Canadian Social Trends* 24 (Ottawa: Ministry of Industry, Science and Technology, Catalogue 11–008E.

———. 1994. *Quarterly Report on Energy Supply-Demand in Canada*. Ottawa: Ministry of Industry, Science and Technology, Catalogue 57–003.

Todd, N.J., and J. Todd. 1994. *From Eco-Cities to Living Machines: Principles of Ecological Design*. Berkeley, Calif.: North Atlantic Books.

Toronto, City of. 1991. *Evaluating the Role of the Automobile: A Municipal Strategy*. Toronto: City of Toronto, Healthy City Office.

Toubier, J.T., and R. Westmacott. 1989. 'Looking Good: The Use of Natural Methods to Control Urban Runoff', *Urban Land* 48, 4: 32–5.

Trushinski, B. 1995. *De-Mystifying Constraint Level One Woodland Buffer Areas*. Waterloo, Ont.: City of Waterloo.

Van der Ryn, S., and P. Calthorpe. 1982. *Sustainable Communities: A New Design Synthesis for Cities, Suburbs and Towns*. San Francisco: Sierra Club Books.

——— and S.S. Cowan. 1996. *Ecological Design*. Washington: Island Press.

Wackernagel, M., and W. Rees. 1996. *Our Ecological Footprint: Reducing Human Impact on the Earth*. Gabriola Island, BC: New Society Publishers. www.newsociety.com

WCED (World Commission on Environment and Development). 1987. *Our Common Future*. New York: Oxford University Press.

Chapter 22

Cities of the Everyday: Socio-Spatial Perspectives on Gender, Difference, and Diversity

Brian Ray and Damaris Rose

The past two decades of feminist-influenced work in urban studies have demonstrated the centrality of gender relations to almost all dimensions of urban form and urban life. The genesis of feminist urban research can be traced to the mid-1970s, when the position of women *vis-à-vis* the labour force and the traditional nuclear family was changing rapidly and being contested.[1] A new research field, initially known as 'women and urban environments', began to unmask the overwhelmingly masculinist, white, middle-class, and 'familialist' biases of theory and research and to challenge their *adequacy* both in understanding the relationships of different groups to built form and social space, and as normative assumptions for planning cities. This work sought to 'make the other half visible'. It documented how women (or subgroups of women) were disadvantaged by urban design and resource allocation mechanisms that failed to take into account specific needs arising from their gendered social roles and responsibilities (Wekerle, 1981; Wekerle, Peterson, and Morley, 1980), the aim being to rectify these inequities, 'enabling women to take their rightful place as full members of society' (McDowell, 1993: 163). Subsequent feminist analysis of the city showed that gender-blind analyses produced false dichotomies (between 'economic' and 'social' processes, between 'public' and 'private' space) and generated inherently incomplete understandings of urban dynamics—in short, bad science.

Feminist theory stresses that gender is a social rather than biological construction. Gender refers not to the biological differences between females and males (usually denoted by the term 'sex'), but to the ways in which social institutions, processes, norms, values, and attitudes, especially those elements particular to urban life, construct differences in what women and men do and experience in our society and cities. However, an individual's identity is seldom singular; it is important, therefore, to consider how gender intersects with other markers of identity, specifically sexuality and ethnicity. How, for instance, does being gay or lesbian, or an immigrant of colour raised in a different gender system, affect one's experience of Canadian gender systems, of social relations generally, and of urban places specifically?

Such questions about social difference have led urban feminist research through a number of transitions in both theory and methodology in recent years. From early studies that strongly focused on the experiences of white middle-class and heterosexual women, the boundaries of feminist work have grown to encompass not only social class distinctions but also broader questions of social difference and of the roles that constructions of gender play in shaping the geographies of everyday experience (Gilbert, 1997a). The plural form 'geographies' signifies that a diversity of gender relations intersects with, structures, and is structured by other social relations of identity and power (Chouinard and Grant, 1995; Kobayashi and Peake, 1994; Ruddick, 1996). This emphasis on social difference and particularity reflects the influence of post-modernism and critical theory, which have challenged notions of universal normative systems, and such an emphasis is also reflected in debates within the women's movement about how to grapple with differences in class, 'race' or ethnicity, sexuality, age, ability, and culture among women (Peet, 1998: ch. 7; Young, 1990). This contrasts with much of the research traditionally conducted within urban geography, and urban studies more generally, which has downplayed the diversity of ways in which urban processes and daily lives are shaped by gender and other forms of social identity.

Our chapter begins with a review of major themes in the literature on gender and urban environments over the past two decades, highlighting the progress of theory and debate from examinations of women and gender as fixed categories to a focus on social constructions of gender and to an increasing concern with 'difference'. Our review departs from other such discussions (e.g., McDowell, 1993; Peet, 1998; G. Rose, 1993) in that we privilege Canadian material wherever possible. The remainder of the chapter presents two 'vignettes' of gendered space in Montreal, chosen to illustrate some of the diverse ways that gender is played out in relation to other forms of identity in the everyday spaces of the city. The principal intent of these vignettes is to illustrate the complexity of social identity. In no way do we wish to suggest that gender is the most important social category to which other categories of social difference are simply tacked on. In fact, our intent is quite the opposite, as such an approach would render simplistic the highly complex and pluralistic experiences of women and men.

The first vignette focuses on the intersections between gender, sexuality, and class in Montreal's 'Gay Village'. Popular understandings of the 'Village' embrace a vision of homosexuality unfettered by gender, but our research demonstrates the intricate ways in which gender and sexual identities among women and men can create very different understandings of an urban space whose social characteristics seem at first to be so self-evident. Building on this illustration of the plural meanings and experiences of neighbourhood, the second vignette examines the everyday geographies of recently arrived immigrant women, their (re)construction of social networks as mediated by particular culture and gender systems, and how these ties in turn con-

tribute to different place-making strategies. We argue that where immigrant women live, who constitutes their networks, and the intersections between different gender systems are all critical aspects of adaptation to life in Montreal and are central to the creation of new hybrid identities as women and immigrants. At best, our vignettes and review of research simply scratch the surface, and function as illustrations, of the various ways that gender shapes the city's forms, spaces, places, and experiences. In this sense, this chapter is intended to spark discussion about social difference and about how analyses sensitive to these influences can improve our understandings of Canadian cities in the twenty-first century.

An Overview of Feminist Urban Research: What's Gender Got to Do With Urban Form?

Until quite recently, urban analysts assumed unquestioningly that it was entirely natural, logical, and rational for industrialized cities to be organized along principles that spatially separated places of employment from places of residence. The former were associated with a 'public sphere' where economic 'production' took place, the latter with a 'private sphere' where most of the activities of 'social reproduction' took place in the homes of families and in surrounding neighbourhoods. The concept of social reproduction refers to the labour performed to ensure the day-to-day material and emotional sustenance of people in the paid labour force, children, and other dependants, as well as the reproduction of the population. In our society much of this 'reproductive work' is unpaid (tasks such as raising children, cooking, cleaning, shopping, caring for elderly relatives, volunteer work in schools) and has primarily been undertaken by women. Because the tasks are unpaid and because of the erroneous assumption that performing them is inherently part of 'natural' gender roles, the fundamental contribution women make has been largely obscured and undervalued. Mirroring the 'separate spheres' logic, it was also presumed equally natural and logical that urban residential space be divided up into zones for 'family' and 'non-family' living, with family households gravitating to suburban environments of single-family housing, green space, and safe streets as they reached the family-formation and child-rearing stage of the life cycle, leaving behind an inner city characterized by congested environments, unstable household forms, marginal social groups, and 'deviant' cultures.

Many empirical studies over several decades have verified these organizing principles of built form and urban social space (Davies and Murdie, 1993; Le Bourdais and Beaudry, 1988; Randall and Viaud, 1994) (see also Chapter 13 in this volume). An important dimension of early 'women and environments' research, however, entailed questioning whether the 'separate spheres' model of urban land use was compatible with women's current roles. Notably, traditional suburbs created logistical difficulties for increasing numbers of 'dual role' women who combined paid work with being wives and mothers (Michelson, 1985, 1988).[2] Feminist work pointed out that urban planning norms helped reinforce the dichotomy between 'public' and 'private' life, the former essentially the primary domain of men as 'workers', the latter the primary domain of women as 'carers'. Feminist geographers argued that this false dichotomy undervalued the reproductive work of women, ignored the fact that production is dependent on, not separate from, women's reproductive work in the home, and rendered impossible holistic understandings of how cities function and how they are experienced by *all* inhabitants (Mackenzie and Rose, 1983; McDowell, 1991; Rose and Villeneuve, 1993).

One key strand in this body of work has dealt with transportation (for reviews and examples of research examining gender differences in commuting patterns and car ownership, see Brais and Chicoine, 1998; England, 1991; Hanson and Pratt, 1995; Preston and McLafferty, 1993; Villeneuve and Rose, 1988; Wekerle, 1981; Wekerle and Rutherford, 1988). Pointing to women's lower rates of access to the private automobile and to the schedules of sub-urban public transit systems oriented towards downtown nine-to-five commuters (most of whom have historically been male), it was shown that urban transportation systems failed to accommodate the different space-time paths of many women, most notably female part-time workers or mothers with multiple-destination trips. Suburban women's trips to work were consistently found to be shorter than those of their male counterparts, domestic responsibilities presumably impinging on the possibility of a longer commute to a more rewarding job and reinforcing their likelihood of working in low-paid 'women's jobs' located closer to home. However, gendered commuting patterns were also found to be influenced by social class: for instance, female clerical workers tend to have long commutes from their modest-income suburbs to the central city, whereas many female professionals working downtown can afford more costly inner-city housing and some, but by no means the majority, opt for this location (Rose, 1989). Importantly, class and gender are affected by social ties, and to the extent that suburban working-class women obtain their jobs through local social networks of women who are themselves in gender-typed occupations, they may continue to opt for jobs close to home (Gilbert, 1997b; Hanson and Pratt, 1995).

While recognizing the importance of documenting how spatial forms were often dysfunctional for women, beginning in the late 1970s some feminists felt that merely to document this was insufficiently critical of existing gender relations. This critique sparked another major body of scholarship, socialist-feminist, that shifted the focus from seeing women as located in a *given* urban environment with a *given* set of gender roles to studies of the processes through which spatial forms and practices *become* gendered as female or male. A key goal was to 'demonstrat[e] the social construction rather than the "naturalness" of the defining characteristics of femininity' (McDowell, 1993: 163). The intent was to provide theorized historical accounts of the social processes by which urban and suburban places, such as office buildings, downtown streets, bars, department stores, suburban shopping malls, houses, and schools, became constructed as places for either women or men, a consequence of gender ideologies and material divisions of labour intimately associated with various phases of capitalist development. This work emphasized that the division of the city into putatively female and male realms could be challenged at a number of levels, ranging from utopian blueprints for non-sexist cities (Hayden, 1981) through to women's day-to-day strategies to overcome their isolation in the domestic sphere (Mackenzie, 1986).

This perspective (typified by Mackenzie and Rose, 1983) shed new light on the historical production of urban spatial form since the Industrial Revolution. It showed how the role of the home, and the work of working-class women within it, changed with urbanization and the development of the factory system. Goods for sale were no longer produced in the home through family labour, and the items that women had traditionally produced for family consumption were supplanted by purchased items produced in the burgeoning consumer goods sector, in which many women now worked for pay (Bradbury, 1993: 164–8; Chambers, 1997). In the late-nineteenth century, the long hours worked in factories by women and children as well as men in exchange for bare subsistence wages, compounded by very poor housing conditions, undermined women's abilities to sustain their families through domestic labour.

This domestic labour (of wives, but also of daughters) was nevertheless 'fundamental to family survival, to the transformation of wages into a reasonable standard of living, and to the reproduction of the working class' (Bradbury, 1993: 151). Perceived threats to the 'reproduction of labour-power'[3] needed for industrial capitalism, as well as to the health and survival of individuals, generated a slew of state measures to improve housing conditions and regulate working conditions and hours, especially those of women and children (Mackenzie, 1980; Prentice et al., 1988: 226–7; Purdy, 1997). They also led to struggles by male-dominated labour unions for a 'family wage' so that women could devote themselves as little as possible to wage labour

and as much as possible to the care of their husbands and children and to ensuring the stability of family life (Connelly, 1982; Newton, 1995: 82-5).

The desire of working-class men to earn sufficient income to create a 'proper sphere' for the wife became an important dimension of masculinity at this time (Bradbury, 1993: 152, 173). It also dovetailed with the concerns of 'urban reformers' of the late-nineteenth and early-twentieth centuries—many of them bourgeois women—to protect the 'morals' of working-class girls and women by isolating them from the public spaces of the central city, which were associated with 'deviant' sexual behaviours and other threats to the ideal of domesticity (Mackenzie, 1980, 1988; Stansell, 1987; Strange, 1996). Both the urban reformers and large sections of the labour movement, along with some women's organizations, saw suburban environments as a safe, insulating solution to these twin threats to patriarchal forms of social reproduction. Suburbs became touted as places where both working-class and middle-class women could practice the new science of home economics and take pride in their housewife role (Harris, 1996: 98–100; Mackenzie and Rose, 1983; Strong-Boag, 1988: 126–7).

Nevertheless, married women of the early- to mid-twentieth century did not simply buy into ideologies of suburban domesticity, nor were they passive victims of corporate mass media sales pitches. Rather, they embraced the family wage and the move to the suburbs for much more pragmatic reasons: it improved their housing conditions—the workplace in which they carried out domestic labour—and reduced the amount of menial labour involved in domestic work, although not the time spent on it (Luxton, 1980; Séguin, 1989; Strong-Boag, 1991). However, for many working-class families in Canadian suburbs, the family wage was either never a reality or they could only marginally afford to purchase even a scaled-down version of the 'suburban dream' without needing wives' earnings, so the women often created their own sources of income, notably by child-minding or taking in boarders (Bloomfield and Harris, 1994; Strong-Boag, 1988: 126).

The gendered principles on which suburbs were constructed nonetheless created major contradictions for married women who increasingly had to join the paid labour force. The very period that saw the peak of ideological promotions of suburban domesticity (1950s–early 1960s) was also the period when married women's rate of labour force participation began a steady increase that was to continue unabated until the 1990s (Strong-Boag 1991). As women criss-crossed the boundaries of the 'separate spheres', they developed their own spaces of the everyday through various individual and collective strategies for overcoming the contradictions and dichotomies between 'work' and 'daily life' in urban social space (Mackenzie, 1986, 1988; see also McDowell, 1991).

Although contemporary Canadian suburbs have very high rates of female labour force participation, more traditional models of child-rearing and socializing and a greater acceptance of conventionally gendered divisions of labour still tend to prevail, especially in low-density developments (see Rose and Villeneuve, 1998). Moreover, in some suburbs zoning based on 'lifestyle' and household type has prevented women from remaining in suburbs after divorce or from renting apartments when alone with children (Fincher, 1998). Feminist scholars have been in the vanguard of research about social equity issues related to suburbanization, but at the same time they have been attentive to the strong ideological polarities that still persist between inner cities and suburbs. This is perhaps most clearly evident in research about the gentrification of inner-city neighbourhoods and the roles played by professional women in this process (Markusen, 1981; Rose, 1984; Séguin and Villeneuve, 1987; Villeneuve, 1991; Wekerle, 1984; for a critique, see also Caulfield, 1994: 179–86; Bondi, 1994).

Gentrification research has highlighted some of the ways in which family and household forms have diversified in recent decades. With the proliferation of divorce, single-parenthood, blended families, delayed childbearing or childlessness, and common-law partnerships, individuals' itineraries through the life course have become less linear and household composition has become more fluid over time. Consequently, researchers have increasingly questioned the usefulness of assuming the main household breadwinner to be male, and thence associating different parts of the city and types of housing with different 'life-cycle' phases, as was traditionally done in urban social geography (Fincher, 1998; Monk and Katz, 1993; Gober, McHugh, and Reid, 1991; Preston and Taylor, 1981). For instance, many of the inner-city high-rises, such as Toronto's massive St Jamestown complex, originally built for a transient group—young, childless baby boomers working downtown (Miron, 1993; Rose, Mongeau, and Chicoine, 1988)—are now home to low-income families of recent immigrants (Vincent, 1995). In inner cities, family households with dependent children are more likely to be headed by a lone parent—generally a woman—than is the case in the suburbs (Rose and Le Bourdais, 1986). Marketing for new condominium developments on redeveloped land close to the downtown core is often targeted to 'empty-nest' couples and sometimes to groups whose lifestyles are perceived to be urban, such as gays and lesbians (see Rose, 1996). These types of changes indicate that the social complexity of the contemporary Canadian city can no longer be grasped adequately by the well-known and observable zonal pattern dominated by either 'family' or 'non-family' households corresponding to a broadly suburban/inner-city divide.

These kinds of household composition changes, as well as problems related to a strict separation of public and private spheres, have served to emphasize some of the shortcomings inherent in socialist-feminist accounts of the production of urban space. Notably, recent work has shown that the *empirical* spatial separations of public and private spheres, even for married women, were overstated in the research (Ryan, 1990; Stansell, 1987; Wilson, 1995). The degree of social isolation and 'entrapment' as a result of the inscription of gendered separate spheres may likewise have been overestimated. Physical isolation did not always mean social isolation (Chambers, 1997; Dowling, 1998; Dyck, 1989; Martin, 1991; Morton, 1995). At the same time, however, researchers have demonstrated that socially sanctioned rights to public space remain profoundly gendered (Duncan, 1996), as the question of women's safety makes abundantly clear. Valentine (1992) argues that the *ideology* of women properly belonging to the domestic, private sphere has increased their vulnerability to male violence in public as well as in the home (see also Klodawksy, Lundy, and Andrew, 1994; Pratt and Hanson, 1994; Whitzman, 1995).

The conceptual dependence of socialist-feminism on the reproduction of labour-power also effectively limited the focus to husband-wife families with children. As a consequence, this perspective could not provide a theoretical framework for the encounters of lesbians, or indeed those of gay men, with urban form and its imbued gender ideologies, beyond a basic contribution to explaining the overall marginalization and 'othering' of those without a classic reproductive role (in the biological sense). Nor did the literature give much empirical attention to the experiences of female-led households defined statistically as 'non-family', including single women and lesbians, living in inner cities or suburbs. This is rather ironic, in the light of feminist vaunting of the cosmopolitan character of the inner city compared to the traditional suburb, which is, of course, a space imbued with only one legitimate form of sexuality—heterosexuality. Moreover, research has been slow to recognize the numerous ethnocultural changes that have occurred in recent years and the implications of many different culturally defined gender systems in Canadian cities (Ng, 1993). In general, while being quite sensitive to the differences between working- and middle-class women's experiences, socialist-feminist perspectives on the gendering of urban forms failed to consider how class differences were conjugated with or constructed through other dimensions of difference. Thus, in the 1990s, feminist-inspired urban research has broadened out to explore how gender differences in access to, experience, and use of urban space and resources are cross-cut, not only by class but by cultural constructions of 'race', ethnicity, and sexuality (Kobayashi and Peake, 1994).

New Directions in Feminist Research: Considering Social Difference

The need to consider the social and cultural diversity that exists among Canadian women and men is an imperative for urban researchers. How do such differences construct their experiences of belonging or marginality in Canadian cities, experiences that we believe to be everyday rather than exceptional aspects of urban life for many people? Little attention has been given to date as to how marginalized people negotiate, understand, and experience the city's opportunities and constraints. It is in this spirit that we now turn to our two vignettes of gendered space in Montreal. Both address cultural difference and the question of belonging in neighbourhood space, but for very different social groups living in different places. Social difference needs to be explored by feminist researchers in a variety of ways, and our illustrations of the difference that sexuality and ethnicity can make in a gendered analysis of everyday urban spaces are intended as simply two paths among many that deserve examination in studies of people on the margins, as well as at the centre, of city life.

Gender, Sexuality, and Class: Living Difference in the 'Village'

The early socialist-feminist perspective could not provide a theoretical framework for the encounters of lesbians, or indeed those of gay men, with urban form and its imbued gender ideologies, beyond a basic contribution to explaining the overall marginalization and 'othering' of those without a classic reproductive role. In recent years geography and urban studies have witnessed a mushrooming of research directed towards understanding how gender and sexuality intersect and construct the urban experience and the various meanings given to places in the city (Beemyn, 1997; Bell and Valentine, 1995; Ingram, Bouthillette, and Retter, 1997a; Knopp, 1990a, 1990b, 1992, 1995; Rothenberg, 1995; Valentine, 1993a, 1993b). Canadian work in this field is still in its infancy and overwhelmingly oriented to understanding those inner-city enclaves where homosexuality has flourished, although there have been a few groundbreaking studies dealing with how gender and sexuality construct the social and material qualities of neighbourhoods and places, as well as the politics of place. Early studies of gay and lesbian histories and politics in Canada, such as Kinsman's (1987, 1996) landmark work, certainly outlined the terrain of political struggle surrounding sexual difference as an overwhelmingly urban one. Inner-city districts were the only spaces where alternatives to identity and community based on the nuclear family could be constructed—although not without danger. Researchers have charted the emergence of gay and lesbian communities in inner-city neighbourhoods and how these gay enclaves functioned, and continue to function, as sites of social network formation, cultural (re)invention, and political action (Bouthillette, 1997; Goheen and Ray, 1994; Grube, 1997). In addition, researchers are also examining in a more critical way the places that make up gay, lesbian, and straight neighbourhoods, highlighting institutions such as bathhouses (Tattelman, 1997), bars (Chamberland, 1997, 1998; Higgins, 1998; Wolfe, 1997), and women's shelters (Grant, 1999) as critical sites where gender and sexual identities intersect and where political discourses constructed by an often homophobic straight community create places of marginality if not outright danger.

However, few authors have explored the *gendering* of space *within* gay male and lesbian neighbourhoods. Bouthillette (1997) is an important exception. Based on case studies of two Vancouver neighbourhoods that have become associated, respectively, with gay men and lesbians, she argues that divergences in social relations and culture give rise to distinct gender-related processes that both create and reinscribe spaces as 'gay' or 'lesbian'. Yet she observes that the line between the two neighbourhoods, defined by the gender of residents, is far from sharp and is increasingly transgressed by members of both communities. Due to high rents in the West End and a public landscape increasingly defined in

terms of hyper-masculine bar culture and consumerism, some gay men have been migrating to the Commercial Drive neighbourhood. At the same time, the West End has started to attract a number of lesbians who seek out housing in its remaining pockets of affordable housing and/or who are attracted to its unambiguously gay composition. Here they feel at greater liberty to express sexual desire and affection as compared to Commercial Drive's more heterogeneous mix of 'ethnic' and 'counter-cultural' groups and identities.

Gender and sexuality are negotiated in particular political, social, and economic contexts, and as a consequence sexual and gender identities depend strongly on place. Gay neighbourhoods, such as Church and Wellesley in Toronto, often emerge out of active contestation of the power of public authority and repression. Based on an analysis of Toronto's bathhouse raids of 1981, Grube (1997: 128) argues that 'the militant presence of gay and lesbian groups in strategic urban open space has tended to be an essential prerequisite to forms of "place-making" that nurture a wide array of activities for specific sexual minorities and their respective networks.'

The intricate weave of place-making (see Ingram, Bouthillette, and Retter, 1997a: 295) is also well illustrated in the genesis and continuing transformation of Montreal's Gay Village. For much of its postwar history Montreal has had a significant number of gay bars and commercial services, although their location in what is now known as the 'Gay Village' (see Figure 22.1), surrounded by the working-class neighbourhood of Centre-sud, is a much more recent development. Since 1982, this area has achieved widespread recognition as the city's 'gay neighbourhood'. Importantly, for many within the gay community and the population at large, the perception of the Village as a gay neighbourhood includes lesbians, although largely by default.

Centre-sud lies some three kilometres east of the centre of downtown Montreal; its commercial heart, and the section most readily identified as the Gay Village, is almost entirely focused around a stretch of Ste Catherine Street East that extends

Figure 22.1   **Montreal's Gay Village and Centre-sud: Location and Gender Composition**

Plateau Mont-Royal

Sherbrooke

Papineau   Centre-sud

St Hubert   The Gay Village

Ste Catherine St.

Legend
▲ 56 to 70% Male
★ 50 to 55% Male

from St Hubert on the west to Papineau on the east. By the 1970s Centre-sud seemed to be more of a 'ghost' neighbourhood than anything else. The area experienced massive deindustrialization and concomitant job losses and population decline (a loss of some 20,000 people, or 36 per cent of the total population, between 1971 and 1991). Today it is one of Montreal's poorest neighbourhoods, where average household income in 1991 was only $24,582, or 57 per cent of that of the Montreal census metropolitan area (CMA), which was $43,405. The unemployment rates of men and women in 1991 were 18.5 and 14.5 per cent, respectively, markedly higher than the rates for the CMA (11.6 per cent for men and 11.8 per cent for women). Nevertheless, the core of Centre-sud has emerged as Montreal's Gay Village, today one of the top five gay tourist destinations in North America, though according to some estimates the resident gay and lesbian population is only a fraction of the total neighbourhood population (Duhaime, 1996). Yet, non-family house-

holds led by males are strongly represented in the neighbourhood, and there is an especially strong concentration of men in census tracts adjacent to Ste Catherine Street (Figure 22.1).

The statistics point to the overwhelmingly male character of the Village, as do the nature of its establishments and public and semi-public street activities. But what does this place embody for people associated with the label 'Gay Village' and for whom it is assumed that the neighbourhood holds significant meaning? To begin to understand this, we undertook interviews with two small subsets of Montreal's gay and lesbian populations: 15 gay men who live in the Village and 18 lesbians who live in adjacent neighbourhoods and use the Village periodically.[4] We sought to understand the multiple meanings of the Village through in-depth interviews with a broad range of individuals.[5]

Contrary to what might be supposed, virtually all the men we interviewed minimize the significance of the neighbourhood as a 'gay' space in their choosing to live in Centre-sud and often seem to create self-consciously a distance between their sexuality and their residential choice. They are not, however, oblivious to the neighbourhood's various reputations, and most certainly not to the significance of sexuality in shaping its residential and commercial spaces. As a first point of reference in describing the neighbourhood, virtually all of the men point to its poverty and social marginality as overarching factors that shape the area's reputation and their everyday experiences of place. As 'Benoît' put it:

> I believe that in the neighbourhood about one-third are gay, one-third are new Quebecers [immigrants, visible minorities], and one-third are on social welfare who I could not classify as families. But watch out, there are also new Quebecers on social welfare and also among gays. So I would say that in the area there are about, well, 50 per cent who live on social welfare. That's really evident the day they receive their welfare cheques. Those days you see cases of beer literally roll down the streets, and drug pushers become active like you have never seen. [translation]

Poverty is also an issue for lesbians who frequent the Village, but it is experienced and expressed in a less personal, more distant manner. Many women describe the area as grimy, seedy, noisy, and unattractive and often discuss the growing prevalence of considerable drug dealing and abuse, as well as prostitution. Only two women commented directly on the experience of poverty in Centre-sud, 'Patricia' noting that, 'often I don't think in terms of the Village but of Centre-sud there, and there you see a lot of poor people who live there ... a lot of poverty ... at the same time as there is money around from gay men, and it's a little rough' [translation]. The fact of social class in structuring the built and social landscapes of Centre-sud and the Village is always present in the perceptions of gays and lesbians. But most respondents, whose levels of education, if not incomes, are substantially higher than

those of long-time Centre-sud residents, juxtapose and intersect this reality with conceptions of their own sexual identities and the ways in which sexuality is marked and experienced on the streets and in particular places, such as grocery stores, restaurants, bars, saunas, clubs, and parks.

Most of the men discussed how sex and sexuality are expressed in the neighbourhood and generally were extremely supportive of the neighbourhood's openness towards difference. 'David' was candid about the kinds of sexuality that find expression in the public spaces of the Village: 'Well, let's face it, I have been living here for three and a half years or so and the first year I realized that the first warm day of spring, when the sun is out and it goes over 20 degrees, half of the men are out there, half-naked in the streets.... And this spreads, it is cruisy everywhere along Ste Catherine Street'. Several men also placed considerable importance on the neighbourhood as a place they use to explore their sexuality. 'Nick' in some ways is typical, recounting at several points during the interview the different ways he used the neighbourhood as a space to develop friendships of all kinds with other gay men and thereby cultivate a level of comfort with his sexuality, although it was never really a place where he sought out sex. The simple presence of other gay men in large numbers allowed him, like other men, to live their difference in an unexceptional manner. As 'Patrice' put it, 'even though I never hid my homosexuality, living here, it's a funny feeling, . . . how can I put it . . . I can live my homosexuality easier here I find, in the neighbourhood more so than elsewhere' [translation].

As important as the Village and its various institutions might be for gay men as places both to explore their sexuality and to develop friendship networks, the space holds different meanings for lesbians. Few are the women who do not go to lesbian and/or gay bars in the Village: many described the area as the one place in the city where they could show physical affection towards other women in public space. Still others defended the neighbourhood as having important symbolic value (for example, as the hub of the annual Divers/Cité parade in which both men and women participate), making a visible statement of difference the straight community could not ignore. Yet these positive aspects of the Village are counterposed by most women with a stark and ever-present sense of the Village as gay male space and exclusive of women.

The words the women use to describe the space are particularly telling in that they refer to it as 'boys' town', 'gay', 'masculine', and of gay men 'owning' the space and constructing the images, both material and social, that make the Village a place. The Gay Village for most of the women is exactly that—gay and male. For instance, as 'Holly' succinctly put it: 'Well, the Village is so boy, it's so strongly gay boy', while 'Anne' says that she 'feels like the gay men own the Village and we rent space.... I always feel like I'm in the minority.' 'Nathalie' also speaks of being only 'allowed' at the margins of the street when she is in the Village: 'I feel like I'm allowed to walk on that one block where Sky or K.O.X. [two mixed bars] is because they have girls' space. I think it's a gay man's space and I feel it's a horrible example of what a community can do.' Other women simply say that the Village is a commercial space and, if you do not have money, you are automatically excluded. As previous research has noted (Adler and Brenner, 1992), this sentiment highlights the economic marginality of lesbians due to their gender (especially in the case of those raising children). The second major way in which lesbians interpret the Village differently from gay men is a function of male violence, which lesbians may experience on account of their sexual orientation as well as their gender (Grant, 1998). Physical danger and 'gay bashing' in the Village are much publicized and complicated (Remiggi, 1998), and many women signal that residential streets off Ste Catherine in Centre-sud are especially fearful and dangerous spaces at night.

Some incidents of discomfort or marginalization reported by women interviewees had nothing to do with 'straight-hate' or fear of violence from an unknown assailant. These incidents instead reflected the public behaviour and attitudes of gay men towards lesbians. Several of the women indi-

cated that gay misogyny often places lesbians at the margins of the Village (see also Cadorette, 1998) and, consequently, constructs the Village as a marginal place in their daily lives. As 'Kim' put it: 'There are a lot of men who go out of their way to be feminist men ... and I feel happy about that, but there is a certain amount of misogyny when people cluster in groups. So I don't feel that it's my space because I feel like I'd have to beat my way in there.' Like many of the women, 'Kim' indicated a much greater level of comfort in public space on major shopping streets in and around the Plateau Mont-Royal (a socially and ethnically diverse part of town reputed for its cosmopolitan ambience and where some gentrification has occurred) and pointed to these as significant spaces of lesbian sociability and personal security (see Podmore, 1998).

It is interesting, and perhaps a little telling, that a place once described as a 'ghost' neighbourhood has emerged in Montreal's post-industrial economy as a paradoxical 'home' to gay men and lesbians. As illustrated by the lesbians and, to a lesser extent, the gay men we interviewed, the Village, this place that the public codes as gay and lesbian, in many ways remains a remote, sometimes liberating, sometimes dangerous, and often quite contradictory landscape. It is a place where distinct versions of gay male culture actively construct social space and where a celebration of 'post-modern difference' or 'unassimilated otherness', to use Iris Young's (1990) term, seems difficult to identify, especially for lesbians (Podmore, 1998). The interplay of gender, sexuality, and class revealed by this research thus relegates lesbians to the margins of a space that at least in the public imagination is objectively supposed to be 'theirs', and underlines the importance of not subsuming lesbians' experience under that of gay men (Chouinard and Grant, 1995).

Difference is expressed and experienced in the Village, and in Montreal more generally, in many different ways. Many gay men and lesbians discussed the city's archetypal French-English linguistic cleavage, as well as ethnic and racial discrimination, as some of the other ways in which Village space is constructed, used, and understood by them in daily life. In the second vignette, which considers difference and gender, we move away from the constructions of sexuality embedded in the social landscape of the Village and turn our attention to the city more broadly to examine the place-making strategies of a group of people too often stereotyped as spatially and socially isolated—immigrant women.

Social Geographies of Everyday Life: Immigrant Women Constructing the Urban Experience

The virtual invisibility of immigrant women in studies of migration, post-arrival settlement, and ethnicity has been a long-standing problem in social science (Ng, 1993). Scant attention has been paid to the specific roles that women play and the work they do, both in cultural conservation and in mediating the challenges inherent in adaptation and integration for themselves, their families, and the larger community (Boyd, 1989; Lamotte, 1991). This section explores some of the ways that immigrant women who have lived in Montreal for several years and who come from two very different cultural backgrounds, in this case Indian and Polish, come to experience and understand their local neighbourhood spaces and the city more generally. The process of developing social networks of friends and family in a new country is one of the important conduits by which all immigrants, women in particular, come to experience and in turn construct a new urban landscape. We argue that by delving into the experiences of these women concerning 'belonging' and 'place', we can gain a strong understanding of adaptation to a new urban society as a multiple and contingent process that is itself gendered.[6]

To provide some context we need to begin with a thumbnail sketch of immigration to Quebec and the geography of immigrant settlement in Montreal. Immigration is primarily an urban phenomenon in Quebec, as elsewhere in Canada. According to 1991 census data, just under 90 per cent of all Quebec-bound immigrants live in the metropolitan Montreal area, and over 70 per cent

of these immigrants live on the Island of Montreal, with most of the remainder in off-island suburbs quite accessible to the urban core. In Montreal, as in other large Canadian cities, we have a good understanding of the residential distribution of immigrants, as well as the kinds of neighbourhoods and housing conditions in which they live (Ray, 1998; see also Chapter 9). Many newly arrived immigrants still gravitate to the urban core: 53 per cent of immigrants who arrived in the metropolitan area after 1981 lived in the City of Montreal, the Island's largest, oldest, and most densely populated municipality. At the same time, however, several suburban municipalities on the Island, such as Ville St-Laurent, Dollard-des-Ormeaux and Pointe-Claire, also have seen a significant increase in numbers of new and long-established immigrants. The residential locations of the Indian and Polish women in fact strongly exemplify this general pattern, with the vast majority living in newer inner-city neighbourhoods (e.g., Côte-des-Neiges) and the inner-suburban municipalities just mentioned (Figure 22.2).

Immigrant adaptation to Canadian society has been a sustained area of research over the decades (Canada, 1974; Ornstein and Sharma, 1981; Renaud, Desrosiers, and Carpentier, 1993), with adaptation to urban life garnering much academic and popular interest throughout this century. Studies have characterized the adaptation experience as one marked by both continuity and change, and have been sensitive to the mediations of class (Harney, 1985; Iacovetta, 1992; Lees, 1979; Mormino, 1986; Mormino and Pozzetta, 1987; Zucchi, 1988). Very few studies have differentiated the experiences of women and men (Iacovetta, 1992) or actively considered how gender might intersect with ethnicity and culture to give rise to a multiplicity of immigrant adaptation experiences and landscapes of settlement.

An important and growing body of research clearly demonstrates that limited access to language training and retraining programs and constraints imposed by child-care and household responsibilities, as well as race and gender discrimination, cre

Figure 22.2   **Place of Residence of Indian and Polish Women Interviewees at Time of Interview**

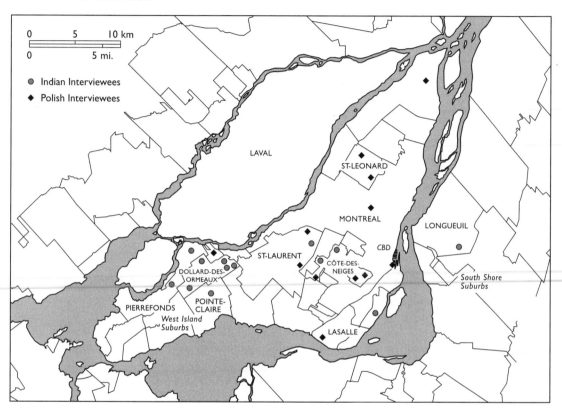

ate significant inequalities for immigrant women. Yet, as in the case of the early feminist orientation to the constraints of suburban living, by emphasizing structural factors and especially constraints we have, as Iacovetta (1992: xxvii) argues, 'learn[ed] little about how the women themselves learned to cope under these conditions and, moreover, how they have given meaning to their lives.'

To this end, learning about immigrant women's social network construction and day-to-day experiences of adaptation to and negotiation with new urban forms and cultures can furnish some key insights into how these experiences are gendered. In our project, semi-directed qualitative interviews were undertaken with a total of 49 women immigrants who had raised young children since their

arrival and who had lived in Montreal for between five and 10 years.[7]

The Indian[8] and Polish women in our study were for the most part either sponsored by family or jointly sponsored by a family member and a community organization. None were refugees, most were living in lower-middle- to middle-class households, and none could be described as wealthy; most of the women and their husbands were still trying to find employment commensurate with their level of education or skills. Only a few of the Indian women were living in owner-occupied housing whereas all of the Polish women were renters, some living in quite crowded and very modest apartments.

A good number of those who comprise the women's social networks live relatively nearby, although none of the women's networks approximate the dense ties of an urban 'ethnic village' (Gans, 1962; Harney, 1985). In general, the women consider that between a quarter and a third of their associates live in the immediate neighbourhood or within walking distance (Chicoine and Charbonneau, 1998). Although the majority of network members live beyond the bounds of the immediate neighbourhood as conventionally defined, a *sense* of neighbourhood was still significant in many women's lives either for social contacts or in the creation of a sense of belonging.

Among the Indian women we sampled, the vast majority of their networks are comprised of other Indian immigrants (82 per cent), followed by a small number of immigrants from other countries (7 per cent) and English and French Canadians (8 per cent and 2 per cent, respectively). The Polish women also tend to have quite large networks that are overwhelmingly dominated by other Poles: out of all possible ties, 77 per cent are with other Polish people and 17 per cent are with other immigrants not from Poland. Relatively few ties are with people identified as French Canadian (4 per cent) or English Canadian (2 per cent). In many ways this high degree of socializing with people from the same ethnic group is not unusual: ethnicity and language strongly delimit the boundaries of relationships (Gurdin, 1996).[9] The propensity to associate with others from one's own ethnic/linguistic group is by no means absolute, but may be more amplified in Montreal among all groups.[10]

The ethnic composition of the Indian and Polish networks thus conforms to our expectations, but while these women arrived in Montreal during the same time period and are at basically the same point in their lives as adult women, how they construct networks of friends and family and come to know and use their neighbourhoods and the city are often remarkably different. These differences begin to reveal some of the ways that gender and cultural backgrounds influence patterns of association. Among the Indian women a high proportion of network associates consist of extended family members (36 per cent). Their social relations are strongly dominated by ties with other women (85 per cent of all associates identified are women) and are frequent (several of the Indian women discussed frequent, if not daily, socializing with extended family members, especially other women). An extended family living close by is a very important part of culture and family life among many Indian migrants, and as a consequence a 'chain migration' process involving sponsorship of brothers, sisters, and parents is often a key element behind long-term settlement plans. In this sense, immigration is a collective rather than individual strategy and is reflected in the composition of social networks and the functions that these networks perform. As Das Gupta (1994) has noted, Indian women frequently regard the reconstituted and often hybrid family in Canada as a source of strength in a society where they experience marginality.

The family does not, however, share a similar structuring force among Polish migrants. Friends and acquaintances overwhelmingly dominate the networks of Polish women (91 per cent of all associates), as close family members and in-laws seldom live in Montreal or elsewhere in Canada. Family ties, while often quite important and maintained by phone calls and letters, are not immediately at hand and generally do not figure into how Polish women come to know Montreal as a city. The Polish networks are also dominated by other women (61 per cent) but by no means to the same extent as those of the Indian interviewees. In part this reflects the importance that the Polish women place upon heterosexual couples as a component of their networks, although their strongest ties are with the female half of a couple rather than both partners. It must also be noted that many people in the Polish networks were initially contacts made through their husbands—27 per cent of all contacts mentioned by the women were in their social networks by virtue of whom their husband knew. To a certain extent this reflects the more 'public' role of men in Polish organizations and social life, which potentially opens up a broader range of contacts with other Polish men and, in turn, couples. As Temple (1994: 50–1) notes, the work of Polish immigrant women in the community is relegated to 'backstage activities' such as cooking and sewing, while the work of men is based on public displays and interactions implicitly regarded as more important and truly 'Polish'. Very much reflective of patriarchal gender relations within Polish families, this interpretation was echoed by several of the women we interviewed, who indicated simply that their husbands' contacts were more important than their own, both to them and to their families.

The differences in network composition and the ways in which gender mediates relationships have an important influence on where Indian and Polish women live in the city and on the kinds of social attachments they form at a neighbourhood level. In this regard, the Indian women frequently discussed the importance of kin, especially female relatives and their families, material aid, and intra-ethnic group socializing as key issues in neighbourhood selection, although these factors could play themselves out in quite different ways between women and across neighbourhoods. On the other hand, for Polish women the neighbourhood and having either friends or kin in the immediate area were generally not very important; instead, the home itself was emphasized as a critical site where members of their extensive friendship networks were brought together for socializing.

Research about immigrant adaptation to a new society and the construction of social networks has generally emphasized the importance of neighbourhood-based contacts in furnishing a sense of belonging and identity (Hagan, 1998; Iacovetta, 1992; Yancey, Ericksen, and Juliani, 1976; Yancey, Ericksen, and Leon, 1985; Zucchi, 1988). Many of the Indian women interviewed did live in broadly defined 'Indian neighbourhoods'. This is perhaps best exemplified by 'Roshni's' social network, which is tightly woven into and around the Côte-des-Neiges neighbourhood, where she has lived since her arrival in Canada in 1987. 'Roshni' and her immediate family live in the second-floor apartment of a duplex they initially rented but now own. Her parents live in the apartment below her, and an additional eight families of relatives with whom she has close con-

tacts live either on the same street or on adjacent streets. It is extremely important for her to have these families living nearby: 'Yeah, and you never know, sometimes I am alone at home. You never know what may happen to me. Sometimes emergency call at my home and I have to leave my child somewhere.' Her network is also organized principally through the lives of other female relatives. 'Roshni' counts on these women to provide mutual aid and minor material support as well as friendship, and she points out that propinquity makes this kind of network and form of socializing possible:

> Because we always have every weekend, weekdays even, mostly, either that family or our family is going, or going to someone's house.... Even not everyone in the same area or same street but at least close enough, not living in DDO [Dollard-des-Ormeaux], LaSalle, or a far area that's hard to [get to]. This is like, you know, 'Can you come over?' and they just come over. If you are living in West Island and you say can you come over, they will say, 'No, are you crazy!'

Most of the other Indian women's associates are more dispersed, although many still stress the significance of neighbourhood-based social ties. For instance, 'Shantha' underlines the importance of living close to her husband's relatives, and in fact they lived with her brother- and sister-in-law in Pierrefonds for seven months after they arrived in Canada. When they looked for their first apartment, they deliberately chose one close to their extended family. They repeated this strategy when they looked for another apartment two years later and again when they bought their first home in 1995. Even after five years in Canada, living very close to the brother- and sister-in-law was a primary consideration. Many women emphasized the dual role that relatives, friends, and a sense of a larger Indian community played in their locational decisions. 'Vira', who now lives in DDO, initially lived with her aunt in St Hubert (a suburban South Shore municipality) and then subsequently followed her aunt to DDO, locating near her aunt's home. 'Vira' also noted that her most important contacts and friends are within the Indian community in and around her neighbourhood: 'All my community people are nearby, live nearby.' Another respondent, 'Hema', who lives in Longueuil on the South Shore, said that she felt a little isolated and lamented the fact that she does not live in an area like DDO, where many of her friends live: 'It's very far from where our friends are. They are mostly in West Island and Brossard and it's more far. Everything is difficult.'

All of the suburban women noted the existence of an informal Malayalee, Gujarati, or broader Indian community in their neighbourhood or on the West Island more generally, which allows them to feel comfortable or 'at home'. For these women, the experience of the Indian community is both highly gendered, in that their roles within it are prescribed by their sex, and intricately tied to suburban neighbourhood space as their social networks, and especially meaningful ties with other Indian women, spill beyond the walls of their homes to streets, temples, schools, and community organizations. In this way, community life in Canada, even in the suburbs, comes broadly to resemble village life in India, and is based on countless small actions and personal encounters between women in everyday neighbourhood spaces. These spaces, in a suburban context dominated by automobile use, can extend to the scale of the municipality. While the daily ties and actions of the Indian women are much less apparent than the often highly public, political, and event-oriented activities of men in community and religious organizations, they are nonetheless critical both to the development of a sense of belonging in Montreal and to the (re)construction of an Indian, Gujarati, or Malayalee identity and community.

Such strong associations between community and neighbourhood spaces are difficult to identify among the Polish women interviewed, but this does not negate the importance of locality or imply that relationships to spaces of socializing are not heavily gendered. Both Polish and Indian cultures are characterized by strongly patriarchal family structures, although the ways in which these create social ties

and a sense of belonging to a neighbourhood and ethnic community are distinctly different. As noted above, friends rather than family dominate the Polish networks, and none of the women really emphasized the neighbourhood as a community space or thought that it was particularly important to live in close proximity to their Polish friends and/or relatives. In contrast to the Indian women, the Poles stressed the importance of the home and were much more likely to crystallize their networks in place by inviting Poles from the same migration wave to their homes for informal and formal socializing. Home spaces are often where friends of friends are first introduced and where associates from other social contexts, such as a husband's work or school, are brought into the fold. Home is one of the most important sites of socializing, and the act of bringing a guest into the home implies a privileged relationship, be it new or old.

Home is certainly the most frequent site of getting together with network associates. Among the women, 76 per cent of interactions with friends took place either in their own homes or in the homes of their friends. For some of the women, all of their relationships took place in home space. The importance of home as a social space was communicated to us in some quite matter-of-fact ways, such as where women would get together to talk, but most emphatically in terms of where important occasions, such as a child's first communion and religious holidays, were celebrated. For example, as 'Magda' explained: 'Christmas is usually spent in a group of six friends.... So we organize Christmas Eve in one home, Christmas Day is spent at another home and the next day we may also meet in yet another home.... So it feels like a family really.' A number of the women echoed her words, highlighting the importance of socializing within homes that are spatially dispersed throughout the city— that these are the sites of *their* Polish community in a city of Poles from several different migration waves and that the relationships created in these spaces take on the dynamic of a surrogate family. 'Wanda', in fact, characterizes her entire network as a family:

Yes, with this group I listed, we spend a lot of time together. In different mixes often because this or that couple may not have time, but they are like a family to me in many ways. We always have a big Christmas Eve supper together. We [the women] organize it together, we all cook, each doing things we do best. And we celebrate together at someone's house.

Wanda's description of socializing is instructive beyond its emphasis on relationships constructed in particular homes. She, like other women we interviewed, noted that get-togethers, whether celebrations such as Christmas, birthdays, or name days[11] or more routine forms of socializing such as watching Polish videos, are usually organized by women but include the entire family. In this sense, the 'community work' these women undertake is largely invisible and strongly associated with their traditional gender roles in Polish households wherein women are principally seen as wives and mothers and their work as 'concerned [with] the "backstage" activities of "Polishness" rather than its public face' (Temple, 1994: 50). But the 'invisible' socializing these women do among friends in dispersed home spaces, while engaged in such 'mundane' activities as collectively preparing for Easter, Christmas, and name days, is crucial to the (re)construction of a Polish community and sense of identity in a culturally diverse city like Montreal. Here we have an excellent example of how the perpetuation of public/private distinctions undervalues immigrant women's contributions to community-building.

Both the Polish and Indian networks reveal important interrelationships among gender, culture, and space. In both groups we find strongly patriarchal family structures, that women's work in community and identity (re)building is usually relegated to the 'invisible' spaces of everyday life, and that networks are often constructed through strongly gendered relationships resulting in a de facto extended family. How these factors manifest themselves in city spaces, however, could not be more different. For Indian women, coming from a culture that emphasizes tight extended family relationships where shar-

ing of tasks among women and reciprocity between households is the social norm (Das Gupta, 1994; Nair, 1998), reconstituting such linkages in Montreal leads to the social construction of 'neighbourhoods'. In contrast, localized neighbourhood spaces are of little consequence to Polish women, whose relationships of friendship and mutual aid are instead focused on spatially dispersed homes across the city. For Polish women a sense of community is strongly rooted in diverse kinds of in-home socializing with other women and their immediate families. It is also a geography that is not constructed out of the often obligatory bonds of kinship but rather through their own acquaintances and friends, as well as those of their male partner, and through the circumstance of being Polish in a new city with few opportunities for interaction with older Polish communities.

The quite different social networks and relationships to local spaces of Indian and Polish women at the very least highlight the fallacy of a generic 'immigrant woman' experience. More importantly, however, they point to the critical role that the nexus between ethnicity and gender can play in elaborating multiple geographies of immigrant women in a city like Montreal. Gender plays an important role both in how these networks are constructed and when the networks of social relationships and, geographies become articulated in space, in shaping how women invest in creating a sense of identity and community. It is important to emphasize, however, that these social constructions also intersect with the material constraints and opportunities of real urban neighbourhoods. In this way, the mingling of the social and material conditions of everyday life gives rise to a tapestry of women's landscapes defined by difference.

Conclusion

Elizabeth Wilson, in *The Sphinx in the City* (1992), draws her readers into the intricate weave between reality and myth surrounding gender in the construction of women's and men's lives in the modern city. The myths and silences of the city are, of course, numerous and we have only broached some of them in this chapter—separate spheres of production and reproduction, the absence of women from public spaces and the workplace, the invisibility and passivity of immigrant women, the assumed inclusiveness of 'gay' spaces for lesbians. Yet these myths of women's and men's urban lives, and of the places and spaces where gendered and sexualized identities can find expression, have shaped our understandings of urban life and contributed to the creation of real material spaces. It is for these reasons that we have looked to historical research that has sought to establish the presence of women in the diverse private and public spaces of the modern city and to examine the real constraints and possibilities of their daily lives. The past reverberates through to the present in city spaces and urban lives. The multiple intersections between public and private space experienced by urban and suburban women over the past century, for instance, reveal the fallacy of the traditional and largely masculinist conception of these spheres as binary. Yet, as we have also argued, and as the everyday experiences of lesbians in Montreal's Gay Village and immigrant women demonstrate, the material power of the ideologies that support the binary myths is such that we should not assume that women's access to public space today—a key dimension of 'social citizenship' (Pratt and Hanson, 1994; Young, 1990)—is equal, equitable, assured, or unproblematic.

Gender gives rise to an array of quite different daily spaces, places, and lives in our cities, but it does so in interaction with a dense web of other social relationships, such as ethnicity, 'race' and racism, sexuality, class. We have suggested here that the expression of *multiple* identities in the everyday spaces of cities and the barriers to their expression pose challenges that all urban researchers will need to consider as we plan socially sustainable cities in the future. As our urban population continues to diversify, and as city dwellers interact across, if not transgress, the boundaries of diversity and difference, the urban myth of a singular identity of a common 'everyday geography'—woman or man, gay or straight, immigrant or Canadian, Francophone or Anglophone—will become ever more tenuous.

Notes

Both authors are equally responsible for this chapter. Suzanne Mackenzie provided vital feedback on our original chapter outline and inspirational reflections on the evolution of feminist debates in urban geography; we hope she would have approved of the final product had she lived long enough to read it. We also thank our research assistants and interviewees, without whom the research about the Gay Village and immigrant women would not have been possible. All errors and misinterpretations are entirely our own.

1. For accounts of the emergence and evolution of different strands of feminism in the Canadian context, see Backhouse and Flaherty (1992).
2. These women with 'dual roles' increased greatly after 1960. Between 1961 and 1991 the proportion of two-earner families among husband-wife families with dependent children jumped from less than 20 per cent to 71 per cent (Rose and Villeneuve, 1998: 123). By 1994, even among women with children under three years old, 56 per cent held paid employment (Statistics Canada, 1995: 64).
3. The Marxist concept of reproduction of labour-power, built on by socialist feminists, fits within the broader concept of social reproduction we referred to earlier, but places the emphasis on capitalist society's structural need for labour to be supplied by willing and able workers. In early industrial capitalism, where there seemed to be an unlimited supply of labourers, employers had virtually no interest in how the health and welfare of workers and their families were maintained. See, *inter alia*, Mackenzie and Rose (1983); Seccombe (1992: 14–22).
4. This research was undertaken by a team of researchers—J. Guindon, J. Podmore, and A. Lebrun from McGill University—led by B. Ray as one of the projects making up a research program called 'Le quartier: espace social, territoire d'intervention'. The research team is coordinated by A. Germain (INRS-Urbanisation)

and includes D. Rose and F. Dansereau (INRS-Urbanisation) and R. Morin (UQAM). (Quebec Ministry of Education, Fonds pour la Formation de Chercheurs et l'Aide à la Recherche [FCAR], Team Grant #97–ER–2605.)

5. For both groups, individuals were selected by snowball sampling. Respondents were identified by means of established contacts that interviewers already had with individuals, usually intermediaries, and several different 'balls' were created to introduce as much diversity into the samples as possible. We also eliminated individuals who were close associates of people we had already interviewed and for whom we knew, based on the earlier interview, that their experiences and social networks strongly overlapped. In the case of gay men, we deliberately sought out individuals who had been living in Centre-sud for at least two years and whose ages ranged from mid-twenties to early fifties. The lesbian respondents were also adults, although none were over 40, and were selected in part because they lived in adjacent inner-city neighbourhoods, namely the Plateau and St Louis/Mile End.

6. Information presented in this vignette originates from a project funded by the SSHRC Strategic Grant Program, Women and Change (no. 816–95–004) and undertaken by the research team of Damaris Rose, Johanne Charbonneau (INRS-Urbanisation), and Brian Ray (McGill University), together with five research assistants: Pia Carrasco, Nathalie Chicoine, Ella Chmielewska, Roopa Nair, and Van Ho.

7. The women were identified by a snowball sampling method in which contacts were made through social service and community organizations, as well as already established contacts with individuals known to the interviewers and researchers. The methodology of creating 'balls' and maintaining independence between respondents is identical to that described above in the study of Montreal's Gay Village. The 5–10-year time period of Montreal residence

recognizes that immigrant adaptation is an ongoing process that extends over a relatively long time horizon, especially so for women who, because of their more marginal economic circumstances and household/family responsibilities, can see their relationships to neighbourhood and other city spaces modified significantly when family and household circumstances change, such as following the birth of a child, a divorce, or when a husband becomes unemployed.

8. The Indian women more specifically belong to the Malayalee and Gujarati communities. Almost all are Hindu, and all are fluent or at least conversant in English. The sample of Indian women is made up of individuals who live either in multi-ethnic inner-city districts, such as Côte-des-Neiges (CDN), or in suburban municipalities, mostly in the West Island, Dollard-des-Ormeaux (DDO), Pierrefonds, and Pointe-Claire being the most important (Figure 22.2). The Polish immigrants also live predominantly on the west side of the Island of Montreal in suburban rental housing in neighbourhoods such as Ville St Laurent and LaSalle (Figure 22.2). With regard to the Polish women, it is also important to note that while many were initially sponsored by the Polish Canadian Congress, none have strong relationships to existing Polish organizations.

9. When a large and heterogeneous sample of Montrealers was asked to identify the ethnicity of their six closest friends, it was found that 'most people chose more of their closest friends from their own ethnic group, although people from all groups chose close friends from groups outside their own as well' (Gurdin, 1996: 98).

10. In contrast to US research pointing to a tendency for people with higher-status occupations to have more friends from outside their own ethnic group, Gurdin (1996) found that in Montreal occupation and education seemed to make very little difference in the ethnic composition of networks. Gurdin attributes this propensity for intra-ethnic group association to

denominational and linguistic affiliation in the education system, tensions around linguistic and identity issues in Quebec, and the real and perceived division of the city into French and English neighbourhoods. To this list we would also add a strong history within Montreal of occupational segregation by ethnicity within the labour force (Olson, 1991).

11. In Eastern Europe, people have two 'birthdays' —one on the day they were born, the other, the name day, on the anniversary of the saint after whom they are named.

References

Adler, S., and J. Brenner. 1992. 'Gender and Space: Lesbians and Gay Men in the City', *International Journal of Urban and Regional Research* 16: 24–33.

Backhouse, C., and D.H. Flaherty, eds. 1992. *Challenging Times: The Women's Movement in Canada and the United States*. Montreal and Kingston: McGill-Queen's University Press.

Beemyn, B., ed. 1997. *Creating a Place for Ourselves: Lesbian, Gay and Bisexual Community Histories*. London: Routledge.

Bell, D., and G. Valentine, eds. 1995. *Mapping Desire: Geographies of Sexualities*. London: Routledge.

Bloomfield, V., and R. Harris. 1994. 'The Journey to Work: An Historical Methodology. II. The Gendered Geography of Work'. Hamilton: McMaster University, Department of Geography, mimeo.

Bondi, L. 1994. 'Gentrification, Work and Gender Identity', in A. Kobayashi, ed., *Women, Work and Place*. Montreal and Kingston: McGill-Queen's University Press.

Bouthillette, A.M. 1997. 'Queer and Gendered Housing: A Tale of Two Neighbourhoods in Vancouver', in Ingram, Bouthillette, and Retter (1997).

Boyd, M. 1989. 'Family and Personal Networks in International Migration: Recent Developments and New Agendas', *International Migration Review* 23: 638–70.

Bradbury, B. 1993. *Working Families: Age, Gender, and Daily Survival in Industrializing Montreal*. Toronto: McClelland & Stewart.

Brais, N., and N. Chicoine. 1998. 'Des banlieues et des femmes', *Relations* 637: 18–22.

Canada, Department of Manpower and Immigration. 1974. *Three Years in Canada: First Report of the Longitudinal Survey on the Economic and Social Adaptation of Immigrants*. Ottawa: Information Canada, Catalogue MP23-37-1974-1.

Cadorette, J. 1998. 'Gay Pride. Female Trouble: The Queer Mix of Lesbian Politics', *Hour* 23 (July): 16.

Caulfield, J. 1994. *City Form and Everyday Life: Toronto's Gentrification and Critical Social Practice*. Toronto: University of Toronto Press.

Chamberland, L. 1997. 'Remembering Lesbian Bars: Montreal, 1955–1975', in V. Strong-Boag and A.C. Fellman, eds, *Rethinking Canada: The Promise of Women's History*, 3rd edn. Toronto: Oxford University Press.

———. 1998. 'La conquête d'un espace public: Les bars fréquentés par les lesbiennes', in Demczuk and Remiggi (1998).

Chambers, D. 1997. 'A Stake in the Country: Women's Experiences of Suburban Development', in R. Silverstone, ed., *Visions of Suburbia*. London: Routledge.

Chicoine, N., and J. Charbonneau, with the collaboration of D. Rose and B. Ray. 1998. 'Le processus de reconstruction des réseaux sociaux des femmes immigrantes dans l'espace montréalais', *Recherches féministes* 10, 2: 27–48.

Chouinard, V., and A. Grant. 1995. 'On Being Not Even Anywhere Near "The Project": Revolutionary Ways of Putting Ourselves in the Picture', *Antipode* 27: 137–66.

Connelly, P. 1982. 'Women's Work and the Family Wage in Canada', in A. Hoiberg, ed., *Women and the World of Work*. New York: Plenum Press.

Das Gupta, T. 1994. 'Political Economy of Gender, Race, and Class: Looking at South Asian Immigrant Women in Canada', *Canadian Ethnic Studies* 26, 1: 59–73.

Davies, W.K.D., and R. Murdie. 1993. 'Measuring the Social Ecology of Cities', in L.S. Bourne and D. Ley, eds, *The Changing Social Geography of Canadian Cities*. Montreal and Kingston: McGill-Queen's University Press.

Demczuk, I., and F.W. Remiggi, eds. 1998. *Sortir de l'ombre: Histoires des communautés lesbiennes et gaies de Montréal*. Montréal: VLB Editeur.

Dowling, R. 1998. 'Suburban Stories, Gendered Lives: Thinking through Difference', in R. Fincher and J. Jacobs, eds, *Cities of Difference*. New York: Guilford.

Duhaime, J. 1996. 'Le Village Rose', *L'Actualité*, 15 Nov.

Duncan, N. 1996. 'Renegotiating Gender and Sexuality in Public and Private Spaces', in Duncan, ed., *Body Space*. London: Routledge.

Dyck, I. 1989. 'Integrating Home and Wage Workplace: Women's Daily Lives in a Canadian Suburb', *Canadian Geographer* 33: 329–41.

England, K.V.L. 1991. 'Gender Relations and the Spatial Structure of the City', *Geoforum* 22: 135–47.

Fincher, R. 1998. 'In the Right Place at the Right Time? Life Stages and Urban Spaces', in Fincher and J. Jacobs, eds, *Cities of Difference*. New York: Guilford.

Gans, H. 1962. *The Urban Villagers*. New York: Free Press.

Gilbert, M.R. 1997a. 'Feminism and Difference in Urban Geography', *Urban Geography* 18: 166–79.

———. 1997b. 'Identity, Space and Politics: A Critique of the Poverty Debates', in J.P. Jones III, H.J. Nast, and S.M. Roberts, eds, *Thresholds in Feminist Geography: Difference, Methodology, Representation*. Lanham, Md: Rowman & Littlefield.

Gober, P., K.E. McHugh, and N. Reid. 1991 'Phoenix in Flux: Household Instability, Residential Mobility and Neighborhood Change', *Annals, Association of American Geographers* 81: 80–8.

Goheen, P.G., and B.K. Ray. 1994. 'Social Control of Public Space in Toronto: 19th Century Sodalities and 20th Century Gay Community', paper presented at the annual meeting of the Association of American Geographers, San Francisco, 29 Mar.–2 Apr.

Grant, A. 1998. 'UnWomanly Acts: Struggling Over Sites of Resistance', in R. Ainley, ed., *New Frontiers of Spaces, Bodies and Gender*. London: Routledge.

———. 1999. 'And Still, the Lesbian Threat: Or, How to Keep a Good Woman a Woman', *Journal of Lesbian Studies* (forthcoming).

Grube, J. 1997. '"No More Shit": The Struggle for Democratic Gay Space in Toronto', in Ingram, Bouthillette, and Retter (1997).

Gurdin, J.B. 1996. *Amitié/Friendship: An Investigation into Cross-Cultural Styles in Canada and the United States*. San Francisco: Austin and Winfield.

Hagan, J.M. 1998. 'Social Networks, Gender, and Immigrant Incorporation: Resources and Constraints', *American Sociological Review* 63: 55–67.

Hanson, S., and G. Pratt. 1995. *Gender, Work and Space*. New York: Routledge.

Harney, R.F., ed. 1985. *Gathering Place: Peoples and Neighbourhoods of Toronto, 1834–1945*. Toronto: Multicultural History Society of Ontario.

Harris, R. 1996. *Unplanned Suburbs: Toronto's American Tragedy, 1900–1950*. Baltimore: Johns Hopkins University Press.

Hayden, D. 1981. *The Grand Domestic Revolution: A History of Feminist Designers for American Homes, Neighbourhoods, and Cities*. Cambridge, Mass.: MIT Press.

Higgins, R. 1998. 'Des lieux d'appartenance: les bars gais des années 1950', in Demczuk and Remiggi (1998).

Iacovetta, F. 1992. *Such Hardworking People: Italian Immigrants in Postwar Toronto*. Montreal and Kingston: McGill-Queen's University Press.

Ingram, G.B., A.M. Bouthillette, and Y. Retter, eds. 1997. *Queers in Space: Communities, Public Places, Sites of Resistance*. Seattle: Bay Press.

Kinsman, G. 1987. *The Regulation of Desire: Sexuality in Canada*. Montreal: Black Rose Books.

———. 1996. *The Regulation of Desire: Homo and Hetero Sexualities*. Montreal: Black Rose Books.

Klodawsky, F., C. Lundy, and C. Andrew. 1994. 'Challenging "Business as Usual" in Housing and Community Planning: The Issue of Violence against Women', *Canadian Journal of Urban Research* 3: 40–58.

Knopp, L. 1990a. 'Exploiting the Rent-Gap: The Theoretical Significance of Using Illegal Appraisal Schemes to Encourage Gentrification in New Orleans', *Urban Geography* 11: 48–64.

———. 1990b. 'Some Theoretical Implications of Gay Involvement in an Urban Land Market', *Political Geography Quarterly* 9: 337–52.

———. 1992. 'Sexuality and the Spatial Dynamics of Capitalism', *Environment and Planning D: Society and Space* 10: 651–69.

———. 1995. 'Sexuality and Urban Space: A Framework for Analysis', in D. Bell and G. Valentine, eds, *Mapping Desire: Geographies of Sexualities*. London: Routledge.

Kobayashi, A., and L. Peake. 1994. 'Unnatural Discourse: "Race" and Gender in Geography', *Gender, Place and Culture* 1: 225–43.

Lamotte, Aleyda. 1991. 'Femmes immigrées et reproduction sociale', *Recherches sociographiques* 32: 367–84.

Le Bourdais, C., and M. Beaudry. 1988. 'The Changing Residential Structure of Montreal, 1971–81', *Canadian Geographer* 32: 98–113.

Lees, L.H. 1979. *Exiles of Erin*. Ithaca, NY: Cornell University Press.

Luxton, M. 1980. *More Than a Labour of Love: Three Generations of Women's Work in the Home*. Toronto: Women's Press.

McDowell, L. 1991. 'Life Without Father and Ford: The New Gender Order of Post-Fordism', *Transactions of the Institute of British Geographers*, New Series 16: 400–19.

———. 1993. 'Space, Place and Gender Relations: Part I. Feminist Empiricism and the Geography of Social Relations', *Progress in Human Geography* 17: 157–79.

Mackenzie, S. 1980. *Women and the Reproduction of Labour Power in the Nineteenth Century City: A Case Study*. Brighton, UK: University of Sussex, Working Papers in Urban and Regional Studies, No. 23.

———. 1986. 'Women's Responses to Economic Restructuring: Changing Gender, Changing Space', in R. Hamilton and M. Barrett, eds, *The Politics of Diversity*. London: Verso.

———. 1988. 'Building Women, Building Cities: Toward Gender Sensitive Theory in the Environmental Disciplines', in C. Andrew and B.M. Milroy, eds, *Life Spaces: Gender, Household, Employment*. Vancouver: University of British Columbia Press.

——— and D. Rose. 1983. 'Industrial Change, the Domestic Economy and Home Life', in J. Anderson, S. Duncan, and R. Hudson, eds, *Redundant Spaces? Studies in Industrial Decline and Social Change*. London: Academic Press.

Markusen, A. 1981. 'City Spatial Structure, Women's Household Work, and National Urban Policy', in C.R. Stimpson, E. Dixler, M.J. Nelson, and K.B. Yatrakis, eds, *Women and the American City*. Chicago: University of Chicago Press.

Martin, M. 1991. 'Communication and Social Forms: The Development of the Telephone 1876–1920', *Antipode* 23: 307–33.

Michelson, W. 1985. *From Sun to Sun: Daily Obligations and Community Structure in the Lives of Employed Women and Their Families*. Totowa, NJ: Rowman and Allanheld.

———. 1988. 'Divergent Convergence: The Daily Routines of Employed Spouses as a Public Affairs Agenda' in C. Andrew and B.M. Milroy, eds, *Life Spaces: Gender, Household, Employment*. Vancouver: University of British Columbia Press.

Miron, J. 1993. 'Demography, Living Arrangement and Residential Geography', in L.S. Bourne and D. Ley, eds, *The Changing Social Geography of Canadian Cities*. Montreal and Kingston: McGill-Queen's University Press.

Monk, J., and C. Katz. 1993. 'When in the World are Women?', in Katz and Monk, eds, *Full Circles: Geographies of Women over the Life Course*. London: Routledge.

Mormino, G.R. 1986. *Immigrants on the Hill*. Urbana: University of Illinois Press.

——— and G.E. Pozzetta. 1987. *The Immigrant World of Ybor City*. Urbana: University of Illinois Press.

Morton, S. 1995. *Ideal Surroundings: Domestic Life in a Working-Class Suburb in the 1920s*. Toronto: University of Toronto Press.

Nair, R. 1998. 'Renegotiating Home and Identity: Experiences of Gujarati Immigrant Women in Suburban Montréal', MA thesis, McGill University.

Newton, J. 1995. *The Feminist Challenge to the Canadian Left: 1900–1918*. Montreal and Kingston: McGill-Queen's University Press.

Ng, R. 1993. 'Sexism, Racism, Canadian Nationalism', in H. Bannerji, ed., *Returning the Gaze: Essays on Racism, Feminism and Politics*. Toronto: Sister Vision Press.

Olson, S. 1991. 'Ethnic Strategies in the Urban Economy', *Canadian Ethnic Studies* 22, 2: 39–64.

Ornstein, M.D., and R.D. Sharma. 1981. *Adjustment and Economic Experience of Immigrants in Canada: 1976 Longitudinal Survey of Immigrants*. Toronto: Institute for Behavioural Research, York University.

Peet, R. 1998. *Modern Geographical Thought*. New York: Blackwell.

Podmore, J. 1998. ' "Allons Cruiser le Saint-Laurent": Lesbian Desire and Interstitial Space in Montreal', paper presented at the annual meeting of the Association of American Geographers, Boston, 25–9 Mar.

Pratt, G., and S. Hanson. 1994. 'Geography and the Construction of Difference', *Gender, Place and Culture* 1: 5–29.

Prentice, A., P. Bourne, G.C. Brandt, B. Light, W. Mitchinson, and N. Black. 1988. *Canadian Women: A History*. Toronto: Harcourt Brace Jovanovich Canada.

Preston, V., and S. McLafferty. 1993. 'Gender Differences in Commuting at Suburban and Central Locations', *Canadian Journal of Regional Science* 16: 237–59.

———— and M. Taylor. 1981. 'Personal Construct Theory and Residential Choice', *Annals, Association of American Geographers* 71: 437–51.

Purdy, S. 1997. 'Industrial Efficiency, Social Order and Moral Purity: Housing Reform Thought in English Canada, 1900–1950', *Urban History Review* 25, 2: 30–40.

Randall, J.E., and G. Viaud. 1994. 'A Gender-Sensitive Urban Factorial Ecology: Male, Female, Grouped, and Gendered Social Spaces in Saskatoon', *Urban Geography* 15: 741–77.

Ray, B. 1998. *A Comparative Study of Immigrant Housing, Neighbourhoods and Social Networks in Toronto and Montréal*. Ottawa: Canada Mortgage and Housing Corporation.

Remiggi, F.W. 1998. 'Le Village gai de Montréal: entre le ghetto et l'espace identitaire', in Demczuk and Remiggi (1998).

Renaud, J., S. Desrosiers, and A. Carpentier. 1993. *Trois années d'établissement d'immigrants admis au Québec en 1989: Portraits d'un processus*. Montreal: Département de sociologie, Université de Montréal and Institut québécois de recherche sur la culture.

Rose, D. 1984. 'Rethinking Gentrification: Beyond the Uneven Development of Marxist Urban Theory', *Environment and Planning D: Society and Space* 2, 1: 47–74.

————. 1989. 'A Feminist Perspective of Employment Restructuring and Gentrification: The Case of Montréal', in J. Wolch and M. Dear, eds, *The Power of Geography: How Territory Shapes Social Life*. Boston: Allen and Unwin.

————. 1996. 'Economic Restructuring and the Diversification of Gentrification in the 1980s: A View from a Marginal Metropolis', in J. Caulfield and L. Peake, eds, *City Lives and City Forms: Critical Research and Canadian Urbanism*. Toronto: University of Toronto Press.

———— and C. Le Bourdais. 1986. 'The Changing Conditions of Female Single Parenthood in Montréal's Inner City and Suburban Neighborhoods', *Urban Resources* 3, 2: 45–52.

————, J. Mongeau, and N. Chicoine. 1999. *Housing Canada's Youth*. Ottawa: Canada Mortgage and Housing Corporation.

———— and P. Villeneuve. 1993. 'Work, Labour Markets and Households in Transition', in L.S. Bourne and D. Ley, eds, *The Changing Social Geography of Canadian Cities*. Montreal and Kingston: McGill-Queen's University Press.

———— and ————. 1998. 'Engendering Class in the Metropolitan City: Occupational Pairings and Income Disparities among Two-Earner Couples', *Urban Geography* 19: 123–59.

Rose, G. 1993. *Feminism and Geography*. Minneapolis: University of Minnesota Press.

Rothenberg, T. 1995. ' "And She Told Two Friends": Lesbians Creating Urban Social Space', in D. Bell and G. Valentine, eds, *Mapping Desire: Geographies of Sexualities*. London: Routledge.

Ruddick, S. 1996. 'Constructing Difference in Public Spaces: Race, Class, and Gender as Interlocking Systems', *Urban Geography* 17: 132–51.

Ryan, M.P. 1990. *Women in Public*. Baltimore: Johns Hopkins University Press.

Seccombe, W. 1992. *A Millennium of Family Change: Feudalism to Capitalism in Northwestern Europe*. London: Verso.

Séguin, A.-M. 1989. 'Madame Ford et l'espace: lecture féministe de la suburbanisation', *Recherches féministes* 2, 1: 51–68.

——— and P. Villeneuve. 1987. 'Du rapport hommes-femmes au centre de la Haute-Ville de Québec', *Cahiers de géographie du Québec* 31, 82: 189–204.

Stansell, C. 1987. *City of Women: Sex and Class in New York, 1789–1860*. Chicago: University of Illinois Press.

Statistics Canada. 1995. *Women in Canada: A Statistical Report*, 3rd edn. Ottawa: Ministry of Industry, Science and Technology, Catalogue 89–503E.

Strange, C. 1996. *Toronto's Girl Problem: The Perils and Pleasures of the City, 1880–1930*. Toronto: University of Toronto Press.

Strong-Boag, V. 1988. *The New Day Recalled*. Markham, Ont.: Penguin Books Canada.

———. 1991. 'Home Dreams: Women and the Suburban Experiment in Canada, 1945–1960', *Canadian Historical Review* 72: 471–504.

Tattelman, I. 1997. 'The Meaning at the Wall: Tracing the Gay Bathhouse', in Ingram, Bouthillette, and Retter (1997).

Temple, B. 1994. 'Constructing Polishness, Researching Polish Women's Lives: Feminist Auto/Biographical Accounts', *Women's Studies International Forum* 17: 47–55.

Valentine, G. 1992. 'Images of Danger: Women's Sources of Information about the Spatial Distribution of Male Violence', *Area* 24: 22–9.

———. 1993a. '(Hetero)sexing Space: Lesbian Perceptions and Experiences of Everyday Spaces', *Environment and Planning D: Society and Space* 11: 395–413.

———. 1993b 'Negotiating and Managing Multiple Sexual Identities: Lesbian Time-Space Strategies', *Transactions of the Institute of British Geographers*, New Series 18: 237–48.

Villeneuve, P. 1991. 'Les rapports hommes-femmes en milieu urbain: patriarchat ou partenariat?', *Cahiers de géographie du Québec* 35, 95: 385–401.

——— and D. Rose. 1988 'Gender and the Separation of Employment from Home in Metropolitan Montréal, 1971–1981', *Urban Geography* 9: 155–79.

Vincent, I. 1995. 'Ethnic Communities Definitely on the Rise', *Globe and Mail*, 1 Nov., A10.

Wekerle, G. 1981. 'Review Essay: Women in the Urban Environment', in C.R. Stimpson, E. Dixler, M.J. Nelson, and K.B. Yatrakis, eds, *Women and the American City*. Chicago: University of Chicago Press.

———. 1984. 'A Woman's Place is in the City', *Antipode* 16, 3: 11–20.

———, R. Peterson, and D. Morley. 1980. *New Space for Women*. Boulder, Colo.: Westview Press.

——— and B. Rutherford. 1989. 'The Mobility of Capital and the Immobility of Female Labor: Responses to Economic Restructuring', in J. Wolch and M. Dear, eds, *The Power of Geography: How Territory Shapes Social Life*. Boston: Unwin Hyman.

Whitzman, C. 1995. 'What Do You Want to Do? Pave Parks?', in M. Eichler, ed., *Change of Plans: Toward a Non-Sexist Sustainable City*. Toronto: Garamond Press.

Wilson, E. 1992. *The Sphinx in the City*. Los Angeles: University of California Press.

———. 1995. 'The Invisible Flaneur', in S. Watson and K. Gibson, eds, *Postmodern Cities and Spaces*. Oxford: Basil Blackwell.

Wolfe, M. 1997. 'Invisible Women in Invisible Places: The Production of Social Space in Lesbian Bars', in Ingram, Bouthillette, and Retter (1997).

Yancey, W.L., E.P. Ericksen, and R.N. Juliani. 1976. 'Emergent Ethnicity: A Review and Reformulation', *American Sociological Review* 41: 391–403.

———, ———, and G.H. Leon. 1985. 'The Structure of Pluralism: "We're All Italian Around Here, Aren't We Mrs. O'Brien?"', *Ethnic and Racial Studies* 8, 1: 94–116.

Young, I.M. 1990. *Justice and the Politics of Difference*. Princeton, NJ: Princeton University Press.

Zucchi, J.E. 1988. *Italians in Toronto: Development of a National Identity, 1875–1935*. Kingston and Montreal: McGill-Queen's University Press.

Chapter 23

Urban Homelessness in Canada

Tracy Peressini and Lynn McDonald

Few contemporary social issues have simultaneously captured the attention of the public, the media, politicians, and social scientists as much as homelessness. With the rapid expansion of the homeless population and its increasing visibility on our streets, in our parks, under our bridges, and in our public spaces, homelessness has surfaced as one of the major urban issues. Yet, for all its saliency, homelessness has not been widely researched in Canada (O'Reilly-Fleming, 1993; Peressini, 1995; Peressini, McDonald, and Hulchanski, 1995). Only a handful of studies have attempted to identify the characteristics of Canada's most vulnerable and disadvantaged population.[1] These studies depict a fluid and diverse population, which has grown as a result of the last two decades' economic and social changes and which continues to expand today. In this chapter we present a review of the contemporary research on homelessness, starting with a description of the issues and complexities involved in studying this phenomenon. Next we introduce the main explanations given to the causes of homelessness. Following this, we paint a portrait of the homeless based on original data collected from a representative and random sample of the homeless population in a mid-sized Canadian city. The chapter concludes with a brief discussion of social policy and research advancements needed to address homelessness.

Studying the Homeless

Defining Homelessness

At first glance, the task of defining who the homeless are appears to be deceptively simple. Obviously, people are homeless when they do not have a home and live on the street. That these individuals are homeless is not debatable. But, what of people who live in emergency shelters, in transitional housing for runaway youths or battered women, in abandoned or condemned buildings, in parking garages, in cars, or doubled-up with family or friends? Are these people homeless? While they are not sleeping on the streets, their shelter is temporary, substandard, or not intended for habitation. Moreover, their housing situation is extremely unstable; they are at any time susceptible to losing their housing, which would leave them with little choice but to live on the street. Should these individuals be included in the homeless category? Finally, what about the housed poor whose economic circumstances are such that a missed paycheque or a health problem would result in the loss of their housing? Again, shouldn't people whose situation is so precarious be considered as nearly homeless?

The research that has been carried out over the last two decades has used a definition of homelessness that encompasses one, a combination, or all the above types of sheltered and unsheltered poor people. In the main, however, most studies adopt the definition of homelessness proposed by the United Nations or present in the Stuart B. McKinney Homeless Assistance Act (US Congress, House of Representatives, 1987).

The UN definition considers that people are homeless when they meet one of two criteria: (1) they have no home and live either outdoors or in emergency shelters or hostels; or (2) they live in homes that do not meet UN basic standards, i.e., protection from the elements, access to safe water and sanitation, affordable price, secure tenure and personal safety, and accessibility to employment, education, and health care (Murray, 1990: 17–18). This obviously is a very comprehensive definition that includes both the 'literally homeless' and the 'precariously housed'[2] (i.e., those who possess some form of housing but who are at risk of becoming homeless) (Hopper, 1995; Jencks, 1994).

The definition specified in the Stuart B. McKinney Homeless Assistance Act (US Congress, House of Representatives, 1987), draws from the UN understanding of the 'literally homeless' but excludes people who are at risk of becoming homeless. This act defines homeless individuals as: (1) persons who lack a fixed, regular, and adequate night-time residence; or (2) persons who have a primary night-time residence that is either a supervised or publicly operated shelter designed to provide temporary living accommodation (including welfare hotels, shelters, and transitional housing for the mentally ill), an institution that provides temporary residence for individuals intended to be institutionalized, or a public or private place not designed or ordinarily used for regular sleeping purposes (Hirschl, 1990: 444–5). This more restrictive definition tends to be the one used to survey the homeless because it is less costly and easier to take a census of the homeless when one relies on a narrow definition of this phenomenon (Jencks, 1994; Koegel, Burnam, and Morton, 1996; Peressini, McDonald, and Hulchanski, 1995).

According to a new breed of definitions, the homeless are not to be viewed as a homogeneous population but, rather, as a series of sub-groups with specialized needs, who require specialized programs, services, and policies in order to address their unique type of homelessness (Wright, 1997: 20). Thus, layered over the definitions outlined above are definitions that highlight the specific circumstances faced by women, men, children, families, runaways, the elderly, older adults, the unemployed, the disabled, the mentally ill, the HIV positive, persons living with AIDS, persons with substance abuse dis-

orders, etc. In other words, these definitions shift the focus from an individual's lack of shelter to circumstances associated with personal problems and demographic characteristics (Blasi, 1990; Blau, 1992; Shlay and Rossi, 1992).

A final dimension of homelessness that needs to be taken into consideration when defining the term is duration of homelessness. At its most basic level, homelessness may be conceived of as simply the loss of one's shelter. In this sense, homelessness is defined as a static event: people lose their shelter, they become homeless, end of story. The reality is, however, more complex. As Blasi suggests, 'homelessness is not an end point but a recurring way station for the very poor' (1990: 208). In other words, homelessness is not a finite or static process, but a fluid and dynamic one, characterized by multiple transitions, role exits, and role entries. One becomes homeless, stays homeless for a period of time, and then (for a variety of reasons), becomes domiciled. Thus, homelessness is a process that occurs, and reoccurs, over time (Allgood, Moore, and Warren, 1997; Breese and Feltey, 1996; Koegel, Burnam, and Morton, 1996; Wong and Piliavin, 1997). The current research literature suggests that the majority of the homeless population experiences multiple spells of homelessness, with initial spells being of a relatively short duration, that is, from seven to 30 days, and the duration of subsequent spells becoming progressively longer, that is, from more than a month to lifetime homelessness (Peressini, 1995; Piliavin et al., 1996). Current findings also suggest that the longer people spend on the street, the more likely they are to remain homeless (Dear and Wolch, 1987; Jencks, 1994). An individual's period of homelessness, then, correlates with the number and duration of previous episodes of homelessness. Thus, expressions such as 'new homelessness', 'chronic homelessness', and 'episodic homelessness' are used to connote the variable nature of the process of homelessness, to differentiate the population based on individuals' positioning in the process, and, finally, to reflect the recurrent nature of homelessness.

Counting the Homeless

As public attention and social awareness about the homeless began to rise during the early 1980s, so did the demand for reliable and accurate information about the extent of the problem. While American social advocates argued that the size of the homeless population numbered in the millions (Hombs and Snyder, 1982), US government officials estimated the numbers to be in the order of 250,000 to 350,000 people (US Department of Housing and Urban Development, 1984). These widely divergent figures are a function of the different definitions of homelessness relied upon in these two cases. Choosing a definition constitutes a statement regarding whose social conditions and circumstances are worthy of public attention and redress, and whose are not. As Peter Rossi has commented, 'disputes over definitions ... involve defining the goals of social welfare policies and hence engage central political values' (1989: 12). In determining who is to be defined as homeless, we set the scope of current and future social programs by delineating their target population. There is thus a social philosophy dimension to debates over definitions and counts. These debates are fundamentally about the degree to which governments are responsible for caring for those who do not have the resources (for whatever reason) to care and provide for themselves (Cordray and Pion, 1991). For example, fiscally motivated governments adopt definitions that focus only on those who are 'literally' homeless. By contrast, social advocates argue that the provision of emergency programs and services is not enough. In their view, the elimination of homelessness requires preventive measures targeted at those who are susceptible to becoming homeless at any given time.

Canadian efforts to estimate the size of the homeless population provide an example of the difficulties inherent in defining and counting the homeless. There have been only two national attempts to estimate the number of homeless people in Canada. The most recent attempt was made by Statistics Canada during the 1991 census (Peressini, McDonald, and Hulchanski, 1995). In an effort to include all Canadians, Statistics Canada supplemented the regular census with an enumeration of the homeless by counting the number of people using soup kitchens in 16 Canadian cities (Begin, 1994: 5). The results of this census, however, have never been made public (Begin, 1994: 6; Peressini, McDonald, and Hulchanski, 1995: 82). Given the lack of detail about their attempt to count the homeless, it is difficult to identify the inaccuracies that prevented Statistics Canada from releasing their estimate of the homeless population in Canada. However, at least one aspect of this count stands out as a potential source of unreliability: the reliance on soup kitchens to count the homeless.

Soup kitchens provide food to a very diverse population, from those who are impoverished to those who are literally homeless. While Statistics Canada did not specify the definition of homelessness underlying the census, there is some indication that the agency intended to count only those who were 'literally' homeless (Statistics Canada, 1990: 1). If this was indeed its objective, counting persons using soup kitchens was not a suitable method because it includes some of those who are at risk of becoming homeless. It is thus not surprising that Statistics Canada concluded that their results were inaccurate and refused to release them.

The only other nationwide attempt to count the homeless in Canada was carried out by the Canadian Council on Social Development (CCSD) in conjunction with the Canada Mortgage and Housing Corporation (CMHC). Observing the International Year of Shelter for the Homeless, the CCSD carried out a national survey of temporary and emergency shelters in the winter of 1987. Using a key informant and 'count-like' strategy (Cordray and Pion, 1991: 588), the CCSD did not actually count the number of homeless, but, rather, contacted service providers and local organizations in 472 facilities across the country and asked them to report on the numbers of persons using their facility. In total, 283 facilities (59 per cent) participated in the study. Based on their findings, the CCSD reported that approximately 7,751 people slept in a shelter or hostel in Canada on any given night in 1987. As shelter users only represent a portion of the total homeless population, the CCSD combined these data with information collected from service providers, the police, and other key informants across Canada to construct their final estimate of the total population. As a result, it estimated that between 130,000 and 250,000 Canadians, representing approximately 0.5 to 1 per cent of Canada's total population, were homeless on any given night in 1987. Keep in mind that the figure of 7,751 represents the estimate of the number of homeless *in shelters* on a given night, whereas the final total is an estimate that consolidates the estimates of shelter, soup kitchen, and social services users as well as those at risk of becoming homeless. This estimate represents the only one of its kind in Canada; there is, therefore, no direct source of information with which to evaluate its accuracy. Given how the CCSD carried out its study, there are, however, a number of reasons to question the accuracy of this estimate.[3]

A comparison with estimates from the United States indicates just how problematic CCSD results may be. Table 23.1 presents a summary of the figures for the total (1991) and homeless (1987) populations of the United States and Canada. When we control for population size, the rate of Canadian

homelessness appears to be 4.5 times larger than that of the US; nine in 1,000 Canadians were homeless, as compared with two in 1,000 Americans.

These findings are, indeed, surprising. We would expect a much lower level of homelessness in Canada, given that the proportion of the population who are destitute has been consistently below that of the United States, thanks to a tighter social safety net. What can account for the disparity in the Canadian and American rates of homelessness? Answering this question brings us back to the matter of definitions. American estimates are the result of a study carried out in 1987 by the Urban Institute. The primary difference accounting for the discrepancy between Urban Institute and CCSD results concerns the definition underlying each study. The Urban Institute employed a literal definition of homelessness, which included only those who did not have a home or a permanent place to live; who resided in a shelter or hotel/motel paid for by a voucher or other instrument; who stayed in an indoor or outdoor space that was not intended for habitation; and who stayed with a relative or friend with whom they did not have a regular arrangement to stay for five or more days a week (Cordray and Pion, 1991: 589–91). The CCSD used the more comprehensive United Nations definition of homelessness cited above, which encompasses those who do not have secure homes, those whose housing is grossly inadequate, as well as those who are literally homeless (McLaughlin, 1987: 2). Thus, the American estimate is based on a more conservative definition, and, therefore, encompasses a smaller range of people than the Canadian one.

There are also considerable differences in how these definitions were operationalized in the two studies. Researchers at the Urban Institute carried out true counts and interviews with homeless adults from the selected sample of shelters or soup kitchens in 20 American cities with populations over 100,000 (Burt and Cohen, 1989). The screening instrument used the conditions in the definition cited above as the criteria given to the respondents, who, themselves, identified whether or not they met the criteria. If they identified themselves as meeting any

Table 23.1   **Canadian and US Total and Homeless Population Estimates**

	United States	Canada
Total population (1991 census)	270,661,877	27,296,859
Homeless population	600,000	250,000
No. of homeless per 1,000 persons	2/1,000	9/1,000

Sources: Burt and Cohen (1989, based on 1987 Urban Institute survey); McLaughlin (1987).

one of these conditions, they were considered to be homeless and included in the study. The CCSD, on the other hand, provided key informants and service providers with the UN definition, but did not provide any guideline as to its interpretation or application. The CCSD simply assumed that any person using the services provided by those contacted for the study was homeless.

The comparison of these Canadian and American estimates underscores problems inherent in attempts to study the homeless. Estimates vary according to definitions, and these reflect diverging philosophies, theories, and political agendas. The Canada–US comparison demonstrates that both the source of the definition and the definition itself affect our knowledge about the homeless at any given time.

Understanding Homelessness

The absence of consensus over definitions of homelessness is accompanied by disagreement about its causes and consequences (Blau, 1992; Jencks, 1994; Piliavin et al., 1996; Wong and Piliavin, 1997). Debates about the causes of homelessness have congealed into two general models or explanations: an individual model and a structural model.[4]

The Individual Model

The individual model focuses on a homeless person's social, behavioural, emotional, and psychological deficits, and emphasizes the role that personal pathology and disabilities play in the process of homelessness. From this perspective, homelessness is the result of personal limitations, of something 'wrong' with an individual (Koegel, Burnam, and Baumohl, 1996). Identified causes of homelessness are: mental or physical illness; physical disability; social disaffiliation (e.g., personal choice); social deviance (e.g., criminal behaviour, juvenile delinquency, drug and alcohol abuse); and human capital deficits (e.g., low or no education, and poor job skills and work experience). In essence, these theories argue that homelessness results from individuals'

inability to care for themselves, either because of incapacitation, choice, or a lack of social and personal resources (Devine and Wright, 1993; Jencks, 1994; Piliavin et al., 1996; Wong and Piliavin, 1997).

Liberal researchers and social advocates view these explanations as perpetuating stereotypes about the homeless (Rubin, Wright, and Devine, 1992). The overriding stereotype is that the homeless are deviants who, for a variety of reasons, have rejected mainstream values in favour of an alternative lifestyle. This model interprets drug and alcohol abuse, mental illness and disability, criminality, juvenile delinquency, unemployment, and even poverty as a matter of free will and individual choice. This perspective was particularly popular during the politically conservative 1980s and was promoted by prominent figures such as Ronald Reagan, who publicly announced that the homeless are, 'well we might say, homeless by choice' (Marcuse, 1988: 86; National Council of Welfare, 1987: 1). This interpretation was echoed by Canadian politicians, such as British Columbia's former Minister of Human Resources, Grace McCarthy, who maintained that the people claiming to be hungry and lining up at food banks are taking advantage of the public's goodwill by patronizing food banks and then spending the money they save on $17 hairdos and skis (Riches, 1986: 48). Thus, over the latter half of the 1980s much research focused on individual and behavioural correlates of homelessness, identifying individual deficits and free will as the primary explanation of homelessness.

While some of the research carried out over the last decade and a half supported these explanations, other work provided evidence to the contrary. For example, researchers have found that if mental illness is, in fact, correlated with homelessness, it only accounts for 10 to 30 per cent of the homeless (Caton et al., 1994, 1993; Linhorst, 1992; Wright, 1990).

Other research has demonstrated that mental illness is as much a consequence of homelessness as it is a cause. Insufficient evidence to support 'blaming the victim' types of explanations (Peressini, 1995; Ropers, 1990; Ryan, 1971) has caused a shift towards exploratory models that seek to uncover the 'risk factors' or 'predictors' associated with becoming, staying, and exiting homelessness (Allgood, Moore, and Warren, 1997; Rocha et al., 1996; Susser, Lin, and Conover, 1991; Wong and Piliavin, 1997). As more scientific research was conducted on homelessness, the emphasis has moved from confirming or refuting the stereotype-based individual model to identifying and describing the various demographic, personal, and behavioural antecedents of homelessness. This change of emphasis has also raised interest in the consequences of homelessness.

The Structural Model

The structural model perceives homelessness as a consequence of the social, political, and economic structures of society (Devine and Wright, 1997; Shinn and Gillespie, 1994). Increases in homelessness are viewed as a function of increased poverty and unemployment, less social housing, social welfare and health-care cut-backs, the globalization and restructuring of the economy, and gentrification (Devine and Wright, 1993, 1997; Rubin, Wright, and Devine, 1992; Shinn and Gillespie, 1994). The structural model can be broken down into two components: explanations that focus on poverty, unemployment, and housing affordability; and explanations that concentrate on gentrification and housing availability.

From the 1981–2 recession, and even more so during the 1989–92 recession, real incomes dropped (Statistics Canada, 1990). Poverty and unemployment rose and housing became less affordable (Economic Council of Canada, 1992; Shinn and Gillespie, 1994). Those who became unemployed as a result of the contracting economy saw their incomes fall precipitously and thus faced serious housing affordability problems (CMHC, 1992). For example, the Canada Mortgage and Housing Corporation reports that during the 1978 to 1986 period, 'while the proportion of income spent on shelter diminished for Canada's highest income households, it increased for the poorest households, pushing the average shelter cost-to-income ratio for

the lowest quintile above today's accepted affordability norm of thirty per cent' (1992: 2).

High unemployment and underemployment left many Canadians with little option but to rely on the social safety net at a time when benefits were being reduced (Begin, 1994; Ecumenical Coalition for Economic Justice, 1993; National Council on Welfare, 1987). This explanation thus pictures homelessness as an outcome of poverty, unemployment, and declining rates of social assistance (Burt and Cohen, 1989; Elliott and Krivo, 1991; O'Reilly-Fleming, 1993; Rossi et al., 1987; Wright, 1990). With no job there is no money, and without money and social support, there is no housing (Blau, 1992; Koegel et al., 1990; Marcuse, 1988).

As low-income households experience a fall in revenue in relation to the cost of living, it is inevitable that some will fall off the edge of the housing continuum into homelessness. But this represents only half of the explanation. The shortage of affordable housing constitutes the other half. Much of the research in this area supports the view that a lack of affordable housing is a significant factor in the rising rates of homelessness in Canada since the 1980s (Fallis and Murray, 1990).

In many Canadian cities over the last 15 years, middle-income households have invaded low-income inner-city neighbourhoods. They have renovated much of the housing stock and transformed these areas into middle-class neighbourhoods (see Chapter 12). The process, called gentrification, is associated with deindustrialization. Deindustrialization refers to the concomitant decline in manufacturing and service-sector growth, the related replacement of blue-collar by white-collar jobs, and increasing proportions of professional, technical, and administrative jobs, many of which locate downtown. Growing downtown employment fuels middle-class demand for high-quality housing adjacent to major cities' central business districts (Fallis and Murray, 1990; Jencks, 1994; Marcuse, 1988; see also Chapter 15).

Gentrification results in the 'displacement of the incumbent population' (Begin, 1994: 10), the poor, the indigent, those who cannot afford to live elsewhere. This displacement is the consequence of a number of factors. First, the gentrification process removes many low-rent dwelling units from the rental market. Converted houses once rented to several households become owner-occupied. Second, apartments are renovated and command much higher rents. And, lastly, apartments and rental houses are demolished and replaced by more expensive housing. This is particularly the case with rooming-houses and residential hotels (Begin, 1994; Blau, 1992; Fallis and Murray, 1990; O'Reilly-Fleming, 1993). The Ontario Task Force on Roomers, Boarders, and Lodgers estimated that, between 1982 and 1986, 1,700 rooms in rooming-houses per year were lost in the City of Toronto as a result of demolition and conversion (Begin, 1994: 10). Some of the poor who are displaced by this middle-class repatriation of the inner city end up in shelters and ultimately on the streets.

Finally, the impact of the removal of low-cost housing is compounded by the few affordable units built in Canada over the 1980s and 1990s by the private sector, the public sector, and the publicly assisted third sector (Begin, 1994; Fallis and Murray, 1990; Filion and Bunting, 1990; O'Reilly-Fleming, 1993). Annual levels of new dwelling units supplied under social housing programs fell during the late 1970s, rose again in 1980–1, declined for a few years, and were up and down, but mostly down, in the late 1980s (Banting, 1990). At present, the federal government and some provinces, such as Ontario, have discontinued all social housing funding. Meanwhile, repeal and relaxation of rent control by some provinces contribute to the disappearance of affordable housing.

Surprisingly, given the large number of researchers adhering to the structural model, empirical support for its propositions is mixed (for example, Blau, 1992; Elliott and Krivo, 1991; Koegel et al., 1990; Ropers, 1991; Rossi et al., 1987; Roth and Bean, 1986; Tucker, 1990). For example, Elliott and Krivo, in a study of 60 major US metropolitan areas, found inconsistent housing availability and affordability effects on rates of homelessness (1991: 122). In addition, a study carried out by Tucker

(1990) could not identify a correlation between the rates of homelessness, poverty, and unemployment across sampled cities. Conversely, Roth and Bean (1986) found that almost a quarter of their sampled homeless persons listed unemployment as the major reason for their homelessness, which led to the conclusion that homelessness is highly correlated with unemployment.

Part of the problem in adducing supporting evidence for structural explanations is the absence of a reliable database, both in Canada and the US, with which to test the structural model. To test the structural explanations of homelessness national-level longitudinal data are required. Such data would make it possible to examine the correlation between rates of homelessness and structural characteristics, such as poverty, unemployment, and housing supply.

In summary, while researchers have amassed a large amount of qualitative, anecdotal, and circumstantial evidence in support of both models of homelessness, the lack of reliable data collected from representative samples has severely limited our understanding of the process of homelessness. Still, the current research literature suggests that each model provides us with a partial explanation of the causes and consequences of homelessness. Thus, to understand homelessness, we must combine the individual and structural perspectives.

A Profile of Canada's Homeless

Canadian society consists of a *mélange* of peoples, each with different characteristics, backgrounds, and histories that have been investigated in great detail. People on its margins remain elusive, however. We have noted that our knowledge of the homeless and of the causes of homelessness is founded on stereotypes, anecdotal observations, and information from small, non-random samples that represent particular subgroups of the homeless, e.g., those with mental health problems, homeless women, homeless people with AIDS, runaways, etc. While these studies focus attention on the issue of homelessness, they have failed to provide a systematic and reliable knowledge base about even the most fundamental facet of the problem: the characteristics of the people themselves.

In this section, we use data collected from a cross-sectional study of the homeless in a mid-size Canadian city to construct a detailed picture of their social backgrounds, demographic characteristics, and history. We present an overview of the demographic and social attributes, as well as of the survival strategies, of a City of Calgary sample of homeless persons.

The Calgary Survey of the Homeless

The Calgary Survey of the Homeless was carried out as part of a larger study of Calgary's East Village community, conducted in 1990-1 by Lynn McDonald (University of Toronto) for the City of Calgary. Based on a sample design developed by Burnam and Koegel (1988) in the study of the Los Angeles skid row area, the sampling frame of the Calgary survey included all homeless adults in Calgary's downtown area who were living temporarily or permanently in shelters, visiting drop-in centres, or served by agencies and community programs providing meals to people in need. A representative sample of the homeless in Calgary's skid row was drawn using a multi-stage design. First, researchers took a census of the homeless using agencies and programs serving this population in the East Village and downtown area, as well as a census of all persons in known homeless indoor and outdoor 'hang-outs' (based on information provided by key informants and services providers). From this information, a set of sampling probabilities was derived based on the type of service provided and the number of persons using the service. This made it possible to determine the number of individuals to be selected at each of the sites across the three sampling strata: shelters, drop-in centres, and food providers. Finally, a systematic random sample within shelters, drop-in centres, and food-providing agencies was selected. Using a literal definition of homelessness, individuals were considered homeless if they did not currently have a room, apartment,

or home, or had not been in their own place within 30 days of participating in the survey (McDonald and Peressini, 1991). A total of 110 men and women were interviewed. The interview protocol included questions about: prior and current homelessness; an array of social, demographic, and background attributes; work and occupational characteristics; educational background; source and amount of income; mental and physical health problems and disabilities; alcohol and drug use; family background; social networks; and social and medical service utilization.

Limitations of the Study

There are three main limitations to the Calgary survey. First, it does not provide any means of verifying the extent to which its observations can be generalized to the homeless population of Canada as a whole. Thus, the data presented here, while representative of the homeless in Calgary in 1991, may not be representative of the total population of homeless people in Canada. Second, since we drew our sample from the population of homeless persons who used temporary or permanent shelters, drop-in facilities, and meal programs provided by community and social service agencies, it is possible that our results do not reflect the social, demographic, and economic characteristics and backgrounds of the homeless who do not rely on such services. According to Burnam and Koegel (1988), this group may encompass as much as 15 per cent of the total homeless population.

Finally, the data presented in the tables below are based on a cross-sectional survey. They pertain to measurements carried out at one point in time and, therefore, cannot be used to address changes in the size and composition of homelessness over time, or to examine the impact of Canada's evolving social, economic, and political structures on the rate of homelessness. As Hirschl notes, 'because of the dynamic nature of the homeless population, the value of cross-sectional study design is limited in comparison to longitudinal design' (1990: 454). In order to go beyond a simple description of the homeless, however, our analysis subdivides this group into two types, new or chronic, based on the length of time an individual reported being homeless. In keeping with most studies, we have chosen six months as the cut-off point for distinguishing between the new and the chronically homeless (Grigsby et al., 1990; La Gory, Ritchey, and Fitzpatrick, 1991).

Homeless Histories

The Calgary Survey of the Homeless contains a series of items about individuals' housing histories and previous experience of homelessness. Table 23.2 presents a summary of selected characteristics of the homeless, broken down by duration of homelessness.

One of most valuable pieces of information collected in the Calgary survey pertains to respondents' self-perception of their homelessness. When asked if they perceived themselves to be homeless, over 85 per cent of the newly homeless answered positively, while a much smaller proportion of the chronically homeless (65 per cent) reported that they thought of themselves as homeless. Of interest here is the change in perception over time. When asked why they did or did not think of themselves as homeless, the newly homeless said that they perceived themselves to be homeless because they did not have a home or place to live (52.7 per cent). In contrast, the majority of the chronically homeless said that they were homeless because of an absence of money or source of income (49.9 per cent). The remaining respondents said they were homeless because they were unemployed (new, 11.9 per cent; chronic, 14.4 per cent) or transient (new, 12.4 per cent; chronic, 3.1 per cent). On the other hand, those who did not see themselves as homeless said it was because their situation was temporary (new, 60.5 per cent; chronic, 27.0 per cent) or because they viewed the shelter as their home (new, 15.9 per cent; chronic, 45.0 per cent).

On average, the chronically homeless have been homeless for 37 months, were older when they first became homeless (37 years old), and have been homeless more often (three times) than the newly

homeless. By contrast, the newly homeless were homeless on average for a period of a month or less, were 28 years of age when they first became homeless, and have been homeless an average of 2.5 times. Essentially, these data suggest that the longer people are homeless, the more likely they are to experience frequent and long episodes of homelessness. In addition, it appears that the older the homeless are, the more frequent and longer are their episodes of homelessness.

Most of the homeless in the Calgary sample have had their own place at some point in their life, although about 5 per cent of the chronically homeless reported never having a place of their own. Reasons given for not presently having one's own place differ significantly according to homelessness status. The majority of the newly homeless reported that they did not have a place of their own because they had no money (48.1 per cent) or job (23.7 per cent), while the majority of the chronically homeless said that they did not have a home because they had no money (32.4 per cent) and because of the poor state of the economy (30.0 per cent).

Both the new and chronically homeless reported that they did pay rent (85.7 per cent and 81.6 per cent, respectively) in their last place of residence. On average, both groups paid around $430 for their place, which is consistent with the average rent for a one-bedroom apartment in Calgary at the time. Of the 15 to 20 per cent who said that they had not paid rent in their last place, roughly three-quarters reported that it was because they lived at home with their parents. The majority of both groups said that the reason they left their last place of residence was because they could not afford the rent (new, 42.7 per cent; chronic, 63.7 per cent).

Despite the fact that they are without a home, Calgary sample respondents seldom sleep on the street. Eighty-five per cent of the newly homeless and 81 per cent of the chronically homeless slept in shelters, and only a very small percentage of both groups reported that they slept on the street (new, 1.5 per cent; chronic, 3.4 per cent). When not sleeping on the street or in a shelter, 7.7 per cent of the newly homeless slept at either a relative's or a

Table 23.2   **Descriptive Statistics for Homeless History and Experiences by Duration of Homelessness, Calgary, 1991**

Variable Description	Newly Homeless	Chronically Homeless
% who perceive themselves to be homeless*:	87.0%	65.2%
Reasons for perceiving self to be homeless*:		
No home or place to live	52.7%	32.6%
No money or source of income	22.9%	49.9%
Unemployed	11.9%	14.4%
Transient	12.4%	3.1%
Duration of current homelessness (mos)*: $\mu(\sigma)$	1.38(1.31)	37.44(60.91)
Age first became homeless (years)*: $\mu(\sigma)$	28.27(10.99)	30.87(11.59)
Number of times homeless*: $\mu(\sigma)$	2.62(2.55)	3.12(2.87)
% who have ever had a place of their own*:	100.0%	95.3%
Main reason for not currently having a place*:		
No money	48.1%	32.4%
No job	23.7%	9.7%
No welfare	1.6%	0.0%
No unemployment insurance	3.1%	3.2%
Family crisis	3.0%	3.4%
Health (mental or physical) problems	4.6%	6.6%
No job skills	0.0%	3.2%
The economy	8.6%	30.0%
No affordable housing	3.1%	6.4%
Don't know anyone to live with	0.9%	1.8%
Don't need or want a place of own	1.6%	0.0%
Transient	1.6%	3.4%
% who paid rent in the last place they lived:	85.7%	81.6%
Reason for leaving last place of residence*:		
Couldn't afford the rent	42.7%	63.7%
Building was torn down or condemned	4.7%	6.4%
Evicted	24.0%	0.0%
Family conflict	15.8%	16.7%
Left to look for work	12.7%	13.1%
Where typically sleeps*:		
Shelter	85.3%	81.1%
Street or river bank	1.5%	3.4%
At a relative's	3.0%	0.0%
At a friend's	4.7%	9.3%
In a hotel or rented room	5.5%	6.2%

Table 23.2   *(continued)*

Where typically eats*:		
Soup line	12.4%	13.1%
At a shelter or hostel	74.7%	68.3%
Buys own food	5.3%	13.8%
At a friend's or relative's	7.6%	4.7%

Note: μ(σ) = mean(standard deviation).
*Significant differences between the newly and chronically homeless at α ≤ 05. Tests of significance calculated using unweighted data.

friend's place, and 5.5 per cent slept in a hotel or rented room. Similarly, 9.3 per cent of the chronically homeless slept at the home of friends and 6.2 per cent in a hotel or rented room.

Not surprisingly, the eating patterns of the homeless are consistent with their sleeping habits. Put simply, the homeless eat where they sleep. For example, roughly 75 per cent of the newly homeless and 68 per cent of the chronically homeless received their meals from shelters. Just over one-tenth of the homeless, either new (12.4 per cent) or chronic (13.1 per cent), ate at the various soup lines and kitchens in the community. The remaining portion of the homeless ate at the homes of either friends or relatives (new, 7.6 per cent; chronic, 4.7 per cent), or purchased their own food (new, 5.3 per cent; chronic, 13.8 per cent).

The Sociodemographic Characteristics of the Homeless

Sutherland and Locke in their 1936 study of the homeless in Chicago first postulated that the primary reason people became and remained homeless was low income and lack of education, job skills, and work experience. Other researchers have suggested that a number of factors predispose an individual to homelessness, and that these factors raise the likelihood of someone becoming homeless while decreasing possibilities of exiting homelessness. These factors include age, gender, marital status, ethnic background, and parental socio-eco-

nomic status, characteristics associated with the availability of the personal resources that influence life chances.

Table 23.3 presents a variety of demographic and economic attributes broken down by newly and chronically homeless status. Characteristics of the Calgary sample are loosely consistent with those observed in previous research. For example, while the average age of the homeless in this study was 33.56, the literature suggests that the homeless tend to fall into the 'young' middle-age category (e.g., 32-9). This figure corresponds exactly to the Canadian population's median age of 33.5 (Statistics Canada, 1992a: 1). The Calgary sample's 9:1 male-female ratio is somewhat higher than the 4:1 to 7:1 ratios reported in the literature.

The Calgary sample is primarily made up of single men, with 84.6 per cent of the newly homeless reporting that they were single, separated, divorced, or widowed, and an overwhelming majority (97.0 per cent) of the chronically homeless fall within these categories (see also Fallis and Murray, 1990). These figures are much higher than the proportion of single Canadians. Statistics Canada (1992a) reports that approximately 46 per cent of the Canadian population (male and female) is single, separated, divorced, or widowed.

The Calgary survey is composed of individuals who were born in the three primary regions of Canada from which people migrate to Calgary: Ontario, the prairies (primarily Alberta), and British Columbia (Dumas and Lavoie, 1992). Calgary find-

Table 23.3   **Descriptive Statistics for Selected Social and Demographic Characteristics by Duration of Homelessness, Calgary, 1991**

Variable Description	Newly Homeless	Chronically Homeless
Age*: $\mu(\sigma)$	31.97(13.10)	36.78(9.77)
Gender*:		
Men	87.4%	97.0%
Women	12.6%	3.0%
Place of Birth*:		
Maritimes	6.2%	6.5%
Quebec	7.7%	3.0%
Ontario	31.8%	26.1%
Prairies	34.3%	50.3%
British Columbia	10.8%	9.4%
NWT	1.6%	0.0%
Outside Canada	7.7%	4.7%
Marital status*:		
Single	64.8%	65.4%
Married	4.5%	0.0%
Separated	1.5%	5.1%
Common-law	10.9%	3.0%
Divorced	16.8%	24.8%
Widowed	1.5%	1.7%
Ethnic background*:		
Canadian	37.5%	43.8%
Aboriginal	11.5%	8.1%
United Kingdom	29.0%	31.7%
W. Europe	9.3%	0.0%
E. Europe	1.6%	11.4%
Other	11.1%	5.0%
Education—years of schooling*: $\mu(\sigma)$	10.92(2.18)	10.37(2.37)
Current Occupation*:[a]		
Professional	1.5%	0.0%
Skilled worker	0.0%	4.9%
Farm worker	0.0%	3.0%
Semi-skilled worker	88.8%	67.2%
Unskilled	9.8%	24.6%
Current labour force status*:		
Unemployed	84.1%	75.0%
Employed seasonally	7.5%	9.5%
Employed part-time	2.3%	3.0%
Employed full-time	6.2%	12.5%

Table 23.3   (continued)

Length of time unemployed (in months): $\mu(\sigma)$	11.73(34.80)	13.24(25.13)
Type of problems finding employment*:		
No jobs available	23.0%	23.1%
Lack of education or work experience	29.2%	27.1%
No transportation	9.0%	25.8%
Too old—no one will hire	9.6%	24.0%
Health problems (mental & physical)	12.4%	0.0%
Recession—economy	6.9%	0.0%
Will not work for minimum wage	10.0%	0.0%
Looked for employment in last year*:	68.7%	55.7%
Weekly income from all sources*: $\mu(\sigma)$	100.27(99.74)	120.29(158.92)*
Source of income per month*:		
Work:	31.0%	54.6%
Social Assistance:	13.3%	9.4%
Unemployment Insurance:	19.5%	4.6%
Bottle Sales:	2.9%	12.5%

Note: $\mu(\sigma)$ = mean(standard deviation).

*Significant differences between the newly and chronically homeless at $\alpha \leq 05$. Significance tests calculated with unweighted data.

[a] Occupational categories, socio-economic status (SES), and social class derived by recoding standard occupational codes using Pineo, Porter, and McRoberts (1977) socio-economic classification of occupations.

ings concerning the ethnic background of homeless persons deviate somewhat from the results of other research. In the Calgary sample approximately 10 per cent of the homeless were of Native ancestry, while other Canadian studies have indicated that anywhere from one-third to one-half of the homeless belong to this group. On the other hand, Aboriginals are overrepresented in the Calgary sample when considered in the light of their 2 per cent proportion of the national population (Statistics Canada, 1992a, 1992b).

The average level of education for the homeless reported in the literature is 10 years (Fallis and Murray, 1990). The Calgary homeless displayed similar levels, with respondents reporting, on average, 10.74 years of education. Looking at educational levels across homeless status, we note that the newly homeless tend to have slightly more formal education, 10.92 years, than their chronic counterparts, 10.37 years. In addition, approximately 40 per cent of the newly homeless and 35 per cent of the chronically homeless reported additional educational training (e.g., job training programs, trade schools). Thus, while the majority of the homeless had not finished high school, many had pursued other avenues of education and training—a finding supported by other research (see Blau, 1992; O'Reilly-Fleming, 1993).

Stereotypes of the homeless as lazy, unemployed, and uninterested in working have lost much of their currency in the literature. Researchers are becoming aware that a majority of the homeless want to work and actively seek employment when out of work (Blau, 1992; Fallis and Murray, 1990; O'Reilly-Fleming, 1993). The data in Table 23.3 confirm this observation by demonstrating that the homeless put considerable time and effort into working or finding work.

Work patterns of the chronically homeless depart significantly from those of the newly homeless. In addition to experiencing longer periods of unemployment, the chronically homeless tended to be employed less often and in multiple jobs that are temporary in nature, lasting anywhere from one day to three weeks. In other words, the longer people are homeless, the less likely they are to find a job, and when they do, the less likely it is that this job will be permanent. It is noteworthy that even though the newly homeless were more likely to be employed than the chronically homeless, both groups spent as much time looking for work. Although a higher percentage of the newly homeless (68.7 per cent) than the chronically homeless (55.7 per cent) reported looking for work in the last year, there is no significant difference between the two in terms of the amount of time devoted to seeking employment. After their last period of employment, both groups of homeless reported spending 16 weeks, on average, looking for work. In addition, roughly the same percentage of respondents in both groups reported that the main problem they experienced in finding work was a lack of education and/or work experience (new, 29.2 per cent; chronic, 27.1 per cent).

When taken in tandem, the data presented here paint a picture reminiscent of the employment pattern described by Fallis and Murray as the 'casual labour syndrome' (1990: 37). This syndrome refers to a downward spiralling process where, because of a lack of marketable skills, education, and experience, the homeless are confined to the casual labour office for their employment search. As Fallis and Murray note, 'escaping the casual-labour syndrome is next to impossible' (ibid.). The longer they are on the street, the less employable are the homeless. They become totally dependent on a day-to-day

fixed income that covers only their primary expenses: food, occasional shelter, and perhaps a few other odds and ends. Their employment situation leaves them with no resource with which to extricate themselves from homelessness.

The data on income presented in Table 23.3 further support these observations. When queried about their income, the homeless, both new and chronic, reported on average one source of income. However, they differed markedly in terms of the nature of their main source of income. Roughly one-third of the newly homeless and well over 50 per cent of the chronically homeless reported work as their main source of income (the corresponding figure for the Canadian population as a whole is 78 per cent [Statistics Canada, 1994: 22]). Moreover, not only did a significantly higher percentage of the chronically homeless report employment as their main source of income, but they also reported significantly more income from this source than the newly homeless did ($365 vs $216 a month). The remainder of the surveyed homeless reported their main source of income as social assistance (new, 13.3 per cent; chronic, 9.4 per cent), unemployment insurance (new, 19.5 per cent; chronic, 4.6 per cent), and bottle sales (new, 2.9 per cent; chronic, 12.5 per cent). Discrepancy in proportions of chronic and newly homeless receiving unemployment insurance payments reflects eligibility rules and time limits on benefits (McGilly, 1990). Not only did fewer of the chronically homeless receive unemployment insurance benefits, but the amount they received is one-sixth of that of the newly homeless. On average, the unemployment insurance benefits for the newly homeless were worth about $103 a month, while the chronically homeless received $16 a month from this source. Finally, the income of roughly 16 per cent of the sample originated from social assistance. Given that the majority of people in this sample were single men aged 18-34, these findings reflect the stringent eligibility rules for social assistance (that is, if you are young and male you are expected to find work).

On average, the newly homeless reported a total weekly income of approximately $100, while the chronically homeless indicated having $120 a week to live on. The incomes of the homeless ranged from $400 to $480 dollars a month, barely enough to cover the rent on a one-bedroom apartment in Calgary during the study time period—$407 a month—let alone other subsistence needs (Sarlo, 1992: 9).

Comparing these figures with the 1991 Canadian Council of Social Development's $280 a week poverty line for a single person in Calgary, we observe that the homeless, regardless of how long they have been on the street, survive on incomes that are two-thirds lower than the poverty line. The large discrepancy between their present incomes and those for the previous year, which were 25 (chronic) to 40 (new) per cent above the poverty line, points to a sharp deterioration in their financial situation. But the positive relationship between income and length of homelessness indicates that incomes increase with the amount of time spent homeless. This underscores the resourcefulness of the homeless; the longer they spend on the street, the better become their skills at 'getting by'.

In summary, these data suggest that the homeless tend to be single, male, poor, undereducated, and unemployed. Some are transient, but many are not. They have lived in a variety of places, but they also tend to 'stay put' in one place for a long period of time. They have had a place of their own for which they paid rent. They often have families and friends; they are not social outcasts who have abandoned mainstream norms and values in favour of a homeless lifestyle. In fact, there is every indication that 'homeless life' holds little attraction for them. Thus, the homeless do not represent a deviant subculture. Rather, they are members of Canadian society who have been abandoned at a time when they most require assistance. Finally, there is much more to the lives of the homeless than being poor, undereducated, and unemployed. The findings contradict the stereotype that portrays the homeless as idle and dependent on welfare and unemployment

benefits. A high proportion of the homeless work, generally on a casual or day-to-day basis, or seek employment opportunities.

Not Only a National Disaster, But a National Disgrace

In this chapter, we have presented an overview of the contemporary research literature on homelessness and of salient issues surrounding this phenomenon in Canada. We have also presented a detailed profile of the homeless. The analysis and data presented in this chapter demonstrate that what we do not know about the homeless in Canada far outweighs what we do know. This is in large part due to the absence of a systematic database that would allow a testing of theoretical perspectives on homelessness. With the passing of a resolution by Toronto City Council declaring homelessness a national disaster (DeMara, 1998) and editorials depicting homelessness not just as a national disaster but as a national disgrace (James, 1998), we do, however, know that homelessness has become an important social issue.

With the enduring nature of homelessness, Canadians realize that contemporary urban homelessness is a problem that is 'large-scale, permanent and independent of the short-term business cycle, a combination never before existing in an advanced industrial society. It represents the inability of the market and the unwillingness of the state to care for the most basic needs of a significant segment of the population' (Marcuse, 1988: 359). This is most apparent in Canada's national legislation, policy, and programs regarding the homeless. As Gerald Daly notes, there is no national legislation, policy, or program pertaining to the homeless in Canada (1996: 25). Thus, as the media lament the lot of Canada's homeless and local governments attempt to meet the needs of the homeless with resources increasingly constrained by senior government downloading (Daly, 1996), the federal government responds to the crisis of homelessness by pondering the possibility of creating a cabinet committee to study the issue (Walker,

1998). Yet, every winter we are reminded by exposure casualties on Canada's streets that homelessness is often a matter of life and death, and not just another political issue requiring a national inquiry.

Notes

1. See, for example: Begin, 1994; Fallis and Murray, 1990; Golden et al., 1998; Hulchanski et al., 1991; McDonald and Peressini, 1991; McLaughlin, 1987; O'Reilly-Fleming, 1993; Peressini, 1995.

2. This concept is similar to the Canadian concept of 'core housing need'. Briefly, core housing need is defined in a two-step process. First, it is established whether the household suffers from one of three basic housing problems: adequacy, suitability, and affordability. Second, if one or more of these problems are present, to qualify a household's income must be insufficient to solve the problem, e.g., inability to find suitable housing for less than 30 per cent of income (CMHC, 1991; Peressini, McDonald, and Hulchanski, 1995). In 1991, CMHC reports that just under two million households lived below one of the above two standards and about one million were deemed to be in core housing need. Within the context of the UN definition of homelessness, then, roughly 4 per cent of the Canadian population was in 1991 'at risk' of becoming homeless.

3. The CCSD study is based only on a partial count of the population (Rossi, 1989: 52–61). The CCSD data include only shelter users, and exclude that part of the homeless population who slept with friends, on the streets, or in low-rent hotels (McLaughlin, 1987). Moreover, the CCSD did not ask key informants to report the actual number of persons using their facility on a given night, but, rather, relied on these informants' knowledge of the population they serve and their estimate of the number of persons using the facility on an average night. Finally, the CCSD combined shelter estimates with a further set of estimates obtained by other key informants about the number of homeless in the communities participating in the survey (McLaughlin, 1987). Apart from its reliance on second-hand sources of information, the CCSD's final estimate is questionable because it was obtained by compounding estimates, which yields results that may or may not be accurate. Martha Burt notes that opinions of key informants (e.g., service providers, social advocates) tend to be unreliable. This is mainly due to the fact that most of the providers and other individuals working with the homeless only have direct contact with those that use their service and, therefore, do not have any reliable knowledge or information about those homeless who do not use their service (Burt, 1991: 24). Thus, the CCSD's estimate amounts to nothing more than a 'guesstimate', or what Rossi has termed a heroic extrapolation from partial counts (1989: 56).

4. For a detailed overview of the structural and individual theories of homelessness, see Burt, 1993; Fallis and Murray, 1990; Jencks, 1994; O'Reilly-Fleming, 1993; Peressini, 1995; Ropers, 1990; Rossi, 1989.

References

Allgood, S., M.L. Moore, and R.S. Warren, 1997. 'The Duration of Sheltered Homelessness in a Small City', *Journal of Housing Economics* 6: 60–80.

Banting, K.G. 1990. 'Social Housing in a Divided State', in G. Fallis and A. Murray, eds, *Housing the Homeless and Poor: New Partnerships among the Private, Public and Third Sectors*. Toronto: University of Toronto Press.

Begin, P. 1994. *Homelessness in Canada*. Ottawa: Minister of Supply and Services.

Blasi, G.L. 1990. 'Social Policy and Social Science Research on Homelessness', *Journal of Social Issues* 46, 4: 207–19.

Blau, J. 1992. *The Visible Poor: Homelessness in the United States*. New York: Oxford University Press.

Breese, J., and K. Feltey. 1996. 'Role Exit from Home to Homeless', *Free Inquiry in Creative Sociology* 24, 1: 67–76.

Burnam, M.A., and P. Koegel. 1988. 'Methodology for Obtaining a Representative Sample of Homeless Persons: The Los Angeles Skid Row Study', *Evaluation Review* 12, 2: 117–52.

Burt, M.A. 1991. 'Causes of the Growth of Homelessness During the 1980s', *Housing Policy Debate* 2: 903–36.

———. 1993. *Over the Edge: The Growth of Homelessness in the 1980s*. New York: Russell Sage Foundation.

——— and B.E. Cohen. 1989. *America's Homeless: Numbers, Characteristics, and Programs that Serve Them*. Washington: Urban Institute Press.

Caton, C.L.M., P.E. Shrout, P.F. Eagle, L.A. Opler, A. Felix, and B. Dominguez. 1994. 'Risk Factors for Homelessness among Schizophrenic Men: A Case-Control Study', *American Journal of Public Health* 84: 265–70.

———, R.J. Wyatt, A. Felix, J. Gruntberg, and B. Dominguez. 1993. 'Follow-Up of Chronically Homeless Mentally Ill Men', *American Journal of Psychiatry* 150: 1639–42.

CMHC (Canada Mortgage and Housing Corporation). 1991. *Core Housing Need in Canada*. Ottawa: CMHC.

———. 1992. 'A Comparison of Housing Needs Measures Used in Canada, the United States and England', *CMHC Socio-economic Series: Research & Development Highlights*. Ottawa: CMHC.

Cordray, D.S., and G.M. Pion. 1991. 'What's Behind the Numbers? Definitional Issues in Counting the Homeless', *Housing Policy Debate* 2: 587–616.

Daly, G. 1996. *Homeless: Policies, Strategies and Lives on the Street*. New York: Routledge.

Dear, M., and J. Wolch. 1987. *Landscapes of Despair: From Deinstitutionalization to Homelessness*. Princeton, NJ: Princeton University Press.

DeMara, B. 1998. 'Relief for Homeless Pledged', *Toronto Star*, 29 Oct.

Devine, J.A., and J.D. Wright. 1993. *The Greatest of Evils: Urban Poverty and the American Underclass*. New York: Aldine de Gruyter.

——— and ———. 1997. 'Losing the Housing Game: The Leveling Effects of Substance Abuse', *American Journal of Orthopsychiatry* 67: 618–31.

Dumas, J., and Y. Lavoie. 1992. *Report on the Demographic Situation in Canada 1992*. Ottawa: Minister of Industry, Science and Technology. Statistics Canada Catalogue No. 91–209E.

Economic Council of Canada. 1992. *The New Face of Poverty: Income Security Needs of Canadian Families*. Ottawa: Minister of Supply and Services.

Ecumenical Coalition for Economic Justice. 1993. *Reweaving Canada's Social Programs: From Shredded Safety Net to Social Solidarity*. Toronto: Ecumenical Coalition for Economic Justice.

Elliott, M., and L.J. Krivo. 1991. 'Structural Determinants of Homelessness in the United States', *Social Problems* 38: 113–31.

Fallis, G., and A. Murray. 1990. *Housing the Homeless and Poor: New Partnerships among the Private, Public and Third Sectors*. Toronto: University of Toronto Press.

Filion, P., and T.E. Bunting. 1990. *Affordability of Housing in Canada*. Ottawa: Minister of Supply and Services. Statistics Canada Catalogue No. 98–130.

Golden, A., W.H. Currie, E. Greaves, and J. Latimer. 1998. *Breaking the Cycle of Homelessness: Interim Report of the Mayor's Homelessness Action Task Force*. Toronto: City of Toronto.

Grigsby, C., D. Baumann, S.E. Gregorich, and C. Roberts-Gray. 1990. 'Disaffiliation to Entrenchment: A Model for Understanding Homelessness', *Journal of Social Issues* 46, 4: 141–56.

Hirschl, T. 1990. 'Homelessness: A Sociological Research Agenda', *Sociological Spectrum* 10: 443–67.

Hombs, M.E., and M. Snyder. 1982. *Homelessness in America: A Forced March to Nowhere*. Washington: Community for Creative Non-Violence.

Hopper, K. 1995. 'Definitional Quandaries and Other Hazards in Counting the Homeless: An Invited Commentary', *American Journal of Orthopsychiatry* 65: 340–6.

Hulchanski, J.D., M. Eberle, K. Olds, and D. Stewart. 1991. *Solutions to Homelessness: Vancouver Case Studies.* Vancouver: UBC Centre for Human Settlements.

James, R. 1998. 'Homeless Get Spotlight They Deserve', *Toronto Star*, 30 Oct.

Jencks, C. 1994. *The Homeless.* Cambridge, Mass.: Harvard University Press.

Koegel, P., A. Burnam, and J. Baumohl. 1996. 'The Causes of Homelessness', in Baumohl, ed., *Homelessness in America.* Phoenix, Ariz.: Oryx Press.

———, ———, and R.K. Farr. 1990. 'Subsistence Adaptation Among Homeless Adults in the Inner City of Los Angeles', *Journal of Social Issues* 16, 4: 83–107.

———, ———, and S. Morton. 1996. 'Enumerating Homeless People: Alternative Strategies and Their Consequences', *Evaluation Review* 20: 378–403.

La Gory, M., F. Ritchey, and K. Fitzpatrick. 1991. 'Homelessness and Affiliation', *Sociological Quarterly* 32: 201–18.

Linhorst, D.M. 1992. 'A Redefinition of the Problem of Homelessness Among Persons with a Chronic Mental Illness', *Journal of Sociology and Social Work* 17, 4: 43–56.

McDonald, L., and T. Peressini. 1991. *The East Village Community Study: Final Report.* Calgary: City of Calgary.

McGilly, F. 1990. *An Introduction to Canada's Public Social Services: Understanding Income and Health Programs.* Toronto: McClelland & Stewart.

McLaughlin, M.A. 1987. *Homelessness in Canada: The Report of the National Inquiry.* Ottawa: Canadian Council on Social Development.

Marcuse, P. 1988. 'Neutralizing Homelessness', *Socialist Review* 1: 69–97.

Murray, A. 1990. 'Homelessness: The People', in G. Fallis and A. Murray, eds, *Housing the Homeless and Poor: New Partnerships among the Private, Public and Third Sectors.* Toronto: University of Toronto Press.

National Council on Welfare. 1987. *Welfare in Canada: The Tangled Safety Net.* Ottawa: Minister of Supply and Services.

O'Reilly-Fleming, T. 1993. *Down and Out in Canada: Homeless Canadians.* Toronto: Canadian Scholars' Press.

Peressini, T. 1995. 'Disadvantage, Drift and Despair: A Study of Homelessness in Canada', Ph.D. dissertation, University of Waterloo.

———, L. McDonald, and D. Hulchanski. 1995. *Estimating Homelessness: Towards a Methodology for Counting the Homeless in Canada.* Ottawa: Canada Mortgage and Housing Corporation.

Piliavin, I., B. Wright, R. Mare, and A. Westerfelt. 1996 'Exits from and Returns to Homelessness', *Social Service Review* (Mar.): 33–57.

Pineo, P.C., J. Porter, and H.A. McRoberts. 1977. 'The 1971 Census and the Socioeconomic Classification of Occupations', *Canadian Review of Sociology and Anthropology* 14: 91–102.

Riches, G. 1986. *Food Banks and the Welfare Crisis.* Ottawa: Canadian Council on Social Development.

Rocha, C., A. Johnson, K. McChesney, and W. Butterfield. 1996. 'Predictors of Permanent Housing for Sheltered Homeless Families', *Families in Society: The Journal of Contemporary Human Services* (Jan.): 50–7.

Ropers, R.H. 1990. *Persistent Poverty: The American Dream Turned Nightmare.* New York: Plenum Press.

Rossi, P.H. 1989. *Down and Out in America: The Origins of Homelessness.* Chicago: University of Chicago Press.

———, J.D. Wright, G.A. Fisher, and G. Willis. 1987. 'The Urban Homeless: Estimating Composition and Size', *Science* 235: 1336–41.

Roth, D., and G. Bean. 1986. 'New Perspectives on Homelessness: Findings from a Statewide Epidemiological Study', *Hospital and Community Psychiatry* 37: 712–19.

Rubin, B.A., J.D. Wright, and J.A. Devine. 1992. 'Unhousing the Urban Poor: The Reagan Legacy', *Journal of Sociology and Social Welfare* 19: 111–47.

Ryan, W. 1971. *Blaming the Victim.* New York: Pantheon Books.

Sarlo, C. 1992. *Poverty in Canada.* Vancouver: Fraser Institute.

Shinn, M., and C. Gillespie. 1994. 'The Roles of Housing and Poverty in the Origins of Homelessness', *American Behavioral Scientist* 37: 505–22.

Shlay, A., and P. Rossi. 1992. 'Social Science Research and Contemporary Studies of Homelessness', *Annual Review of Sociology* 18: 129–60.

Statistics Canada (Methodology Branch, Social Survey Methods Division). 1990. *Census Test of Enumeration in Soup Kitchens*, Working Paper # SSMD–90–006 B. Ottawa: Statistics Canada.

Statistics Canada. 1992a. *Age, Sex and Marital Status: The Nation*. Ottawa: Minister of Industry, Science and Technology.

———. 1992b. *Profile of Census Divisions and Subdivisions in Alberta—Part A*. Ottawa: Ministry of Industry, Science and Technology.

———. 1994. *Profile of Census Divisions and Subdivisions in Alberta—Part B*. Ottawa: Ministry of Industry, Science and Technology.

Susser, E.S., S.P. Lin, and S.A. Conover. 1991. 'Risk Factors for Homelessness Among Patients Admitted to a State Mental Hospital', *American Journal of Psychiatry* 148: 1659–64.

Tucker, W. 1990. *The Excluded Americans: Homelessness and Housing Policies*. Washington: Regnery Gateway.

United States Congress, House of Representatives. 1987. *Stewart B. McKinney Homeless Assistance Act, Conference Report to Accompany H.R. 558, 100th Congress, 1st Session*. Washington: U.S. Government Printing Office.

United States Department of Housing and Urban Development (Office of Policy Development and Research). 1984. *A Report to the Secretary on the Homeless and Emergency Shelters*. Washington: Department of Housing and Urban Development.

Walker, W. 1998. 'Ottawa May Tackle Homeless', *Toronto Star*, 4 Nov.

Wong, Y., and I. Piliavin. 1997. 'A Dynamic Analysis of Homeless-Domicile Transitions', *Social Problems* 44: 408–24.

Wright, J.D. 1990. 'Poor People, Poor Health: The Health Status of the Homeless', *Journal of Social Issues* 46, 4: 49–64.

Wright, T. 1997. *Out of Place: Homeless Mobilizations, Subcities and Contested Landscapes*. New York: State University of New York Press.

Chapter 24

Power and Decision-Making in the City: Political Perspectives

Paul Villeneuve and Anne-Marie Séguin

This chapter examines power relations in Canadian cities over the last 50 years.[1] It first articulates the notions of social category, territory, conflict, and strategy into a framework that highlights the role of class, gender, and ethnicity in the exercise of power at the municipal level. This framework distinguishes three broad political phases in Canadian cities since World War II. It relates transitions in power relations on the municipal scene to prevailing national economic and policy contexts.

The first phase, that of the late industrial city, extends roughly to the mid-1960s. Power relations were then influenced by postwar prosperity and by the industrial character of Canadian urban areas. The emphasis was on efficient city management and the predominant view was that cities should be run like businesses. During the late sixties and the seventies, the importance of tertiary activities grew at the expense of manufacturing. This evolution prompted changes in class, gender, and ethnic relations, which in turn gave rise to the transition in urban politics that characterizes the second phase. The political climate shifted as citizen participation in urban affairs challenged the pure efficiency-based approach to municipal policy-making. A leading role in municipal politics was taken by a new middle class whose growth was associated with the rise of the tertiary sector and that conveyed feminist and environmental values. Expansion in public-sector intervention capacity encouraged pressures for new and enlarged programs. More recently, during the eighties, the welfare state, whose national and provincial development was partly a response to the politics of the new middle class, was strained

by globalization tendencies. This situation ushered in a third phase in urban politics, characterized by a search for renewed forms of local decision-making giving prominence to public-private partnerships. To be sure, the precise timing and configuration of each of these three broad phases vary somewhat from city to city, but similarities across cities reflect the impact of broad economic and policy-making tendencies.

Power: An Elusive Concept

Defining Power

Strictly speaking, power is not possessed, it is exercised (Foucault, 1976). In its broadest understanding, it is present in every social relation, whether between individuals, groups, or institutions. Max Weber defined power as 'the chance for persons or groups to realize their will even against the opposition of others' (Clark and Lipset, 1991: 399). Researchers increasingly recognize that an element of power is present even in family relations. But the capacity to achieve one's will in these circumstances relies on strategies different from the ones used, say, by a group of citizens opposing an urban renewal project, or by a municipal political party fighting an election. The level of organization of collective actors exercising power is highly variable: corporations are more tightly organized than municipal political parties and the latter are usually more structured than citizens' associations. It is noteworthy that Weber's definition includes the notion of 'chance'. This explains the frequently unpredictable effects of power relations. For example, outcomes of conflicts, such as strikes, are often difficult to anticipate. Although most power relations appear to be asymmetrical, with certain individuals and groups repeatedly yielding to others' will, there is always the possibility that successful strategies can reverse such relations. After all, this is what politics is all about.

In this chapter, we limit our discussion of power to its exercise in the political sphere. In *The Vertical Mosaic*, John Porter defined political power as 'the recognized right to make effective decisions on behalf of a group of people' (Porter, 1965: 201). Power relations strongly influence decisions made by all urban actors, including households, firms, governments, and various institutions, and thus drive urban change (Clark, 1996). Due to media coverage, power relations are more apparent during overt conflicts. These conflicts involve actors struggling over stakes. Most of the debates around power relations revolve around attempts by actors to justify their stands and social values. Some conflicts, such as strikes and lockouts, are regulated by laws. Other types of struggles are less institutionalized. This is the case of struggles over urban life issues, the object of this chapter.

Social Constituents of Power: Class, Gender, and Ethnicity

Persons living in cities belong to a number of social categories. In their efforts to understand the evolution of cities, researchers rely on three basic categorizing factors. The first, socio-economic groups, refers to individuals' access to material resources. The second factor concerns households, their type, size, life cycle. The third factor, ethnicity, involves values, language, eating habits, religious practices, and identity. As discussed in Chapter 9, in its effort to map residential social space, factorial ecology ranks neighbourhoods on a number of socio-economic, household, and ethnic status scales.

If useful from a descriptive point of view, these factors are limited in their capacity to throw light on social geographical processes of change. Such a purpose requires a rethinking of social, family, and

ethnic status in terms of class, gender, and ethnic relations.[2] These relations can be more or less asymmetrical and conflicting. They are always expressions of the relative power exercised by the individuals and groups involved (Foucault, 1976; Raffestin, 1980). To understand urban change, researchers must move beyond the mere description of the social profiles of neighbourhoods to concentrate on these power relations. Pretty much all expressions of power within the city can be traced to class, gender, and ethnic relations: class covers all struggles over the distribution of resources and urban space between income groups; gender pertains to issues related to women's participation in different aspects of society and to the delivery of services needed to enhance this participation; and ethnicity relates to the expression of identity and issues of segregation.

We need to view class, gender, and ethnicity relationally to understand how social categories can produce 'purposeful actors'. This concept refers to individuals' capacity to interpret their situation and deploy strategies to advance the status of their category and/or improve their own living conditions therein. Such a perspective underscores the importance of considering individuals' perception of the power relations in which they are involved in order to understand their behaviour. For example, analysts may consider that residential segregation between social classes dominates North American cities because of such broad factors as the putative propensity of all decision-makers to maximize utility within income constraints. This perspective would lead researchers to model residential location without probing deeper into the motivations of the actors involved. On the other hand, if individuals are depicted as capable of interpreting their situation and as possessing complex sets of motivations and intentions derived from their position in society and their interactions with others, other factors besides utility maximization become relevant. Residential location is then perceived as the outcome of strategies derived from the context of class, gender, and ethnic relations in which individuals partake. Locational choices can no longer be reduced to an abstract calculus of utility maximization; actors must be queried about their intentions. For example, the exploration of gentrifiers' motivations by Caulfield (1994) has portrayed gentrification as an urban social movement, involving as well as pure utility, identity, feelings, and a full range of aspirations.

With this perspective on power in the city, we enter the realm of urban political economy. Actors are no longer viewed as isolated, autonomous decision-makers, as is the case in economic models. Rather, they are portrayed as social beings who associate in various ways and co-operate or fight over norms, values, and the production of the space in which they live.

Urban Spheres of Power

Cities can be viewed as *localized* systems of social and political actors. Therefore, strategies of special interest to urban researchers are location and territorial strategies. The social categories to which individuals belong influence, in complex ways, their territorial strategies. This complexity derives from the combined effect of intra- and inter-category relations, of individuals' interpretation of their position within society and attempts to improve it, and of the influence of broad economic and policy contexts. To make sense of this complexity, we now trace the broad historical developments that have contributed to our understanding of urban spheres of power. These developments originate in nineteenth-century social thought, especially in the theories of social class of Karl Marx and Max Weber.

The Urban Political Process

Class, ethnicity, and gender form the social matrix in which our urban political institutions have historically been constituted and have evolved. We may start summarizing this evolution by asking the following question: If power is the right to make decisions on behalf of people, what individuals possess this right? When and how did they achieve it? In Canada, political power is exercised by three main levels of government: federal, provincial, and local.[3]

They all make decisions that affect residents of cities. Why are there three levels of government and how are the various decision-making domains allocated among the levels? Without going in detail on this key political issue,[4] it is important to note that municipalities were introduced in Canada in the first half of the nineteenth century when state decentralization was viewed as a means of approaching the liberal ideal (see Chapter 18). The liberal ideal was (and still is) concerned only with the logistics of representative democracy, a limited form of democracy; it is not to be equated with the democratic ideal, which involves much broader participation in the political process.[5] Liberals also viewed majority rule as central to the democratic process. But majority rule can curtail minority rights.

A solution is to create units of representation that permit minorities at a given geographical scale to become majorities at another scale. A variant of this solution entails geographical mobility. If a person suffers from being in a minority in one place, she or he can move to another place to become part of a majority. The expression 'voting with one's feet' describes such behaviour. Households leaving central cities, where taxes are high, for low-tax suburbs vote with their feet. There are serious downsides to such behaviour, however. When performed at a large scale, it can contribute to social segregation—for example, stark socio-economic discrepancies between rich and poor municipalities. In fact, three broad strategies are available when disagreeing with local rule: suffer, exit, or voice (Orbell and Uno, 1972). People can either suffer in resignation, move away, or organize to try to change things. Sociologist Werner Sombart (1976), in a classical study first published at the turn of the century, attributed the absence of important socialist movement in the United States to workers' option to move away ('go west') when dissatisfied with eastern industrial cities' work and living conditions, rather than organizing and challenging the bourgeoisie.

Another important aspect of the urban political process concerns the institutionalization of territoriality. The principal way of managing territorial power relations is their 'domestication' into *property relations.* A distinguished Canadian political scientist, C.B. Macpherson (1978), made fundamental contributions to the analysis of property. Macpherson observed that property was not a thing, but a right, the right either to exclude, or not to be excluded, from the enjoyment of particular goods, including space. He then considered three types of property relations: (1) private property, defined as the right to exclude; (2) common property or the right not to be excluded; and (3) public property, defined as the right, delegated to the state, to exclude. 'No trespassing' signs are visible expressions of private property rights. Oceans beyond territorial limits are common property domains, as are living-rooms for family members. Municipalities prohibiting access to parks outside certain hours exert their public property right to exclude. Urban areas are aggregations of private, common, and public spaces regulated by countless norms, rules, and laws, which are debated in the political arena. The role of property at the municipal level is further enhanced by municipalities' primary dependence on property taxes for their revenues. This accounts for their overwhelming concern over property matters and for the close relationship that prevails between municipal politics and the property industry (see Chapter 18).

These are some of the basic concepts used to describe the sociopolitical aspects of urban life. In any city, the exercise of power is shaped by territorially constructed class, gender, ethnic, and property relations. Conversely, these relations are modified by the outcomes of the political decisions resulting from the exercise of power. These innumerable events aggregate into circular and cumulative processes, sometimes producing breaks and discontinuities, and yielding patterns detectable in time and space.

Class and the Grounding of Democracy

Marxism has been influential in shaping our thinking about power relations. As a political economist, Marx analysed the economic relation between capital and labour, which dominated the history of industrialization. For Marx, economic and political power are closely intertwined. Until some decades ago, Marxian analysis had been almost exclusively concerned with capital-labour relations within the industrial sector. Authors such as Lefebvre (1968, 1974) and Harvey (1973, 1985) have shown how this method can extend to social relations having to do with *living*, and not only working, in cities. Instead of confronting employers and employees (as in classic Marxist struggles), these relations involve social categories such as citizens, government officials, landowners, and developers. They usually concern living conditions, which are influenced by working conditions, but also by numerous other factors. These other factors received a fuller treatment at the turn of the century from the German sociologist Max Weber than from Marx. Weber considered a wider array of influences on social stratification, including cultural factors. He also focused on the various forms taken by interest groups and collective action.

In the contemporary city, many (but by no means all) power struggles find their way to the municipal political scene. The notion of 'citizenship', derived from the very notion of 'city', is crucial to understanding the political process at the local level. Citizens can exercise rights, the right to vote being one of the most significant in representative forms of democracy. This right is territorially grounded; voters are registered at their place of residence and the exercise of political power is largely related to residential location patterns. Votes are usually compiled by electoral districts or wards, although in all cities and towns in Canada the mayor is elected at large, and in some of them, so are councillors (Higgins, 1986: 324). By virtue of this territoriality, representative democracy tends to mirror uneven spatial socio-economic, household type, and ethnic distribution. But voting is not alone in regulating power relations between social categories. Citizens also use the right to associate and act collectively to defend and promote their interests. Analysis of locational conflicts in cities indicates that they frequently involve residents defending their turf against distant and powerful actors. This is the case for the results reported on Table 24.1

Table 24.1   **Distribution of Locational Conflict Activity by Broad Categories of Opponents, Quebec Metropolitan Area, 1988–1991**

Opposers:	Citizens' Groups	Governments	Private	Total
Proposers:				
Citizens' Groups	3	4	6	13
Governments	27	5	7	39
Private Corporations	41	6	1	48
Total	71	15	14	100

Note: Conflict distribution is evaluated by percentage of press coverage in the regional daily *Le Soleil*. Coverage is measured in square centimetres, excluding photographs. For example, of the total coverage of locational conflicts during the four years, 4 per cent involved citizens' groups as proposers of a new land use and governments as opposers to the change.
Source: Côté (1993: 66).

(Côté, 1993). The press coverage of the 142 land-use conflicts that occurred in the Quebec City metropolitan area during the 1988–91 period indicates that more than two-thirds of the conflicts involved citizens' groups opposed to changes proposed either by various levels of government (27 per cent, including municipal government) or by private and quasi-public organizations (41 per cent, including religious, health, and educational institutions). These defensive struggles by residents can at times be viewed as selfish (e.g., when opposing a day-care centre) or on other occasions as vehicles for progressive social change (e.g., when opposing a nuclear plant). Another source of struggle among groups of citizens involves attempts to obtain local public services such as parks or day-care centres. Frictions between adversarial interest groups within the same neighbourhood complicate municipal political processes.[6]

Upper-class households (as well as corporations) are in a strong position to influence municipal policy-making by virtue of their capacity to move to other jurisdictions and thus take away their fiscal contribution. Local administrations readily adopt measures to prevent their departure, thereby favouring the wealthy at the expense of lower socio-economic categories. Moreover, it is well known that property owners (who generally belong to middle- and high-income groups) are more likely than tenants (who tend to be poorer) to organize politically, vote at municipal elections, and, consequently, influence local governments. To a large extent, therefore, class divisions on the municipal political scene correspond to housing tenure.

Ethnicity, Territory, and Identity Formation

Identity and consciousness constitute a second important territorial constituent of power relations. Ethnicity is perhaps the main factor in identity formation. It is thought of as a 'boundary phenomenon between groups, a set of markers by which one group differentiates itself from another' (McCall, 1990: 98). In simple terms, identity refers to the strength of the bonds linking individuals who belong to a group, while consciousness expresses the capacity to make an adequate reading of the position of one's group in the system of power relations. Territoriality plays an important role in the formation of identities, not only because proximity between members facilitates bonding, but also because it clarifies boundaries between groups engaged in power relations and constitutes one of the most pregnant markers of ethnic identity. Thus, it is with regard to ethnicity that identity, consciousness, and territoriality reinforce each other most strongly. Indeed, a number of sociology and geography studies have shown that in Canadian metropolitan areas residential segregation between ethnic groups is stronger than it is between social classes, household types, or life-cycle stages.[7] On this basis, we would expect ethnicity to play an important role in urban politics. It probably does, but we cannot say for sure because the role of ethnicity in Canadian municipal politics remains very much understudied.

Gender Relations and Urban Space

As was pointed out above, urban researchers now recognize that gender relations are at the heart of household and family life.[8] A number of authors have shown that gender relations have always contributed to the structuring of cities, although this went largely unnoticed. For example, England (1991) has argued that gender is central in the allocation of resources and opportunities in cities, and Coutras (1996) has demonstrated that urban space is fundamentally gendered, especially as regards the articulation of private space and public space. Storrie (1987: 1) uses the expression 'ecology of gender' to evoke a social and physical landscape 'marked by a specific spacing of women and men' in which 'men, as a group, can move more freely than women.' This suggests that in our explorations of urban political dynamics the notion of gender relations should receive priority over that of family status. Attention should be given to the fact that the feminist movement, a most important social movement of the last decades, reverberates at the household level, modifying relations within couples and thereby influencing location processes. For example, among employed couples where occupational asymmetry between partners is minimal, women have more weight in the decision-making process, including residential location decisions, than is the case among couples where the male partner's occu-

pational rank is higher than that of his female partner (Villeneuve, 1991).

Phases in the Political Structuring of Canadian Cities

There have been three phases in the evolution of postwar urban power relations in Canada—the late industrial (1945–65), post-industrial (1965–82), and post-welfare (1982–present) periods. These phases highlight the determining effect of national and international economic transitions and of major federal and provincial policy shifts on the exercise of power within cities. Economic trends and changes in governments' priorities are reflected in the evolution of public expenditure. Spending by all levels of government in Canada expressed as a percentage of gross domestic product (GDP) can be taken as an indicator of the evolution of the relative importance of the state between 1929 and 1995 (Figure 24.1a). Five periods can be identified quite clearly. Over the first two, the Great Depression and the war years, strong government action was called for. Figure 24.1a shows that state expenditure, as a share of GDP, grew moderately between the late forties and the early sixties. Then, growth accelerated until the early eighties, and decelerated thereafter, while showing a great deal of fluctuation. Straight lines, fitted separately for each period, show distinct slopes. Each of these three postwar periods is considered in more detail below.

Expenditures can be broken down by level of government. Figure 24.1b shows federal, provincial, and local governments' constant dollar per capita expenditures. It depicts the tremendous increase in the importance of government in our lives. Prior to World War II the three levels together spent less than $1,000/year per Canadian (in 1986 dollars), while this amount has exceeded $9,000/year since the beginning of the nineties. Almost half of the Canadian economy flows through government. Ours is, without doubt, a 'political' economy. But what is the relative importance of local governments in all of this? Figure 24.1b demonstrates clearly that local government spending rose much more slowly than either federal or provincial expen-

Figure 24.1   **Evolution of the Importance of the State in Canadian Society**

a) Government Expenditures as a Percentage of GDP

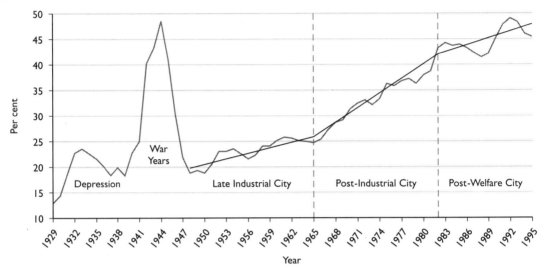

b) Government Expenditures Per Capita in Constant Dollars

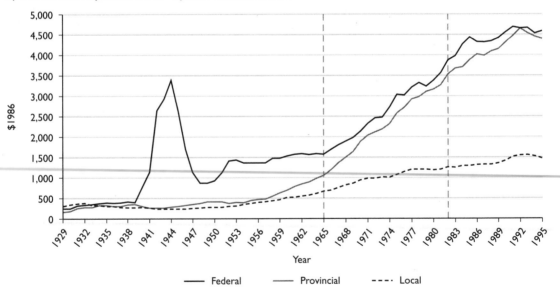

ditures. This suggests a municipal loss of importance and autonomy relative to upper levels of government. As we will see below, it is ironic that while the municipal level was extending the practice of democracy, first by taking steps towards universal voting franchise and more recently by introducing forms of participatory decision-making and co-management, it was experiencing a reduction in its capacity of intervention by comparison to that of other government levels (Villeneuve, 1992).

These three postwar periods coincide with changes in cities' socio-economic structure and decision-making processes. As we will see, during the late industrial city phase, municipalities were still viewed as administrative rather than political entities and the style of decision-making was over-whelmingly 'managerial'. During the following post-industrial phase managerialism was contested as the public became aware of the 'political' nature of municipal decision-making. In the most recent phase, that of the post-welfare city, awareness of the political nature of municipalities remains high and groups emerging from civil society increasingly take part in local government decision-making.[9] The cash-strapped local state enters into partner-ships with different kinds of organizations, ranging from voluntary groups to private firms.

As depicted in Table 24.2, each of the three phases has presented specific configurations and dis-tinct political manifestations in regard to class, gen-der, and ethnic relations. Existing literature supports certain parts of this table more firmly than others. While the urban reform movement and the associ-ated rise of a new middle class during the post-industrial city phase have been abundantly discussed, surprisingly few Canadian studies have been carried out on the role of ethnic relations in local politics.[10] Although the dates and the nature of these phases vary from city to city, this sequencing helps us to understand the complex historical processes leading to present urban circumstances.

Managerialism and the Late Industrial City, 1945–1965

The decades after World War II have been variously described as 'Les trente glorieuses' (Fourastié, 1979), the golden age of capitalism (Lipietz, 1986: 26), or the years when Keynesian policies could deliver prosperity (Wallace, 1990: 103). These were also years of rapid urban growth. To accommodate this growth, especially in western Canada, central cities annexed surrounding municipalities, and in Toronto a second-tier administration (Metro) was estab-lished in 1953. By contrast, municipal fragmentation in Quebec and Atlantic Canada persisted, due partly to slower growth and a longer, more entrenched municipal history.

Until the first oil crisis in 1973, advanced in-dustrial countries appeared to have found policies capable of securing stable economic growth. The rapid rise over the mid-1960s in public expenditure as a percentage of Canada's GDP was largely due to increasing provincial expenditures, which started to grow faster than federal spending (Figure 24.1). The rapid expansion of collective consumption spend-ing, especially in health and education, which are primarily the responsibility of provinces, accounted for this situation.

Clientelism and patronage inherent in populist municipal politics, sometimes grounded in deep-rooted ethnic identities, persisted in certain cities, such as Montreal, until the 1950s. But the late indus-trial city was more likely the scene of modernist reforms introduced in the name of efficiency by political élites recruited among local merchants and professionals. The 'social contract' associated with Fordist prosperity resulted in relative stability throughout society. For example, growing industrial wages and strong political and ideological control created a situation where work conflicts were scarce.[11]

In the late industrial city, gender relations were largely dominated by the 'family wage ideology'. According to this ideology, the husband's income should be sufficient to support a family, thus allow-ing the wife to devote herself entirely to household chores and the family. The postwar years were also a period of high immigration, and ethnic relations gradually rose on the federal agenda. Recently arrived groups, such as Italians and Greeks, were much more distant culturally from the British than previous immigrants, Germans and Scandinavians, for example. The politics of ethnicity developed in a totally different direction from the United States, where the melting-pot ideology and the remnants of slavery and overt racism produced a profound and long-lasting social divide. John Porter (1965) coined the expression 'vertical mosaic' to illustrate the placement of different ethnic groups on the Canadian occupational and political ladder.

Table 24.2   **Evolution of the Social Geographical Bases of Political Power in Canadian Cities**

Dimensions Underlying Power Relations and Urban Politics	Late Industrial City (Managerialism: 1945–1965)	Post-Industrial City (Government: 1965–1982)	Post-Welfare City (Shared Governance: 1982–present)
Class Relations	Low work conflicts and low environmental conflicts	High work conflicts and rising environmental conflicts	Decreasing work conflicts and high environmental conflicts
Political Correlate	Low working-class political representation	Urban reform movement led by disparate 'new middle class'	Public-private partnerships and inter-class local politics
Gender Relations	Prominence of the 'family wage' ideology	Acceleration of women's labour force participation	Restructuring of relations between domestic and employment spheres
Political Correlate	Consolidation of the feminist movement's gain of right to vote	Ties between the feminist movement and the urban reform movement	Very slow increase in percentage of elected women
Ethnic Relations	The 'mosaic' metaphor is developed as an alternative to the 'melting pot'	Federalism and multiculturalism reinforce each other	Confrontation of police with visible minorities in largest cities
Political Correlate	Moderate segregation and low representation	Segregation as a base for representation*	Decreasing segregation and increasing political participation*

*Indicates tentative, less documented interpretations.

During the period from World War II to the mid-1960s, Canadian metropolitan areas witnessed profound changes, suburbanization probably being the most prominent. During this period, the single-detached house and the low-density residential neighbourhood became the norm; they were perceived as most appropriate for family life. The desire to own a detached suburban home became so pervasive during these years that older inner-city neighbourhoods, where housing no longer conformed to aspirations in terms of domestic environments, were seen as obso-

lete (Séguin, 1989, 1996). Thus, during the 1950s and early 1960s, urban renewal appeared to be an acceptable way of updating older sectors. The removal of aging housing made room for non-residential uses of valuable centrally located land or for dense housing, including public housing, more in line with new domestic norms. Projects such as Regent Park in Toronto, Habitations Jeanne-Mance in Montreal, and the redevelopment of Parliament Hill in Quebec City enjoyed broad public support (Choko, Collin, and Germain, 1986, 1987; Séguin, 1996).

Strategies deployed by municipal politicians must be viewed in this general context. During the 1950s and 1960s, Canadian municipal politics was characterized by boosterism, a reflection of the necessity for municipal politicians to promote policies designed to make their city 'more prosperous and more appealing than competing cities' (Sancton, 1983b: 293; see also Mollenkopf, 1978). Competition *between* cities tended to de-emphasize class and ethnic conflicts *within* cities. (Gender was not yet on the municipal agenda.) Politicians of the late industrial city era often adopted populist approaches to issues. For instance, Jean Drapeau was elected mayor of Montreal by appealing to the French-Canadian ethnic vote, but this did not prevent him from working closely with the English-Canadian business élite. In reality, he did not have any choice insofar as he had to attract large urban redevelopment projects, and their associated fiscal benefits, in order to respond to the pressing social needs of a large urban proletariat at a time when provincial welfare state measures were still rare.

During the postwar years, the main competitors of central cities were increasingly their own suburban municipalities, where extensive tracts of single-family houses were built with the financial support of the Central (now Canada) Mortgage and Housing Corporation. This rapid residential expansion was associated with industrial and commercial deconcentration as well as with the construction of expressways. To preserve their tax base, central cities concentrated on urban functions requiring high levels of centrality, such as office towers, especially corporate headquarters, large hotels, cultural attractions such as museums, concert halls, and stadiums, and high-rise apartment buildings.

These activities had the capacity to displace less intensive uses, a process encouraged by municipal administrations through changes in zoning by-laws and by provincial transportation investments that had the effect of increasing the potential rent of central sites. The federal government also played a role (which extends to the present) in supporting the clearing or redevelopment of central land through such large-scale operations as the removal of rail yards and the redevelopment of port areas into leisure and recreation-oriented districts. Clearly, in attempting to counter the effects of the flight to the suburbs, central cities sought to create political conditions favouring urban investments capable of producing large tax returns.

Central city policies favourable to urban renewal did not necessarily mean that municipal politicians entered into an exclusive alliance with the real estate industry, although documented cases of collusion are legion.[12] Rather, these policies resulted from municipalities' insufficient control of landownership, because most land was in private hands, and from their dependence on the volume of real estate investments made on their territory to serve adequately the needs of their citizens (Offe and Ronge, 1984). All municipalities, and especially central cities facing obsolescence costs, had to become attractive to investors and 'sell themselves' (Andrew, Bordeleau, and Guimont, 1981; Ézop-Québec, 1981; Filion, 1987). The construction of large public infrastructures aimed at attracting private real estate investors and creating jobs was consistent with the Keynesian approach favoured at the time.

Until the mid-1960s, there was little organized citizen opposition to large-scale urban renewal in Canada. On the contrary, wide segments of civil society, including trade unions, churches, and the intellectual élite, tended to support such modernization and its counterpart, the sprawling suburb, although early efforts were made to document the social and environmental costs of this type of urban development (Langlois, 1961). At the time, economic growth, which sustained urban expansion, was seen as highly desirable since many had lived through the Great Depression and now hoped to enjoy the fruits of prosperity. The function of municipalities was seen as administrative, not political. In this view, their role was to administer the urban component of economic growth for the benefit of home-owners, viewed first and foremost as ratepayers. Few municipal politicians during this period achieved electoral success by appealing to class, ethnic, or even neighbourhood solidarity. Most successful were the ones best able to convince voters of their capacity to promote growth.

Things began to change in the 1960s. Paralleling conflicts in the production sphere, struggles arose in the consumption sphere. This is illustrated by Figure 24.2, which shows the evolution of work and locational conflicts. Locational conflicts were fought largely over consumption issues, including environmental quality. The number of work conflicts reached a peak in the province of Quebec during the mid-1970s, while the number of locational conflicts in the Quebec City CMA tended to increase moderately until the mid-1980s and rapidly thereafter. Housing and collective services became the objects of demands on the part of citizens' groups and often, but not always, were associated with trade unions, churches, or political parties. These demands resulted from the realization that not everybody partook in the benefits deriving from the pro-growth institutional arrangements, sometimes referred to as the 'Fordist compromise' (Filion, 1995).

Poorer households, bypassed by postwar growth, were left behind in the older neighbourhoods. These households had to endure a deterioration of neighbourhood livability due to urban renewal and population erosion and saw the closing of public

and private services, such as primary schools and grocery stores. These circumstances led to the emergence of neighbourhood organizations (Hamel, Léonard, and Mayer, 1982).

In summary, the 1945–65 period was characterized by a broad consensus over the need for cities to accommodate rapid economic growth. Power was in the hands of politicians, bureaucrats, and developers, all of whom were involved in the transformation and expansion of cities—hence, the focus was on efficiency and only limited debate occurred over policy orientations. The climate was unfavourable to the mounting of a large-scale opposition to this growth coalition. Still, as the period progressed, the adverse side-effects of prevailing forms of development and redevelopment (in particular, expressways and urban renewal) became a source of mobilization among inner-city neighbourhood residents and low-income households.

The Post-Industrial City and the Politicizing of Urban Life, 1965–1982

The late 1960s and the 1970s were a period of rapid expansion in the share of the GDP taken by gov-

Figure 24.2 **Evolution of Locational and Work Conflicts**

ernment expenditures. This period also witnessed a considerable rise in the service-sector proportion of the GDP accompanied by a decline in manufacturing. The growing employment gap between the two sectors was even more pronounced, a reflection of advancing automation within manufacturing establishments. The rapid growth of the service sector resulted in a heightened demand for white-collar workers.

Professional and skilled workers of the information economy formed a broad new social category referred to as the 'new middle class'. What distinguishes this new middle class from the old middle class is that it is composed principally of salaried workers rather than self-employed professionals or business owners. Members of the new middle class belong to the large public, but also private, bureaucracies created over the post-industrial period. These individuals tended to promote collective solutions to social problems and contributed to the development of a culture that values quality of life, urbanity, and hedonism. The pre- and early baby-boom cohorts, composed of persons born roughly between 1940 and 1950, formed the first contingents of the new middle class. These age groups benefited from an advantageous job market and promoted state programs as a remedy to various social problems. Of course, the rapid expansion of government activities was a major contributor to the growing size and political influence of this new middle class, which piloted provincial social, health, and education interventions based on universality principles. These included the creation of a number of new universities and of institutions such as community colleges and health clinics, and, in Quebec, CLSCs (Centres locaux des services communautaires) and CEGEPs (Collèges d'enseignement général et professionnel).

This period marked the massive entry of women in the job market. A number of interrelated factors account for the feminization of the labour force. A first factor has to do with the expansion of the sectors of employment that traditionally employed women, particularly sectors that involve caring and nurturing activities (Coutras, 1996). This

was obviously the case of nursing and kindergarten and elementary school teaching. In Montreal during the 1970s, 35 per cent of professional workers in education, health, and welfare services were women, while in no other broad economic sector did this figure exceed 20 per cent (Rose and Villeneuve, 1994: 142). Office employment, another sector where women were overrepresented, also experienced rapid expansion over this period (Bernard, 1982; Oppenheimer, 1985). Perhaps the most significant factor accounting for the feminization of the labour force was the necessity to maintain households' purchasing power, especially as employment income growth slowed down in the 1970s and became negative over subsequent decades. For numerous families, the suburban way of life turned out to be a costly proposition forcing many women, including mothers of small children, to take jobs, often part-time or unskilled, in sectors such as retailing and personal services.

Another crucial source of feminization of the labour force came from the changes initiated by the feminist movement. Successful challenges to patriarchal gender relations, defined as male domination both in the private and public spheres, involved enhancement of the personal autonomy that ensues from sufficient education and earnings (Foord and Gregson, 1986). Struggles for equity took place both at home and at work in a context where access to higher education increased, as did the supply of tertiary jobs. Alongside these transformations, a number of demographic and family changes took place. Divorce and separation rates rose, fertility fell, marriage and childbirth were delayed. Double-income couples formed an increasing share of the total number of households and, in certain inner-city neighbourhoods, one-person households accounted for as much as 60 per cent of the total. The residential preferences and needs of such households were different from those of families with children. Inner-city neighbourhoods frequently offered the accessibility and amenities people were looking for: proximity to work, the presence of services within walking distance, cultural events, etc. (Alonso, 1982).

The combination of these economic and socio-demographic transformations accounts largely for the process of gentrification whereby members of this diversified and partly feminized new middle class rented or bought housing in centrally located working-class neighbourhoods. Gentrification, although it did not in most cities mobilize very large numbers of people, is perhaps the most significant transformation of the post-industrial city. It generated a new pro-urban discourse emphasizing the advantages, cultural and otherwise, of a central residential location and criticizing traditional forms of urban renewal involving demolition and reconstruction (Ley, 1994). Gentrifiers often joined forces with incumbent residents and their community organizations to resist large urban renewal projects endangering neighbourhood livability. As a result, the incidence of activism and locational conflicts increased in central neighbourhoods relative to older and peripheral suburbs, as can be seen from an analysis of press coverage for the Quebec City CMA (Figure 24.3). Although new and incumbent residents joined forces to combat 'aggressions'

against their neighbourhood, they often disagreed on the type of improvements that should take place. Generally, new residents promoted the recycling of old structures for cultural and heritage purposes, while incumbent residents favoured socially oriented projects such as retirement homes and co-op housing. The arrival of higher-income gentrifiers often had socially adverse consequences. It fuelled a considerable rise in property values, which generated needed tax revenues for central cities but placed housing in gentrified neighbourhoods out of the reach of lower-income residents.

Citizens' associations in gentrified neighbourhoods, fighting as they were over issues of livability, often found themselves in sympathy with other community organizations, such as environmental, feminist, peace, and gay and lesbian groups.[13] A vast sociological literature refers to these as 'new social movements' (Offe, 1985) to distinguish them from other more traditional interest groups, such as chambers of commerce and trade unions. These new social movements were usually less organized than traditional interest groups. Most of them shared a common view of the world, which can minimally be described as anti-growth, and were as much concerned with changing decision-making processes as they were with the outcomes of these processes (Habermas, 1981; Higgins, 1986). They contributed to make political practice more accommodating to public participation. These movements owed much of their credibility to the impression they projected that they were defending idealistic causes rather than their own narrow self-interest. This set them apart from traditional interest groups. Nonetheless, new social movements occasionally joined ranks with unions (a product of the industrial city).

This mobilization around urban issues had a significant impact on the political landscape of a number of Canadian metropolitan areas. A new breed of municipal party or political coalition driven by new social movements and occasionally by senior-level political parties (usually the NDP) emerged on the political scene of many Canadian central cities (Sancton, 1983b). Their program

Figure 24.3   **Press Coverage of Locational Conflicts, Quebec CMA**

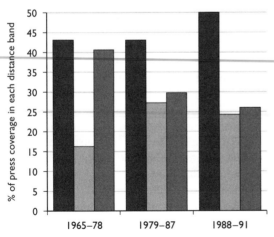

% of press coverage in each distance band

Coverage in square centimetres in daily newspaper Le Soleil

■ 0–4km   ■ 4–10km   ■ +10km

largely reflected the agenda of new social movements: public participation, the conservation of inner-city neighbourhoods, pro-transit policies, and the like. In many cases, these parties and coalitions also championed social measures targeted at lower-income groups. Collectively, the new political organizations were referred to as the 'municipal reformist movement'. They challenged the pro-development and *laissez-faire* stand of traditional municipal politicians (Higgins, 1986: 340). These parties and coalitions often enjoyed their highest support in gentrifying neighbourhoods (Ley and Mills, 1986). This was the case of Vancouver's The Electors Action Movement (TEAM), the Montreal Citizens' Movement (MCM), and Quebec City's Rassemblement Populaire (RPQ). Many reform municipal parties found it difficult to function as political parties.[14] They experienced considerable internal tensions around the issue of whether they should be primarily dedicated to winning elections or to the promotion of community organization and mobilization (Racicot, 1980). When they gained power, as TEAM did in 1972, the MCM in 1986, and the RPQ in 1989, they experienced the severe constraints within which central cities must operate, which prevented the implementation of large chunks of their programs (on the MCM's experience, see Thomas, 1997). Competition with suburbs and other metropolitan areas greatly impeded their capacity to control the development industry. When confronted by regulations they perceived as too rigid, developers could threaten to pursue their activities in suburban municipalities. What is more, insufficient senior-level government co-operation impeded the implementation of reformist parties' social agenda, which included public housing and day-care development.

The limited power of cities with regard to social policies was a direct consequence of the loss of municipal autonomy that came with the development of the Keynesian welfare state (Lustiger-Thaler, 1993; Villeneuve, 1992). But the welfare state was itself coming under strong pressures from globalization processes, including fierce inter-city competition not only from neighbouring suburbs or national rivals but increasingly from far-away cities. We identify the economic recession of the early 1980s, which exacerbated governments' fiscal difficulties, as the event that launched the subsequent post-welfare period.

To summarize, the 1965–82 period was one of growing demands in a context of government expansion. At the urban level, the new middle class took a leading role in municipal politics and became instrumental in opening decision-making processes to public participation and in securing the built environment of inner-city neighbourhoods. These are the major transitions that distinguish this from the previous period.

Governance and Partnerships in the Post-Welfare City, 1982-present

Without the benefit of hindsight, the social and political configuration of the post-welfare city does not lend itself easily to characterization. Since the beginning of the 1980s, the share of government activities in the Canadian economy has varied considerably, reaching all-time highs during the recessions of the early 1980s and early 1990s and falling markedly in between and over the mid- and late 1990s. These movements are in themselves indicative of the strong stabilizing effects of the state. One can only imagine the turmoil in the lives of Canadians had it not been for government deficit-spending capacity during these two recessions. However, most Canadians would now agree that an accumulated public debt as large as the present one seriously curtails government action and that it has to be reduced. But how is this to be achieved without destroying the social security net that has become, during the last decades, an enduring feature of Canadian citizenship rights? And what of the impact of these issues on city politics?

One way of dealing with a retrenchment of the welfare state is to involve community organizations in the delivery of services, thus taking advantage of the diffusion of power achieved over the previous period by the new social movements. These movements have indeed reversed somewhat the 'passive citizenship' inherited from the welfare state (Simard, 1979; Lustiger-Thaler, 1993). Social rights, including some form of minimum income and access to a variety of public services, were considerably advanced by the welfare state. But, in the long run, socializing the costs of economic growth simply proved to be too expensive. When deficits went out of control and senior governments started to cut deep into social spending, protest from new social movements and trade unions failed to reverse the shrinking of the welfare state.

Confronted with the reduced capacity of the welfare state to secure, on its own and from above, a sufficient redistribution of wealth, certain communities engaged in local development efforts to make up for waning transfer payments. In many instances, the contribution of new social movements to these efforts marked the evolution of their role from one of political protest to that of agents of local socio-economic development, which resulted in their involvement in various forms of self-help initiatives (Favreau, 1989; Hamel, 1991). The creation of local economic development corporations in inner-city neighbourhoods is perhaps the most visible aspect of this new approach to social and economic development. These corporations have been supported by all three levels of government. Indeed, partnerships with local citizens' groups have now become inherent in the regular functioning of the state. Expressions such as 'co-production' and 'entrepreneurial state' aptly evoke this form of co-operation (Hasson and Ley, 1997). Andrew, Houle, and Thériault (1992) note how weaker controls and practices such as networking and partnerships seem to be replacing more rigid and hierarchical forms of social program management. Sometimes, these partnerships amount to no more than the subcontracting of services once rendered by public agencies to voluntary groups or low-paying firms. In other circumstances, however, these partnerships involve a genuine sharing of decision-making with groups and minorities not previously part of the 'Keynesian social compact' (Hasson and Ley, 1997: 52). Seen in this light, the political challenge in the post-welfare city is to

achieve co-operation between civil society groups that are capable of experimentation and social innovation and a state that should give as much support to these groups as it does to private corporations.

The retrenchment of the local state resulting from precarious fiscal circumstances has also contributed to enhance the influence of the private sector at the expense of the public sector. Eager to maintain their fiscal base in a deteriorating economic context, municipalities are engaged in a ferocious competition to attract investments. In these circumstances, municipal administrations are often willing to offer advantageous conditions to potential investors. Also, to provide costly infrastructures, fiscally strapped governments increasingly resort to partnerships with private enterprise. For example, in the Greater Toronto Area, Highway 407 is owned and operated by private enterprise.

This period is also characterized by a diversity of power-related issues. What were defined at the outset as class conflicts often became something else. Urban social movements contributed to bring into the public sphere the unequal gender relations that prevail in the domestic sphere. Male participants to these movements often lived through consciousness-raising processes. As for female participants, they contributed to the enhancement of gender awareness and paved the way for the increased presence of women in the formal municipal political process (Gidengil and Vengroff, 1997; Tremblay, 1996). To be sure, there are still relatively few women elected on municipal councils. In 1996, among the central cities of the 25 Canadian CMAs, their presence ranged from none of the 20 seats in Halifax to half of the 10 seats in Saskatoon and Vancouver and half of Victoria's eight seats. More generally, women occupied 77 (22.4 per cent) of the 344 seats in the 25 central cities. Smaller, high-density, rapidly growing CMAs, prairie CMAs, and those with larger numbers of municipalities and less seats in their central city council tend to have larger percentages of women on municipal councils.

Although ethnicity has been the object of little formal research, there is evidence that its influence on the local political scene has grown over the present period. While there is generally little residential segregation by gender at the neighbourhood level, ethnic groups can be quite concentrated in urban space (and thus in wards), which favours the election of ethnic representatives on city councils. One exception to the poor documentation of the involvement of ethnic minorities in urban social movements and municipal politics is Calliste's (1996) work on the anti-racism mobilization of Blacks in Halifax, Montreal, and Toronto. Pointing out interactions between racism and gender and class inequality, she depicts the politicization of racial consciousness associated with increased Black immigration to Toronto and Montreal in the late 1960s. Another exception is the study by Tate and Quesnel (1995) on differences between Toronto and Montreal in the way municipal services are delivered to their respective ethnic populations. They note that the arrival of the MCM to power in 1986 marked a significant improvement in Montreal's policy of *interculturalism* towards its ethnic minorities, but they also stress that awareness of ethnic affairs remains lower in Montreal than in Toronto, where a somewhat different policy of *multiculturalism* prevails. This policy difference in large part results from the ethnic composition of Canada's two largest cities. With one charter ethnic group, Toronto easily conforms to the federal multicultural policy, which has recently come under strong criticism (Bissoondath, 1994). With its French charter group more separated from ethnic groups than is the case in Toronto, and with the historical tendency for immigrants to integrate into the English group, the City of Montreal tends to follow the provincial policy of linguistic integration of immigrants into the Francophone majority and to give more attention to helping ethnic communities adapt to the municipal system rather than modifying the way services are offered to these groups.

In brief, the retrenchment in public-sector spending over this period has had a major impact on cities. Social measures were curtailed, as evidenced in the abandonment of social housing construction programs by different jurisdictions. At the same time, infrastructure development did not keep pace with growth, thus causing bottlenecks in expanding metropolitan regions, while everywhere, maintenance standards fell. To alleviate the consequences of fiscal retrenchment, community groups have become involved in the delivery of certain services. The opening of the municipal political system to public participation over the previous period encouraged such forms of delivery. The period equally has witnessed mounting private-sector presence in areas of intervention previously under exclusive public-sector responsibility. Finally, over these years, women have taken a larger role on the municipal political scene and more attention has been given to the special needs of ethnic groups.

Conclusion

Power relations and decision-making processes have changed considerably in Canadian cities during the second half of the twentieth century. We have argued in this chapter that underlying transformations in class, gender, and ethnic relations account for a good share of these changes. First, we have sketched a simple conceptual framework shedding light on complex urban political processes. Second, we have recalled a few key elements in the Canadian history of local government and politics. Relying on these conceptual and historical prerequisites, an outline of the evolution of urban politics since 1945 has been presented.

A first phase, late industrialism, extends to about 1965. The industrial city had produced a style of urban decision-making that emulated the reputed efficiency of business managers and attempted to be 'non-political'. Certain aspects of this form of decision-making can still be found in cities across Canada. During this period, gender was almost non-existent on the municipal agenda. As for ethnicity, it is well known that French-English relations played a major part in city politics in Montreal, but little academic research has focused on the local political role played by other ethnic groups in that city or, for that matter, in other Canadian metropolitan areas.

A few decades after World War II, urban managerialism was challenged by important transformations in the social and economic fabric of Canadian cities, especially larger central cities. The rise of a new middle class associated with post-industrialization produced urban social movements that viewed municipal decision-making as 'political' rather than solely 'managerial'. These movements promoted participatory democracy and opposed perceived collusions between developers and more traditional municipal politicians. Meanwhile, the development of the welfare state at the provincial and federal levels had reduced the autonomy of municipalities to the extent that when politicians originating from the new middle class were elected, they found it difficult to carry out their political agenda.

With the shrinking of welfarism during the 1980s and 1990s, grassroots democracy in urban neighbourhoods constitutes one of the few vehicles through which citizenship rights can be exercised and extended. Co-production agreements and partnerships between government agencies at all three levels and community groups introduced a form of governance characterized by weaker controls and a diffusion of power. Many of these recent changes are associated with the transformations of the social space we live in. These include public spending cutbacks and technological advancements that cause a redefinition of the relations between the local and the global (Castells, 1989; Mitchell, 1996). Economic globalization signifies that, increasingly, Canadian cities are competing or co-operating not only with neighbouring cities but also with distant ones. In this context, new forms of inter-city politics are developing that could, as we enter the twenty-first century, further modify urban power relations and decision-making.

Notes

1. As will become clear, it is not easy to generalize about urban politics in a country as diverse as Canada. Our goal is simply to sketch a broad interpretation of the joint evolution of the social fabric and the political sphere at the urban level in Canada. We rely heavily on research published by colleagues on various cities across the country and on our own work on Quebec City and Montreal. We would like to thank the Social Science and Humanities Research Council of Canada and the Quebec FCAR Fund for financial support.

2. For examples of studies where these interrelationships are taken into account, see Clement and Myles (1994), Hanson and Pratt (1995), McCall (1990), and Preston and Giles (1997). By moving from 'household status' to 'gender relations', we suggest that the primary locus of social change in the domestic sphere is currently the interactions between women and men, although we also have to recognize that these interactions are far from limited to the domestic sphere. This implies that we have to move beyond the notion of 'spatial independence' between the factors found in factorial ecologies and study the relationships of class, gender, and ethnicity.

3. Unlike the senior levels, local or municipal governments do not have a constitutional existence of their own. Constitutionally, municipalities are creations of provinces and operate under tight provincial laws.

4. Authors such as Clark and Dear (1984), Higgins (1986), and Stelter and Artibise (1986) discuss this matter.

5. For a more detailed discussion of these issues as they relate to the Canadian municipal context, see Villeneuve (1992).

6. See Hasson and Ley (1994) for a thorough analysis of political processes at the neighbourhood level in Jerusalem and Vancouver.

7. See Hill (1976) for the most systematic among these studies. Using 1971 census data pertaining to the census tracts of all the Canadian metropolitan areas of the time, Hill finds an average overall segregation index of 0.136 between age groups, of 0.199 between family income classes, and of 0.309 between ethnic groups. To be sure, insofar as members of ethnic groups tend to integrate with time into the larger society, these differences may diminish if immigration changes. We may surmise that changes in immi-

grant countries of origin since 1971 may have decreased residential segregation tendencies, because the groups arriving from developing countries are not as large as those that originated from such countries as Italy and Greece in the postwar years. Newer immigrant groups, therefore, often did not reach the size threshold for the development of ethnic institutions and services, a factor known to favour spatial concentration, as Breton (1964) demonstrated years ago.

8. This is obvious in the case of female-male couples, but since gender relations are socially constructed it is also the case for same-sex couples and for single-person households.

9. 'Civil society' is a key notion in social science. Most definitions include the idea that social life (that is, the multitude of daily interactions among individuals) exists quite autonomously from the various political institutions associated with the state. Civil society is composed of numerous overlapping informal social networks, whereas the state is formed of hierarchically structured institutions. Social change often emerges from civil society before being incorporated into institutions. In this sense, the notion of civil society is important for understanding processes of 'development from below' (see Thériault, 1985).

10. Exceptions include Sancton (1983a), who documents the role of English-French relations in the evolution of municipal politics in Montreal, and Driedger (1995), who studies how concentrations of Mennonites in urban areas influence their political participation.

11. According to the *Labour Gazette* of Canada, the number of strikes and lockouts jumped from 244 on average per year between 1946 and 1965 to 878 between 1966 and 1981.

12. For examples, see articles in *City Magazine*, a leftist periodical.

13. A number of chapters in Caulfield and Peake (1996) discuss the interaction between new social movements and urban issues.

14. See Quesnel (1996) on the debates around the desirability of party politics at the municipal level, and Quesnel and Belley (1991) for a thorough analysis of party politics in Quebec City, with special emphasis on the 1989 election won by the RPQ.

References

Alonso, W. 1982. 'The Population Factor and Urban Structure', in L.S. Bourne, ed., *Internal Structure of the City*. New York: Oxford University Press.

Andrew, C., S. Bordeleau, and A. Guimont. 1981. *L'urbanisation: une affaire: l'appropriation du sol et l'État local dans l'Outaouais québécois*. Ottawa: University of Ottawa Press.

———, F. Houle, and J.Y. Thériault. 1992. 'La définition du local dans les nouvelles stratégies de développement', *Canadian Journal of Regional Science* 15: 457–75.

Bernard, E. 1982. *The Long Distance Feeling: A History of the Telecommunications Workers Union*. Vancouver: New Star Books.

Bissoondath, N. 1994. *Selling Illusions: The Cult of Multiculturalism in Canada*. Toronto: Penguin Books.

Bourne, L.S. 1989. 'Are New Urban Forms Emerging? Empirical Tests for Canadian Urban Areas', *Canadian Geographer* 33: 312–28.

Breton, R. 1964. 'Institutional Completeness of Ethnic Communities and the Personal Relations of Immigrants', *American Journal of Sociology* 70: 193–205.

Calliste, A. 1996. 'Anti-racism Organizing and Resistance: Blacks in Urban Canada, 1940s–1970s', in J. Caulfield and L. Peake, eds, *City Lives and City Forms: Critical Research and Canadian Urbanism*. Toronto: University of Toronto Press.

Castells, M. 1989. *The Informational City: Information Technology, Economic Restructuring and the Urban-Regional Process*. Oxford: Basil Blackwell.

Caulfield, J. 1994. *City Form and Everyday Life: Toronto's Gentrification and Critical Social Practice*. Toronto: University of Toronto Press.

———— and L. Peake, eds. 1996. *City Lives and City Forms: Critical Research and Canadian Urbanism*. Toronto: University of Toronto Press.

Choko, M.H., J.-P. Collin, and A. Germain. 1986. 'Le logement et les enjeux de la transformation de l'espace urbain: Montréal, 1940–1960, Première partie', *Urban History Review* 15: 127–36.

————, ————, and ————. 1987. 'Le logement et les enjeux de la transformation de l'espace urbain: Montréal, 1940–1960, Deuxième partie', *Urban History Review* 15: 243–53.

Clark, G.L., and M. Dear. 1984. *State Apparatus: Structures and Language of Legitimacy*. Boston: Allen and Unwin.

Clark, T.N. 1996. 'Structural Realignments in American City Politics: Less Class, More Race, and a New Political Culture', *Urban Affairs Review* 31: 368–403.

———— and S.M. Lipset. 1991. 'Are Social Classes Dying?', *International Sociology* 6: 397–410.

Clement, W., and J. Myles. 1994. *Relations of Ruling: Class and Gender in Postindustrial Societies*. Montreal and Kingston: McGill-Queen's University Press.

Côté, G. 1993. 'Esquisse d'une géographie des conflits de localisation dans la région métropolitaine de Québec', MA essay in Aménagement du territoire et développement régional, Université Laval.

Coutras, J. 1996. *Crise urbaine et espaces sexués*. Paris: Armand Colin.

Driedger, L. 1995. 'Ethnic Urban Dominance: Demographic, Ecological and Institutional Patterns', *Canadian Journal of Urban Research* 4: 207–28.

England, K. 1991. 'Gender Relations and the Spatial Structure of Cities', *Geoforum* 22, 2: 135–47.

Ézop-Québec. 1981. *Une ville à vendre*. Montreal: Éditions coopératives Albert Saint-Martin.

Favreau, L. 1989. *Mouvement populaire et intervention communautaire de 1960 à nos jours: continuités et ruptures*. Montréal: Le centre de formation populaire et les Éditions du fleuve.

Filion, P. 1987. 'Core Redevelopment, Neighbourhood Revitalization and Municipal Government Motivation: Twenty Years of Urban Renewal in Québec City', *Canadian Review of Political Science* 20: 131–47.

————. 1995. 'Fordism, Post-fordism and Urban Policy-making: Urban Renewal in a Medium-size Canadian City', *Canadian Journal of Urban Research* 4: 43–71.

Foord, J., and N. Gregson. 1986. 'Patriarchy: Towards a Reconceptualisation', *Antipode* 18: 186–211.

Foucault, M. 1976. *Histoire de la sexualité, 1: La volonté de savoir*. Paris: Gallimard.

Fourastié, J. 1979. *Les trente glorieuses ou la révolution invisible de 1946 à 1975*. Paris: Fayard.

Gidengil, E., and R. Vengroff. 1997. 'Representational Gains of Canadian Women or Token Growth? The Case of Québec's Municipal Politics', *Canadian Journal of Political Science* 30: 512–37.

Habermas, J. 1981. 'New Social Movements', *Telos* 49: 33–7.

Hamel, P. 1991. *Action collective et démocratie locale: les mouvements urbains montréalais*. Montréal: Les Presses de l'Université de Montréal.

————, J.-F. Léonard, and R. Mayer. 1982. *Les mobilisations populaires urbaines*. Montréal: Nouvelle optique.

Hanson, S., and G. Pratt. 1995. *Gender, Work, and Space*. London: Routledge.

Harvey, D. 1973. *Social Justice and the City*. Baltimore: Johns Hopkins University Press.

————. 1985. *The Urbanization of Capital*. Oxford: Basil Blackwell.

Hasson, S., and D. Ley. 1994. *Neighbourhood Organizations and the Welfare State*. Toronto: University of Toronto Press.

———— and ————. 1997. 'Neighbourhood Organizations, the Welfare State, and Citizenship Rights', *Urban Affairs Review* 33: 28–58.

Higgins, D.J.H. 1986. *Local and Urban Politics in Canada*. Toronto: Gage.

Hill, F.I., ed. 1976. *Croissance du Canada urbain, Vol. II: Tendances au niveau des métropoles*. Toronto: Copp Clark.

Langlois, C. 1961. 'Problems of Urban Growth in Greater Montréal', *Canadian Geographer* 5: 1–11.

Lefebvre, H. 1968. *La vie quotidienne dans le monde moderne.* Paris: Gallimard. Translated, 1971. *Everyday Life in the Modern World.* London: Allen Lane.

———. 1974. *La production de l'espace.* Paris: Anthropos. Translated, 1991. *The Production of Space.* Oxford: Basil Blackwell.

Ley, D. 1994. 'Gentrification and the Politics of the New Middle Class', *Environment and Planning D: Society and Space* 12: 53–74.

——— and C. Mills. 1986. 'Gentrification and Reform Politics in Montréal, 1982', *Cahiers de géographie du Québec* 30, 81: 419–27.

Lipietz, A. 1986. 'New Tendencies in the International Division of Labour: Regimes of Accumulation and Modes of Regulation', in A.J. Scott and M. Storper, eds, *Production, Work, Territory.* Boston: Allen and Unwin.

Lustiger-Thaler, H. 1993. 'Social Citizenship and Urban Citizenship: The Composition of Local Practices', *Canadian Journal of Urban Research* 2: 115–29.

McCall, C. 1990. *Class, Ethnicity and Social Inequality.* Montreal and Kingston: McGill-Queen's University Press.

Macpherson, C.B., ed. 1978. *Property: Mainstream and Critical Positions.* Toronto: University of Toronto Press.

Mitchell, W.J. 1996. *City of Bits: Space, Place and the Infobahn.* Cambridge, Mass.: MIT Press.

Mollenkopf, J.H. 1978. 'The Postwar Politics and Urban Development', in W.K. Tabb and L. Sawers, eds, *Marxism and the Metropolis.* New York: Oxford University Press.

Offe, C. 1985. 'New Social Movements: Challenging the Boundaries of Institutional Politics', *Social Research* 52: 817–69.

——— and C. Ronge. 1984. 'Theses on the Theory of the State', in Offe, ed., *Contradictions of the Welfare State.* Cambridge, Mass.: MIT Press.

Oppenheimer, M. 1985. *White Collar Politics.* New York: Monthly Review Press.

Orbell, J.M., and T. Uno. 1972. 'A Theory of Neighborhood Problem Solving: Political Action Versus Residential Mobility', *American Political Science Review* 66: 471–89.

Porter, J. 1965. *The Vertical Mosaic: An Analysis of Social Class and Power in Canada.* Toronto: University of Toronto Press.

Preston, V., and W. Giles. 1997. 'Ethnicity, Gender and Labour Markets in Canada: A Case Study of Immigrant Women in Toronto', *Canadian Journal of Urban Research* 6: 135–59.

Quesnel, L. 1996. 'Media and Urban Politics: The 1991 Civic Elections in Toronto', *Canadian Journal of Urban Research* 5: 220–51.

——— and S. Belley. 1991. *Partis politique municipaux: Une étude de sociologie électorale.* Montréal: Editions Agence d'Arc.

Racicot, P. 1980. 'Le Rassemblement populaire de Québec et les comités de citoyens', *Revue internationale d'action communautaire* 4, 44: 129–33.

Raffestin, C. 1980. *Pour une géographie du pouvoir.* Paris: Libraries techniques.

Rose, D., and P. Villeneuve. 1994. 'Gender and Occupational Restructuring in Montréal', in A. Kobayashi, ed., *Women, Work and Place.* Montreal and Kingston: McGill-Queens University Press.

Sancton, A. 1983a. 'Montreal', in W. Magnusson and Sancton, eds, *City Politics in Canada.* Toronto: University of Toronto Press.

———. 1983b. 'Conclusion: Canadian City Politics in Comparative Perspective', in W. Magnusson and Sancton, eds, *City Politics in Canada.* Toronto: University of Toronto Press.

Séguin, A.-M. 1989. 'Madame Ford et l'espace: lecture féministe de la suburbanisation', *Recherches féministes* 2, 1: 51–68.

———. 1996. 'La construction sociale d'un compromis (1945–1970): prélude à la rénovation urbaine dans le quartier Saint-Jean-Baptiste de Québec', *Urban History Review* 24, 2: 12–24.

Simard, J.-J. 1979. *La longue marche des technocrates.* Montréal: Éditions coopératives Albert Saint-Martin.

Sombart, W. 1976. *Why Is There No Socialism in the United States?* London: Macmillan.

Stelter, G.A., and A.F.G. Artibise, eds. 1986. *Power and Place: Canadian Urban Development in the North American Context.* Vancouver: University of British Columbia Press.

Storrie, K. 1987. *Women: Isolation and Bonding. The Ecology of Gender.* Toronto: Methuen.

Tate, E., and L. Quesnel. 1995. 'Accessibility of Municipal Services for Ethnocultural Populations in Toronto and Montréal', *Canadian Public Administration* 38: 325–51.

Thériault, J.-Y. 1985. *La société civile ou la chimère insaisissable.* Montréal: Québec/Amérique.

Thomas, T.L. 1997. *A City with a Difference: The Rise and Fall of the Montreal Citizen's Movement.* Montreal: Véhicule Press.

Tremblay, M. 1996. 'Conscience de genre et représentation politique des femmes', *Politique et Sociétés* 15, 29: 93–137.

Villeneuve, P. 1991. 'Les rapports femmes-hommes en milieu urbain: patriarcat ou partenariat?', *Cahiers de géographie du Québec* 35, 95: 385–401.

———. 1992. 'Les vicissitudes des partis politiques municipaux au Canada', in G. Boismenu, P. Hamel, and G. Labica, eds, *Les formes modernes de la démocratie.* Montréal and Paris: Les Presses de l'université de Montréal and les Éditions l'Harmattan.

Wallace, I. 1990. *The Global Economic System.* London: Unwin Hyman.

Urban Definitions, Statistics Canada, 1996[1]

Census Agglomeration [CA]

Concept and General Criteria

The general concept of a census agglomeration area (CA) as a geographic area is one of a large urbanized area (urban core), together with adjacent urban and rural areas (urban and rural fringes) that are highly integrated socially and economically with that of the urban core.

A CA is defined with an urban core population of at least 10,000 based on the previous census. If the urban core population of a CA falls below 10,000, based on the previous census, the CA is retired. However, if a CA attains an urban core population of at least 100,000, based on the previous census, it is eligible to become a census metropolitan area (CMA).

Consolidated and Primary Census CAs

A CA with an urban core of at least 50,000 based on the previous census is subdivided into *census tracts*. These census tracts are small geographic units representing urban or rural neighbourhood-like communities created in CAs and CMAs. These tracts are maintained for CAs even if the population of the urban cores subsequently falls below 50,000. A CA may be consolidated with adjacent CAs (as consolidated CA), or several CAs may be consolidated with a larger CA. The CAs are evaluated for inclusion based on the following criteria:

- if they are socially and economically integrated;

- if the total commuting interchange between two CAs is equal to at least 35 per cent of the employed labour force living in the smaller CA.

After consolidation, the components of the original CAs become *primary census agglomerations* (PCAs) under the consolidated CA. In order to ensure spatial contiguity, a CA is delineated by *census subdivisions* (CSDs) as building blocks if the CA meets at least one of the following rules that are ranked in order of priority.[2]

1. *The Urban Core Rule.* The CSD falls completely or partly inside the urban core. A core hole is a CSD enclosed by a CSD that is at least partly within the urban core and must be included to maintain spatial contiguity.

2. *The Forward Commuting Flow Rule.* Given a minimum of 100 commuters, at least 50 per cent of the employed labour force living in the CSD work in the *delineation urban core* as determined from commuting data based on the place of work question in the 1991 census. In setting CSD limits, the *delineation urban core* has at least 75 per cent of its census subdivision's population residing within the urban core.

3. *The Reverse Commuting Flow Rule.* Given a minimum of 100 commuters, at least 25 per cent of the employed labour force working in the CSD live in the delineation urban core as determined from the commuting data based on the place of work question in the 1991 census.

4. *The Spatial Contiguity Rule.* CSDs that do not meet a commuting flow threshold may be included in a CMA or CA and CSDs that do meet a commuting flow threshold may be excluded from a CMA or

CA. Two situations determine whether a CSD is included or excluded from a CA or CMA:

- Outlier: A CSD with sufficient commuting flows (either forward or reverse) is enclosed by a CSD with insufficient commuting flows but which is adjacent to the CA (or CMA). If this situation occurs, the CSDs within the enclosing CSD will be grouped to create a minimum CSD set for inclusion in the CA (or CMA). The total commuting flows for the minimum CSD set are then considered for inclusion in the CMA or CA. If the minimum CSD set has sufficient commuting flows (either forward or reverse), then all of its CSDs are included in CA (or CMA).
- Hole: A CSD with insufficient commuting flows (either forward or reverse) is enclosed by a CSD with sufficient commuting flows, and which is adjacent to the CA (or CMA). If this situation arises, the CSDs within and including the enclosing CSD are grouped to create one unit as a minimum CSD set that will then be considered for inclusion in the CA (or CMA). The total commuting flows for the minimum CSD set are then considered for inclusion in the CA (or CMA). If the minimum CSD set has sufficient commuting flows (either forward or reverse), then all of its CSDs are included in the CA (or CMA).

5. *The Historical Comparability Rule.* In order to maintain historical comparability of a CA or a CMA that is subdivided into census tracts (based on previous census), CSDs are retained even if the commuting flow percentages fall below the commuting flow thresholds. An exception to this rule is made if the CSDs are subject to legislated reorganization or changes to their boundaries.

Census Metropolitan Area [CMA]

Concept and General Criteria

The general concept of a census metropolitan area (CMA) as a geographic area is one of a very large urbanized area (urban core) together with adjacent urban and rural areas that have a high degree of social and economic integration with the urban core.

A CMA is defined as having an urban core population of at least 100,000 based on previous census. Once an urban area becomes a CMA, it is retained even if the urban core population declines below 100,000. All CMAs are subdivided into census tracts.

Consolidated CMAs

A CMA may be consolidated with adjacent CAs (consolidated CMA) according to the following criteria:

- if they are socially and economically integrated;
- if the total commuting interchange between a single CMA and adjacent census agglomerations (CAs) is equal to at least 35 per cent of the employed labour force living in the CA.

The calculation of the total percentage commuting interchange is shown below:

$$\frac{\begin{array}{l}\text{Total resident} \\ \text{employed labour} \\ \text{force living in} \\ \text{smaller CA and} \\ \text{working in larger} \\ \text{CMA/CA}\end{array} + \begin{array}{l}\text{Total resident} \\ \text{employed labour} \\ \text{force living in} \\ \text{larger CMA/CA} \\ \text{and working in} \\ \text{smaller CA}\end{array}}{\begin{array}{c}\text{Resident employed labour} \\ \text{force of smaller CA}\end{array}} \times 100\%$$

Based on this consolidation, the components of the original CMA and CA(s) are called primary census metropolitan area (PCMA) and primary census agglomeration (PCA). A CMA may not be consolidated with another CMA. The delineation rules, as described in the preceding paragraphs for CAs, are applied for CMAs to allow statistical comparison of PCMAs and PCAs and to ensure spatial contiguity according to:

- the urban core rule;
- the forward commuting flow rule;

- the reverse commuting flow rule;
- the spatial contiguity rule;
- the historical comparability rule.

For CMA and CA delineation purposes, a delineation urban core is based on CSD limits that require at least 75 per cent of a census subdivision's population who reside within the urban core. The delineation of these areas (CMAs and CAs) are then used for statistical analysis as comparable levels of geography.

Urban Area

As a geographic term used in the 1996 census, an urban area has a minimum population concentration of 1,000 and a population density of at least 400 people per square kilometre, based on the previous census population counts. All territory outside urban areas is considered rural.

Rural Area

As a geographic term used in the 1996 census, a rural area has sparsely populated lands lying outside urban areas.

Urban Core, Urban Fringe, and Rural Fringe

The terms 'urban core', 'urban fringe', and 'rural fringe' distinguish between central and peripheral urban and rural areas within a CMA, PCMA, CA, and PCA.

An urban core is a large urban area around which a CMA or CA is delineated. It must have a population, based on the previous census, of at least 100,000 in the case of a CMA, or between 10,000 and 99,999 in the case of a CA. Urban fringe is the urban area within a CMA or CA that is not contiguous to the urban core. Rural fringe is all territory within a CMA or CA not classified as urban core or urban fringe.

Notes

1. Definitions in this appendix are from Statistics Canada, *1996 Census Dictionary* (Ottawa: Minister of Industry, 1997, Cat. No. 92–351–XPE) and Statistics Canada, *Population and Dwelling Counts* (Ottawa: Minister of Industry, 1997, Cat. No. 93–357–XPB).

2. The term 'census division' (CD) is a general term applied to areas established by provincial law that are intermediate geographic areas between the municipality (census subdivision) and the province level. 'Census subdivision' (CSD) is a general term applied to municipalities (as determined by provincial legislation) or their equivalent, e.g., Aboriginal settlements and reserves (Statistics Canada, *1996 Census Dictionary*).

Appendix B: **Selected Data on Canada's Census Metropolitan Areas, 1996**

Rank CMA	1 Population 1996 (000s)	2 Population Change 1991–1996 (%)	3 Population Change 1971–1991 (%)	4 Recent Immigrants, 1991–1996 (% of population 5 years and over)	5 Foreign-Born (% of population)	6 Less than Grade 9 (% of population 15 years and over)	7 University Degree (% of Population 15 years and over)	8 Labour Force Participation Rate (%)	9 Unemployment Rate (%)	10 Labour Force Engaged in Manufacturing (%)	11 Labour Force Engaged in Finance, Insurance, Real Estate, and Government Service (%)	12 Average Income ($)*	13 Incidence of Low Income (%)**
1. Toronto	4,263	9.4	48.1	7.9	41.5	10.2	19.0	67.2	9.1	16.1	12.2	28,980	21.1
2. Montreal	3,326	3.7	13.9	3.5	17.6	16.0	15.3	63.6	11.2	16.7	10.4	24,625	27.3
3. Vancouver	1,831	14.3	48.0	9.8	34.6	7.2	17.4	67.3	8.6	9.9	11.4	27,450	23.3
4. Ottawa–Hull	1,010	7.3	52.8	3.6	16.0	8.0	22.6	69.4	8.8	6.3	23.7	29,749	18.9
5. Edmonton	862	2.6	69.4	2.9	18.3	7.0	14.4	71.1	8.2	9.4	11.3	25,728	21.3
6. Calgary	821	9.0	87.0	4.1	20.7	5.3	18.5	74.0	6.6	9.2	9.5	28,963	19.8
7. Quebec	671	4.1	34.3	1.0	2.5	12.9	15.9	64.4	10.4	8.4	19.8	24,382	22.8
8. Winnipeg	667	1.0	20.7	2.3	16.7	9.0	14.7	67.2	7.9	12.7	12.9	24,184	23.0
9. Hamilton	624	4.1	20.2	2.4	23.3	9.7	13.0	64.9	8.1	19.6	9.6	27,556	19.0
10. London	398	4.5	33.2	2.4	19.0	7.0	15.5	67.3	9.3	15.4	10.3	26,756	17.3
11. Kitchener	382	7.4	57.5	3.0	21.6	10.1	13.5	70.5	8.1	26.1	9.4	27,074	14.6
12. St Catharines	372	2.2	20.1	1.5	18.0	10.9	9.7	62.0	9.9	19.0	8.0	24,565	16.1
13. Halifax	332	3.7	44.1	1.7	7.1	6.4	19.0	67.7	8.6	5.9	20.2	25,135	17.8
14. Victoria	304	5.7	47.1	3.2	18.9	4.4	17.8	64.7	7.5	4.8	6.5	27,369	15.4
15. Windsor	278	6.3	1.5	1.1	20.4	9.9	12.5	64.7	8.1	27.8	6.9	28,053	15.7
16. Oshawa	268	11.9	100.0	1.8	16.4	7.2	9.5	68.7	9.0	21.2	10.7	29,202	12.4
17. Saskatoon	219	3.8	66.6	1.6	7.5	8.2	15.5	69.5	7.5	9.2	9.9	24,215	21.4
18. Regina	193	1.0	36.4	0.8	7.8	7.9	14.4	69.9	7.3	6.2	16.7	25,820	17.6

Appendix B: (continued)

Rank CMA	1 Population 1996 (000s)	2 Population Change 1991–1996 (%)	3 Population Change 1971–1991 (%)	4 Recent Immigrants, 1991–1996 (% of population 5 years and over)	5 Foreign-Born (% of population)	6 Less than Grade 9 (% of population 15 years and over)	7 University Degree (% of Population 15 years and over)	8 Labour Force Participation Rate (%)	9 Unemployment Rate (%)	10 Labour Force Engaged in Manufacturing (%)	11 Labour Force Engaged in Finance, Insurance, Real Estate, and Government Service (%)	12 Average Income ($)*	13 Incidence of Low Income (%)**
19. St John's	174	1.3	30.5	0.5	2.9	8.9	14.2	63.4	14.2	4.7	16.0	23,145	19.5
20. Sudbury	160	1.8	1.2	0.5	7.4	12.4	10.2	62.5	12.0	6.1	11.6	26,088	17.3
21. Chicoutimi–Jonquière	160	–0.3	3.2	1.5	0.7	14.7	9.6	57.9	13.4	14.8	12.2	22,675	20.7
22. Sherbrooke	147	4.7	—	0.5	4.2	15.3	14.4	63.6	10.3	17.4	7.7	22,603	22.8
23. Trois-Rivières	139	2.7	—	0.3	1.6	16.8	11.4	59.1	12.0	17.2	8.3	22,307	23.4
24. Saint John	125	–0.1	16.9	0.7	3.9	10.4	11.0	62.3	13.1	12.2	9.9	23,012	20.0
25. Thunder Bay	125	0.5	10.7	0.7	12.1	10.6	11.6	64.8	10.7	10.6	10.4	26,463	14.5

*Average income ($) is computed from total income of population 15 years and over per CMA.

**Incidence of low income (%) is based on Statistics Canada low-income cut-off (LICO), the minimum necessary to sustain an average-size household in each locality. The incidence of low income (%) means the proportion of economic families or unattached individuals below LICO.

Sources: Statistics Canada, 1971 Census of Canada, Population: Cities, Towns, Villages, Census Metropolitan Areas and Census Agglomerations (Ottawa: Minister of Industry, Trade and Commerce, 1971, Catalogue No. 92–708); Statistics Canada, Profile of Census Metropolitan Areas and Census Agglomerations (Ottawa: Minister of Industry, 1998, Catalogue No. 95F0182XDB, diskette).

Index